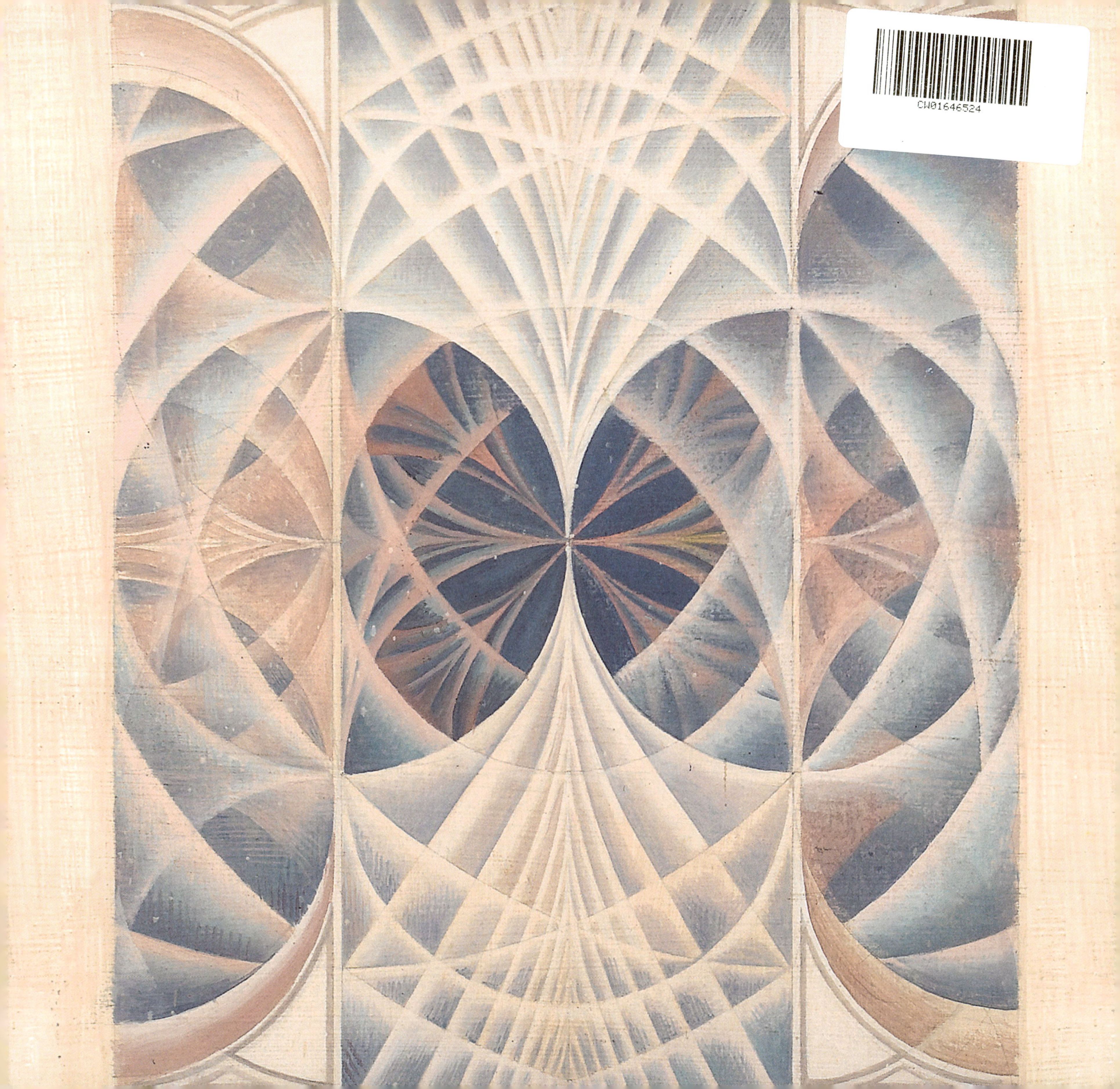

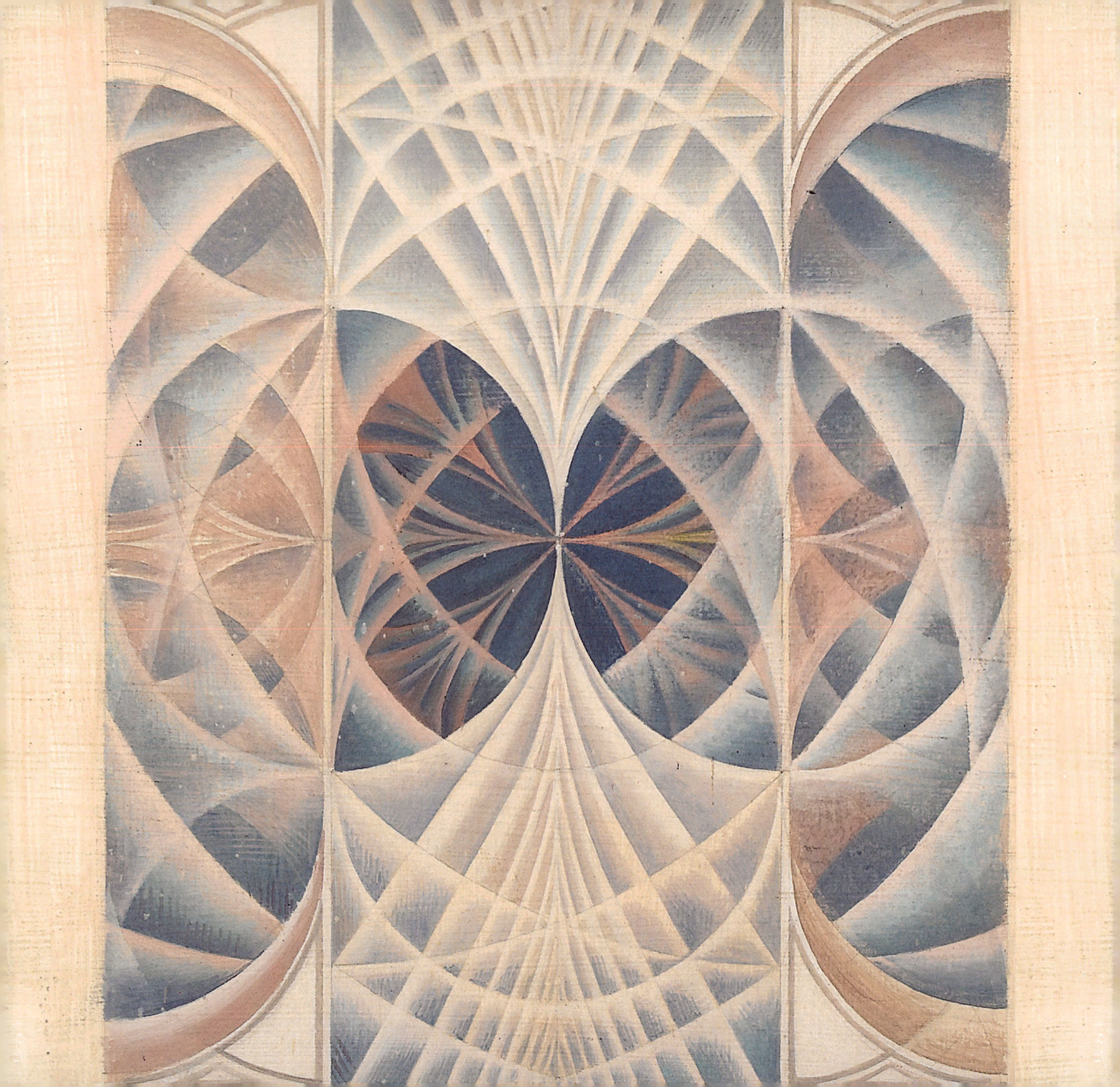

British Murals
&
Decorative Painting

1920 - 1960

Rediscoveries and New Interpretations

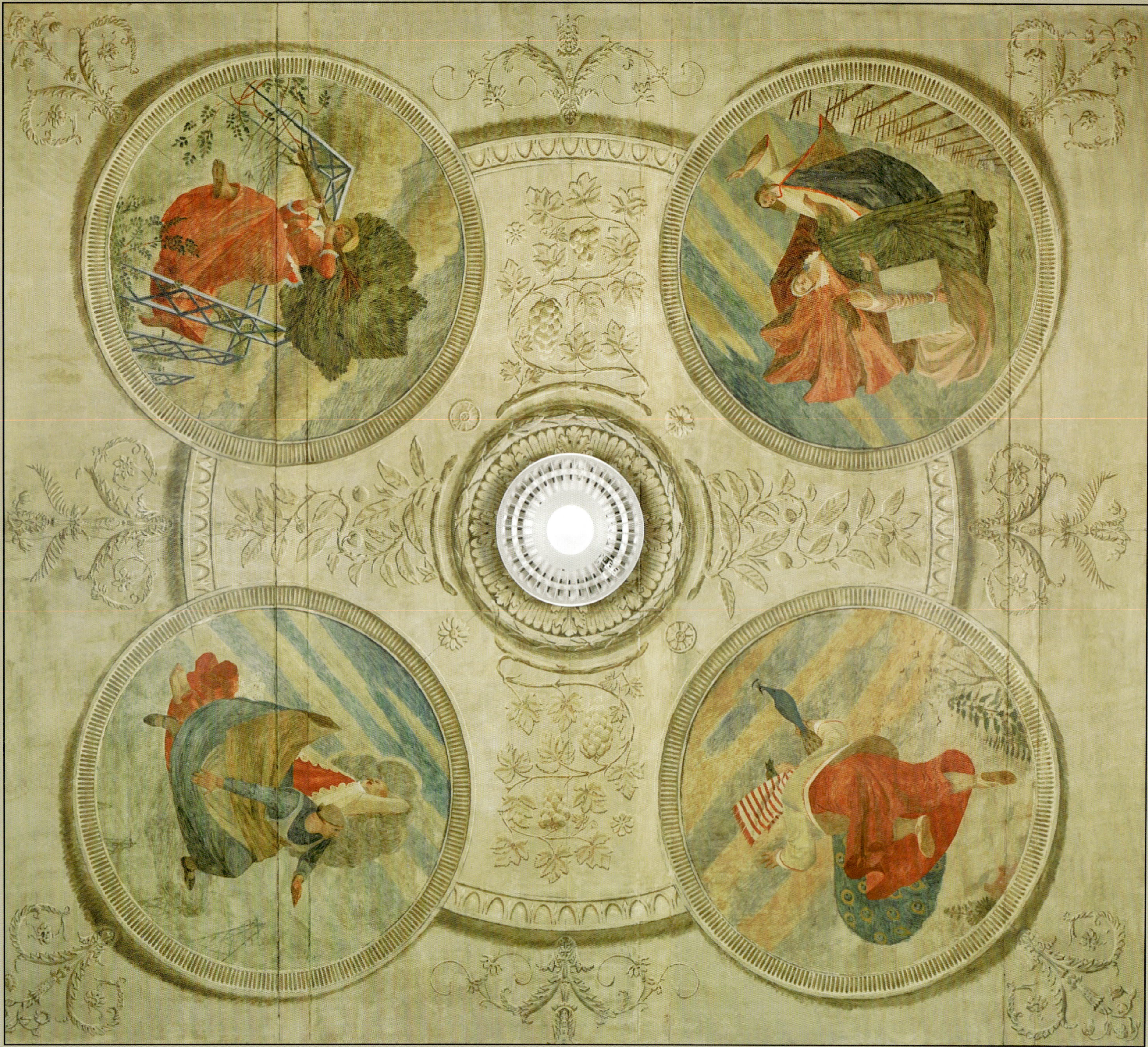

British Murals
&
Decorative Painting

1920 - 1960

Rediscoveries and New Interpretations

Sansom & Company

First published in 2013 by Sansom & Co.,
81g Pembroke Road, Bristol BS8 3EA

www.sansomandcompany.co.uk
info@sansomandcompany.co.uk

ISBN: 978-1-908326-23-2

British Library Cataloguing-in-Publication Data
A catalogue record for this book is available
from the British Library

Design and typesetting by David Maes
Printed and bound by Zenith Media

For Evelina, Maude & Blanche

Contents

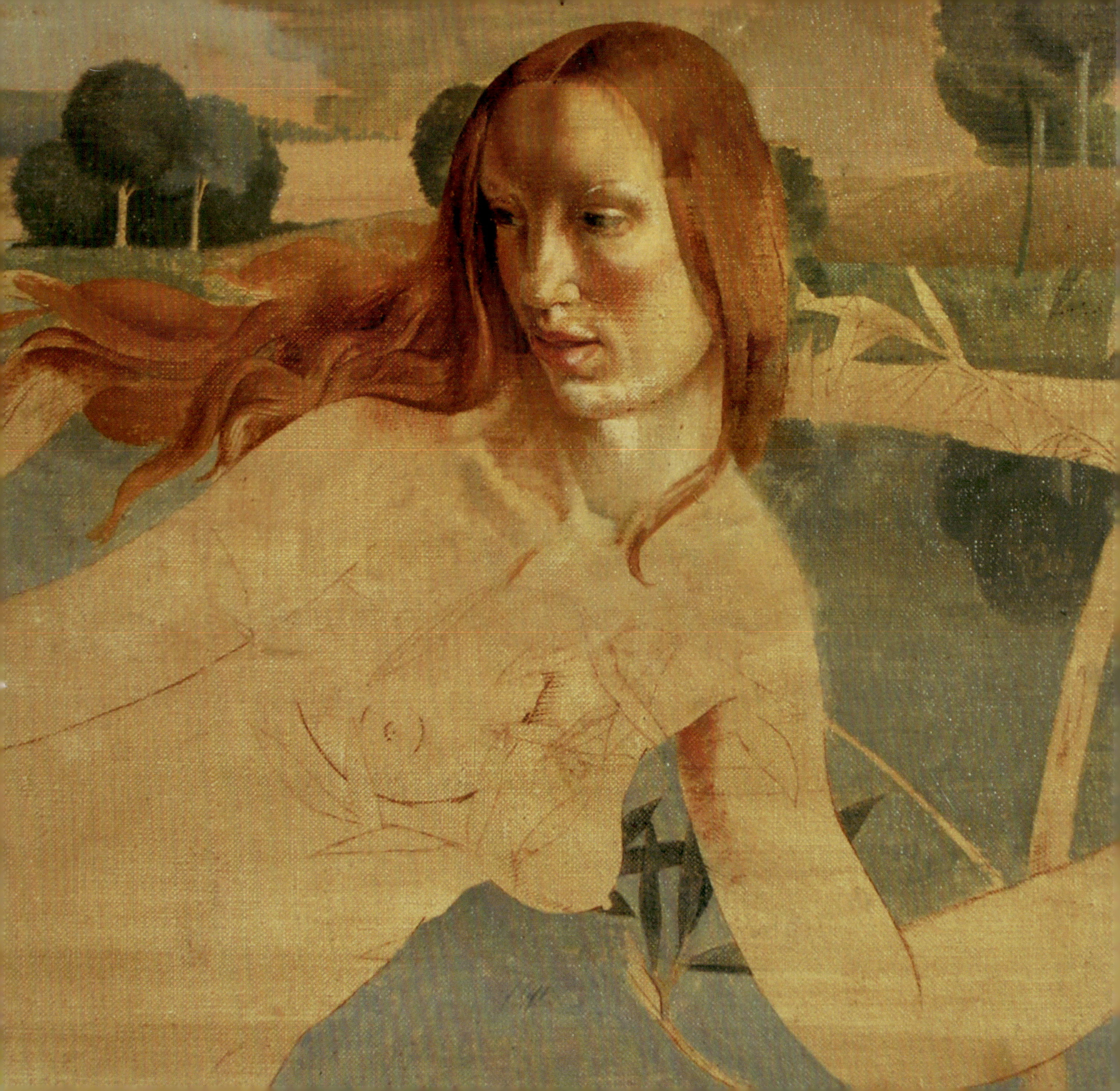

Preface

Paul Liss

This book is illustrated with a series of specially commissioned photographs that record some of the least known but most remarkable mural cycles in Great Britain. In the vast majority of cases these works have previously only been reproduced in black and white if at all.

Today murals are rarely seen as the artist intended. Often they are partially obscured, especially where there has been a change of building use. Frequently works are completely covered up or painted over – examples include murals by Mary Sargent Florence, Mary Adshead, Eric Ravilious, Dora Carrington, William Roberts and Gilbert Spencer. Where murals survive they are more often than not displaced works. Historic photographs showing John Piper's *The Englishman's Home* at The Festival of Britain, *in situ* on the river side of the Homes and Gardens Pavilion on Belvedere Road, come as a revelation (see page 290); a digital reconstruction of Frank Brangwyn's *Empire* panels for The House of Lords, seen *in situ* as they were originally intended, gives a dramatically more favourable impression than their final installation in The Brangwyn Hall, Swansea. (see page 82)

Murals suffer from the anonymity of public art – central London alone boasts remarkable but little known works by Edward Bawden, Jean Cocteau, George Clausen, Edward Halliday, Alfred Kingsley Lawrence, Colin Gill, Charles Sims, William Rothenstein, Rex Whistler, D.Y. Cameron, Hans Feibusch, and Ivon Hitchens.

At a Morley College dinner in 1938 it is recorded that Sir William Rothenstein, having pointed to the Charles Mahoney murals at the back of the stage (which he declared to be 'the finest in this country since Ford Madox Brown decorated the Manchester Town Hall'), finished his speech by recalling that Max Beerbohm, looking at the same murals, 'had grown very angry: in any other country there would be a stream of people waiting to see these enchanting paintings.' (see pages 204-209) Just two years after this speech Mahoney's murals were destroyed by enemy bombing, along with the better known mural cycles of Edward Bawden and Eric Ravilious in the same building. (see page 41) Ironically more often than not the vandalism has been self-inflicted. In October 1951, when the Conservative government was elected, Winston Churchill's very first instruction was to clear the South Bank of that 'three-dimensional socialist propaganda'. This sealed the fate of Keith Vaughan's epic mural *The Beginning of Time/Thesus* – considered too large to store or sell off it was destroyed. Edward Bawden's *Country Life In Britain* (see pages 246-247) for the Lion and Unicorn Pavilion fared little better – earmarked as one of the murals which should be saved for the nation it was put into a Ministry of Works store which itself was later demolished. The fate of John Armstrong's murals for the Telecinema is unknown and they are assumed to have been destroyed. (see page 285)

Thomas Monnington
Study for *Allegory*, c. 1925
(detail)
see page 171

Not all, however, is lost. The inspiration for this publication was the re-emergence of two remarkable Festival of Britain murals – by John Piper and Alan Sorrell – and two of Mary Adshead's murals commissioned for Lord Beaverbrook's dining room, which were previously listed as destroyed. (see pages 176-181) Likewise, Fyffe Christie's epic *Christ Feeding the People*, for the Iona Community's canteen in Glasgow, (see pages 88-89) re-emerged some decades after it was assumed to have been lost when removed from the building in the late 1970s. Might Edward Bawden's *Country Life in Britain* one day re-emerge? Is it possible that John Armstrong's Telecinema murals were removed before the first National Film theatre was demolished when the lease on the site expired? A remarkable number of important murals might still be uncovered: The Pavilion Tearoom Mural in Colwyn Bay by Mary Adshead and Eric Ravilious is in the process of being restored, having been previously painted and plastered over. Murals painted in 1912 for Bishop Creighton House, Lillie Road, include designs by William Roberts, Dora Carrington and Colin Gill which are no longer visible having been painted over after the Second World War. Gilbert Spencer's *Scholar Gypsy*, 1957, remains obscured by a layer of paint at the University of London Students Union. Mary Sargant-Florence's main mural cycle, at Oakham School, still survives but was panelled over in 1994.

In 1923, Eugenie Strong, Assistant Director of the British School at Rome (1909-1925), wrote to *The Times* to make an impassioned plea for 'initiating on a generous scale the publication of … all those mural paintings in our churches and cathedrals which have either been overlooked or forgotten for centuries or else only recently come to light again.' This, she went on to say, was 'not only a patriotic duty and national responsibility but would fill a deplorable gap'. So long as murals and decorative paintings are poorly documented and largely unprotected they will remain a part of Britain's artistic heritage that is at risk. As Alan Powers points out, while high standards of conservation are imposed for works in museum collections, murals have to take their chance. There is as yet no coordinated photographic recording of murals, surely an important task following the model set by the Public Sculpture and Monuments Association and the Public Catalogue Foundation?

This book is divided into two sections. Part one seeks to define murals and decorative paintings within their historic context. Although the term 'Decorative Painting' has largely been written out of accounts of twentieth-century British art, it had wide currency in the first half of the century and informed the aims and aspirations of a large number of artists. Alan Powers' survey of the major events and significant dates in mural and decorative painting describes the background out of which the mural revival of the early twentieth-century emerged and the role played by its main patrons, artists, art schools, and institutions. It offers important re-interpretations of some of the best-known schemes and draws attention to others which deserve to be better known. It argues for a more inclusive view of twentieth-century British art generally, and with it a more developed understanding of the role of murals in the lives of artists and in society during this period.

Part two of this book consists of 15 essays – written by experts in the field – which provide in-depth case studies of selected works, as well as considering the careers of specific artists as muralists. This section gives a special emphasis to murals which are less well-known and in many cases have only recently been rediscovered. Four of the case studies highlight the work of the first generation of Rome Scholars – artists who produced some of the most enduring decorative paintings of the interwar years – Colin Gill, Winifred Knights, Thomas Monnington and Edward Halliday. These essays offer a fascinating account of the role played by the British School

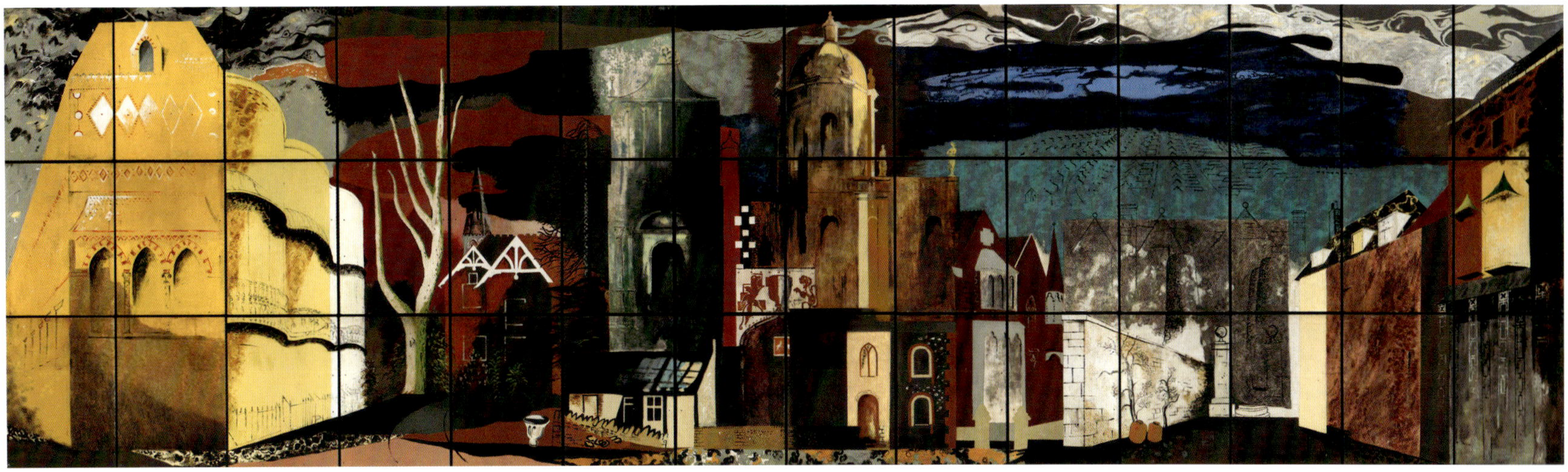

John Piper – *The Englishman's Home*, 1951, oil on plywood, 42 panels, each panel 159 x 119 cm (62 ½ x 46 ⅞ in.), overall size: 477 x 1547 cm (187 ¾ x 609 in.) see pages 292-293

at Rome immediately after the First World War in promoting mural and decorative painting. Case studies on Edward Bawden, Alan Sorrell, John Piper, John Armstrong and '60 Paintings for 51' focus on significant newly discovered works from the Festival of Britain – Alan Sorrell's mural for the Nelson Bar of the HMS *Campania* (reproduced for the first time in colour), John Piper's *The Englishman's Home*, Charles Mahoney's *The Garden,* Gilbert Spencer's *Hebridean Memory* and John Armstrong's *Storm*. Barbara Jones' *Man at Work – a century of technical and social progress* was considered by the artist to be her masterpiece and after the Turin exhibition she paid to have it repatriated. It spent the next 50 years hidden behind a studio wall and it too is reproduced in this book in colour for the first time. Of the 36 murals Jones painted during her lifetime less than ten percent of her work is extant – this is probably representative of the survival rate of murals for many artists. Charles Mahoney's murals have fared better than most – two of his three major mural schemes have survived – Brockley School and Campion Hall – but neither scheme to date has been well-documented. At the same time, the loss of the Morley College murals – his most significant early work – has undoubtedly held back public appreciation of his *oeuvre*.

As a consequence of remaining out of the public domain murals often end up being written out of the accounts of the lives of the artists who created them – notwithstanding the fact that for sheer size and scale it might be assumed that they counted amongst the most ambitious projects they ever undertook. Covering a surface area of over 800 square feet, John Piper might have been expected to employ a team of assistants to rapidly and schematically complete *The Englishman's Home* – instead he chose to paint the mural with almost no help, in his garden at Fawley Bottom, through the long and hard winter of 1950-51.

This book is not intended to be comprehensive or conclusive. It is hoped, however, that it will contribute to a debate about heritage and about murals that have been lost and murals that might still be recorded and be saved. It will hopefully serve to inspire a more inclusive account of twentieth-century British Art in which murals and decorative paintings are fully accounted for.

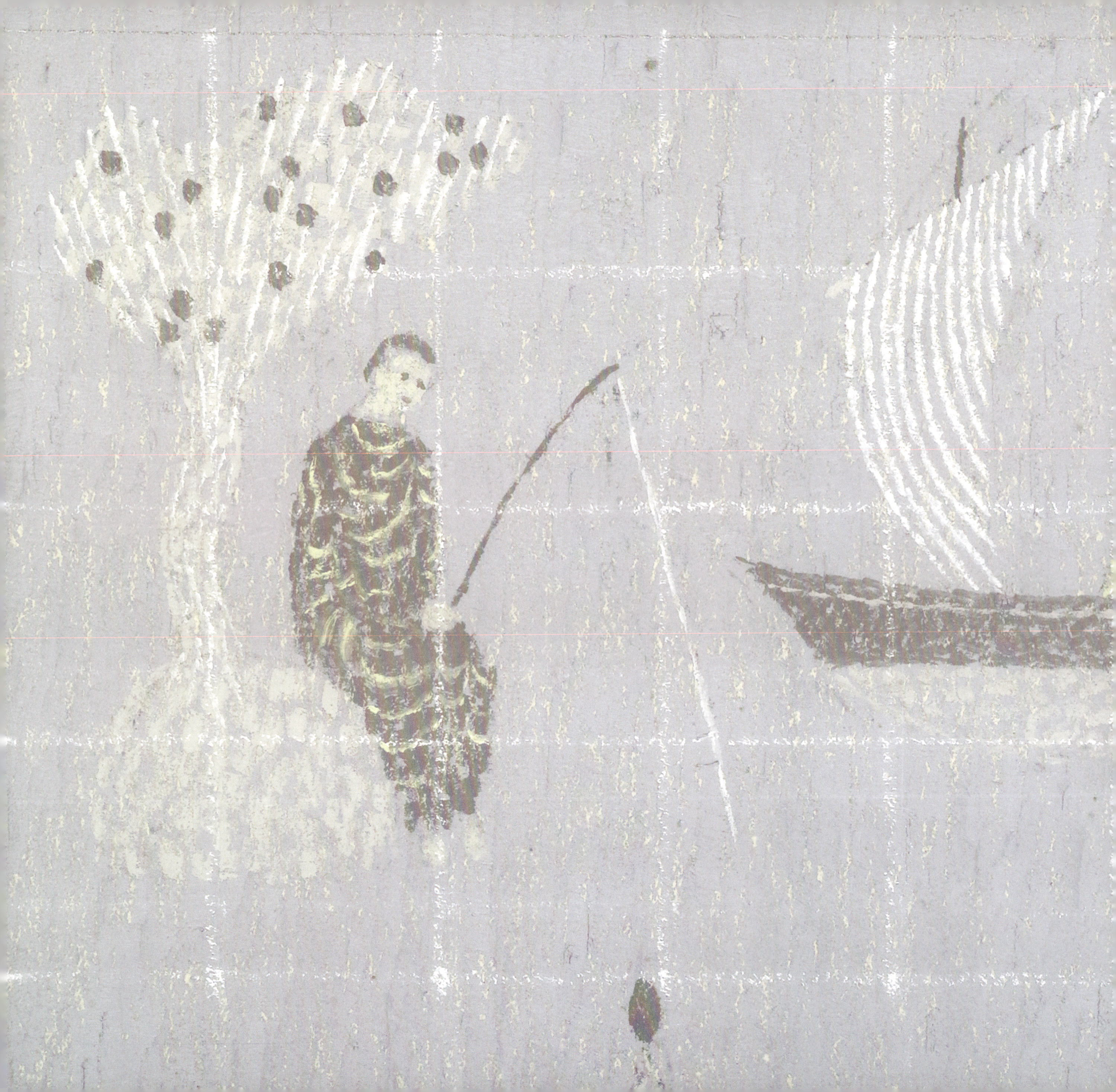

Acknowledgements

The contributors would like to thank:

Barbara Adams
Elaine Andrews
Annette Armstrong
Kate Austin
Nicholas Bagshawe
Ian Beck
Edward Bettella
Sylvester Bone
Quentin Bone
Patrick Bourne
Cordelia Bourne
Roger Bowdler
Erica Brandl
David Brangwyn
Sue Breakell
Nick Bridgland
Elizabeth Bulkeley
Sarah Bull
Louise Burley
Dinah Casson
Emma Chambers
Eleanor Christie-Chatterley
Glynn Clarkson
Matthew Clough
Gordon Cooke
Nicola Costaras
Country Life
Susie Cox
Therese Crawley
Paul Deaton
Sasha Devas
Rod Dorling
Daniel Dullaway
Simon Edsor
Andy Ellis
Amy English
Hugh Fowler-Wright
Andrea Fredericksen
David Gear
Willoughby Gerrish
Jonathan Gibbs
Alessandra Giovenco
Gill Clarke
Nigel Green
Harry Moore Gwyn
Charlotte Halliday
Stephen Halliday
Debbie Hickmott
Justin Hobson
Clara Hudson
Neil Jennings
Kelly Lean
Anton Liss
Barrie and Marion Liss
Evelina Llewellyn
Jonathan Makepeace
John McKenzie
John Monnington
Rowena Morgan-Cox
Conor Mullan
Vivienne Palfreyman
Lynn Pearson
Robyn Pender
Jane Powell
Tony Raymond
Mary Rose Rivett-Carnac
Susan Ross
Andrew Saint
John Sansom
Valerie Scott
Andrew and Kathleen Simon
Graham Snow
Chris Stephens
Barbara Taylor
Brian Webb
Clare Willsdon
Neil Campbell Wilson

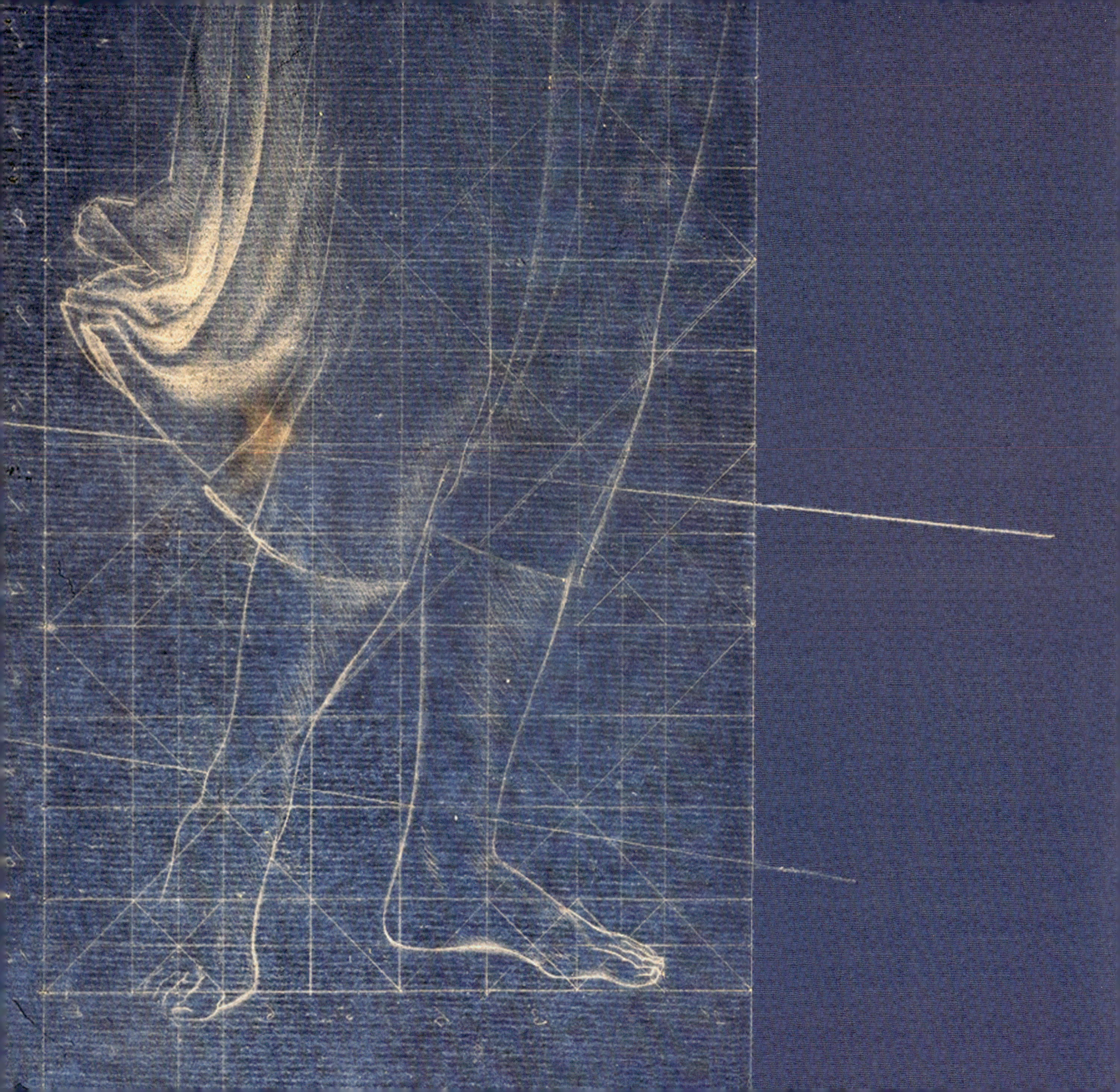

PART I

Murals & Decorative Painting in Britain

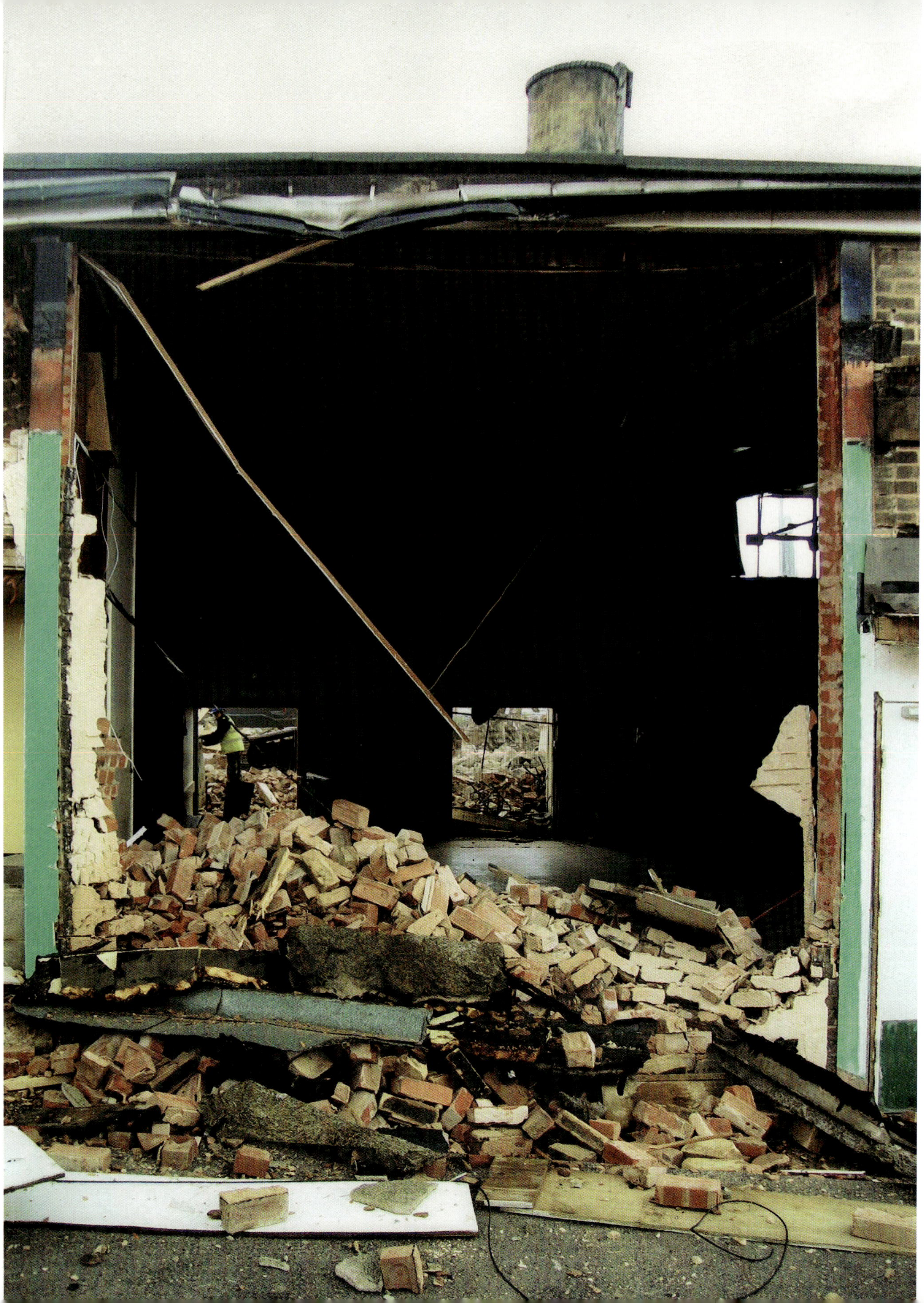

1a & 1b
Demolition of Barbara Jones' 1959 mural *Adam Naming the Animals,* Yew Lane School, Sheffield

The Mural Problem

Alan Powers

1b 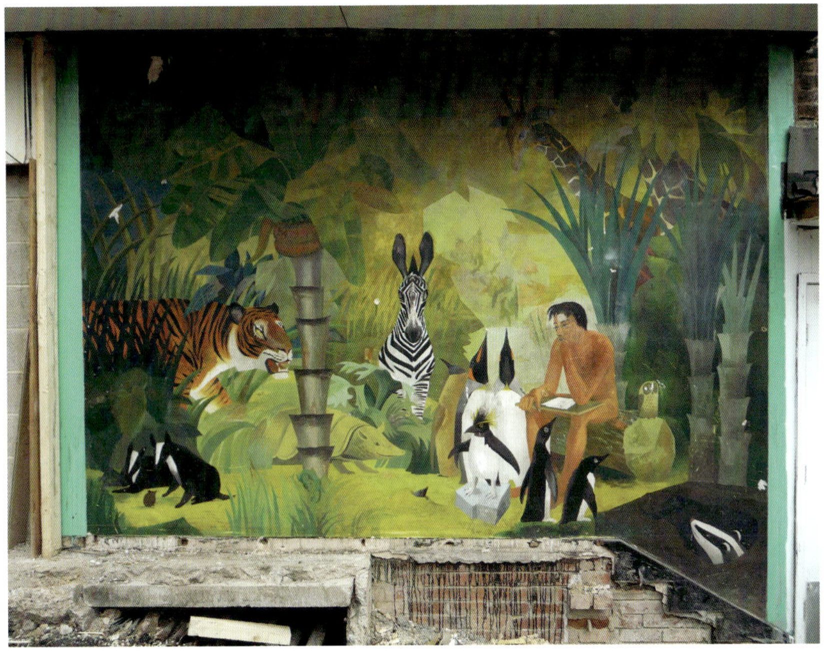

Murals are an odd category of art. No artist seeking a quiet existence would choose to paint them, for they are usually a taxing and unprofitable undertaking, yet during the twentieth century, many artists ignored the penalties of long hours of work and produced a wonderful and still largely unknown body of work. That is the mural problem as seen from the production point of view.

Murals present different kinds of problems to posterity. One is a physical problem, for unlike normal works of art they are vulnerable because they are unwieldy and can only be moved with difficulty, if at all, although the later owners and occupiers of the buildings they are in often have no wish to see them. They are apt to become dirty or damaged because their surfaces are unprotected. They cannot be kept in a controlled environment, and are subject to deterioration from environmental conditions. When conserving is needed, unless they are on moveable panels, they must be conserved *in situ*, which is more costly than studio work. While these constraints are understood in relation to earlier mural paintings, twentieth-century ones tend to come lower in the hierarchy. Yet, whether or not murals are by well-known artists, they have left a responsibility to posterity that is often neglected and much work has been carelessly destroyed, covered over or saved only by chance or last-minute intervention.

The problem for posterity is also one of knowledge and interpretation. Knowledge of where murals exist is fragmentary, with no coordinated photographic record or even a database of locations. The Public Sculpture and Monuments Association and the Public Catalogue Foundation have set examples for this basic fact-gathering that need to be applied to murals of the twentieth century, especially since no organization takes responsibility for advising their owners of and investigating salvage options if destruction threatens. The national amenity societies have intervened where possible in their different roles, and the Twentieth Century Society, the most relevant for the works in this book, while primarily concerned with buildings, has achieved a few successes with murals and regularly organizes visits to buildings which contain them. In 2008, the Society set up an online campaign with the Tiles and Architectural Ceramics Society. The Decorated School research project, led by Dr Catherine Burke, was stimulated by the loss of a mural by Barbara Jones at a school in Sheffield that was demolished and replaced by a new building. [1a & 1b] In a few cases, buildings have been listed primarily for the sake of the murals they contain, but even so, the subject as a whole has not enjoyed the same level of research as public sculpture.[1]

This book includes photographs of many works never before published, or seen only in poor quality images. Sadly, some murals disappeared before adequate records could be made. At the same time that the physical salvaging of the original works or reproductions of them is an important task, their poor treatment reflects the need for an intellectual and aesthetic salvage effort to re-evaluate an area of art that has never lost the interest of the general public. An important beginning was made when Clare Willsdon published the comprehensive survey, *Mural Painting in Britain 1840-1940: Image and Meaning*, in 2000, collecting a great deal of information and pictures of murals. Even so, the period from the end of the First World War into the early post-war decades is a self-contained period in its own right in which the nature of art was further explored and debated, and murals were part of the transition between the ideals of the Victorians and the visual languages of Modernism.[2]

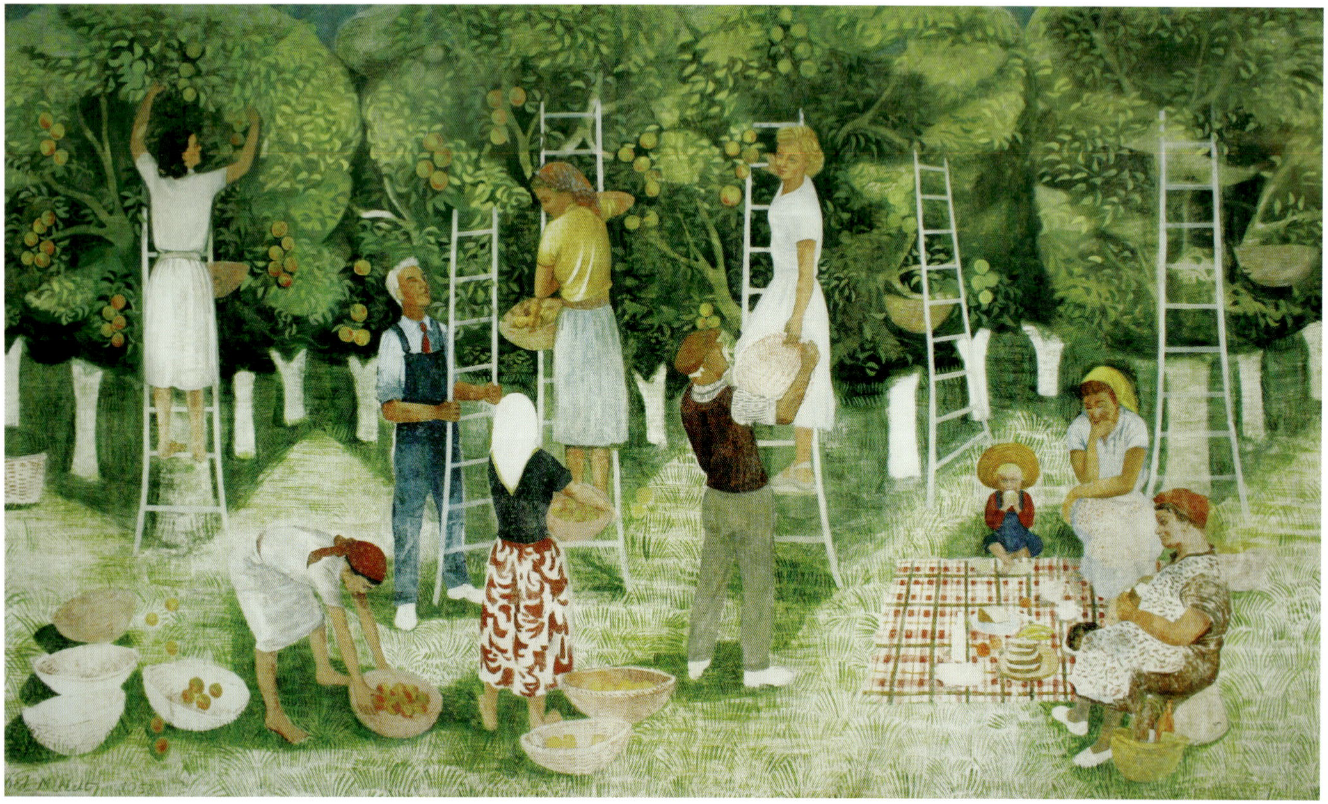

2
Fred Millett, *Summer*, 1953, St Crispin's School, Wokingham

Murals are always deemed newsworthy as Radio 4's coverage of the uncovering from several layers of later overpainting of Fred Millett's *Summer*, 1953, at St Crispin's School, Wokingham in 2011 showed.[3] Millett painted two more walls in this Secondary Modern School, designed by the Ministry of Education's in-house architects to be a model of modern spaciousness and light. The interest in *Summer* led in 2012 to fundraising for the uncovering of the companion piece, *Autumn*. [2 & 3] However, it seems that art fixed in buildings presents not only physical problems but cognitive ones – paintings become over-familiar and on some level we fail to understand what they are doing there, hence the risk of over-painting or complete destruction. Often only with some form of rediscovery, highlighting their existence, can they become contemporary again and arouse new excitement. Something of this kind has recently happened when parents at Greenside School, Hammersmith, 'rediscovered' the mural by Gordon Cullen from behind a curtain.

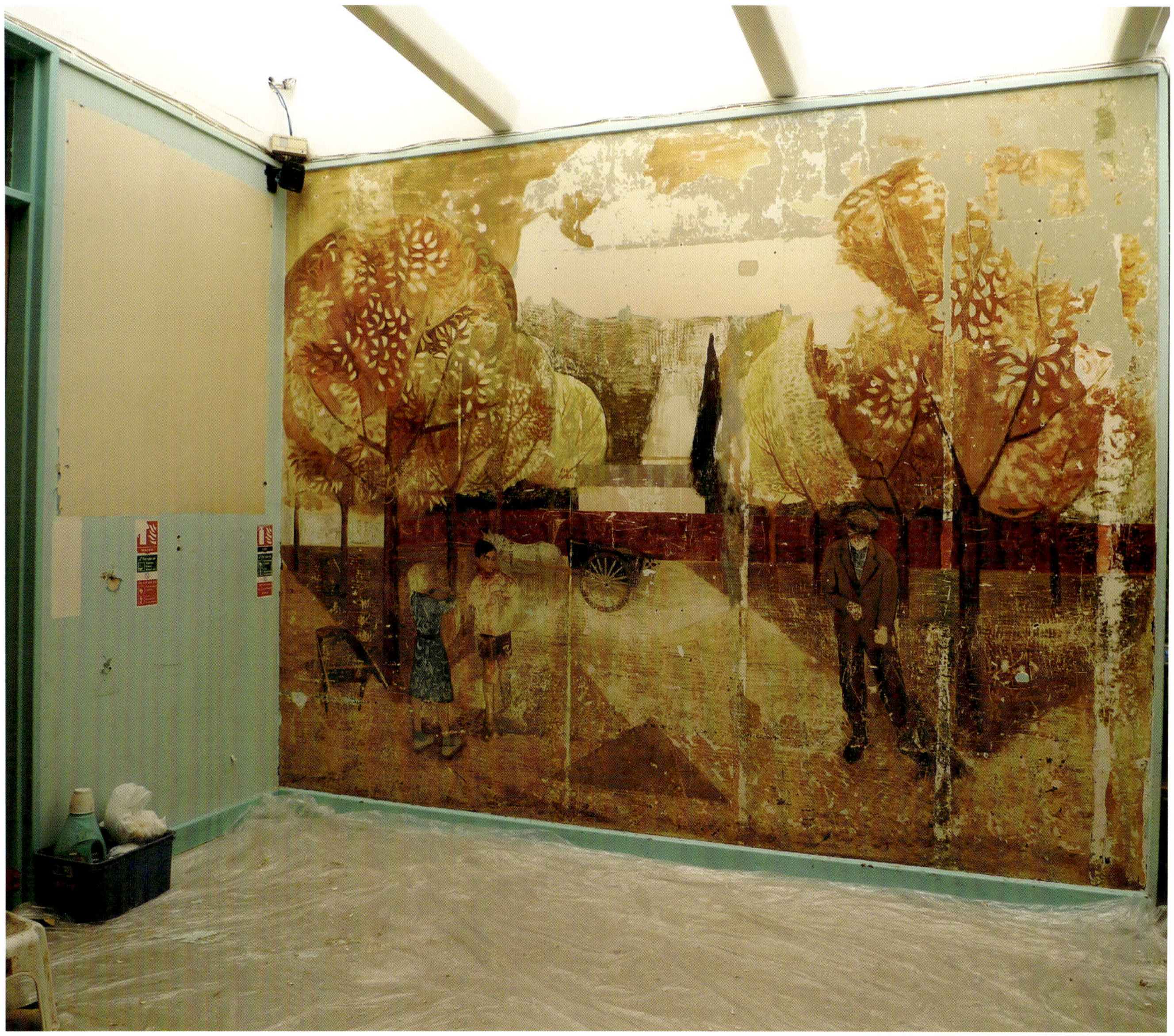

3
2012 restoration of Fred Millett's *Autumn*, St Crispin's School, Wokingham

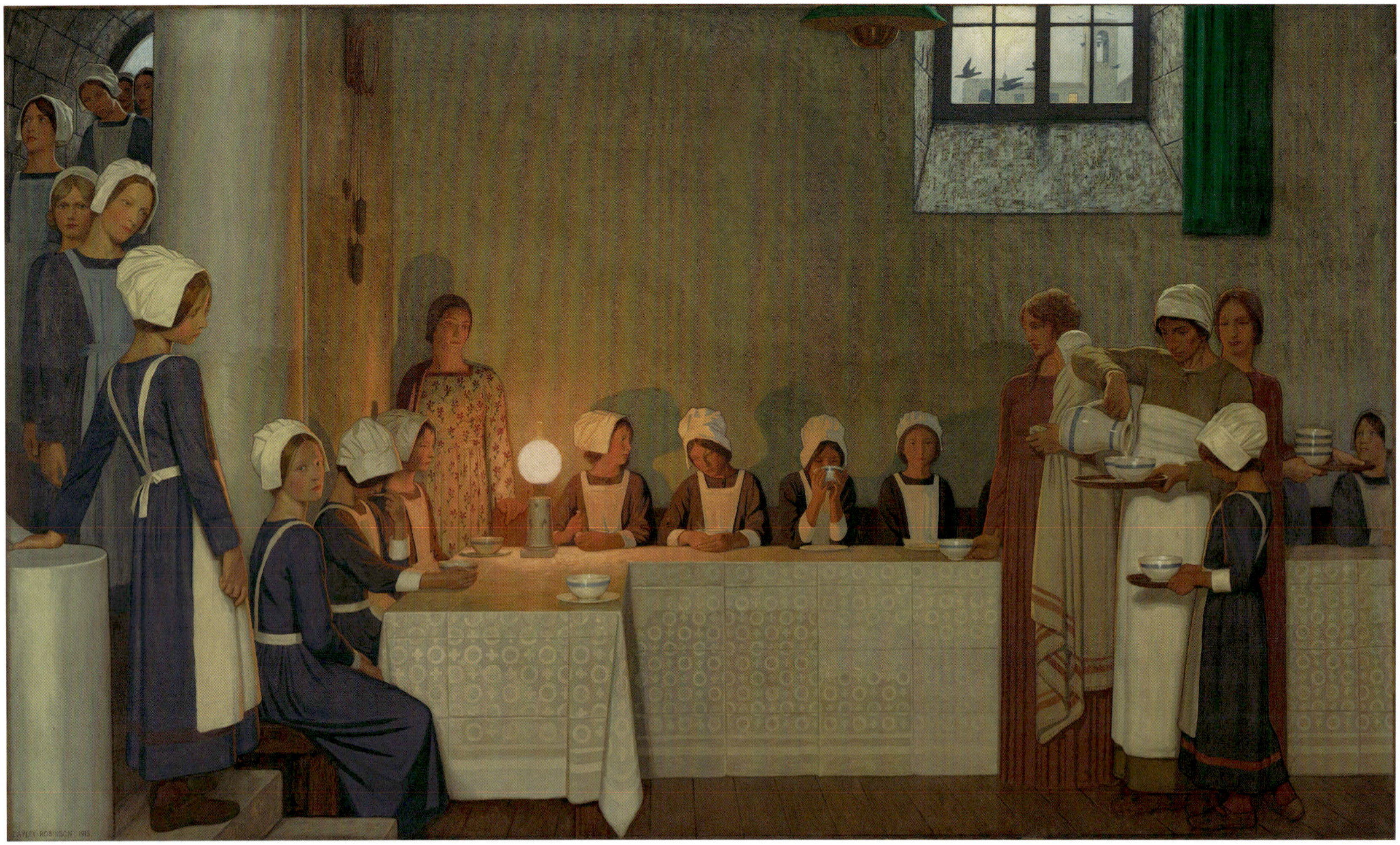

4a Frederick Cayley Robinson, *Orphan girls entering the refectory of a hospital.* signed and dated lower left "Cayley-Robinson, 1915", oil on canvas, 199 x 339 cm (78 ⅜ x 133 ½ in.), from *The Acts of Mercy,* 1915-20, Courtesy of the Wellcome Collection

From the viewpoint of knowledge and interpretation, it must be acknowledged that not all murals are necessarily great works of art. All but the most incompetent are likely to enhance the experience of a building in some way, if only by adding another layer to its history, so that they may exceed more conventional forms of painting in this respect, while almost invariably acquiring additional interest from their social context, patronage, and any other reasons for their existence.

The field of twentieth-century British art is still relatively under-appreciated as a whole, with the exception of the established names, and most mural painters come below that level of recognition. Since the canon has to a great degree been formed in relation to pictures hanging in public collections, a painter specializing in murals is apt to lose out. Mary Sargant-Florence presents this problem, for her main mural cycle, at Oakham School, was threatened with complete destruction, against which no sanctions existed, and only as a concession was it agreed to conceal the painted walls behind heavy panelling.[4] Apart from her murals, little of her other work has

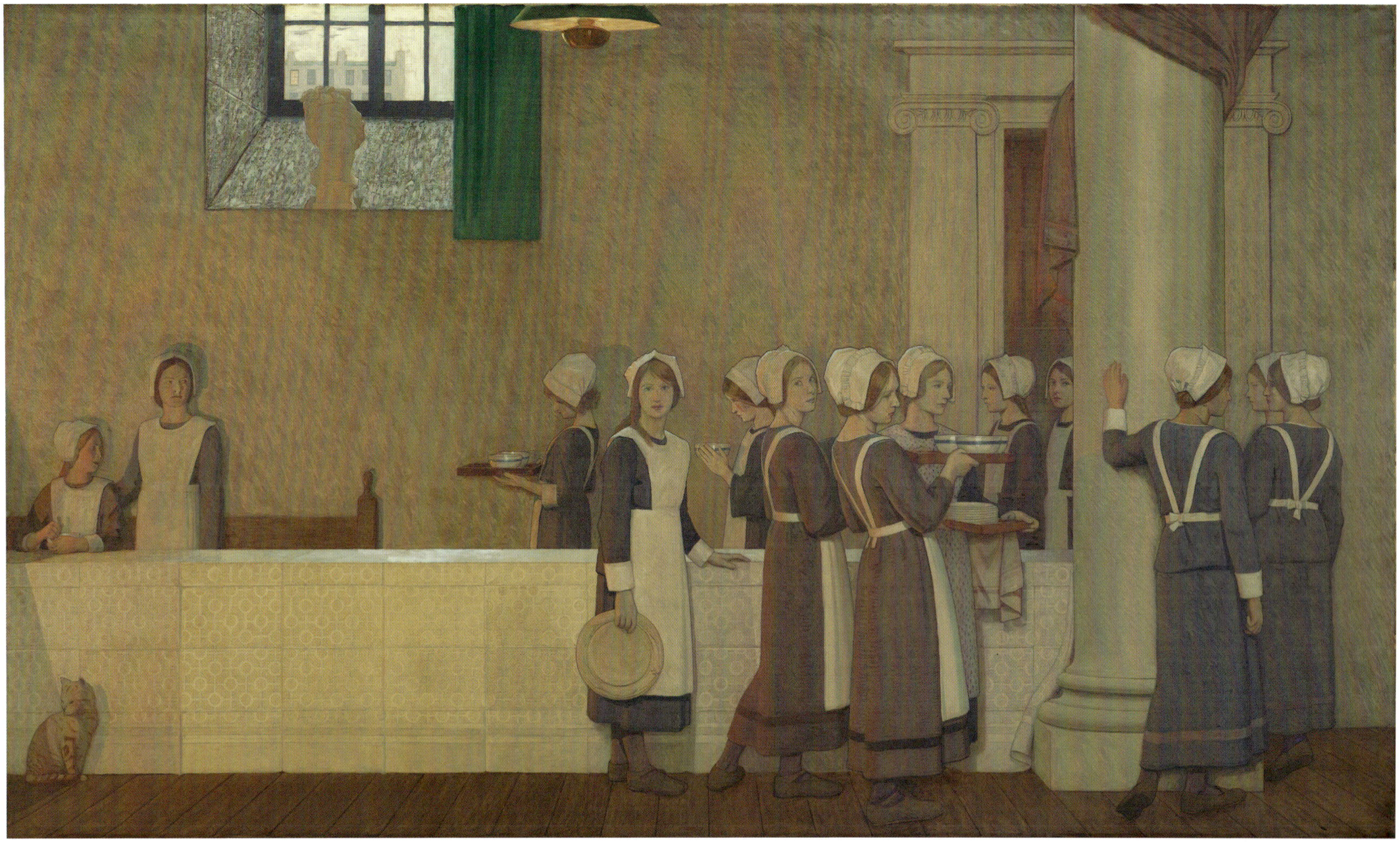

4b Frederick Cayley Robinson, *Orphan girls in the refectory of a hospital, proceeding around the end of a table towards their seats,* not signed or dated, oil on canvas, 198.7 x 339 cm (78 ¼ x 133 ½ in.), from *The Acts of Mercy,* 1915-20, Courtesy of the Wellcome Collection

been located following its dispersal after her death, and as a result, even though she is a major woman artist of her time, there is still little scholarship on her.

Even recognized figures whose work forms part of the canon can have their mural work ignored for years unless some exceptional event brings it to wider attention. An extreme case of transformation from invisibility while in clear sight to national exposure occurred with Frederick Cayley Robinson's set of four paintings *The Acts of Mercy* which had been on public view almost continuously since 1920 in a central London location, the Middlesex Hospital, just north of Oxford Street, apparently without being noticed. They could have been sold abroad or lost to view in a private collection in Britain without comment after the hospital put them on the market in 2007, but fortunately they were bought for the Wellcome Collection and when shown on loan at the National Gallery in 2010, they received many appreciative newspaper and magazine reviews, calling for more published information on the artist.[5] [4a & 4b]

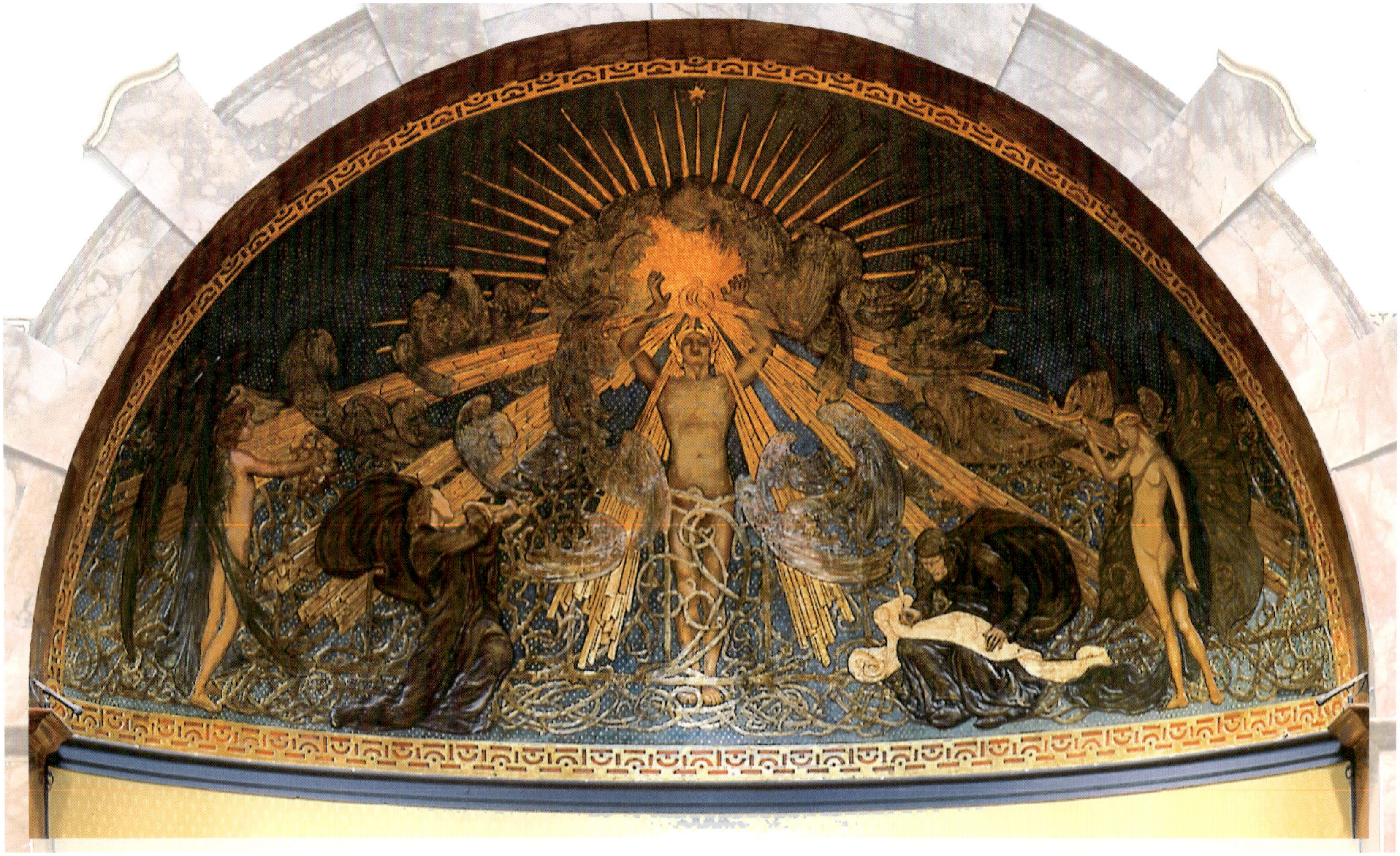

5 Gerald Moira and F. Lynn Jenkins, *The Spirit of Harmony* over the stage of the Wigmore Hall, 1900, courtesy of Wigmore Hall

A minor problem exists in defining murals. There is a general understanding of what the word means, but the boundaries are harder to fix. Mosaic pictures, decorative tiles and sculptural reliefs are usually excluded, but a painted relief, such as Gerald Moira and F. Lynn Jenkins' *The Spirit of Harmony* over the stage of the Wigmore Hall, made in 1900, is harder to determine. [5] Does the work need to be integral with the wall, like a fresco or other painting applied directly to the plaster, brick or concrete, or does it include a canvas stuck on, or a panel lightly fixed, as in the case of Cayley Robinson's work? The tendency is to include all of these. In terms of artistic content, a mural can range from a frivolous bathroom to a chapel. In style, it can cover the most traditional and academic to pure abstraction, with everything in between. For the present purpose, we are confining murals to work made with paint, but this does not close the debate. The most general definition would be that the work was made for a particular place ('site specific') even if it is no longer in that place, and this covers a wide spectrum of media.

The idea of the mural in modern British art

In the history of mural painting, there is no absolute starting point. Medieval buildings were covered in coloured imagery, painted either onto plaster, which was universal in churches or in the form of painted cloth hangings for domestic spaces. Tapestries played a similar role as a high-value form of portable decoration for secular spaces that also helped rooms to retain heat, although we tend only now to see these buildings with bare stone walls. Painting chapels, rooms and ceilings was seen as a natural role for art in the Renaissance and the fact that this way of working, in addition to more constrained altar pieces and panels, brought out the talents of some of the greatest artists, including Michelangelo, Raphael and Leonardo, was a powerful inducement to later campaigns for restoring the scale and prestige of painting in this way.

In England, the full force of European baroque arrived when Rubens painted the panels in the ceiling of Inigo Jones's Banqueting House, Whitehall, between 1619 and 1622, demonstrating that the greatest talents can be applied to site-specific work. Later in the century, Sir James Thornhill developed a robust home-grown baroque style at St Paul's Cathedral and Greenwich, although commissions for country house or London staircases over the next century tended to go to Italian artists. James Barry's neo-classical paintings at the Royal Society of Arts of 1777 indicate the beginning of a new seriousness about mural painting, which in Barry and, in the next generation, Benjamin Robert Haydon, amounted to a form of mania.[6]

The fire in the Palace of Westminster in 1835 and the need to rebuild the Houses of Parliament marked a new stage in earnestness about mural painting as a proper way of representing the nation's history and values, while elevating the skills of its artists and bringing completeness to a building already rich in symbolism.[7] The new seriousness of intention was hard to sustain and has remained a challenge. When cartoons submitted by artists for the competition to decorate the new building were displayed in 1843, the word was subverted by John Leech in *Punch* magazine and applied to scenes of modern life that were anything but heroic.[8]

Viewing the past as a challenge and a standard for emulation, later mural painters fell easily into reworking historical styles and subjects that also suited their patrons. Stanley Spencer remarked when awarded the commission for the Sandham Memorial Chapel at Burghclere, 'What ho, Giotto!'[9] His work there, which resembles Giotto's chiefly in the creation of an intimate space with paintings on three sides like the Arena Chapel in Padua, lacks nothing in originality and emotional depth. The pleasure that drives artists to mural painting, despite the many disadvantages of the task, could be related to the enhanced sense of power over space that it can bestow, as reflected in the almost pathological mural painting of the character Gulley Jimson, sometimes supposed to be modeled on Spencer, in Joyce Cary's novel, *The Horse's Mouth*, 1944. Murals can also offer opportunities for collaboration between artists working side-by-side or in the relationship of master and assistant, unlike the solitude of the studio.

The urges of individual artists existed in a wider context and one must ask what other purposes murals served and who else was involved? If murals were the answer, what was the question? Various possibilities are considered here, coming from the individual artist or representatives of the artistic community, from the architect of a new building, from an interior decorator, and from a client or patron, whether corporate or personal. These factors often overlapped, but they help in understanding the many motives behind mural painting.

Decorative and Mural painting – education and civic ideals

However much artists looked back in time, those with a social mission were engaged in the present. After work at the Palace of Westminster faltered in the 1860s, relatively few murals were attempted in public buildings, the most notable being Ford Madox Brown's in Manchester Town Hall (1879-93), the product of his later years. The idea of mural painting was carried forward by the Arts and Crafts Exhibition Society, established in 1888 as part of a continuing reaction against the exclusiveness of the Royal Academy, which called for an artistic and social revival through varied forms of decorative practice, largely inspired by John Ruskin's social and spiritual ideals among which the nobility of mural painting was included.[10]

The Arts and Crafts movement was dedicated to breaking down the distinction between fine and decorative arts, demystifying painting and at the same time raising other forms of practice. In France the term 'Decorative Painting' developed in the years of the Third Republic after 1871. It remains, as Nicholas Watkins wrote in 2001, 'one of the most important but least understood issues in late nineteenth- and early twentieth-century art. It is an area fraught with contradictions and misunderstandings, particularly for an English-speaking audience.'[11] In French terms, a 'décoration' carried all the weight of 'history painting' on a grand scale, while also encompassing both the conservative and the avant-garde. The word implied a consciously designed painting, whose structure tended towards a shallow pictorial space with figures arranged as a frieze. Thus while these figures could be a continuation of the Renaissance tradition, the term developed in the 1880s to include those artists, especially of the Nabis group, who were moving towards abstraction. Maurice Denis, one of the leaders of the 'Decorative' movement, famously wrote in 1890, 'Remember that a painting – before it is a battle horse, a nude model, or some anecdote – is essentially a flat surface covered with colours assembled in a certain order.'[12] Jan Verkade, a minor member of the Nabis, recalled the mood of the 1890s in his memoirs, writing that they believed, 'there are no paintings, but only decorations.'[13]

The word Decorative thus potentially includes all murals within its scope, while also covering a category of paintings with common properties that were conceived in the same spirit as murals without being destined for a particular place. It also covers, especially in its English usage, the lightweight and frivolous, whether or not applied directly to walls. Through the range of meanings in the word, we can understand the wide variety of style and intention within the canon of murals. In the time that they were working, as Morna O'Neill writes, decorative was 'a word that could be applied equally to James McNeill Whistler's tonal nocturnes and to the political allegories of [Walter] Crane.'[14] While the Aesthetic Movement is sometimes thought to have turned away from public engagement, many painters linked to it desired to exercise their skill for the benefit of an audience that might never step inside an art gallery. G. F. Watts hoped to paint *The Progress of Cosmos* in the ticket hall of Euston Station, while Burne-Jones, whose only actual mural was at the beginning of his career, in the Oxford Union, still dreamed of 'big things to do and vast spaces, and for common people to see them and Oh! – only Oh!'[15] Leighton carried his enthusiasm for murals forward from his lunettes in the Victoria and Albert Museum in the 1870s to his leadership of the cycle of historical murals in the Royal Exchange, which started in 1894. He also encouraged the adoption of murals as a training method in art schools, valuing the demands they imposed on skills of drawing, organization, and the ideal of social service they implied.

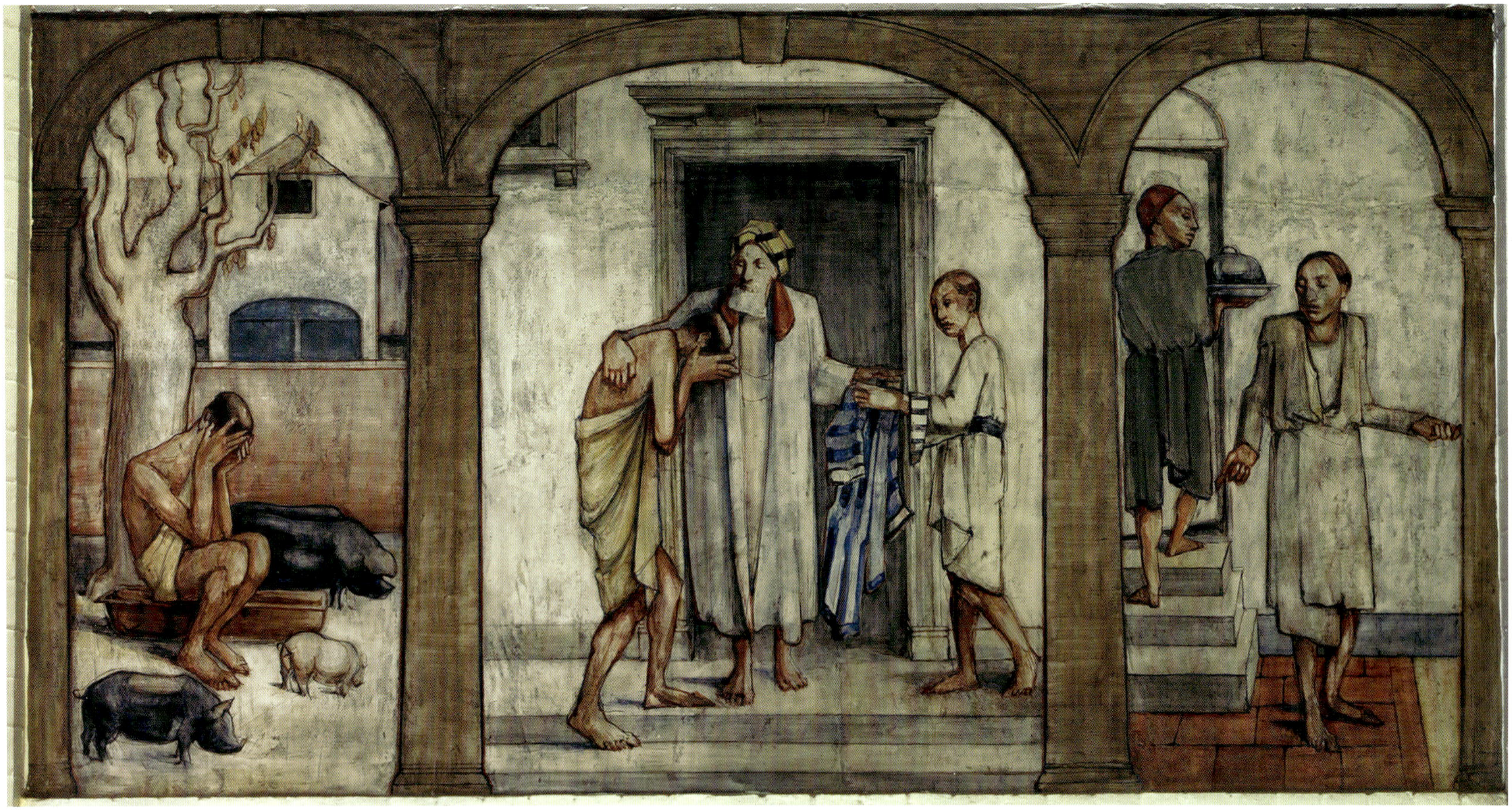

6a Mary Creighton, *The Prodigal Son*, panel from mural cycle in fresco with Mary Sargant-Florence at Bournville Junior School, Birmingham, c. 1914

Edward Armitage, lecturing to Royal Academy students, described Decorative painting as 'moral figure painting' but failed to give much more weight to this idea.[16] Nonetheless, it grew and developed into the twentieth century becoming in Morna O'Neill's words, a 'political theory of decoration' in the Edwardian period, in which the decorative was 'a cultural product that represented a collective impulse and a civic ideal.'[17] It was a time of transition and readjustment, with a shift in the global economic order that threatened to detach art from society, despite the efforts of the previous generation to link them. This situation stimulated a renewed public role for art, with a search for appropriate content and form that could lead in conservative and modernist directions that initially were almost indistinguishable from one another.

Because the style and aims of mural and decorative painting were continuous with each other, the reformed Royal College of Art in 1900 coupled them together, offering 'Mural and Decorative Painting' as its only painting course. The title carried the message that this state-funded school considered that this conjunction of mural and decorative implied a higher form of art than ordinary painting. The principal of the College from 1919, Sir William Rothenstein, proclaimed his support for murals as Professor of Civic Art at Sheffield in 1916, and continued to value the link that murals made between art and society. Appealing for public support of

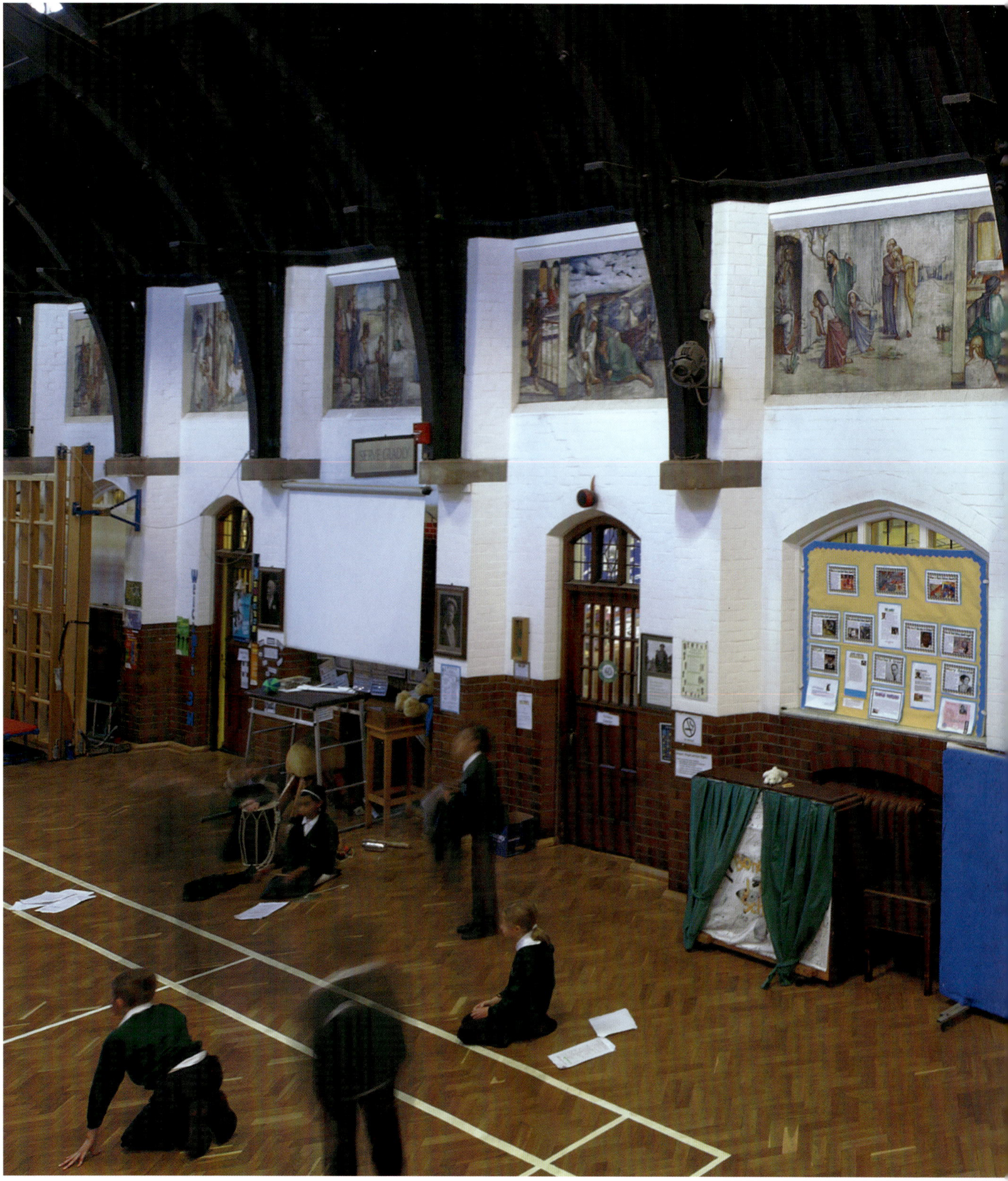

6b
Mary Sargant-Florence
and Mary Creighton,
mural cycle in fresco at Bournville
Junior School, Birmingham,
c. 1914

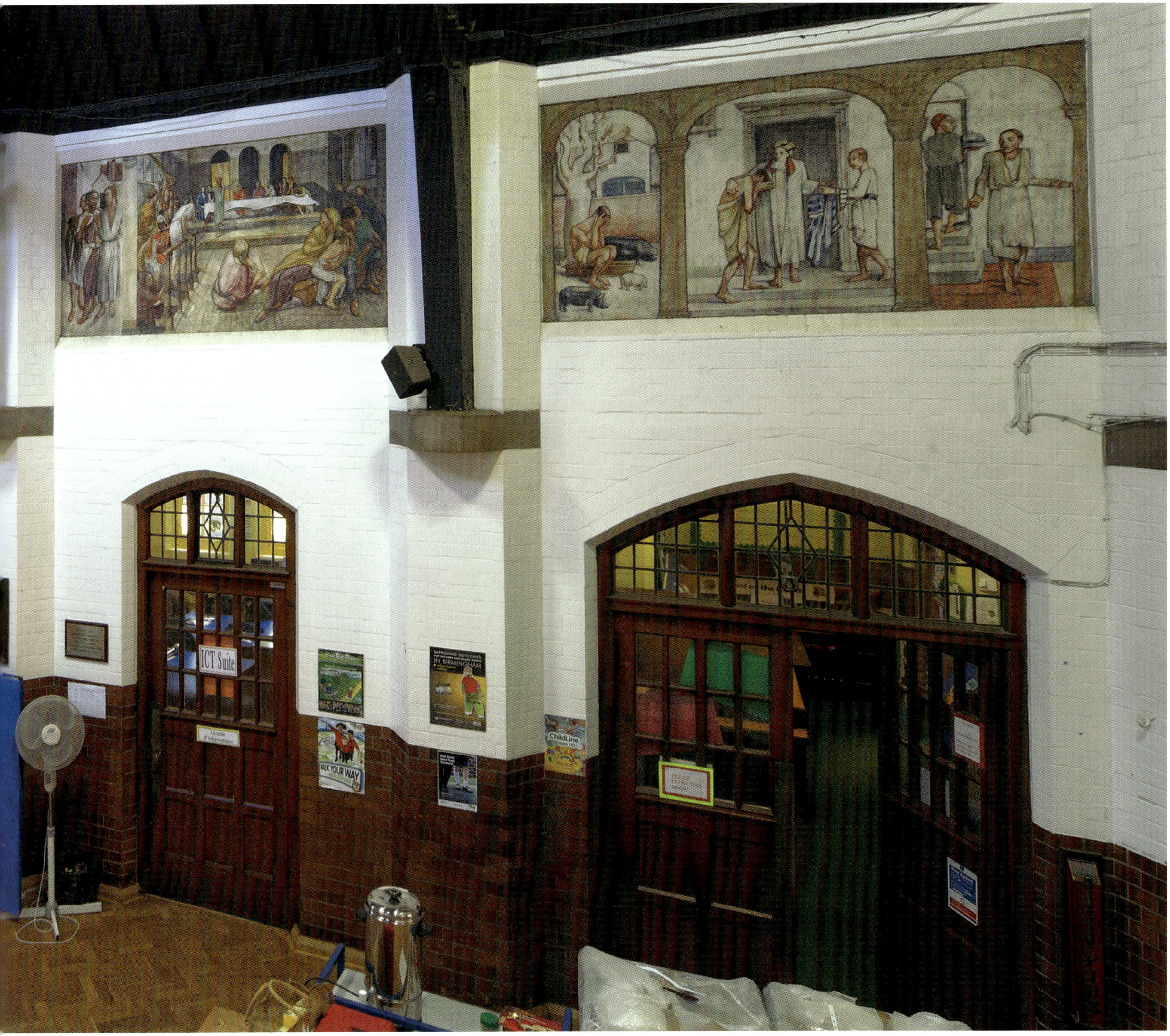
ICT Suite
WALK YOUR WAY
IN BIRMINGHAM
ChildLine

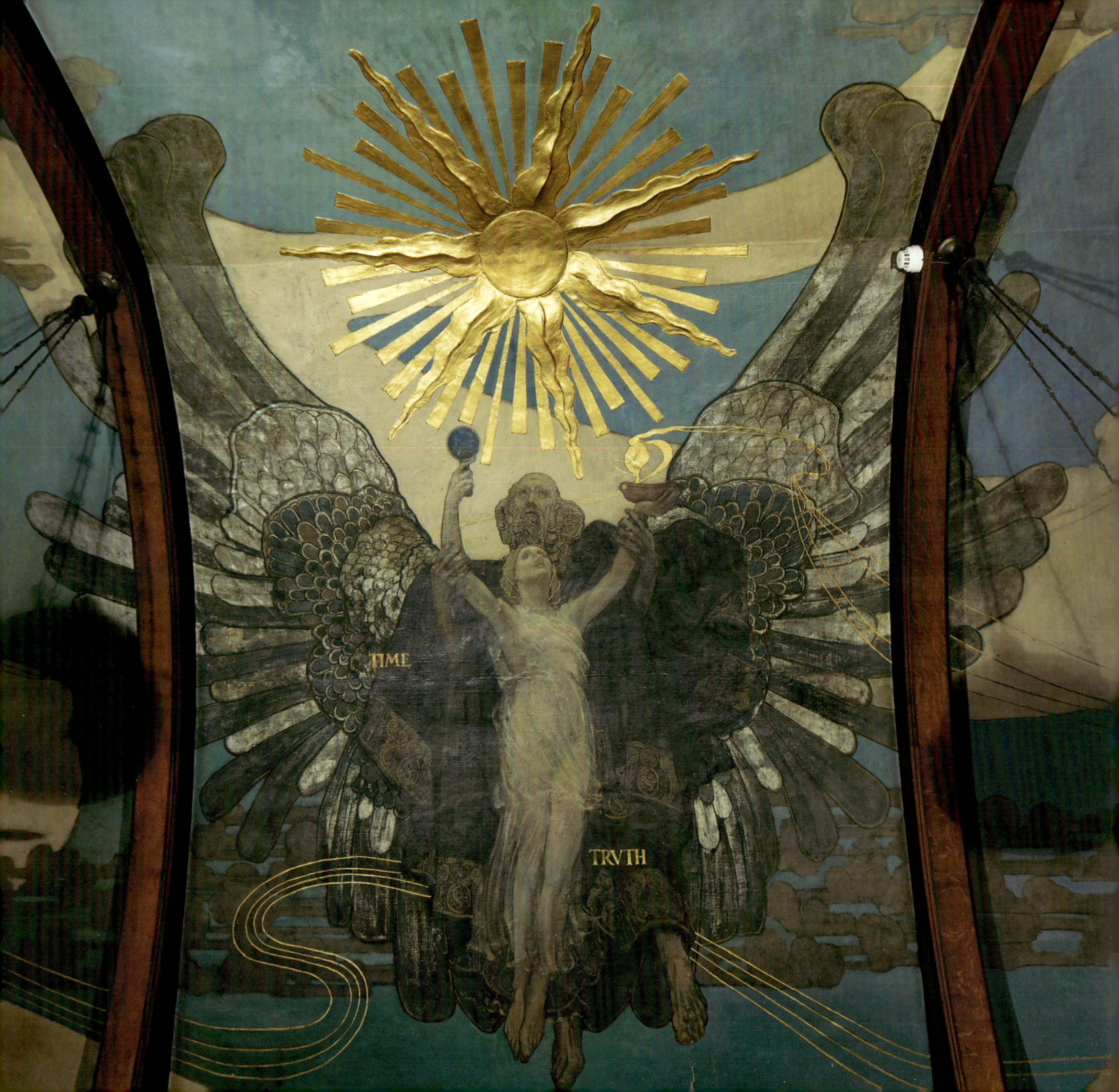
TIME
TRVTH

mural painting in 1933, he explained that 'painters and sculptors were ashamed of being dependent on rich people, and they felt that somehow their services to the community should be other than that of parasites.'[18]

For all the promotion of Decorative Painting, the definition remained more a convention of art school practice than a familiar or well-understood term. In his book, *Modern Mural Decoration*, 1902, A. Lys Baldry deplored the 'misapplication of the term "decorative," which mars so much of present-day criticism.'[19] The solution, he argued, required that pleasing the public with anecdotal subjects (as he believed most of the Royal Exchange artists had done) should give way to more exacting principles. When Walter Bayes, an artist and educator, published *The Art of Decorative Painting* in 1927, he failed to reach a clear definition, considering fitness the key word, whether in terms of location or audience, with an additional quality of self control, intellectual awareness and application of appropriate technique.[20]

Murals acquired particular prominence in the culminating stages of the Arts and Crafts Movement, within whose outlook their moral and social role could be seen as a counterbalance to increasingly mechanized and dehumanizing trend of modern life. Additionally, murals were a fertile field for the reconstruction of lost techniques. Arts and Crafts Movement artists used texts of Cennino Cennini for research into ancient pigments, binders and supports for painting.[21] Conventional oil painting was considered unsuitable for murals because of the reflections from the surface and many artists deserted it entirely. Thomas Gambier-Parry's 'Spirit Fresco' was an alternative medium favoured in the nineteenth century but by 1900 some artists, finding this a particularly damaging misnomer, wanted to rediscover the technique of genuine fresco – painted in pure pigment on wet lime plaster that had long been considered a sort of unattainable Holy Grail owing to the many failures experienced in its use from the Palace of Westminster onwards. Its priestess in the early 1900s was the energetic and rather eccentric artist Mary Sargant-Florence, whose mural cycle at Oakham School, followed by another at Bournville School, showed how it could be done properly.[22] [6a & 6b] She wrote eloquently of the liberation to be enjoyed by the fluidity of the medium and its brightness and purity of colour.[23]

Egg tempera, the other technique associated with the early Renaissance, was valued for purity of colour and matt surface, although it was difficult to use on a large scale. Some modern artists in the 1920s and 30s, notably Edward Wadsworth and Augustus Lunn, used these techniques for modernist subject matter. The alliance of these activities was represented in the addition of 'Mural Decorators' to the Society of Painters in Tempera.[24]

The first Professor of Mural and Decorative Painting at the RCA, Gerald Moira, was active as a member of the Art Workers Guild and embodied the idea of collaboration with work in the Trocadero Restaurant and Wigmore Hall, both works painted in relief with the sculptor F. Lynn Jenkins and commissioned by the architect T. E. Collcutt. Perhaps his most original work is his least known, the ceiling in the Library of the Unitarian Church in Ullet Road, Liverpool, a Symbolist work showing *Truth Uplifted by Time*, in which the great thinkers of all ages were shown receiving golden rays of inspiration from the lamp of truth.[25] [7]

7
Gerald Moira,
Truth Uplifted by Time,
ceiling in the Library of the Unitarian Church in Ullet Road, Liverpool,
1902

Unitarians were representative of the kind of civic leaders, often linked by dynastic connections, who helped to create a new feeling about the future around 1900. They were active in health and social reform, and in many cities they took pride in supporting new public buildings with appropriate decoration. The Birmington painter Joseph Southall, a Quaker, taught in the municipal art school. He was commissioned to fill a panel in fresco at the head of the stairs in the Birmingham Art Gallery, and his painting *Corporation Street, Birmingham in March 1914* is a rare example of the historic technique being used for a modern life subject. Working after the outbreak of the First World War, Southall painted recognizable people involved locally in the arts, as a form of quiet protest against the effects of the war on this hopeful moment.[26] [8]

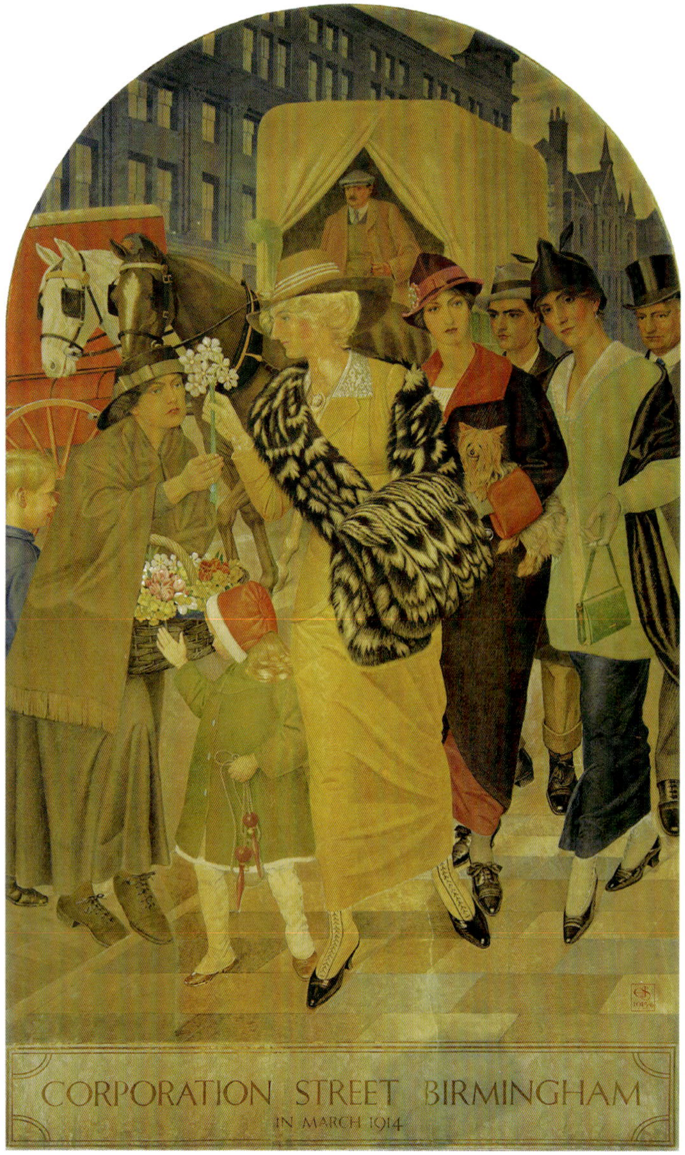

8 Joseph Southall, *Corporation Street, Birmingham in March 1914*, Museum and Art Gallery, Birmingham

In the first three decades of the century, the Slade School of Art in London outshone its rivals under the direction of Henry Tonks and nurtured a remarkable group of young artists working in a 'decorative' manner. Stanley Spencer is the most famous of these, but work by his contemporaries is not so much influenced by him as a growth from a common stem. Slade students competed for an annual 'Summer Composition' prize, of which Spencer was a winner in 1912 with a most unusual treatment of the set subject, 'The Nativity' [9] in an outdoor summer setting. Other Summer Compositions, like William Orpen's *Play Scene from Hamlet*, 1899, similarly take liberties with their subject matter, as if this were almost a way of teasing the viewer, a feature found among many of the narrative artists working well into the second half of the century.

Arts and Crafts ideals, reinterpreted in classical terms, inspired the Rome Scholarship in Decorative Painting in 1912, one of a trio of awards for painting, architecture and sculpture that were offered in imitation of the French Academy in Rome, with the intention that young artists could thereby be groomed for public commissions in which they would instinctively wish to collaborate. The first painting scholar was Colin Gill, a student from the Slade, which between the wars competed with the Royal College in putting forward their top students. Gill fulfilled the expectation of the award by contributing to St Stephen's Hall and other public schemes,

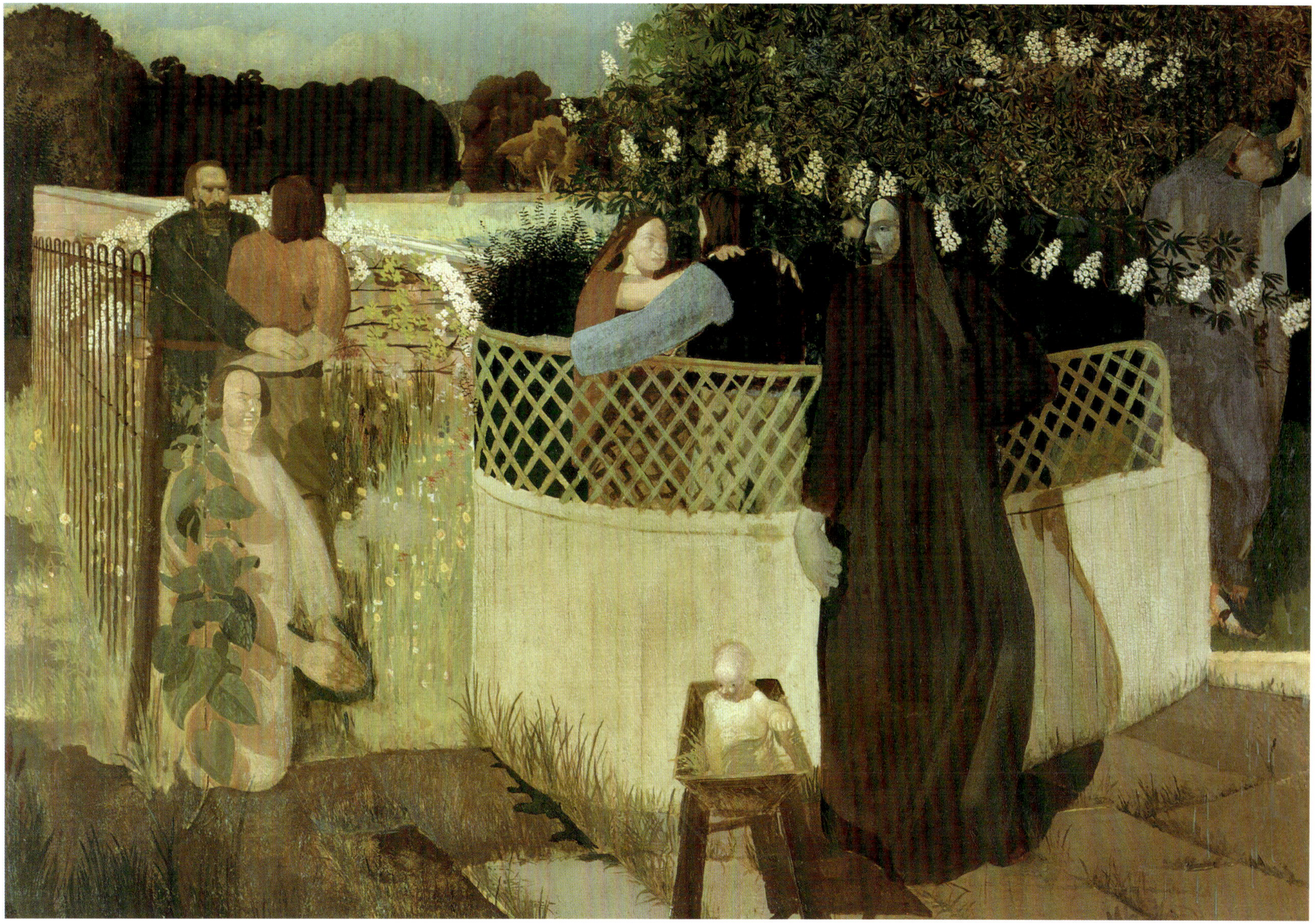

9 Stanley Spencer, *The Nativity,* 1912, oil on canvas stuck onto plywood panel, 101.2 x 152.4 cm (39 ⅞ x 60 in.)

although he never recaptured the frozen lyricism of his *Allegro*, taking its name from one of a pair of poems by John Milton, but far from being a literal illustration, was painted as the final submission at the end of the scholarship in 1921. (see pages 138-157) The Rome Scholarship scheme was effective in achieving collaborations as much through the social contacts that were made in Rome as through the rather ill-defined pedagogic programme, although Alan Sorrell (RCA) was one of the few painting scholars who collaborated with an architect scholar on a joint scheme for an imaginary building with murals.

The two or three years before the outbreak of war in 1914 were significant for the outbreak of a native avant-garde in London, consisting of the Omega Workshops, the Vorticists and the Rebel Art Centre. With overlapping and frequently quarrelling personnel, these movements had a shared commitment to using art to create imaginative spaces with bold colours and forms. Sadly almost none of this work remains in its original position, but can still be justly celebrated as an extraordinary if short-lived manifestation of Modernism, arising out of the existing trend towards highly formal and composed paintings which might or might not become murals.[27] [10]

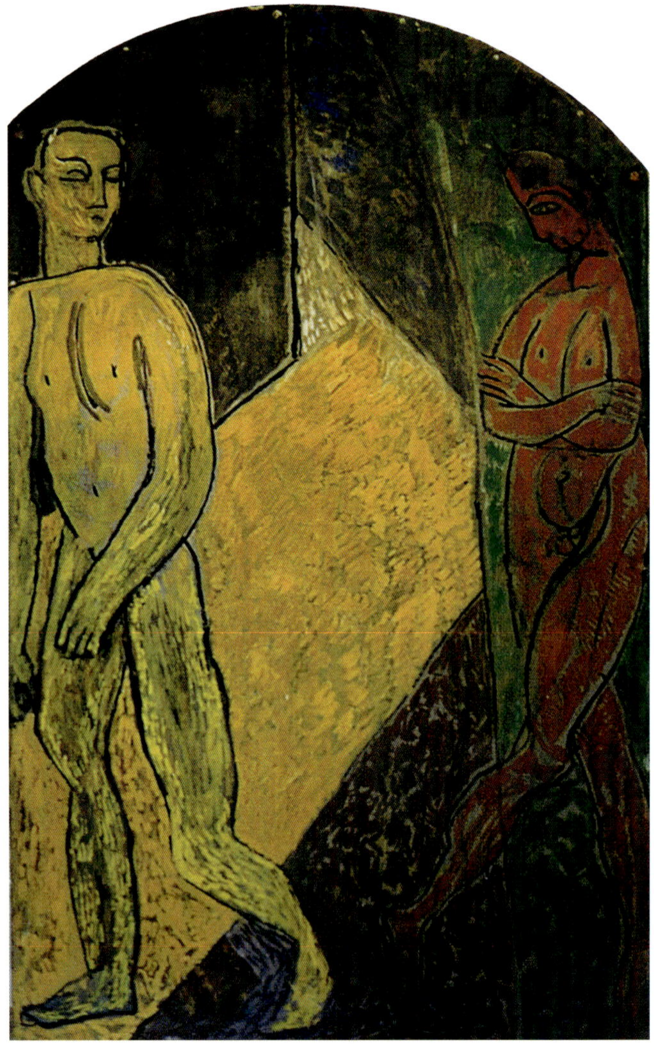

10
Duncan Grant,
painting at Durbins,
Guildford, c. 1911-12

1912 also saw the 'Exhibition of Mural Designs for the Decoration of Schools and other Institutions' organized by Patrick Geddes at Crosby Hall, Chelsea, the medieval relic moved from Bishopsgate to become part of a group of student halls of residence. Geddes invented the term 'Civics' as a branch of study and practice, making his reputation as a thinker and urban activist in Edinburgh Old Town where he inspired mural schemes by Phoebe Traquair and other artists. The *avant-garde* was not represented at Crosby Hall, but prizes were offered for particular commissions, including the Middlesex Hospital and the never-to-be-built Gallery of Modern Art in Dublin sponsored by Sir Hugh Lane, who also commissioned two frieze panels from Augustus John, *Lyric Fantasy* and *Mumpers* for the hall of his house in Chelsea.

During the war, attention was turned again to the civic role of murals by the major exhibition staged at the Royal Academy in 1916 by the Arts and Crafts Exhibition Society, led by the architect Henry Wilson.[28] The upper parts of several gallery spaces were handed over to Maurice Greiffenhagen [11], Charles Sims and others, while the largest gallery was fitted out like a church as 'The Hall of Peace' and Henry Payne, Joseph Southall, Gerald Moira [12] and others referred to the war. The most sensational contribution was Augustus John's vast frieze *Galway* (Tate), while the most peculiar was William Rothenstein's two canvasses showing some of the famous young Oxford and Cambridge graduates killed in the war (Rupert Brooke among them) in a procession with linked hands. Three years later, Rothenstein was appointed as Principal of the Royal College where he continued the mural painting tradition.

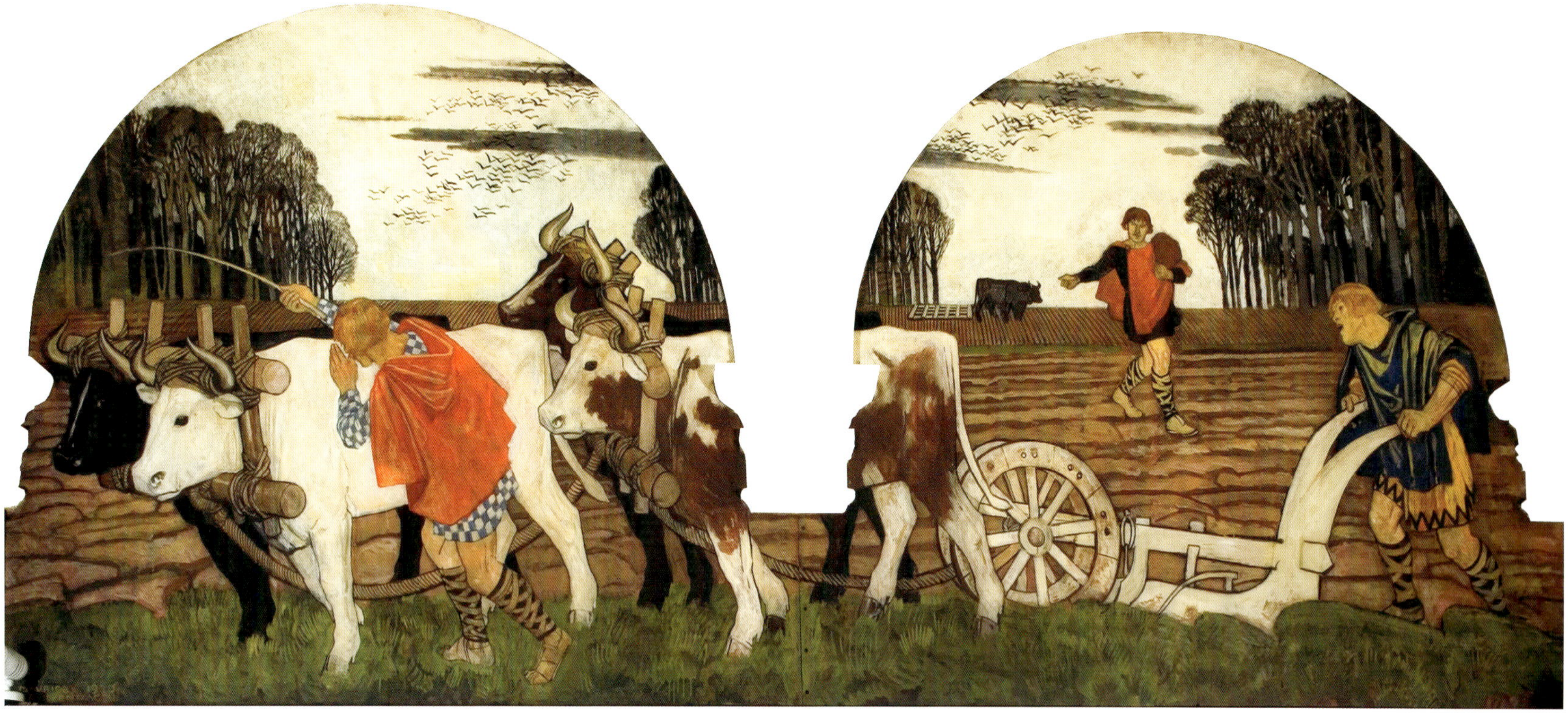

11 Maurice Greiffenhagen, *Ploughing and Sowing in Saxon Times*, one of the panels from the Council Chamber's vaulted ceiling of the Braintree Town Hall, c. 1929-30.

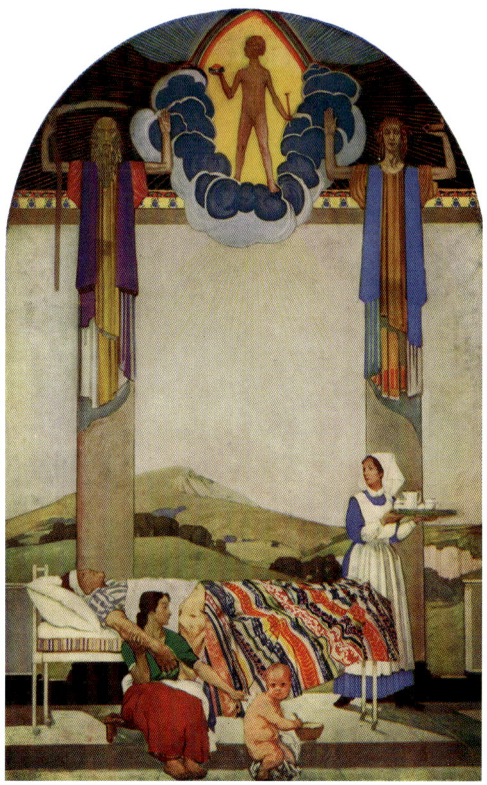

12
Gerald Moira,
A War Allegory, 1916

A number of paintings were made as war memorials, including the Victory Hall at Balcombe, East Sussex by Neville Lytton [13] and the little-known panels at Heanor School, Derbyshire by F. Cayley Robinson. [14] These continued the elegiac feeling of loss and regret conveyed by the 1916 exhibition pieces. Their locations in community buildings were a fulfilment of the idea of murals being an art of the people. The Balcombe scheme was promoted by a local resident, Lady Denman, who in 1915 introduced the Canadian idea of the Women's Institute to Britain, one of its aims being a democratization of art and craft. The artist was a member of the liberal aristocracy and an Olympic bronze medallist in real tennis in 1908. War memorial subjects are otherwise relatively rare in murals, owing perhaps to the preference for sculpture in outdoor locations.

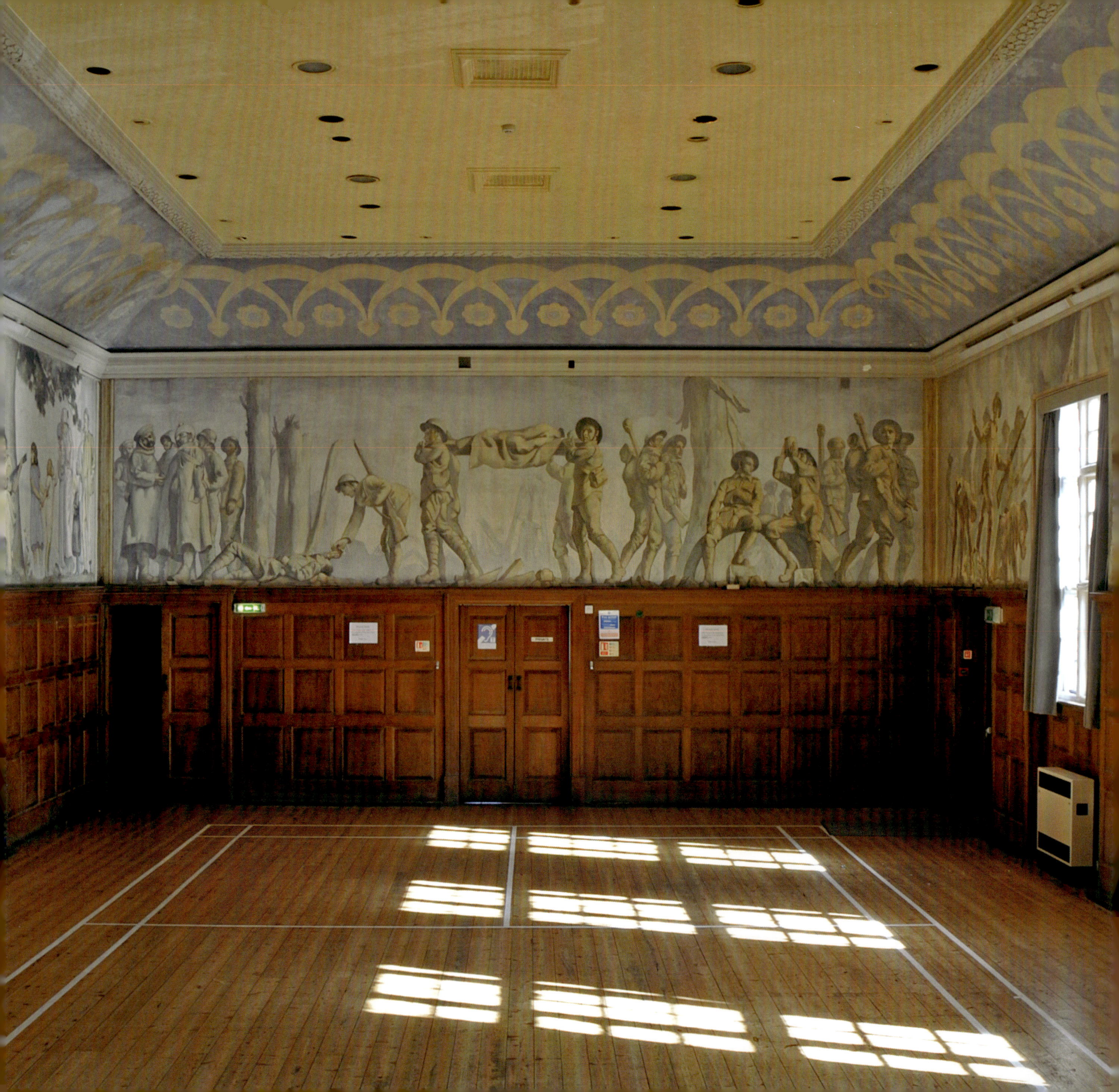

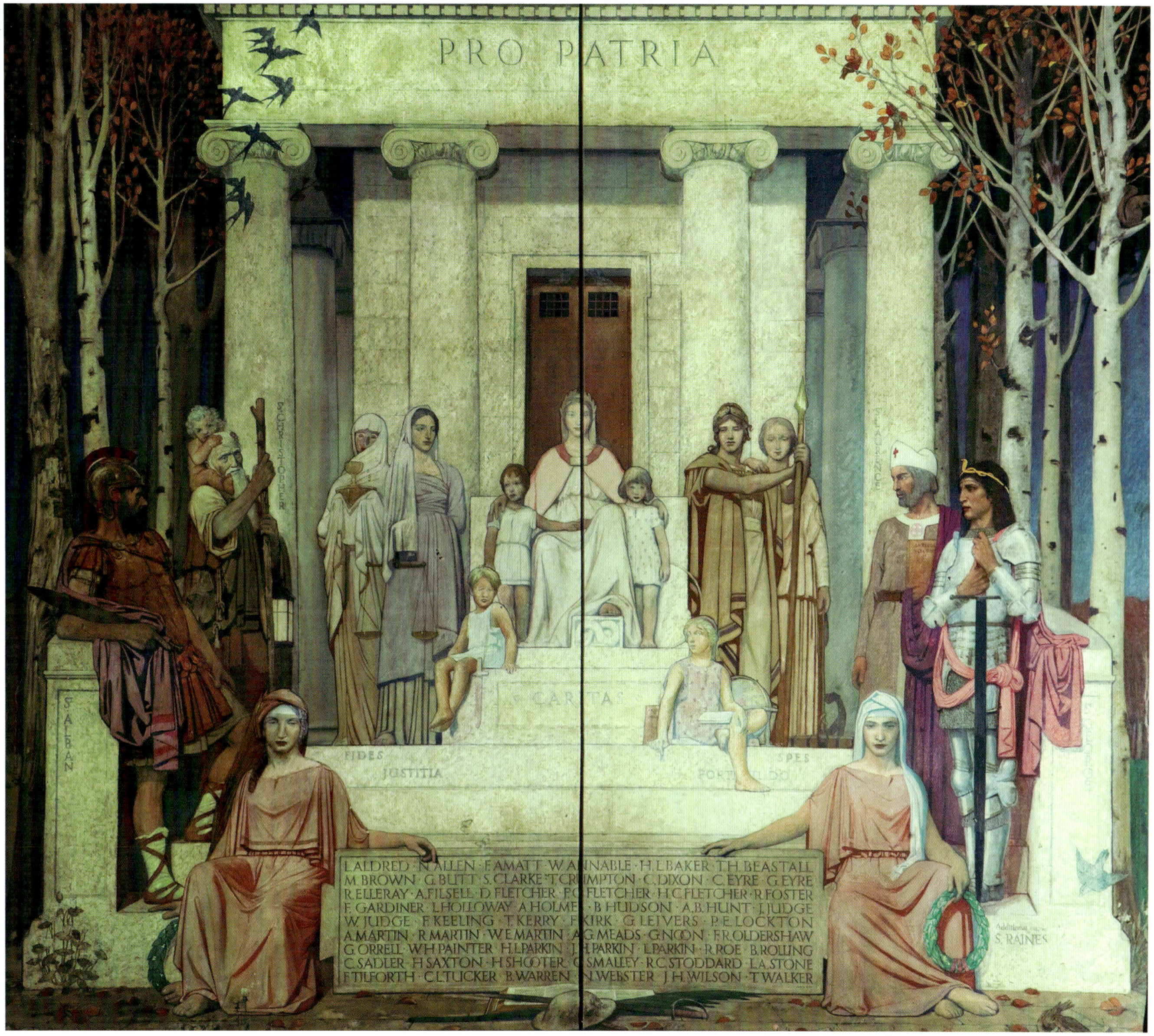

14
Cayley Robinson,
War Memorial, c.1919
tempera on board,
255 x 288 cm
(100 ⅜ x 113 ⅜ in.) (estimated)
Heanor School/ Derby College,
Collection:
Derby College
Public Catalogue Foundation

From village halls and small town schools, murals extended up the scale of national politics to buildings of local and national government such as Braintree Town Hall and Essex County Hall in Chelmsford, both supported by Sir Samuel Courtauld and featuring the work of Rome Scholars A. K. Lawrence and Colin Gill, and St Stephen's Hall, Westminster, where these two artists were also represented. [15]

13
Neville Lytton,
mural cycle for
Victory Hall at
Balcombe, East Sussex,
c. 1923

Everything described up to this point is the background to the period covered in this book. It is important to understand the situation that existed in 1920, however, in order to see that a momentum had been building up from several directions. Despite many setbacks and the severe shortage of money for public projects in the two inter-war decades, the impetus continued. There were also failures during this period. A set of

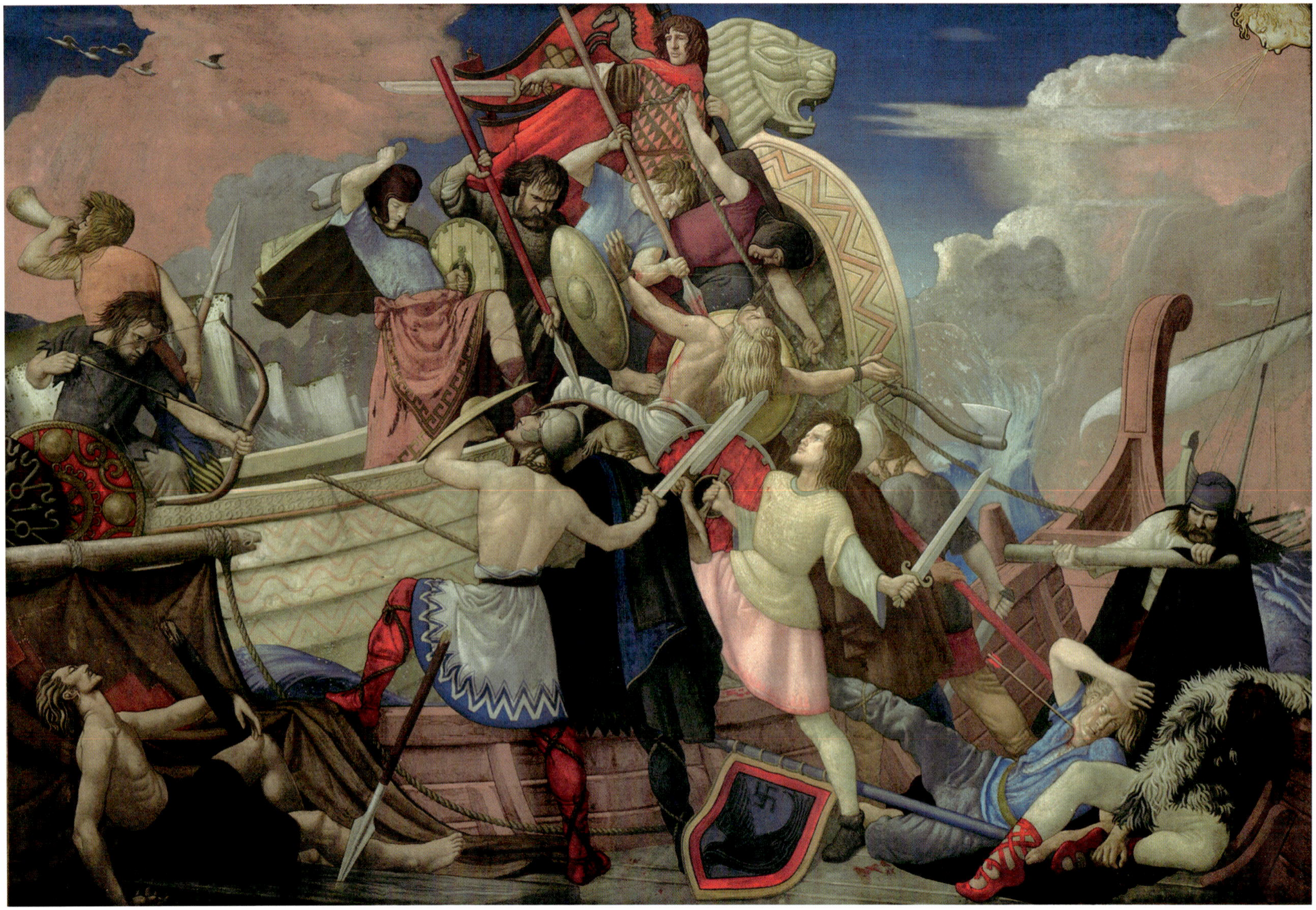

15 Colin Gill, *King Alfred's long-ships defeat the Danes 877*, 1925-27, St Stephen's Hall, Westminster

proposed murals for the LCC County Hall commissioned from students at London art schools in 1921 was never implemented.[29] In the same year, at Leeds, the University Vice-Chancellor, Sir Michael Sadler, instigated a scheme of murals for the Town Hall by artists including Edward Wadsworth, Paul and John Nash, based on local scenery. These were among the few of the period that showed a continuation of pre-war British Modernism, combined in this case with a commentary on the sublime but shocking devastation caused by industry. Given this dual unconventionality, it is not surprising that the project foundered.

Murals had been used to create a more stimulating atmosphere in educational spaces from early in the century, with the scheme led by Roger Fry for the Borough Polytechnic canteen in 1911, another rare case of murals stemming from the avant-garde, even though the treatment of their themes of sports and recreations would have seemed more naïve than shocking.[30] [16] Before the 1930s, there was little possibility for funding murals in schools, although the mural of 1938 by Eve Garnett in the Children's House, Bow was created for a child welfare organization.[31] [17] Art students were encouraged to try their hands on a variety of schemes for mission halls and other socially useful buildings. Thus Rex Whistler's first mural was painted while he was at the Slade for the Highways Club, Shadwell (funded through Eton College) [18], where his fellow student Mary Adshead shared the work with him.[32] This was followed by Whistler's Tate Gallery Restaurant, funded by Lord Duveen at the instigation of Henry Tonks, setting the tone for a new and typically 1920s frivolity and breaking the mould of 'Decorative painting' with its deep landscape setting and small-scale figures. Mary Adshead went on to become one of the most dedicated mural painters into her old age in the 1980s.

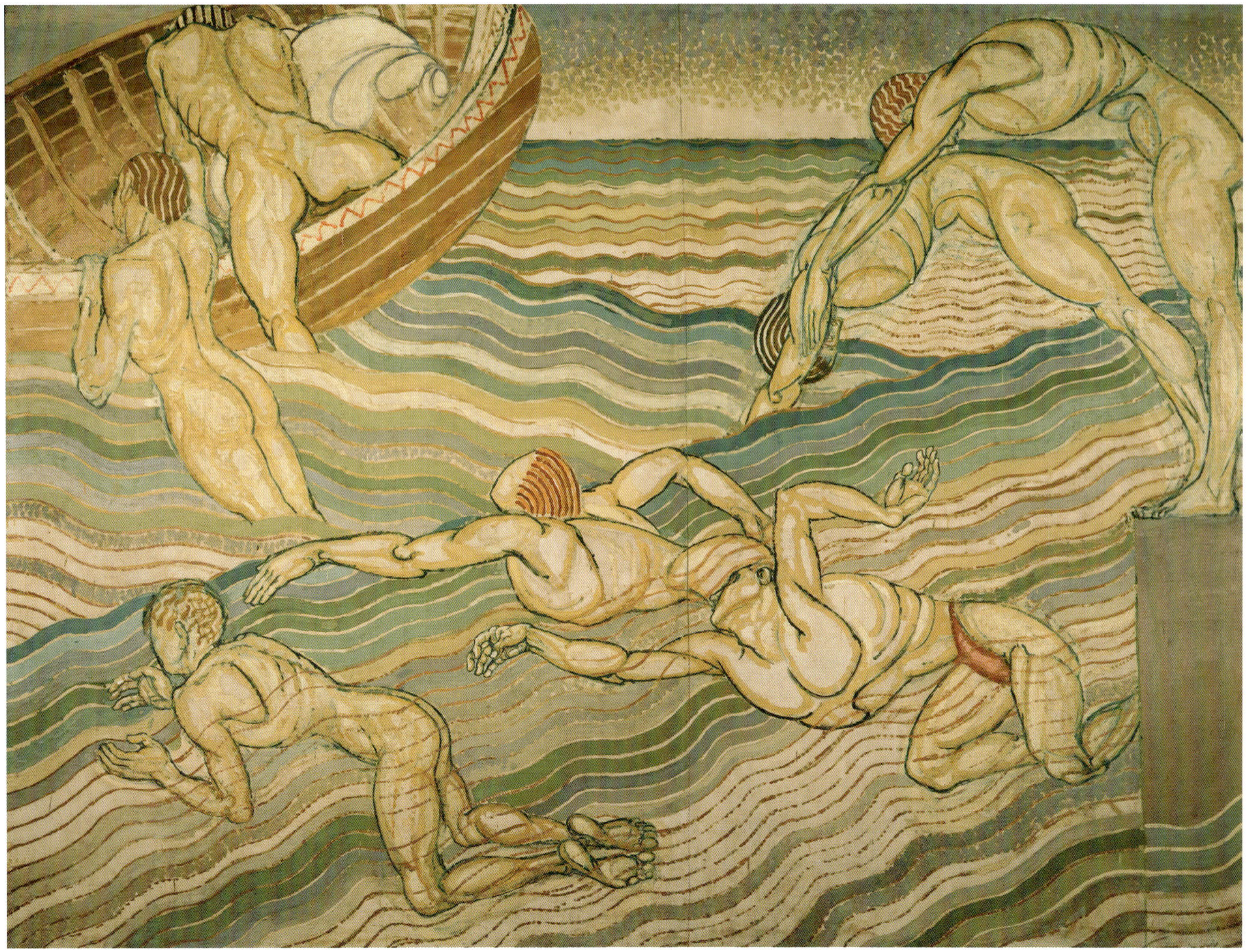

16 Duncan Grant, *Bathing,* 1911, oil on canvas, 228.6 x 306.1 cm (90 x 120 ½ in.) ©Tate, London 2012

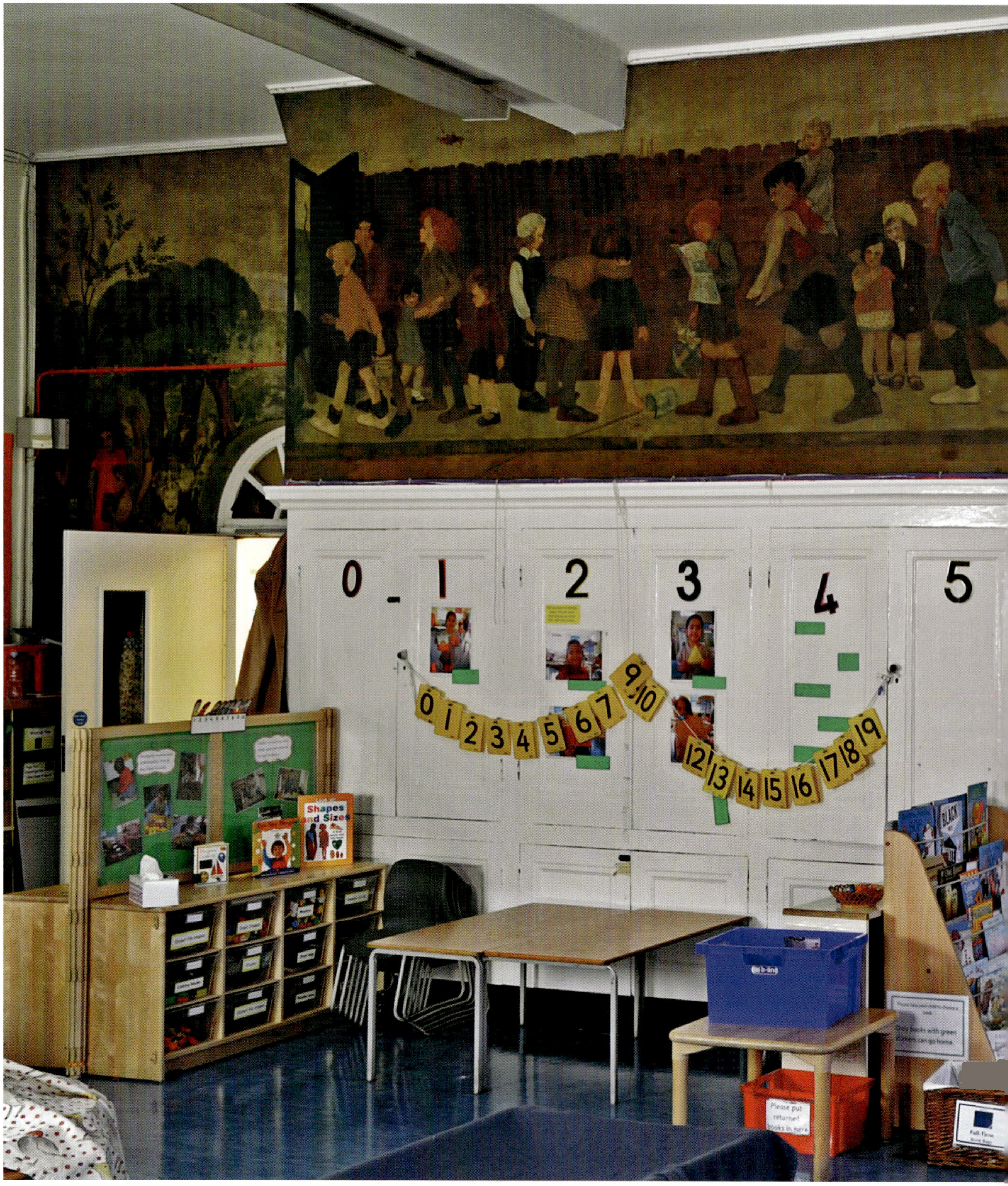

17
Eve Garnett,
murals in the
Children's House, Bow,
1938

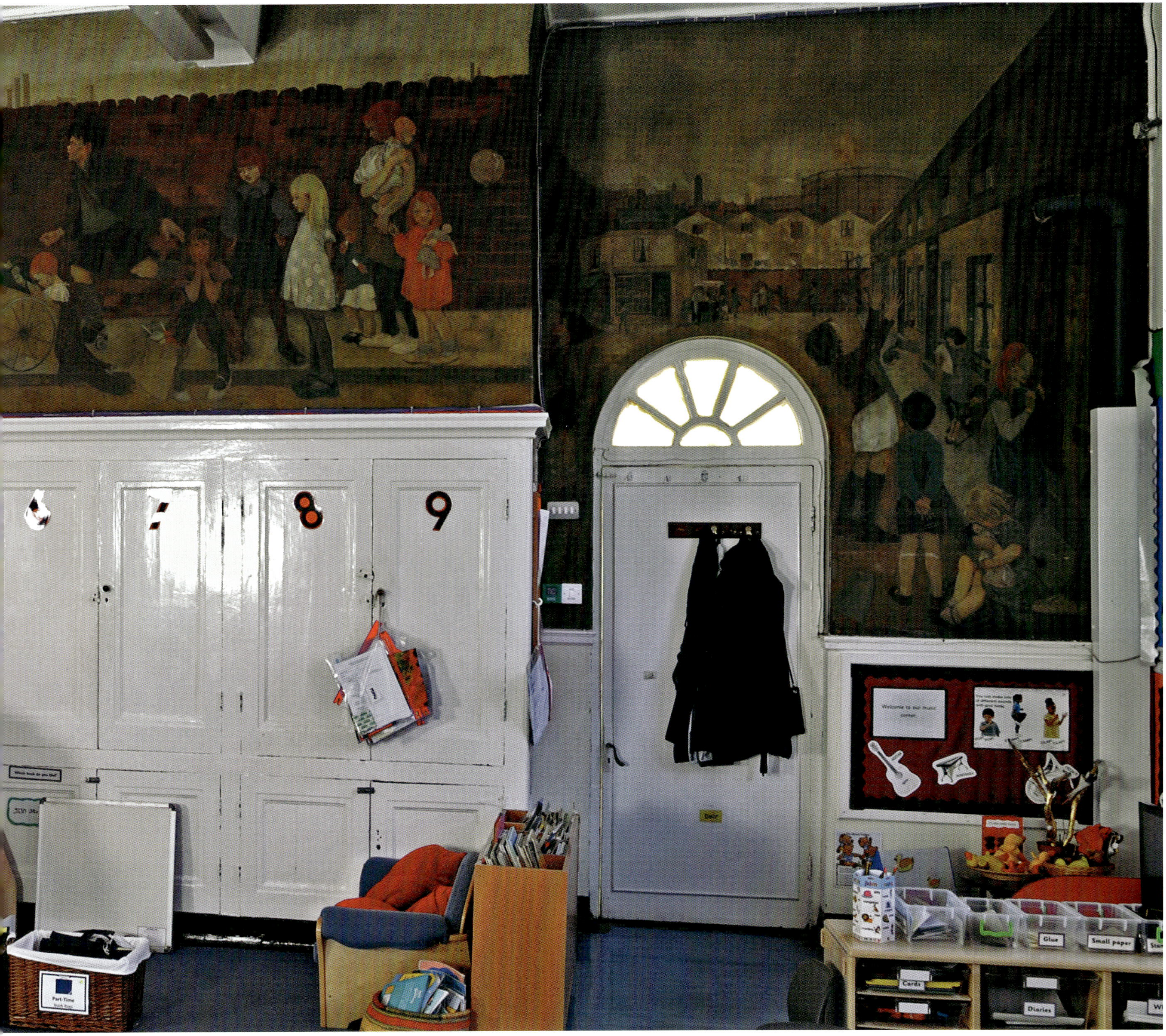
8
9
Door
Glue
Small paper
Cards
Diaries

These schemes were forerunners to the Morley College murals of 1928-30, painted in the famous adult education institute in Lambeth by artists selected from recent RCA students by a committee that included William Rothenstein. The Refreshment Room walls, painted direct on the plaster by Eric Ravilious and Edward Bawden, [19 & 20] remain the most famous despite being destroyed by a bomb in 1940. The subjects were deliberately light-hearted in order to cheer up the students who in most cases came to evening classes after a day's work. Ravilious made mural painting his special subject for the RCA Diploma in 1925, and both he and Bawden went on to paint more examples, including, in Bawden's case, the *Canterbury Tales* murals which replaced the bombed ones in the 1950s and can still be seen in the canteen. The lunette over the stage in the theatre by Charles Mahoney, a gentle pastoral that some critics preferred at the time, tends to be overlooked by posterity, but was the first of Mahoney's distinguished series of murals.[33] [21] These murals were opened by the former and future Prime Minister, Stanley Baldwin and widely reported in the press.

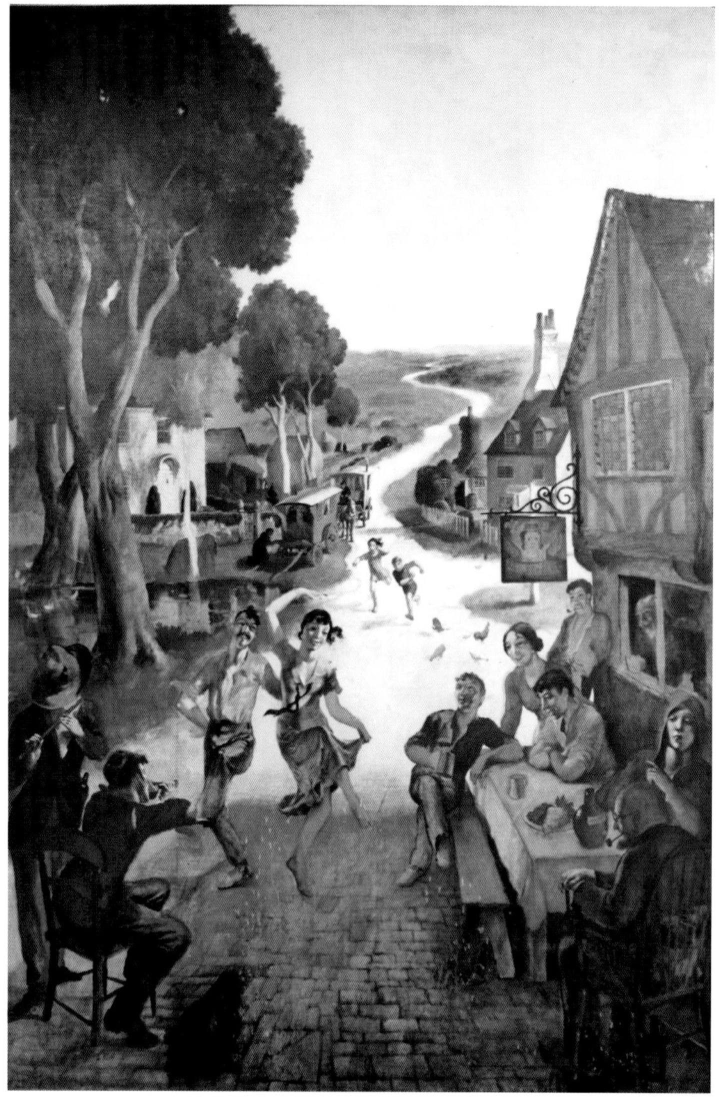

18
Rex Whistler,
Rustic Scene: Villagers Dancing,
1925,
oil on canvas, 332 x 227 cm
(130 ¾ x 89 ⅜ in.),
painting from Highways Club, Shadwell
(Slade Collection, UCL)

Rothenstein kept looking for opportunities for his students to repeat this triumph. In 1930, Robert Baker and Edward Payne were offered the village hall at Woodgreen in Hampshire, where they painted local people involved in their daily work. [22] This project, funded by a Liberal politician Vaughan Nash, was in line with ideas of the special value of rural life at the time. These paintings are well preserved and cherished. Baker was given another commission, instigated by the powerful political insider Thomas Jones, for murals and a set of detached panel paintings at the Welsh working men's college, Coleg Harlech.[34] Here, although the paintings survive, the room they are in is crowded with furniture and the paintings almost inaccessible, while the series of framed paintings depicting a young Welsh miner preparing to leave home and arriving to study at the college, unrecorded in any accessible photographs, are no longer in the building but kept in storage. The third commission was Brockley School (now Prendergast School) in Lewisham, where the headmaster was inspired by a broadcast by Rothenstein to make an offer. Charles Mahoney led a team consisting of Evelyn Dunbar, Mildred Eldridge and Violet Martin. These murals were the reason for listing the building in 1992. [23]

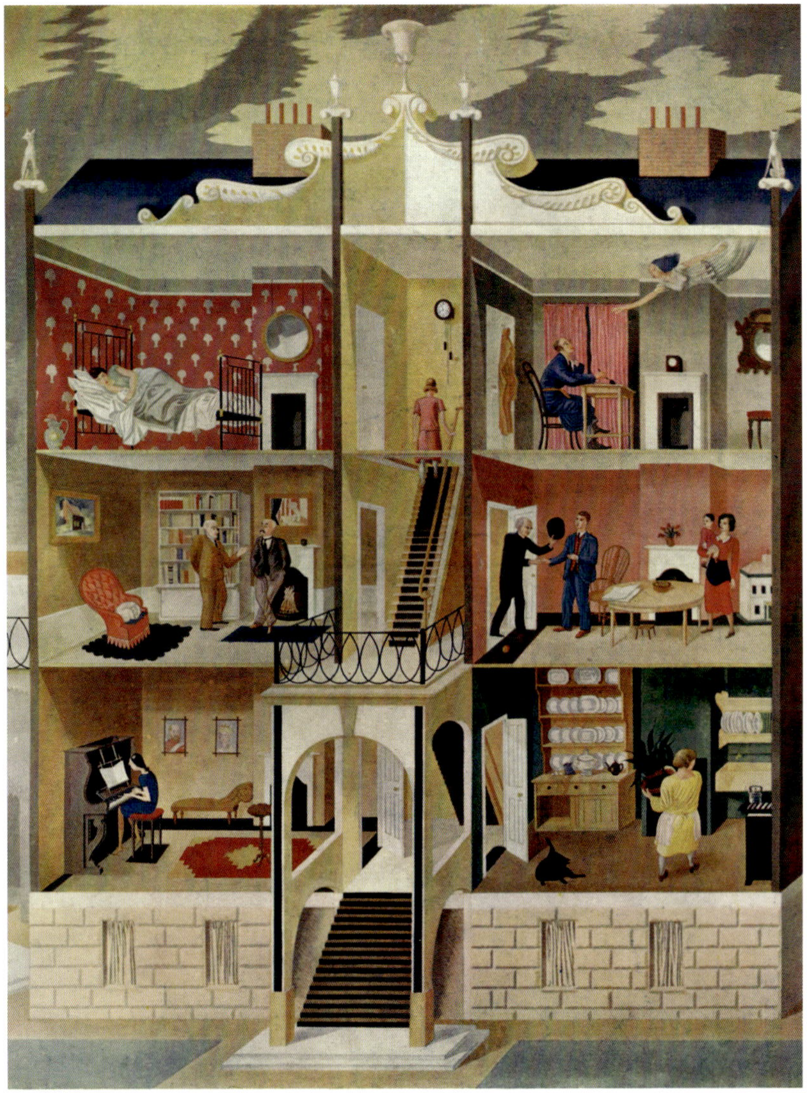

19 Eric Ravilious, *Doll's House* from Morley College, Lambeth, 1928-30. Destroyed in 1940

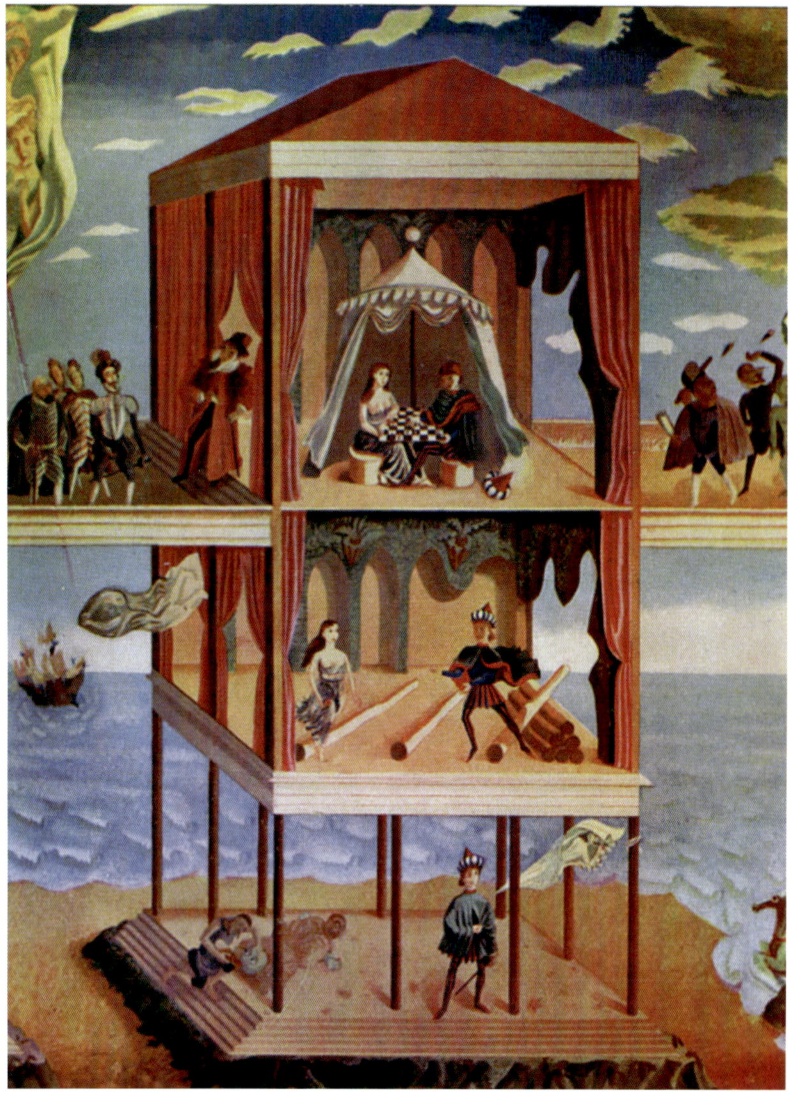

20 Edward Bawden, *The Tempest* from Morley College, Lambeth, 1928-30. Destroyed in 1940.

Compared to mainland Europe, there was a lack of theoretical or political thinking about murals during this time. In France and Italy, by contrast, as described by Romy Golan in *Muralnomad* (2009), a much greater significance was attributed to the activity as a representation of national values and as an alternative to conventional art forms, especially in relation to a division between artistic concepts of north and south, and the role of murals in state buildings and exhibitions under Mussolini. Social changes in the eighteenth and nineteenth centuries shifted patronage away from church, state and aristocracy towards a market in paintings sold at exhibitions. This was seen as a threat to the integrity of the artist and a temptation to trivialize his work for financial gain. Some artists resisted by developing difficult and unconventional subjects and styles that we recognize as modernist, but the decorative painting movement managed to include the most avant-garde as well as the most conservative in an attempt to recover the social significance of art and its role in creating an immersive

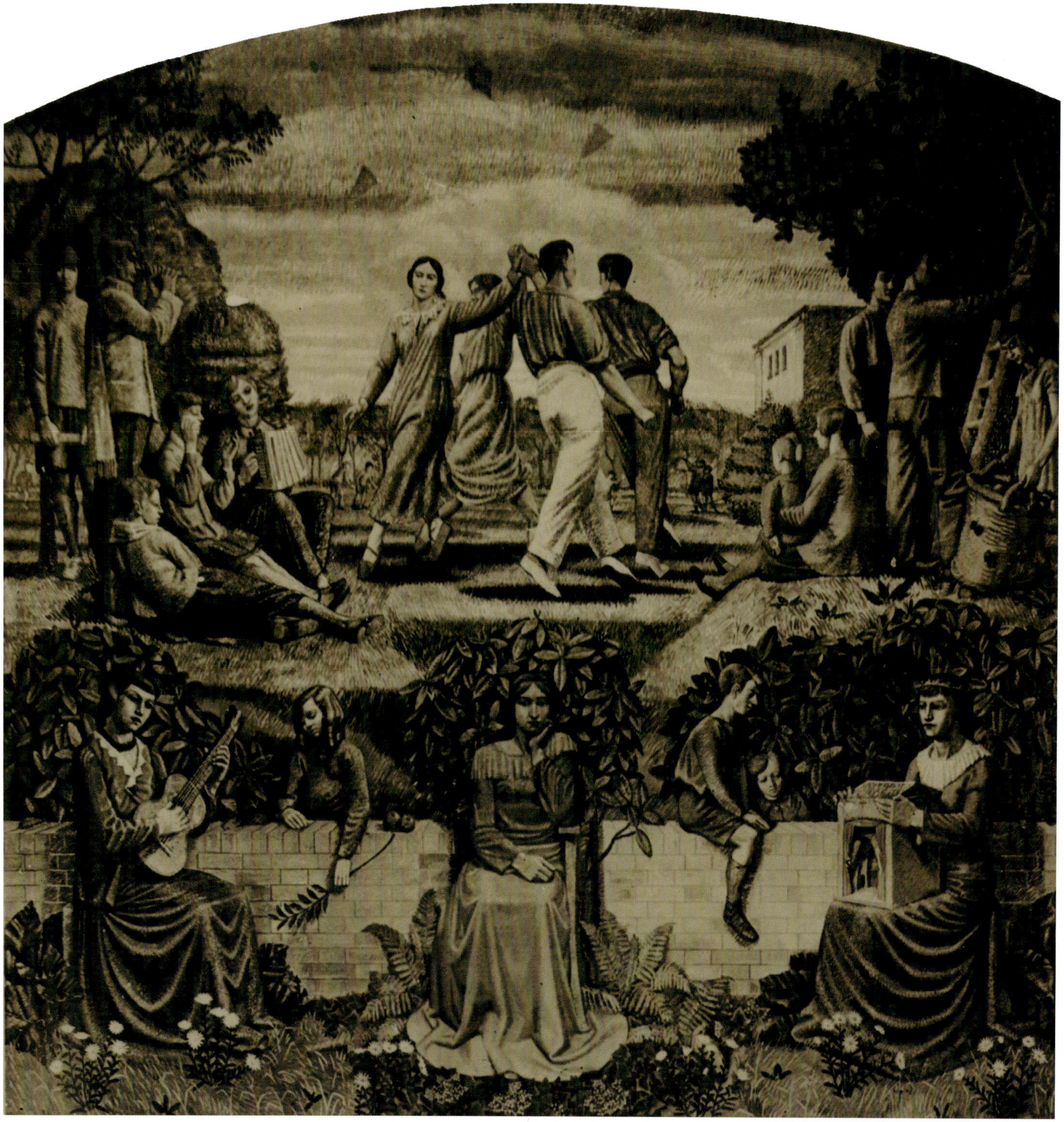

21 Charles Mahoney, *The Pleasures of Life*, Morley College, Lambeth, 1928-30 (central section detail). Destroyed in 1940.

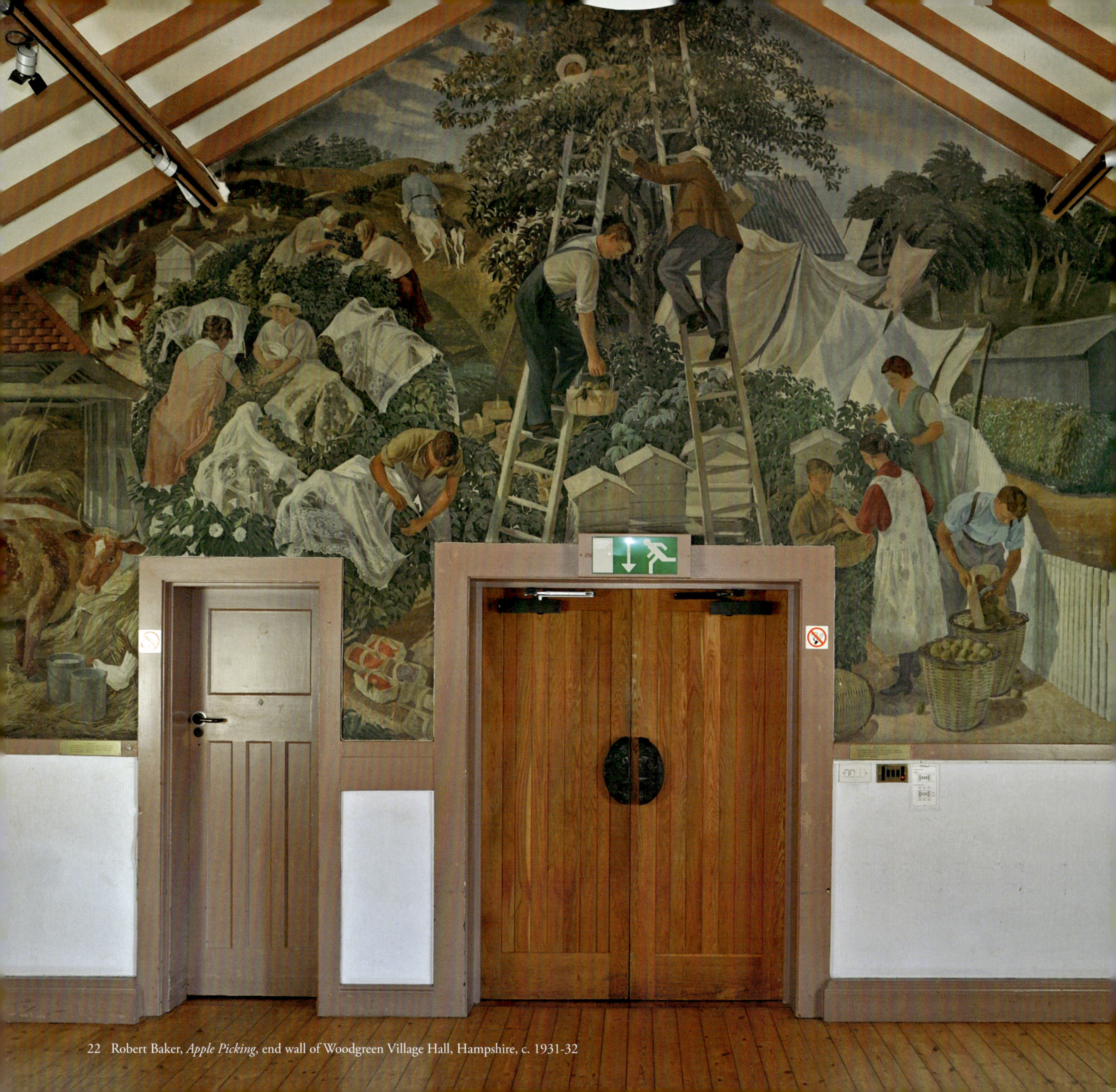

22 Robert Baker, *Apple Picking*, end wall of Woodgreen Village Hall, Hampshire, c. 1931-32

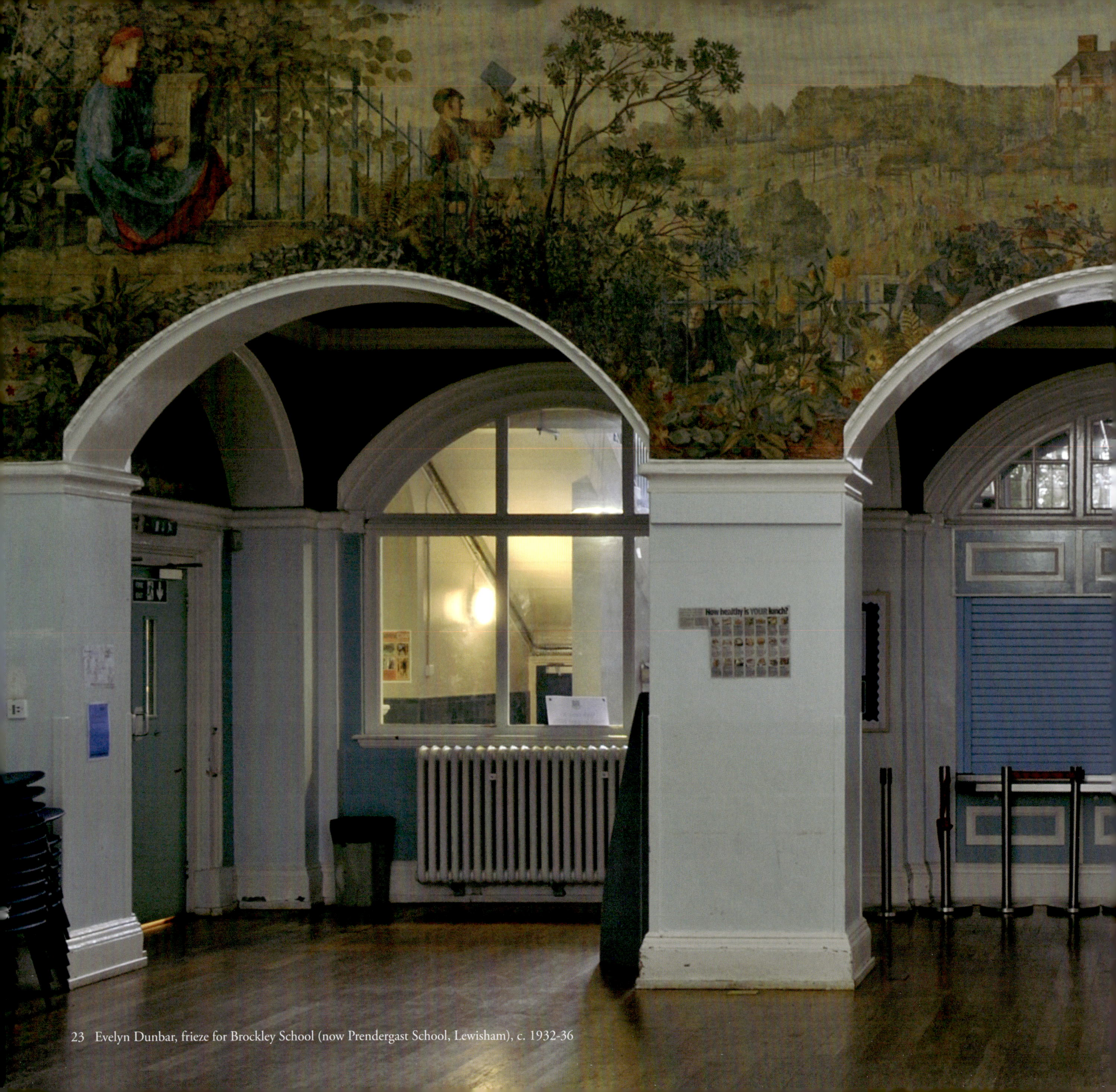

23 Evelyn Dunbar, frieze for Brockley School (now Prendergast School, Lewisham), c. 1932-36

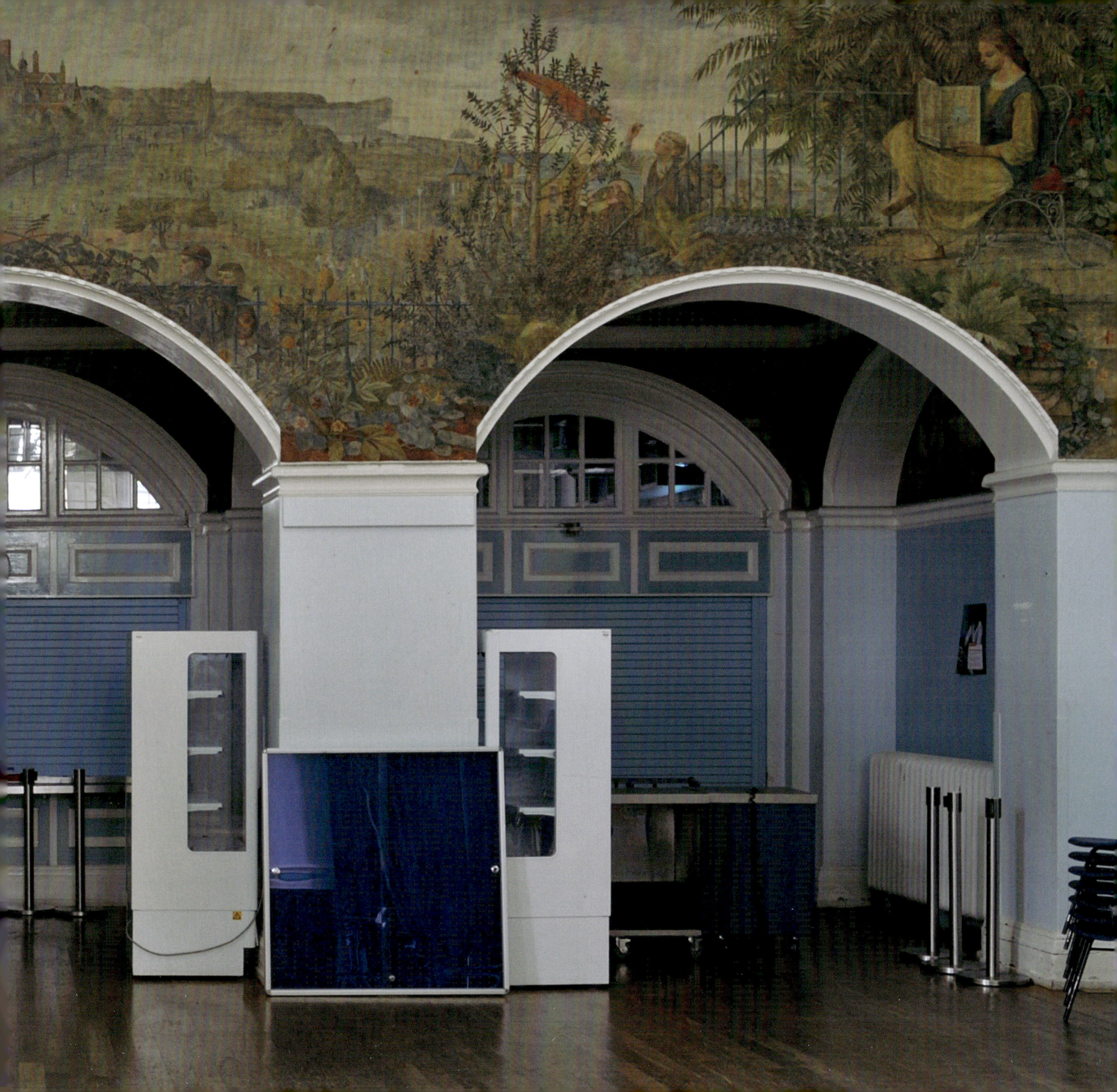

environment.[35] The closest equivalent in Britain can be found in the left-wing Artists International Association, founded in 1933. This was active in staging exhibitions of realist art on themes from modern life, but while the members admired the political murals in Mexico and the American New Deal, it was hard to find appropriate commissions in the 1930s, although several AIA members went on to paint murals in British Restaurants during the war and afterwards in schools, Fred Millett of the Wokingham murals being one of them. Sketches were made by Graham Sutherland for a mural at Impington Village College, Cambridgeshire, a building by Walter Gropius, but the project did not proceed owing to the outbreak of war. The most overtly political painting from the period, almost naïve in its directness, was by a pupil of Diego Rivera, Jack Hastings who painted *The Worker of the Future Disrupting the Chaos of the Present* in fresco at the Marx Memorial Library in Clerkenwell, 1935. [24] Rather incongruously, the other main work by Hastings (who inherited the title of Earl of Huntingdon) from the pre-war years is a set of paintings in the barrel vault of a garden building at Buscot House, Oxfordshire, showing the estate staff at work, painted for the Socialist peer Lord Faringdon.

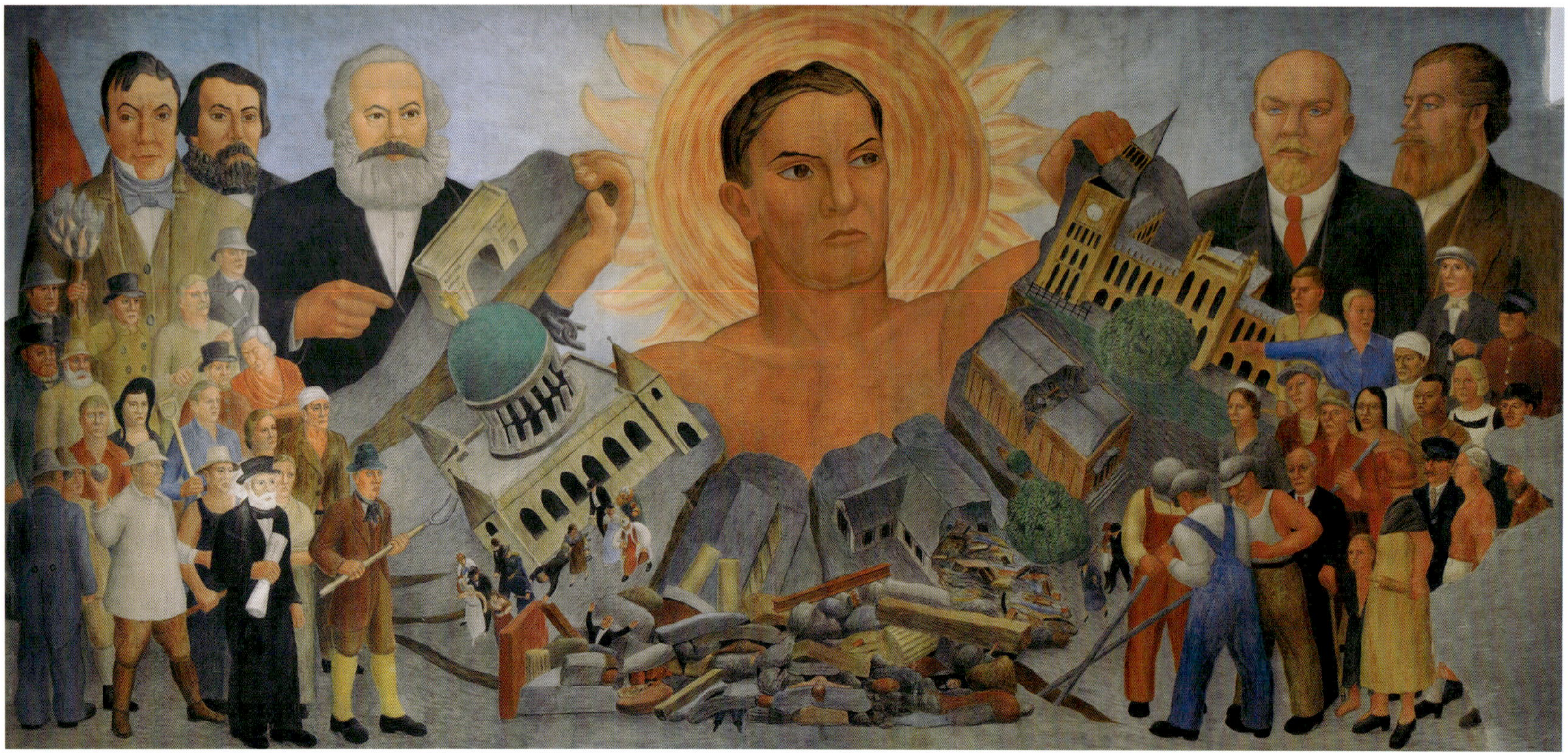

24 Jack Hastings, *The Worker of the Future Disrupting the Chaos of the Present*, 1935, fresco at the Marx Memorial Library in Clerkenwell

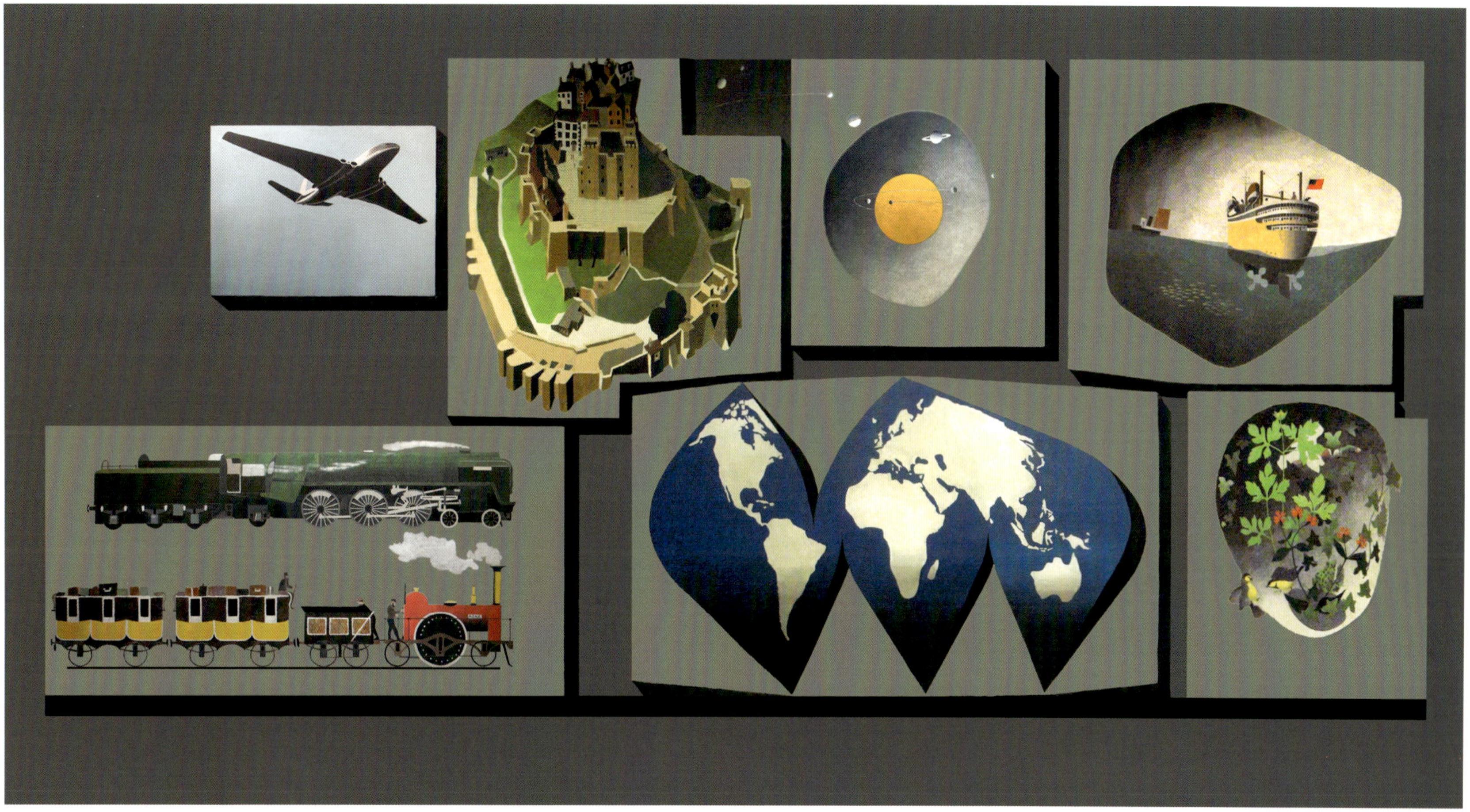

25 Gordon Cullen, mural for Greenside School, Hammersmith, 1953

Among the many schools built by county councils after the war, murals were not an inevitable occurrence, but there was a climate in their favour and often places were specially designed to receive a painting with appropriate indirect light from above, as with Pat Tew's paintings of Russian tales at Templewood School, Welwyn Garden City in 1952, part of the Hertfordshire 'Art for All' programme. [26a & 26b] This was part of an inspired movement across much of the country, which encompassed the more traditional mural of *The Seasons* at Warwick by Alan Sorrell of 1954. Gordon Cullen's mural in Ernö Goldfinger's Greenside School, Hammersmith, 1953, is another notable example by an architect-artist, currently the subject of a fundraising project for conservation. [25]

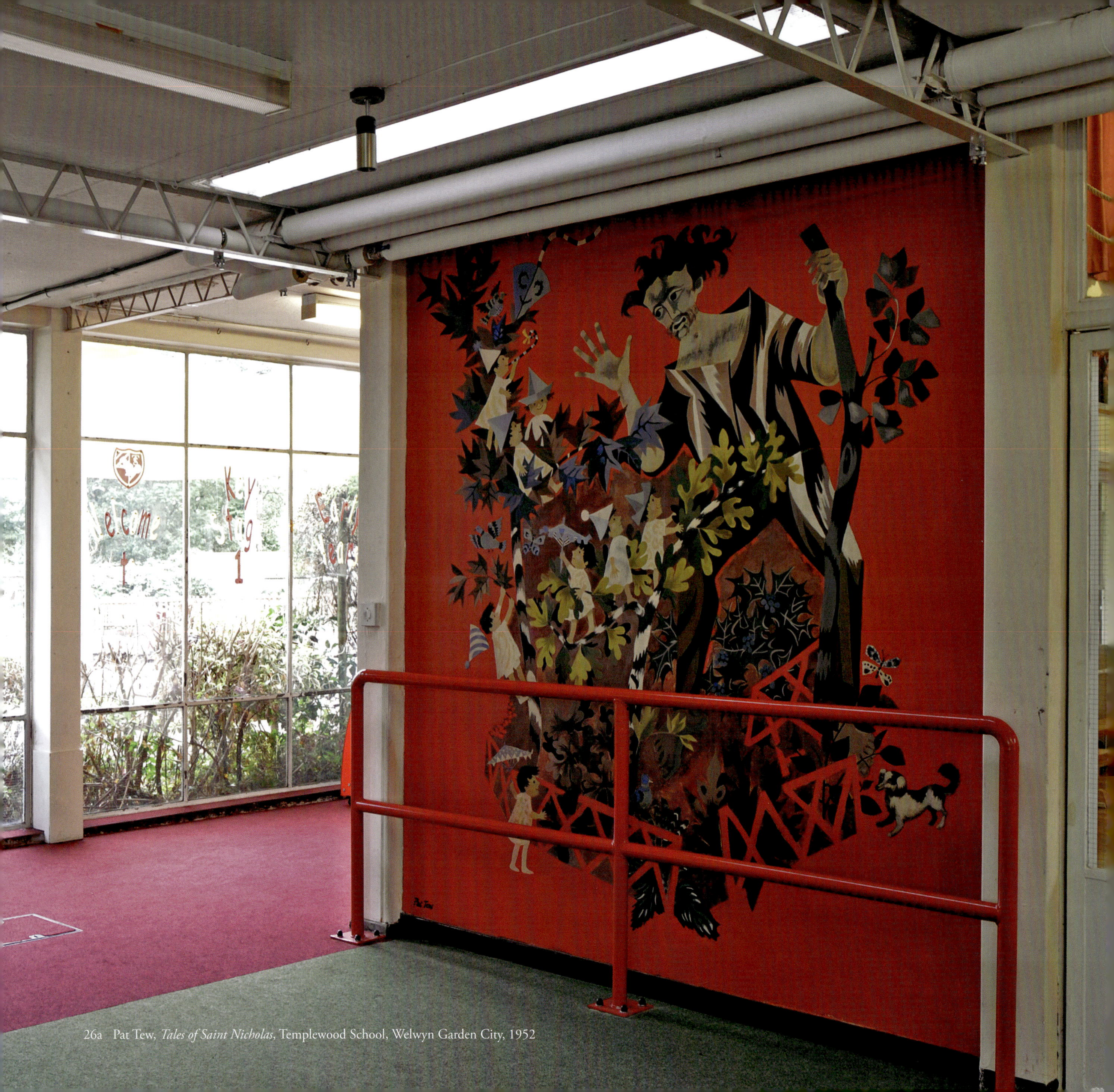

26a Pat Tew, *Tales of Saint Nicholas*, Templewood School, Welwyn Garden City, 1952

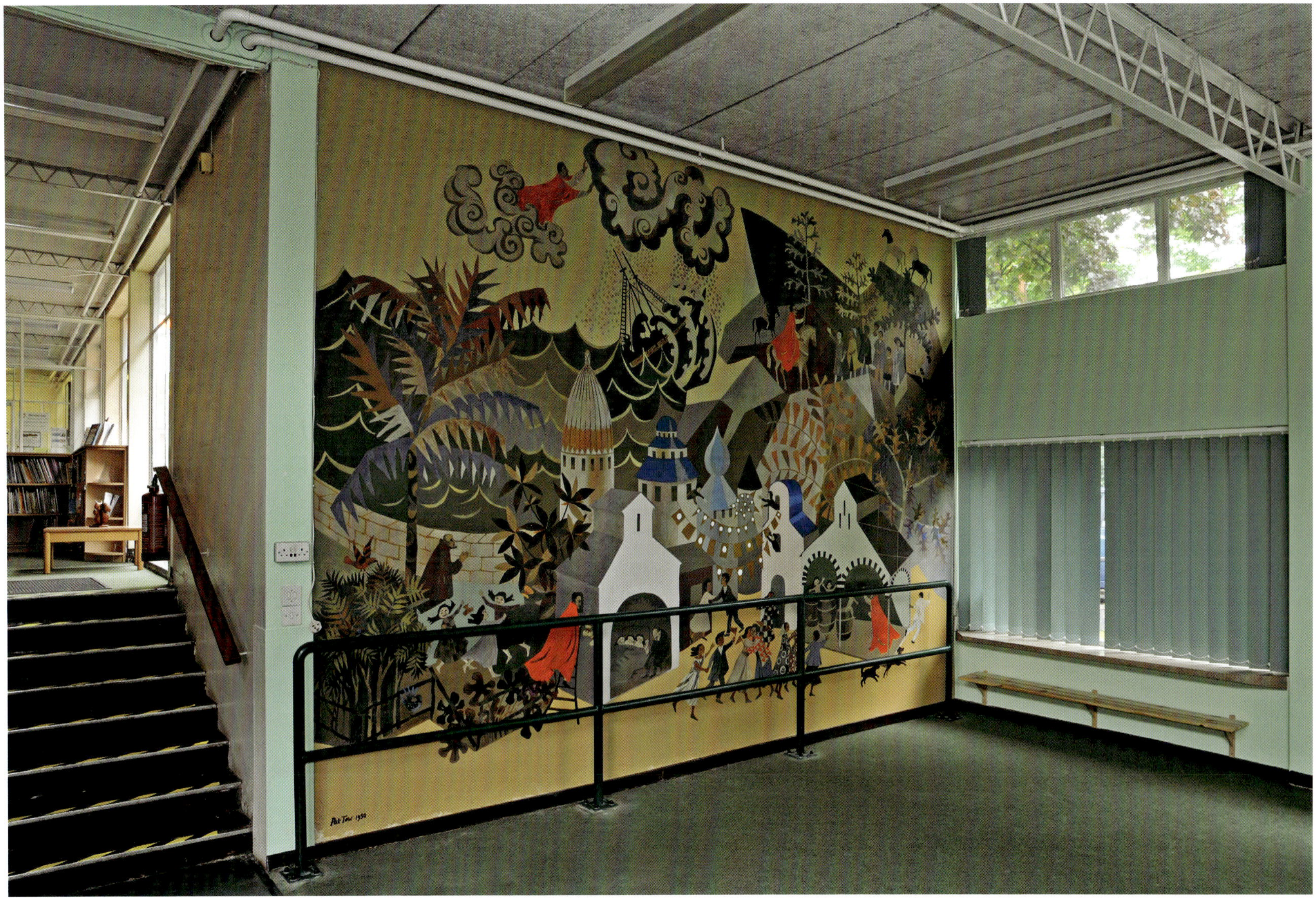

26b Pat Tew, *Tales of Saint Nicholas*, Templewood School, Welwyn Garden City, 1952

There were precedents from the 'Schools Beautiful' programme in Edinburgh before the war, where a new freshness of subject and approach was seen in John Maxwell's *Children's Games* at Craigmillar School, 1934-35 [27] and in Robert Westwater's scenes from *Alice in Wonderland* at Wardie School, 1938.[36] [28] Before the war, places of higher education were financially constrained and little mural painting was done. One notable exception was the Common Room at Holywell Manor, an outlying building developed by Balliol College, Oxford, and painted round all four walls by Gilbert Spencer in 1938. [29] Art students continued to undertake projects for which they could offer work for nothing, such as the children's section of the Wimbledon Public Library, painted by students at the local art school in 1947.[37]

Following pages: 27 John Maxwell, *Children's Games*, Craigmillar School, 1934-35

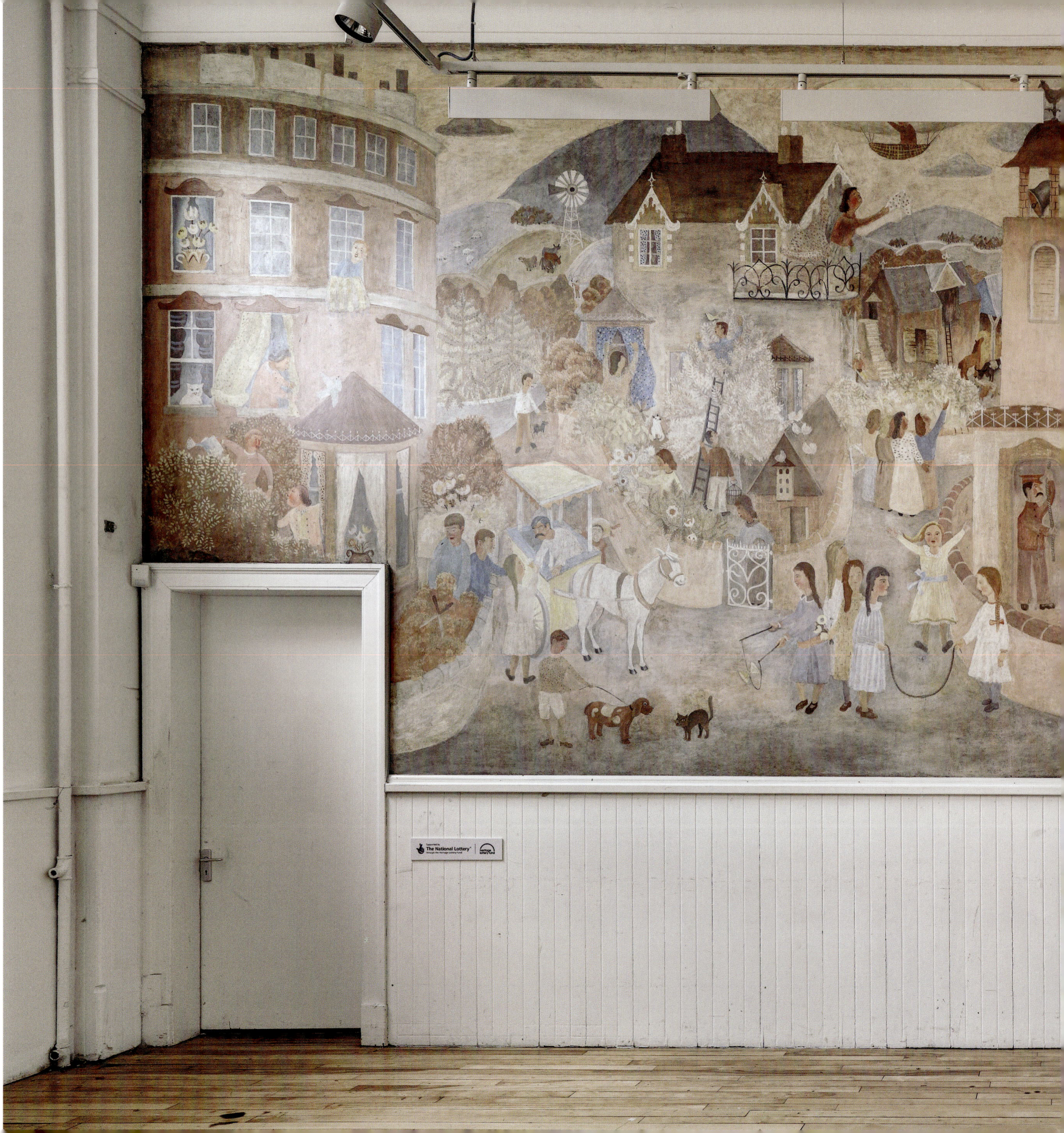

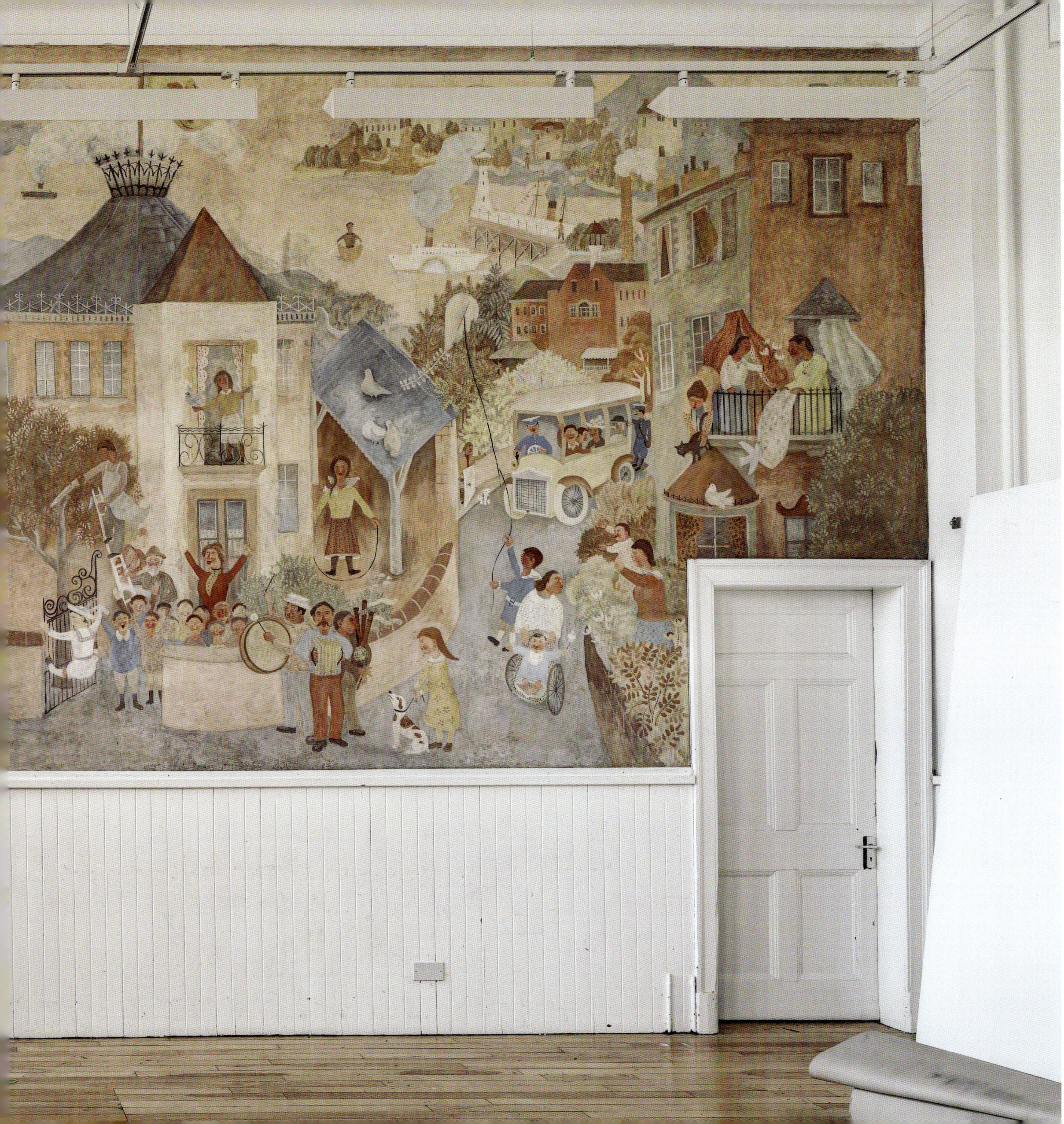

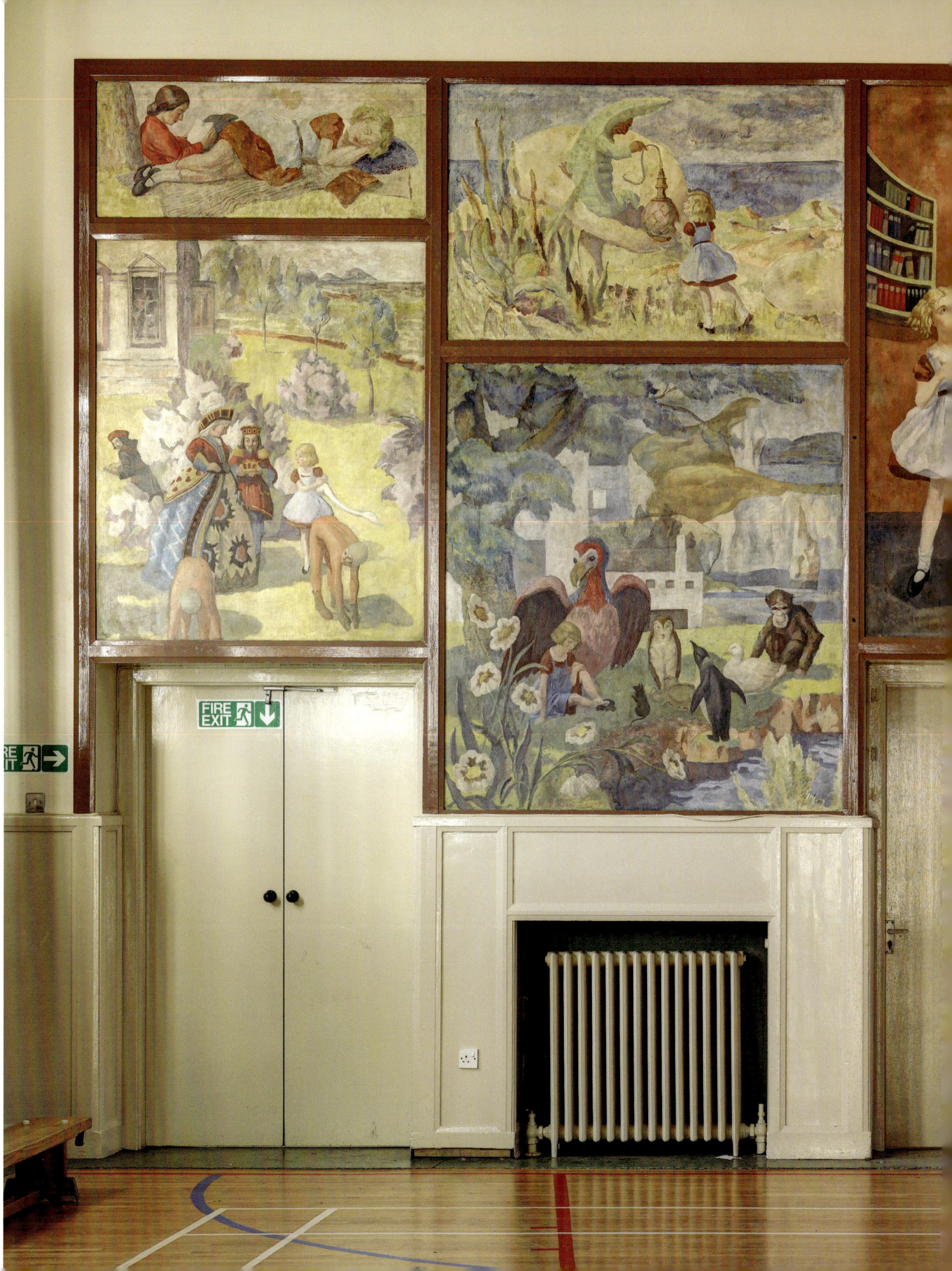

28 Robert Westwater's mural of scenes from *Alice in Wonderland* at Wardie School, 1938

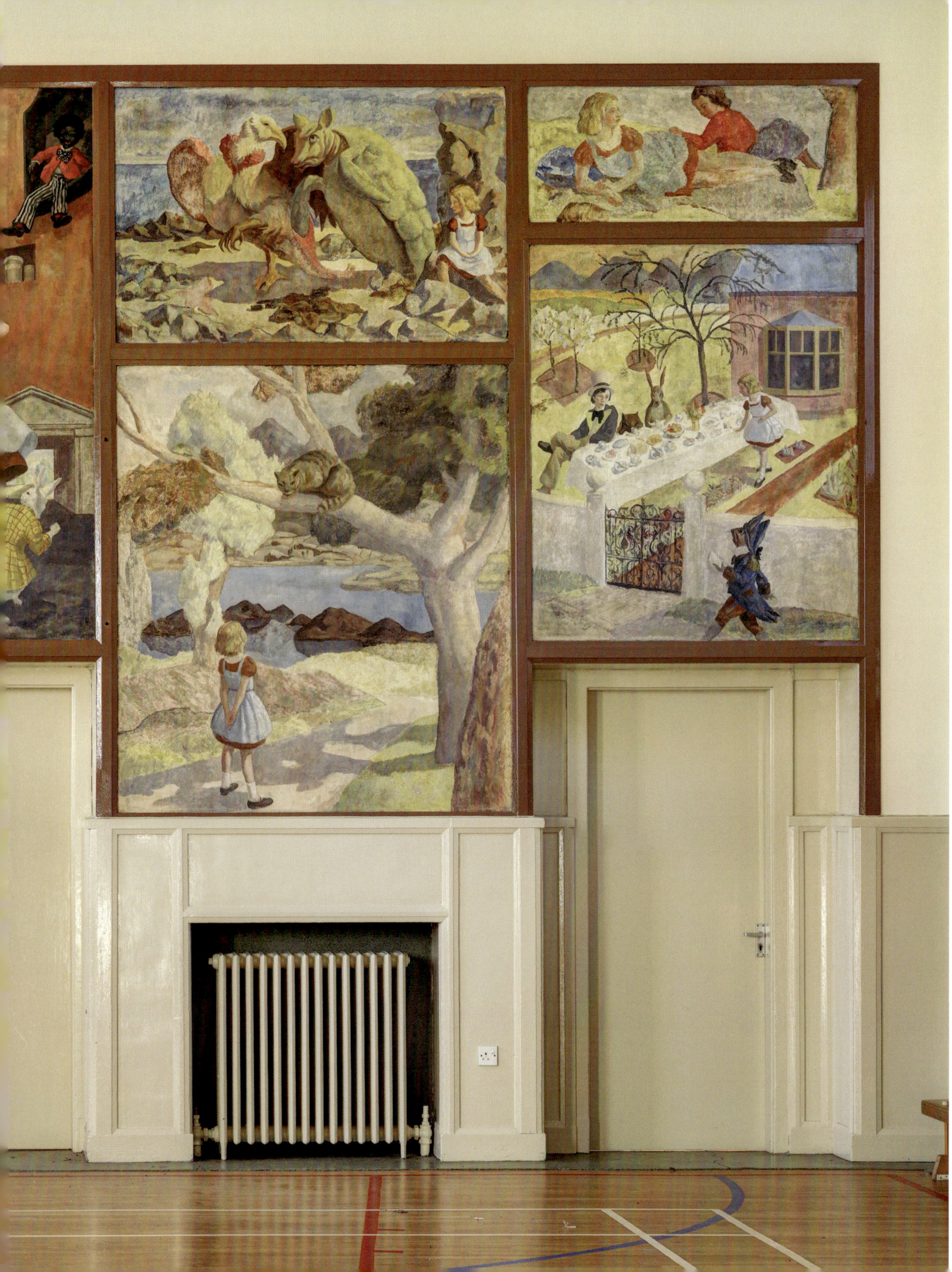

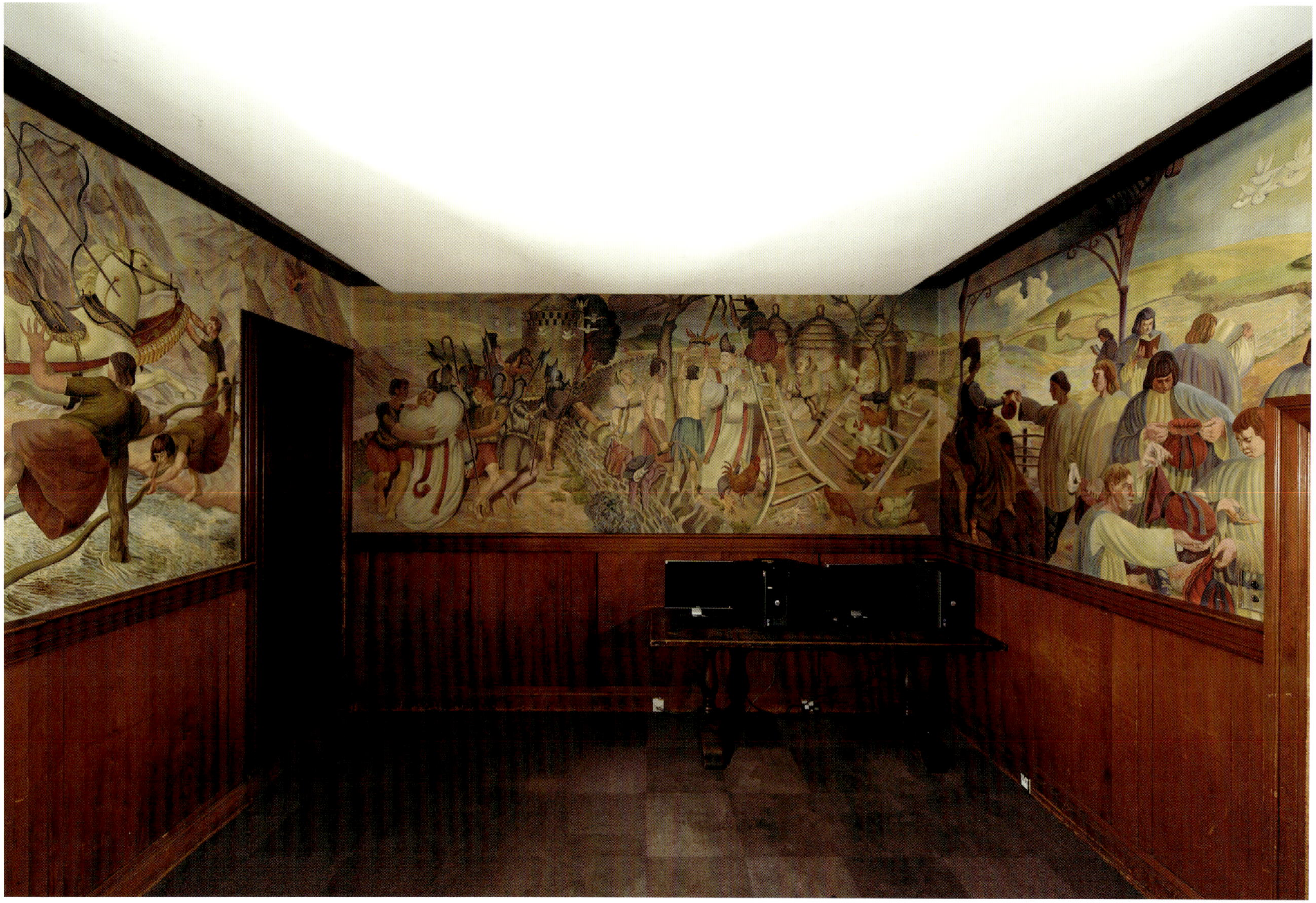

29 Gilbert Spencer, *The Foundation of Balliol College,* Common Room, Holywell Manor, Balliol College, 1938, © Estate of Gilbert Spencer, All rights reserved DACS 2012

There was a resurgence of public art of all kinds after the war, with a gradual widening of the stylistic range. Vincent Harris, designer of large buildings in a continuation of a Georgian classical style, commissioned the murals in Bristol Council House from Thomas Monnington (who displayed his new abstract style here for the first time to a wide public) [30] and John Armstrong in the early 1950s. [31a & 31b] Monnington also contributed to The University of London Students' Union in Malet Street, where his work, as well as that of Gilbert Spencer and Clive Gardiner, has been destroyed or covered up.[38] Both of these schemes were commissioned through the Edwin Austin Abbey Trust Fund, set up by Abbey's widow to support murals in public buildings. The building owners made the application, and the committee decided which artist would be suitable, favouring the work of younger artists, some of whom went on to become Royal Academicians, including the imaginative figurative artists Leonard Rosoman and Richard Eurich.[39]

30
Thomas Monnington, ceiling at Bristol Council House, 1953-54

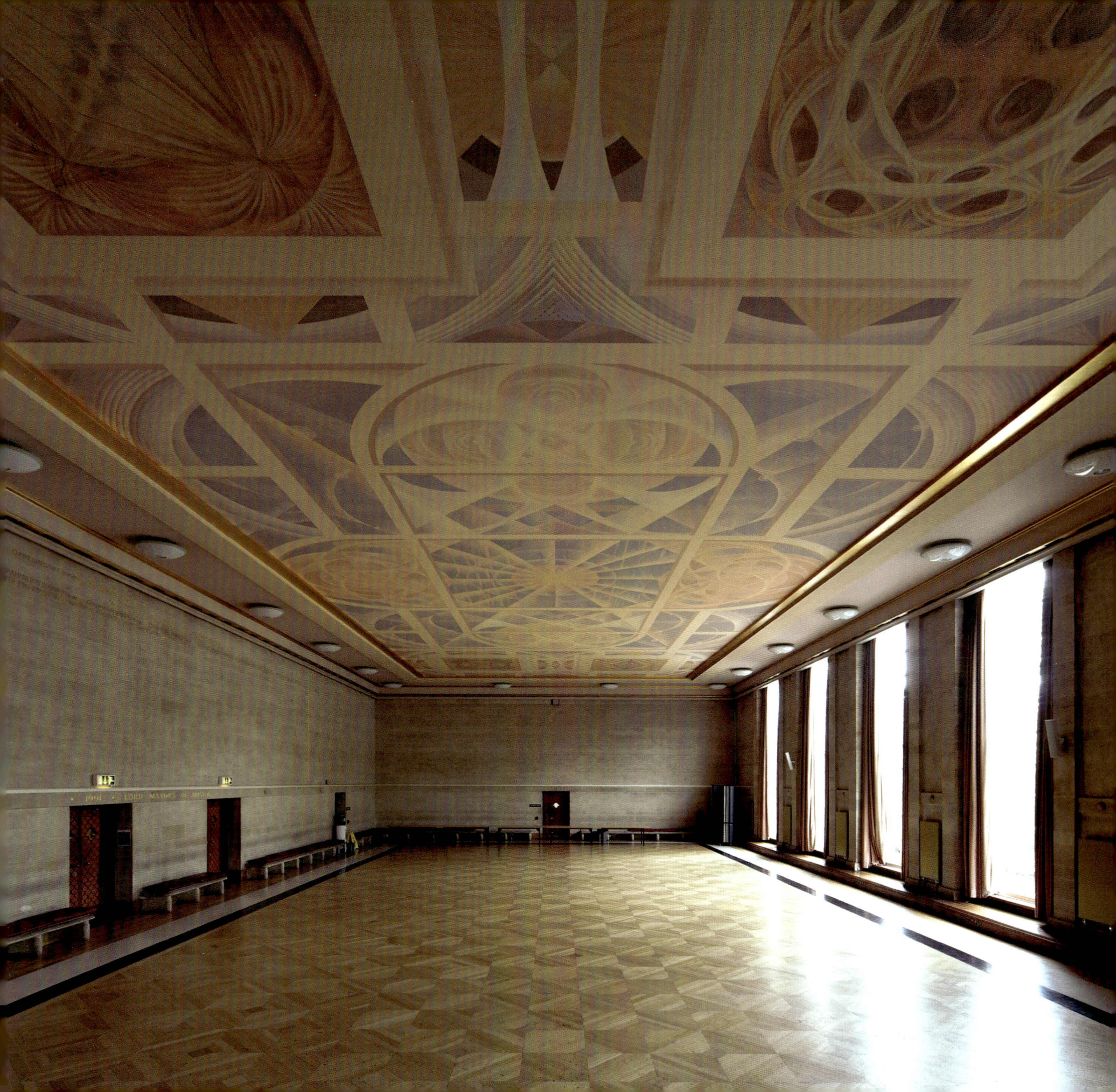
1991 • LORD MAYORS OF

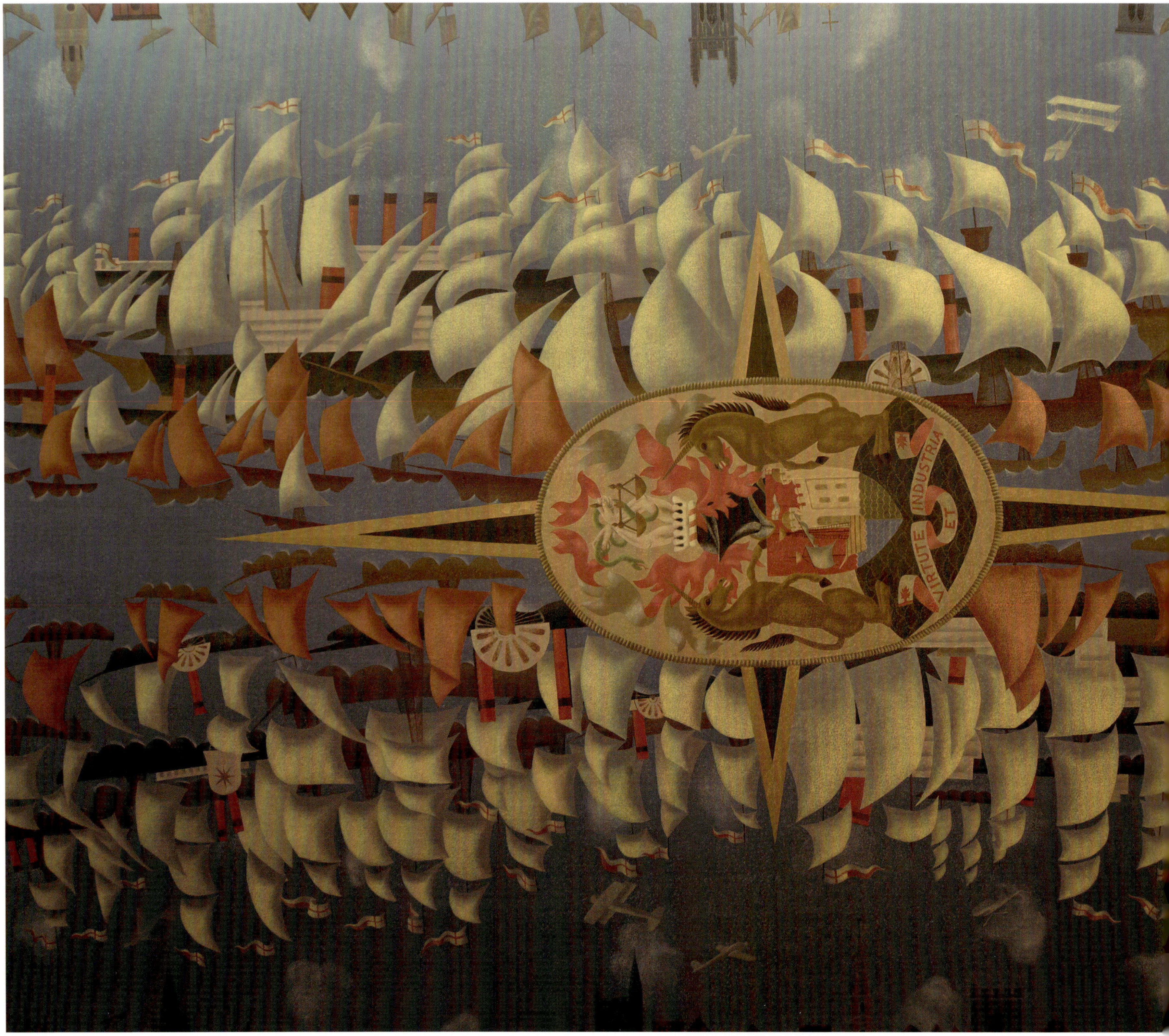
VIRTUTE ET INDUSTRIA

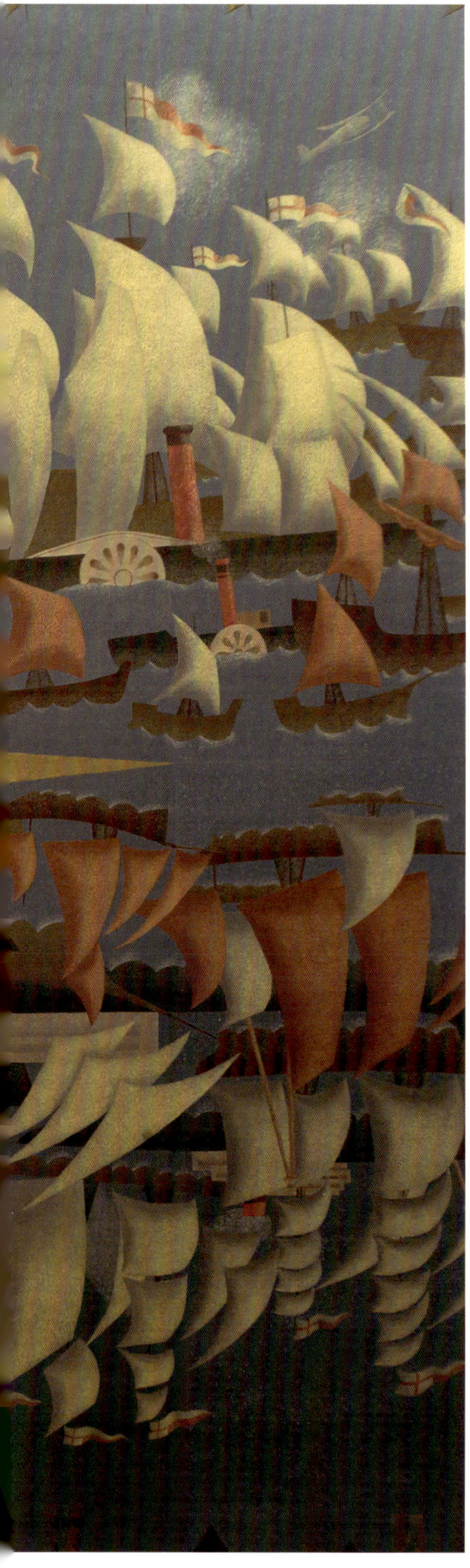

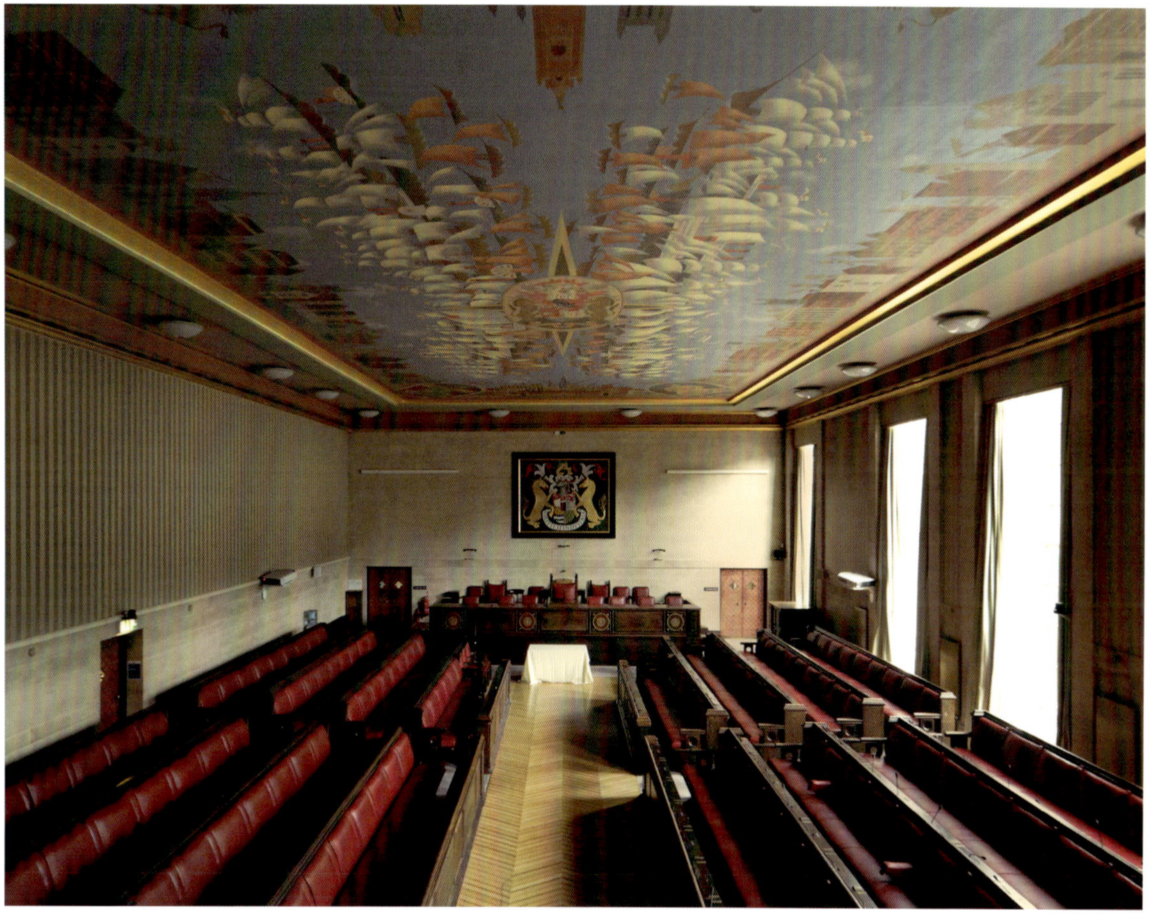

31b John Armstrong, ceiling at Bristol Council House, 1953-54

31a John Armstrong,
ceiling at Bristol Council House, 1953-54,
(detail)

The Festival of Britain [32] provided many opportunities for muralists, continuing the link between large-scale art and exhibition sites established at the turn of the century but with a new range of styles and techniques. Ben Nicholson, whose abstract work was much admired by modern architects, painted a panel for the Riverside Restaurant, one of his few site-specific works. Victor Pasmore had recently turned to abstraction and painted *Spiral Motif* on tiles. Apart from these works, figurative pieces prevailed, with indoor and outdoor work by artists on the South Bank and at the Festival Pleasure Gardens in Battersea, including Edward Bawden (page 244), John Armstrong (page 285), Betty Swanwick, Barbara Jones, John Hutton and, the largest of the few survivors, John Piper's *The Englishman's Home.*[40] (pages 292-293)

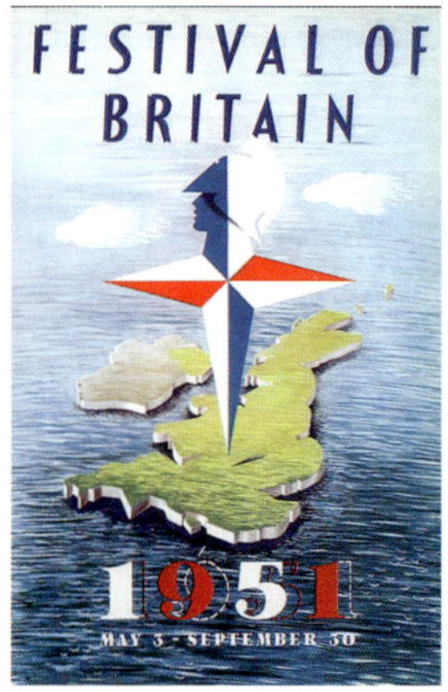

32
Poster for Festival of Britain, 1951

In the summer of 1951, the international congress of modern architecture, CIAM, met in Hertfordshire to talk about the 'core of the city', stressing the need for more public art in post-war rebuilding that would help people to identify with the otherwise unfamiliar modern architecture.[41] This discussion can be seen as a continuation of the civic impulse from the beginning of the century, still owing much to the influence of Patrick Geddes, coming with new force in the more democratic society of the Welfare State. It picked up the growing enthusiasm for murals in new buildings from before the war, and played out during the 1950s with schools and other public buildings before the artistic impulse began to fade or transfer into other media after 1960. One of the later manifestations was Plymouth Civic Centre by the architects Jellicoe, Ballantyne and Coleridge, containing engraved glass by John Hutton and murals by Hans Tisdall [33] and Mary Adshead. [34] [42]

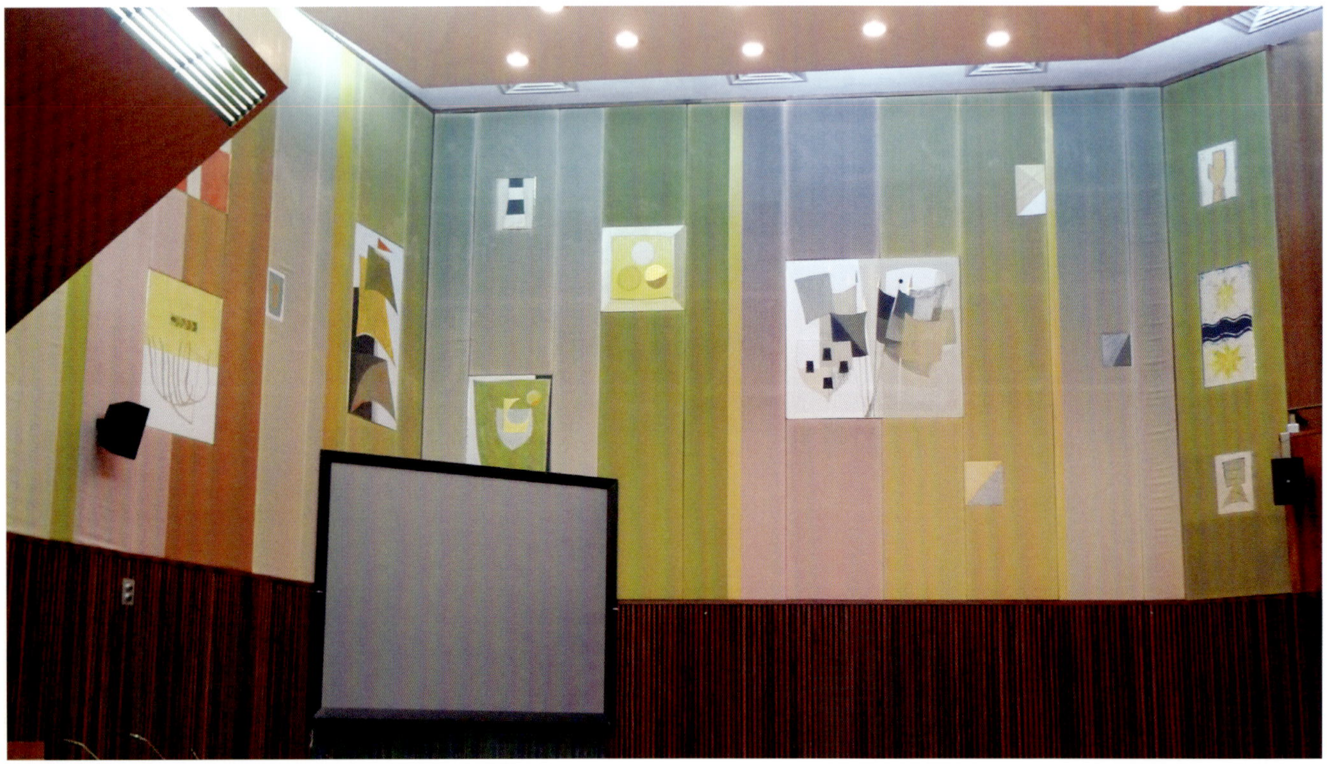

33
Hans Tisdall,
Council Chamber, Plymouth Civic Centre,
c. 1962

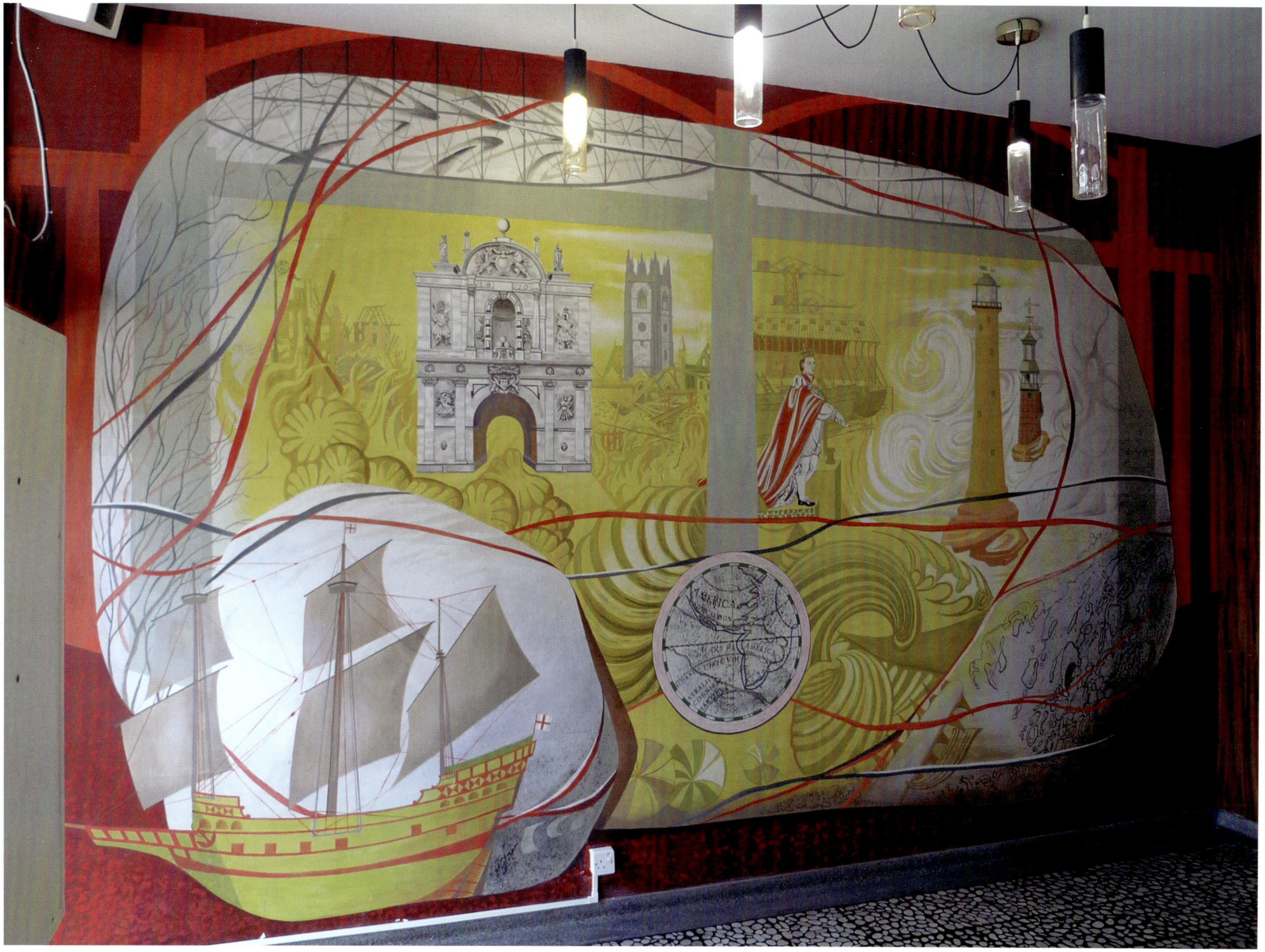

34 Mary Adshead, *Plymouth Landmark Events*, Plymouth Civic Centre, c. 1962-63

The year 1960 was not a specific end date, but as Romy Golan notes, the artistic climate began to move against murals in the previous decades. In Coventry Cathedral, among the many forms of decoration and art, murals were not included. This was not just in relation to abstraction but more specifically because artists became sensitive to the idea of the 'decorative' in its derogatory sense and felt that site-specific commissions and direct involvement in trying to meet the requirements of specific social groups, including children, would threaten their independence.

The design of murals for architectural spaces

The idea that a mural could complete an interior space was a long-standing one, crossing over between the work of the fine artist and that of the 'trade painter', a distinction that became more pronounced from the mid-nineteenth century onwards. The 'Decorative' painting idea was in some ways an attempt to rebuild the connection, with fine artists expected to work in specific, often domestic, settings without compromising their standards. In France, it was part of the mural painter's professional equipment to be able to adapt two-dimensional art to the viewer's angle and the lighting conditions of a particular space, and to judge the relationship between his work and its context, even if for an English critic such as A. Lys Baldry the results, with the exception of the work of Puvis de Chavannes, were too opulent.

The idea of the integrated decorated room was explored in England by James McNeill Whistler in the Peacock Room for Frederick Leyland of 1876-7, although the work could not be described as murals. The ninth Earl of Carlisle's interiors at 1 Palace Green, with Burne-Jones's *Cupid* and *Psyche* paintings set in the frieze of the morning room in a complete interior scheme by Morris & Co from 1869 onward, were still being admired in 1902.[43] In the 1890s Decorative Painting took on a more radical turn in Scotland as both interior decoration and painting became less intricately detailed, with the collaborations of Charles Rennie Mackintosh and Margaret Macdonald, while in Europe Klimt, Bonnard and Vuillard were prominent avant-garde artists who believed in the 'Decorative' incorporation of paintings into the design of domestic spaces.

Some artists showed themselves particularly adept at finding the right form of expression for an existing building at a variety of scales. Churches often presented ready-made spaces to be filled by painters, and Phoebe Traquair's design for the former Catholic Apostolic Church in Mansfield Place, Edinburgh in the 1890s used bands of figures as a way of structuring the large vertical sides of the chancel arch with an inverted circle of angels above to counteract the larger curve.[44] [35] Frank Brangwyn's tempera paintings in the chapel of Christ's Hospital, Horsham, 1912, were similarly effective in the space provided by Sir Aston Webb, and in their bright mosaic of broad colour strokes come close at times to the work of Bonnard, Klimt and Duncan Grant.[45] [36a, 36b, 36c & 36d] Grant and his fellow members of the Bloomsbury Group were enthusiastic about Byzantine mosaics, which led them to work at times with tesserae-like patterns of colour.[46] For a brief period, both these artists were among the few in Britain before 1930 to produce completely abstract works.

It is much easier for a single artist to achieve a satisfying unity of form and colour across a series of panels, but a number of schemes in the early twentieth century involved several artists with one of them acting as coordinator. For the House of Commons East Corridor, this was Edwin Abbey, remarking that 'artists were difficult cattle to drive in a team', although the size of the figures, the vanishing points and the dominant colour palette were agreed in advance.[47] Sir D. Y. Cameron fulfilled the role for St Stephen's Hall, where there were doubts more about the choice of subjects than the treatment by carefully selected artists in sympathy with Rome School classicism. For later schemes of this kind in new buildings, an architect was in charge, and Sir Herbert Baker seems to have enjoyed this role at India House, South Africa House and the Bank of England.

35
Phoebe Traquair,
The Worship of Heaven,
Mansfield Place Church,
Edinburgh, 1893-94.
Courtesy of
Mansfield Traquair Trust

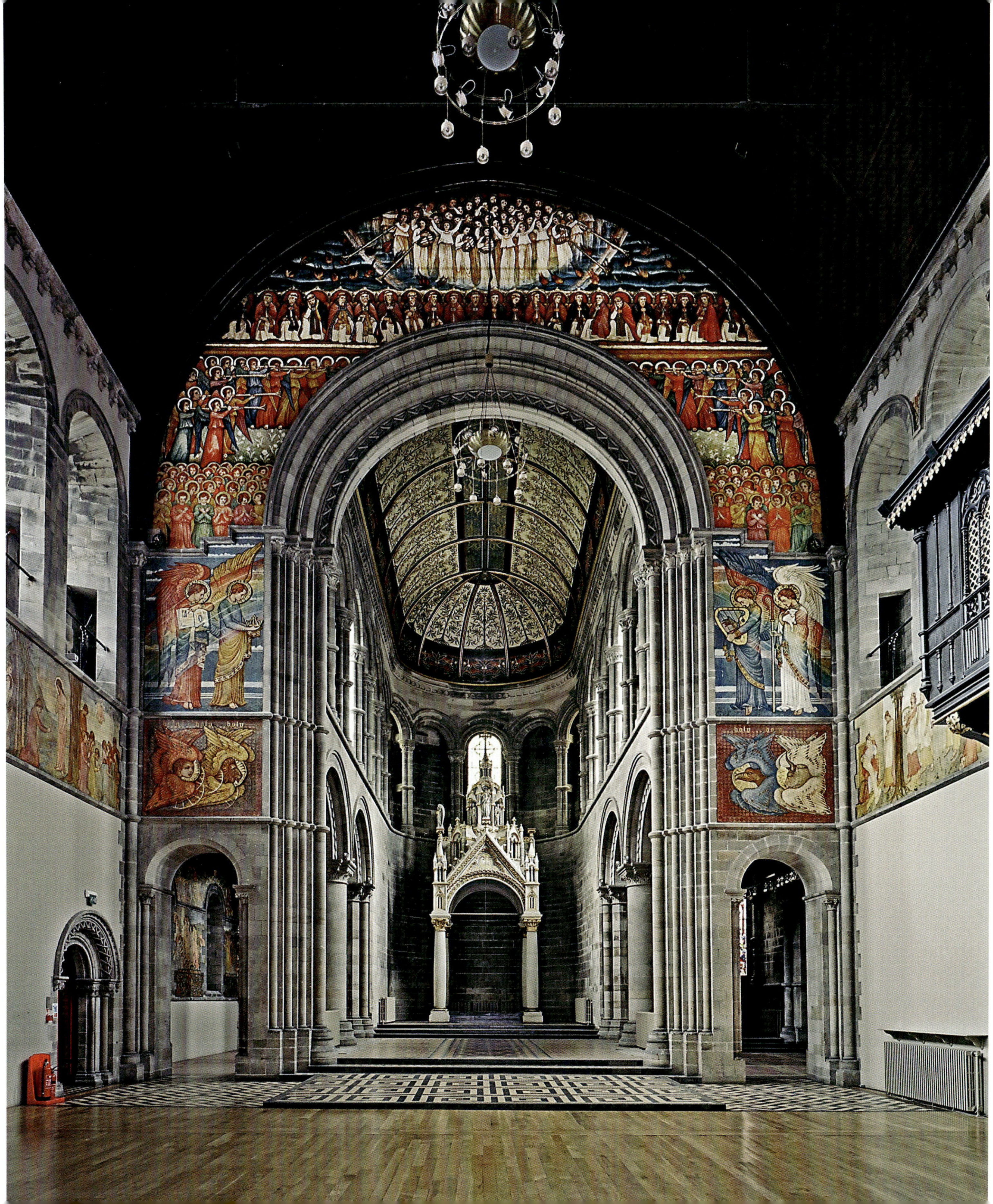

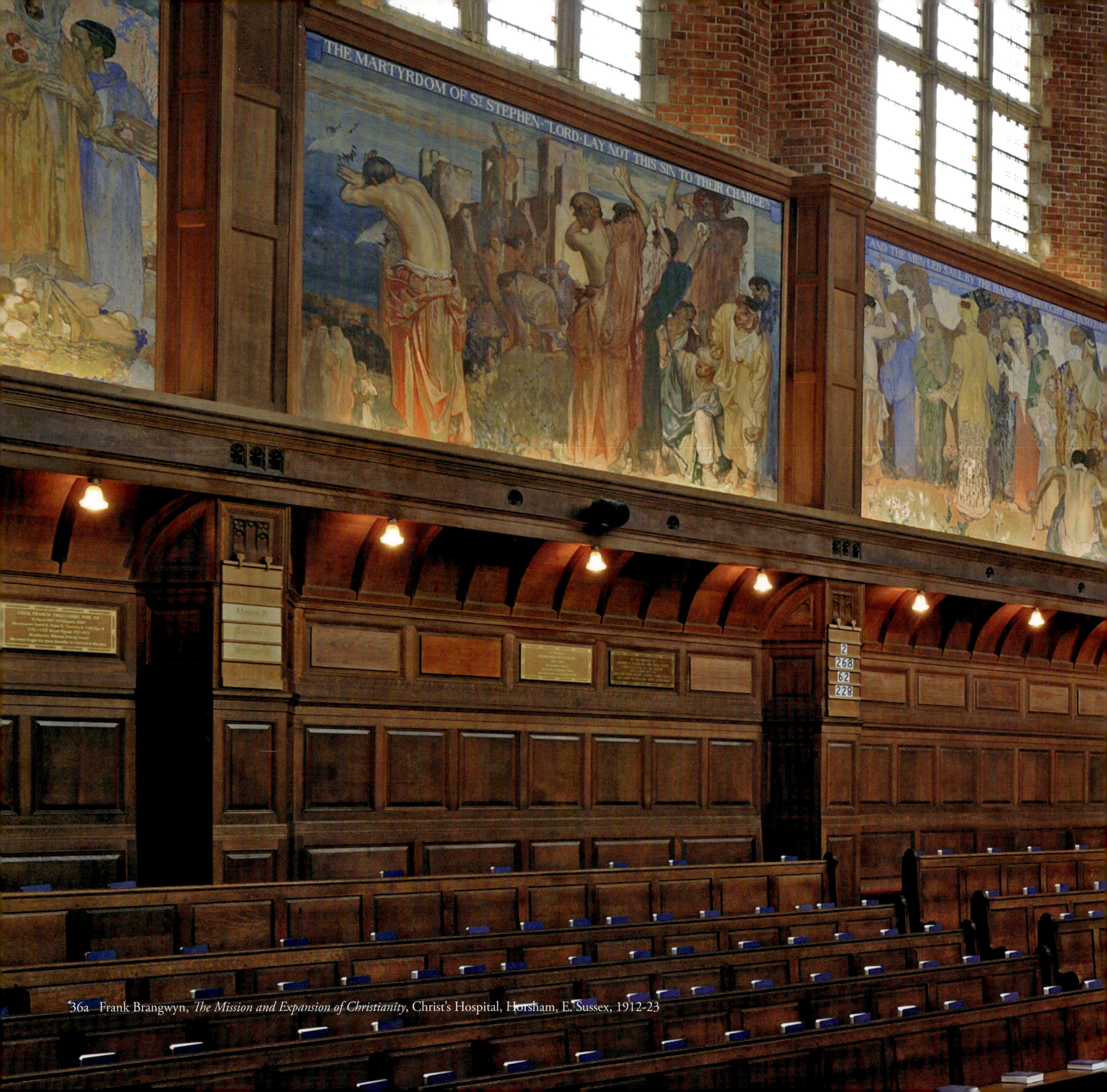

36a Frank Brangwyn, *The Mission and Expansion of Christianity*, Christ's Hospital, Horsham, E. Sussex, 1912-23

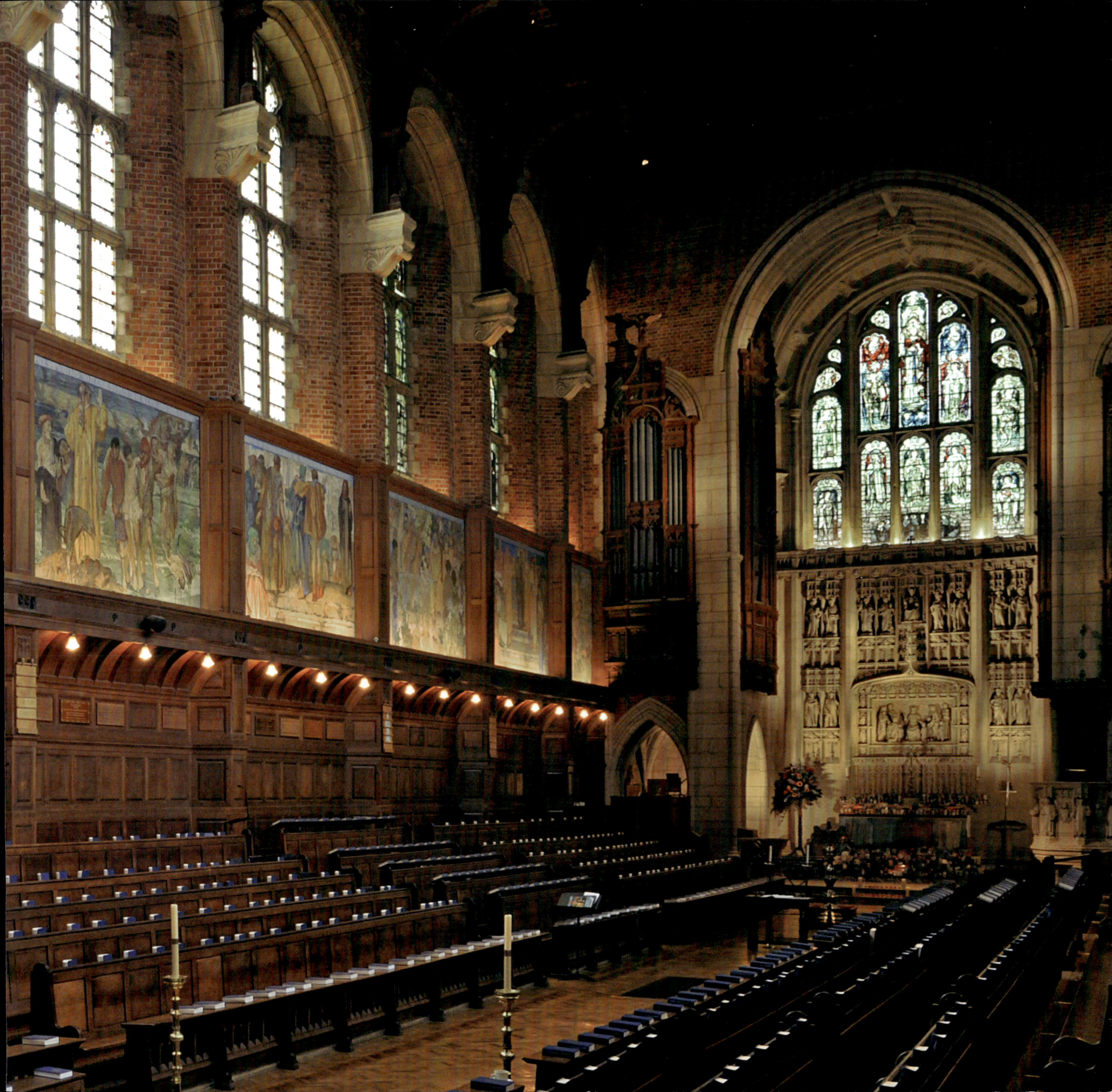

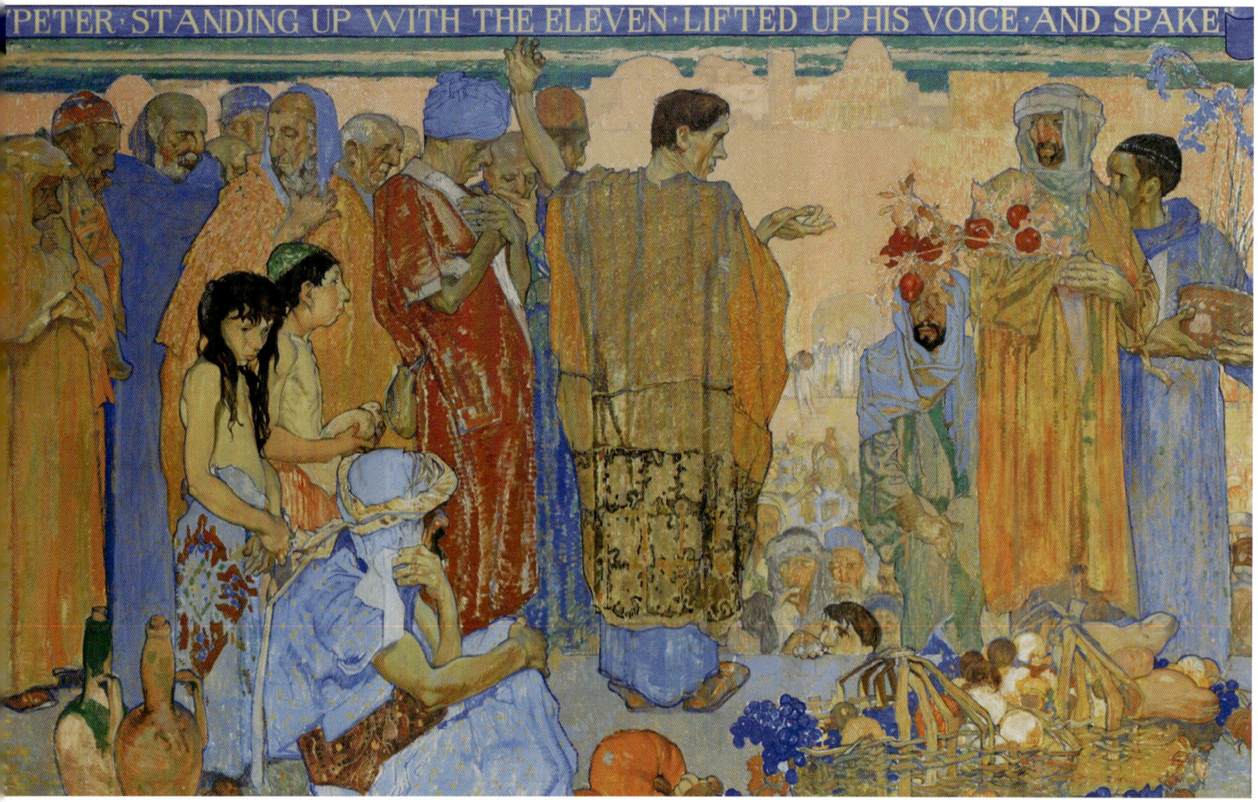

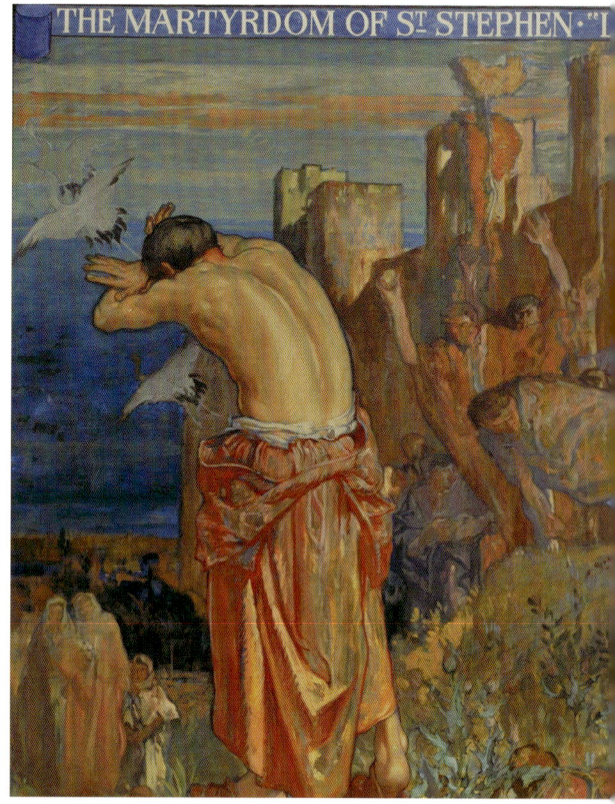

36b, 36c & 36d Frank Brangwyn, three of the 16 panels in Christ's Hospital, Horsham, 1912-23, egg tempera on canvas, each panel 243.8 x 426.7cm (8 x 14 ft.)

The idea that art, decoration and architecture would become indistinguishable from each other was transferred to the avant-garde movements of the 1920s. In 1924 the manifesto 'Vers une Construction Collective' in the Dutch *De Stijl* magazine declared, 'We have established the true place of colour in architecture, and we declare that painting without architectural construction (that is, the easel painting) has no further reason for existence.' One of the authors, Theo van Doesberg, realised his vision at the Café de l'Aubette in Strasbourg in 1927, providing one of the inspirations for post-1945 attempts to maintain this 'Constructivist' way of treating an interior. The Bauhaus, where a non-pictorial style of colour decoration was taught, was relatively little known before 1930 in Britain, but in 1932, Eric Mendelsohn, Henrik Wijdeweld and Amedée Ozenfant were meeting in London with Serge Chermayeff and Eric Gill to plan a European Academy of the Mediterranean, with a similar idea of the unity of the arts, described by some as a 'Bauhaus on Sea'.[48] Ozenfant, who painted a mural in Mendelsohn's house in Berlin, was to teach this subject. The Académie never opened, but the decade continued to dream and occasionally to act. The presence in London in the mid-1930s of the former Bauhaus teacher Laszló Moholy-Nagy stimulated the idea of radical spatial transformation, but little was produced for an English audience.[49] Shortly before leaving for America in 1937, Moholy-Nagy took part in a discussion with Serge Chermayeff and Naum Gabo in which Chermayeff declared of the artist and architect that 'Their relationship and spiritual alliance must be a working alliance if they were to enjoy to the full the creative existence to which they are entitled. We must form a united front everywhere, continually to sweep away the aesthetic and technical confusion which is our immediate heritage.'[50]

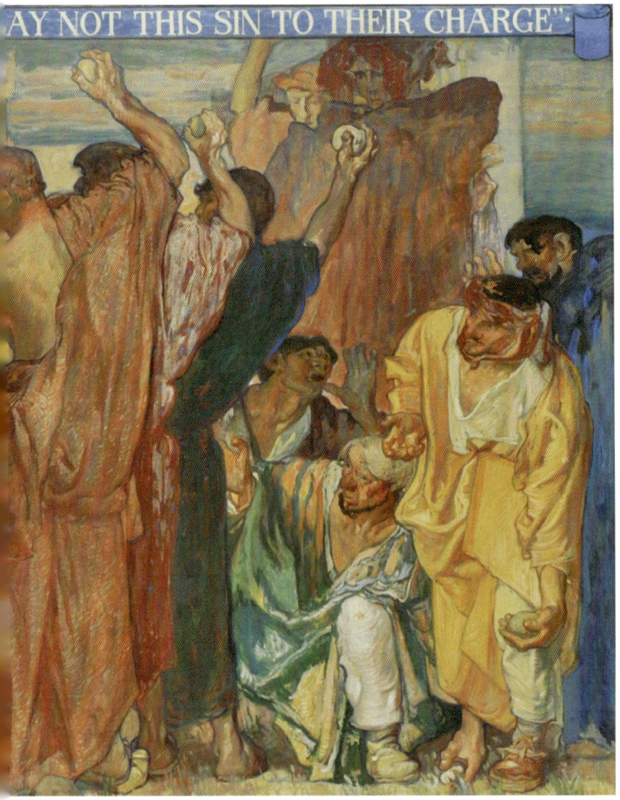

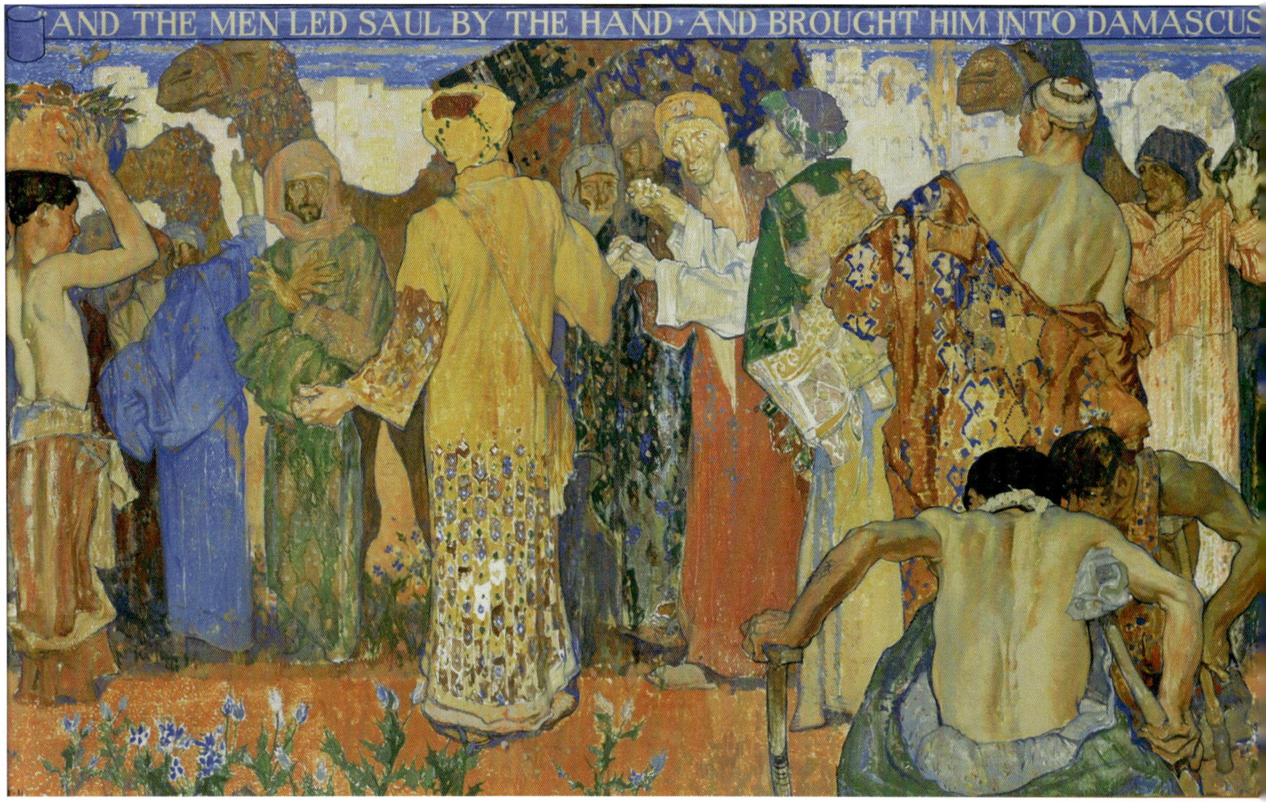

More commonly, artists in the 1920s and 30s chose to revert to a more historical style, influenced perhaps by the same direction taken by Picasso, Matisse and Gino Severini (who painted murals for the Sitwell family at the Castello di Montegufoni in Tuscany), responding to what the multi-talented Jean Cocteau (himself a muralist on several occasions, including a little-known work in the French church off Leicester Square) called *Le Rappel à l'Ordre* or *The Call to Order*.[51] This movement gave much more value to composition than to subjects and encouraged theatrical content, in line with the huge popularity of Diaghilev's Ballets Russes with its decorative adoption of the styles of modern art.

If the given room had few architectural features, one solution was to invent some in paint. Trompe l'oeil architecture like that painted by the architect Baldassare Peruzzi in the salon at the Villa Farnesina in Rome, 1510, was developed by Veronese at Palladio's Villa Barbaro, Maser in 1560, and became a staple device in Italy and in Baroque painting everywhere. In twentieth-century Britain, the obscure painter George Murray deserves credit for reintroducing it in his murals for the Institute of Chartered Accountants Council Chamber in the City of London, 1914, appropriately for the 1890 neo-Baroque setting by the architect John Belcher, but it was Rex Whistler who gave it wider currency in the 1920s, making invented buildings and cities a large part of his subject matter. In the panoramic murals at the Tate Gallery Restaurant he skilfully made the arched windows and the doorways into architectural features in their own right. The way he reversed the real perspective of the corner where the city of Epicuranea recedes on walls which are actually coming towards the spectator was particularly

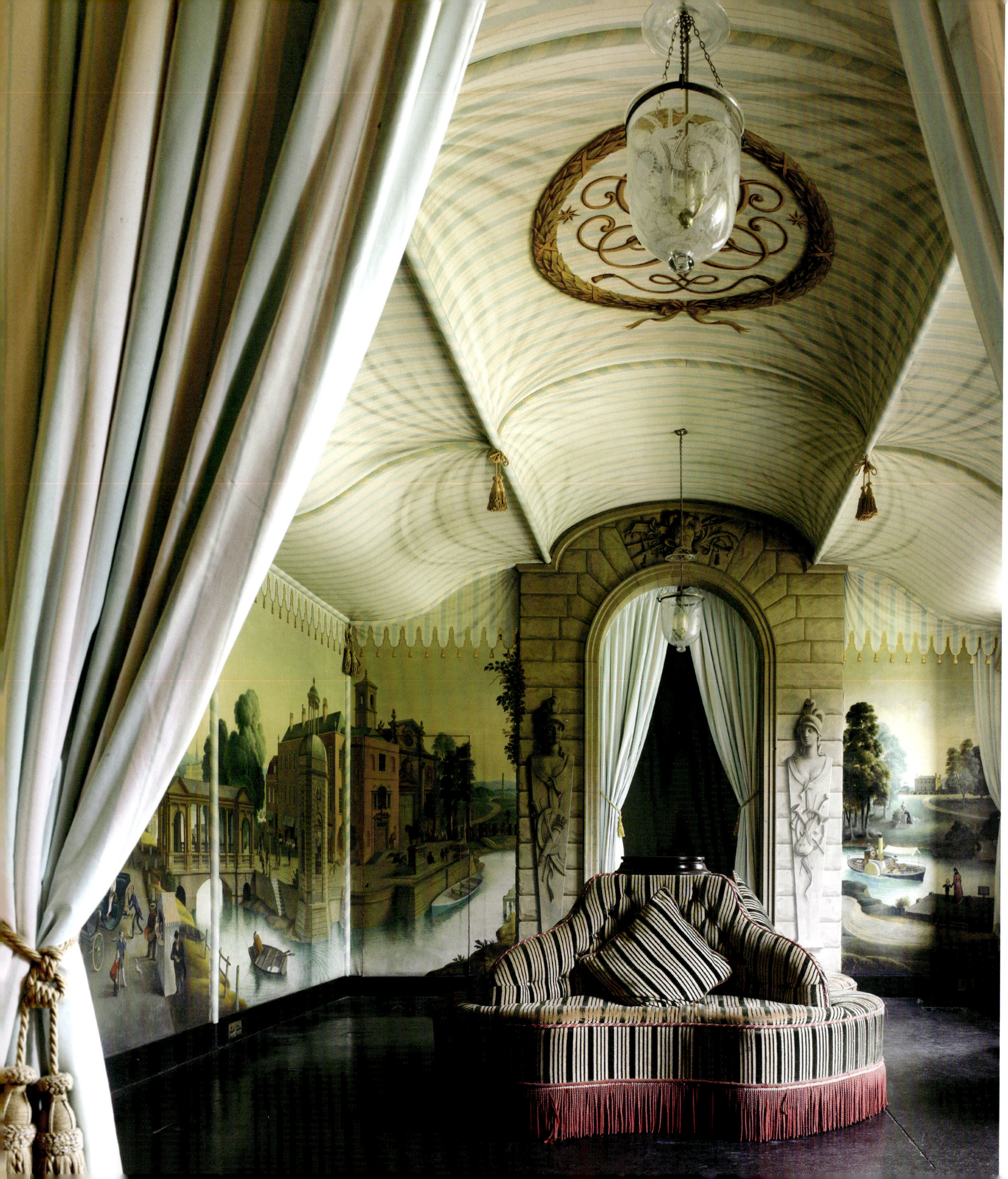

37
Rex Whistler
murals at Port Lympne,
Kent, 1930-32,

Courtesy of *Country Life*

adroit. Further imaginary cities are depicted in his painted rooms at Port Lympne [37] and Plas Newydd, while at Mottisfont Abbey he made the fictive architecture of the wall decoration the subject of the mural. In these works Whistler was able to blend historical periods and national references with extraordinary skill, making haunting dream-like visions that, more than any other murals of their kind, can almost engulf the viewer in an imagined world.

It became relatively common for architects to set aside spaces suitable for murals. Many examples could be cited, but Edward Halliday's panels in the library of the Liverpool Athenaeum (designed by Harold A. Dod in 1927) show how the confident neo-classical scheme of painting and architecture was conceived as whole.[52] (see page 199) Fitting into existing buildings could be more difficult, and when Sir Herbert Baker commissioned Winifred Knights in the 1930s to paint a canvas of St Martin in Canterbury Cathedral, a side panel was added to accommodate a column near the left-hand end and mouldings with scooped curves. The painting was removed during the war and repositioned, without the side panel, and with a frame made to include matching shapes cut out at the upper corners. [38a & 38b]

With the rare opportunity of having a purpose-made building, Stanley Spencer specified the arrangement of the dense mass of upper and lower rows of scenes in the Sandham Memorial Chapel at Burghclere, a scheme deriving from examples such as the Arena Chapel rather than from any architectural principles. [39] The idea of painting itself having a structure related to architectural form was conducive to establishing a more direct form of relationship both of colour and composition than was common in the nineteenth century.

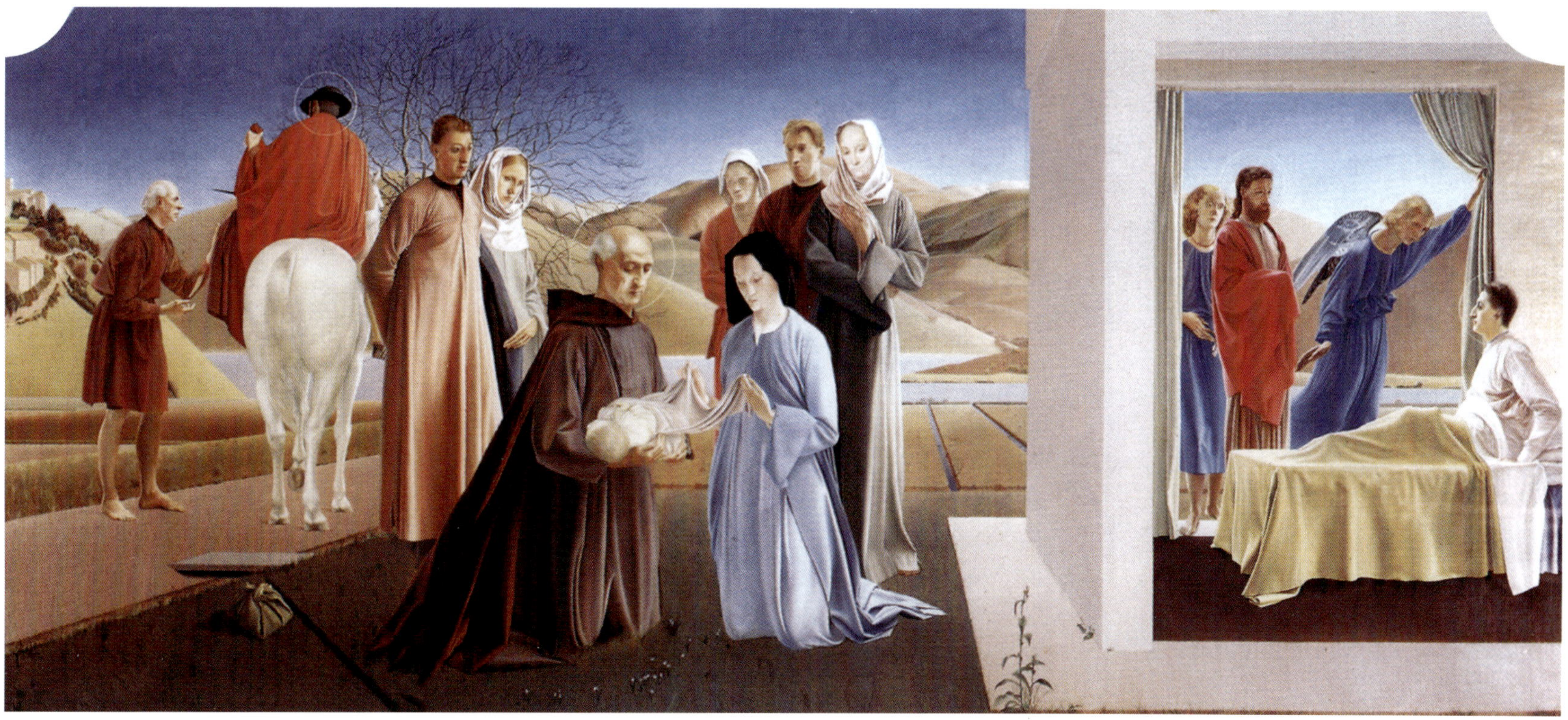

38a Winifred Knights, *Scenes from the Life of St Martin of Tours*, 1928-1933, oil on canvas, 76.5 x 189.5 cm (30 ⅛ x 74 ⅝ in.), Milner Memorial Chapel, Canterbury Cathedral

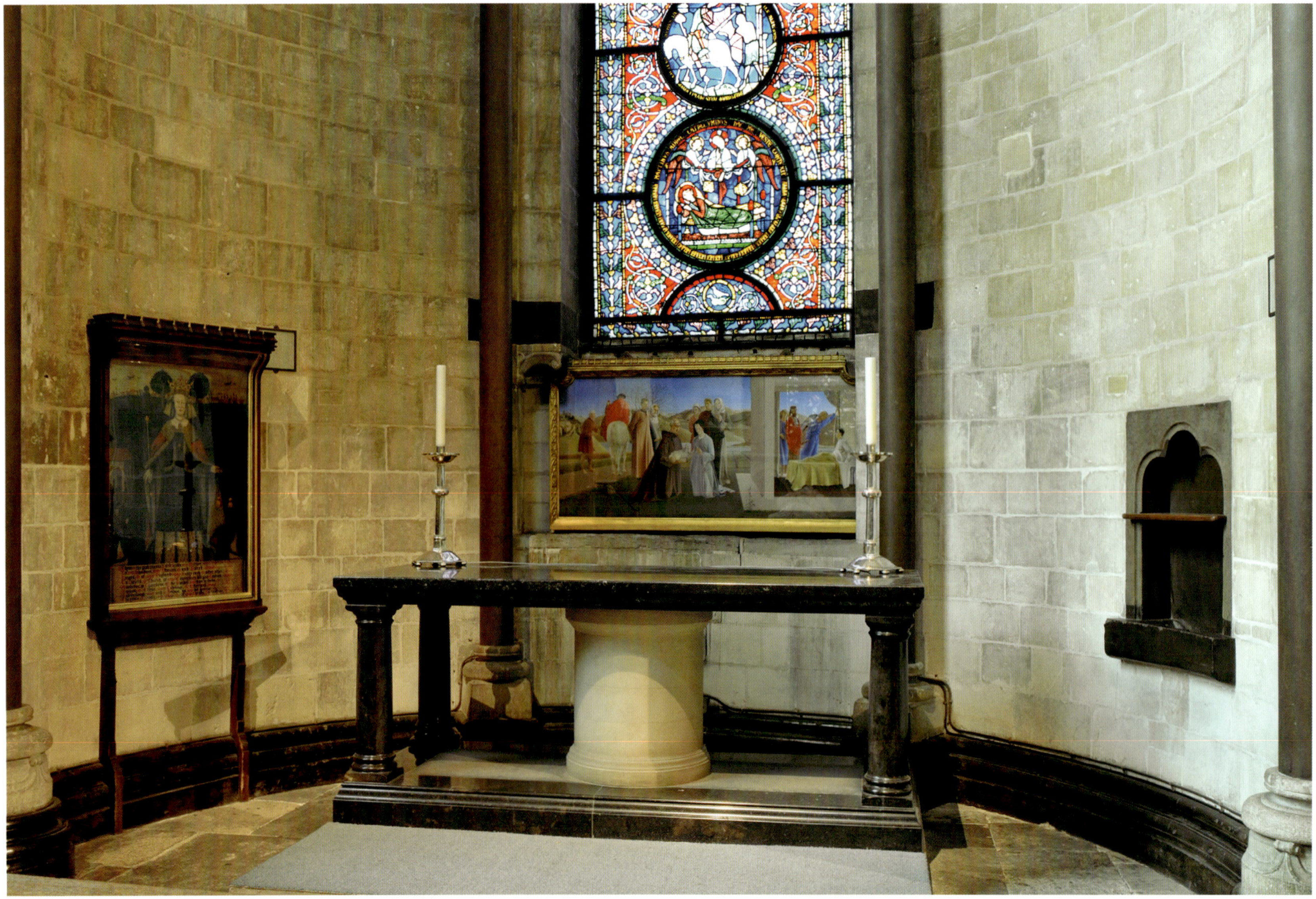

38b Winifred Knights, *Scenes from the Life of St Martin of Tours*, 1928-1933, Milner Memorial Chapel, Canterbury Cathedral

Even the 'salon' Cubism of the 'Section d'Or' group could be integrated into the academic tradition of the Renaissance. One of the group members, André Lhote, founded a personal academy in Montparnasse in 1922, where one of his pupils was the young German painter Hans Feibusch, who came to England in 1933 and soon became a highly prolific specialist in murals. Prior to this date, the example of the Baroque combination of painting and architecture had been despised in Britain as too Catholic and in poor taste, but by blending this with Lhote's teaching, Feibusch was able to give mural painting a new sense of architectural possibility.

Feibusch's book *Mural Painting*, published in 1946, laid emphasis on the compatibility of past and present. He wrote of 'the mysterious quality of colour to suggest various degrees of depth' that he attributed to Matisse,

39
Stanley Spencer,
Resurrection Scene from
Sandham Memorial Chapel,
Burghclere, Hampshire,
1928-29,

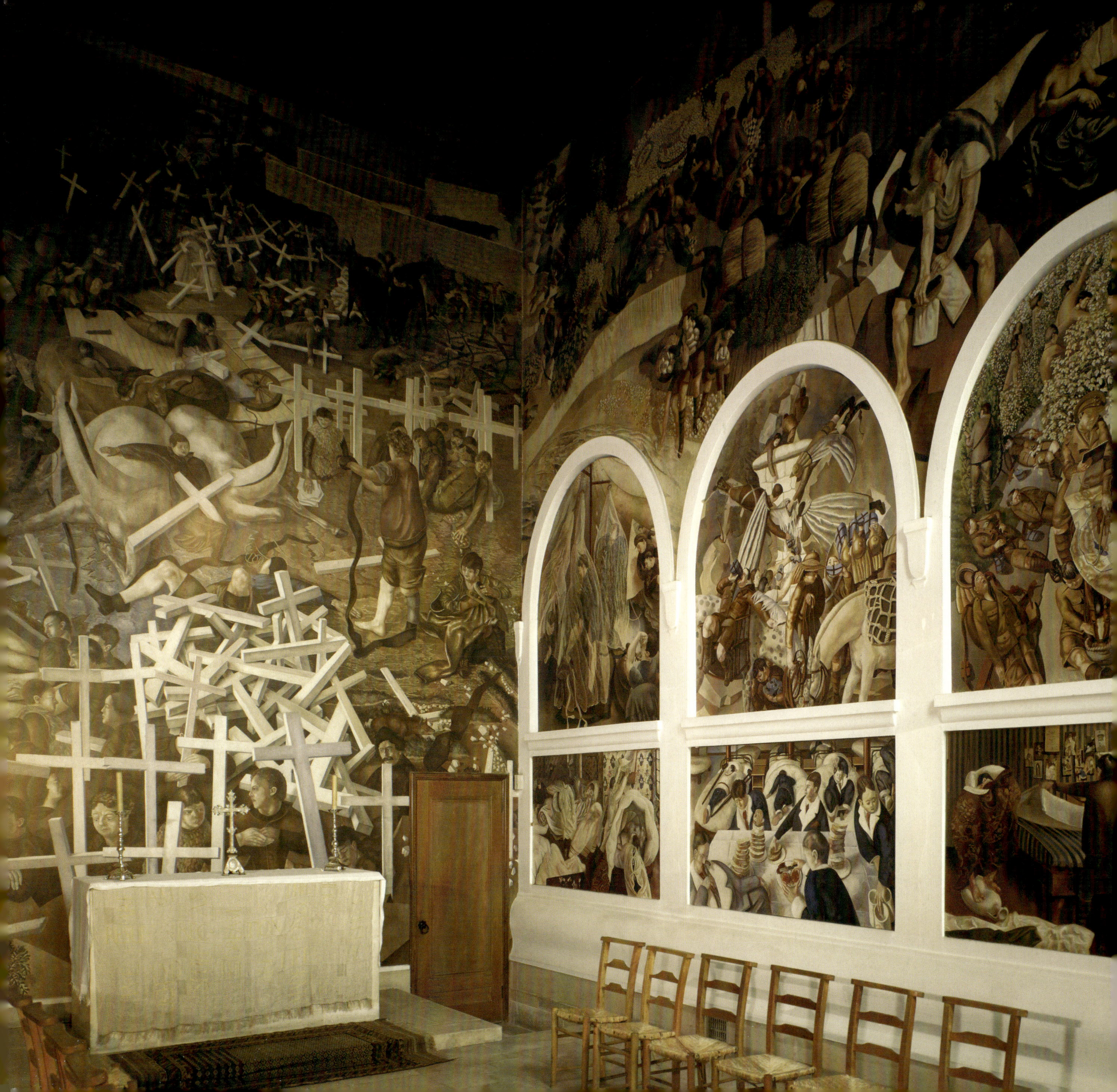

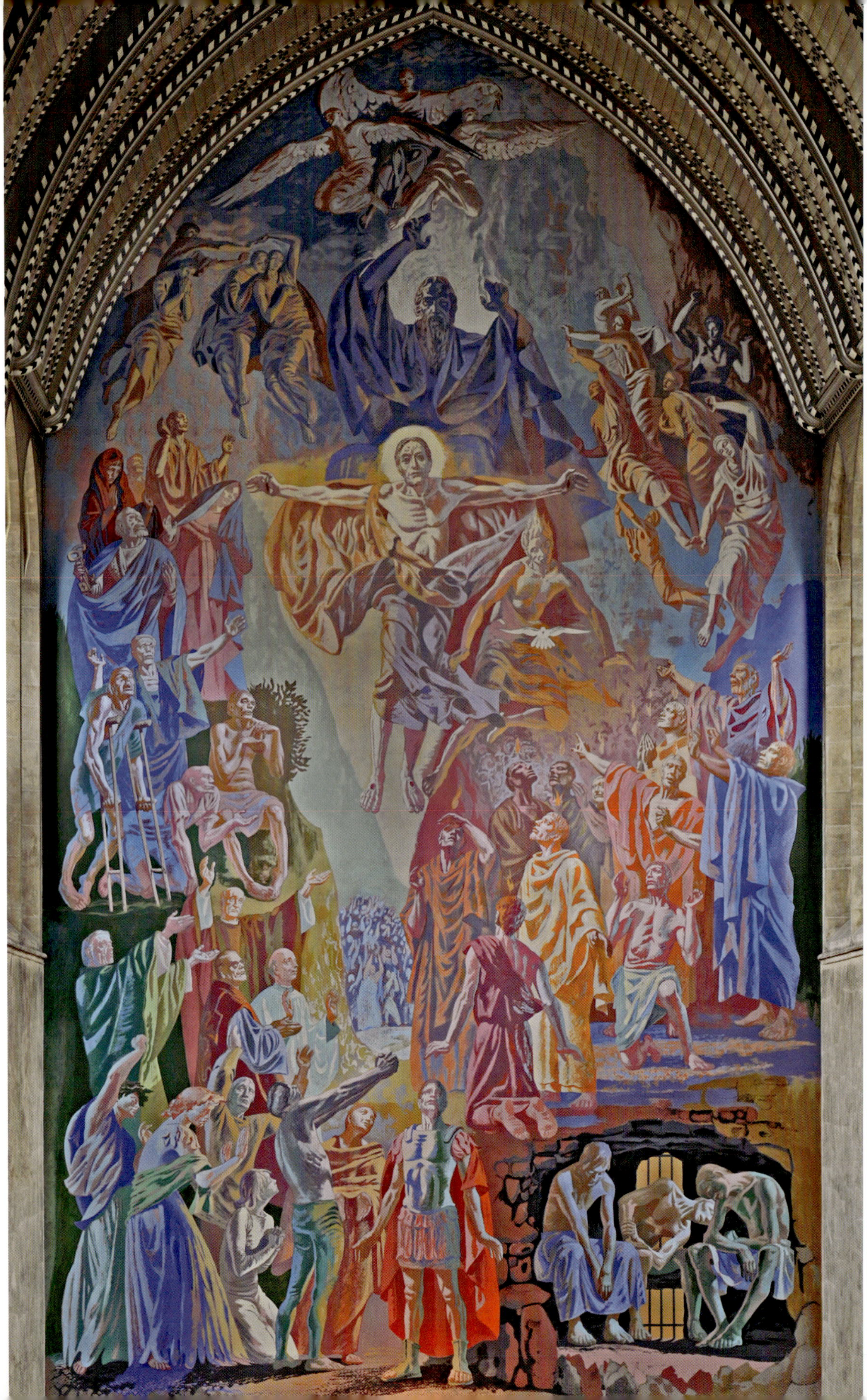

40a
Hans Feibusch,
The Trinity in Glory,
oil mural,
1520 x 880 cm (50 x 29 ft.)
Church of St Alban's,
Holborn, 1966

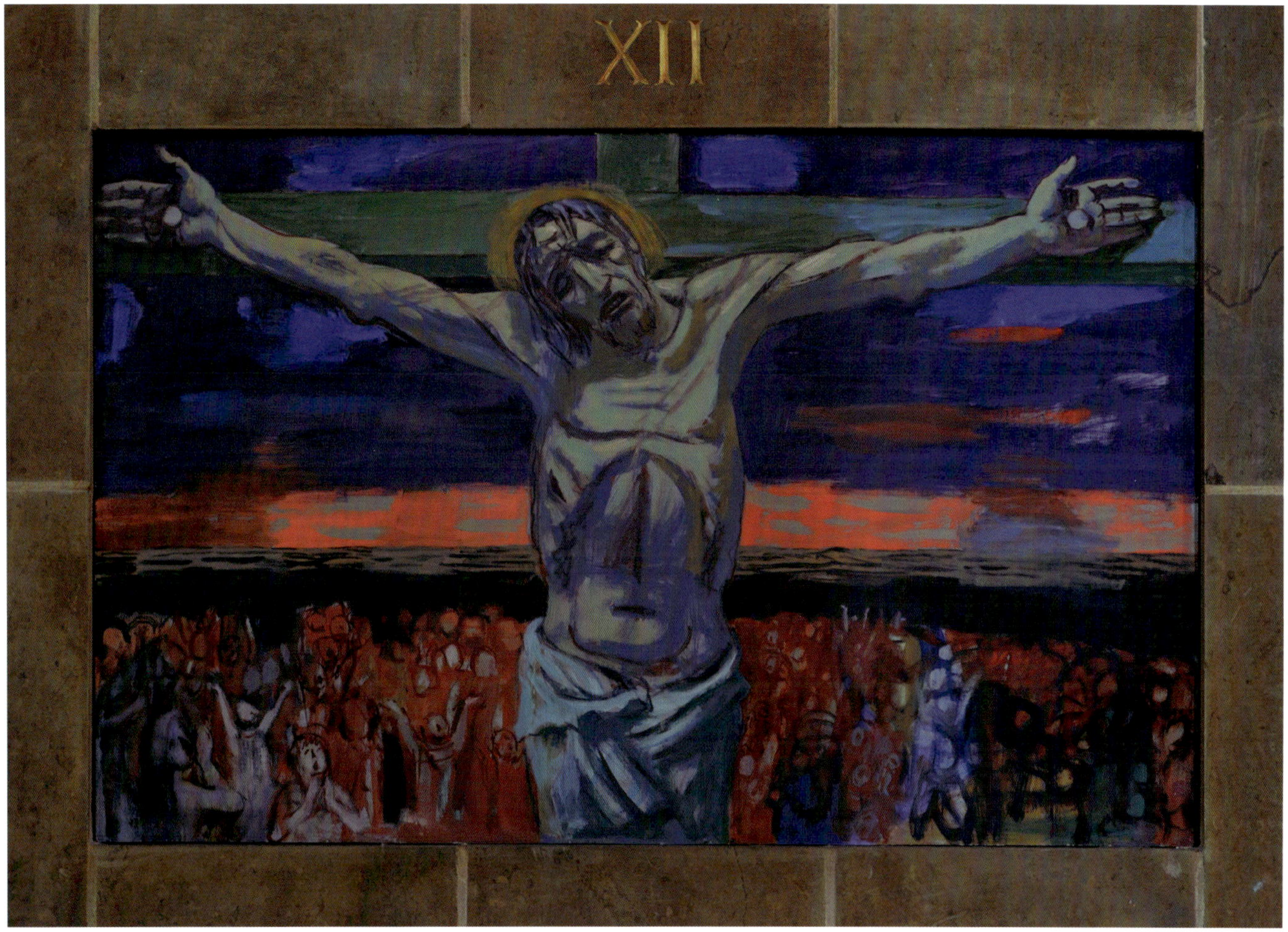

40b
Hans Feibusch,
Twelfth Station,
Church of St Alban's,
Holborn, 1966

which in his view made it no longer necessary to use perspective depth.[53] His description of Cézanne's construction of pictures 'not with Renaissance perspective but with planes, flat shapes lying behind each other, so that objects are shown not so much as curving away towards the back but rather flattened out sideways to their full silhouette and separated from the ones behind them by an outline or shadow' is a description that might apply to John Piper's method in *The Englishman's Home*.[54]

Feibusch's work as a painter stands out after 1950 rather as Brangwyn's did in the first half of the century for its un-English energy and scale, aspects of which made both artists able to respond to architectural settings, as Brangwyn did for the ill-fated Royal Gallery murals in the Palace of Westminster, carefully controlled in relation to the existing lighting and the vast compartmentalized spaces but sadly only partially installed on a trial basis before being refused and sent to Swansea. Both artists had little time for conventional good taste, and while Feibusch's ability to deal with a large undifferentiated wall surface is well displayed in the east wall of the rebuilt Victorian church of St Alban's, Holborn in 1966, the non-naturalistic pastel colours are almost shocking in their unfamiliarity and strength. [40a & 40b]

Several artists welcomed the arrival of a more abstract form of modern architecture, believing that it would offer greater freedom for painters as well as making their work more necessary when conventional forms of decoration were stripped away. Feibusch executed several commissions in modern buildings for Maxwell Fry, making his paintings blend into the surrounding white wall as a form of vignette. As early as 1922, Gerald Moira wrote hopefully that the need for enforced economy 'will bring about the birth of a new period in architecture for the very simple reason that it will compel, in many cases, the use of cheaper materials. Concrete and steel will perhaps after all be our salvation and will give the mural decorator his great chance.'[55] As a lifelong advocate of fresco, Mary Sargant-Florence in 1936 quoted a 'modern artist' who said that the 'unequalled trinity of modern construction – steel, glass and concrete – would in itself be the best reason for the birth of fresco in our day if fresco were not already as ancient as the first buildings in which man employed mortars on a base of lime.'[56] In fact, fresco did not experience a revival, but new paints such as Keim Mineral Paints and Stic B were developed to give a good range of colours and grounds that were non-glossy and weather-resistant for outdoor work.[57] [41]

The idea that architects could be the instigators of mural schemes was transferred without interruption from the earlier academic styles used in Britain. In reality, owing to economic stringencies, there were few Modernist public buildings in the 1930s, and little money to pay for murals in them. The Midland Hotel, Morecambe, designed for the LMS railway by Oliver Hill, was completed in 1933, and the modern construction methods saved enough money in comparison to conventional building that some of the fixed budget was left over for works of art. On the curved tea-room wall Eric Ravilious painted sparkling visions of 'Night and Day', [42] with the same fictive architecture on the edge of the water. The work looked splendid in photographs, but the wall had not dried out properly and the painting decayed, even after a restoration by the artist the following year. Works in the hotel in painted plaster relief by Eric Gill and Denis Tegetmeier [44] fared better, however, and remain in place in the recently restored building.[58] Geoffrey Jellicoe's Caveman Restaurant in Cheddar Gorge (1934-5) had a mural by Eliot Hodgkin showing 'primitive man at play', in an updated cave painting style.[59] [43]

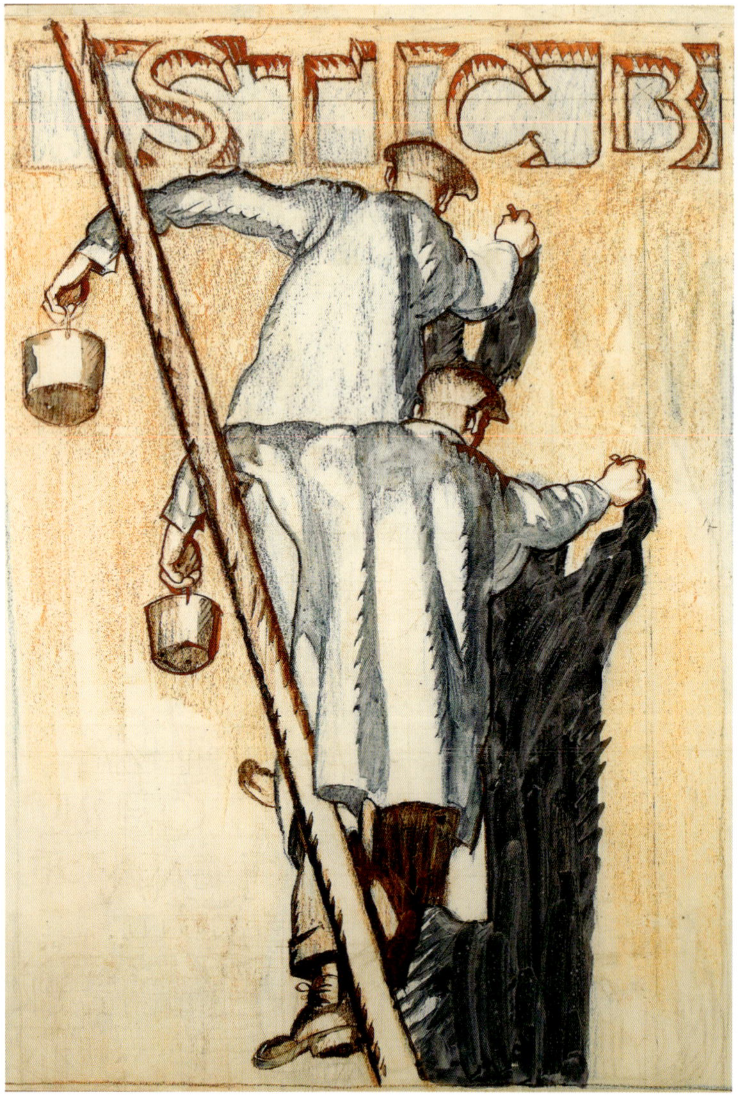

41
Frank Brangwyn,
Stic B, Design for a Poster,
c. 1920,
signed with monogram & inscribed 'Small tail',
watercolour and pastel,
71.1 x 50.8 cm (28 x 20 in.)

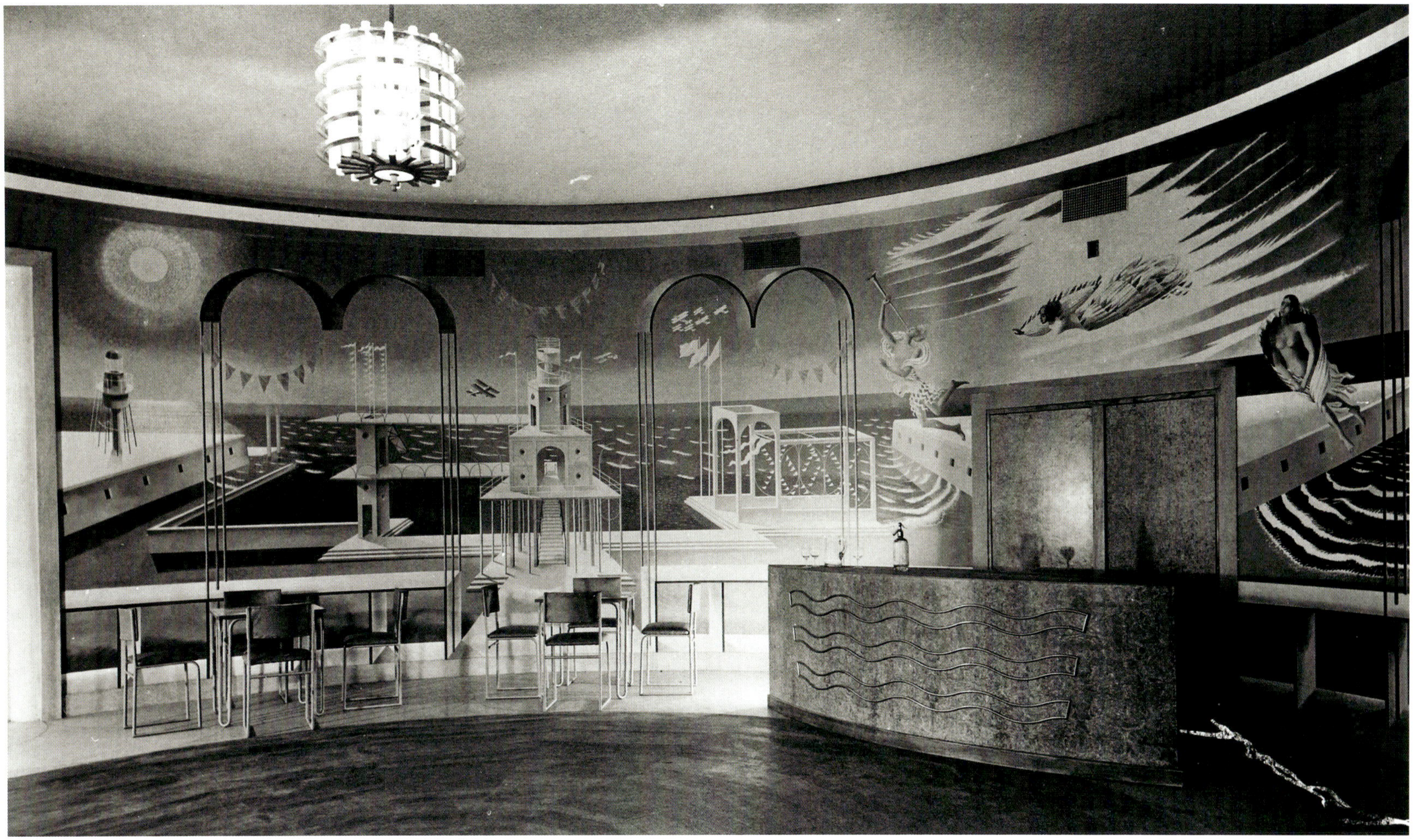

42 Eric Ravilious, *Day*, Midland Hotel, Morecambe, Lancashire, 1933. Courtesy of the RIBA Library Photographs Collection (destroyed c.1935)

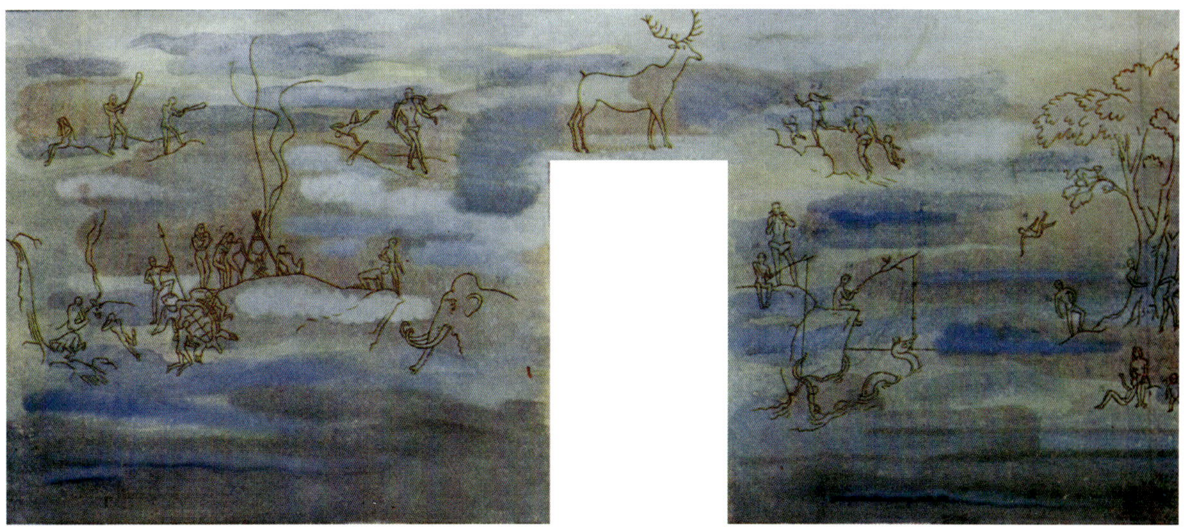

43
Eliot Hodgkin,
mural for Geoffrey Jellicoe's
Caveman Restaurant in
Cheddar Gorge, 1934-35

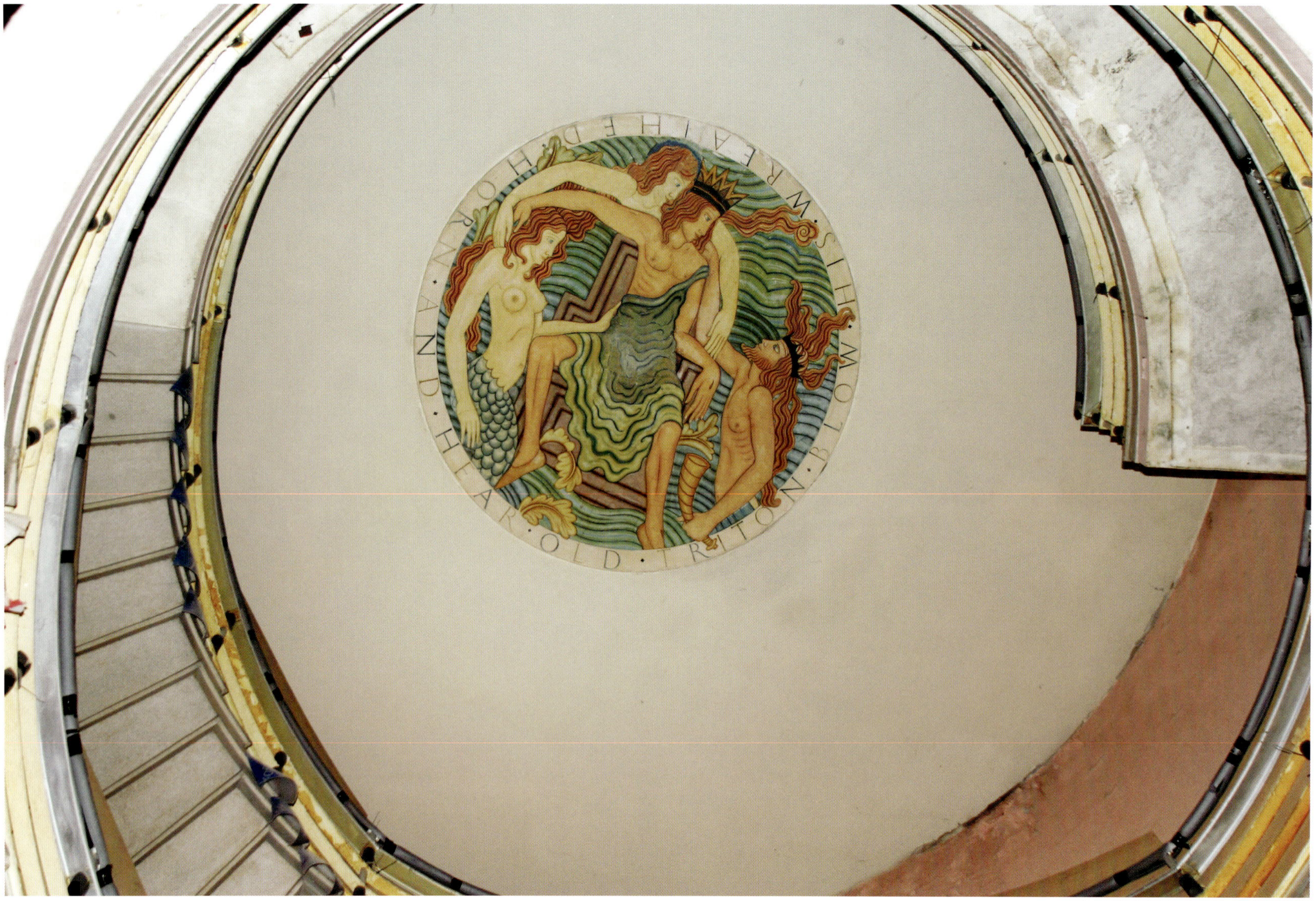

44 Eric Gill and Denis Tegetmeier, *Neptune*, painted ceiling relief, Midland Hotel, Morecambe, Lancashire, c. 1933

Both these buildings were showcases not only for new architectural styles but for the revival of tourism with an international image. Ravilious was considered for a mural commission at the De La Warr Pavilion in Bexhill-on-Sea in 1935, the most famous of the modernist public buildings commissioned as the slump began to wear off, designed by Mendelsohn and Chermayeff, but the commission went to Edward Wadsworth, probably because as a man of independent means he did not charge a fee.[60] [46] The greatest scope for combining murals with modern architecture came in exhibition buildings, such as those at the Empire Exhibition in Glasgow in 1938, where the artists included Eric Fraser, [45] MacDonald Gill, John R. Barker and Clive Gardiner.[61] Photomurals became a popular medium in the 1930s, achieved either by making an enlargement from a photomontage, or by projecting onto a light-sensitive emulsion laid onto the wall in darkroom conditions.[62]

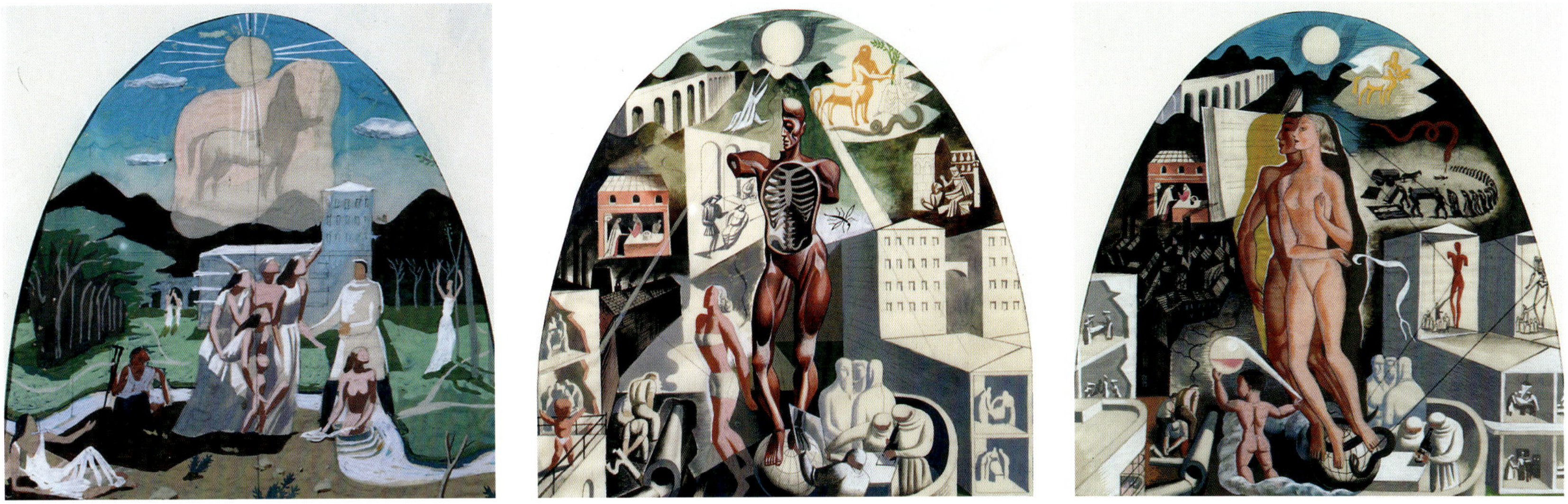

45 Eric Fraser, studies for murals for 'Fitter Britain' display, Empire Exhibition, Glasgow, 1938

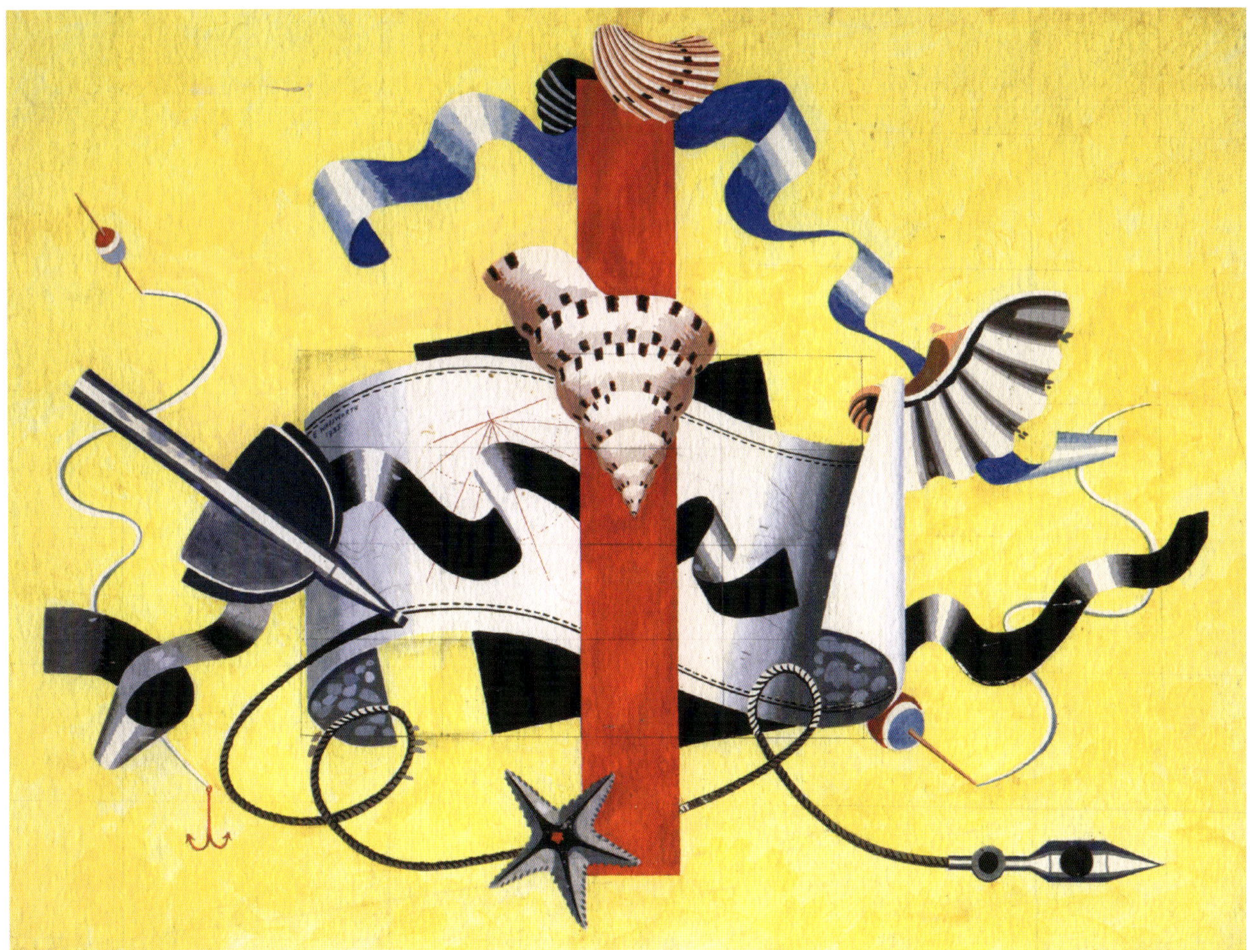

46
Edward Wadsworth,
study for mural at
De La Warr Pavilion,
Bexhill-on-Sea, 1935,
58.4 x 78.7 cm (23 x 31 in.)

The Festival of Britain took this work much further in 1951, promoting the idea that murals and sculpture might make up for the loss of decoration in modern architecture. The re-emergence of John Armstrong's studies for the mural in the Telecinema (see page 285) not only add to our knowledge of the Festival, but also mark the endpoint of his collaboration with the architect Wells Coates, whom he met in the 1920s at Elsa Lanchester's cabaret club in Fitzrovia, The Cave of Harmony, where Armstrong acted as the barman.[63] Ben Nicholson painted a curved panel in the Regatta Restaurant, and many other murals were interspersed among the buildings, including John Hutton's for the Sea and Ships Pavilion, [47] in collaboration with the architect Basil Spence that pre-dated his role in the west window of Coventry Cathedral.

One of the overlooked artists of the Festival was J. C. Stephenson, a veteran of 1930s abstract art in Hampstead and a neighbour of Ben Nicholson, Mondrian and Henry Moore among the 'nest of gentle artists' so named by Herbert Read. Although older than these famous figures, Stephenson turned to abstractions at the beginning of the 1930s and by taking a teaching job in an architecture school made contact with a number of architects. He painted a large ceiling for the Industry Pavilion at the Festival with a design of overlapping frames in the colours of the spectrum on a black ground, [48] before going on to execute several large panels in the 1950s using laminated glass, including one for the British Pavilion at the Brussels Exhibition in 1958.[64] [49]

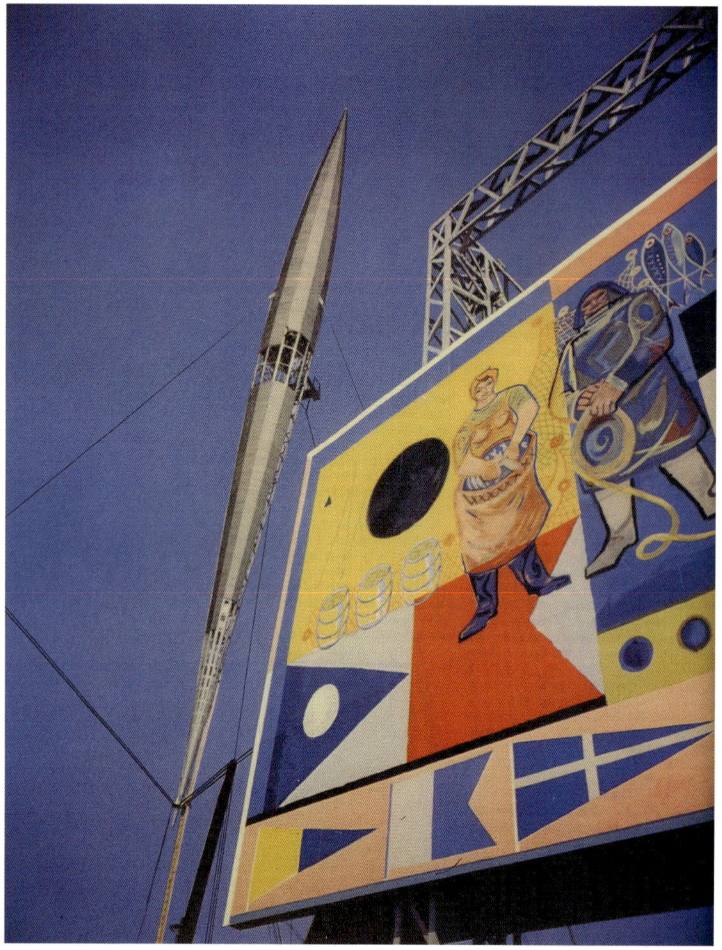

47
John Hutton,
mural for the Sea and
Ships Pavilion,
Festival of Britain, 1951

Occasionally architects themselves painted murals. Notable in this respect was Le Corbusier in France, and one of his former atelier staff, Peter Yates who practised in Newcastle in the 1950s and 60s, and painted one of his earliest murals for another employer, Berthold Lubetkin, at the Bevin Court flats in Finsbury, in a top-lit space specially allocated for the purpose by the entrance.[65] [50] Lubetkin also commissioned Gordon Cullen to paint a propaganda mural at the Finsbury Health Centre in London in 1938 (long lost beneath coats of paint) and one of the relatively rare murals by Feliks Topolski (also lost) at the post-war Priory Green Flats, not far from Bevin Court.

48
John Cecil Stephenson
painting the fluorescent mural
for the Festival of Britain,
April 5, 1951

John Piper painted his first mural, an abstract, for Freddie Skinner, a partner in Lubetkin's firm, Tecton, on a wall outside his flat in the famous Highpoint block in Hampstead.[66] Piper went on to work in both

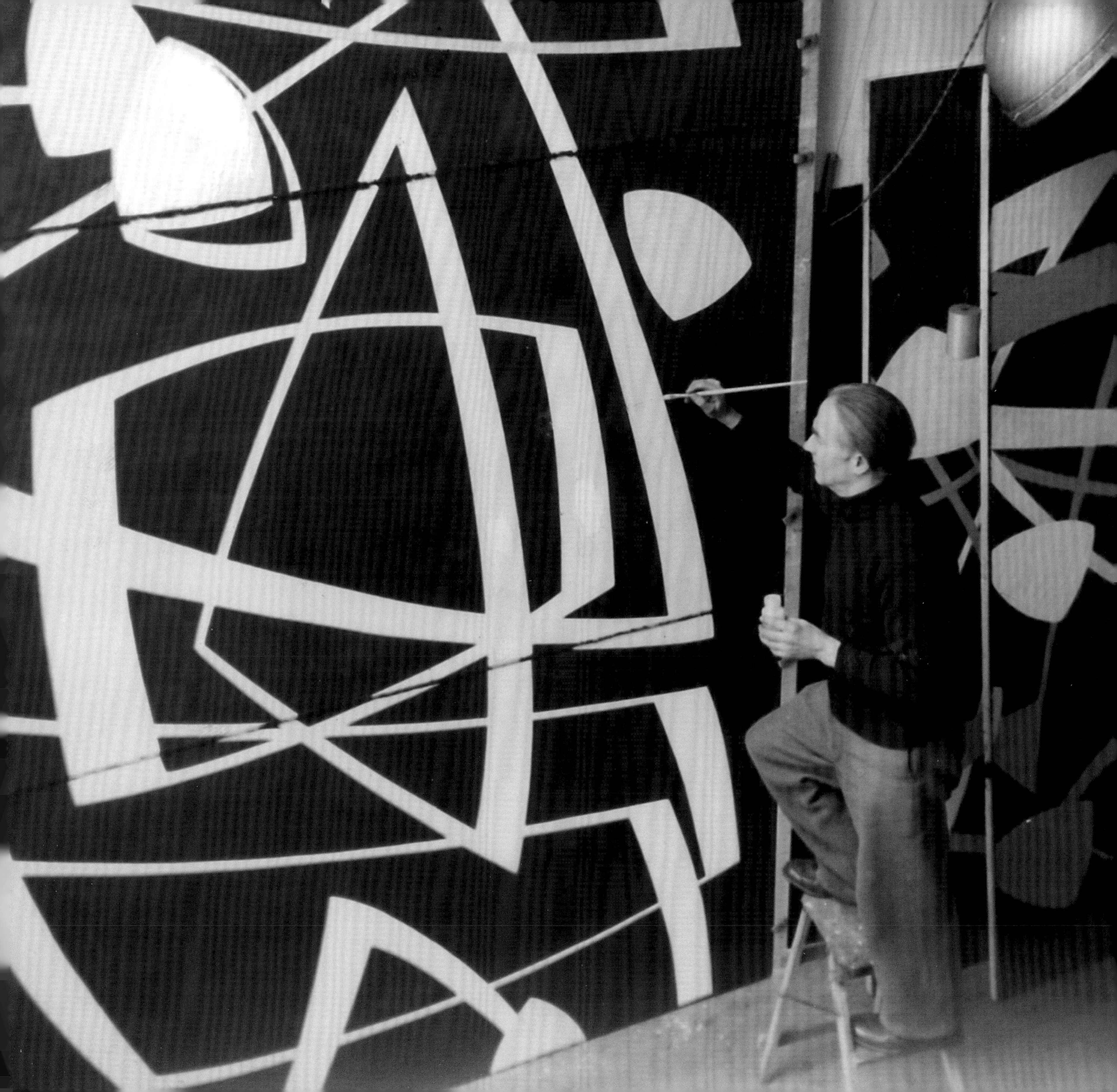

representational and abstract styles, and on his fibreglass panels for the North Thames Gas Board building in Fulham, 1962, [51] the gestural brush marks helped to give vitality to an otherwise conventional 'podium and slab'. As David Fraser-Jenkins writes, 'the blandness of this office block was echoed but turned into a riot of Miro-like dancing shapes in playing-card colours by his long wall of decorations, taken in fact from his studies of rocks on the beach at Britanny.'[67] Fred Millett, who also worked in cast concrete relief later in his career, also turned from the social realism of his paintings at Wokingham of the early 1950s to varieties of Op Art, including an array of coloured stripes at the King of Wessex School, Cheddar, Somerset, 1964.[68]

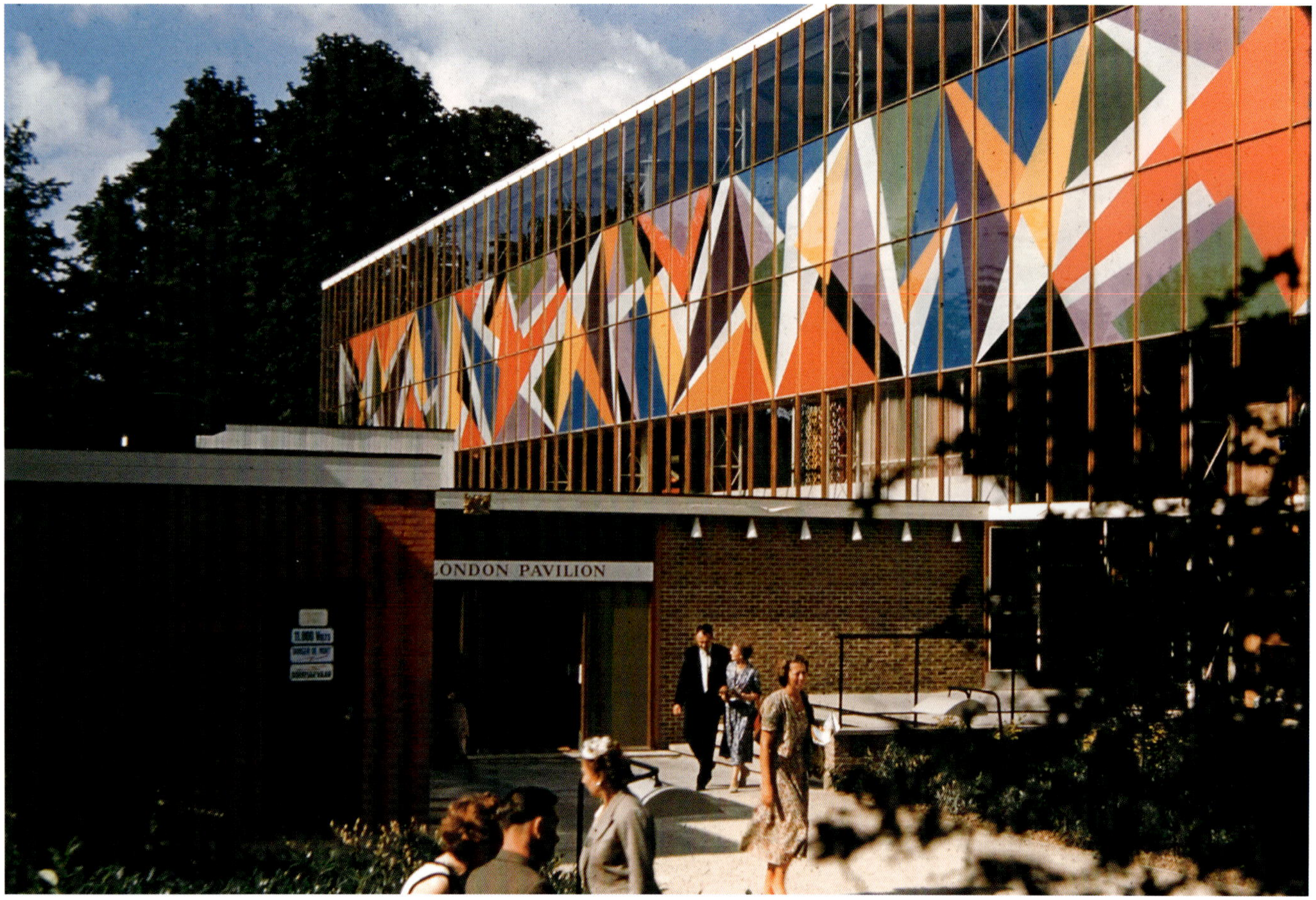

49
John Cecil Stephenson, mural for British Pavilion at the Brussels Exhibition, 1958

Should fibreglass, laminates and low-relief concrete or metal wall panels count as murals? The intention of constructivist artists was to break away from the conventional definition of a mural. In the 1950s Richard Hamilton and Victor Pasmore made the Newcastle University Department of Fine Art a place for progressive education and created a joint installation called *An Exhibit*, 1957, at the Hatton Gallery, consisting of coloured panels hanging in space. The was a reversion to the ideas of van Doesberg in the 1920s, an immersive environment of a kind that prefigured the shift from murals to other ways of introducing art into specific spaces. Having made his first large-scale abstract work for Kingston Bus Garage in 1950, Pasmore made wall reliefs for the Rates Hall at Newcastle Civic Centre, opened in 1968 [52], and went on to act as a consultant for the new town at Peterlee in

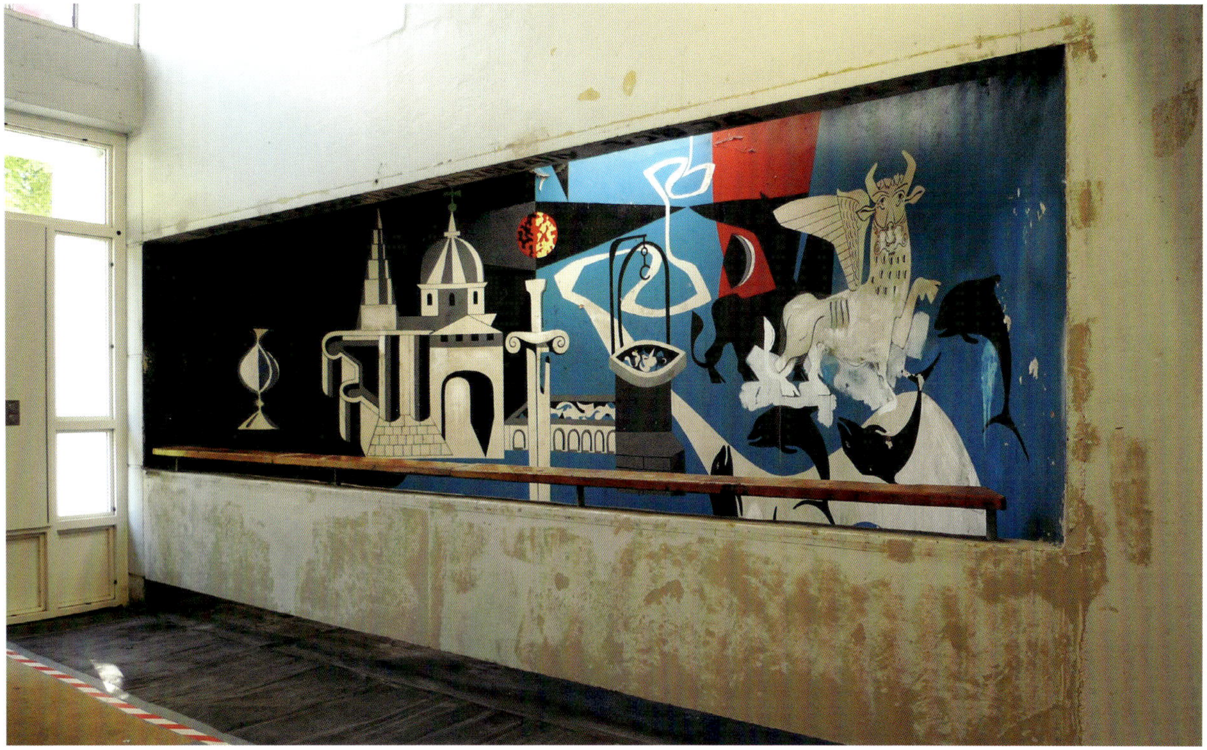

50
Peter Yates,
mural at
Bevin Court flats,
Finsbury,
1953

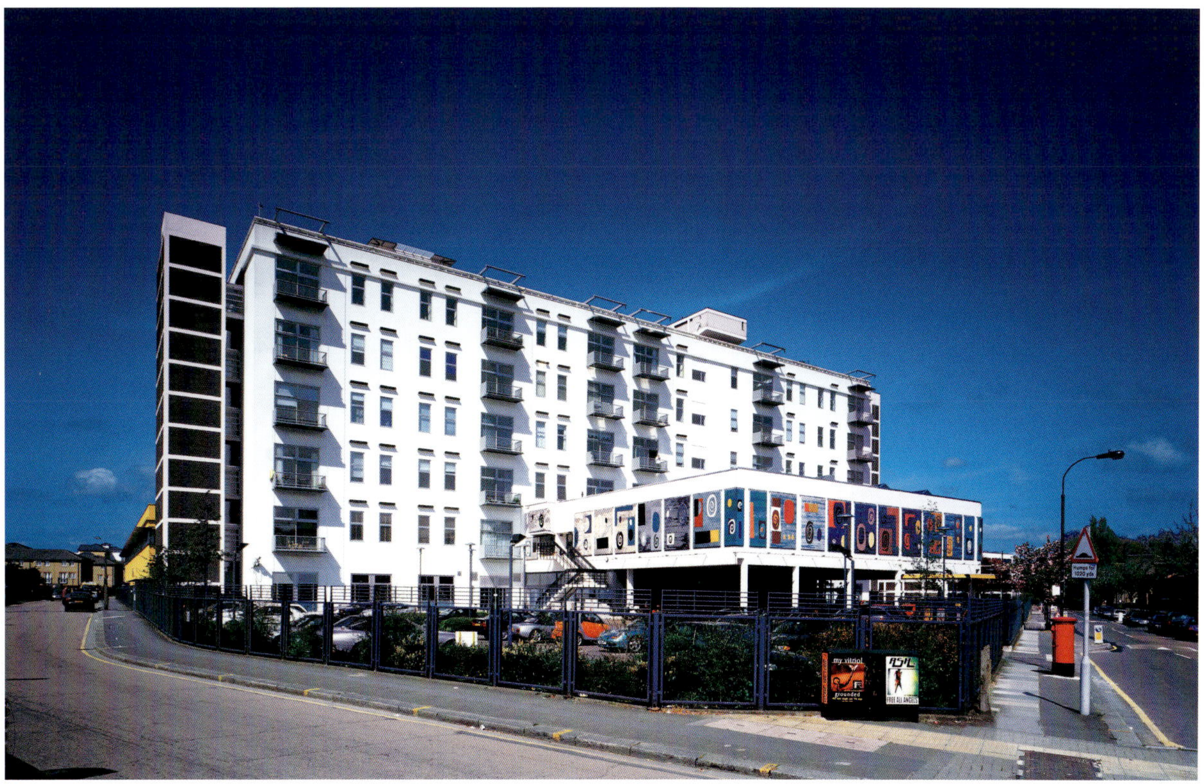

51
John Piper,
panels for
North Thames
Gas Board, Fulham,
(now Piper Building),
1963

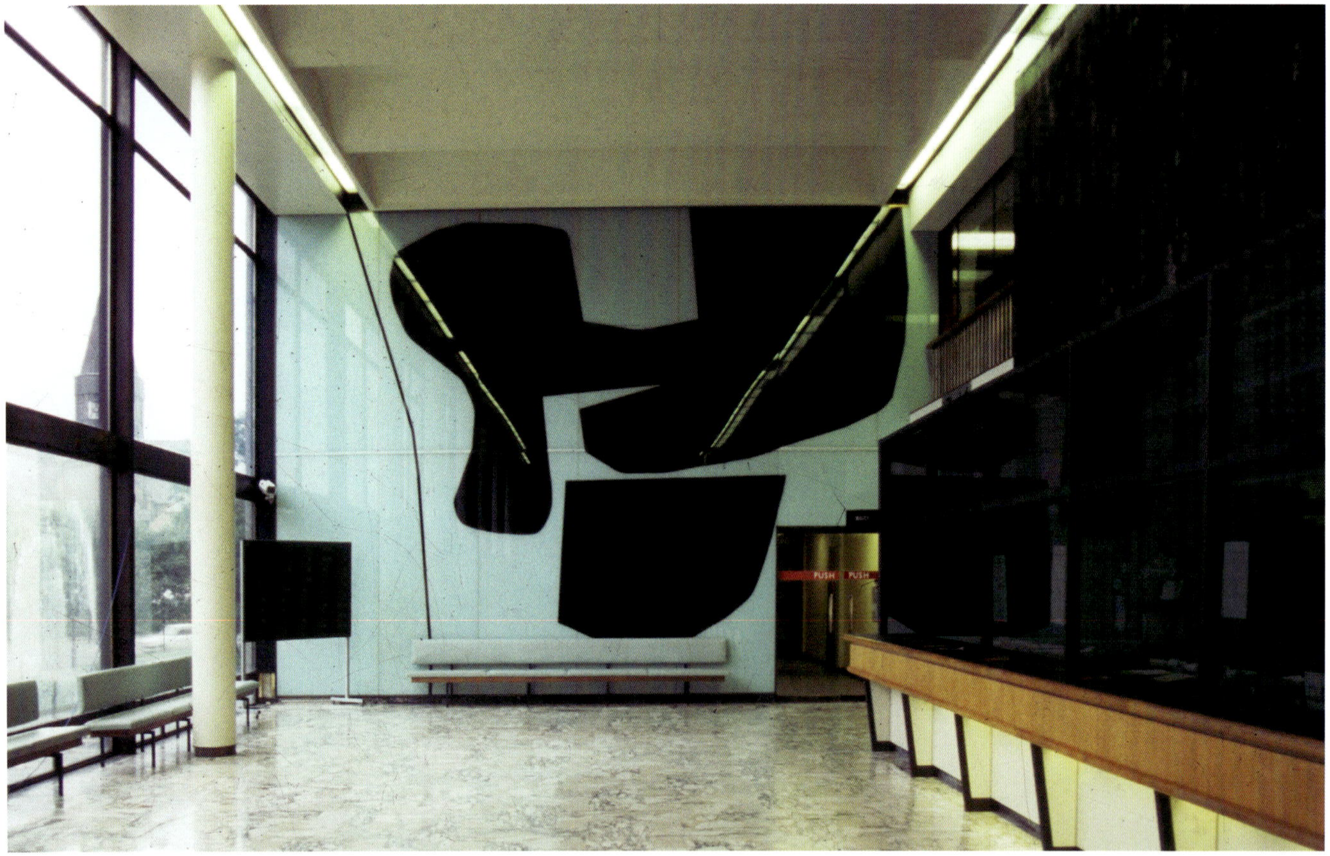

52
Victor Pasmore,
murals in Rates Hall,
Newcastle Civic Centre, 1968

County Durham in the 1960s, trying to create three-dimensional kinetic experiences from the arrangement of the house fronts as seen when driving, a well-intentioned gesture that failed to communicate strongly enough to register. His final legacy to Peterlee, the Apollo Pavilion, was something between sculpture and architecture, but a long way from his origins as a painter. [53] A group of English Constructivists remained active in London and Paris, and a notable work by a member, Gillian Wise, was the staircase installation at the Barbican Arts Centre of 1983 which with angled surfaces reflected in mirrors makes going down into the depths of the building a joyful experience, a work that reflected the continuation of a long-running theme of pure abstraction as a way of exploring interior space in three dimensions.

Despite its potential and short period of public exposure, the Constructivist tradition never gained a strong hold in Britain, and its attempt to merge art and architecture in formal abstract terms now seems a long way from the intensely narrative-based trend in contemporary art. The apparent dead end of what was previously thought to be the single authentic line of progressive art has had an effect on how we think about the many artists of the twentieth century who declined to fall into step with what the critics demanded of them and continued to paint figurative and narrative subjects within the long tradition of the Renaissance. Mural and decorative painting is largely, although not exclusively, made up of these. Critical opinion is still trying to work out an attitude to them, and so far as they have been rehabilitated, they have become valued more for what they depicted in terms of content and subject, in a reflection of the values of current art, than for what probably counted most for them, which was skill in building up a painting from its constituent elements and displaying craftsmanship at all levels. Perhaps we can be allowed to accept and enjoy both these aspects of their work, as we do with writers of poetry and fiction, among whom craftsmanship, content and expression are not required to be continually renewed by originality, but whose ability to command our attention and sympathy is considered enough to justify their place in the canon.

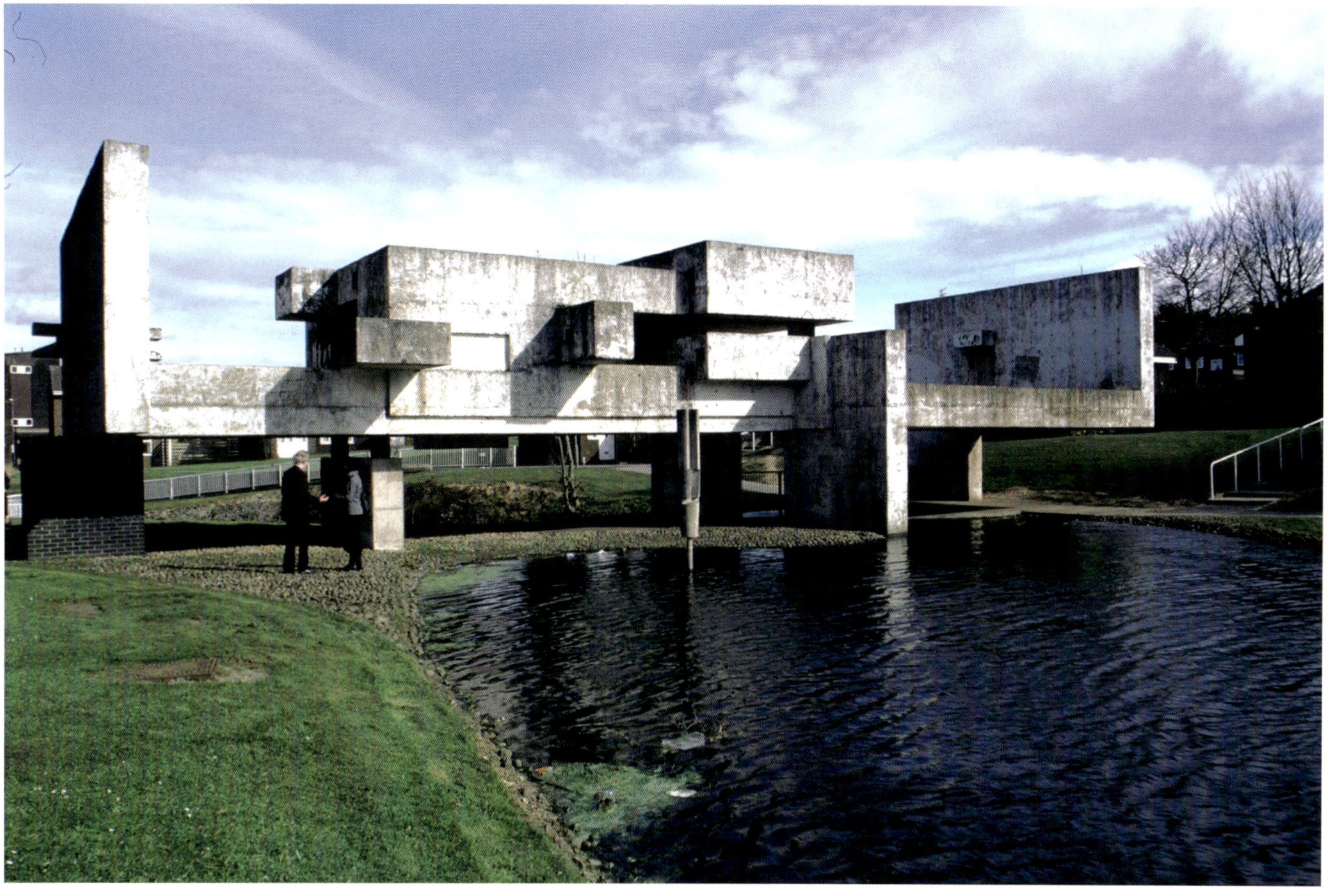

53
Victor Pasmore,
Apollo Pavilion,
Peterlee, County Durham,
1969

Despite the considerable development in the study of twentieth-century British art in the past 25 years towards a greater pluralism, the world of the earlier muralists still seems remote and hard to understand. How could Tom Monnington have laboured so long on so many unpromising subjects with painstaking technique with what sometimes seems a misplaced sense of duty while the modern world took a different course? Monnington's apparently conservative art, like that of his wife, Winifred Knights, was shot through with flashes of genius, most readily apparent during the long gestation of the major works through drawings, colour studies and cartoons. It is revealing that several of their works were left unfinished, as if too much 'finish' could smother the life in them. In the midst of Modernism, they chose to inhabit a different sphere, and even Monnington's turn to abstraction after the war was out of step with the Abstract Expressionist freedom of approach coming from America during the same years.

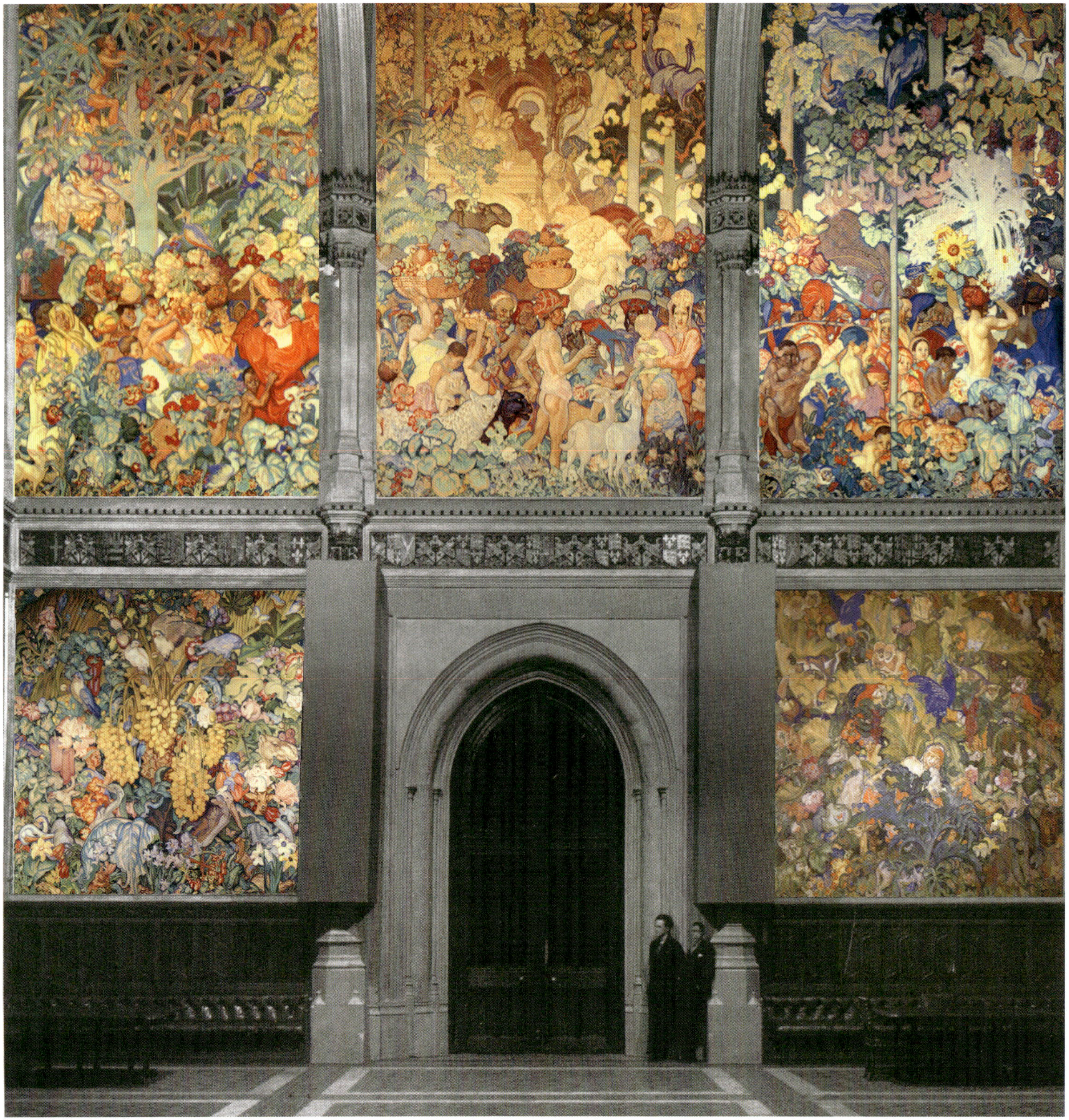

54 Frank Brangwyn, British Empire panels as they would have looked in place, oil and tempera on canvas, total painted surface: 300 m² (3000 sq. ft.)

Patronage

Unless, like the exiled Kurt Schwitters and his Merzbarn in Ellerdale in the Lake District, they are given access to a building and are prepared to work without payment, the counterpart to any artist's hope of making art in a permanent space depends on a patron.[69] Several of these have been mentioned already, since it is impossible to separate one strand of mural parentage from another.

Patronage can have a modifying effect on what artists are able to achieve. It can be an essential enabler, and a good patron will help an artist to surpass their previous work and go in new directions. It was possible for institutions to organize themselves in order to convey a message, and Clare Willsdon's studies have drawn attention to possible political links between the Liberal peers who paid for the East Corridor panels in the House of Commons in 1906, which were seen at the time as 'Coals of Fire', a form of reproof from the Lords towards the Commons at the time of their unveiling in 1910, after the General Election, when a constitutional crisis threatened over the role of the House of Lords in blocking progressive social legislation.[70] This scheme set a pattern for direct selection of artists rather than the competitions that were favoured in France and Germany. However, as Willsdon remarks, 'it is questionable, in fact, whether the artists ever fully appreciated the political purposes of their patrons.'[71] Sometimes an artist was moved to donate their work but needed the protection of a patron, as when Sigismund Goetze painted the upper landing of the grand stair in the Foreign Office between 1912 and 1920, producing work that so displeased Lord Curzon as Foreign Secretary that nearly succeeded in having it removed on its completion.

Frank Brangwyn was less fortunate, for his initial patron for the Royal Gallery Scheme [54], Lord Iveagh, died early on and his successor, Lord Lincolnshire, found that things had begun without enough detailed discussion about who was in charge. Brangwyn kept his work private until a late stage and the project fell foul of the Royal Fine Art Commission partly on grounds of the exuberance of the content, although the visual discrepancy between Brangwyn's bright colours and the subdued work of William Maclise on the lower levels of the side walls was the formal grounds for objection. Brangwyn was luckier in his early patrons, notably R. H. Kitson, an artist of private means from Leeds who commissioned a variety of work including the mosaics at St Aidan's Leeds (1916) and the painted dining room at his Sicilian villa, the Casa Cuseni, Taormina, 1909-10, a survival of a complete painted interior with furniture designed for it by the artist unmatched in mainland Britain.[72] [55]

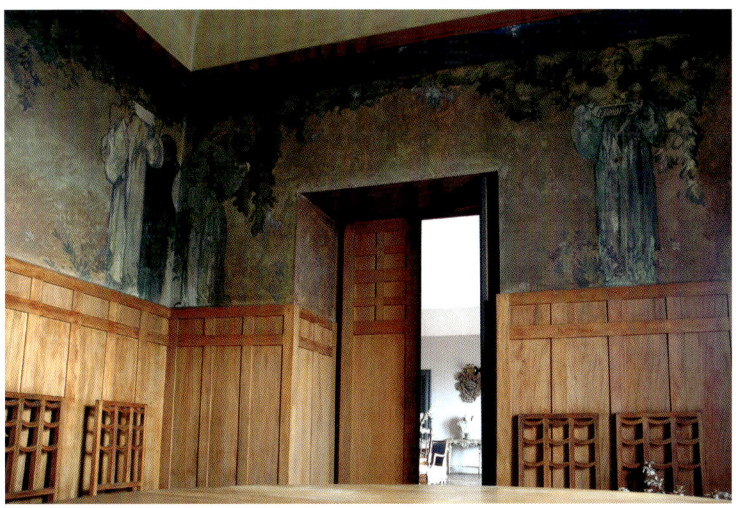

55
Frank Brangwyn, Casa Cuseni, Taormina, Italy, 1909-10

From time to time, public appeals were made for donors to come forward in relation to specific schemes. The heads of the two principal London art schools, Henry Tonks and William Rothenstein, cultivated

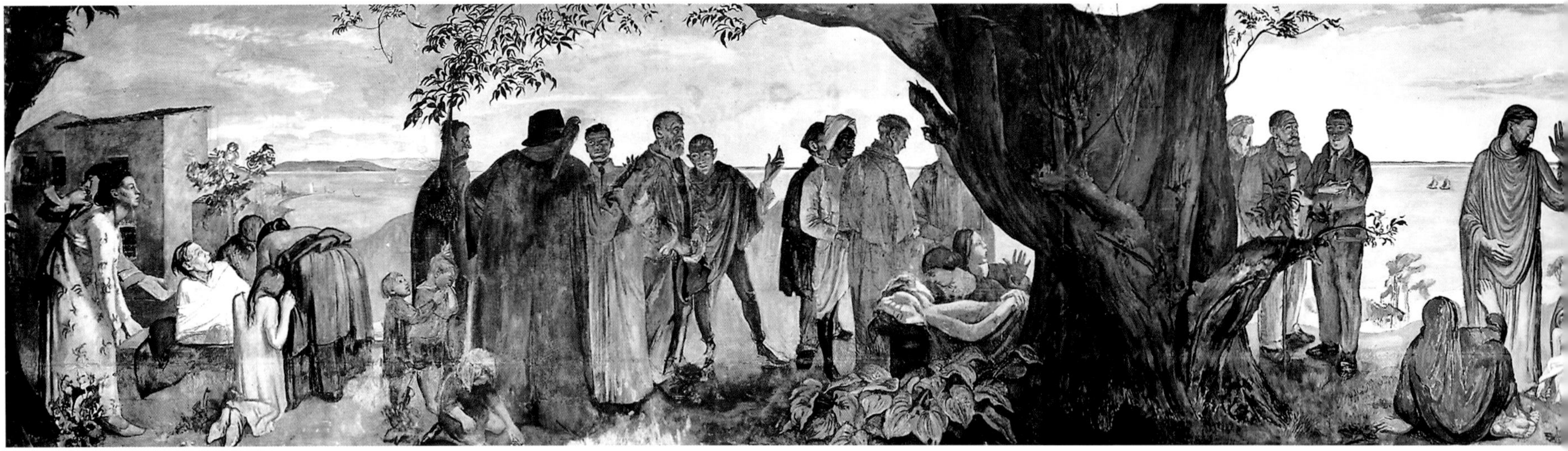

56 Daphne Pollen, murals from the Church of All Hallows, Poplar, 1923-32 (destroyed by bombing)

potential connections. Tonks persuaded the celebrated American art dealer, Joseph Duveen, initially to fund Rex Whistler and Mary Adshead's work at the Highways Club, Shadwell (itself a charitable venture by Eton College) in 1924. Two years later, after Whistler had completed the Slade course, Tonks, having dissuaded him from applying for the Rome Scholarship, worked with Sir Charles Aitken, the Director of the Tate Gallery, to secure further funding from Duveen for him to paint the Refreshment Room at Millbank. When this proved a great public success on completion in 1928, Duveen was willing to fund another scheme by students of the Royal College of Art, and Aitken contacted Rothenstein for suggestions. Morley College for Working Men and Women, a pioneer of evening classes in a wide variety of subjects, had just moved into new premises in Lambeth and Eva Hubback, the principal, had already approached Duveen with a proposal, and from six artists who submitted, Mahoney, Bawden and Ravilious were selected and received a total of £1,200 between them based on a rate of £1 per day, half of which appears to have been contributed by Duveen.[73]

Completely private patronage can be either a blessing or a curse. In 1925, Mary Adshead completed a dining room for one of her architect father's colleagues, the Professor of Architecture at Liverpool, Charles Reilly, and was able to indulge her fantasy with a picnic in a jungle. (see page 186) Not long after, she was commissioned, via another architect, Robert Atkinson, to paint a dining room for the Newmarket house of Lord Beaverbrook. Her 1928 set of canvasses *An English Holiday* for the four walls of the room was full of incident and recognizable friends of Beaverbrook's, but when the paintings were completed, he was persuaded by Lady Diana Cooper that he would probably quarrel with most of them and that the paintings, although paid for, should therefore not be installed. After a brief outing at Peter Jones store in 1930, (see page 185) the paintings were lost to view. The artist retained some rolled up in the attic and they were sold in the 1980s, with some further canvases reappearing at a later date.[74]

Adshead argued in 1927 that the demand for mural painting ought not to come from municipalities (as the civic model proposed) but from 'the private individual, business firms, hotel and restaurant proprietors, shipping companies, and, above all, from the smaller and more individual shop owners.'[75] She followed these precepts

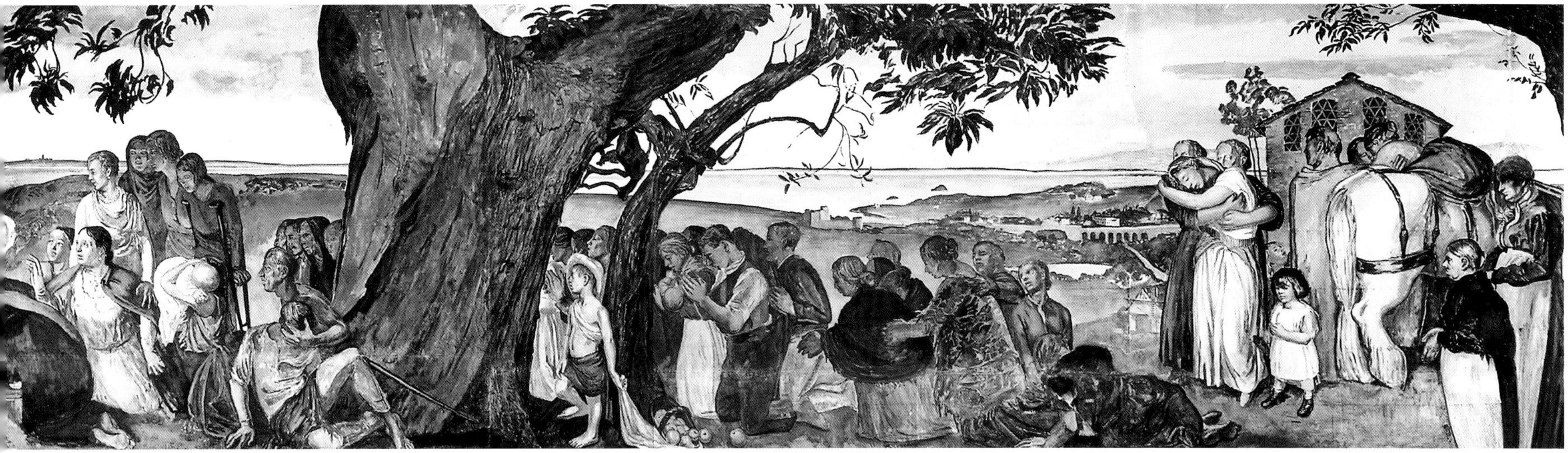

and became a specialist in painting murals for the restaurants in department stores, including Selfridges and Lewis's in Bristol and Leicester. At St Christopher, Withington, near Manchester, 1931-5, she painted a large figure of the Ascending Christ in the east end, [57] a design organized in a way that strikingly resembles Graham Sutherland's *Christ in Majesty* tapestry in Coventry Cathedral. The church was demolished in the 1990s, but fortunately the painting found a home at another church, St Columba, Anfield, near Liverpool, by the same architect, Bernard Miller. Other church commissions followed, including a powerful rendering of the Crucifixion on the east wall at St Francis, Luton, 1960.

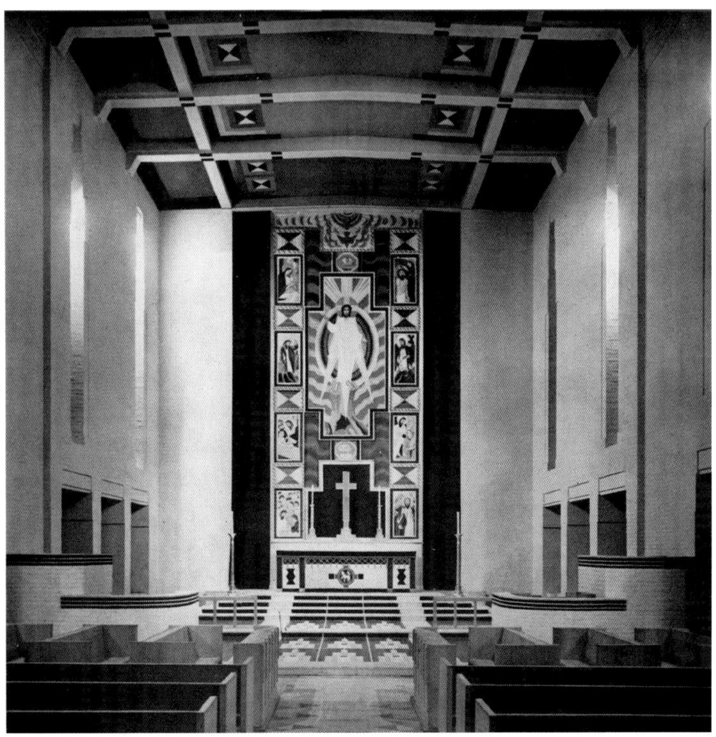

57
Mary Adshead,
Altarpiece from
St Christopher,
Withington,
1931-35,
(in original setting)

The tradition of painted walls in churches was revived in the nineteenth century, but in cities there was a risk of air pollution and in the country a risk of damp.[76] Some painters have had strong religious convictions of their own, including Daphne Pollen [56] whose 60ft-long murals (destroyed by bombing) in the church of All Hallows, Poplar, from 1923-32, aroused the admiration of Henry Tonks for his pupil. 'I was bowled over,' he wrote to a friend, 'such drawing, such large conception. Never have I had such a woman at the Slade and few men….'[77] The artist almost certainly gave her services free for this work, which as a member of the Baring banking family she was well able to do. Charles Mahoney's paintings for the Lady Chapel at Campion Hall (see pages 232-243) were financed by a fund of £600, the royalties from Evelyn Waugh's life of

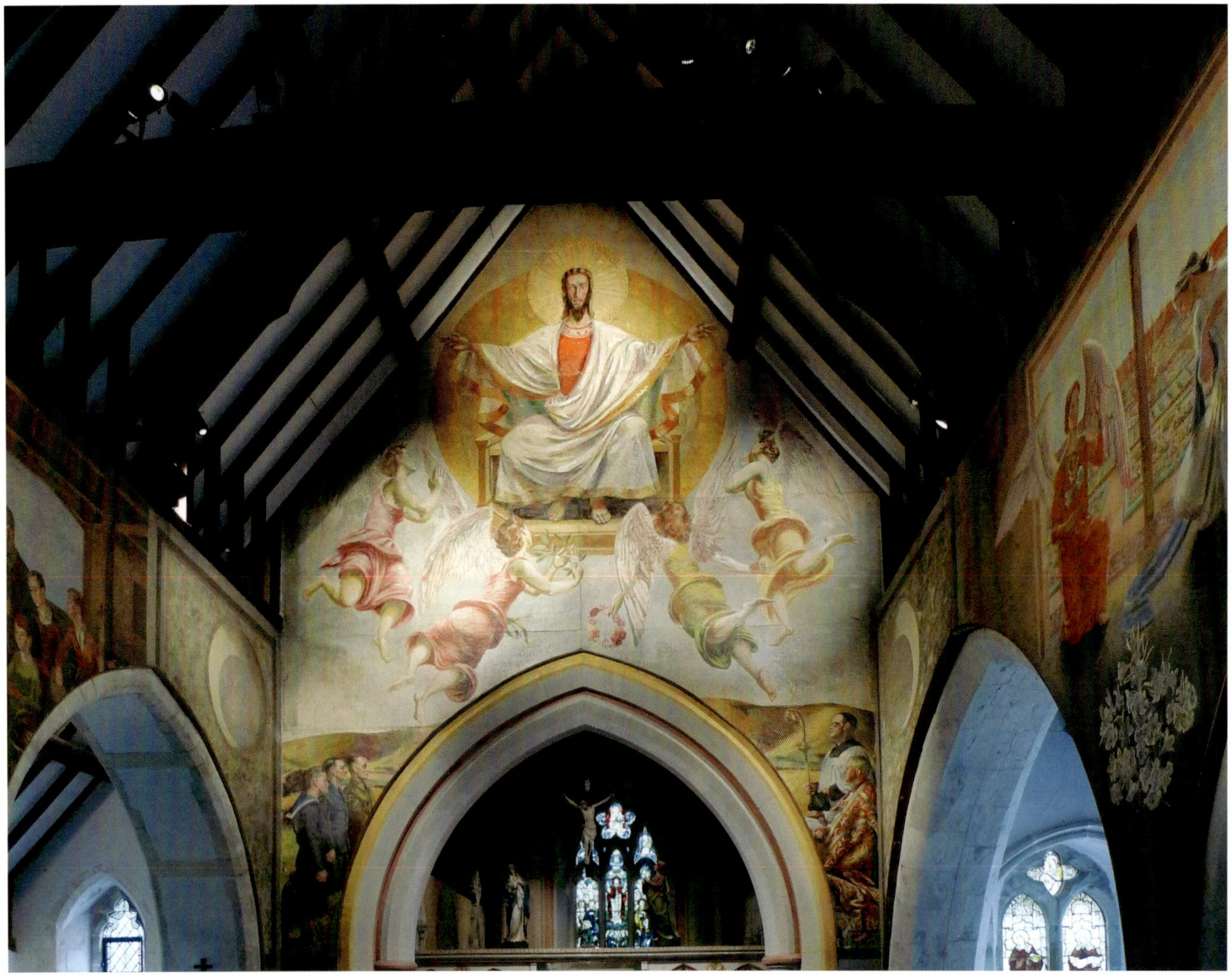

58
Duncan Grant and
Vanessa Bell,
Berwick Church, Sussex,
1941

Edmund Campion, 1935. The commission was awarded in 1941, and the work continued until it was nearly completed in 1952. As John Rothenstein commented later, '£600 … would in any case have been very modest remuneration, but during the previous ten years it had lost much of its value. The Hall supplemented his pay on a modest scale, but he believed it could have afforded more.'[78] Mahoney was certainly not driven by thoughts of money, but the work involved was out of proportion to the fee, and he later regretted that he had not worked on canvas in his studio, rather than on site in the poorly lit space.

Paintings in churches could easily become controversial in terms of subject matter, or their very existence even could still be theologically divisive. The Protestant Truth Society was loud in denunciation and even conducted a damaging raid on the medieval church of St Hilary near Marazion in Cornwall where the high church vicar employed members of the local artists' colony at Newlyn and Lamorna in the 1920s to paint the choir stalls and other items.[79]

One notable patron in the Church of England in the mid-century was Bishop George Bell of Chichester, who encouraged the performance of modern plays in churches and cathedrals (he commissioned T. S. Eliot's *Murder in the Cathedral* for Canterbury) and the broadcasting of services. Discussing 'The Church and the Artist' in the *Studio* magazine he asked, 'why should not the present age also make its contribution? Is it not essential that it should do so?'[80] Bell became interested in murals as extension of his social and sacramental mission, in 1939 writing to Sir Kenneth Clark, then the most influential source of patronage in Britain, for recommendations.[81] Through this channel, he met Hans Feibusch who had already painted one Methodist church mural. Bell was actively concerned about the plight of opponents of Nazism, and under his influence Feibusch joined the Church of England, executing several commissions in the Chichester diocese.[82] George Bell helped in the commissioning of murals by Alan Sorrell at St Peter's, Old Bexhill (1951) and Augustus Lunn at the newly-constructed Bishop Hannington Memorial Church, Hove (1938-41, architect Edward Maufe). He is best remembered for his support of Vanessa Bell and Duncan Grant when they proposed to donate paintings to Berwick Church, near their Sussex home, Charleston, in 1941.[83] [58]

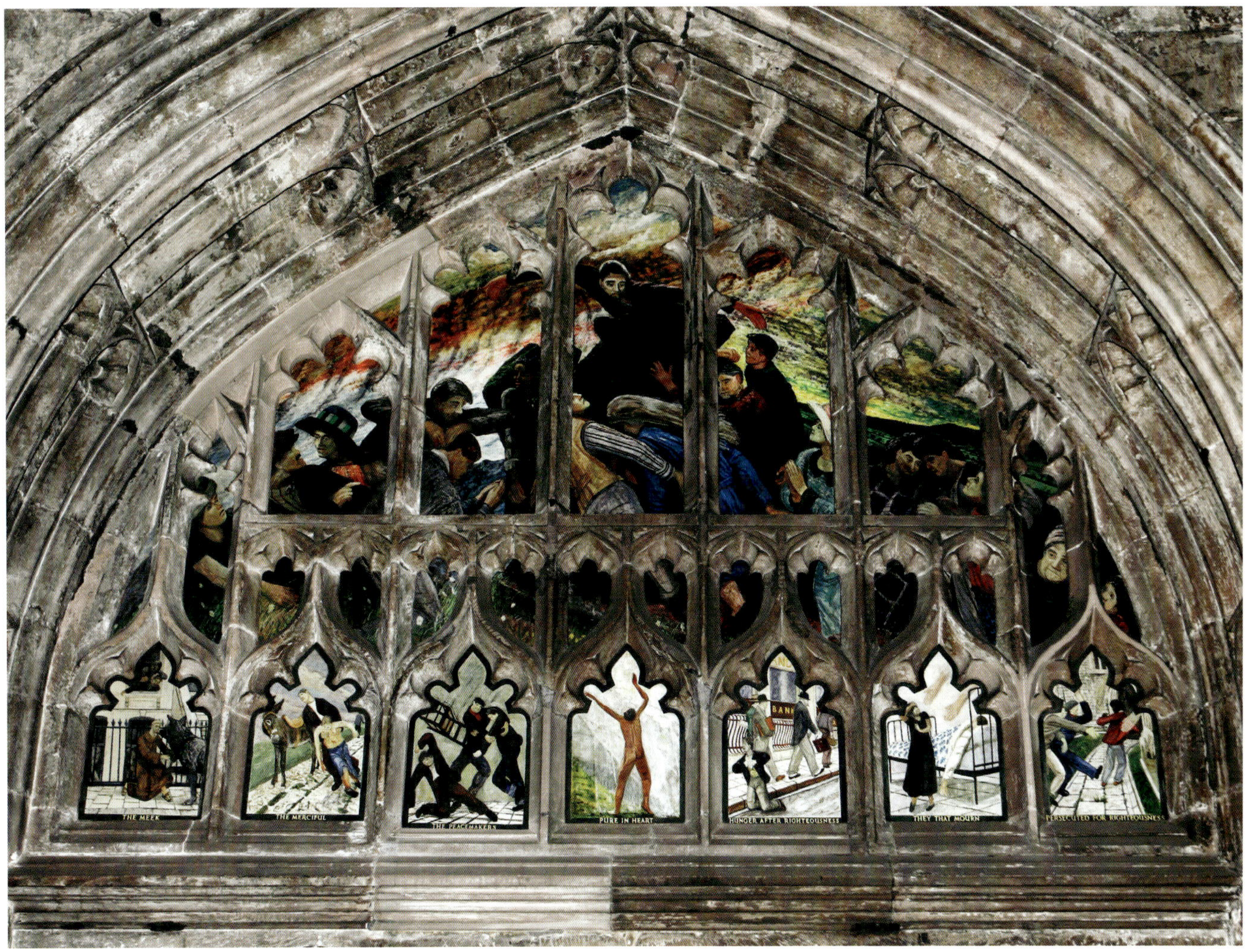

59
Carel Weight,
Christ and the People,
Manchester Cathedral,
1963

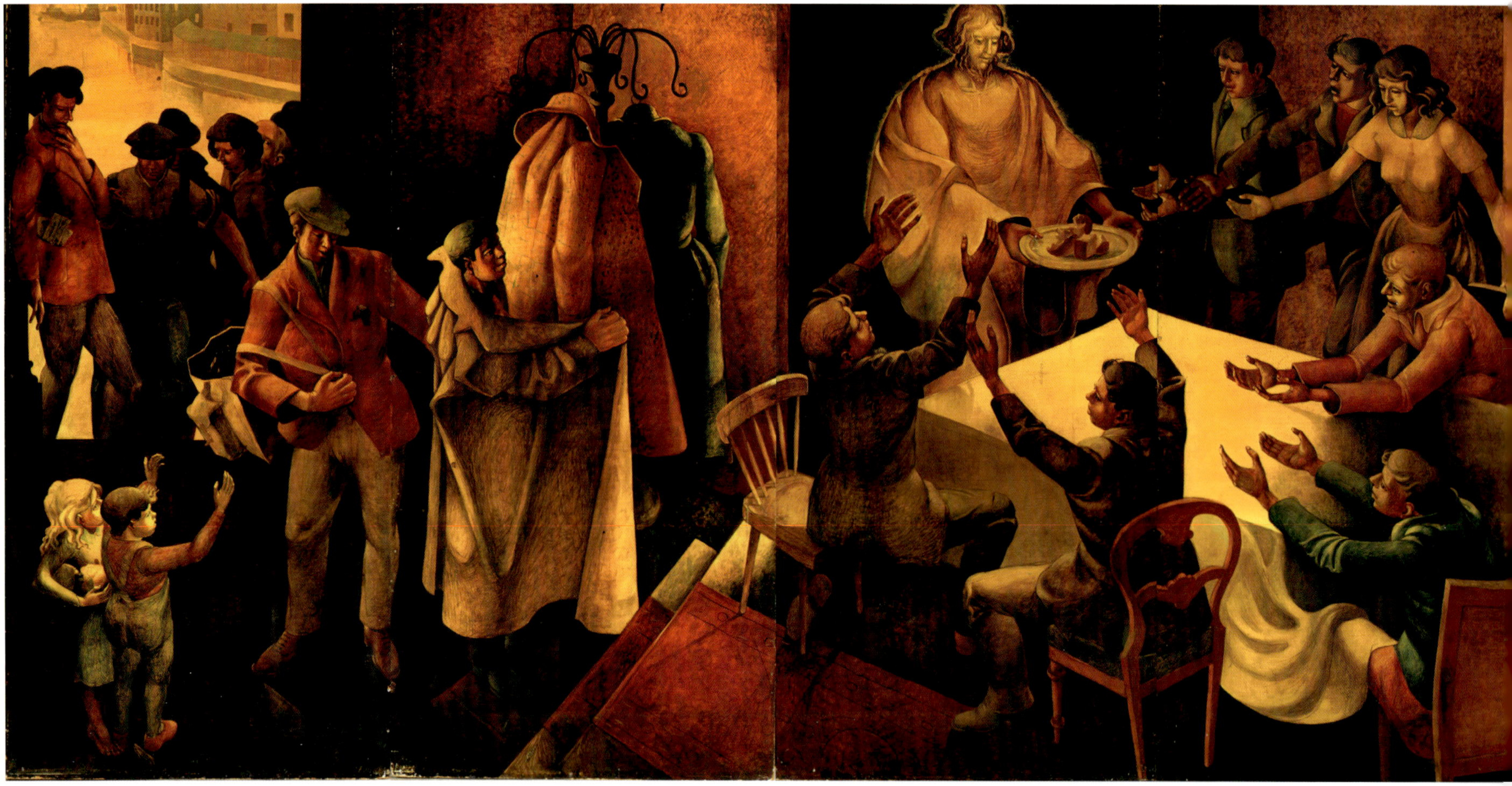

60 Fyffe Christie, *Christ Feeding the People*, mural for the café set up in Glasgow by the Iona Community, signed and dated, oil on board, eight panels: 243.8 x 975.2 cm (96 x 384 in.)

By overcoming opposition, Bell and others prepared the way for a more extensive use of artists in churches after 1945. War damage payments given in respect of stained glass destroyed by bombing had to be used for replacement art, but it was agreed that this could take the form of murals, and proved to be a valuable source of patronage for Feibusch among others. The active patrons could be the clergy or the architects, and the Edwin Austin Abbey Trust Fund, set up by the widow of the American painter Abbey, himself a pioneer of murals in Boston Public Library and Harrisburg State Capitol. The Abbey Trust Fund supported murals by Duncan Grant at Lincoln Cathedral and Carel Weight's 1963 *Christ and the People* at Manchester Cathedral, both in existing architectural spaces.[84] [59] The Abbey Trust Fund also supported the murals painted by John Ward, a local resident, in the chancel of St Cosmas and Damian, Challock, Kent. These delicate scenes from the life of Christ, showing recognizable local people in modern dress, continue the Spencer tradition of updating and localizing religious themes, but with a different aesthetic closer to book illustration.

When church art after the war is discussed, it is usually the modern artists, such as Graham Sutherland and John Piper, who are mentioned, often in connection with the patronage of Canon Walter Hussey, first at St Matthew's, Northampton and then at Chichester Cathedral, where he served as Dean during George Bell's time

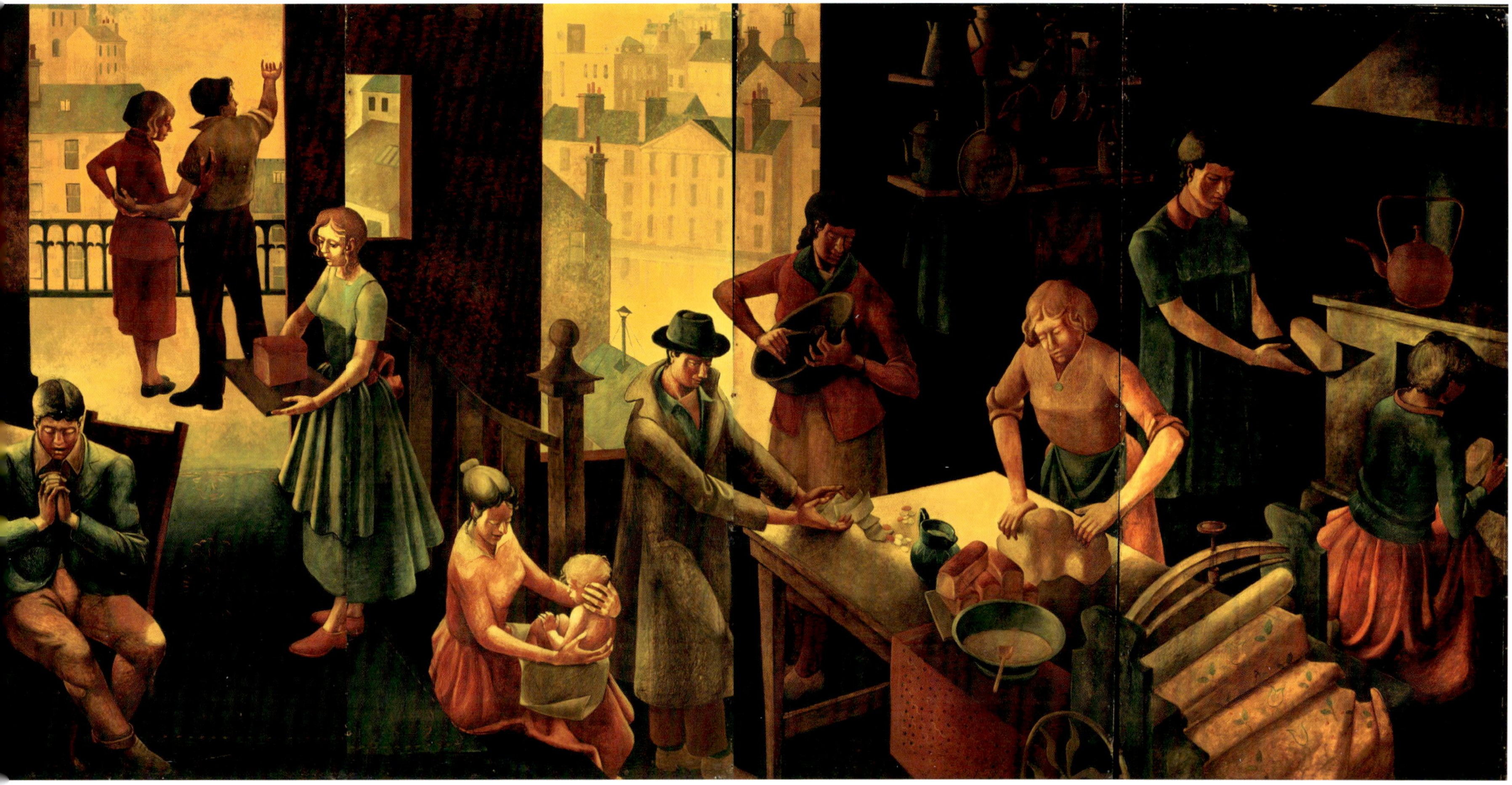

as Bishop. Neither of these artists produced mural paintings as such, which may have been a practical move to allow them to work off site. Sutherland preferred to work on framed canvases hung in the conventional way, and at Coventry Cathedral followed the French revival of tapestry, while Piper worked in stained glass and mosaic.[85]

Leon Underwood painted murals in two newly built Oxford churches immediately after the war, working with the architect Lawrence Dale. His large altarpiece at St Alban's, Cowley, showing a nearly-nude saint meeting the risen Christ, is a striking work with more strength of feeling than many church paintings, conveyed by its scale and by the contorted figures. The parishioners disliked its nudity from the beginning and concealed it behind a curtain, helping in the process to protect its light tempera colours from the light. This work came towards the end of Underwood's career, and although it did not continue his avant-garde trajectory from the 1920s, when he was valued as a teacher by Henry Moore and others, it is a vigorous and surprising piece.

The Scottish artist Fyffe Christie painted many murals, including a large set of panels in 1950-51 for the café set up in Glasgow by the Iona Community [60], where the poor and homeless were welcomed. It had the appropriate subject of *Christ Feeding the People*. Despite a widespread demand for it to enter a public collection in the 1990s, the panels entered a private collection.[86] Christie moved to London and taught art in Ilford and Barking. At the Little Ilford Baptist Tabernacle, he painted a major mural of *A Modern Pilgrim's Progress* in 1961. His work has been compared to Stanley Spencer, but was largely unknown until the publication of a monograph in 2004.[87]

One of the categories mentioned by Mary Adshead in 1927 was ships, and up to the launch of the *QE2* by Cunard in 1969, they remained an important source of patronage for artists. A light approach was considered appropriate in creating an atmosphere similar to a hotel, and French and German ships led in the 1920s in moving from a heavily 'period' look towards a middle-of-the-road Modernism. For Cunard's RMS *Queen Mary*, 1936, paintings by Duncan Grant were rejected as unsuitable, but others by Doris Zinkeisen, Alfred Thompson and Edward Wadsworth remain to this day in Long Beach, California. In 1934 the Orient Line launched the RMS *Orion*, with interiors by the architect, Brian O'Rorke, who was selected by a young director of the company, Colin Anderson. While the *Orion* contained only one painted mural by Tristram Hillier, successor ships in for the Australia and New Zealand service (all with names beginning 'Or-') included paintings by Edward Bawden, Robert MacBryde, John Piper, [61] Ceri Richards and Humphrey Spender.

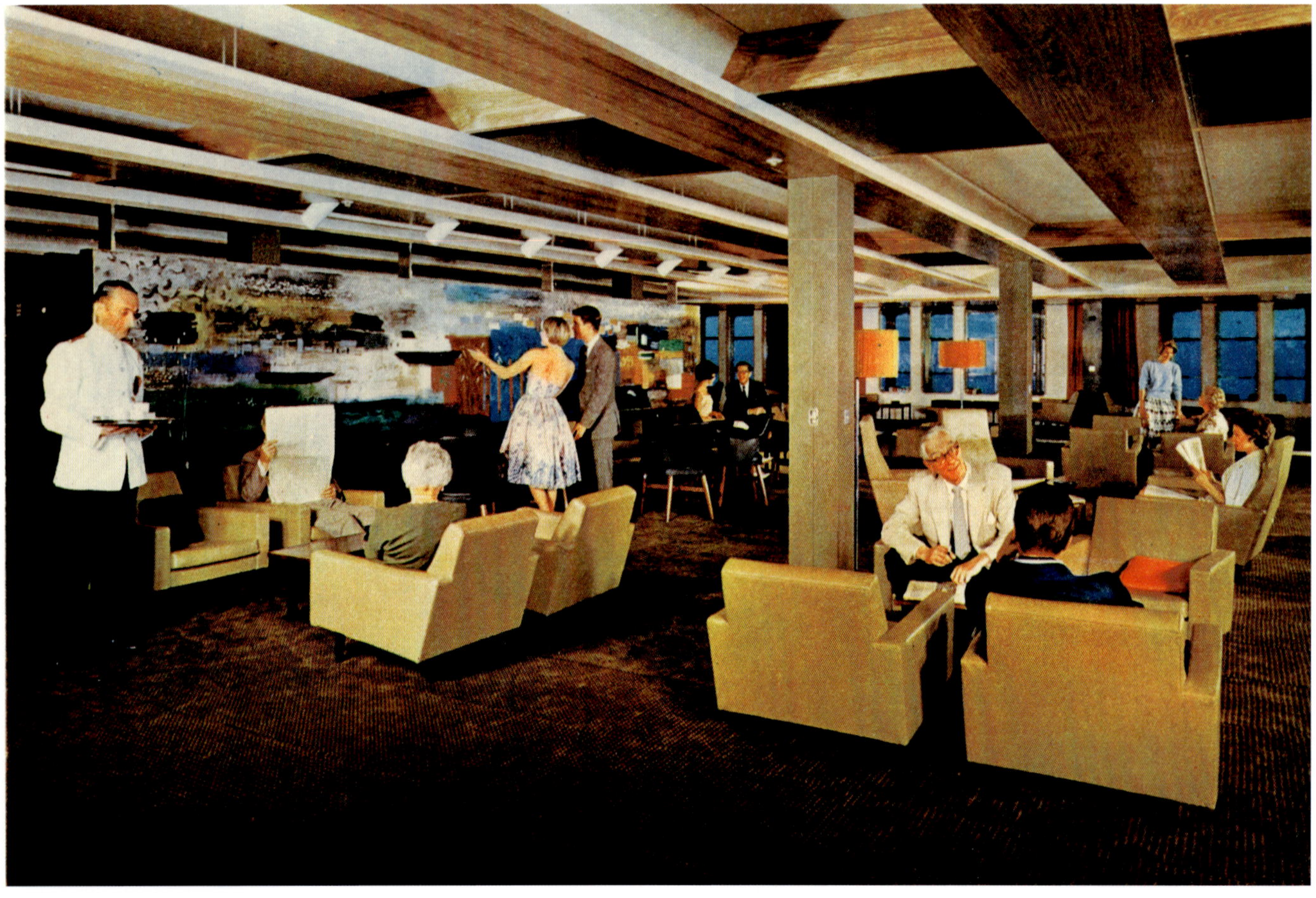

61
John Piper,
Landscape of the Two Seasons, Princess Room,
SS *Oriana*, 1959

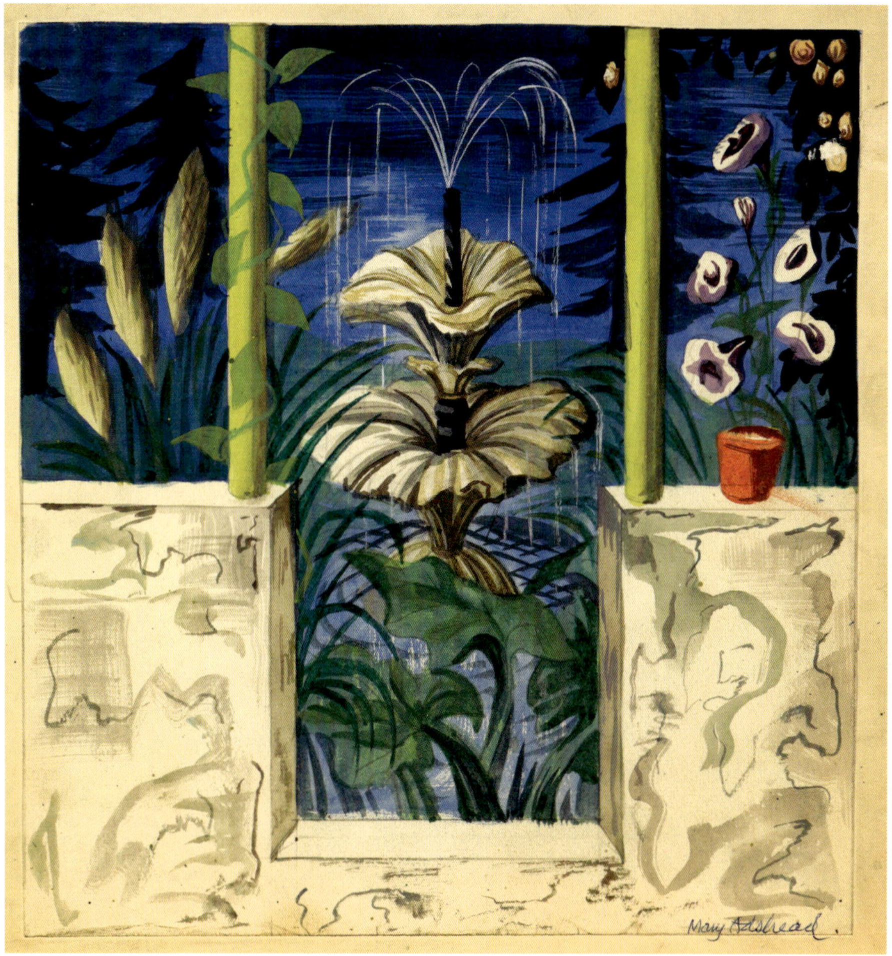

62
Mary Adshead,
study for mural for
tea room,
Luton Hoo,
Bedfordshire, c.1949,
signed, gouache over
pencil on card,
27 x 26 cm (10 ½ x 10 ⅜ in.)

Restaurants and pubs have often had murals, although apart from notable exceptions such as Rex Whistler's Tate Gallery work, these have tended not to survive. Department stores, which often contain a lot of windowless walls in their deep plans, were keen on restaurant murals, and Mary Adshead painted a long jungle scene (one of her favourite subjects) for Selfridges in the 1950s, as well as murals for Lewis's stores in Bristol and Leicester, and a tea-room for Luton Hoo, the country house near Bedford. [62] At the Barcelona Restaurant in Soho, Beatrice Playne, who studied fresco both with Mary Sargant-Florence and Diego Rivera, entertained the staff by painting the ceiling of her panorama of Catalonian buildings, running from table top to table top with a paintbrush in her outstretched arm.[89] Edward Bawden, Hans Aufseeser (who changed his name to Tisdall during the war) and John Armstrong shared the decoration of a short-lived trade federation headquarters, The International Building Society Club in 1939, with Bawden's mural suitably depicting a summer alfresco banquet.[90] [63] The list could continue, but an outstanding survivor is the Morritt Arms, a Georgian stone hotel and pub at Greta Bridge, North Yorkshire (the building appears in the famous watercolours of this spot by John Sell Cotman). Here in 1936, the artist John Gilmour, famous for his Guinness advertisements featuring toucans, painted a panorama of late Georgian jollity in a way that avoids the sentimentality of so much backward-looking commercial art of the time.

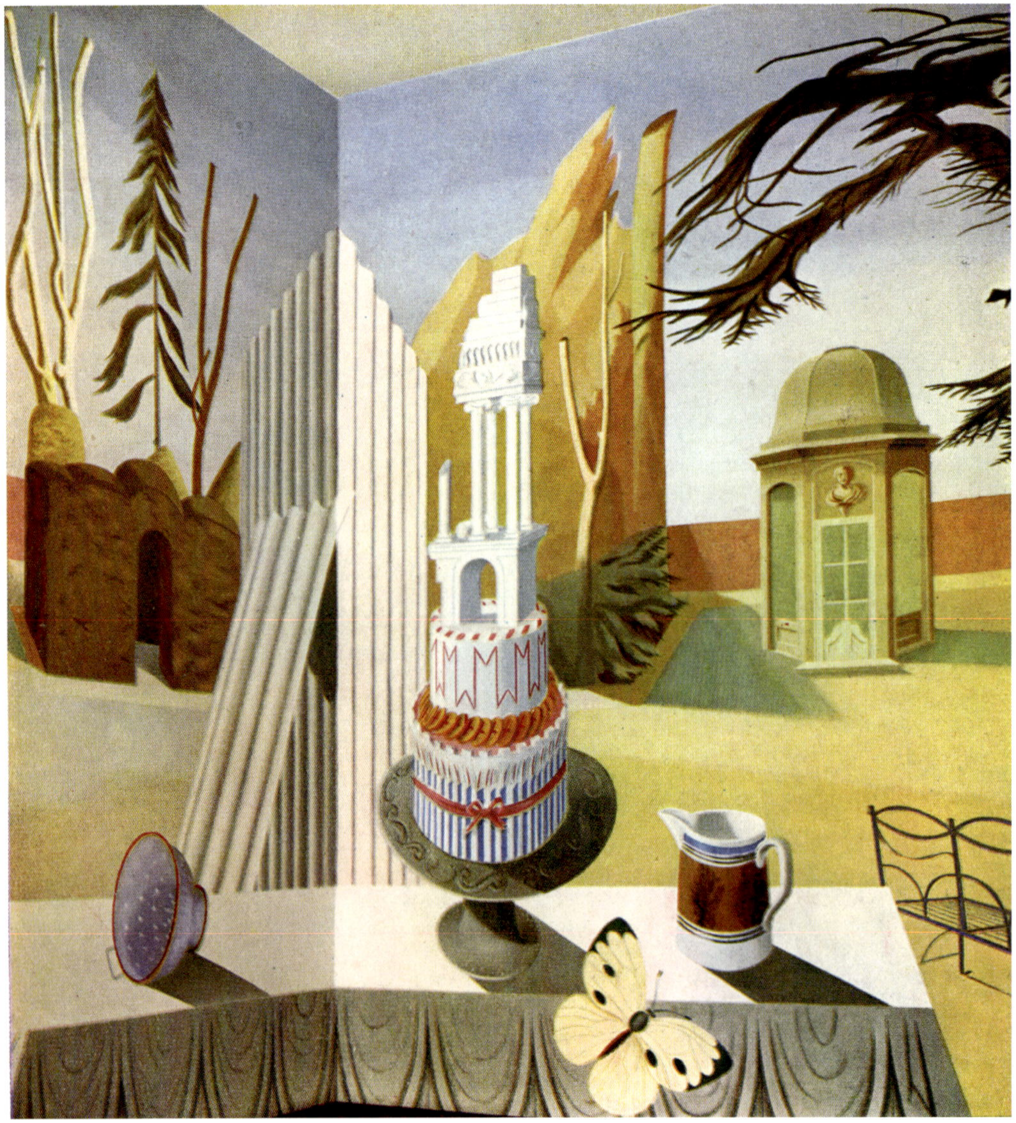

63
Edward Bawden,
mural for International
Building Society Club,
London, 1939 (destroyed)

A more high-minded note entered into the murals painted for British Restaurants, a government scheme to convert existing buildings for temporary use as canteens during the war. None of these murals survives, but there are photographs of work by John Piper, Kenneth Rowntree [64a & 64b] and others.

Frivolity

Frivolity is an important aspect of mural painting which was lost to view in the nineteenth century. Even the Edwardians would have understood wall decoration of a lighter kind as belonging in the domain of the high-class trade decorator, providing backgrounds of putti trailing garlands across fluffy clouds in the Louis Seize painted ceilings of the Ritz Hotel or the town house ballroom in Brook Street that is now part of the Savile Club. Even before 1914, however, a few examples showed how the aesthetic mood was shifting. Theatricality

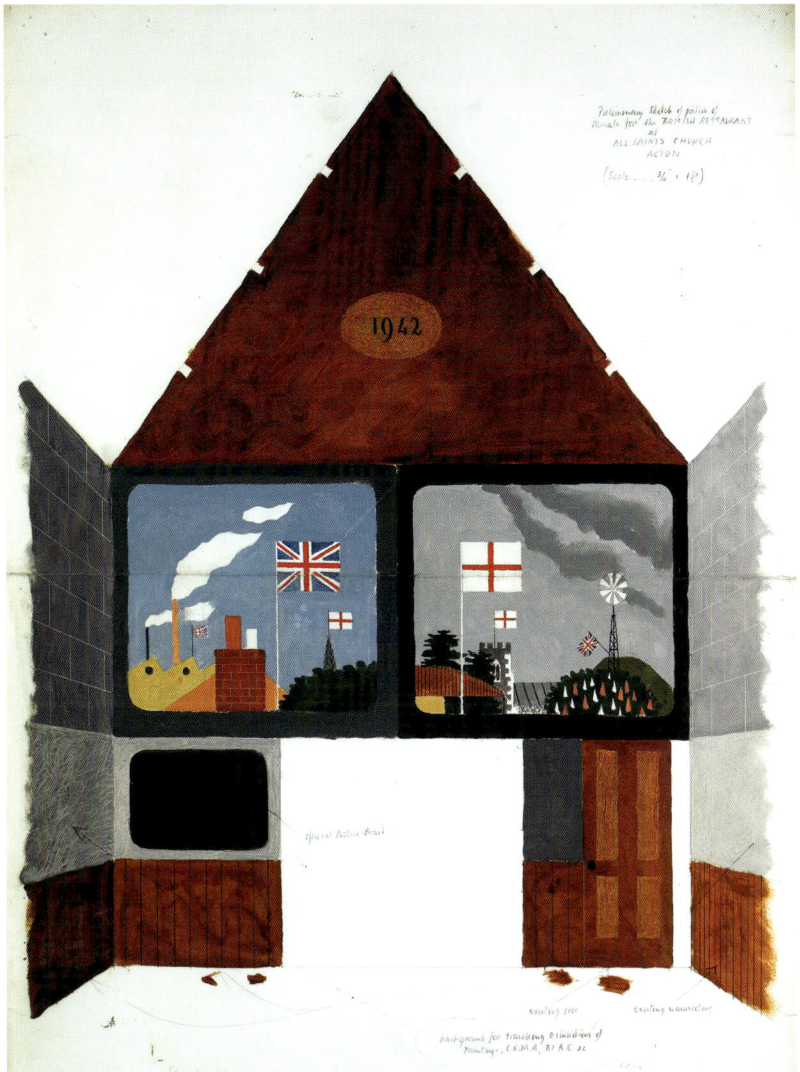

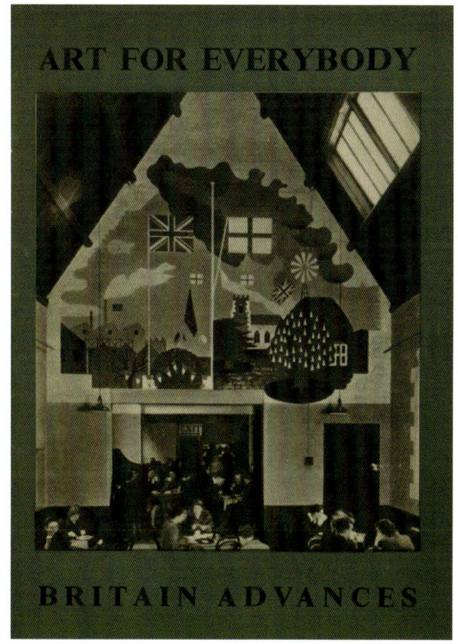

64a
Kenneth Rowntree,
study for mural
in British Restaurant,
Acton, Middlesex, 1943
(destroyed)

64b
Wartime booklet with
photograph of Rowntree's
mural *in situ*

became a ruling principle not only on the stage but in decoration, whether in the black drawing room commissioned by Lady Hamilton, the wife of a General, from Wyndham Lewis, or in the glass paintings created in Paris in 1913 by William Nicholson for the playwright Edward Knoblock, originally installed in an apartment in the Palais Royal. These show vast ruins under a dark blue sky, not in itself a frivolous theme, but with the inclusion of the artist's sardonic self-portrait and in the context of neo-classical furniture in which Knoblock installed them at Beach House, Worthing, in the early 1920s, they acquire a quality of camp that was lacking from earlier aesthetic interiors and heralds a new era of taste. [65] During the war, Nicholson painted the dining room at Folly Farm, Berkshire, a house designed by his friend Sir Edwin Lutyens, with a semi-*trompe l'oeil* of scarlet window frames opening onto a background of meerschaum colour, inhabited by parrots and other exotica.

The change of mood appears to have coincided with the first appearance of the Russian Ballet brought to London by Serge Diaghilev in the Coronation season of 1911. The seed was sown before the First World War,

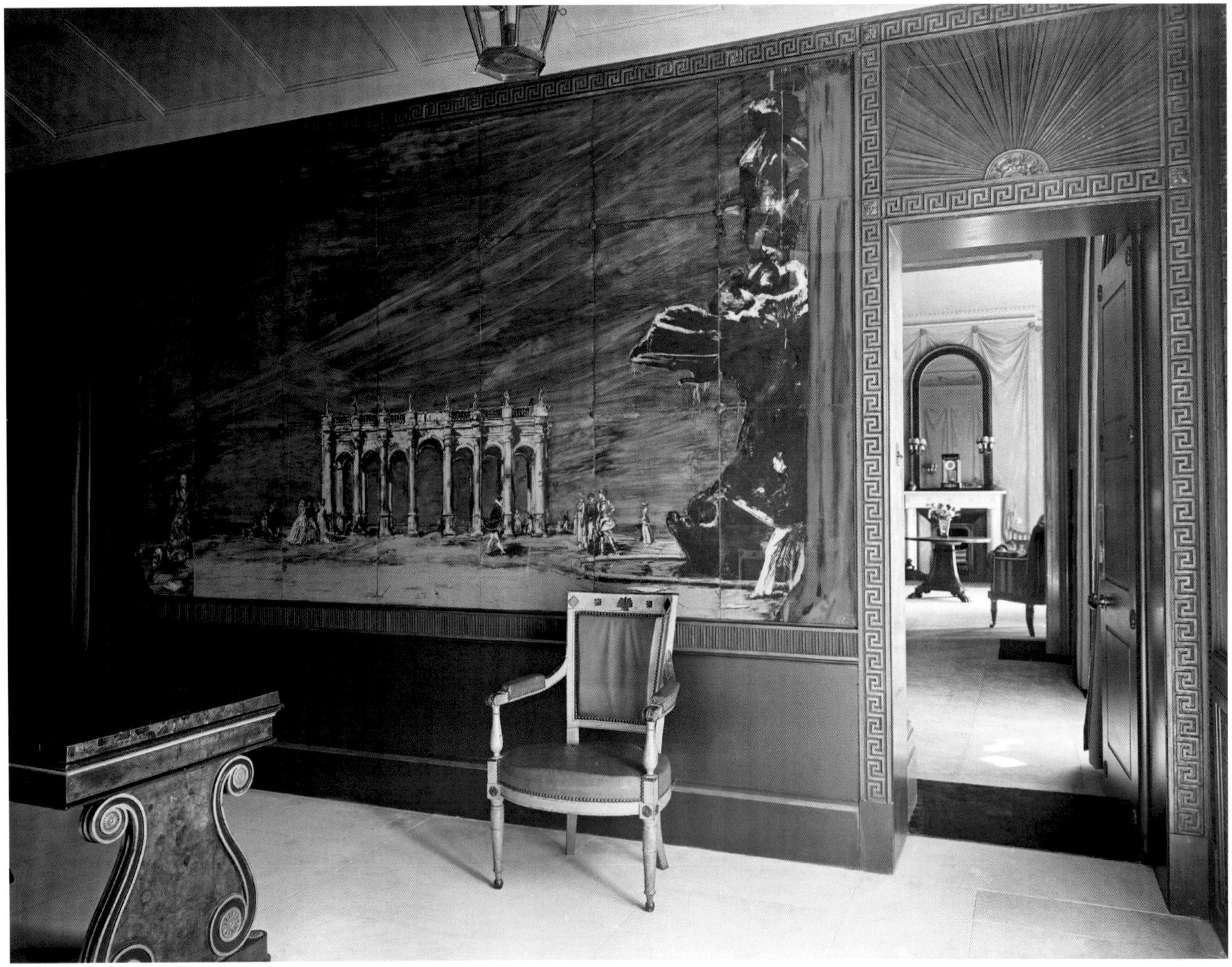

65
William Nicholson, painting on glass for Edward Knoblock, Beach House, Worthing, early 1920s
Courtesy of *Country Life*

and rather than being extinguished in the pain and sorrow of war, it seems to have become an antidote, part of the widespread change in dress, behaviour and values that was a form of anaesthesia against what had happened so recently. The tragic and the comedic were sometimes placed in uncomfortable proximity. In Paris in 1925, at the exhibition which gave the term 'Art Deco' to later decades, the British Pavilion close to the Seine contained A. K. Lawrence's now-lost mural, *The Altruists*, [66] one of the more literal borrowings from Piero della Francesca by a recent Rome Scholar, showing First World War soldiers and a selection of robed figures grouped on either side of a risen Christ, a serious attempt to sublimate the losses of war. Maurice Greiffenhagen's frieze *Empire*, installed in the British Section of the Galerie des Invalides, with elephants and other exotic creatures in procession against a black background, was an attempt to recapture the Edwardian sense of confidence. Among the work of French painters, *Les Perruches* (*The Parakeets*) by Jean Dupas, installed in the panelling in the furnished suite of the Hôtel d'un Collectioneur designed by Emil-Jacques Ruhlmann, with rather pert robotic female nudes, was particularly admired, indicating a lightweight, elegant form of Modernism separated from any kind of social reality or sentiment, a *tour de force* of classically-derived technique.[91] [67]

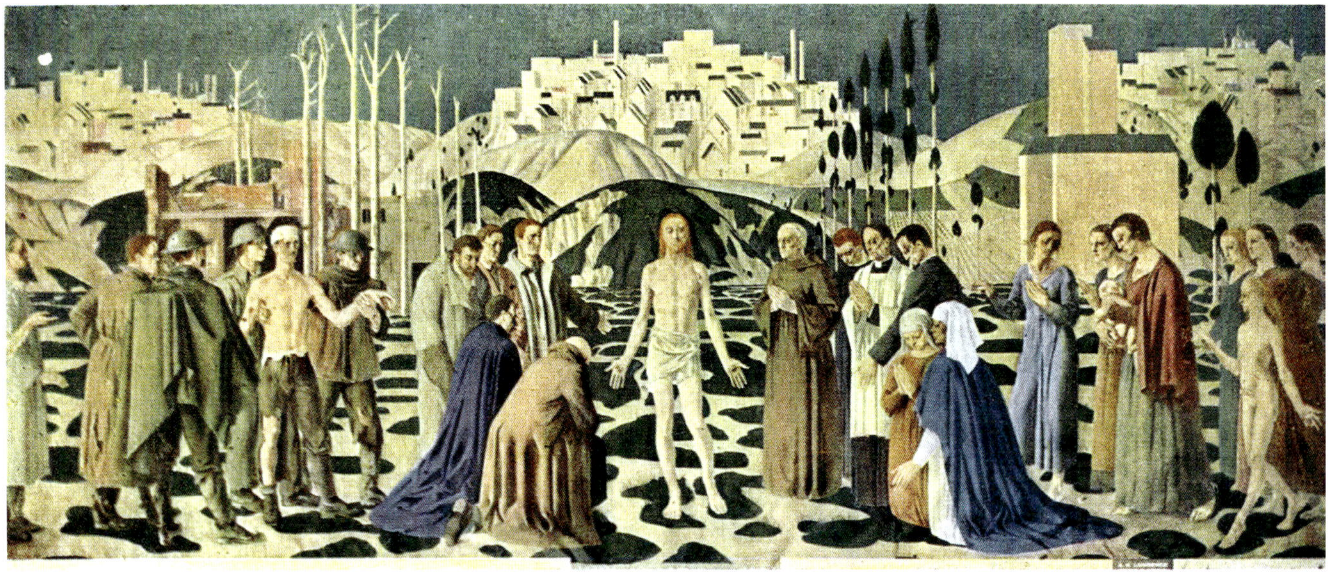

66
A.K. Lawrence,
The Altruists,
British Pavilion,
1925 Paris Exhibition
(first exhibited at
British Empire Exhibition,
Wembley, 1924, mural lost)

In London, the early 1920s occasioned a burst of colour on the stage, where Claud Lovat Fraser led the way with *The Beggar's Opera* production of 1921 at the Lyric Theatre, Hammersmith, followed by similar evocations of the eighteenth century by William Nicholson, Albert Rutherston, George Sheringham and Charles Ricketts, whose use of whimsical and exaggerated historical forms and novel colours was in contrast to the realist conventions of professional designers. Book illustration and posters, often by the same artists, picked up and disseminated the youthful, stagey, rather 'arch' look.

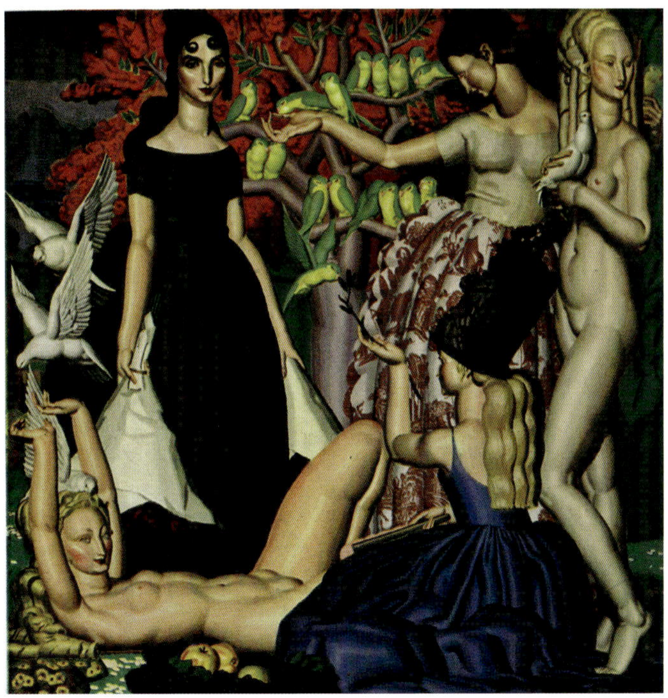

67
Jean Dupas,
Les Perruches,
panel installed in the
suite of the Hôtel
d'un Collectioneur,
Paris, 1925

Frivolity in murals is usually occasioned by a conjunction between patronage and certain kinds of room uses, predominantly social rooms in houses or hotels where some kind of fantasy was thought appropriate to lift the spirits of a party. Interestingly, dining was seen as a potentially frivolous activity in the 1920s almost for the first time, as instanced in the murals by Rex Whistler and Mary Adshead already mentioned. Whistler and Adshead's Slade contemporary, Nan West, transferred the light modern pastoral *genre* into a public space with her murals for the Royal National Orthopaedic Hospital in Bolsover Street, Marylebone, 1926-8. Inserted into panels in a long top-lit waiting hall, her cycle of the seasons includes picnics, reclining lovers and other such details.[92]

Decorators in the inter-war period limited the

number of framed paintings as a way of cleaning out the clutter of the previous generation and responding to a new aesthetic of simplicity and colour harmony. Murals could sweep all framed paintings aside, as in the drawing room at Mulberry House, Westminster, [68] created for Henry Mond and his wife Gwen by the painter Glyn Philpot in a Franco-American Art Deco style, with Charles Sargent Jagger's relief *Scandal* over the fireplace.[93] Bathrooms were also becoming showpieces no longer of hygienic hydraulic engineering but of suggestive luxury, with Roman-style marble tubs set into niches in the wall and co-ordinated colour schemes in which the lady of the house might be imagined as the coy centerpiece. Lady Juliet Duff, one of the supporters of the Diaghilev Ballets Russes, had a bathroom with a painted recess in baroque style by the Spanish artist José Maria Sert, one of Diaghilev's circle, who also painted the drawing room at Port Lympne for Philip Sassoon.

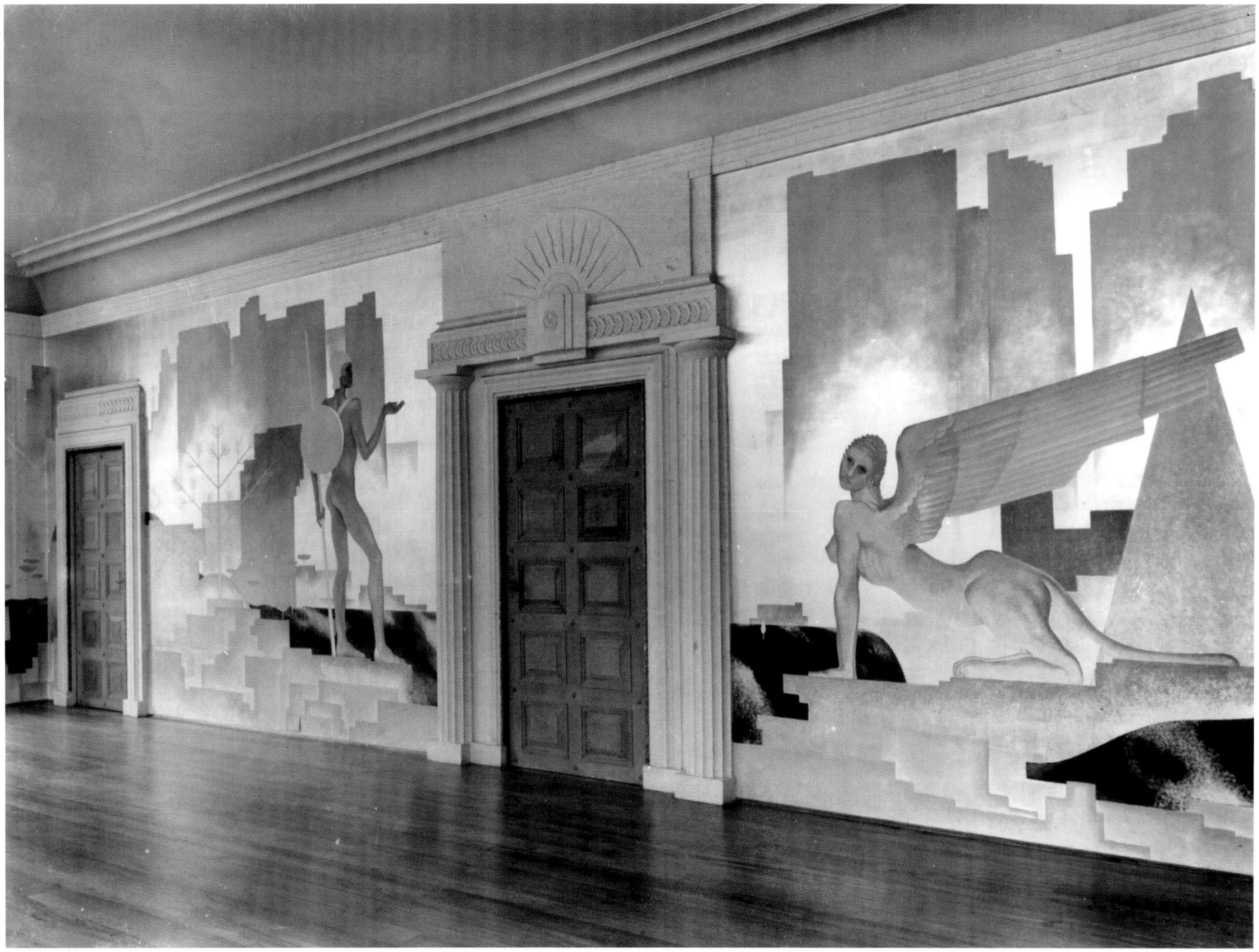

68
Glyn Philpot,
Oedipus and the Sphinx,
Drawing Room,
Mulberry House,
Westminster, 1931.
Courtesy of *Country Life*

John Armstrong, a painter with many theatrical associations, executed a bathroom at Home House in Portman Square for Sir Samuel Courtauld that later served Anthony Blunt when he was the living-in director of the Courtauld Institute. Armstrong was representative of a number of painters, including Edward Wadsworth and Tristram Hillier, who can be seen in the context of both surrealism and abstraction but confined to neither label.

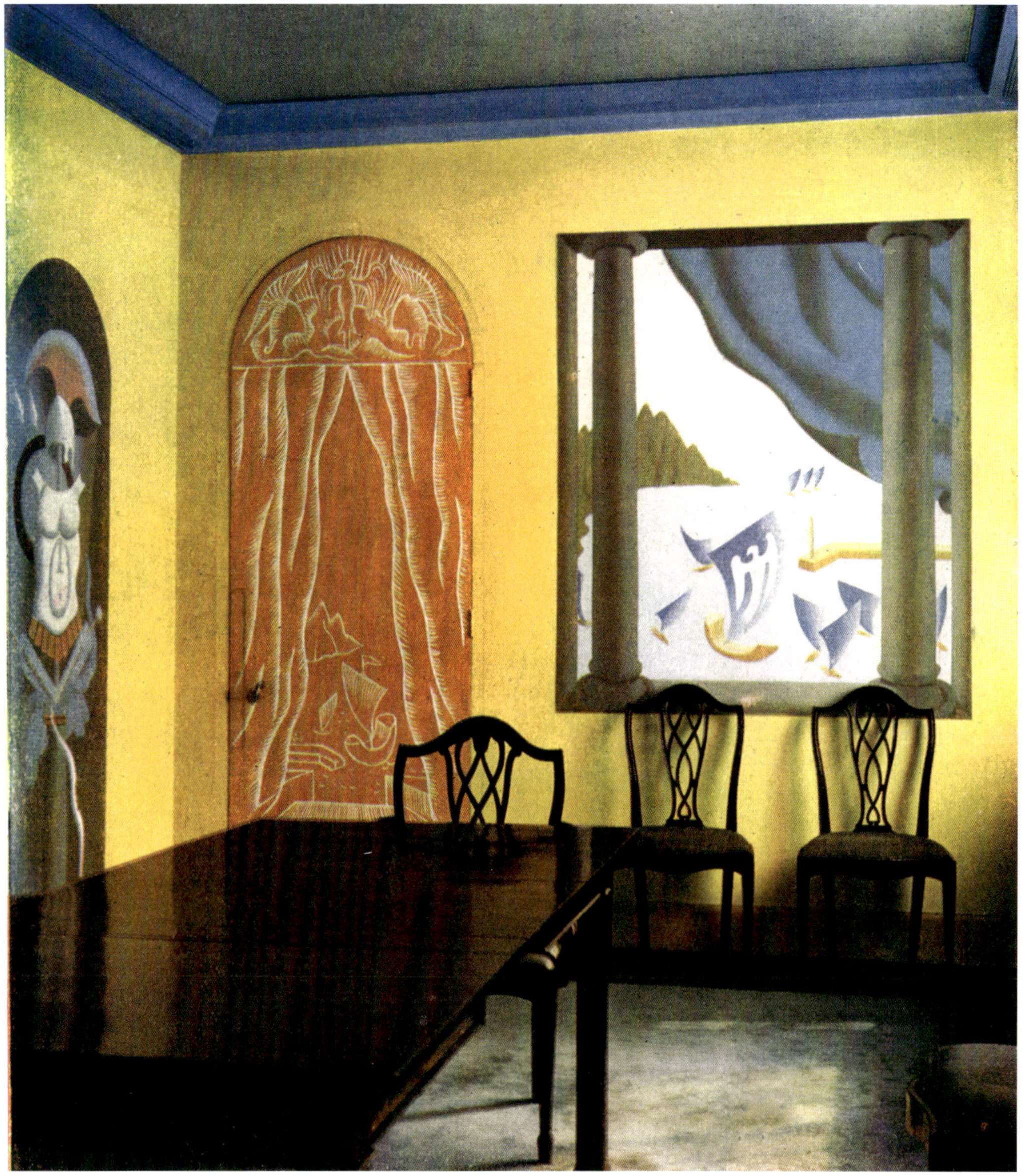

69
John Armstrong,
Dining Room for
Sir Geoffrey Fry,
Portman Square,
1920s (destroyed)

Theirs was a form of poetic modernism whose graphic simplicity and clarity of form was well adapted to mural decoration. Armstrong was active in this field, decorating rooms in modern flat conversions by Wells Coates, a dining room for Sir Geoffrey Fry in a flat in Portman Square [69] that also included panels of tennis players by Eric Ravilious. In Scarborough, Armstrong painted the bar of the Pavilion Hotel and a function room mural for the Royal Hotel, both for the notable patron and collector Tom Laughton. After the effort of painting the Bristol Council House ceiling, Armstrong's personal touch of fantasy returned in his final delightful fit of mural painting exuberance, *The Fantastic Park* for the entrance hall of the Royal Marsden Hospital, 1961-2. [70] The latter, supported, as were the Bristol ceilings, by the Edwin Austin Abbey Trust Fund, disappeared in less than 20 years, although a study for it conveys its jollity. The artist wrote a description of the subject, which ends thus:

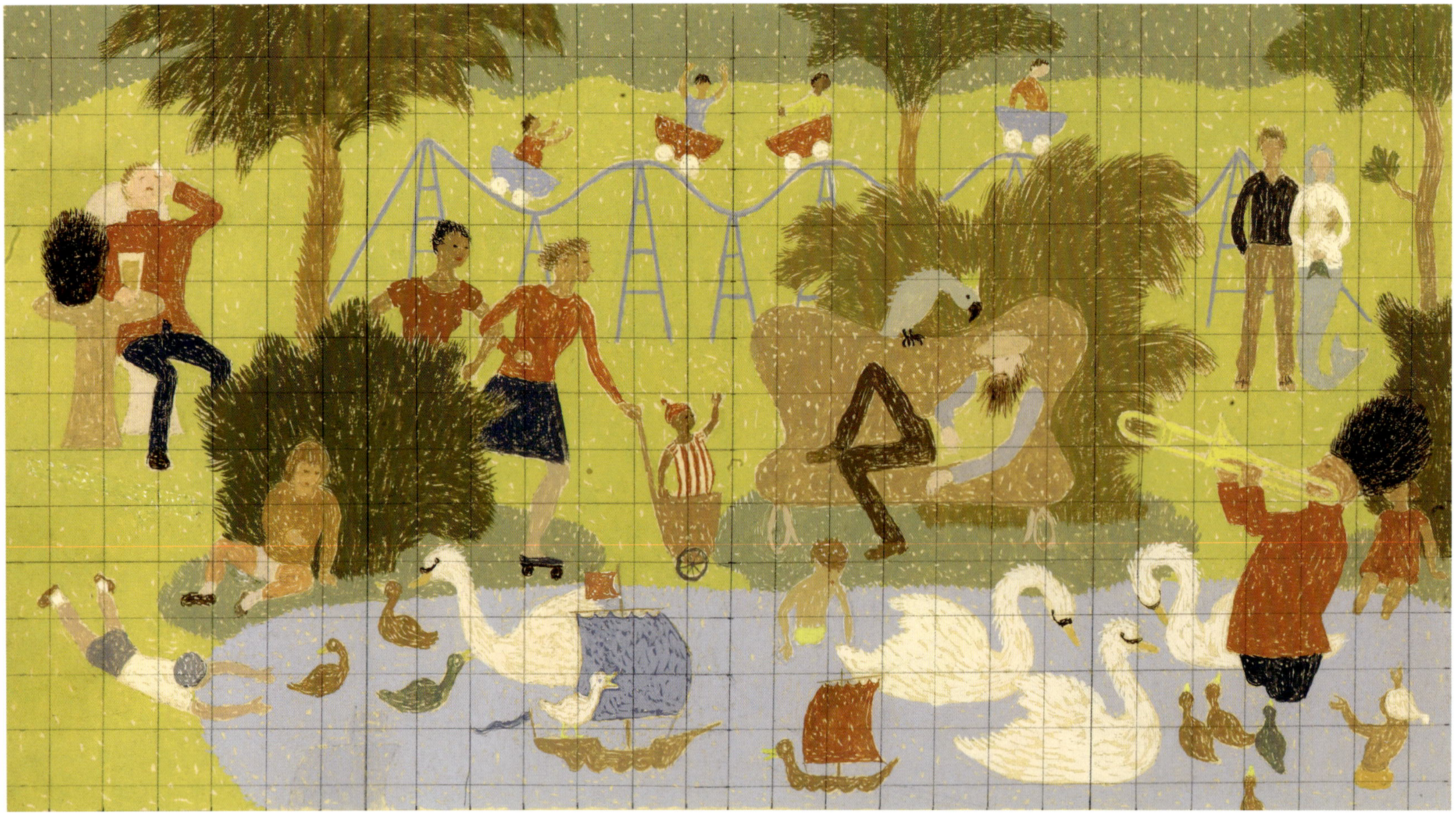

70 John Armstrong, *The Fantastic Park*, study for murals for Royal Marsden Hospital in Sutton, Surrey, 1961, gouache on paper, 25.5 x 34 cm (10 x 13 ⅜ in.)

> On the left, a bandsman gives up and wipes his forehead. He has got a pint from somewhere. Children feed the swans and ducks, and girls and children come to admire the trombonist who for coolness is playing in the lake. The lake mermaid has come out to have a better look and has found a boy-friend. On a seat the poet and his muse meditate.[94]

Relatively few schemes survive that could be described as Art Deco, but among them are George Sheringham's panels in the drawing room at Leweston Manor, Dorset, where there was also an elaborate indoor folly in the form of a 'gilded cage', commissioned by the owner when his wife complained that the interiors of the Georgian house converted by the architect Maxwell Ayrton were exactly that. It consists of a literal domed gilded cage, set in a circular recess with *chinoiserie* decoration by Sheringham.[95] Another eccentric millionaire at the end of the 1930s was Sir Julien Cahn, who converted Stanford Hall, Nottinghamshire to include a private cinema with wall decorations by Beatrice McDermott and a gymnasium with illusionistic landscapes.

Cinemas offered scope for fantasy decoration of several kinds, sometimes in paint and sometimes with colour applied to plaster relief. The Regent Cinema, Brighton, designed by Robert Atkinson, 1924, was considered a superior example with Commedia dell'Arte paintings of carnivals by Walter Bayes in a curved band over the proscenium. This was often undertaken as part of a complete package by decorating firms rather than by individual artists, although the two large panels by F. H. Baines at the Longford Cinema, Stretford near Manchester, 1936, showing the film industry, were rare in their time. Although the building has been closed since the 1990s the paintings have apparently been preserved owing to its listing.[96]

In his book, *Bloomsbury Rooms*, Christopher Reed helpfully revived the term 'The Amusing Style' from the 1920s to provide a collective description of a variety of styles that existed in a zone between Art Deco and Modernism, represented pre-eminently by the Bloomsbury Group artists' reawakening to historical sources in folk art and Baroque. In fact, the quality of being 'amusing' was widespread, including at the more stylistically conventional end of the scale the dream-like hyperrealism of Rex Whistler and the surrealism that was not far removed from it. Being amusing was less about a specific artistic language but more about the intention to subvert in different ways and become a subject for conversation, for which murals seemed to offer good opportunities. Much of this work could be described as camp, and if one follows the explanation of camp given by Susan Sontag in the 1960s, this helps us to understand the theatricality and apparent insincerity as a defence against the intrusions of modern life.[97]

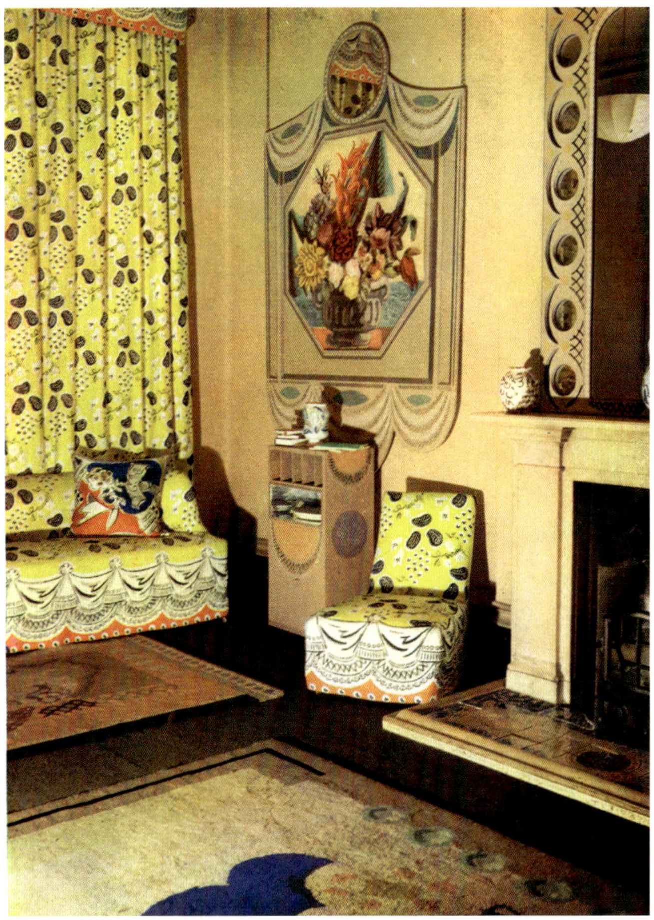

71
Duncan Grant and Vanessa Bell, Music Room, gallery installation for Alex, Reid & Lefevre, 1932

The work of Duncan Grant and Vanessa Bell in this new vein was illustrated in *The New Interior Decoration*, a book by the *Vogue* editor Dorothy Todd and the literary critic Raymond Mortimer, sitting oddly alongside the hardest-edged examples of European modernism.[98] [71] Much of this form of decoration, in college rooms and rented London houses, was ephemeral by nature, yet the survival of Charleston Farmhouse, the home of Vanessa Bell and Duncan Grant, unknown to the public before the 1970s, has left a valuable record of the improvisational gaiety of artists at a time otherwise remembered for conventional good taste in interiors or Modernist austerity. For Grant and Bell, a blank wall, fireplace or piece of furniture was an irresistible temptation to decorate with pattern or figures, with paintings whose butterfly delicacy and lack of solid technique make them so expressive of the brief interval of defiant hedonism in which they were created.[99]

This was the high period of *trompe l'oeil*, which is sometimes understood as a synonym for all mural painting. High-minded Victorians were suspicious of *trompe l'oeil's* theatricality and associations with Catholic churches and London gin palaces, which was all the more reason for their rebellious children of the 1920s to favour it. With his ability to create an imaginary architectural framework for a room, Rex Whistler seems to have done most to revive the Renaissance and Baroque tradition.

In *Brideshead Revisited*, 1945, Evelyn Waugh created a fictional muralist, Charles Ryder, who appears as if he were a posthumous tribute to Whistler, who was killed in action during the D-Day landings the previous year. In real life, Waugh might even have known how Whistler played a role in a complex episode in the lives of the Paget family at Plas Newydd. A few years later, Waugh wrote about Whistler, 'he made a dream world of his own and threw it open to all who would to share.'[100] Already by 1939, the Whistler manner, in the hands of imitators, was in danger of being overworked and out of touch with the grim realities of the time. 'This is all very well for a restaurant,' wrote the wood engraver Gwen Raverat, 'but I should get very tired of such decorations in my own home.'[101] Owing to its qualities of imagination and execution, combined with his brother Laurence's faithful guardianship of his flame, Whistler's work has never disappeared from public view and continued to provide a standard to which muralists in similar vein such as Roland Pym, Martin Battersby, William McLaren and Felix Kelly [72] aspired with varying levels of success.[102] Since the 1960s other artists such as Richard Shirley Smith and Graham Rust have carried on working in the same vein, usually for private clients.

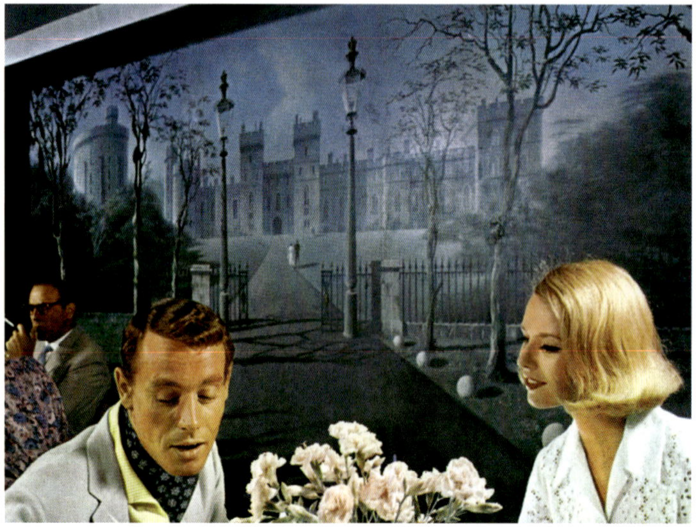

72
Felix Kelly,
mural on board
SS *Windsor Castle*,
1959-60

Despite Raverat's views, a writer in *The Times* in 1938, noting the influence of the Paris exhibition of the previous year, had no hesitation in promoting frivolity in murals: 'They are especially suited to public places such as restaurants, hotel foyers, cocktail bars and shops such as hairdressers and shoe shops', he wrote. 'All these offer blank wall spaces for decoration that may with advantage be satirical or charming and imaginative.' With the rise and diversification of interior decorating in the 1930s, murals were often introduced by decorators and promoted by them as a novelty. A case in point was the thriving interior decoration department at Fortnum and Mason, directed by G. Hayes Marshall and Ronald Fleming, who was responsible for staging an exhibition of mural designs at the Georgian Carlisle House in Soho, the premises of the decorators Keebles, in 1932.[103]

The quality of lightness of mood was revived at the time of the Festival of Britain and carried on during the 1950s, with a different way of visualizing and working to either the loose brushwork of Bloomsbury or the smooth finishes of Whistler and his followers. From the work of Ravilious and Bawden stemmed something harder-edged and less literally illusionistic, partaking of the quality of illustrations writ large and less theatrical in quality. This would include the work of Laurence Scarfe, Humphrey Spender and Barbara Jones, the latter

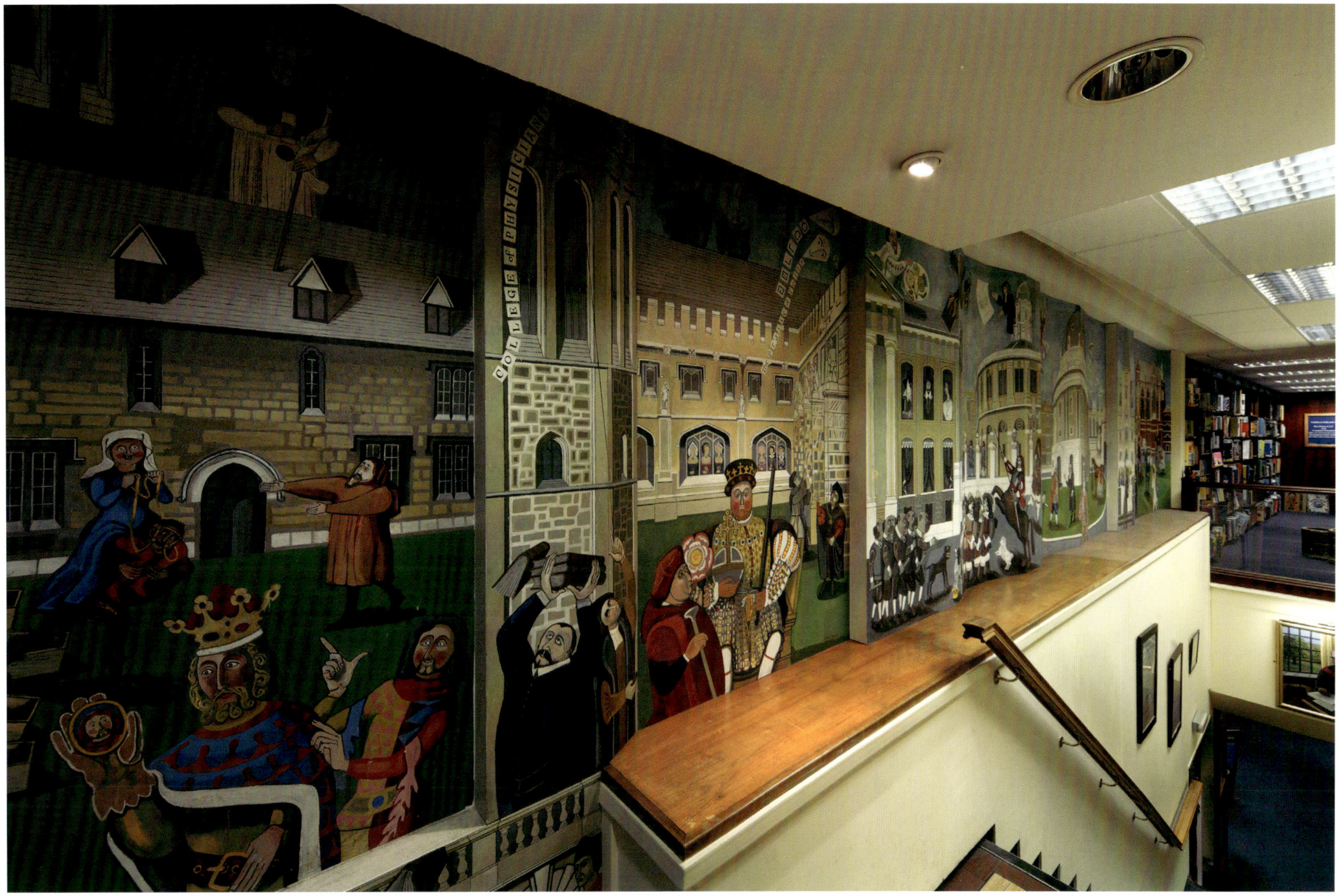

73 Edward Bawden, mural for Blackwell's Bookshop, Oxford, 1973

notable for a wild and occasionally surrealist imagination.[104] Bawden himself remained very active as a mural painter into the 1970s, with a surprising range of styles, from the abstract paintings for the Physics Building at Hull University, 1963 (funded by the Abbey Trust Fund), the replacement of the Morley College murals with a new cycle based on the *Canterbury Tales*, 1958, big paintings for BP, 1966 (showing Islamic architecture) and Morgan Crucible, 1957 (showing industrial processes) (see page 254) a mural made of nails for Carr's Lane Congregational Church, Birmingham, 1971, and his final painted mural for Blackwell's Bookshop, Oxford, 1973. [73] The latter shows all his mischievous and learned sense of humour with episodes from the history of Oxford in which humans and animals are often transposed. Thus the Scapegoat paints a portrait of William Holman Hunt outside the chapel of Keble College where Hunt's *The Light of the World* hangs, and the English Civil War is enacted by Cavalier spaniels and Cromwellian pugs.

From the mid-1930s to the 1950s, Hans Tisdall was another artist, working also as a textile designer, who played a significant role in mural painting, with a major contribution to the Festival Pleasure Gardens at Battersea. By the 1960s, this mood was channelled into Pop Art, especially in the paintings of Peter Blake, but by then the enthusiasm for murals was fading.

The rise of the frivolous mural and the amusing style between the wars has apparently little connection with the serious civic and academic commitment of the fresco painters, Rome Scholars and avant-garde artists, although to work successfully in either vein required physical stamina and good training in the design of paintings. Murals cover a wide spectrum of intention and when the Society of Mural Painters was set up in connection with the 1939 exhibition at the Tate, one of its aims was to demystify the subject and make it seem more available for patrons. The architect Maxwell Ayrton had been calling for muralists to advertise their prices by the square foot, with scales of payment adjusted to their fame and experience and *The Times* noted that 'there can be no doubt that the popularity of mural painting is hindered by the terrifying association of the word, which suggests something solemn, everlasting and expensive. There is no reason why mural painting should not be done light-heartedly, comparatively inexpensively, and on the principle of "rub it out and do it again" if you get bored with it.'[105] The illustrated brochure produced by the Society around 1960, *Eyes on the Wall*, included a loosely inserted scale of charges of this kind.

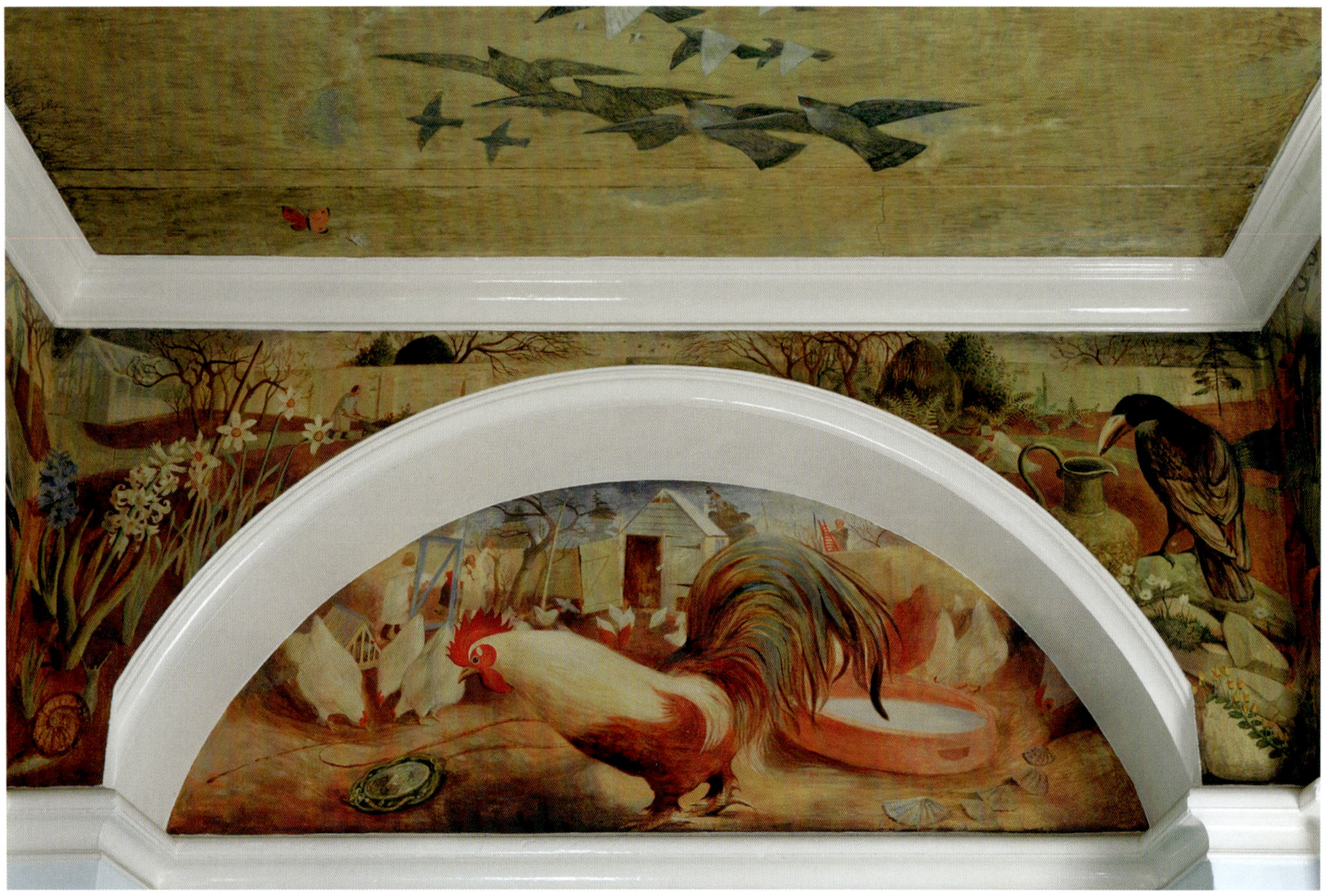

74
Evelyn Dunbar,
left to right:
The Butterfly, the Snail and the Bee,
The Cock and the Jewel,
The Crow and the Pitcher,
murals at Brockley School (now Prendergast School, Lewisham),
c. 1932-36

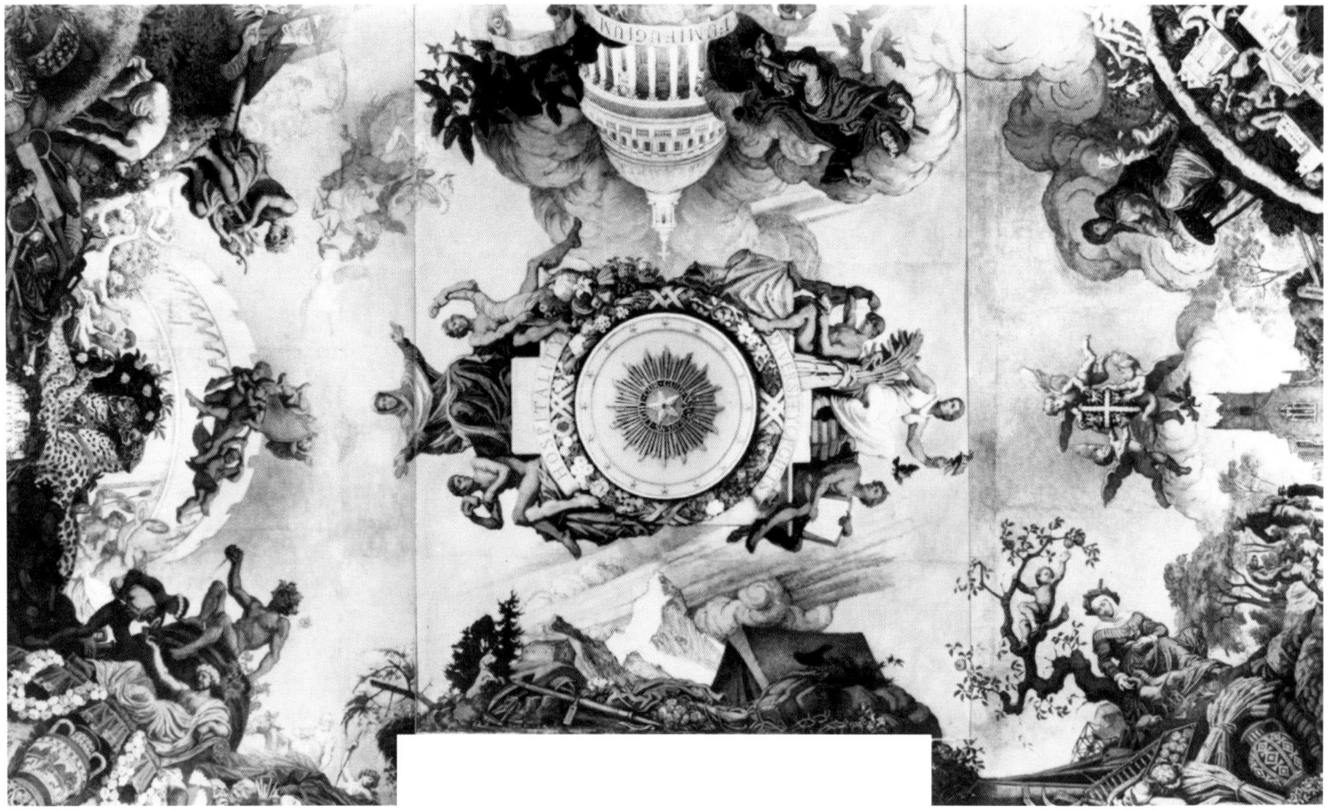

75
Brian Thomas,
ceiling for Templewood,
Northrepps, Norfolk,
1964

This split has made the presentation of a unified history of mural painting during these years a complex matter, and those coming to the subject need to understand the different ends of the spectrum in which it was operating. One unintended result of the 'high art' murals of the time was that the attempt to present some of the subjects seriously risked absurdity, as with the *Punch* cartoon that showed Monnington's mural of modern life in the Bank of England, 'The Governor of the Bank announcing the Bank Rate to the Directors – "No Change" with the caption "It's a boy"'.

Some artists switched between the two modes in different commissions or achieved the difficult act of balancing in the middle. Gilbert Spencer's cycle of murals on the foundation of Balliol College seem to promise a worthy narrative, but the nature of the story that attracted him was its potential comedy, involving some robbery with violence against a bishop and a severe punishment, followed by an indignant wife insisting that her guilty husband, John Balliol, should redress his wrongdoing with a cash payment. Towards the end of the cycle of paintings going round a small room, the first Balliol students are shown loading bundles onto a wagon which will take them to Oxford. Their luggage includes imaginary medieval versions of tennis rackets and cricket bats, a deliberate anachronism of a kind not allowed, for example, in the Palace of Westminster but perhaps needed there to relieve the solemnity. At Prendergast School, Brockley, there are two moods in the work. The major panel paintings of fables and the front of the gallery are relatively serious, but beneath the gallery a lighter mood prevails. The fables shown here in the spandrels are chiefly concerned with birds, beasts and insects, while in the ceiling panels, figures in Victorian clothing are seen taking off into the air.

Brian Dick Lauder Thomas was a Rome Scholar from the early 1930s who dedicated himself to murals, stained glass and teaching. He was perhaps the only Rome Scholar to feel thoroughly comfortable with the Baroque, and made good use of his studies for church work. Apart from the unusual degree of swagger in his work, his sense of humour had little opportunity to break through except in a commission to paint the ceiling at Templewood in Norfolk for his friend and patron, the architect Paul Paget. In a fine double-height room designed by Paget (with his partner, John Seely) for his uncle, Sir Samuel Hoare, in 1938, Thomas created a mock-heroic sequence of events from the life of Paget after he inherited the house, a lesson in composition and perspective rooted in the masters of the genre. [75]

The Anxious Pastoral

The categories for murals discussed so far have only approached subject matter obliquely as a function of patronage or other *genre*. The 'Anxious Pastoral' is a newly invented category that describes a type of subject matter common among British twentieth-century narrative painters, several of whom happened also to be muralists. It was a prevalent and enduring theme, which for many of them seems to have defined what they wanted to convey to the world about their own perception of the times through which they were living. Artists who chose pastoral subjects between the wars have since been dismissed by some critics as escapist or over-conventional, but much as we might wish that they had chosen modern urban life more often as a subject, their preference for rural subjects and the mood in which they portrayed them deserves to be investigated and understood. Many chose to live in the country, if only because it was cheaper and healthier than living in a city. The reasons must have run deeper, however. In the previous generation, around 1900, there was a sense of crisis and loss about rural life and customs that gave urgency to the realist paintings of Herbert La Thangue and George Clausen, but this did not translate into an imaginative *genre*.

The Pastoral is a poetic form derived from ancient Greece in which simple country people are given voices to convey moral and spiritual lessons to readers who are assumed to be more sophisticated in their understanding, yet who may be at risk of losing the intuition and closeness to nature and divinity that poetry seeks to remind them of. It is a complex game of masks and acting that could degenerate into conventional whimsy, but in the hands of Theocritus or Virgil gave to Western literature and art a special form of sensitivity that in England contributed to the rise of the Romantic Movement at the end of the eighteenth century. The element of anxiety or worry was implicit in the pastoral, since rural peace has always been threatened by destructive forces of weather and war. Politics also enters in, with the enclosure of common land in England that provoked Oliver Goldsmith to write *The Deserted Village* and caused John Clare to lament the passing of old attachments to place and people. While Romantics could be sentimental, there was a fierceness in many of them that challenged the disruptive forces of modernity as a form of injustice and a denial of humanity. Some of the representatives of romantic reaction in art, such as Samuel Palmer, remained almost unknown before the twentieth century, but the same feelings were conveyed by the Pre-Raphaelites in many paintings by placing subjects concerned with moral ambiguity and difficult choices within natural settings, or even by making landscapes without figures emblems of insecurity and threat.

These paintings were eagerly collected and displayed in galleries, so that as early as 1912, when the reaction against the Victorians was supposed to be at its height, we find an enthusiasm among certain young artists for the Pre-Raphaelites.[106] Thus Dora Carrington, who was painting frescos at Ashridge Park, Hertfordshire for Lord Brownlow at the time, wrote in 1913 to John Nash, responding to an enthusiastic letter from him, 'How exciting the pre-Raphaelites being back again … Oh isn't *The Hireling Shepherd* amazing! I really think they got there. Wouldn't you like to do a real picture like that?'[107] In this pastoral by William Holman Hunt of 1851-2, the shepherd neglects his flock while courting a maiden, holding a death's head hawk moth in his hand. It is a painting in which the beauty of natural observation is at odds with the narrative, itself intended as a commentary on the decline of the Church of England. When William Rothenstein encouraged his pupils and lecture audiences to respect these artists rather than rejecting them from a Modernist standpoint, he may have thought primarily about their observational technique, but the haunted quality of their subject matter, with its depictions of sexual yearning, loss and regret, seem equally to have resonated through the inter-war years. The Pre-Raphaelites are thus the direct precursors of much twentieth-century figurative painting in which similar themes were explored.

The element of anxiety was conveyed in differing registers. In Spencer, it seems to arise out of the distortions of the human figures and their expressions, including the comic and grotesque, as seen in *The Resurrection, Cookham*, 1924-27, but his energetic optimism shines through. Spencer was also a leader in presenting the ordinary physical features of a country village in a way that makes them unmistakably significant, although their meaning is unclear. A simple iron railing, for example, in his Slade School *Nativity*, 1912, can suggest a permeable spatial barrier between the everyday world and the miraculous or divine. A wall, with trees overhanging, becomes a symbol of a paradise just out of reach. This form of the physical uncanniness of the built environment can often be found in Pre-Raphaelite paintings and in the wood-engraved illustrations of the 1860s by them, which enjoyed a revival in the 1920s.

While it is not difficult to understand the continuing interest in pastoral subjects among the painters of the early twentieth century, does this explain or justify their adoption for large-scale works such as murals and decorative compositions, when Palmer, for example, painted some of his most intense visions on panels or paper no bigger than a laptop screen? The answer may lie in the potential for murals to create an immersive experience in painting through their size. With the advent of colour films, the possibility of feeling oneself transported by a large image became much more commonplace. Before the Second World War, large paintings and stage sets were the only way to project the imagination and live up to the challenge of Renaissance painted rooms and chapels with their intoxicating sense of walking into another world.

The transposition of mythological and Bible subjects into modern settings, for which Spencer is particularly known, was practised by many other artists, including those associated with the Rome School. While Winifred Knights had chosen a modern life urban subject for her Slade Summer Composition, she had to respond to 'The Deluge' for the Rome competition, and her magnificently dark vision of the threat of natural destruction was justly recognized by the selection panel. [76] (see pages 118-137) Even an anodyne subject such as 'winter' produced a haunting and sinister image from Tom Monnington in the same circumstances, a group of figures among whom a narrative seems implicit and is all the more powerful for being ambiguous. [77] (see pages 158-163)

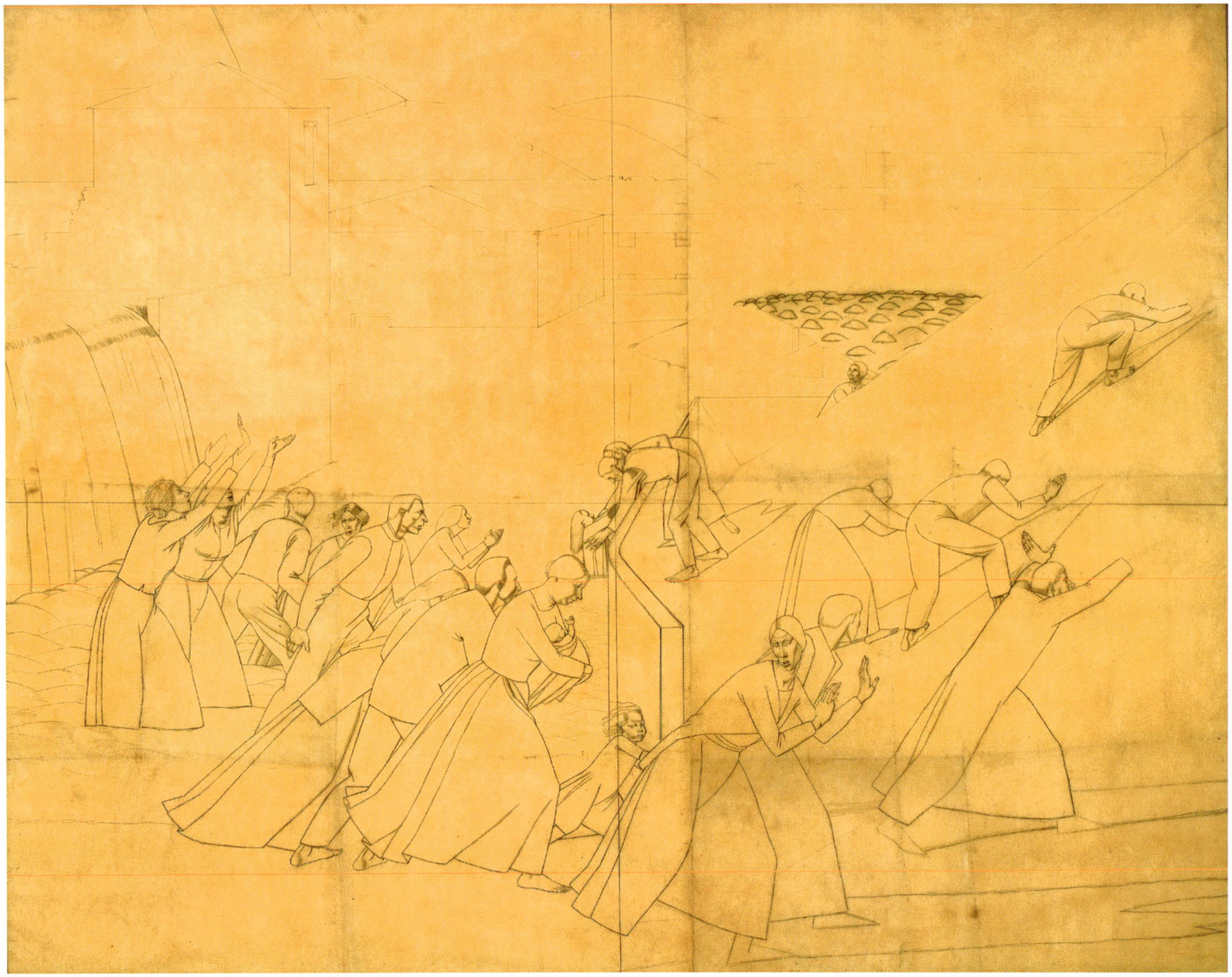

76
Winifred Knights,
cartoon for
The Deluge, c. 1920,
pencil on tracing paper,
152.9 x 183.5 cm
(60 ⅛ x 72 ¼ in.)

Not all painters who chose rural imagery chose the anxious pastoral mood. The Woodgreen Village Hall paintings are beautiful in their evocation of visually stimulating subjects such as apple picking, but seem to convey no mystery or sense of loss. By contrast, the team that Charles Mahoney, himself a dedicated pastoralist, gathered for Prendergast School included two women artists who made significant contributions to the *genre*, Evelyn Dunbar, whose potential for creating images of strangeness was already developing as a student, and Mildred Elsie Eldridge. When asked about the interest of the group of artists in nature and the country, she replied that the only thing they had in common was that they all hated London.[108] Eldridge went on to create what is arguably the most moving large-scale mural work after Spencer's chapel, a post-war creation of the imagination to balance his pre-war achievement and to act as a benchmark for mural painting at the highest level. This is the cycle of paintings, a frieze of 120ft in length, created for a most unlikely location, the canteen of a nurses' home at the Robert Jones and Agnes Hunt Orthopaedic Hospital at Gobowen, near Oswestry on the Welsh border. The artist, married to the poet and Anglican vicar R. S. Thomas, was suggested by Dr C. E. Salt, whom she had known when teaching at the nearby Moreton Hall School some years before. She received

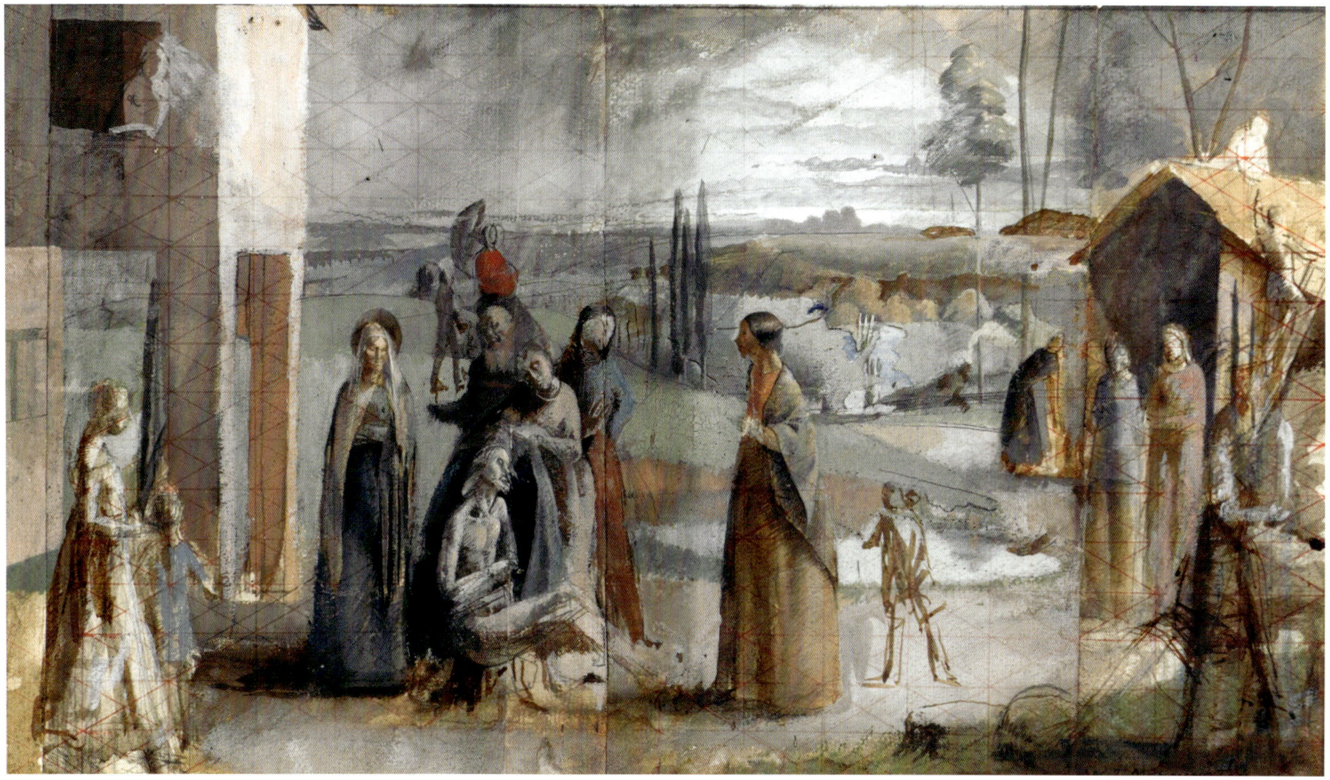

77
Thomas Monnington,
Study for *Winter*, c. 1922,
signed and dated,
pencil and gouache
on paper, squared,
21 x 37 cm
(8 1/4 x 14 1/2 in.)

a payment of £1,500 for the work, which took three years to complete in the early 1950s. Having been in store following the demolition of the original building, the canvas panels were reinstalled in 2009 at Glyndwr College, Wrexham and for the first time achieved widespread acclaim.[109] [78a & 78b]

These paintings, called *The Dance of Life*, do not follow any conventional iconography but are the artist's personal vision of the alienation caused by modern life, starting with a pre-lapsarian vision of Yugoslavian peasants dancing and 'telling the bees', based on pre-war travels.[110] The sequence goes on to show a variety of coastal scenes with the growth of self-consciousness and its perils for mankind. Observed subjects such as the navigation buoys become metaphors for the cages in which children's innocence is trapped as they grow up. The artist's son, Gwydion, was a small child and his 'turnip head' with hair in a variety of shades, featured often in the painting. The final panels of the painting are not apocalyptic, as one might expect, but ambiguous, with 'a masked figure indicating the duality of man's nature, for as he destroys so he seeks to relieve … the right side of the panel shows the "Relief" or "Mercy planes" which carry help and relief in various forms to stricken areas guided by the radio stations indicated by black crosses on the map in the background.'[111] Parachutes appeared in a pre-war painting by Eldridge, titled *Foundation, or the Exploitation of the Country*, made for the Ibis Sports Club at Chiswick, for the Prudential Assurance Company. Recorded only in photographs, this showed pastoral figures in a landscape threatened by a row of parked cars, while parachutes descend on the hills beyond.[112]

Following pages: 78a Mildred Elsie Eldridge, *The Dance of Life*, created for the canteen of a nurses' home at the Robert Jones and Agnes Hunt Orthopaedic Hospital at Gobowen, near Oswestry, completed c. 1955 (*in situ* at Glyndwr College Wrexham, 2012)

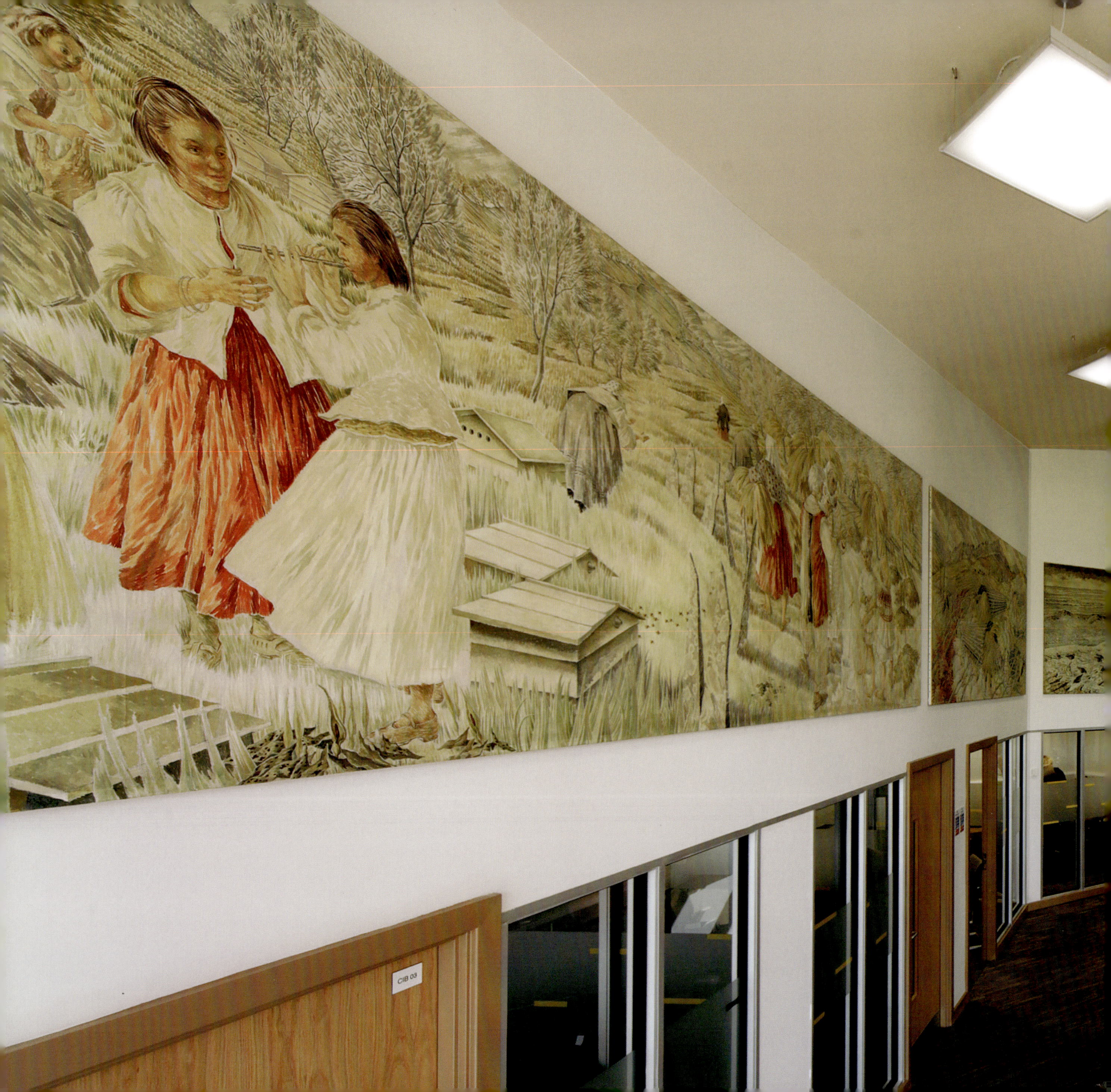
CIB 03

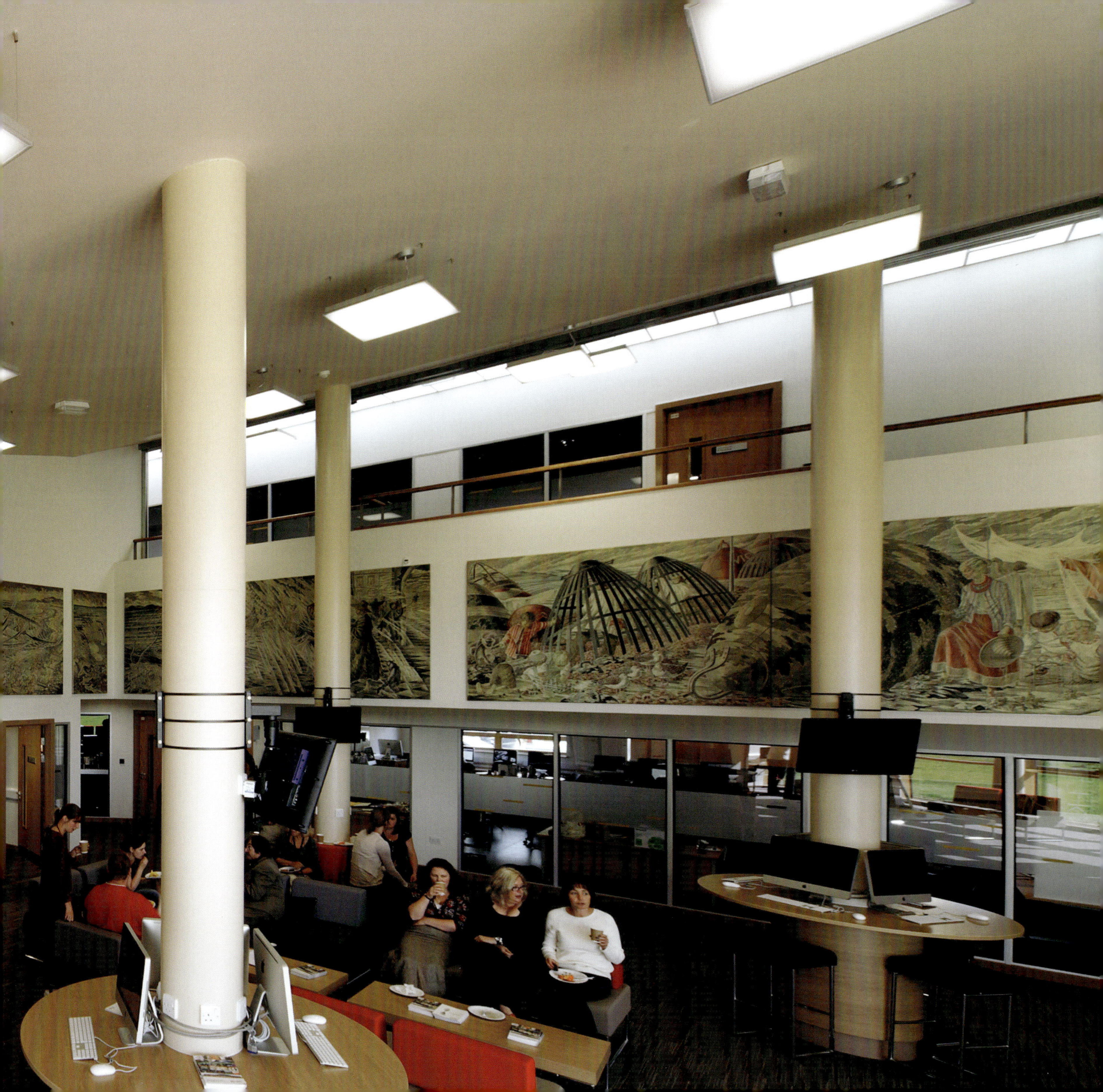

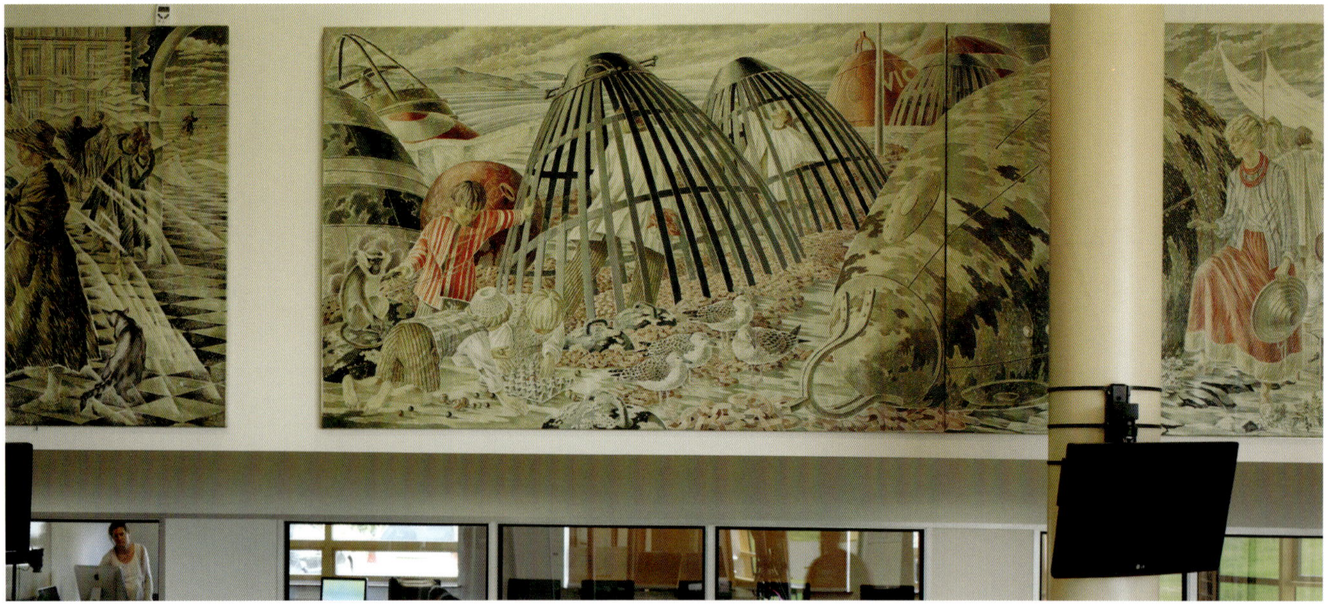

78b
Mildred Elsie Eldridge,
The Dance of Life,
Glyndwr College Wrexham

The comparison with Spencer seems especially apt, since Louis and Mary Behrend, who were neighbours of Eldridge and Thomas in Eglwsfach, near Macchynlleth, took Stanley Spencer to see the paintings in 1958. He was profoundly impressed and left a set of photographs of the mural on his drawing room table to show to his visitors, writing to Eldridge, 'people are amazed at it as I was.'[113] The letter continues, showing how beneath the surface depiction of loss and distress, Spencer saw an affirmative message:

> Although there is the coming war in the theme yet somehow it maintains a joy that stems from the perhaps loveliest of the panels, namely the first one. But all the others are equal. The land & the people & anything else in it are all one thing all doing things to each other. And with this extraordinary degree of unity you can ramify into all places near or far & maintain the import and special meaning & atmosphere … All is safely gathered in to that meaning, nothing is left out in the 'cold' that is to say nothing is without the meaning you meant it to have.
>
> The technique which is born out of the conception is terrific. I feel when I look at the scheme that you hold much the same beliefs as I hope I have in painting: namely that imagination is found in the basest reality & that is what I think is exciting. What we see – because of ourselves & associations mixing & becoming one with it – is a part of ourselves. You are those hills, you are the directions they take, you are the thing that keeps the wind off those sheep you are the scudding sky you are the world and this fact can only be known by your mastery in composition. … because where the composition is a real creation a real conception which in turn means that a fine marriage has come about with every thing every part & item & moment in your pictures.[114]

Spencer's letter not only helps us to understand *The Dance of Life* but also to understand his own attitude to painting. Being convinced, despite the mishaps of his own life, that there would be redemption, he did not dwell on the threatening and sinister aspect of the painting, but recognized the genuine identification with nature and landscape that Eldridge had made which caused her justifiable fears for the future.

Conclusion

It is never easy to declare the end of one phase and the beginning of another. Murals experienced a revival of interest in the 1980s, but there was by then a break in continuity. For the first time, outdoor paintings, usually with political themes, on gable ends and other neglected walls, became popular in London and other cities where funding was available, and were linked to a revival of interest in the Mexican muralists of the 1930s, with their bold legible subjects and crowded political compositions.[115] This trend did not last into the 1990s, however, and the impulse to create public art murals during the past 20 years has taken other forms. Should any artist wish to work with colour on a flat surface today on a large scale, they would find that digital printing saved the labour of paints and brushes, as when a painting by Howard Hodgkin was enlarged to fill the exterior glazing around the Imax cinema at Waterloo from its opening in 1999 until 2006. This has since been replaced by a series of advertisements to raise revenue for the British Film Institute, and one may ponder whether the value ascribed to an artist's own handwork on a mural, had it been produced in the traditional way, might have maintained this space as a giant art gallery instead of it being converted to commerce.

Perhaps it is not surprising that art history has difficulty with murals, given the diversity of style and intention that they represent, as well as the difficulty of gathering visual and documentary information about them. Their relative neglect is regrettable, if only because it has allowed so much destruction of work, especially that in the public realm, which was produced by artists at some cost to themselves in order to provide future generations with windows out of the everyday into some form of imaginative vision. The gradual and overdue recognition that single narratives in the selection of history are a weakness of scholarship and criticism rather than a strength should give support to a more inclusive view of twentieth-century British art generally, and with it a more developed understanding of the role of murals in the lives of artists and in society during this period.

As with so many other things in recent years, murals are special because people aren't making them any more. While this is not an absolute truth, the painstaking building up of skills in design and execution that supported the mural and decorative painters between 1920 and 1960 now represents a lost world. It leaves us with much to enjoy, to wonder at and to cherish.

ENDNOTES

1 Examples include Prendergast School, Brockley and Cecil Sharp House, Camden. A research project, The Decorated School, is currently collecting information, http://thedecoratedschool.blogspot.co.uk/.

2 Clare A. P. Willsdon, *Mural Painting in Britain 1840-1940: Image and Meaning*, Oxford University Press, 2000.

3 BBC Radio 4 'Making History', October 11, 2011.

4 This took place in 1994. At her own house, Lord's Wood, Marlow, there was an earlier fresco on a subject from Maurice Maeterlinck, and this was regrettably destroyed in the 1970s.

5 The hospital buildings were demolished for redevelopment. The entitlement of the Hospital Trust to offer the paintings for sale was questioned at the time. They were consigned for auction but did not go under the hammer. The paintings are illustrated (without the story of their perilous journey to safety) in William Schupbach, *Acts of Mercy: The Middlesex Hospital Paintings by Frederick Cayley Robinson*, London, Wellcome Library and National Gallery, 2010.

6 See Edward Croft-Murray, *Decorative Painting in England, 1537-1837*, London, *Country Life*, 1970 for a survey of these years.

7 See the contribution on painting by T. S. R. Boase in M. H. Port, ed., *The Houses of Parliament*, London, Yale University Press, 1977, pp.268-81 and Willsdon, op.cit.

8 John Leech's *Cartoon No.1: Substance and Shadow* appeared in *Punch* in July 1843.

9 George Behrend, *Stanley Spender at Burghclere*, London, Macdonald & Co., 1965, p.6.

10 Walter Crane lectured on mural painting for the Arts and Crafts Exhibition Society in 1893 and 1896, praising Madox Brown's Manchester work: 'Of Decorative Painting and Design' in *Arts and Crafts Essays by members of the Arts and Crafts Exhibition Society*, London, Longmans, Green & Company, 1893, pp.39-51 and 'Of the Decoration of Public Buildings' in *Art and Life and the Building and Decoration of Cities: A Series of Lectures by members of the Arts and Crafts Exhibition Society*, delivered at the fifth exhibition of the Society in 1896, London, Rivington, Purcell & Co., 1897, pp.111-66. See also *Transactions of the National Association for the Advancement of Art and its Application to Industry*, Liverpool Meeting, 1888, London, 1888; Edinburgh Meeting 1889, London, 1890; Birmingham Meeting 1890, London 1891 for discussion of the social role of art by figures of the Arts and Crafts Movement.

11 Nicholas Watkins, 'The Genesis of a Decorative Aesthetic' in Gloria Groom and others, *Beyond the Easel: decorative painting Bonnard, Vuillard, Denis and Roussel, 1890-1930*, Art Institute of Chicago, 2001, p.2.

12 Maurice Denis, 'Definition du neo-traditionism', *Art et Critique*, August 23, 1890.

13 Dom Willibord Verkade, OSB, *Yesterdays of an Artist-Monk*, translated by John L. Stoddard, New York/London, 1930, p.88, quoted in Watkins, op.cit., p.1.

14 Morna O'Neill, Walter Crane, *The Arts and Crafts, Painting and Politics, 1875-1890*, New Haven and London, Yale University Press, 2010, p.7.

15 Lady Burne-Jones, *Memorials of Edward Burne-Jones*, London, Macmillan & Co., 1912, vol.II, p.13.

16 Edward Armitage, *Lectures on Painting delivered to students of the Royal Academy,* New York, G. P. Putnam's Sons, 1883, p.207. The lectures were delivered between 1876 and 1882.

17 Morna O'Neill, 'A Political Theory of Decoration, 1901-1910' in Morna O'Neill and Michael Hatt, eds. *The Edwardian Sense: Art, Design and Performance in Britain, 1901-1910*, New Haven and London, The Yale Center for British Art, 2010.

18 Sir William Rothenstein speaking at the annual dinner of the Faculty of Architects and Surveyors, reported in *The Times*, December 9, 1933, p.6.

19 A. Lys Baldry, *Modern Mural Decoration*, London, George Newnes, 1902, p.3.

20 Walter Bayes, *The Art of Decorative Painting*, London, Chapman and Hall, 1927, Chapter 1.

21 See *A Treatise on Painting, by Cennino Cennini*, translated by Mrs [Mary Philadelphia] Merrifield, London, Lumley, 1844 (Merrifield also wrote *The Art of Fresco Painting*, London, Charles Gilpin, 1846); *The Book of the Art of Cennino Cennini, translated, with Notes on Mediaeval Method* by Christiana J. Herringham, London, George Allen, 1899.

22 See Alan Powers, 'The Fresco Revival in the Early Twentieth Century', *Journal of the Decorative Arts Society*, 12, [1986], pp.38-46.

23 See Mary Sargant-Florence, 'Fresco Painting' in *Papers of the Society of Painters in Tempera*, vol.1, 1901-1907, [1907], 2nd edition 1928, pp.54-69.

24 The Society of Tempera Painters was founded in 1901 by Christiana Herringham. Three volumes of the edited papers of the combined Society were published in 1907, 1925 and 1936. It held exhibitions, including one in 1914 at the Art Workers Guild and one in 1946.

25 See Harold Watkins, *The Art of Gerald Moira*, London, E. W. Dickens, 1922.

26 See George Breeze, *Joseph Southall 1861-1944 Artist-Craftsman*, Birmingham Museums and Art Gallery, 1980, pp.87-91.

27 See Richard Cork, *Art beyond the Gallery in early 20th century England*, London and New Haven, Yale University Press, 1985 and Christopher Reed, *Bloomsbury Rooms: Modernism, Subculture and Domesticity*, Yale, 2004. The murals by Duncan Grant and Vanessa Bell at Roger Fry's house, Durbins, Guildford, 1912, are the only pre-1914 examples surviving.

28 The inspiration for using artists to decorate an exhibition in this way came from the major Decorative Arts Exhibition in Munich in 1908. See Alan Powers, 'Murals of the Arts and Crafts movement at the 1916 Exhibition', in *Craft History I*, 1988, pp.23-30 and *The Studio*, vol. LXIX, 1917, pp.66-77, 120-30, 189-92.

29 See *Architectural Review* vol.53, February 1923, pp.37-9; *The Times*, February 9, 1924, p.6 and *Survey of London Monograph 19*, County Hall, http://www.british-history.ac.uk/report.aspx?compid=118182.

30 The artists were Roger Fry, Bernard Adeney, Frederick Etchells, Macdonald Gill, Duncan Grant, and Albert Rutherston. The canvases are in the Tate collection.

31 Eve Garnett (1900-91) is chiefly famous for her book *The Family from One-End Street*, 1937. The 40ft long mural survives at 92 Bruce Road, Bow, see http://www.childrenshouse.towerhamlets.sch.uk.

32 The canvas panels were salvaged after bombing and are in the collection of the Slade School of Art, University of London. See *The Times*, September 24, 1924, p.7.

33 The three presentation drawings by Ravilious were reproduced together for the first time in Alan Powers, *Eric Ravilious, Imagined Realities*, London, Philip Wilson, 2003 and 2012. Fragments of Bawden's equivalent drawings survive after wartime storage down a well at his house in Essex.

34 See Alan Powers, 'True Portraits of Village Life' *Country Life* , October 11, 1984, pp.1066-1068; Ted Ellis, T.J.: *A Life of Thomas Jones*, CH, Cardiff, University of Wales Press, 1992.

35 Romy Golan, *Muralnomad: The paradox of wall painting, Europe 1927-1957*, New Haven and London, Yale University Press, 2009, gives a useful background.

36 The scheme was the work of Hubert Wellington, former Registrar at the RCA under Rothenstein and later head of Edinburgh College of Art. See http://thedecoratedschool.blogspot.co.uk and Philip Long, *John Maxwell 1905-1962*, National Galleries of Scotland, 1998.

37 See G. J. Howling, 'Mural Decorations in a Children's Library', *The Builder*, April 30, 1948, pp.510-11.

38 Spencer's marouflaged canvas of *The Scholar Gypsy* should be discoverable in future beneath a layer of styrofoam near the base of the rear staircase. The other works appear to have been destroyed in the 1980s and '90s.

39 The illustrated record book of the Abbey Fund commissions is held in the archives of the Royal Academy of Arts, London.

40 See Mary Banham and Bevis Hiller, eds., *A Tonic to the Nation*, London, Thames & Hudson, 1976 and Elain Harwood and Alan Powers, eds., *Festival of Britain*, London, Twentieth Century Society, 2001 and 2011.

41 Two books help to record the products of the worldwide movement for the Synthesis of the Arts: Eleanor Bitterman, *Art in Modern Architecture*, New York, Reinhold Publishing Company, 1952. and Paul Damaz, *Art in European Architecture*, Reinhold, 1956.

42 The presence of these works of art contributed to the listing of the Civic Centre in 2008.

43 See Baldry op.cit. Walter Crane assisted in completing the paintings in situ in the mid-1870s. They were subsequently removed and dispersed to different public collections.

44 See Elizabeth Cumming, *Phoebe Anna Traquair 1852-1936*, Edinburgh, Scottish National Portrait Gallery, 1993.

45 See Herbert Furst, *The Decorative Art of Frank Brangwyn*, London, Bodley Head, 1924 and Alan Powers, 'The murals of Frank Brangwyn' in Libby Horner and Gillian Naylor, eds. *Frank Brangwyn, 1867-1956*, Leeds Museum and Art Galleries, 2006.

46 See Richard Shone, *Bloomsbury Portraits*, London, Phaidon, 1976 as a pioneering study, and more recently, Christopher Reed, *Bloomsbury Rooms*, London, Yale University Press, 2004.

47Abbey to Lord Carlisle, October 10, 1910, Castle Howard Archives, J22/84, cited in Willsdon op.cit., p.97.

48 See Ita Heinze-Greenberg, 'The Mediterranean Academy Project and Mendelsohn's Emigration' in Regina Stefan, ed. *Erich Mendelsohn 1887-1953*, New York, Monacelli Press, 1998.

49 Moholy-Nagy's relief photomural for the Electricity Showroom, Regent Street, 1936, is well illustrated in 'Murals and Photomurals', *National Builder*, September 1938.

50 Serge Chermayeff 'Modern Art and Architecture', discussion with Laszlo Moholy-Nagy, Naum Gabo and Herbert Read, RIBA, December 9, 1936, reported in *RIBA Journal*, January 9, 1937, p.209-.

51 See Elizabeth Cowling and Jennifer Munday, *On Classic Ground: Picasso, Léger, de Chirico and the New Classicism 1910-1930*, London, Tate Gallery, 1990.

52 See Ann Compton, *Edward Halliday, Art for Life, 1925-1939,* University of Liverpool Art Gallery, 1997.

53 Hans Feibusch, *Mural Painting*, London, A & C Black, 1945, p.44. On Feibusch generally, see David Coke, ed. *Hans Feibusch, the Heat of Vision*, Chichester, Pallant House Gallery Trust with Lund Humphries, 1995 and Paul Foster, ed. *Feibusch Murals, Chichester and Beyond*, Chichester Institute of Higher Education, Otter Memorial Paper No.8, 1997.

54 Feibusch, op.cit., p.49.

55 Watkins, op. cit., p.43.

56 Editor [Mary Sargant Florence] 'Preface', *Papers of the Society of Mural Decorators and Painters in Tempera, Third volume, 1925-1935*, Brighton, The Dolphin Press, 1936.

57 See Golan op.cit. p.79. Stic B was a French product, launched in the late 1920s.

58 See Alan Powers, 'The Stone and the Shell, Eric Gill and the Midland Hotel, Morecambe', *The Book Collector*, Vol.46, spring 1998, pp.43-66.

59 See Alan Powers, 'In Search of the Caveman Restaurant', *Thirties Society Journal V*, 1985, pp.18-23. Hodgkin's cartoon for the mural is reproduced in colour in *The Artist*, August 1935, p.192.

60 The painting was executed by Charles Howard to Wadsworth's design and was originally on the end wall of the café and dance hall on the ground floor. The version currently in the Pavilion is a reconstruction on a panel dating from 1962.

61 See *Architectural Review*, vol. LXXXIV, July 1938, special issue on the exhibition.

62 Golan op.cit. pp.131-62 illustrates many European photomurals from exhibitions. The projecting process was developed in Britain by the architect-decorators Eugene Mollo and Michael Egan, in collaboration with Paul Lamboit and John Gabriel. See Eugene Mollo, 'Decorating by Photography', *Design for Today* vol. IV, April 1936, pp.163-4. The photomural by E. McKnight Kauffer at Embassy Court, Brighton, designed by Wells Coates, was made by projection. Michael Egan wrote in 1997, 'The snag was that it was very difficult to do, so that in spite of architects' and designers' support and heroic efforts, it was uncertain and costly: we lost money.' (letter to author, September 16, 1997).

63 See Elizabeth Darling, *Wells Coates*, London, RIBA Publishing, 2012. Armstrong painted decorations for two flats designed by Coates at 1 Kensington Palace Gardens (for George and Patricia Strauss) and 34 Gordon Square (for Charles Laughton and Elsa Lanchester).

64 See Simon Guthrie, *John Cecil Stephenson*, Grange-over-Sands, Cartmel Press Associates, 1997, and Conor Mullan, *John Cecil Stephenson 1889-1965, Pioneer of Modernism*, Durham, DLI Museum and Durham Art Gallery, 2012.

65 See Rutter Carroll, *Ryder and Yates*, London, RIBA Publications, 2009; John Allan, *Berthold Lubetkin*, London, Merrell, 2002, p.119.

66 Illustrated in *John Piper*, Tate Gallery, 1983, p.44.

67 David Fraser Jenkins, 'Piper for Now', in *John Piper 1903-1992*, London, The Fine Art Society, 2012, p.10.

68 See Eugene Rosenberg, *Architect's Choice: art and architecture in Great Britain since 1945*, London, Thames & Hudson, 1992, p.50.

69 The principal interior wall of the Merzbarn was removed and installed in the Hatton Gallery, Newcastle-upon-Tyne, through the intervention of Richard Hamilton.

70 'Coals of Fire from the Lords to the Commons', *Illustrated London News*, November 5, 1910.

71 Willsdon, op.cit., p.97.

72 See David Boswell, 'Frank Brangwyn and his patrons' in Horner and Naylor, eds. op.cit., pp.156-85.

73 Tate Archive. Charles Aitken papers, Morley College file. Hubert Wellington to Charles Aitken (Director of the Tate Gallery), 24 July 1929. Ibid., Aitken to Duveen, October 12, 1928. The cost at this point was estimated as £150 each for Ravilious and Bawden, with £200 for Mahoney.

74 See Matthew H. Clough & Ann Compton, eds. *Earthly Delights: Mary Adshead 1904-1995*, University of Liverpool Art Gallery, 2004, pp.36-45.

75 Mary Adshead, 'Modern Decorative Painting', Lecture at Liverpool School of Architecture, *Architect and Building News*, March 25, 1927, vol.117, p.515.

76 See Willsdon, op.cit., Chapter 8, 'Ecclesiastical Murals', pp.213-54.

77 Henry Tonks to A. M. Daniel, quoted in Joseph Hone, *The Life of Henry Tonks*, London, William Heinemann, 1939, p.187l.

78 See Sir John Rothenstein, *Charles Mahoney, A Tribute on the occasion of a Memorial Exhibition,* London, Michael Parkin, 1975.

79 See Bernard Walke, *Twenty Years at St Hilary*, London, Methuen, 1936.

80 Find reference (Bishop Bell in *Studio*, probably vol.124, pp.91-2).

81 See Paul Foster, 'Introduction' to Paul Foster, ed. *Feibusch Murals, Chichester and Beyond*, Chichester, Chichester Institute of Higher Education, Otter Memorial Papers, 8, 1997, pp.11-14.

82 See Bishop Peter Walker, 'Hans Feibusch and George Bell' in David Coke, ed., *Hans Feibusch, The Heat of Vision*, London and Chichester, Lund Humphries in association with Pallant House Gallery Trust, 1995.

83 Charles Reilly, by then retired from Liverpool University and living in Brighton, was the first to propose the commission. Although the scheme was passed at the various levels of the church's internal decision-making process, an appeal was lodged at the Consistory Court, with Bell intervening to declare a judgment in favour of the murals.

84 See Edward Mayor and Judith Robinson, *The Duncan Grant Murals in Lincoln Cathedral,* Lincoln Cathedral Publications, nd.

85 See Patricia Jordan and Joanna Cartwright, eds. *John Piper and the Church*, Dorchester, The Friends of Dorchester Abbey, 2012.

86 Sold at Bonhams March 27, 1997. They were exhibited at St Mungo's Museum of Religious Life and Art, Glasgow, May 1–July 11, 1999.

87 See David Buckman, Ludmilla Jordanova and Robert Radford, *Nature and Humanity, the work of Fyffe Christie, 1918-1979*, Bristol, Sansom & Co., 2004.

88 See Ruth Artmonsky, *Shipboard Style: Colin Anderson of the Orient Line*, London, Artmonsky Arts, 2010.

89 In conversation with author, late 1980s.

90 See *The Times*, January 28, 1939, p.10.

91 See George Sheringham, 'French Mural Decorations', *Studio*, March 15, 1926, pp.155-61 and George Sheringham, 'Mural Decoration' in *Report on the Present Position and Tendencies of the Industrial Arts*, London, Department of Overseas Trade, 1927, pp.51-60.

92 See G. D. Schott, 'Nan West's Murals in the Royal National Orthopaedic Hospital', *British Medical Journal*, December 19-26, 1998. The murals were restored in 1996, listed in 1998 and removed prior to installation in a reconstructed version of the original waiting room, now forming a commercial development on the site. Public access to the room is not permitted.

93 See Charles Reilly, *Country Life*, June 6, 1931, pp.736-38. The paintings are lost, but the C. S. Jagger relief and original firebasket were acquired by the V&A in 2005.

94 Quoted in Andrew Lambirth, *John Armstrong, the Paintings*, London, Philip Wilson, 2009, p.138, where studies for a number of murals are illustrated. See also Elizabeth Darling, *Wells Coates*, London, RIBA Publishing, 2012, for interiors of 1 Kensington Palace Gardens (George and Patricia Strauss) and 34 Gordon Square (Charles Laughton and Elsa Lanchester).

95 See Alan Powers, 'Rhythm in Design', *Country Life*, April 18, 1991, pp.116-7.

96 See Richard Gray, *Cinemas in Britain*, London, Lund Humphries, 1996, where Baines's safety curtain at the Gaumont Palace, Wood Green, 1934 is illustrated on p.89.

97 Susan Sontag, 'Notes on Camp' in *Against Interpretation*, London, Eyre & Spottiswoode, 1967.

98 Dorothy Todd and Raymond Mortimer, *The New Interior Decoration*, London, Batsford, 1929.

99 Richard Shone's *Bloomsbury Portraits*, London, Phaidon, 1976, was the first book to explore the full range of work by these artists, in conjunction with biography.

100 Evelyn Waugh, review of The Königsmark Drawings by Rex Whistler, *Time and Tide*, December 6, 1952, p.1456.

101 Gwen Raverat, review of exhibition of mural painting at the Tate Gallery, *Time and Tide*, March 11, 1939.

102 On Felix Kelly, see Donald Bassett, *Fix: the art and life of Felix Kelly*, Darrow Press, 2007.

103 See Alan Powers, 'Ronald Fleming and Vogue Regency', *Decorative Arts Society Journal* No.19, 1995, pp.51-58.

104 On Laurence Scarfe, see Stella Beddoe, 'The Designs of Laurence Scarfe: The Archive presented to Brighton Museum in 1983' in *Journal of the Decorative Arts Society*, 15, 1991; on Barbara Jones, see Ruth Artmonsky, *A Snapper up of unconsidered trifles: a tribute to Barbara Jones*, London, Artmonsky Arts, 2008.

105 'Mural Painting: Exhibition at Tate Gallery', *The Times*, June 1, 1939, p.12.

106 See Elizabeth Prettejohn, 'The Pre-Raphaelite Legacy' in Tim Barringer, Jason Rosenfeld and Alison Smith, *Pre-Raphaelites: Victorian Avant-Garde*, London, Tate Publishing, 2012.

107 Dora Carrington to John Nash, July 22, 1913. Tate Gallery Archive, quoted in Ronald Blythe, *First Friends*, Huddersfield, The Fleece Press, 1997, p.40.

108 Letter to author, 1985.

109 See Alan Powers 'Wards and Walls', *Country Life*, March 17, 1988, pp.96-7. The life of the artist is described in part in Byron Rogers' biography of R. S. Thomas, *The Man who went into the West*, London, aurum, 2006.

110 Notes on the paintings were written by Louis Behrend, photocopy in author's collection.

111 From Louis Behrend's notes on Panel 6.

112 The painting appears to be lost. A photograph of it is in the Tate Archive, from the records of the 1939 mural exhibition, and it was published in *The Builder*, April 7, 1939 (title page).

113 Stanley Spencer to Mildred Eldridge, November 14, 1958. Author's collection.

114 Ibid.

115 See Ray Walker, catalogue for exhibition at the Royal Festival Hall, May 17-June 16, 1985, London, Coracle Press, 1985. Walker painted the still extant mural of *The Battle of Cable Street*, 1982-83, in Cable Street E1. An exhibition of the murals of Diego Rivera was held at the Hayward Gallery, October 1987-January 1988.

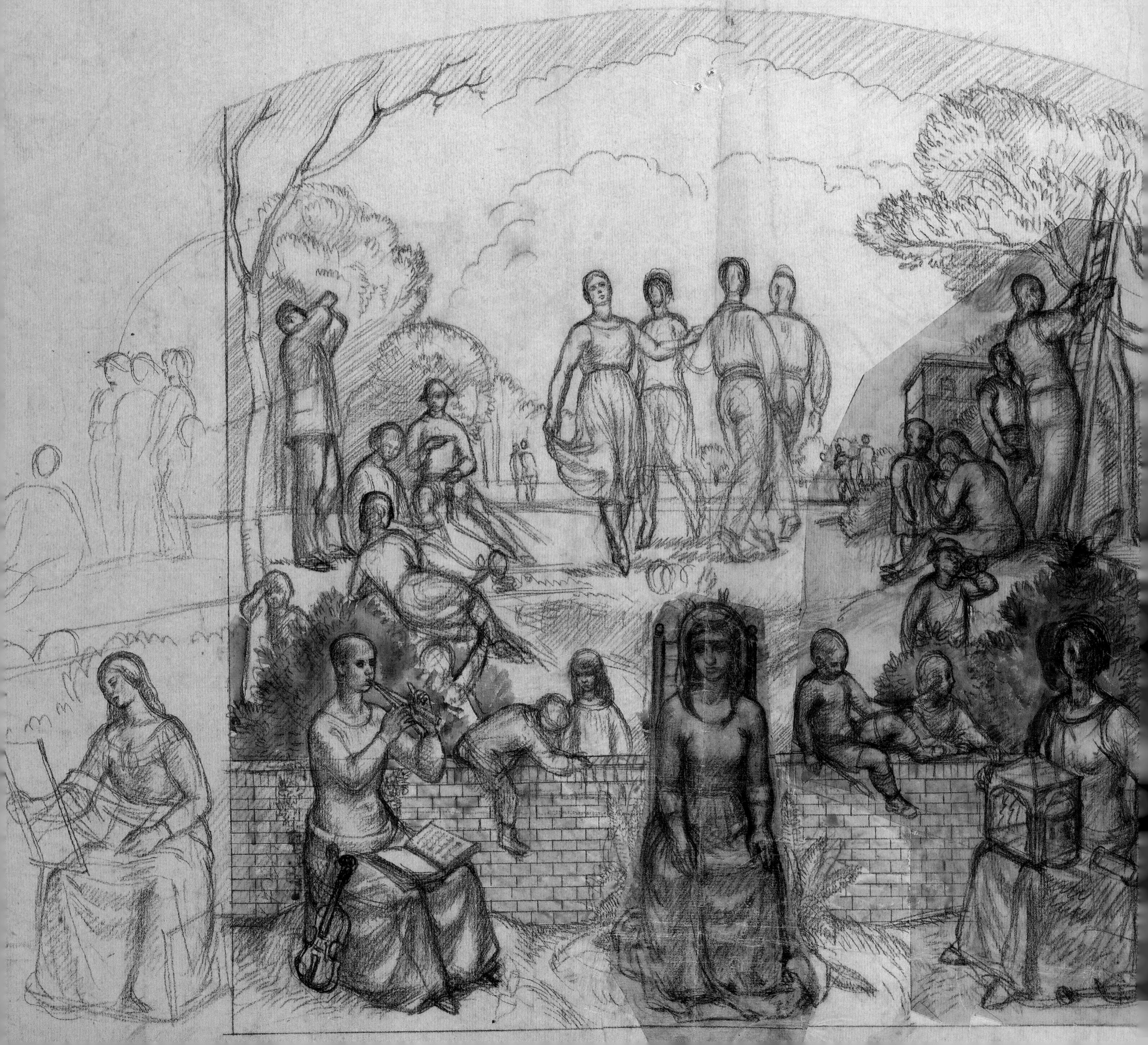

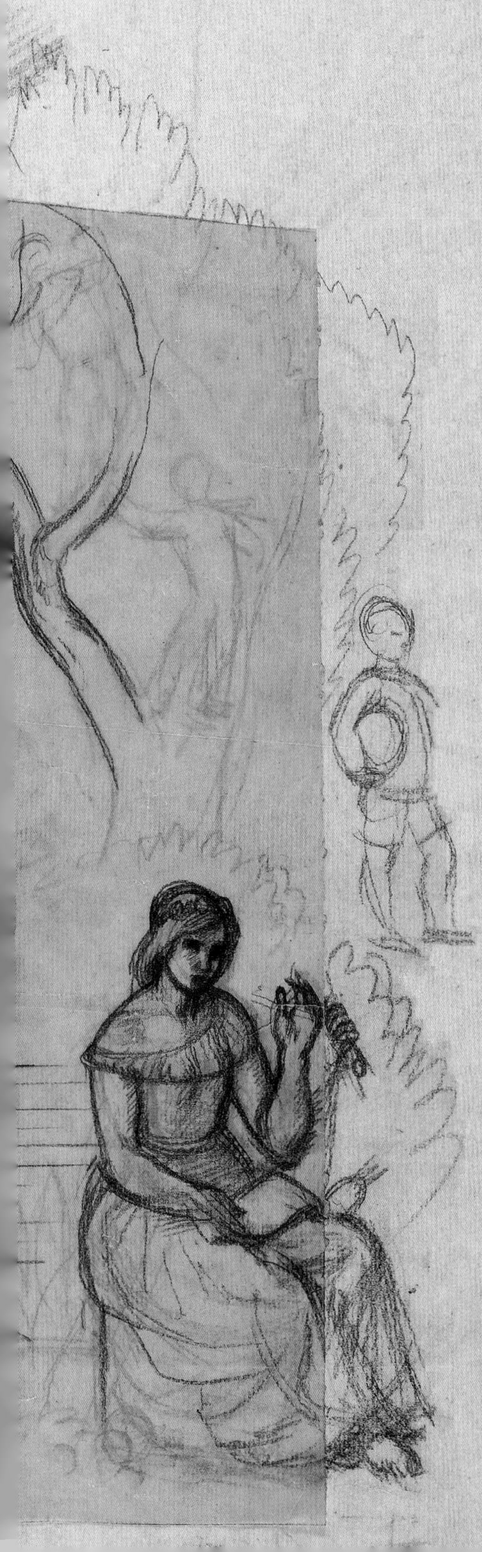

PART II

Case Studies

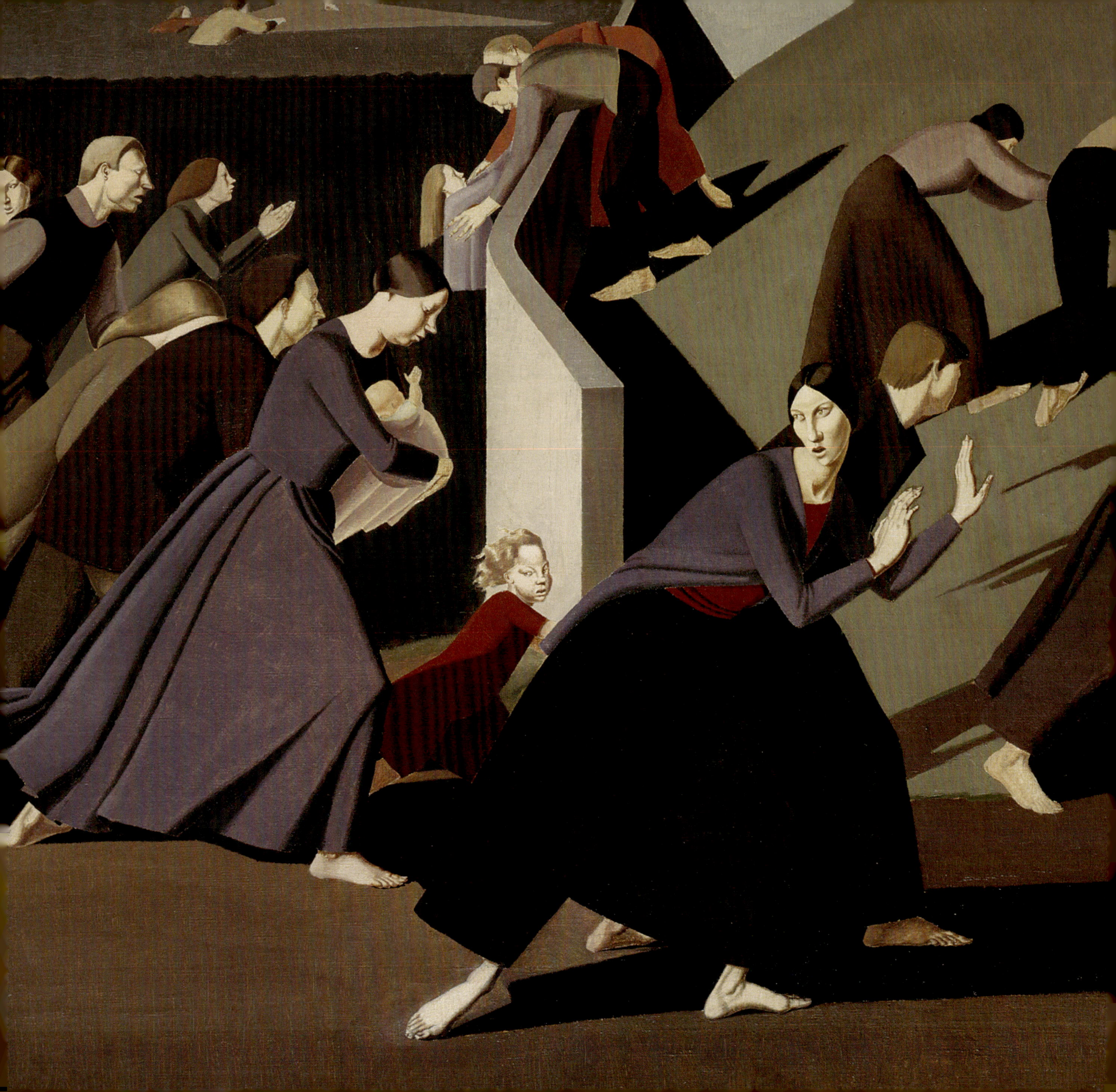

Winifred Knights
The Deluge, 1920

Sacha Llewellyn

In 1920, Winifred Knights won the Rome Scholarship in Decorative Painting, considered at the time to be 'the highest distinction of its kind in the Empire'.[1] Her winning entry, *The Deluge*, was exhibited at the Royal Academy in February 1921 to wide-spread critical acclaim, and Winifred Knights, the first woman to win the scholarship and nine years younger than the three other finalists, was declared to be 'a genius'.[2] This essay will consider the context out of which Winifred Knights produced the most enduring competition painting for the Rome Scholarship throughout its duration.

Winifred Knights attended the Slade School of Art from 1915-1917, and from 1918-1920, and these four years proved definitive in terms of her artistic development. The early influences of Robert Anning Bell and John Byam Shaw and the illustrative work of Jessie King, Charles Ricketts and Walter Crane were broadened by exposure to a much wider spectrum of art. Slade students were encouraged to study the prints and drawings at the British Museum and at the Slade Fine Art Library, to view the paintings at the National Gallery and to use the library at the Victoria and Albert Museum. Early on Knights began to collect black-and-white prints, as well as cuttings from newspapers, of drawings and paintings that she admired, mostly from the early Italian Schools but also nineteenth- and twentieth-century French and English paintings, Flemish painting, and the graphic works of Durer and Cranach.[3]

Her drawings and notebooks from this period bear witness to the rigorous academic training that she received, which was centred around the close observation of the model and accompanied by courses on 'Fine Art Anatomy', 'Perspective and Fine Art Geometry' and 'Ornamental Design', as well as lectures on the 'History of Art'.[4] Since its foundation in 1871, the Slade had placed life-drawing at the centre of its curriculum and Henry Tonks, who taught at the Slade from 1892, first as Assistant Professor and then as Slade Professor from 1918, built upon the tradition of linear constructive drawing expounded by his two predecessors, Edward Poynter and Alphonse Legros.[5] Slade students were not expected to produce a finished academy drawing, but rather to use drawing as a means of expressing form: 'drawing is concerned only with the expression of form and its arrangement to further the design: any attempt to make it do more than this weakens it'.[6] The quality and surety of Knights' drawings from this period, with their sense of completion extending outwards from a detail and with shade and light being the only adjustments made, reflect the teaching that she received.[7]

79
The Deluge,
© Tate, London 2012
(detail)

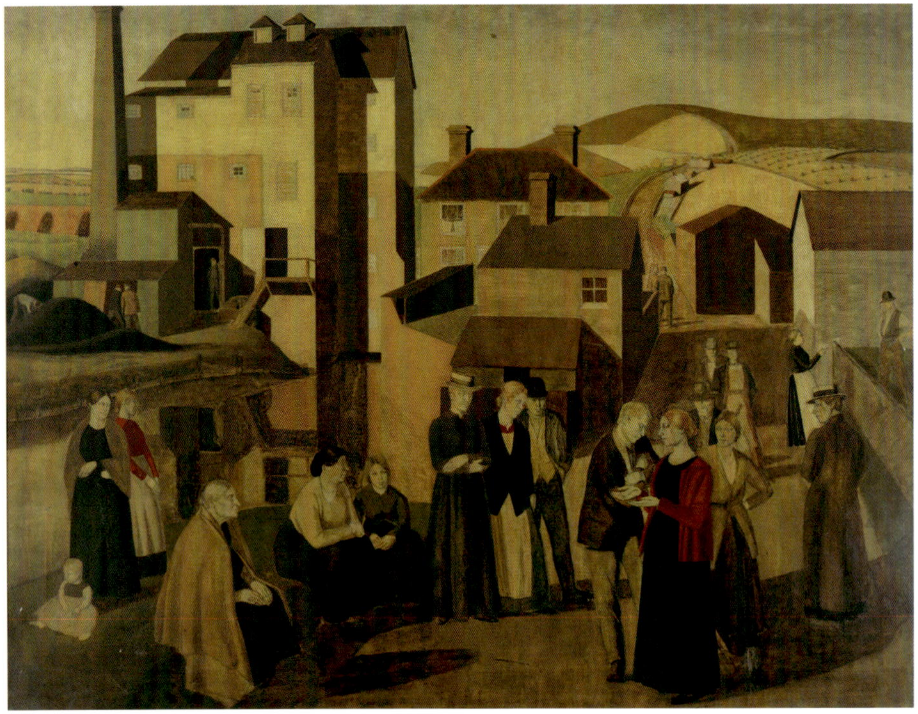

80
A Scene in a Village Street with Millhands Conversing, 1919,
Tempera on canvas relined on board,
91.4 x 122 cm (36 x 48 in.)
Courtesy of UCL Art Museum,
University College London

When a certain level of proficiency had been achieved in drawing, students were allowed to begin to paint from life and 'Sketch Club Subjects' were set monthly to provide practice in composition, ('Special Figure', 'Figure', 'Animal' and 'Landscape');[8] in 1917, Knights won second prize for 'Figure Drawing' and in 1918 she developed her drawing for the 'Special Figure' subject *Design for Wall Decoration* into a substantial painting (private collection).[9] In 1919, she jointly won the prestigious Slade School Summer Composition Competition with *A Scene in a Village Street with Millhands Conversing*.[10] This prize-winning picture, along with *Design for Wall Decoration*, employed the conventions of decorative painting.[11] As an aesthetic category, decorative painting was determined by the exigencies of placing a work within an architectural setting and was seen to be the means of developing in students the traditional skills of drawing, compositional design and the handling of materials such as oil and tempera.[12] By the early twentieth century, decorative painting had also come to denote, as Walter Crane explained in his book *Ideals in Art* of 1905, a 'mural feeling in a picture', comprising 'a certain flatness of treatment with choice of simple planes, and pure and low-toned colours, together with a certain ornamental dignity or architectural feeling in the structure of forms and lines of composition'.[13] Italian Trecento and Quattrocento art, which was seen to so perfectly embody these qualities, was reaching new heights of popularity at this time. For the pre-war generation of Slade students, the Italian Primitives and Modern French Painting were being discovered together, encouraged by Roger Fry who in his Slade lectures from 1909 preached his gospel of Giotto and Cézanne as the way forward to a new formalist future. Knights attended the lectures of Tancred Borenius, a Finnish art-historian and specialist in Italian Art, who succeeded Roger Fry at the Slade in 1914 as Lecturer in the History of Art. His series of lectures, such as 'the Florentine Art of the Renaissance', were accompanied by lantern-slides, and were centred on the study of composition.[14] Good composition was seen primarily to be the 'the architectonic one of the Quattrocento, with rigorous symmetry and co-ordination of the figures which are presented if possible in composed attitudes'.[15]

81
The Illustrated London News,
February 12, 1921

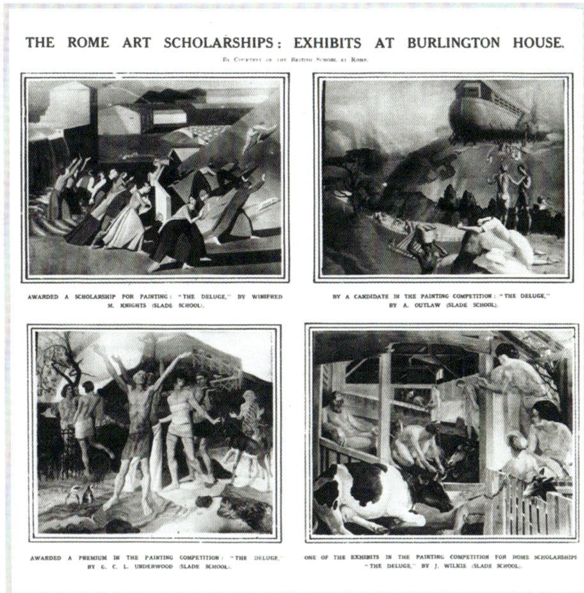
THE ROME ART SCHOLARSHIPS: EXHIBITS AT BURLINGTON HOUSE.

AWARDED A SCHOLARSHIP FOR PAINTING: "THE DELUGE," BY WINIFRED M. KNIGHTS (SLADE SCHOOL).

BY A CANDIDATE IN THE PAINTING COMPETITION: "THE DELUGE," BY A. OUTLAW (SLADE SCHOOL).

AWARDED A PREMIUM IN THE PAINTING COMPETITION: "THE DELUGE," BY G. C. L. UNDERWOOD (SLADE SCHOOL).

ONE OF THE EXHIBITS IN THE PAINTING COMPETITION FOR ROME SCHOLARSHIPS "THE DELUGE," BY J. WILKIE (SLADE SCHOOL).

82
Figure from Life, 1920
oil on canvas,
courtesy of UCL Art Museum,
University College London

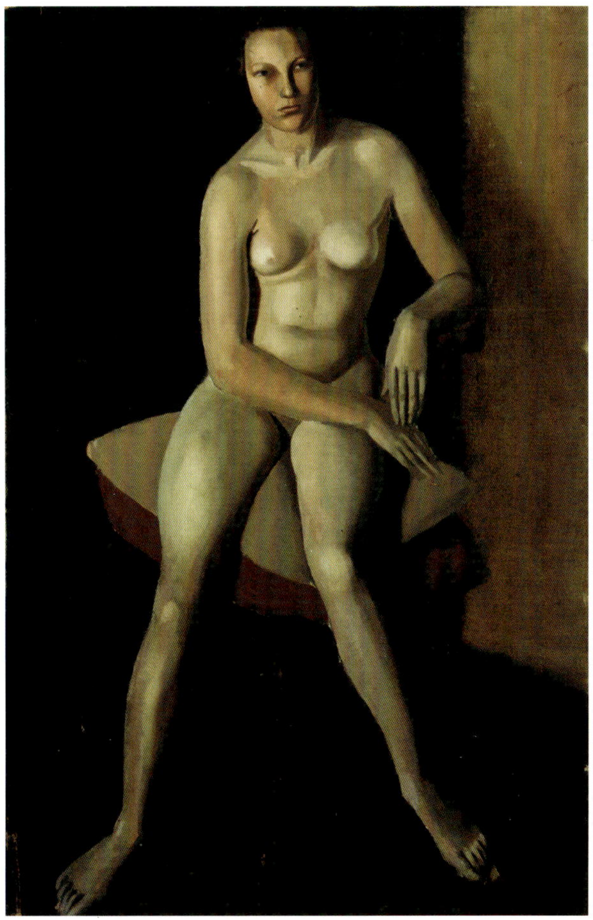

At the end of January 1920, Winifred Knights, along with eight other Slade students, was encouraged to enter the Competition for the Rome Scholarship in Decorative Painting. The Rome Scholarships in Architecture, Sculpture and Decorative Painting had been established in 1912 to 'promote the study of monumental art of which Italy possessed a unique collection, especially in her mural painters'.[16] Modelled on the ideals of the French Grand Prix de Rome, the scholarships aimed to give 'an impetus to artistic training throughout the Empire'.[17] Reflecting the call for art to become 'in a true sense public', the aim was to produce a body of artists to undertake government commissions in Great Britain and its Empire.[18] In a period in which Imperialism was a prevailing force in British politics, the British School at Rome could function therefore as a 'National and Imperial centre of culture and the study of the Arts'.[19]

The first stage of the competition was an Open Qualifying Examination in which the candidates had to submit up to twelve works, to include figure compositions in colour 'suitable for wall decoration', 'sketches of designs and architectural studies for decorative purposes' as well as a full-sized uncoloured cartoon, and a figure from life and life drawings.[20] These criteria were established to demonstrate that the painter 'already possesses a fair understanding of the problems to be dealt with in the execution of a mural painting' and as such were easily accessible to a Slade student.[21] Eight of the seventeen candidates were from the Slade, and the four candidates selected for the final competition were all Slade students: J. Wilkie, A. Outlaw, G. C. L. Underwood, and Winifred Knights.[22] Knights is known to have submitted for the competition a *Figure from Life*, and designs and decorations depicting 'a modern setting of factories and workmen's dwellings'. It is interesting that critics singled Knights out for the sincerity and originality of her designs, which were based on 'primitive simplification and direct expressiveness' as well as 'subtle refinement in colour arrangements', qualities that would distinguish her final competition painting.[23]

Although the final stage of the Rome Scholarship was close in character to a Slade Summer Composition Competition, with a set subject and an eight-week time limit, the conditions were stricter; each candidate was allocated a studio in which to carry out their work, open six days a week from 9am to 7pm, and were forbidden to admit any unauthorised person except for models, for whom a £6 allowance was provided.[24] In a letter to her aunt Knights attributed these disciplined working conditions in part to her success: 'I loved the hard work when I was doing my thing'.[25] On the morning of July 5, 1920, Winifred Knights was handed the terms and conditions for the Final Competition: the subject was the Deluge, and she was to 'produce a painting in oil or tempera and a cartoon…the size of the painting shall be 6 ft by 5ft'.[26]

The Rome Scholarships had been suspended since 1914 and it was hardly a coincidence that the Board would have chosen the Deluge as the set subject in the direct aftermath of the war; the Biblical story was frequently used metaphorically in literature, politics and the arts to refer to the Great War.[27] While Knights would have been aware of the Genesis narrative of the Flood (6:9-8:22), the accepted meanings, the punishment of the guilty and salvation of the faithful, play no part in her interpretation; her men and women are not portrayed as unheroic and sinful, but as terrified, innocent victims who help each other to safety.[28] Rather, Knights' interpretation of the Old Testament story can be read as an analogy of her own emotional response to the war. At the Slade, Tonks encouraged his students to call on their 'subconscious imagination' when interpreting a subject for a painting, which he defined as 'the power to make use at the present moment of something put away in the past.'[29] In January 1917, having experienced at first hand the explosion of a munitions factory in Silvertown from the top deck of a tram, Knights was in 'a terrible state of shock' and by October 3rd she had left London for a year to stay with cousins at Lineholt Farmhouse in Ombersley, Worcestershire, due to her 'fear of the air raids'.[30] For her father, the 'nervous tension' from which his daughter was suffering was a direct result of 'this dreadful turmoil and devastation'.[31] That the finished painting made reference to the war was certainly evident to contemporary critics; the *Manchester Guardian*'s correspondent described the disposition of figures as 'splitting out in sharp lines as if there had been an explosion'.[32] By including her self-portrait twice in the painting (as the two figures looking backwards), as well as that of her sister Eileen (holding the baby) and her close friend Arnold Mason (1885-1963) (the figure climbing the hill and fifth figure from the left), the context becomes deeply personal.[33]

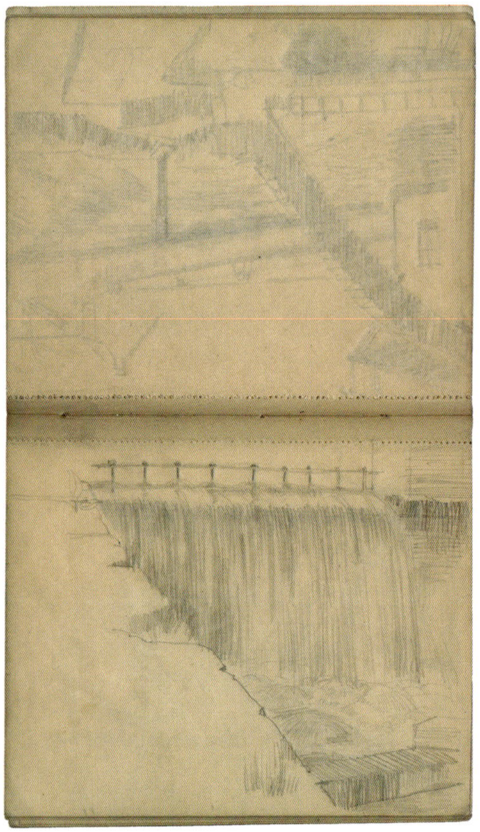

83 *Waterfall at Roydon Weir*, 1920, 'Book of Studies for the Rome Scholarship'

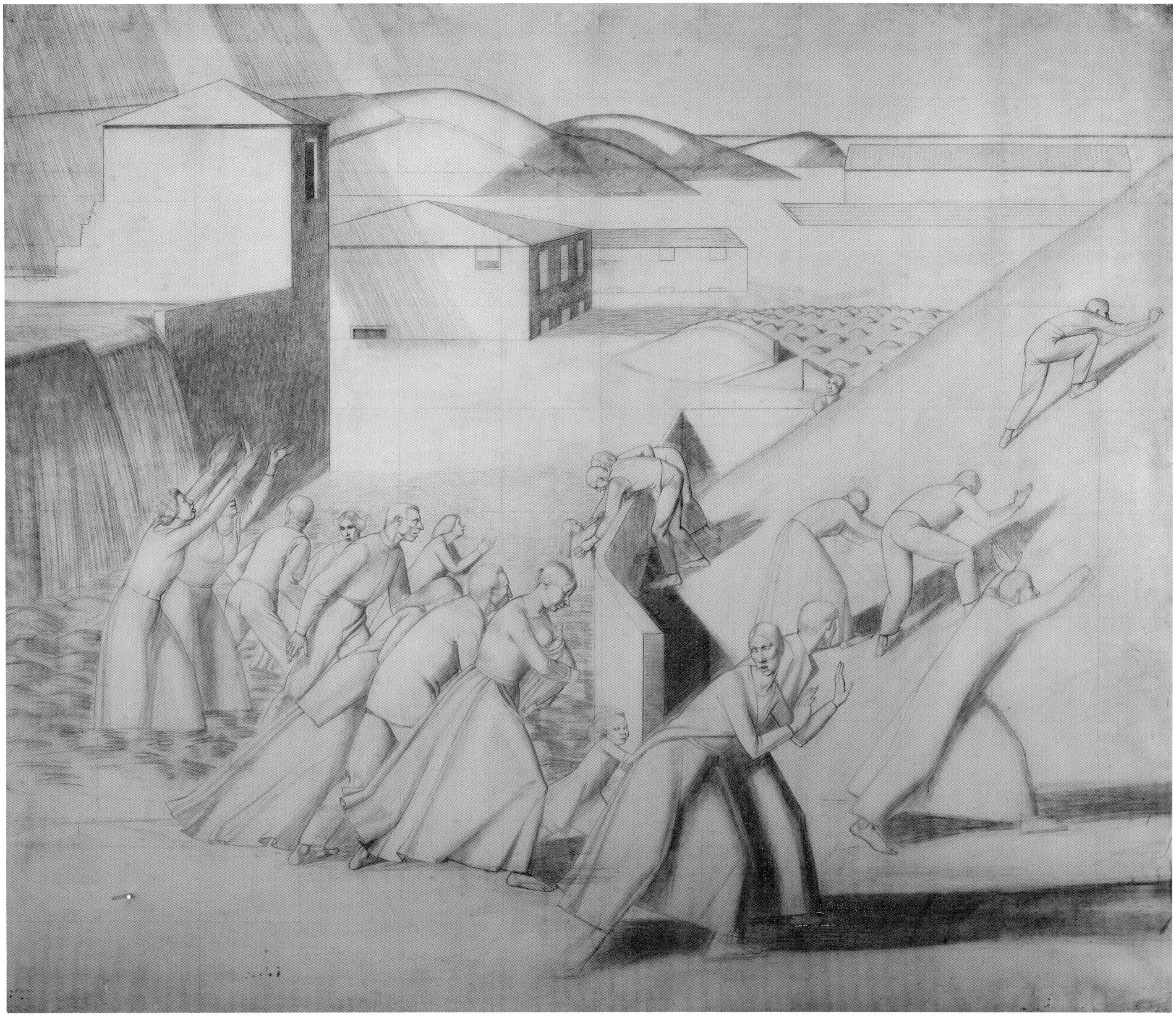

84 Full-scale drawing for *The Deluge*, pencil on paper, 152.9 x 183.5 cm (60 ⅛ x 72 ¼ in.) With the permission of The Wolfsonian – Florida International University (Miami, Florida)

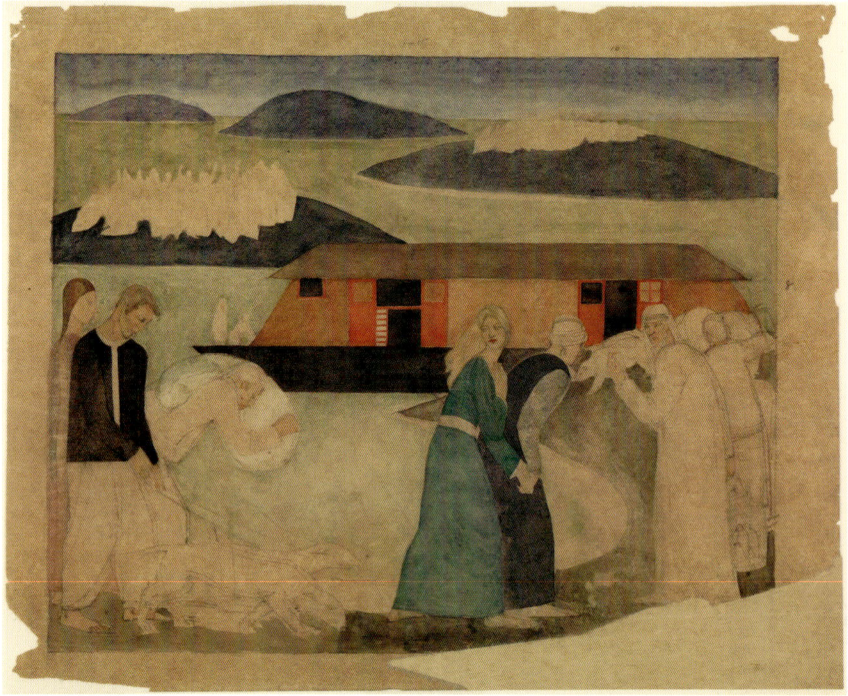

85
Early study for *The Deluge*,
pencil and watercolour,
23.2 x 29.1 cm (9 ⅛ x 11 ½ in.)
Courtesy of the UCL Art Museum,
University College London

The technique that Knights used for *The Deluge* was the standard academic one taught at the Slade and well suited to the production of a 6ft x 5ft painting. Initially, she made numerous studies from life. Central to Tonks' doctrine of 'truth to nature' was his belief that 'if we have exhausted the world about us, we have come to the end of our art'.[34] Knights' 'Book of Studies for the Rome Scholarship, 1920' includes life studies of hands and feet, portraits and self-portraits, as well as detailed landscape drawings and a waterfall, sketched at Roydon Weir. Knights next made colour studies in oil or watercolour, to resolve the relationship of tone, colour and form. Tonks placed great emphasis on 'colour harmonies' at the Slade, and these preliminary colour studies show that Knights attained an increasingly sombre palette in which the flat colours of dark reds, greys, browns and aubergine in the final painting serve to unify the composition.[35] The final resolved composition was scaled up using a traditional grid system.[36] The resulting highly finished full-scale drawing, and a cartoon, were then squared up for transfer on to the canvas.[37] Although Knights had shown her technical ability to paint in tempera with *Millhands Conversing*, she elected to paint *The Deluge* in oil, which she applied thinly to achieve a translucent effect.[38]

Knights' early compositional designs for *The Deluge* show a frieze of calm figures in the foreground with horizontal bands of landscape and water behind. While the figures evoke the work of Robert Anning Bell, in spirit the designs have much in common with the children's illustrations of Walter Crane.[39] A subsequent compositional study shows the beginnings of a dramatic change in both the mood and treatment of the subject, with a noticeable darkening of palette, emphasis on diagonal lines and simplification of form.

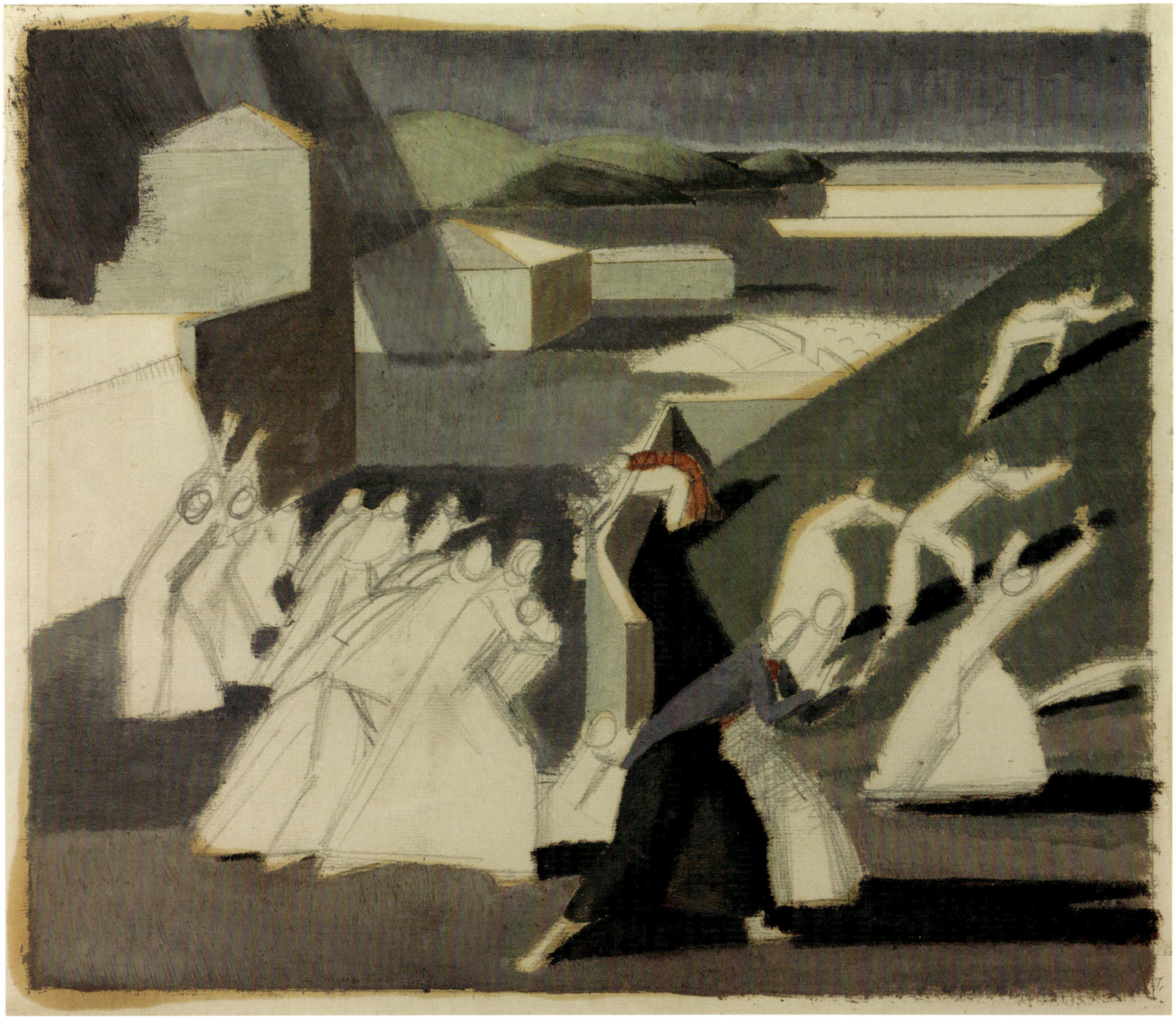

86 Study for *The Deluge*, 1920, oil over pencil on paper, 32.5 x 26.5 cm (12 ¾ x 10 ⅜ in.), courtesy of the UCL Art Museum, University College London

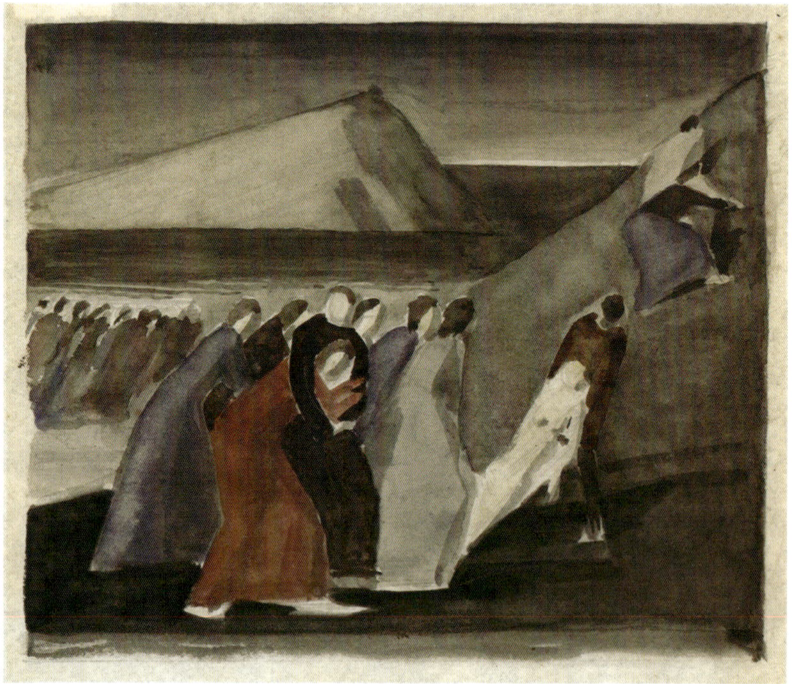

87
Compositional study for *The Deluge*,
pencil and watercolour,
12.5 x 19 cm (5 x 7 ½ in.)

To resolve the composition, Knights looked for inspiration to the most renowned historical depictions of the Deluge. From Michelangelo's celebrated composition (1508-9, Sistine Chapel) she might well have adopted the notion of figures escaping to high land as well as the stranded victims of the flood. Turner's *Deluge* (1805-13, Tate Gallery) may have been the inspiration for the sombre palette and expressive contrasts of light and shade. Of most significance to Knights, however, was Nicholas Poussin's *Le Déluge* from the Louvre Cycle of *Les Quatre Saisons* (1660-4).[40]

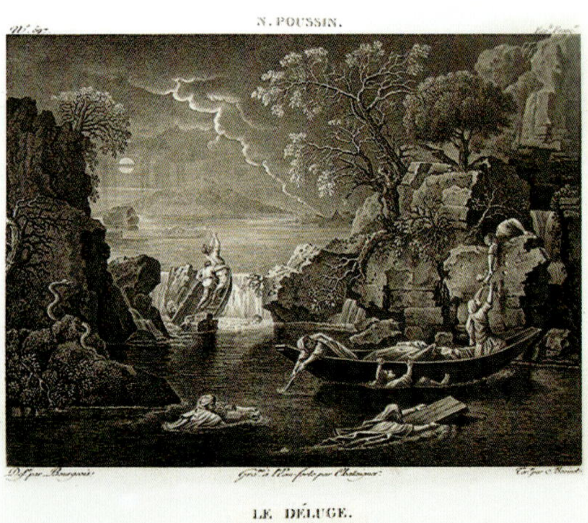

88 After Nicolas Poussin, *Le Déluge,* c. 1810

Contemporary art critics frequently referred to Poussin's influence on modern artists. For Tancred Borenius it was the 'supremely monumental and logical design' that rendered his work so compelling.[41] Charles Ricketts believed it was the 'constructive element' that appealed to Puvis de Chavannes, whom he saw at the Louvre, 'one of the last to leave, before *Le Déluge*, that masterpiece of Poussin'.[42] The flooded landscape in Knights' *The Deluge*, divided into two levels and joined by a waterfall, is a compositional device that she has reproduced, and the motif of a child being pulled from the water, the gesture of raised hands imploring salvation as well as the depiction of the submerged figures, all show a close affinity with Poussin's *Le Déluge*.

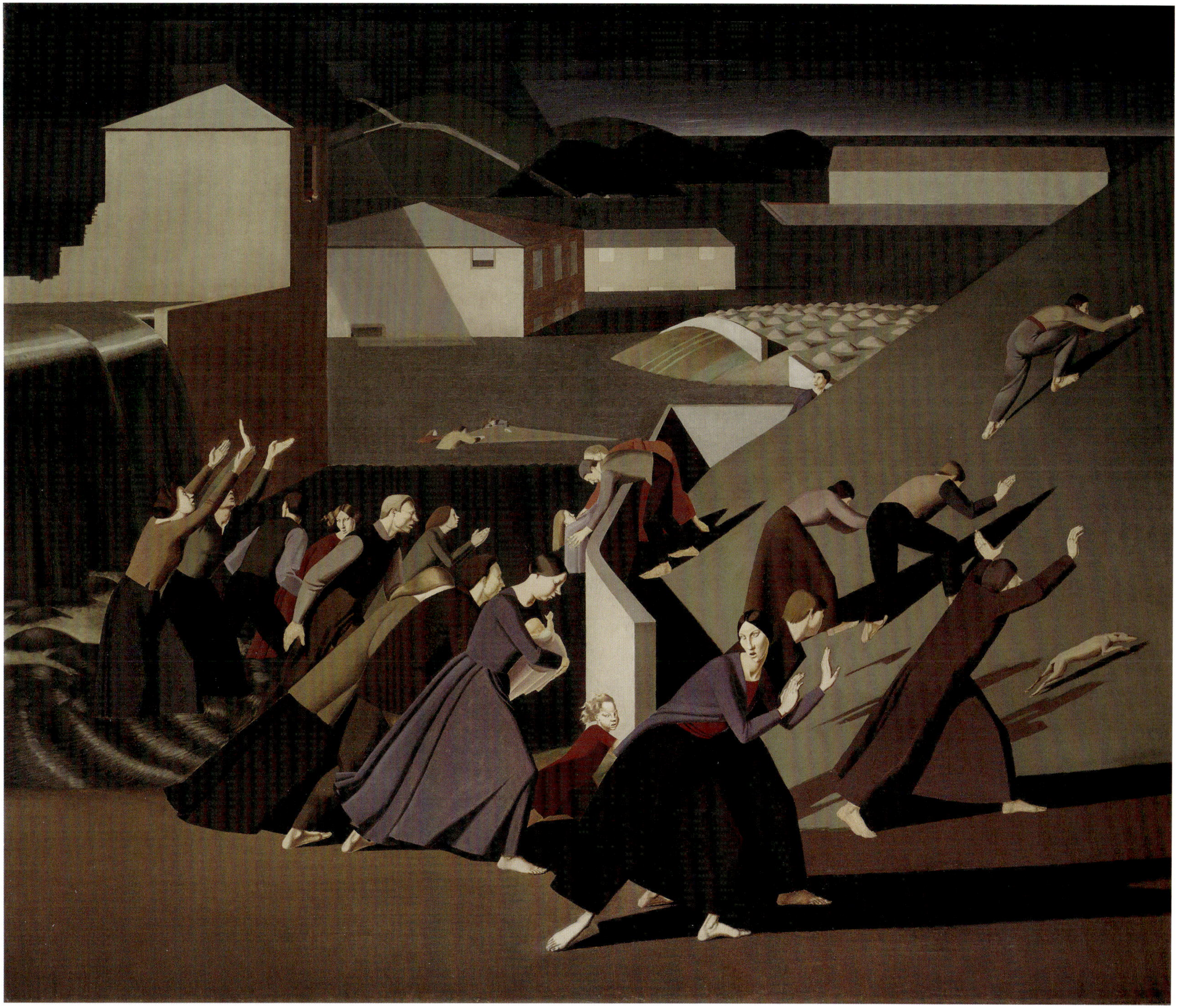

89 *The Deluge,* 1920, oil on canvas, 152.9 x 183.5 cm (60 ⅛ x 72 ¼ in.), © The Estate of Winifred Knights / © Tate, London 2012

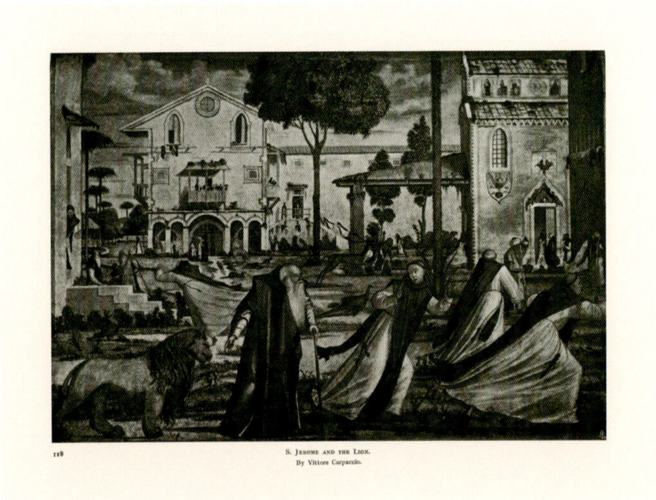

90 From *The Life and Works of Vittorio Carpaccio* by P. Molmenti and G. Ludwig, 1907

The inspiration for Knights' figures fleeing from the rising waters came directly from Vittorio Carpaccio's *St Jerome and the Lion* (c. 1502, Scuola di San Giorgio degli Schiavoni, Venice). The similarity between the complex arrangement of the three central figures in *The Deluge,* and that of the terrified monks fleeing the lion in the Carpaccio panel, is manifest. The monks' slanted, forward thrusting pose, with the front leg bent and the back leg stretched out, was a motif that Knights used for several of her figures. The symbolic gesture of the central monk, who raises his hands upwards whilst looking backwards, was also employed by Knights for her central figure, and serves in both paintings as an artistic device to direct the viewer to the cause of the terror. The revival of interest in Vittorio Carpaccio in England at this period was largely due to the translation in 1907 of Molmenti and Ludwig's monumental *Life and Works of Vittorio Carpaccio*, in which *St. Jerome and the Lion* was illustrated.[43] For the authors, it was the 'expression of fear' that made the painting so remarkable, and set it apart from the simple and lyrical gesturalism of most Quattrocento painting. Roger Fry recognised Carpaccio as 'one of the first artists to give this instantaneous quality of actual life'.[44]

Knights' 'Book of Studies for the Rome Scholarship' shows that for the central child in the painting, she had made drawings from a plaster cast of Andrea Verrocchio's *Putto with Fish*, which she described as 'that beautiful little babe with the Dolphin', and which had been acquired by the Victoria and Albert Museum in 1888.[45] The frequent depiction of greyhounds in Renaissance painting in a variety of settings from sacred to secular, with an emphasis on the hunt, may also have provided a model for the dog in Knights' painting.[46]

When *The Deluge* was exhibited at the Royal Academy in February 1921, critics described it as 'based on the study of the primitives, flat in treatment [and] angular in design'.[47] They also approved the contemporary rendering of the subject with its 'modern concrete buildings' and 'present day men and women'.[48] What characterises the contemporary criticism, however, is the struggle to categorize the painting within recent developments in the visual arts:

> The picture might be Cubist or Futurist, but the critics will not have it that it is either. Some describe it as an example of anarchy in art, original, tragic and inspiring [and] as something distinctly new and compelling in its treatment of a great theme.[49]

While *The Deluge* does not embrace the radicalism and extremism of pre-war modernist avant-garde production, it is clear, however, that Winifred Knights sustained the gains that this modernism had accrued.

In her response to modern French painting, Knights reflected the canon of education expounded by Henry Tonks, that however innovative an artist was he should 'still come under the discipline of his day'.[50] She therefore rejected Picasso, as he 'was not such a great one at drawing' and disliked the young French painters who, 'while trying hard to be like old masters…turn up their noses at Leonardo'. Of greater relevance to Knights was the modernism of the previous generation of Slade painters, which included the Vorticists David Bomberg, Edward Wadsworth, William Roberts and Christopher Nevinson but more significantly the artists Paul Nash, Henry Lamb and Stanley Spencer, whom Knights considered to be 'the most wonderful painter in England, not even excepting John'.[51] She particularly admired his *Nativity* (1912) (see page 31), which Tonks had hung in a prominent position at the Slade, alongside Knights' own painting of *Millhands Conversing*, to demonstrate his 'belief in the sufficiency of the old traditions for equipping [Slade students] to deal with the contemporary world'.[52]

The formal innovations of British Modernism were easily translated to represent the profoundly destructive narrative of *The Deluge*, and the war paintings of these artists, the most significant of which were on show at an Exhibition of the Nation's War Pictures at Burlington House (December 12, 1919-February 7, 1920), became particularly relevant to Knights. In an article for the *Manchester Guardian*, Charles James Holmes, the Director of the National Gallery, considered the paintings in this exhibition to mark 'the arrival of a new artistic movement', in which the formal experimentation of the pre-war years had at last been absolved by its relevance to represent the monumentality of war. He attributed the triumph of the exhibition to the younger and more radical artists who worked in a decorative rather than an illustrative manner, 'the best of which were actual products of the Slade School…or men who have worked more or less on lines similar to those laid down in Gower Street'.[53] Firm, rigid design was seen to be the means through which these paintings had incorporated a modernist vocabulary and thereby reflected Tonks' conjecture that 'all great painters are designers, they could not be great painters if they were not'.[54]

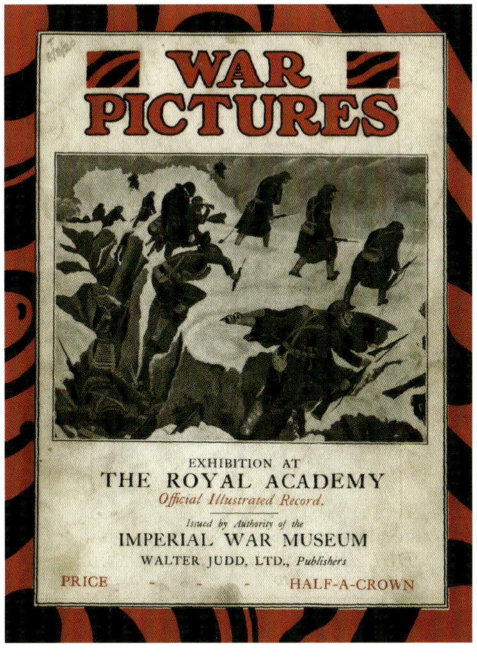

91 Cover of catalogue for 'War Pictures' showing *Over the Top* by John Nash, 1918.

In its equation of the terrifying power of nature to war, Paul Nash's *Menin Road* (1919, Imperial War Museum) seems to have been of particular significance to Knights; the beams of light streaking downwards from the sky was a motif she might easily have borrowed, and the treatment of the buildings in *The Deluge* echo the simplified concrete repoussoir blocks in Nash's painting. There is also a correlation with the tilted figuration in John Nash's *Over the Top* (1918, Imperial War Museum) although the treatment in Knights' painting is more acute, with the figures forming an oblique, diagonal movement right across the canvas. Knights particularly esteemed Stanley Spencer's *Travoys Arriving with Wounded at a Dressing Station at Smol, 1916* (1919 Imperial War Museum).[55] Admired by critics for its 'harmonious range of colours', the palette in *The Deluge* seems to have much in common with Spencer's painting.

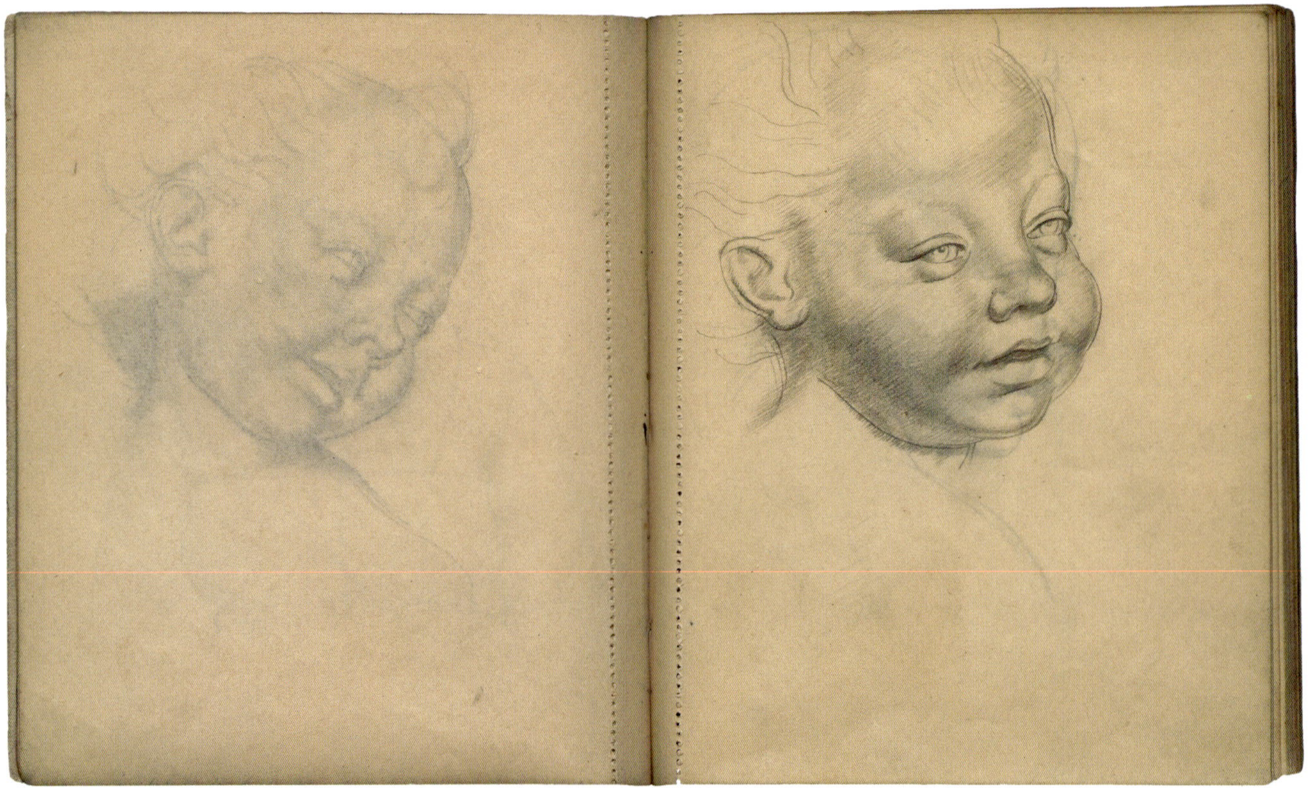

92
Study of Andrea Verrocchio's plaster cast *Putto with Fish,* 1920,
'Book of Studies for the Rome Scholarship'

In his book on *Landscape Painting from Giotto to Present Day* (1924), the writer and art-historian C. Lewis Hind included Knights' *The Deluge* in his chapter on 'Britain in the Twentieth Century'. Although not strictly a landscape, Hind justified its inclusion in the book because it displayed 'an ingenious and surprising adaptation of Cubism'.[56] Since 1918, Knights' landscapes had shown a marked reduction of form but in *The Deluge* this simplification is developed even further, with nature requisitioned to assist the form and intricacy of the design. The geometric construction of the architecture and the ark occupy and transfigure the landscape, and reduce the nature around to a subordinate role. The only surface modulation is provided by the haycocks, which are used as a formal device to create through shadow a sense of depth and contour. A recurrent motif in Knights' *oeuvre*, they possibly recalled happy moments spent haymaking in Worcestershire during the war. In *The Deluge*, they seem to symbolise a traditional and rural way of life against a sweeping modernity.

On September 21, 1920, while staying in Ludlow at Arnold Mason's studio, Winifred Knights learnt that she had become the winner of the Prix de Rome. Frederick Brown considered her success as 'a triumph for you and incidentally for the Slade School' and Henry Tonks judged her painting to be 'by far the best illustration of the subject, and a very interesting composition'. [57] It is not difficult to see why the faculty awarded Winifred Knights the scholarship, for the integrity of her design allied to its emotional content made the other three entries seem very 'vague and piecemeal' in comparison.[58] Her fellow student Alan Gwynne Jones deplored their 'lack of a coherent figure design' whereby the figures had no relation to each other 'besides that of being placed at a becoming distance'.[59]

Press reports about Knights' success focussed on the fact that she was the first woman to win the Rome Scholarship. Although the Slade had roughly three times as many female students as male in 1920, as a woman finalist and later prize-winner, Winifred Knights felt disadvantaged by the prejudicial behaviour of her fellow male students. Leon Underwood and Arthur Outlaw colluded to prevent the granting of extra time to Knights, who had been in bed with a 'septic sore throat' from July 22 for ten days, an act which elicited the fury of Alan Gwynne Jones: 'what swine those other two are it makes me hot every time I think of it'.[60] However, in a letter to her aunt Millicent Murby, Knights declared that this unjust treatment had in fact 'made me feel rather hard'. She went on to disclose that 'people seem to be sorry for the other men (especially men) why should they be, they had just the same chances as I and more.' This hostility continued on her arrival in Rome, where J. Benson, the Rome Scholar in Painting for 1914, was extremely rude, because 'he doesn't like a woman getting the scholarship...and does not respect women'. Knights found some consolation in her female status at the School writing: 'I always sit on the honoured guest's right hand because I am the first woman painter to gain the scholarship and the school is very proud of me'.[61] Knights' claim to equality and positive self-regard was strengthened at this time by a deep fascination with the writings and discourse of Edward Carpenter, the Socialist philosopher and defender, amongst other causes, of women's emancipation, to whom she had been introduced by her Aunt Millicent who lived close to him at Millthorpe.[62] In works such as *Love's Coming of Age*, Carpenter promoted the sexual and economic liberation of women within a just and equal society.[63] Knights also admired the works of D. H. Lawrence, who shared Carpenter's empathy to women's claim to freedom, and criticized those 'philistines [who] say he is sexual & immoral and all sorts of damned rot'.[64]

Before setting out to Rome, Knights wrote to her aunt, 'I'll soon see Massacio and Giotto and all the rest of the blessed company'.[65] As soon as she was able to escape from the confines of Classical Rome and the British School, Knights travelled throughout Italy to discover for herself the early Italian frescos and paintings that she had only seen in books. She found that the countryside in the background of these paintings, peopled by rustics and peasants, still existed, unchanged. Spending long summers roaming the countryside of the Abruzzi region, she was deeply affected by what she perceived to be a lotus land, and she began increasingly to recoil from modern life and its symbols. Whilst always retaining the conventions of decorative painting in her art, she would never again employ the modernist vocabulary of *The Deluge*.

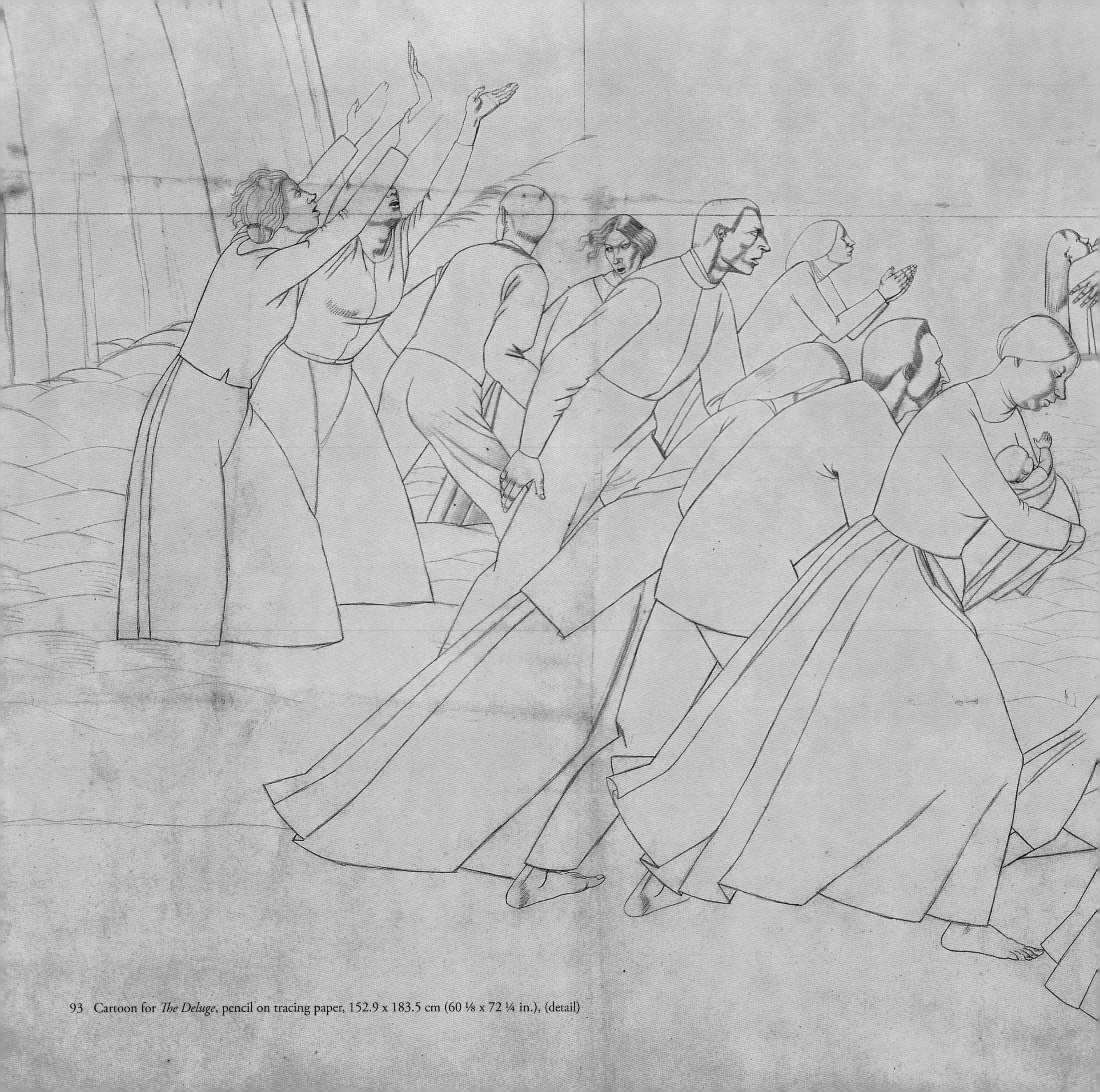

93 Cartoon for *The Deluge*, pencil on tracing paper, 152.9 x 183.5 cm (60 ⅛ x 72 ¼ in.), (detail)

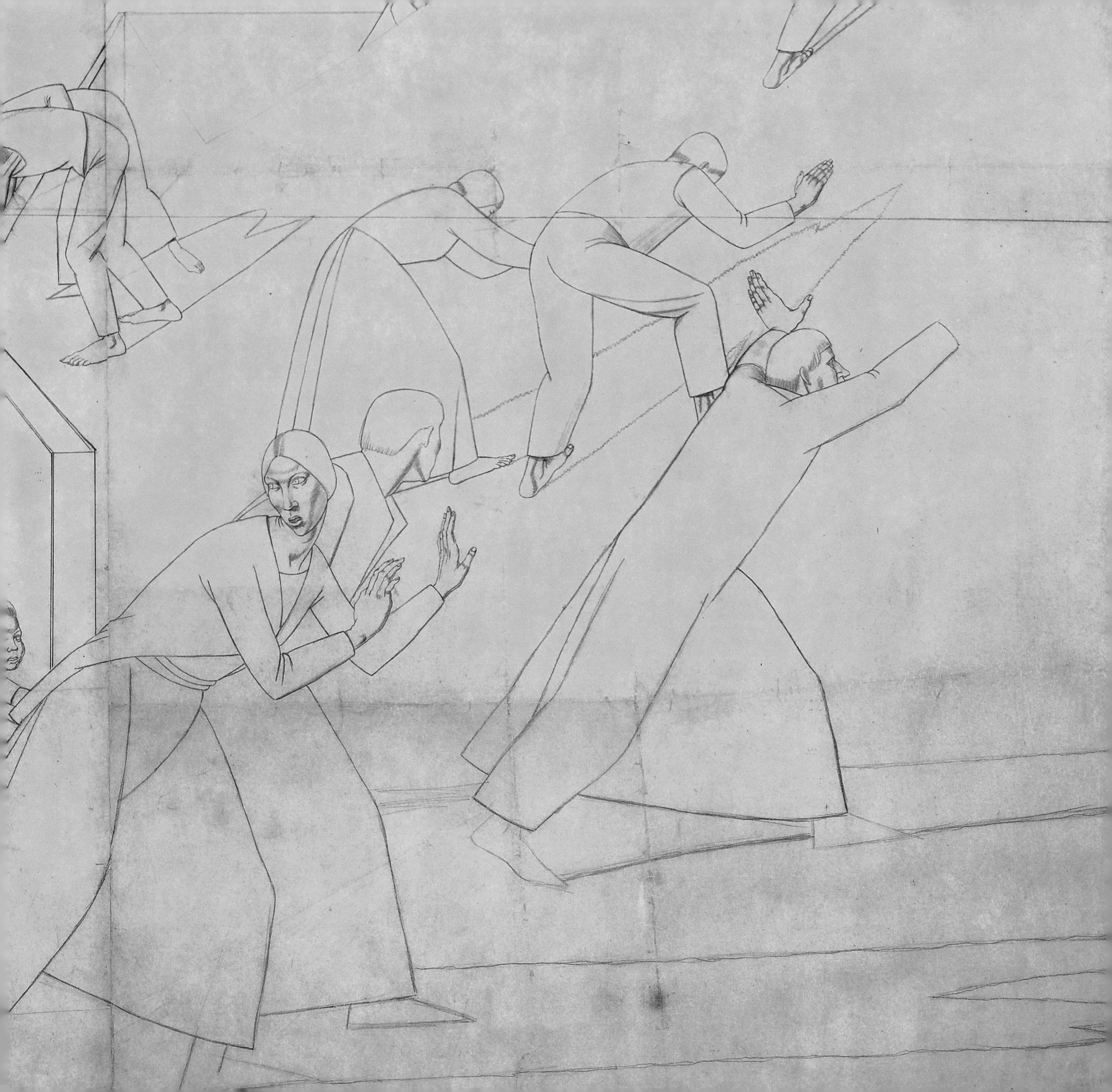

ENDNOTES

1 Press communication to the *Daily Mail*, September 21, 1920, British School at Rome Historic Archives.

2 *Daily Graphic*, February 8, 1921.

3 Winifred Knights added to these collections throughout her life. Many show the marks of pinholes suggesting that she displayed the works for reference. Private Collection.

4 University College Department of the Fine Arts, Courses of Study, Session 1919-1920, p.2.

5 Henry Tonks supported Knights throughout her time at the Slade, and they retained a close friendship until his death in 1937.

6 Henry Tonks, *Catalogue of a Collection of Drawings by Deceased Masters*, Burlington Fine Arts Club, London 1917, p.7.

7 Knights' draughtsmanship was greatly admired at the Slade. In 1920, Alan Gwynne Jones wrote to Knights, 'Oh how I envy you your draughtsmanship, you would just take the pencil and do it so directly and well'. Alan Gwynne Jones to Knights, April 1920, Private Collection.

8 Henry Tonks believed that 'when the student begins to paint he will soon perceive the relation of drawing to paint', quoted in J Hare, *The Life of Henry Tonks*, London 1939, p.173.

9 Henry Tonks was described as 'deeply interested in wall decoration, anxious to see it used, and fully aware that unless the artist is caught young he will never succeed at it'. *The Times*, September 24, 1924.

10 James Wilkie was the joint winner of the Competition with *Reconstruction* (UCL no. PC 5268). Other winners of the Summer Composition Competition include Stanley Spencer for *Nativity*, 1912 (UCL no. PC 5245) and Gilbert Spencer for *Summer*, 1914 (UCL no, PC 5512).

11 Emma Chambers notes a move away from the conventions of history painting towards decorative painting in the Slade Summer Composition student works from around 1905. Emma Chambers, 'Redefining History Painting in the Academy: The Summer Composition Competition at the Slade School of Fine Art, 1898-1922', in *Visual Culture in Britain*, Volume 6, Number 1, summer 2005, p.80. For a summary of the revival of Decorative Painting in England in the early twentieth century, see Alan Powers, 'Decorative Painting in the Early Twentieth Century – A Context for Winifred Knights 1899-1947', in The Fine Art Society and Paul Liss, *Winifred Knights*, Exhib. Cat., 1995, pp.13-17.

12 The aims of the Summer Composition Competition within the Slade curriculum are set out by Hubert Wellington in, 'The Slade Summer Compositions since 1893', in John Fothergill, ed., *The Slade: A Collection of Drawings and Some Pictures done by Past and Present Students of the London Slade School of Art 1893-1907*, London: Slade School of Fine Art, 1907, p.21.

13 Walter Crane, *Ideals in Art*, London 1905, p.267.

14 Helen Lessore, 'Henry Tonks as I Remember Him', in Lynda Morris (ed.), *Henry Tonks and the Art of Pure Drawing*, Norwich School of Art Gallery, 1985, p.10.

15 Tancred Borenius, *The Painters of Vicenza, 1480-1550*, London MCMIX, p.17.

16 Royal Commission for the Exhibition of 1851 Archives RC/44/12.

17 Evelyn Shaw, *The British School at Rome, a Note on the School and its Scholarships*, 3rd Issue, 1931.

18 In 1913, Laurence Binyon called for an alternative to Post-Impressionism based on 'public' art, which he defined as the unification of 'architecture, sculpture, painting and every form of decoration harmonized as part of a single, magnificent language'. Laurence Binyon, *The Art of Botticelli*, London 1913, p.21.

19 Royal Commission for the Exhibition of 1851 Archives RC/44/4 memorandum.

20 Rome Scholarship in Decorative Painting offered by the Commissioners for the Exhibition of 1851 (pamphlet), 1920.

21 Evelyn Shaw, 1931, p.11.

22 'Exhibition of Works submitted in the Open Examinations for the Rome Scholarships in Architecture, Sculpture, Decorative Painting, and Engraving and for the Henry Jarvis Studentship in Architecture, together with Examples of Works executed by Scholars of the British School at Rome', Grafton Galleries, February 1920. *The Observer's* correspondent attributed the Slade's monopoly of the scholarship since 1913 to Henry Tonks and 'the really good work his Department is doing', *The Observer*, February 22, 1920.

23 *The Observer*, February 22, 1920.

24 Minute Book Faculty of Painting, 'Subjects and Conditions for the Final Competition 1920', BSR Historic Archive.

25 Letter from Knights to her Aunt Millicent Murby, September 29, 1920, Slade Archive, UCL Library Services, Special Collections.

26 Unlike the first competition held in 1913, whereby candidates had to execute a site-specific design for a decorative painting, with even the size of the painted figures specified, the Board resolved for the 1920 competition to give 'the competitors as much freedom as possible in carrying out their work: and they be restricted only as to the actual size of the painting'. BSR Historic Archive, Minutes of the Meeting of the Faculty of Painting, p.8 and p.26.

27 See for example, Robert Bridges 'Wake Up, England', published in *The Times*, August 8, 1914, in which the cleansing effect of the shedding of blood in battle is compared with the salvation achieved in the Biblical Flood. Addressing fellow M.Ps in 1922, Winston Churchill referred to the Great War as engendering 'violent and tremendous changes in the Deluge of the World', quoted in A.T.Q. Stewart, *The Narrow Ground: Aspects of Ulster, 1609-1969,* London 1977, p. 14. See also Michael Curtiz's *Noah's Ark* (Warner Bros), 1928, which compares the Old Testament Deluge to the flood of blood in World War 1.

28 By the time Knights had joined the Slade, she had probably already abandoned the Sunday morning Anglican Service that formed part of her childhood ritual, and she would never again implore God or demonstrate any evidence of internal prayer. However, she would have been aware of the Genesis narrative of the flood from an early acquaintance with the Bible, which was taught at school and would have formed part of the Sunday Service. John Monnington, WMK, 2012, unpublished manuscript, Private Collection.

29 Henry Tonks, 1917, p.8.

30 Seventy-three people were killed and more than four hundred injured in the 'Silvertown Explosion', which took place in West Ham on January 19, 1917. Graham Hill & Howard Bloch, *The Silvertown Explosion London 1917*, (Stroud 2003); In 1917, Knights suffered bereavement when a close school friend 'Clarke' and her cousin Edward Murby were both killed in action. Eileen Palmer, *Reminiscences of My Sister*, November 16, 1993, Private Collection; Mabel Gertrude Knights *Interesting Events in My Life from 1874*, Private Collection.

31 Letter to Knights from her father June 4, 1918. Private Collection.

32 *The Manchester Guardian*; February 11, 1921, p.14.

33 On July 27, 1920, Alan Gwynne Jones wrote to Knights that he had heard that she had purchased 'a long mirror' for her studio, 'as you are using yourself as a model for a figure in your picture', Private Collection. As early as 1915, a drawing assistant at the Slade noted how frequently Knights called on her 'own likeness'. Letter from Knights to Awdry, January 26, 1915, Slade Archive, UCL Library Services, Special Collections.

34 Henry Tonks, 1917, p.8.

35 In 1915, Knights had read Lawrence Binyon's treatise on Chinese Painting, *The Flight of the Dragon* (1911), in which a whole chapter was dedicated to the expressive potential of colour. Rather than 'acquiesce in the colours of nature as they find them', artists were encouraged to use colours 'expressive of the mood evoked in themselves'.

36 The painter Robin Guthrie (1902-1971) described this process in a letter to Knights: 'I am making considerable efforts to copy my sketch… putting in a little piece at a time in something like your way'. Robin Guthrie to Knights, April 13, 1932, Private Collection.

37 The final painting reveals pencil drawing and pinholes in the ground and canvas.

38 Knights' choice of oil was possibly due to the time constraints, tempera being a more painstaking medium. The desired palette and solid plains of dark colour would also have been difficult to achieve in tempera.

39 See, for instance, Walter Crane's *Noah's Ark Alphabet* published by Routledge in 1874.

40 Poussin's *Deluge* inspired many of the best-known tempests and deluges from Vernet to Turner, and was arguably the prototype of them all. For a discussion of the influence of Poussin's *Deluge* on subsequent artists' rendering of the subject see Richard Verdi, 'Poussin's "Deluge": the Aftermath', in *Burlington Magazine*, vol. 123, no 940, July 1981, pp 338-401. The painting was frequently engraved, and Knights would have been able to study four examples in the collection of the British Museum's Print Room in 1920: 1874,1212,313; 1859,0806,529; 1874,0808,1787; 1856.0308.1066.

41 Tancred Borenius, 'A Great Poussin in the Metropolitan Museum', in *Burlington Magazine*, volume 59, 1931, p. 208. In *Vision and Design*, Roger Fry examined Poussin's influence on Cézanne, particularly citing the 'discretion and subtlety of his rhythm'. Roger Fry, *Vision and Design*, London 1920, p.139.

42 Charles Ricketts, 'Puvis de Chavannes: A Chapter from "Modern Painters"' in *Burlington Magazine*, Vol. 13, no.61, April 1908 p.12.

43 P. Molmenti and G. Ludwig, *The Life and Works of Vittorio Carpaccio*, translated by R. H. Cust, London 1907, p.124.

44 *The Burlington Magazine*, Vol. XXI, April to September 1912, p.95.

45 Knights letter to her mother, March 16, 1921, Slade Archive, UCL Library Services, Special Collections.

46 Knights would have been able to see Paulo Uccello's *The Hunt* at the exhibition of Florentine Paintings at the Burlington Arts Club in June 1919, (*Burlington Magazine*, vol 34, no.195, June 1919, plate III).

47 *The Observer,* February 13, 1921.

48 *The Daily Graphic*, February 8, 1921.

49 Ibid.

50 Letter from Henry Tonks to Tom Monnington, June 1934, Private Collection.

51 This commentary on modern art is found in a letter from Knights to her Aunt Millicent, (undated) British School at Rome Historic Archive, (photocopy).

52 Lessore, 1985, p.8.

53 *Manchester Guardian*, December 12, 1919.

54 Henry Tonks, letter to *The Times*, May 23, 1933.

55 Knights expresses her admiration for Spencer's *Mules and Stretchers* in a letter to Meredith Monnington, March 1926, Private Collection.

56 C. Lewis Hind, *Landscape Painting from Giotto to the Present Day*, Volume 2, London 1924, p.307.

57 Frederick Brown to Knights, October 20, 1920; Henry Tonks to Knights, September 23, 1920, Private Collection.
58 See the article in the *Manchester Guardian* for February 11, 1921, which compares and contrasts the finalists' paintings.

59 Alan Gwynne Jones, letter to Winifred Knights, September 20, 1920, Private Collection.

60 Alan Gwynne Jones, letter to Winifred Knights, August 18, 1920, Private Collection.

61 Letter from Knights to her aunt, September 29, 1920; Letter from Knights to her mother, undated; letter from Knights to her aunt, February 21, 1921, Slade Archive, UCL Library Services, Special Collections.

62 Knights attended Carpenter's lectures at Millthorpe, given under the auspices of the Union of Democratic Control, with her aunt from 1917. On her arrival in Rome in 1920, she recommended his books to Colin Gill.

63 Edward Carpenter, *Love's Coming of Age, a Series of Papers on the Relations of the Sexes*, New York and London, 1911 edition, pp.59-77.

64 Winifred Knights, letter to her aunt, October 13, 1928, British School at Rome Historic Archives (photocopy).

65 Knights, letter to her Aunt Millicent, September 29, 1920, Slade Archive, UCL Library Services, Special Collections.

Winifred Knights (1899-1947)

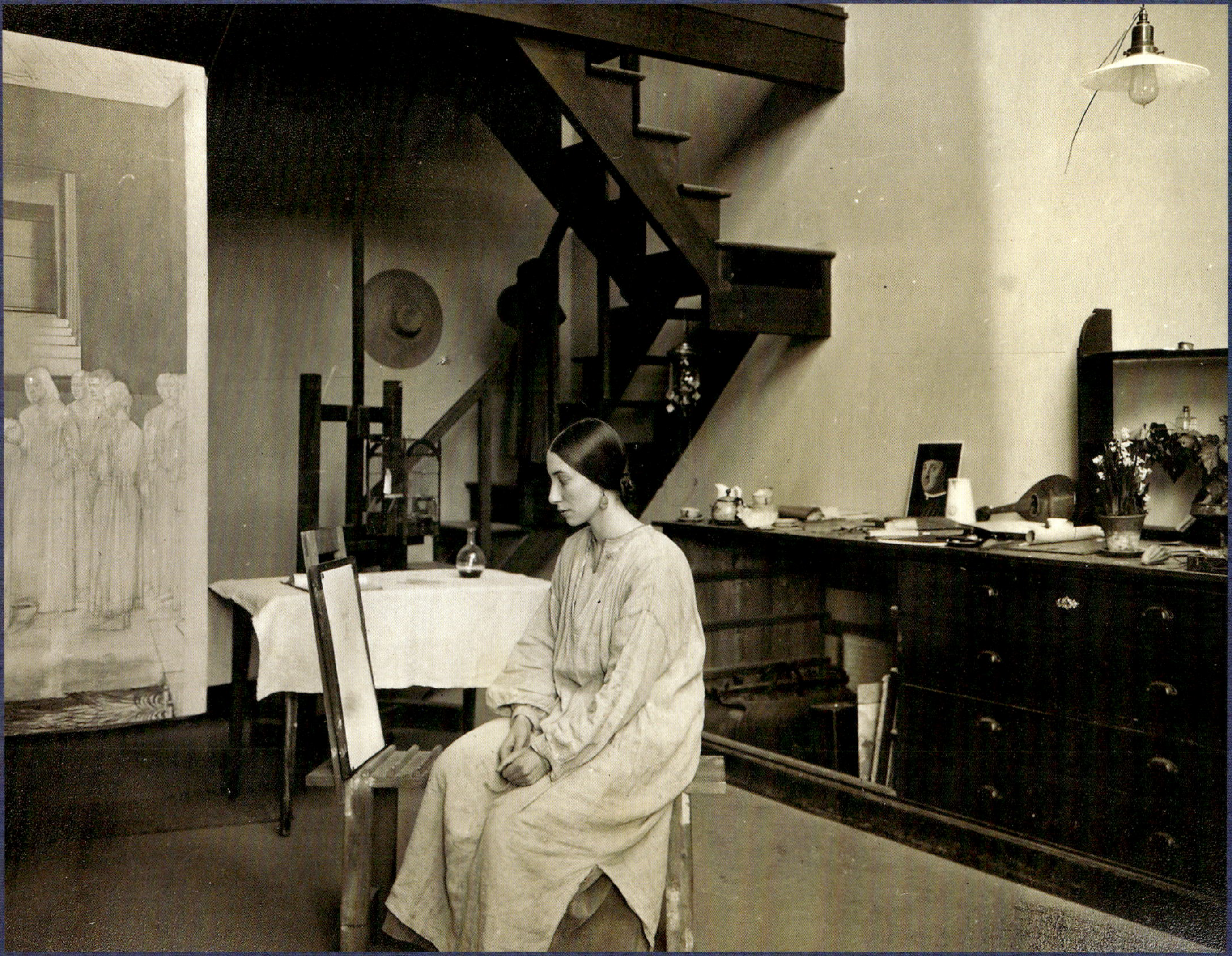

94 Winifred Knights in her studio at the British School at Rome

WINIFRED KNIGHTS. Born Streatham, London, died London. Painter and Draughtswoman. Studied Slade School of Art (1915-17, 1918-20, 1926-27). Won the Rome Scholarship in Decorative Painting (1920) and worked at the British School at Rome (1920-26). Married fellow student Thomas Monnington (qv) (1924). In 1928 she was commissioned to paint the *St Martin's Altarpiece* for the Milner Memorial Chapel, Canterbury Cathedral (1928-33). Elected to the New English Art Club (1929). Principal museum collections: Tate Gallery, London; UCL Art Museum, London; British Museum, London; Fitzwilliam Museum, Cambridge; Te Papa Tongarewa, Wellington, New Zealand; Wolfsonion, Florida International University, Miami Beach, USA.

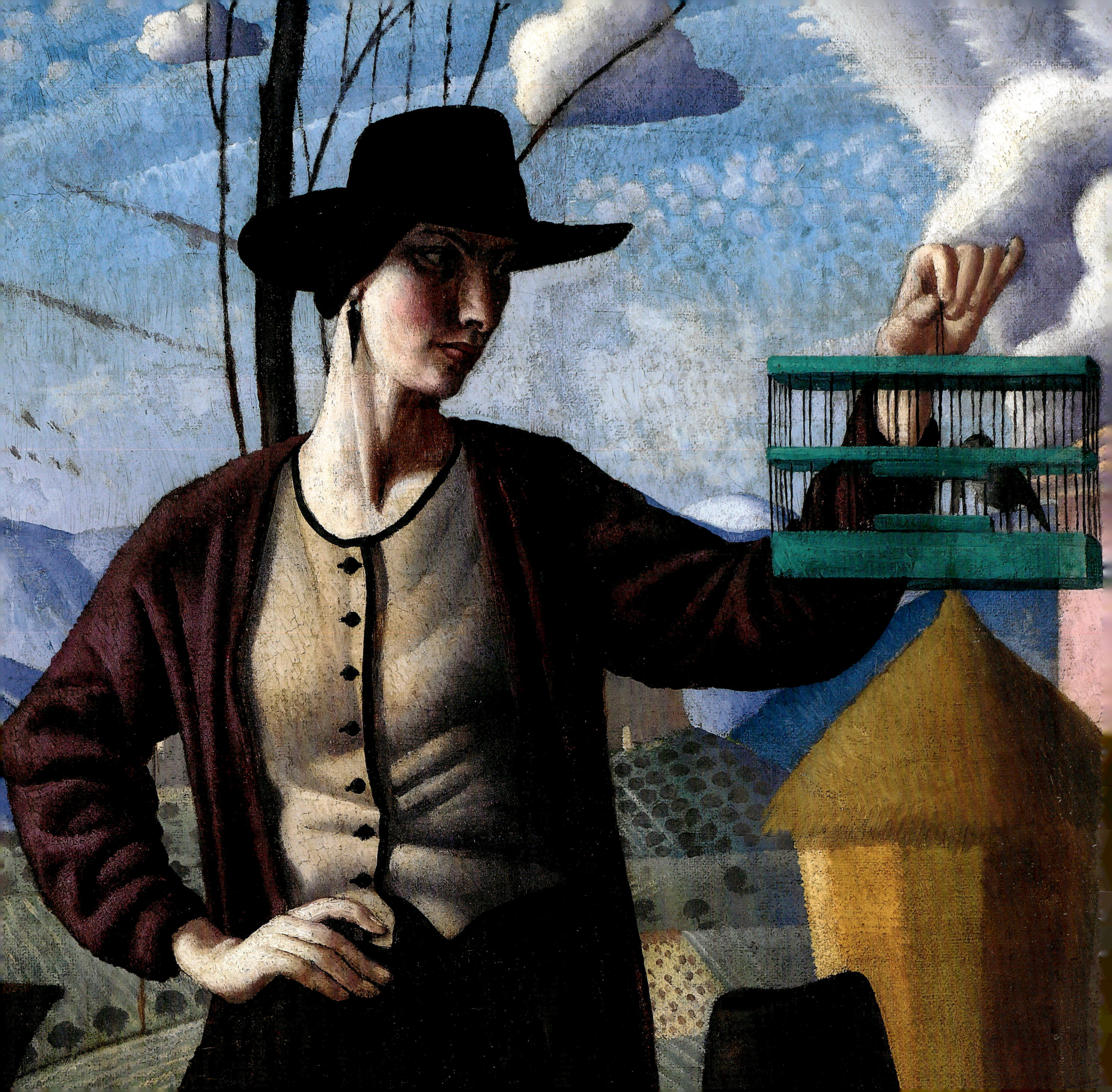

Colin Gill
Allegro, 1921

Sacha Llewellyn

Allegro (1921) was Colin Gill's final submission at the end of his three-year Rome Scholarship in Decorative Painting. The faculty of the British School at Rome considered it 'an able work which shows that he has made good use of his opportunities during the tenure of his scholarship'.[1] When the painting was exhibited at the Grosvenor Galleries in June 1922, the *Manchester Guardian*'s critic admired 'the rhythm of the forms' and the 'gripping quality of draughtsmanship', although he doubted if anyone could follow 'the Allegory of nude and semi-nude figures and ladies with birdcages, and Italian peasants, and donkeys and children'.[2] While an absence of narrative content and a focus on pictorial effects was a defining quality of decorative painting at this time, this essay will show that *Allegro* was also a poetic expression of Colin Gill's own thoughts and sentiments which were bound up with idealisation and reparation in the immediate aftermath of the war.[3]

Colin Gill worked as an apprentice for the artist and illustrator W. H. Caffyn, before joining the Slade School of Art in 1910. In 1911 he was awarded a Slade Scholarship followed the next year by a British Institution Scholarship. He had already shown a keen interest in mural painting before joining the Slade, encouraged by his parents who allowed him to paint a 'brilliant cock-and-hen mural' around the kitchen of their farmhouse in Cudham, Kent.[4] In 1911, Henry Tonks obtained permission to decorate the walls of Bishop Creighton House in Fulham and Colin Gill was one of six Slade students, including Dora Carrington, William Roberts and Elsie MacNaught, who took part in the scheme, producing a composition in egg-tempera on paper, which was stretched onto the walls.[5]

Colin Gill attended the Slade at a vibrant time; dressed in 'dramatic, bohemian clothes' he frequented the Café Royal, dining in the ground-floor room with his 'exalted artist friends' including Augustus John.[6] While never formally associated with the self-styled Slade 'Neo-Primitives', Gill shared a close friendship with Mark Gertler and William Roberts.[7] These artists, nourished by the cumulative effect of a series of important exhibitions of early Italian painting held in London before the war and Roger Fry's Post-Impressionist exhibitions in 1910 and 1912, worked in varying degrees towards a synthesis of contemporary French and early Renaissance painting in the search for a new visual language through which modern art could be addressed.[8] The only known painting by Gill from this period, *Flora*, 1912, shows that while he was obliquely related to this process, by resisting the more modernist experiments of his peers, his paintings came to be deemed as 'archaic in a way the others are not'.[9] Gill, who was among the 132 exhibitors

95
Allegro, 1921,
oil on canvas,
117 x 228.5 cm
(46 x 90 in.),
private collection
(detail)

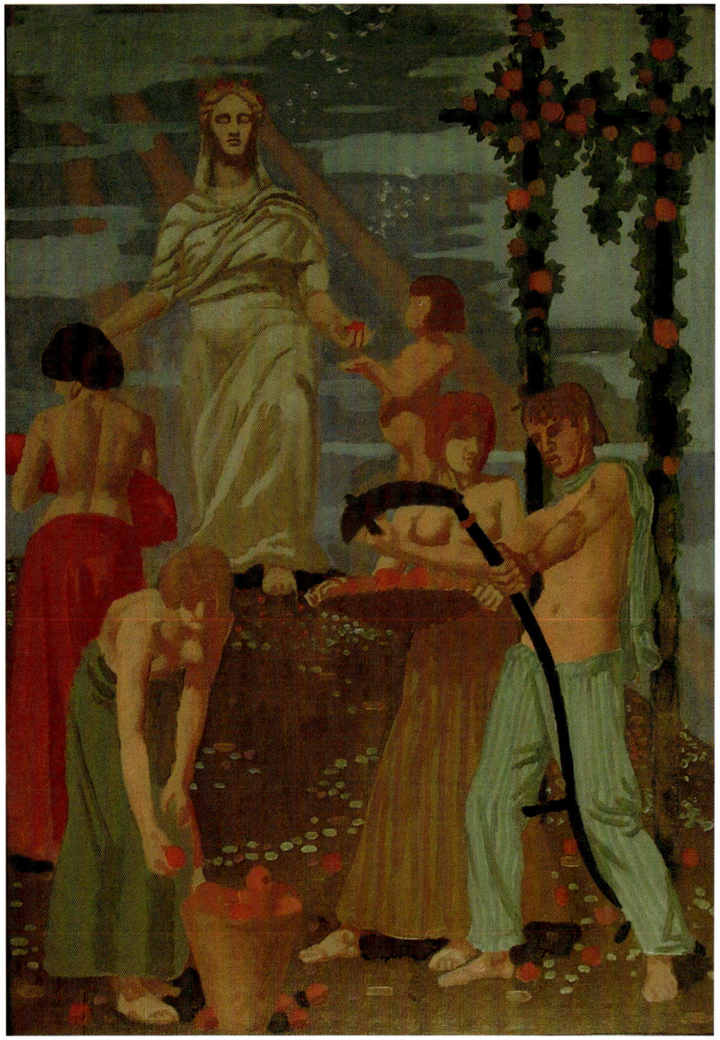

96 *Flora*, c. 1912, oil on canvas, 76.2 x 55.9 cm (30 x 22 in.)

in the Whitechapel Art Gallery's Summer Exhibition of 1914, 'Twentieth Century Art: A Review of Modern Movements', is likely to have been classified under the 'second group' of modern painters who, under the influence of Augustus John, Puvis de Chavannes and Alphonse Legros (the Slade tradition), produced 'imposing decorative design by the creation of commanding human types and appropriate attitudes and gestures.'[10]

In applying for the newly established Rome Scholarship in Decorative Painting, Gill was affirming his commitment to mural painting and in November 1913, he was awarded the inaugural scholarship 'on the unanimous recommendation of the Faculty'.[11] The three other finalists, Gerald Leslie Brockhurst, Lillian Lancaster and James Williams were all artists working within a conventional framework; the British School at Rome's appeal to classical tradition may not have attracted artists working in a more modernist idiom. Indeed, since its establishment in 1912, the question had been raised as to whether 'Rome was a suitable art centre for the environment and mental development of young British Students'.[12] Mark Gertler discouraged Dora Carrington from applying for the Scholarship in 1914, as 'one must always live in cities that have a future, not merely a past – one mustn't be out of things'.[13] The Faculty would respond to this criticism by arguing that 'although a changed outlook and modern conditions may make the masterpieces of Italian Painting less directly useful to the student, he cannot fail to be stimulated and inspired by an intelligent and careful study of them'.[14]

Colin Gill arrived in Rome in February 1914. The studios in Lutyens' new building in the Valle Giulia had not yet been built, and finding it impossible to hire a large studio, Gill set off on a travelling expedition with the Royal College of Art's travelling scholar, Charles F. Collins, to 'discover Italian painting and Italy itself'.[15] They travelled north as far as Ravenna, visiting along the way Spoleto, Assisi, Perugia, Montepulciano, Siena and Florence. Rome Scholars were encouraged to travel, particularly in their first year, for the Faculty believed that it was only by 'studying the works of the great Italian Masters in their own land and often in their original setting' that scholars could understand 'the devotion of the Great Masters to their work for its own sake and their attitude of reverence

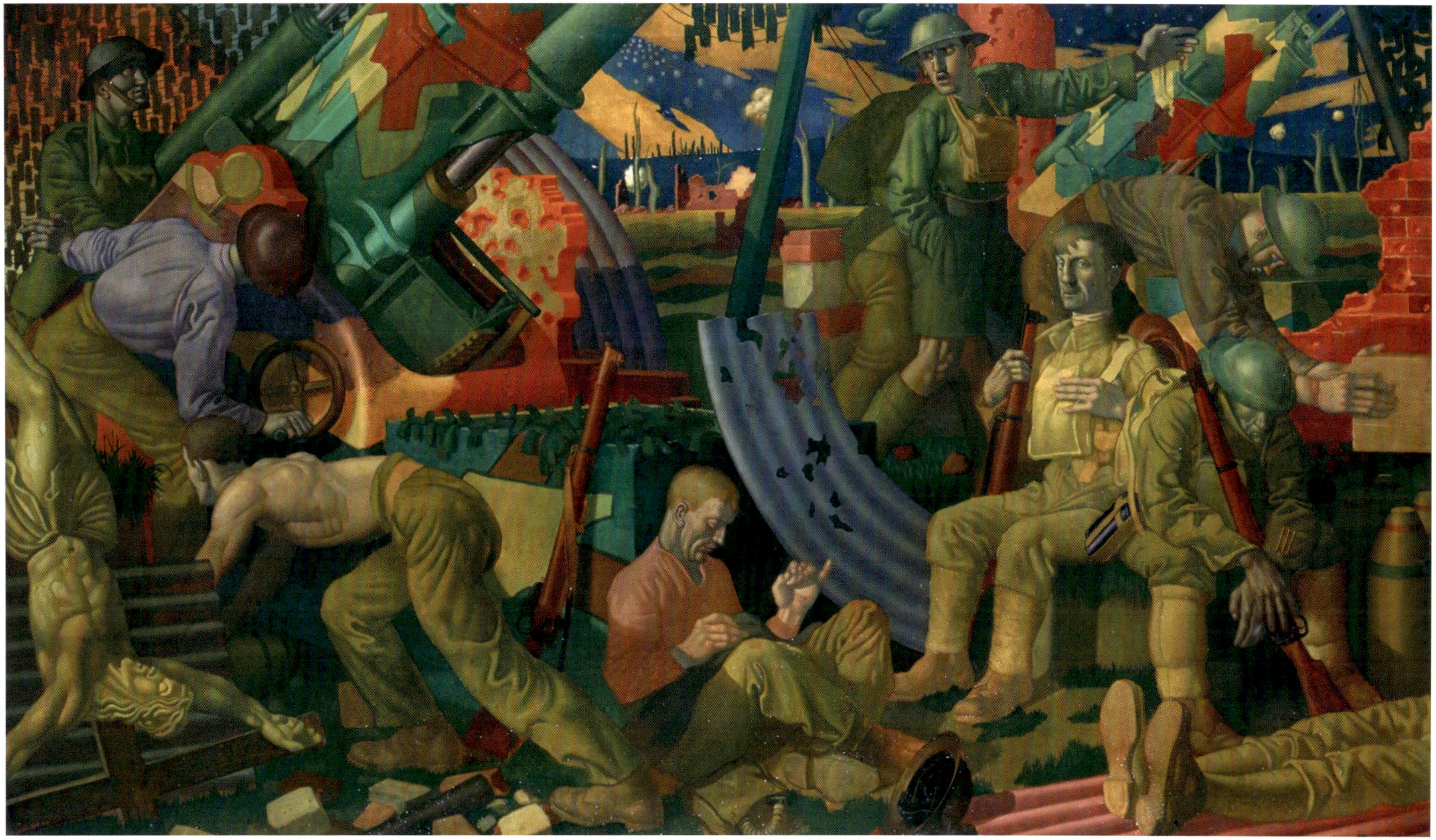

97 *Heavy Artillery,* 1919, oil on canvas, 182.8 x 317.5 cm (72 x 125 in.), © Imperial War Museums

for and searching enquiry into nature'.[16] During these travels, Gill made architectural and landscape studies, and filled several sketchbooks with notes and drawings of the decorations and mosaics that he most admired.[17]

In December 1914, four months after Britain had declared war on Germany, Gill suspended his scholarship to volunteer for the Royal Garrison Artillery and by October 1915, he had been sent to the front in France as a Second Lieutenant of the 17th Heavy Battery. In 1916 he was seconded to the Royal Engineers to work as a camouflage officer before being invalided out with severe gas poisoning in April 1918. After spending several months convalescing at the Hospital for Officers on the Isle of Wight, Gill was appointed an Official War Artist to the Ministry of Information. While the few extant letters that Gill sent to his sister Marjory from the front only hint at the hardships that he endured, his later war pictures are evidence that he had in fact witnessed the horrors associated with active service.[18] *Heavy Artillery*, 1919, was one of a series of paintings commissioned by the British War Memorials Committee as part of a scheme to build a Hall of Remembrance.[19]

The picture, which has as its subject a view of a heavy artillery position, depicts the impact of industrialised warfare; the imposing, camouflaged 9.2 Howitzers, the scattered sheets of corrugated iron, and the ruined

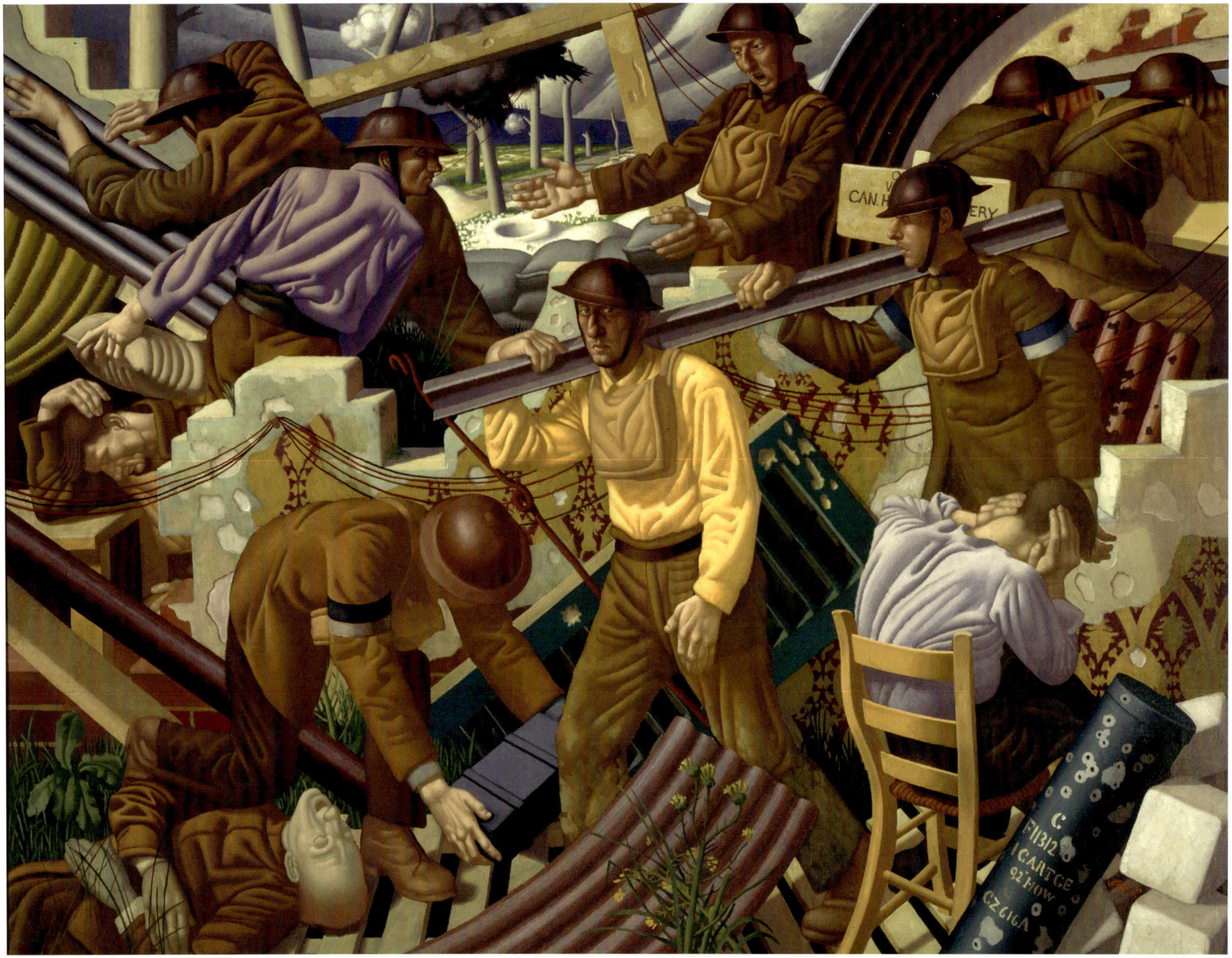

98 *Canadian Observation Post*, 1920, oil on canvas, 185.5 x 243 cm (73 x 95 ⅝ in.), © Canadian War Museum

village and bomb-damaged walls are set within a war-torn landscape, like the one Gill had witnessed on his return to the front at Mons in November 1918, hours after it had been retaken by the Allies at the end of hostilities: 'desolate and encumbered with the debris of battle'.[20] The broken roadside Calvary, which has been overturned by a shell-explosion, is a metaphor for the fallen soldier, a theme explored by Wilfred Owen in his poem 'At a Calvary near the Ancre', 1918. When the painting was exhibited at an 'Exhibition of the Nation's War Pictures at Burlington House', (December 12, 1919-February 7, 1920), the critic P. G. Konody described it as 'a Paolo Uccello with Howitzers' and 'a decorative scheme of massive design, elaborate but not confused, rich and sober at once in colour'. He found it fortunate that Gill, 'who has already gained the Prix de Rome, was given this great opportunity at the beginning of what promises to be a brilliant career'.[21]

In the autumn of 1919, Gill received a commission from the Canadian War Records Office to paint *The Widow's House* or *Canadian Observation Post*, and wanting to return to Rome to resume his scholarship, he was given permission to carry out the work in his new studio at the British School.[22] The painting shares much in common with *Heavy Artillery*, but the message is even more harrowing; a feeling of deep melancholy pervades the scene, which is dominated by a fallen crucifix. The soldiers show visible signs of exhaustion and shell shock.

Towards the end of the war Gill had married a childhood friend, Phyllis, and some time towards the end of 1919 they travelled together to Rome. Some months later their son Peter was born, 'grinning charmingly and making curious noises'. In contrast to the devastation of the war years, Rome seemed like a wonderland. Gill had 'some heavily paying pupils as well as a big commission from the Canadian Government and my scholarship…we are rapidly becoming disconcertingly wealthy. Rome is full of colour and sunshine, and chiccheria (a word meaning the wealthy well-dressed and beautiful, if possible with a title or two)'.[23] For the summer months of 1920, Gill, his wife and child rented a villa in the hilltop village of Anticoli Corrado where he began to make studies and work out the composition for *Allegro*.

The beautiful village of Anticoli Corrado, which appears in a simplified form in Gill's final composition, was an established artists' colony situated in the Latium about twenty-five miles north east of Rome. The women from Anticoli were renowned for their beauty, and in the summer months artists came from all over Europe to work with the models and sketch the dramatic Sabine mountains and the richly cultivated valley below. The British painter Frank Hyde (1849-1937) was one of sixty artists who spent the summer of 1911 there. Describing Anticoli as 'the home of the artist's model', he admired the girls who came in the evening 'to the fountain in the Piazza, carrying their wonderful-shaped copper pitchers, each girl waiting her turn, laughing and joking with the artists who assemble there to choose their models. Such colour! Such marvellous types! All with a natural grace that defies description.' During the day the painters worked out of doors, 'painting the nude in the open air under the vines' and in the evenings, revelries and carnivals took place:

> Try to picture to yourself those groups of fauns, satyrs and nymphs scattered about under the olives, the warm air heavy with the scent of flowers and grain and crowds of natives in their own picturesque costume dancing a wild dance to the weird music of the old Shepherd's sampone.[24]

Gill had a deep love of poetry and literature, and the arcadia that he discovered in Anticoli must have evoked in his mind John Milton's poem *L'Allegro* (1645) from which he borrowed the title and decided to base his composition.[25] 'L'Allegro' means the 'cheerful man' and the 152-line poem takes as its theme the casting off of melancholy in order to take part in the delights of a spring day: 'to many a youth, and many a maid/Dancing in the chequer'd shade/And young and old come forth to play/On a sunshine holyday.'(lines 95-98). Some of these delights were provided by nature in a pastoral setting: 'Mountains on whose barren breast/The labouring clouds do often rest/Meadows trim with daisies pied,/ Shallow brooks, and river wide./ Towers, and battlements it sees/ Bosom'd high in tufted trees.'(lines 73-78).

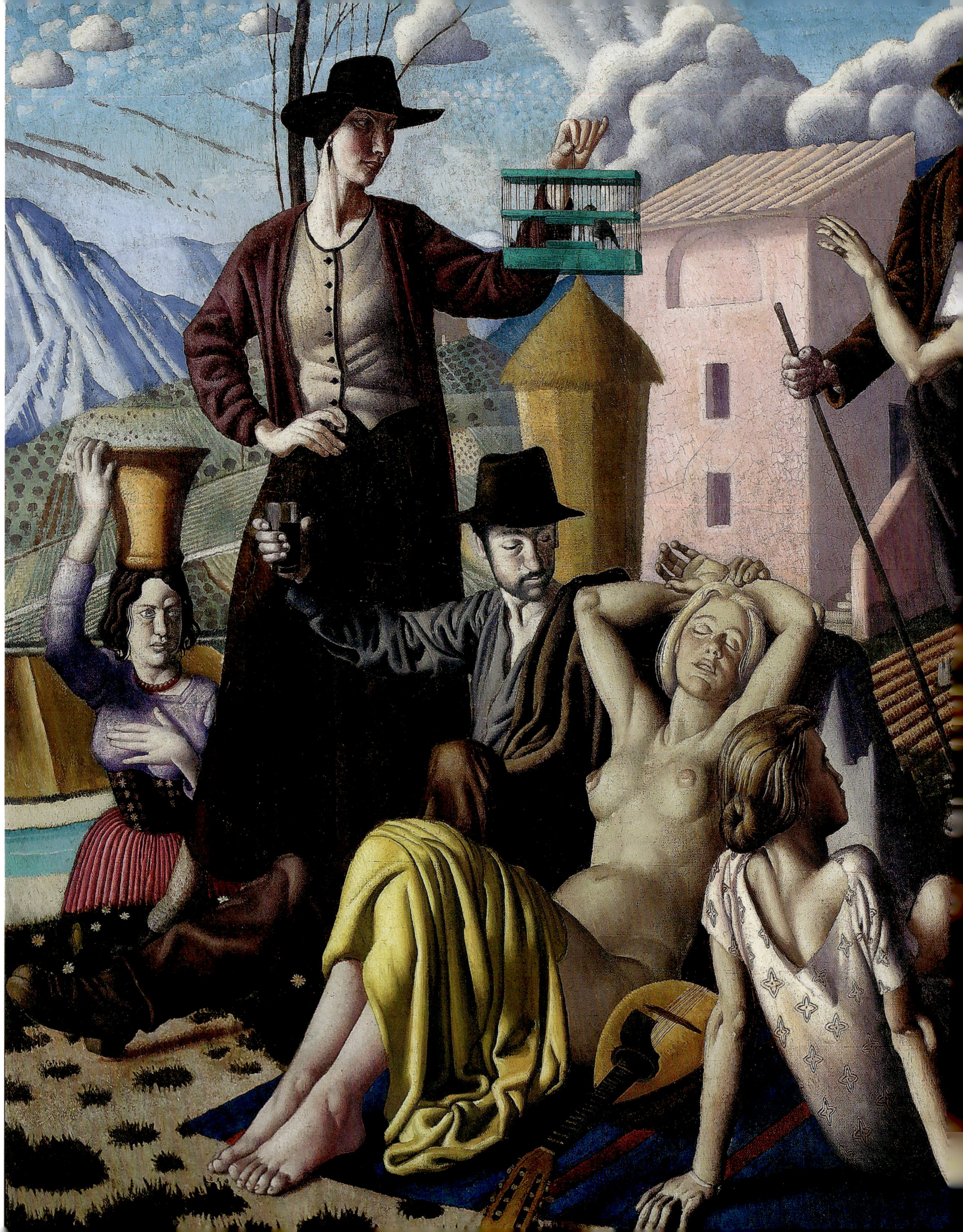

99
Allegro, 1921
signed and dated,
oil on canvas,
117 x 228.5 cm
(46 x 90 in.)

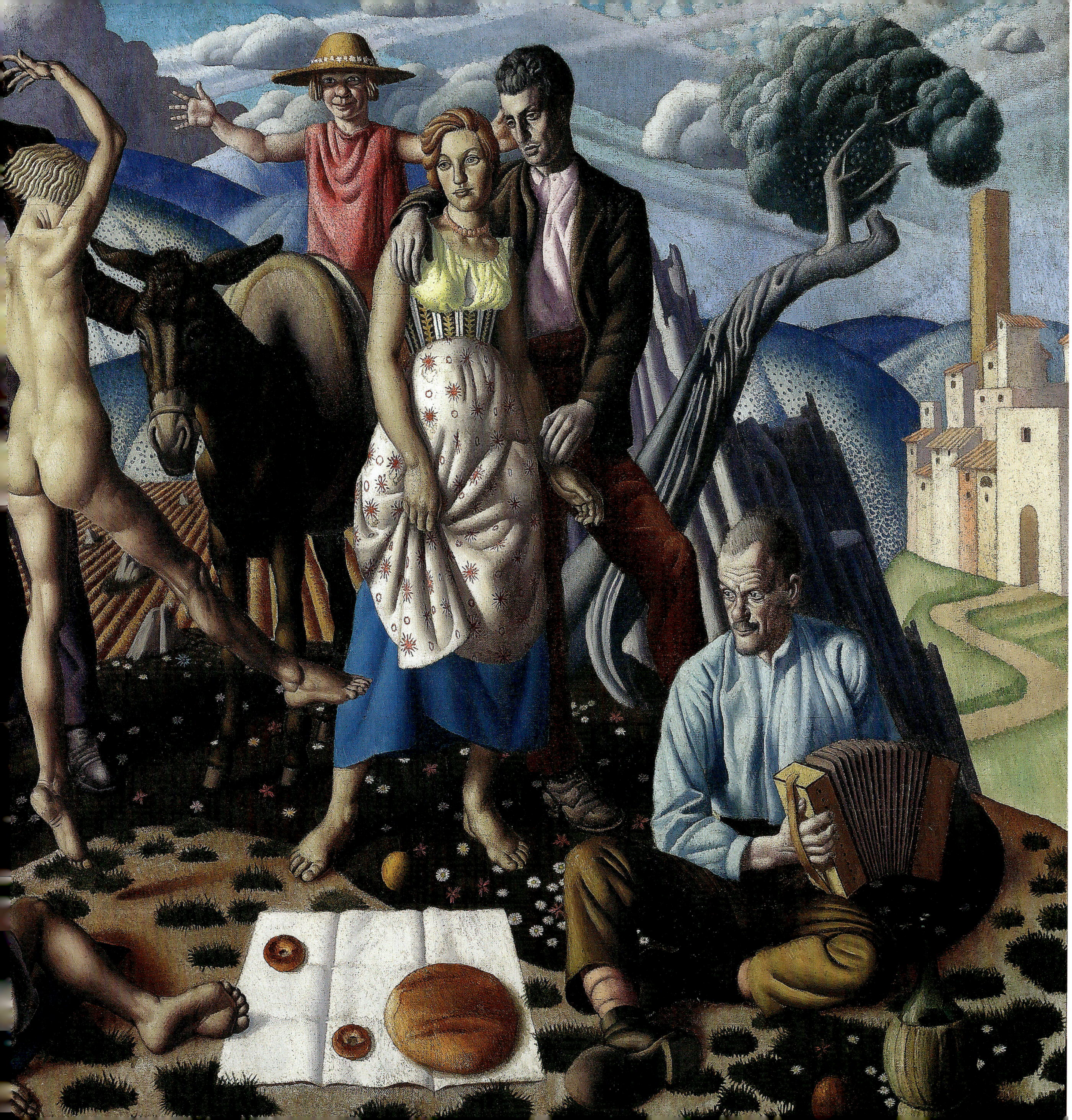

The poetry of Milton had found a new impetus in recent art-theory. In his book *Art* (1913), the art critic Clive Bell used the example of Milton's poetry to develop his theories on 'aesthetic emotion'.[26] In his 1918 lecture on 'English Poetry in its Relation to Painting and the Other Arts', the poet and scholar Laurence Binyon discussed the pictorial nature of Milton's poetry: 'as he sings, we see'. He paralleled his 'vast prospect' and the 'organ music of his rhythm' to Michelangelo and Veronese, although in contrast to these artists, Milton did not 'disdain the softer elements of human surroundings, verdure and foliage, nor the ampler setting of mountains, seas and rivers'.[27]

Throughout the summer of 1920, Gill worked on his painting, and at the end of July he asked Eugenie Strong, the Deputy Director of the British School, to come up to Anticoli Corrado to give her opinion on the composition and help him to advance his ideas. A photograph of Gill in his studio shows that his original composition had included a large Calvary on the left of the canvas. A symbol of suffering and defeat in his earlier war paintings, here it became a symbol of resurrection and salvation.

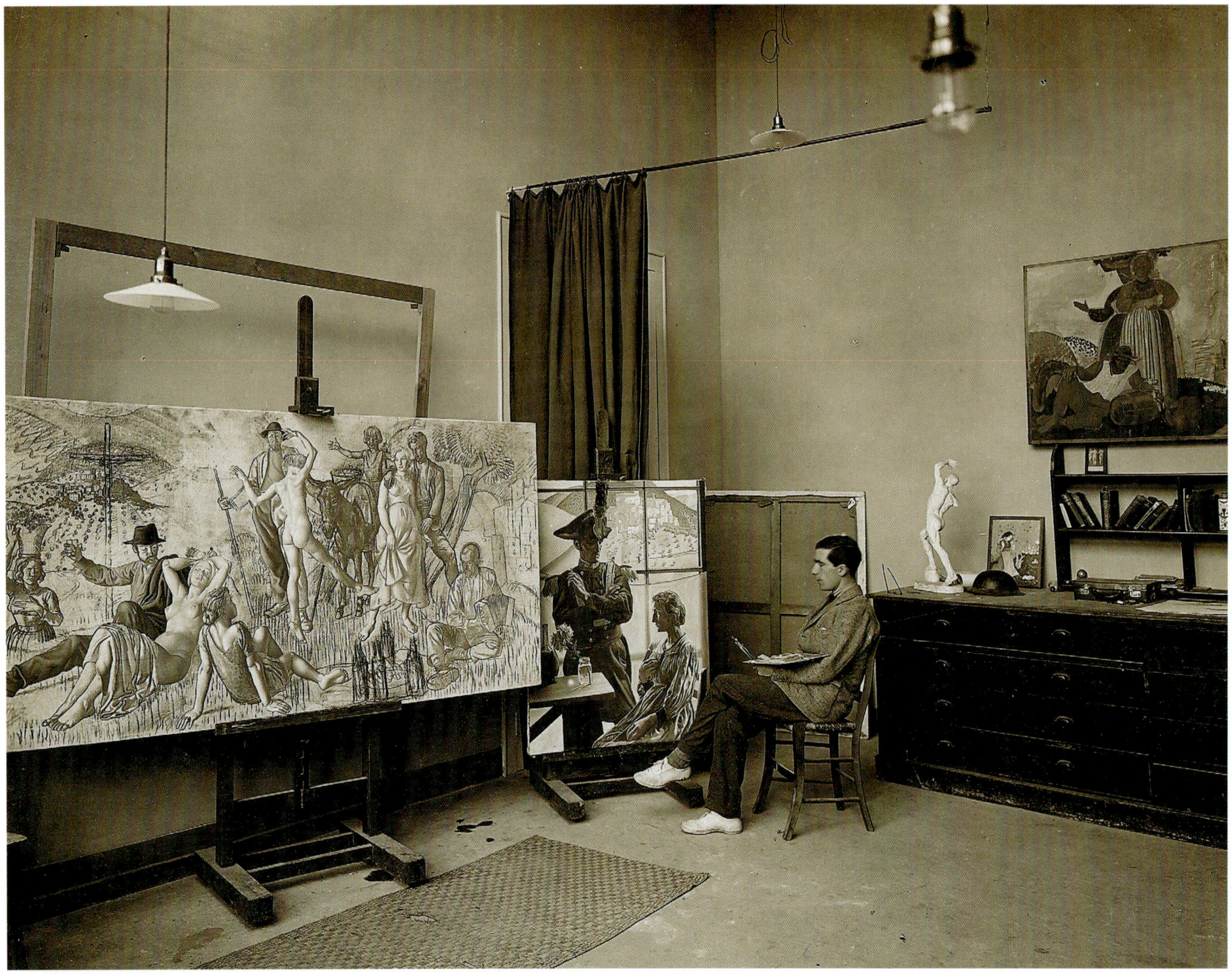

100
Colin Gill in his studio at The British School at Rome, 1920

In October 1920, Gill's wife and child returned to England, and in that same month he received news from the British School at Rome's secretary, Evelyn Shaw, that Winifred Knights would soon be arriving in Rome: 'I am sure I can rely on you…to be very kind to her'.[28] On her arrival in Rome, Winifred Knights wrote to her mother that 'Gill is very nice and seems pleased to see me, as his wife is in England'.[29] During Knights' first few months at the British School, Colin Gill introduced her to Rome and its historic sites and monuments, and together they attended fancy-dress balls, the Russian Ballet and Opera, visited flower markets, ate in Gill's favourite restaurant at Trajan's Forum and made trips to Tivoli and the seaside. In March 1921, accompanied by Gill's sister Marjory, they set off on a walking expedition in the countryside north west of Rome, and then travelled by bus to Viterbo, Orvieto, Assisi, Perugia and Florence. On their return to Rome in April, having clearly developed a passionate love for Winifred Knights ('Jane') which he recorded in *Ode,* 1921, Gill scraped back the crucifix on his painting, and replaced it with her full-length portrait holding a bird-cage:[30]

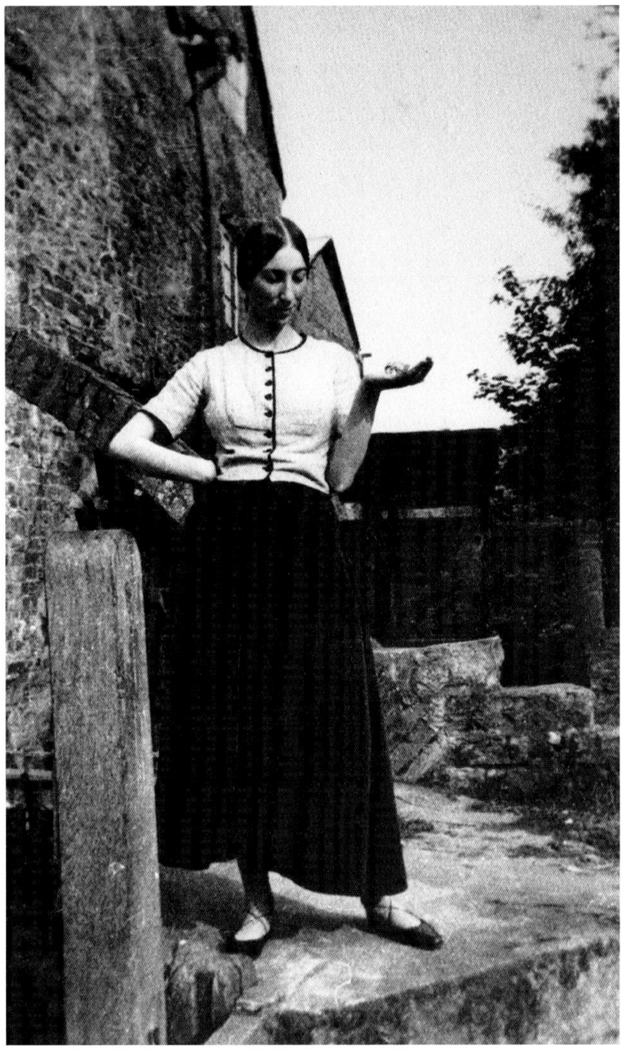

101
Photograph of
Winifred Knights,
September 1920

You were near me at tea
And the light
Fell on your throat and the corals around it, the red
And the white
And I thought, this is she.

This is she holds my heart like a bird in a cage
For so
My spirit is bound by a word that I said in a dream,
Long ago

Dreams. But perhaps to the south there's an isle
Of white sand,
Like your throat
And around it a pink coral band
Afloat
On the plum-coloured sea

If so – it is you
You are she…[31]

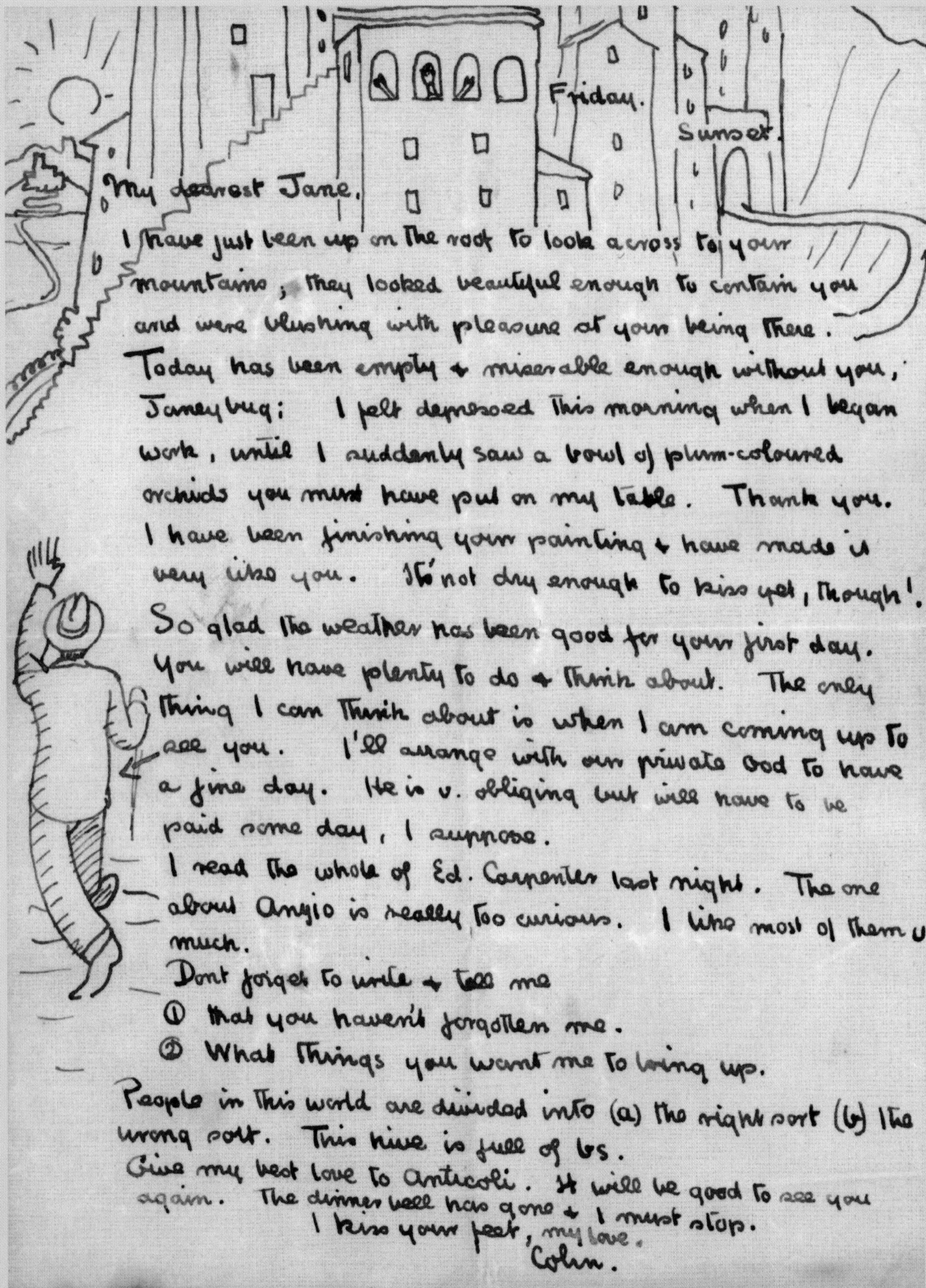

Friday.

Sunset.

My dearest Jane,

I have just been up on the roof to look across to your mountains; they looked beautiful enough to contain you and were blushing with pleasure at your being there.

Today has been empty & miserable enough without you, Janeybug: I felt depressed this morning when I began work, until I suddenly saw a bowl of plum-coloured orchids you must have put on my table. Thank you.

I have been finishing your painting & have made it very like you. It's not dry enough to kiss yet, though!

So glad the weather has been good for your first day. You will have plenty to do & think about. The only thing I can think about is when I am coming up to see you. I'll arrange with our private God to have a fine day. He is v. obliging but will have to be paid some day, I suppose.

I read the whole of Ed. Carpenter last night. The one about Angio is really too curious. I like most of them v much.

Dont forget to write & tell me

① that you haven't forgotten me.

② What things you want me to bring up.

People in this world are divided into (a) the right sort (b) the wrong sort. This hive is full of bs.

Give my best love to Anticoli. It will be good to see you again. The dinner bell has gone & I must stop.

I kiss your feet, my love.

Colin.

102
Letter from
Colin Gill to
'Jane'
(Winifred Knights)

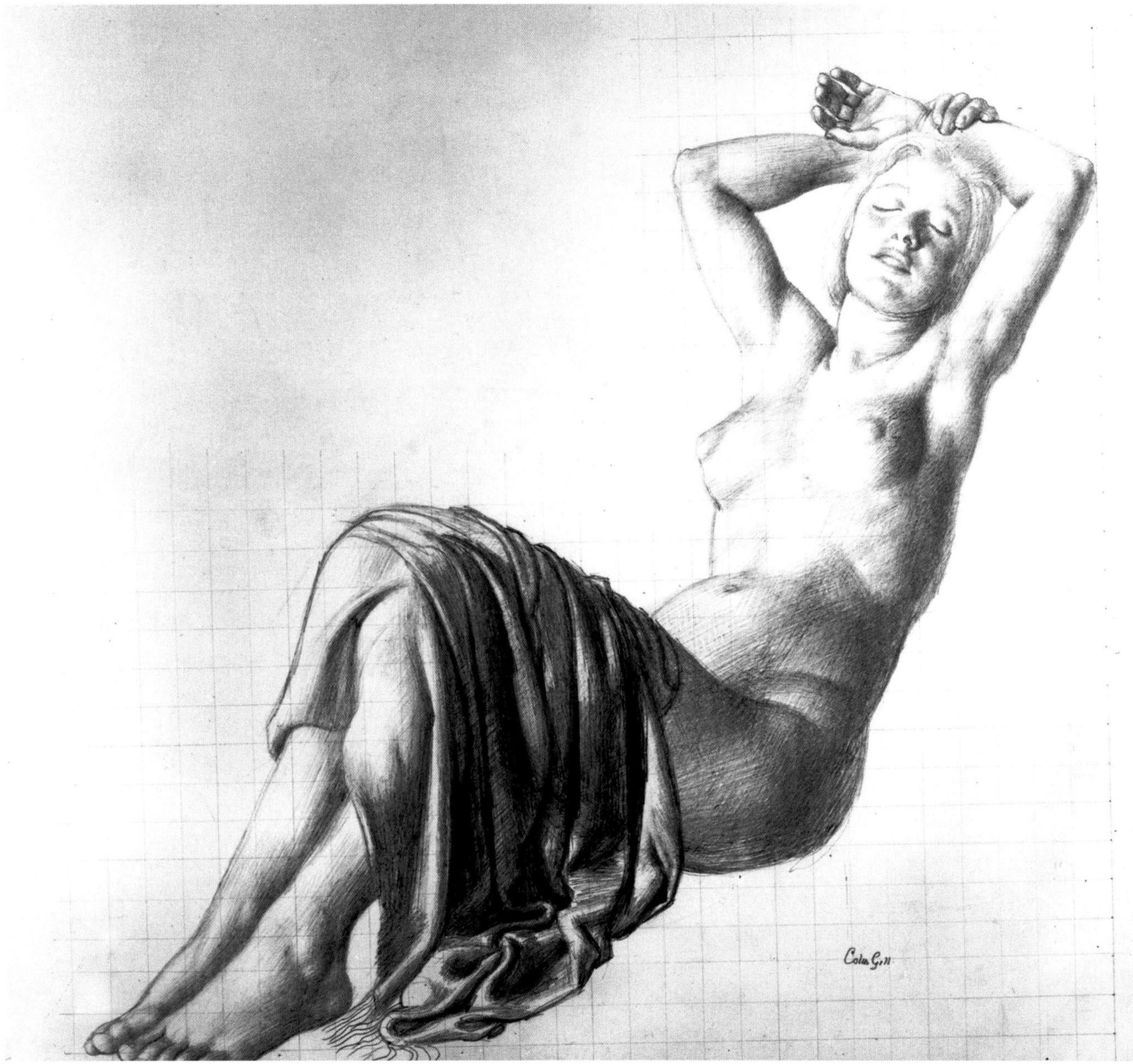

103
Study for Allegro, (sleeping nude), 1921, signed, pencil on card, 54.6 x 61 cm, (21 ½ x 24 in.)
© Tate, London 2012

The final composition of *Allegro* shows a frieze-like arrangement of eleven figures set within a shallow, stylised landscape. In addition to Winifred Knights, Gill included in his painting the Rome Scholar for Engraving, Job Nixon (standing far right) and the Rome Scholar for Sculpture, Alfred Hardiman and his wife, Violet (either side of Winifred Knights).[32] As such, *Allegro* includes the portraits of all three Rome Scholars for 1920. Other models appear to be from Anticoli Corrado, the women wearing the local dress and coral necklaces. A study for the child on the donkey is entitled *La Siciliana* (unknown location). Augustus Daniel (later Director of the National Gallery, 1929), who saw Gill's *Allegro* on a visit to the British School in May 1921, described it as, 'thoroughly worked out and befitting his Slade training' but he felt it lacked '"subject" or purpose

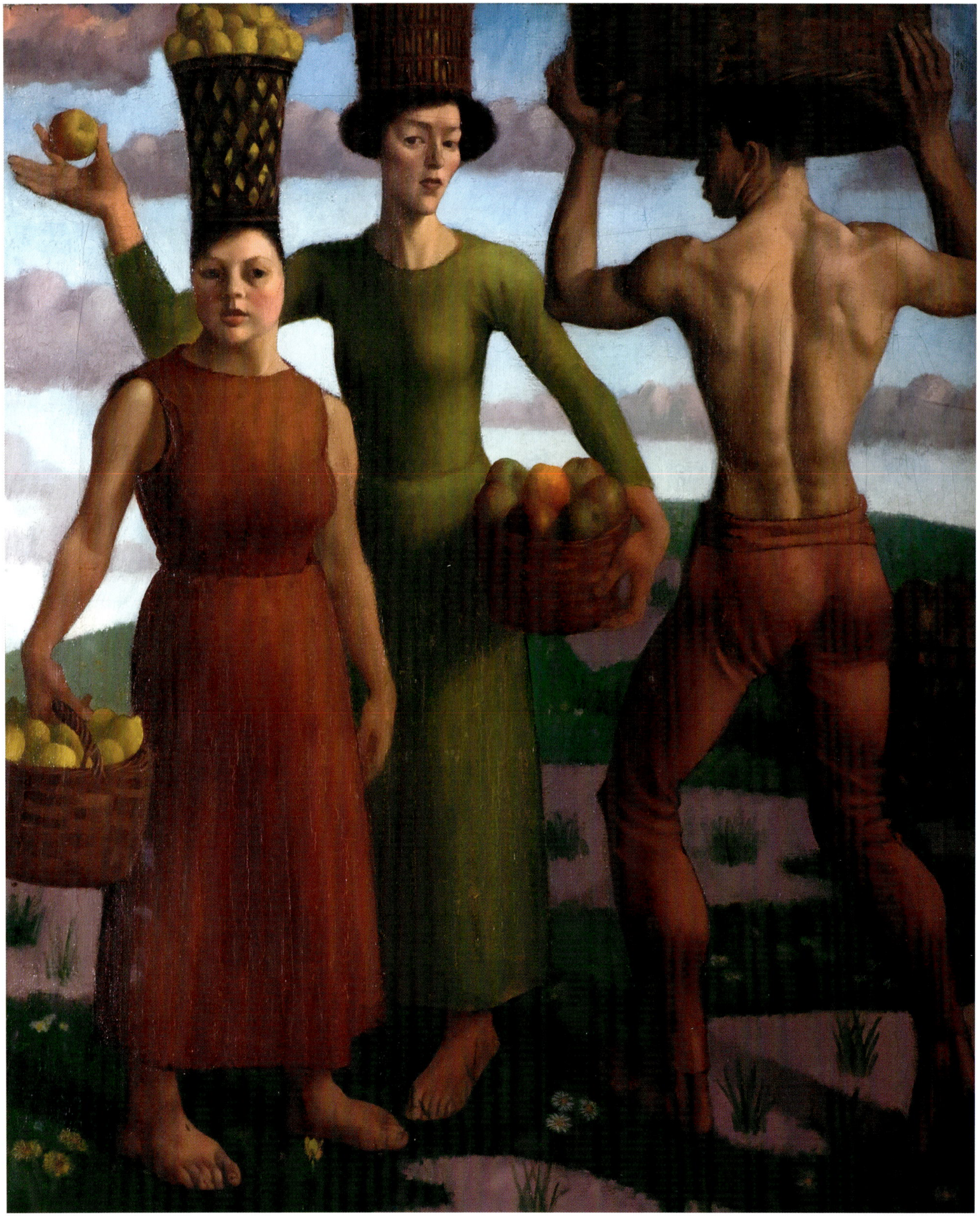

104
Mark Gertler,
The Fruit Sorters, 1914,
oil on canvas,
76.2 x 63.5 cm,
(30 x 25 in.),
courtesy of Leicester Arts
and Museums Service

for the meeting of so many figures and the colour was not pleasant'.[33] Certainly *Allegro's* palette of strong blues, greens and browns, with highlights of yellow, red, pink and purple contrasts with the more restrained colours characteristic of First World War paintings and Slade compositions of this period.

Allegro was Gill's first major painting since the completion of *Canadian Observation Post* and the rural dynamism of the picture seems to compensate for the violent chaos of his war paintings. The treatment of sky, however – intense blue punctuated with billowing clouds and diagonal lines reminiscent of the trajectories left behind by tracer bullets and explosives – refers back to his war canvases.[34] The twisted, blasted tree in *Allegro*, which was a common metaphor for the war dead in much English poetry of the First World War, is another device transported by Gill into the landscape of *Allegro*.[35]

For a large, landscape-format pastoral composition, Gill had many prototypes from which to draw inspiration. The most famous of these, Botticelli's *La Primavera* (*Allegory of Spring*), which like *Allegro* was probably inspired by a poem, he had studied at first hand in Florence.[36] The critic P. G. Konody described Gill's composition as having 'something of the spirit of Botticelli…he has taken from the early Italians as much as he could without falling into an affected primitivism'.[37] *Allegro* also has an affinity with the Golden Age dreams of Puvis de Chavannes, whose work, which Gill had seen in Paris during the war, was profoundly influential on decorative art in England at this time.[38] A more contemporary influence is likely to have come through Gill's friend, Augustus John; of particular relevance is his *Lyric Fantasy*, c.1913-4 (Tate Gallery). There are also striking similarities between *Allegro* and Mark Gertler's Slade composition, *Allegory*, 1910 (private collection) and *Fruit Sorters*, 1914 (New Walk Museum & Art Gallery, Leicester). Inspired by his new-found love of the English countryside, Gertler's *Fruit Sorters* was much brighter in colour and lighter in mood than most of his work from this period.

Gill is certain to have been aware of the recent developments in Italian art that resulted in the founding of Novecento Italiano in 1922. The name of this movement was a deliberate reference to Italian art of the past, the Quattrocento and Cinquecento, and Gill would have empathised with the group's desire to revive the tradition of large-format history painting in the classical manner. Through his friendship with Paul-Albert Besnard, the director of the French Academy in Rome, Gill would also have been conscious of developments in French decorative painting of the period and the work of the French Rome Scholar, Jean Dupas, seems to have been of particular relevance; Dupas' celebrated painting *Les Perruches*, 1925 (private collection) (see page 95) bears a close stylistic affinity to *Allegro*. Indeed, Gill's *Allegro* anticipates many of the qualities that characterised Continental painting in the second half of the 1920s; the fact that it was exhibited at the seminal Exposition des Arts Décoratifs in Paris, 1925, suggests that it was still considered to be representative of British contemporary art some four years after it was painted.

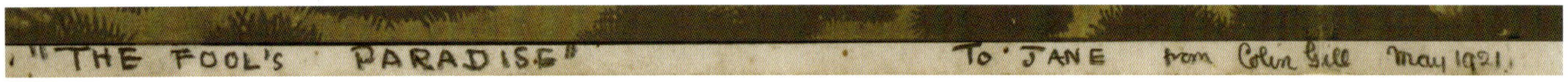

105 Colin Gill's dedication to Winifred Knights (Jane) inscribed on a photographic reproduction of his *Allegro*, May 1921, private collection

When Gill returned to England in May 1921, Knights wrote to her aunt: 'I miss Gill very much now, we have become very good friends. We are very much alike & have had some very good times together.'[39] Gill sent Knights a photographic reproduction of *Allegro* inscribed with the words 'the fool's Paradise'. With a failing marriage at home, and no commissions for paintings, Gill wrote a despondent letter to Evelyn Shaw: 'The French Pensionnaires at the Villa Medici on their return to France are given Government commissions as a matter of course, and know that they can look forward to these as a means of living….a painter returning home and finding no opportunities for Decorative Painting will naturally have to give it up and take to painting portraits, exhibition pictures, or even cheap commercial work, as mural painting on a large scale is obviously not possible unless there are definite jobs to be done'.[40] In June 1922, the *Manchester Guardian* ran an article entitled 'The Plight of the Mural Decorator'. Calling for 'a public art to serve the community', the critic thought 'Mr. Gill a good example of a new school of artists, many of them with Prix de Rome experience, who are growing up with the desire and capacity to decorate our public buildings. Has the time not come for the community to avail themselves of this supply?'[41] Gill received his first major mural commission two years later, in 1924, when he was asked to provide thirteen panels for the Great Hall of Northampton Town Council depicting kings and local great men. Prestigious commissions followed, including St Stephen's Hall, Westminster, 1927 (see page 36) and three lunettes for the Bank of England, 1932.

In 1932, in a letter to Gill's sister, by now Lady Allen of Hurtwood, Winifred Knights reported that 'she had met Colin a little while ago and thought he did not look very happy…it is awful to think that there are three of us who think that that Rome-Florence walk was the happiest time'.[42] Through *Allegro* Gill had attempted to paint out the horrors of four years lost to the war but he was ultimately unable to regain the sense of youth and optimism promised by Milton's poem.

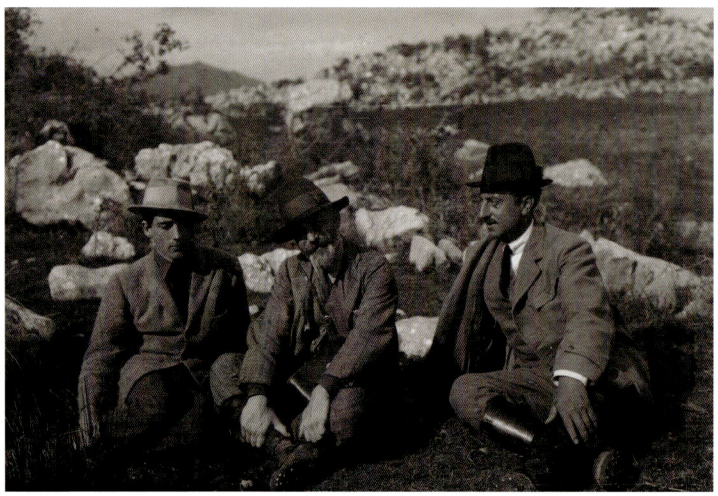

106 Colin Gill, Thomas Ashby and unidentified man in the Italian campagna, c. 1920

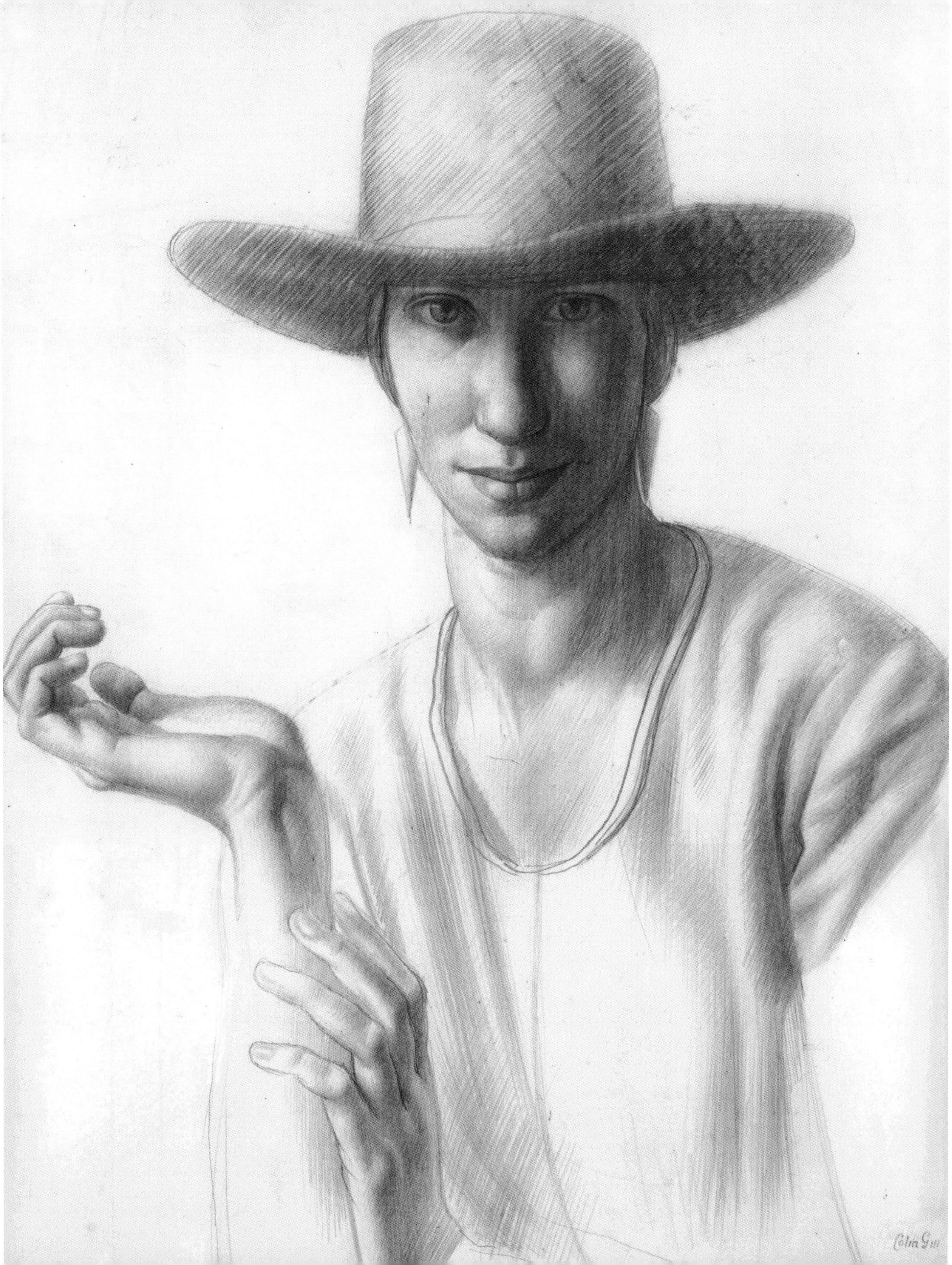

107
Portrait of Winifred Knights, 1921, signed and inscribed 'Jane' on the original backboard, pencil on paper, 43.8 x 32.4 cm (17 ¼ x 12 ¾ in.)

ENDNOTES

1 Minutes of the Faculty of Painting, October 11, 1921, BSR Historic Archives.

2 *The Manchester Guardian*, June 19, 1922.

3 Alan Powers suggests that the defining quality of decorative painting was 'subject matter removed from everyday life and given a classical or primitive treatment'. Alan Powers, 'Decorative Painting in the early Twentieth Century – a Context for Winifred Knights', in *Winifred Knights*, the Fine Art Society and Paul Liss, 1995, p.14.

4 Lady Allen of Hurtwood, *Memoirs of an Uneducated Lady*, London 1975, p.32.

5 These murals were already in need of some restoration in 1923, and when they were further damaged during the Blitz in 1940, it was decided to paint over them. John Sheppard, *Bishop Creighton House 1908–2008: One Hundred Years of Work in the Community*, London, 2008, p.36. In an article in *The Times* (September 24, 1924), Henry Tonks was described as 'deeply interested in wall decoration, anxious to see it used, and fully aware that unless the artist is caught young, he will never succeed at it'.

6 Lady Allen of Hurtwood, (1975), p.52.

7 For Gill's friendship with Mark Gertler, see Lady Allen of Hurtwood (1975) pp. 52 and 67; For Gill's friendship with William Roberts see Andrew Gibbon Williams, *William Roberts: An English Cubist*, London, 2004, pp.19 and 56.

8 'Manet and the Post-Impressionists', Grafton Gallery, November 1910; Second Post-Impressionist Exhibition, Grafton Galleries, January 1912; For a list of the exhibitions of Italian Painting held in London during this period, see Carolyn Leder, *Stanley Spencer: the Astor Collection*, London 1976, pp.16-17.

9 *The Manchester Guardian*, March 23, 1920.

10 For an analysis of this exhibition, see Lisa Tickner, *Modern Life and Modern Subjects*, New Haven and London, 2002, pp.1-9. The introduction to the exhibition catalogue divided the field of modern art between four main groups. For a list of the 132 exhibitors to the exhibition, including Colin Gill, see Anna Gruetzner Robins, *Modern Art in Britain 1910-1914* (exh. cat.), London: Merrell Holberton in association with the Barbican Art Gallery, 1997, pp.184-5.

11 Minutes of the Faculty of Painting, 1913, BSR Historic Archives.

12 Lionel Cust 'The British School at Rome', *Burlington Magazine*, XXI June 1912, p.148.

13 Quoted in David Boyd Haycock, *A Crisis of Brilliance*, London 2009, p.152.

14 *Memorandum on the Course of Study for Rome Scholars in Painting*, October 12, 1925, BSR Historic Archives.

15 Letter from Colin Gill to Evelyn Shaw, June 25, 1914, BSR Historic Archives.

16 Memorandum (1925).

17 Letter from Colin Gill to Evelyn Shaw, June 25, 1914, BSR Historic Archives.

18 See for example the following pictures in the collection of the Imperial War Museum: *Observation of Fire*, 1919 (IWM ART 2297); *The Captive*, 1918 (IWM ART 1209); *Evening after a Push* (IWM ART 1210).

19 As part of the war art scheme, the British War Memorials Committee planned a Hall of Remembrance devoted to 'fighting subjects, home subjects and the war at sea and in the air'. This was to be a record and a memorial to the Great War through paintings commissioned from British artists, including Percy Wyndham Lewis, Stanley Spencer and John Singer Sargent. However, because of a lack of funding after the war, the Hall of Remembrance was never built, and the collection of paintings was given to the Imperial War Museum.

20 Quoted in Roger Tolson, *Art from the First World War*, Imperial War Museum, 2008, p.11.

21 *The Observer*, December 14, 1919.

22 Lord Beaverbrook sponsored the Canadian Scheme and at the close of the war a considerable number of large-sized pictures were commissioned to hang round the walls of the planned special memorial hall, which in the end was never realised. The artists commissioned for this scheme included Gill, Nevinson, Lewis, Roberts, Paul Nash, Sims and Augustus John.

23 Modern Records Centre, University of Warwick, Mss.121/F/3/4/8.

24 Frank Hyde, Anticoli Corrado, *The International Studio*, Volume 47, no.185-188, 1912.

25 'L'Allegro' was published along with its companion piece 'Il Penseroso' in *Poems of Mr. John Milton both English and Latin, Compos'd at Several Times*, in 1645.

26 Clive Bell, *Art*, 1913, p.266. In this book Bell wrote that, 'the value of the greatest art consists not in its power of becoming a party of common existence but in its power of taking us out of it – the lover of poetry shuts the door of his chamber and takes down a volume of Milton with the deliberate intention of getting himself out of one world and into another'.

27 Laurence Binyon, 'English poetry in its relation to painting and the Other Arts' in *Proceedings of the British Academy*, VIII, 1918, pp. 381-402.

28 Letter from Evelyn Shaw to Colin Gill, October 15, 1920, BSR Historic Archives.

29 Letter from Winifred Knights to her mother, November 5, 1920, Slade Archive, UCL Library Services, Special Collections.

30 Ruth Bubb, Interim Conservation Report, September 25, 1989, p.2 (unpublished). This report records that 'the standing woman with the bird-cage appears to have been added at a late stage, as she is thinly painted over the existing landscape'.

31 *Ode to Winifred Knights* by Colin Gill, 1921, Private Collection.

32 I am grateful to Janice Hardiman for the identification of her parents.

33 Letter from Augustus Daniel to Henry Tonks, May 2, 1921, The Harry Ransom Research Center, University of Texas, Austin. I am grateful to Sabina ffrench Blake for this information.

34 During the war, in 1916, Gill had learned to fly and recorded that he always felt 'very exhilarated and godlike whilst among the clouds'. Letter from Gill to his sister, Marjory, July 16, 1916, Modern Records Centre, University of Warwick, mss.121/F/3/4/3.

35 Edward Thomas, Richard Aldington and Harold Monro were all poets who identified trees with the war-dead in their poetry.

36 The Uffizi was one of Gill's favourite places to study paintings. A reproduction of Francesco Morandini's *Three Graces* from the Uffizi can be seen on the bookshelf in the photograph of Gill in his studio [100] Poetic sources for *La Primavera* possibly include Ovid's *Fasti* and Lucretius's *De Rerum Natura*.

37 *The Observer*, February 19, 1922.

38 The motionless figures set within an ideal, shallow landscape, which characterise many of Chavannes' paintings such as *Pleasant Land*, 1882 (Musée Bonnat, Bayonne), bear a close affinity to Gill's *Allegro*.

39 Letter from Winifred Knights to her Aunt Millicent Murby, undated, BSR Historic Archives (photocopy).

40 Letter from Colin Gill to Evelyn Shaw, November 14, 1920, BSR Historic Archives.

41 *The Manchester Guardian*, June 19, 1922.

42 Modern Records Centre, University of Warwick, Mss. 121/F/3/10/2.

MURALS AND DECORATIVE PAINTINGS BY COLIN GILL

1913 – *Music*, winning submission for the first Rome Scholarship in Decorative Painting

1919 – *Heavy Artillery*, oil on canvas, Imperial War Museum

1920 – *Canadian Observation Post*, oil on canvas, Canadian War Museum, Ottawa, Canada

1921 – *Allegro*, oil on canvas, private collection

1924-25 – 13 panels of kings and local great men in Great Hall representing famous men connected with the town, Northampton Town Hall

1925 – *The Colonists*, Apse in the Basilica, Cassis, 34 x 14 ft.

1928 – *King Alfred Defeating the Danes off Swanage*, St Stephen's Hall, Westminster, 10 x 15 ft.

1929 – Mural, Fishmongers Hall, Capitol Theatre

1930 – *Amphitrite in Cassis*, mural 96 x 66 ft.

1932 – Three lunettes for the Bank of England: *Weighing gold, Old Weighing Room*; *Receiving bullion, Old Bullion Yard, Lothbury*; *Moving gold, Old Gold Vault*
Portraits (set into pine panelling) for Glyn Mills & Co, Lombard Street

1938 – *Boadicea after Storming the Roman Fortress at Camulodunum*, decoration for the Council Chamber, Essex County Hall

1939 – *Captain Carl von Brandis, and Louis Trichardt* (unfinished), Magistrates' Court, Johannesburg. Gill died there 16 November 1940 before completing them.

Colin Gill (1892-1940)

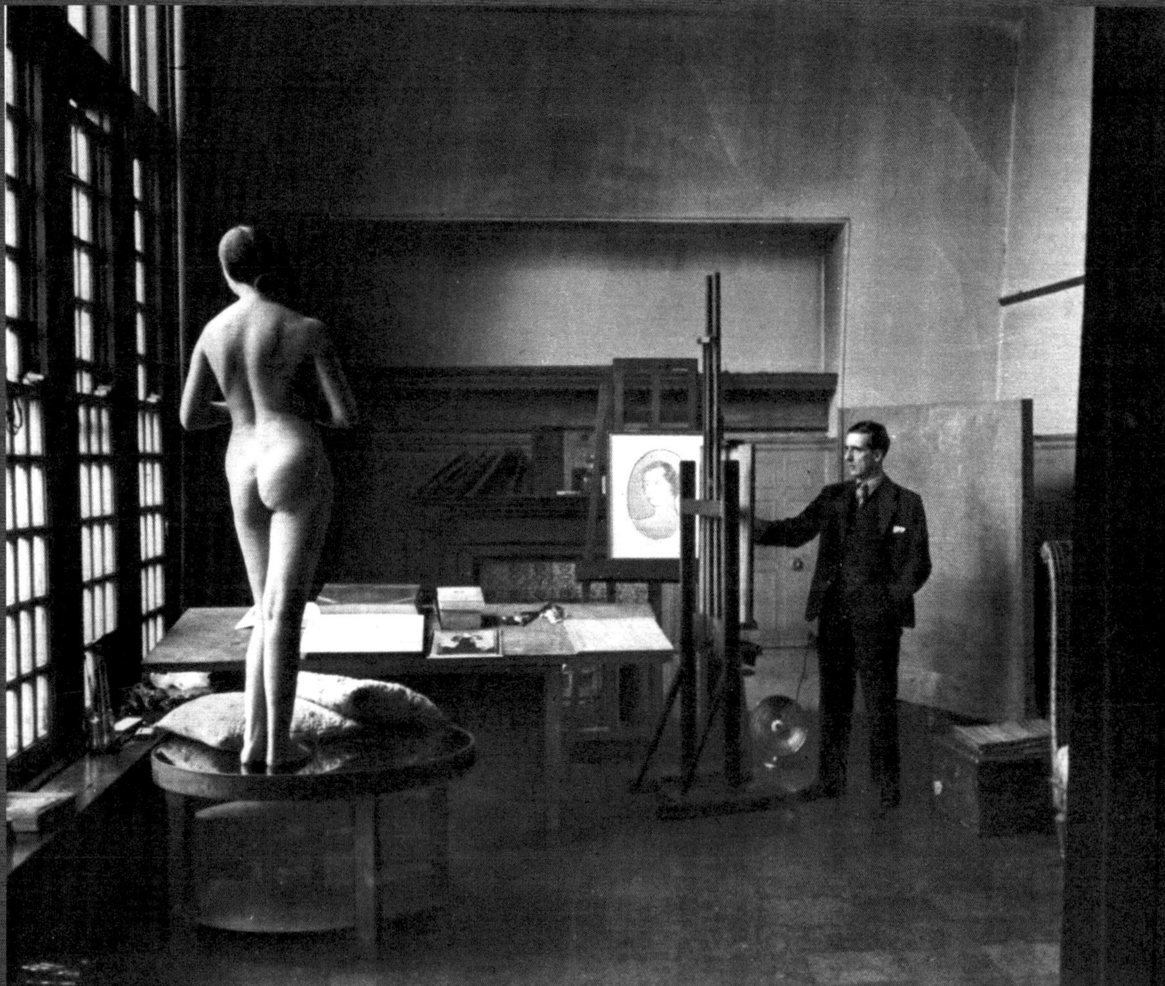

108 Colin Gill working in Whistler's old studio in Tite Street, Chelsea, c. 1938

COLIN GILL N.E.A.C. Born Bexley Heath, Kent, died Johannesburg, South Africa. Decorative, mural and genre painter. Studied Slade School of Art (1910-1913), Slade Scholarship (1911), British Institution Scholarship (1912), Rome Scholarship (1913), Official War Artist (1919-1920), Instructor in Composition, R.C.A. (1922-1925). Exhibited at the N.E.A.C. from 1914 (member 1926) and at the R.A. from 1924. Carried out mural commissions including *Defeat of the Danes* in St Stephen's Hall, Westminster, 1927, and decorations in the Bank of England, Essex County Hall, Chelmsford, and Northampton Town Hall. Went to South Africa in 1939 to paint decorations in the Magistrates' Court, Johannesburg, and died there 16 November 1940 before completing them. Joint author with his wife Una Long, under the name 'Richard Saxby', of *Five Came to London,* 1938. Memorial exhibition at the Argus Gallery, Cape Town, 1941.

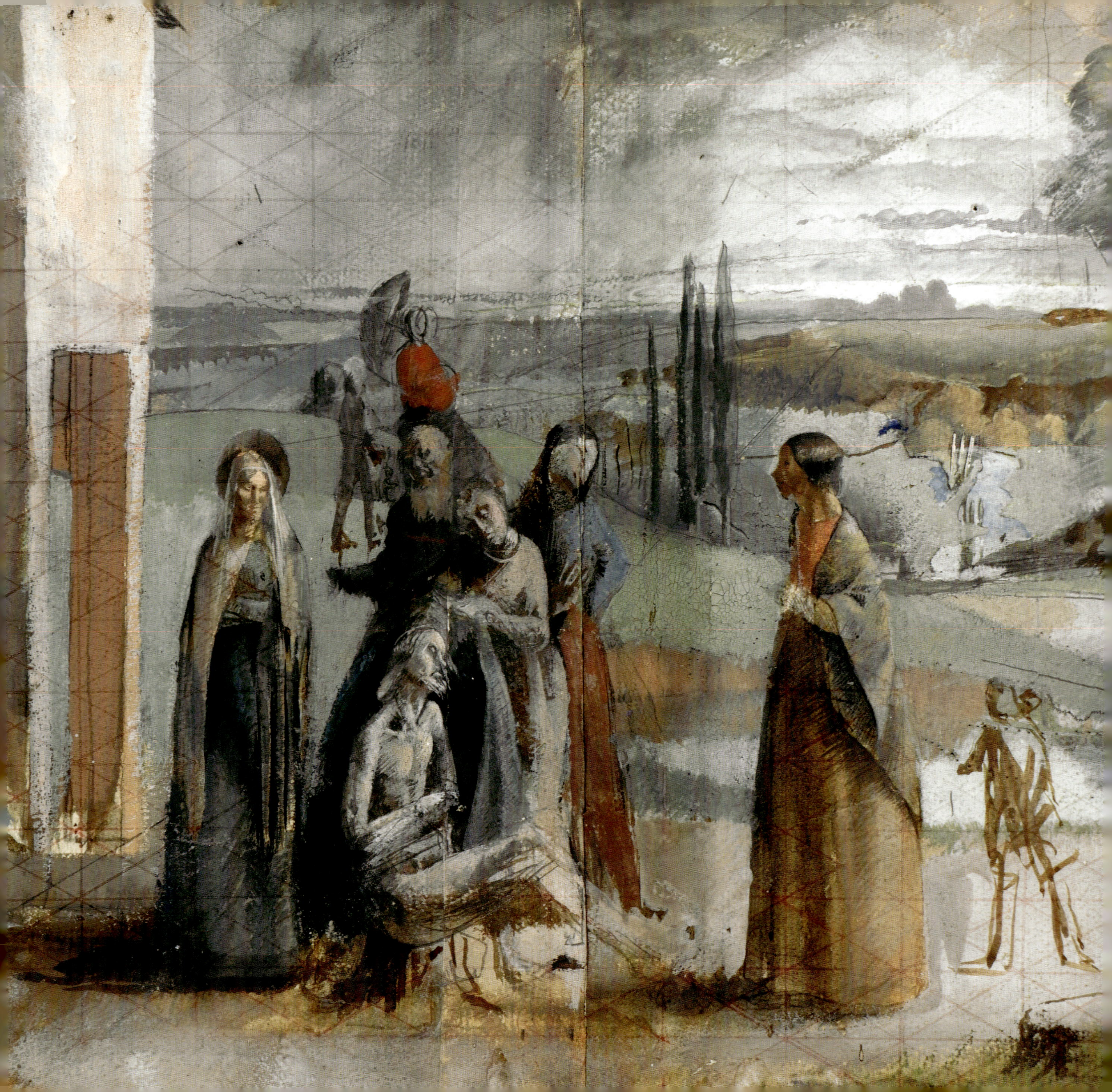

Thomas Monnington
Winter, 1922 & *Allegory*, 1925

Sam Smiles

Thomas Monnington enrolled at the Slade in January 1918, aged fifteen. A talented student, his abilities were first formally recognised with the award of the prize for Figure Painting in 1921. He was nineteen when he began work on *Winter*, his winning submission to the 1922 competition for the British School at Rome's Scholarship in Decorative Painting.[1] The finished canvas and the study for it were included in the Exhibition of works submitted in the final competitions for the Rome Scholarship of 1922, held at the Royal Academy in February 1923.

The background of this painting was derived from landscape studies Monnington had made in 1921, in the Wiltshire countryside near the prehistoric site of Clearbury Rings, a few miles from Salisbury, when he was staying with his cousin Dr. R.C. Monnington. The extensive prospect shows copses of trees in a fold of the downs to the right, while to the left a winter squall breaks upon the fields. Nearer to us, a shelter is being thatched, while in front of it a young man with an axe stands next to the tree he has recently felled. At the centre a ragged old man is offered a cloak as protection from the cold, and food or drink for him is carried in from the left. The clothing of these protagonists is clearly antiquated, their gestures stylised, and this, together with the symbolism of the actions, suggests that Monnington has tied together traditional seasonal occupations with more metaphysical concerns, alluding perhaps to the traditional Christian corporal acts of mercy: feeding the hungry, giving drink to the thirsty, clothing the naked and sheltering the homeless. The choreographed behaviour and frieze-like presentation of the main figure group, all of whom are situated in a relatively shallow space, coupled with the schematic architecture of the building on the left, adds to this perception of ritual.

109
Study for *Winter*, c. 1922
signed and dated,
pencil and gouache
on paper, squared,
21 x 37 cm,
(8 ¼ x 14 ½ in.)
(detail)

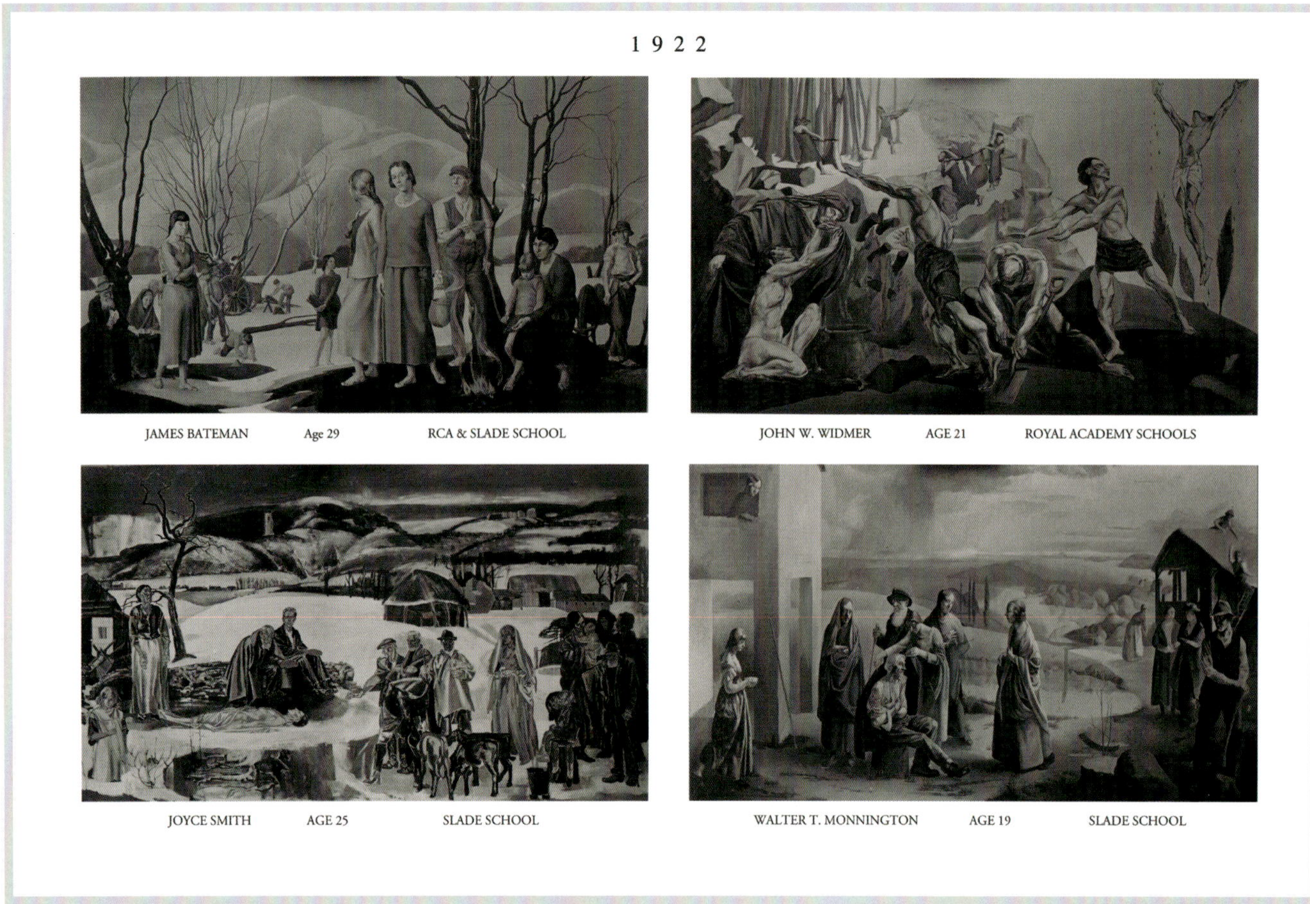

110
Works of the four finalists for the Rome Scholarship in 1922: James Bateman, John W. Widmer, Joyce Smith and Walter T. Monnington

Monnington's artistic inspiration here is clearly taken from Quattrocento painting. This was a life-long preoccupation for him; indeed, he later declared that it was his seeing Piero della Francesca's *Adoration of the Christ Child* in the National Gallery, when he was still a boy, that determined him to become an artist. As a student at the Slade Monnington would probably have been aware of a similar interest which had developed there in the early 1910s, especially among a group of students called the Neo-Primitives, whose ranks included Stanley Spencer, Roberts, Nevinson, Gertler and Currie.[2] This enthusiasm for the Renaissance among the rising generation of artists was echoed in a similar tendency among British art critics of this period, who championed the possibility of maintaining early Renaissance qualities of pictorial design in contemporary art.[3] Roger Fry, for example, made this

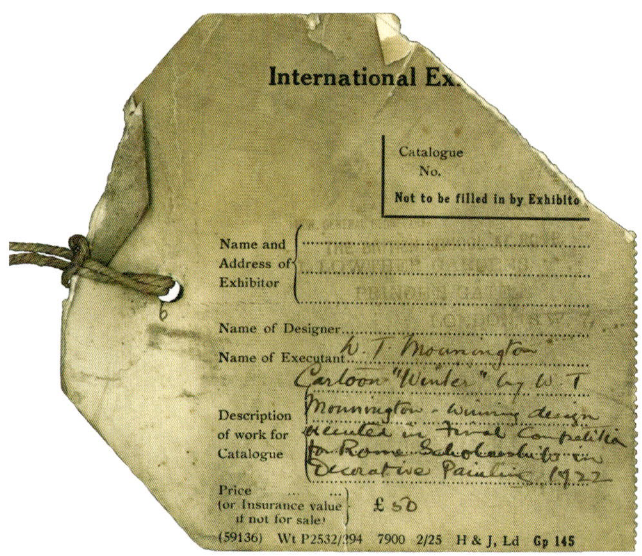
International Ex
Catalogue No.
Not to be filled in by Exhibito
Name and Address of Exhibitor
Name of Designer
Name of Executant W.T. Monnington
Description of work for Catalogue Cartoon "Winter" by W.T Monnington - winning design executed in final competition for Rome Scholarship in Decorative Painting 1922
Price (or Insurance value if not for sale) £50
(59136) Wt P2532/394 7900 2/25 H & J, Ld Gp 145

111 Exhibitor's label for *Winter*

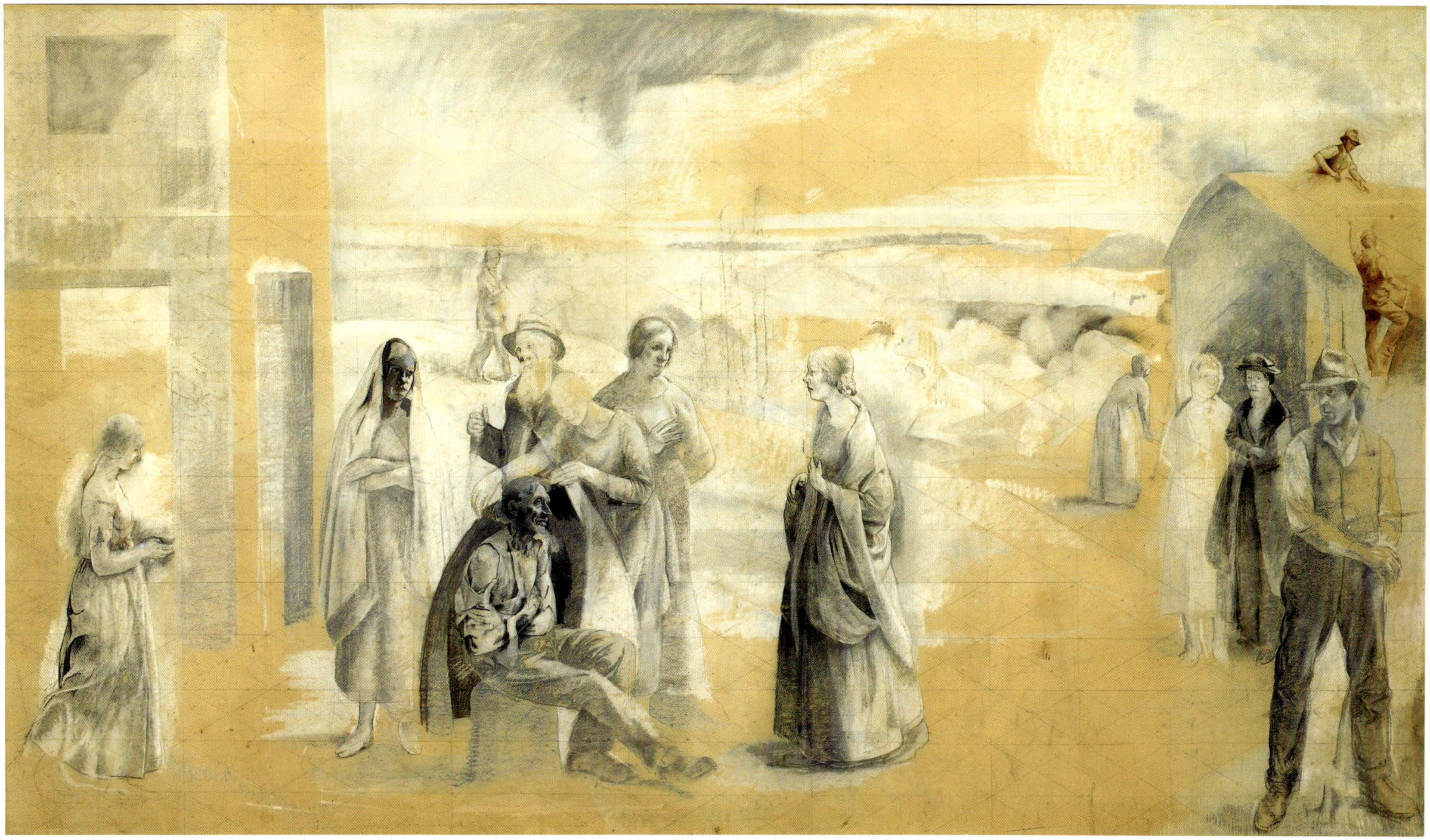

112 Cartoon for *Winter*, c. 1921, chalk and gouache on brown paper, 122 x 216 cm (48 x 85 in.)

claim before the First World War and R.H.Wilenski was to assert in 1926 that a study visit to Italy was essential to a modern painter's development.[4] So when the Italophile critic P. G. Konody praised *Winter* for being 'steeped in the best traditions of the Italian Renaissance. His colour is dull, but there is a marked sense of style in his design,' his remarks found a context in this debate about the appropriate use of the Italian Renaissance in modern British artistic culture.[5]

Monnington left for Rome in January 1923. As part of his first-year studies he was required to copy a suitable work and in May he chose Titian's *Sacred and Profane Love* (Borghese Gallery, Rome) for this purpose. By August, however, he had changed his mind and sought the permission of the painting faculty to copy instead an early fifteenth-century painting by an anonymous artist of *The Entombment*, on display in the museum at Spoleto. Again, his predilection for the Quattrocento had made itself felt.

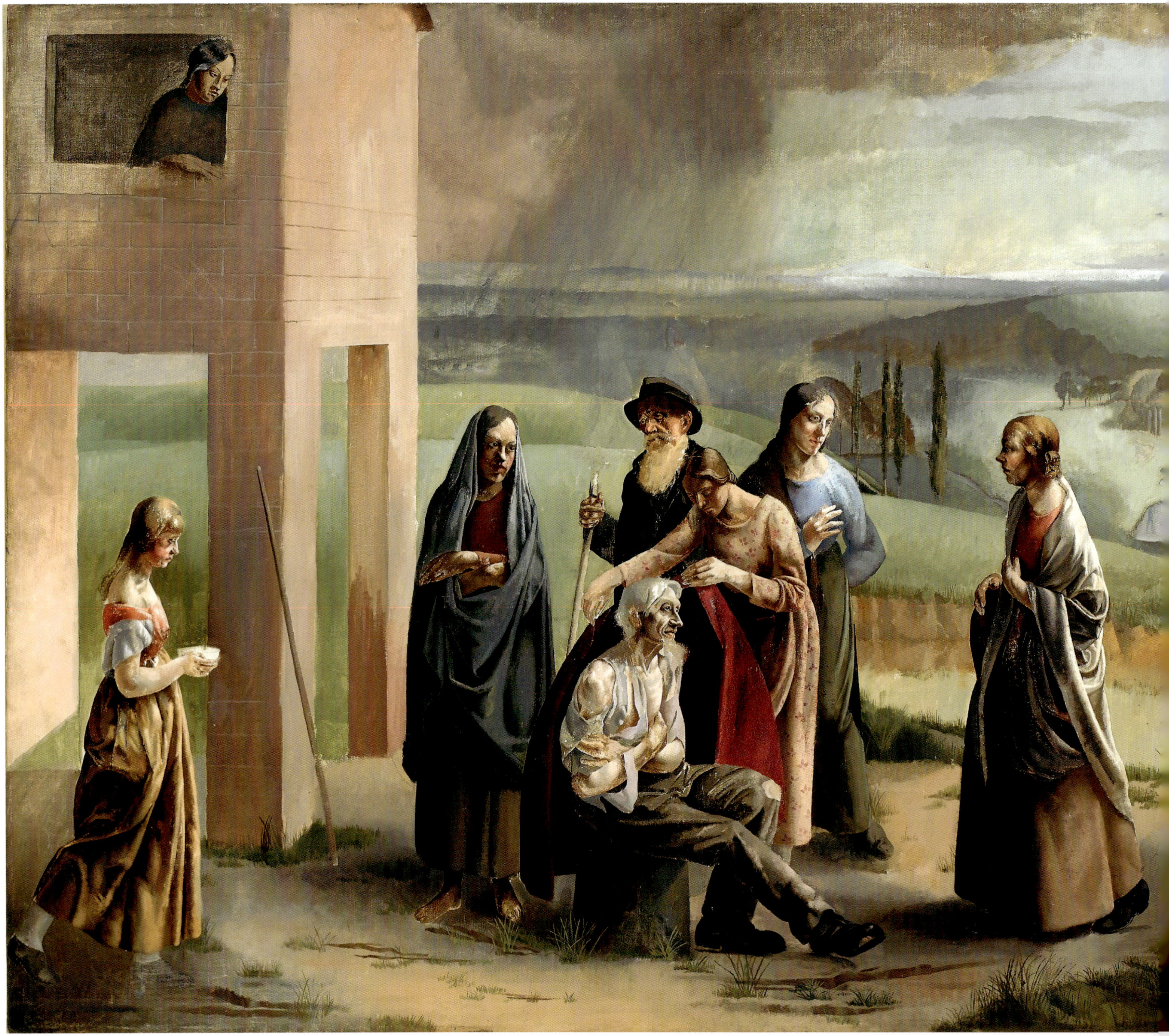

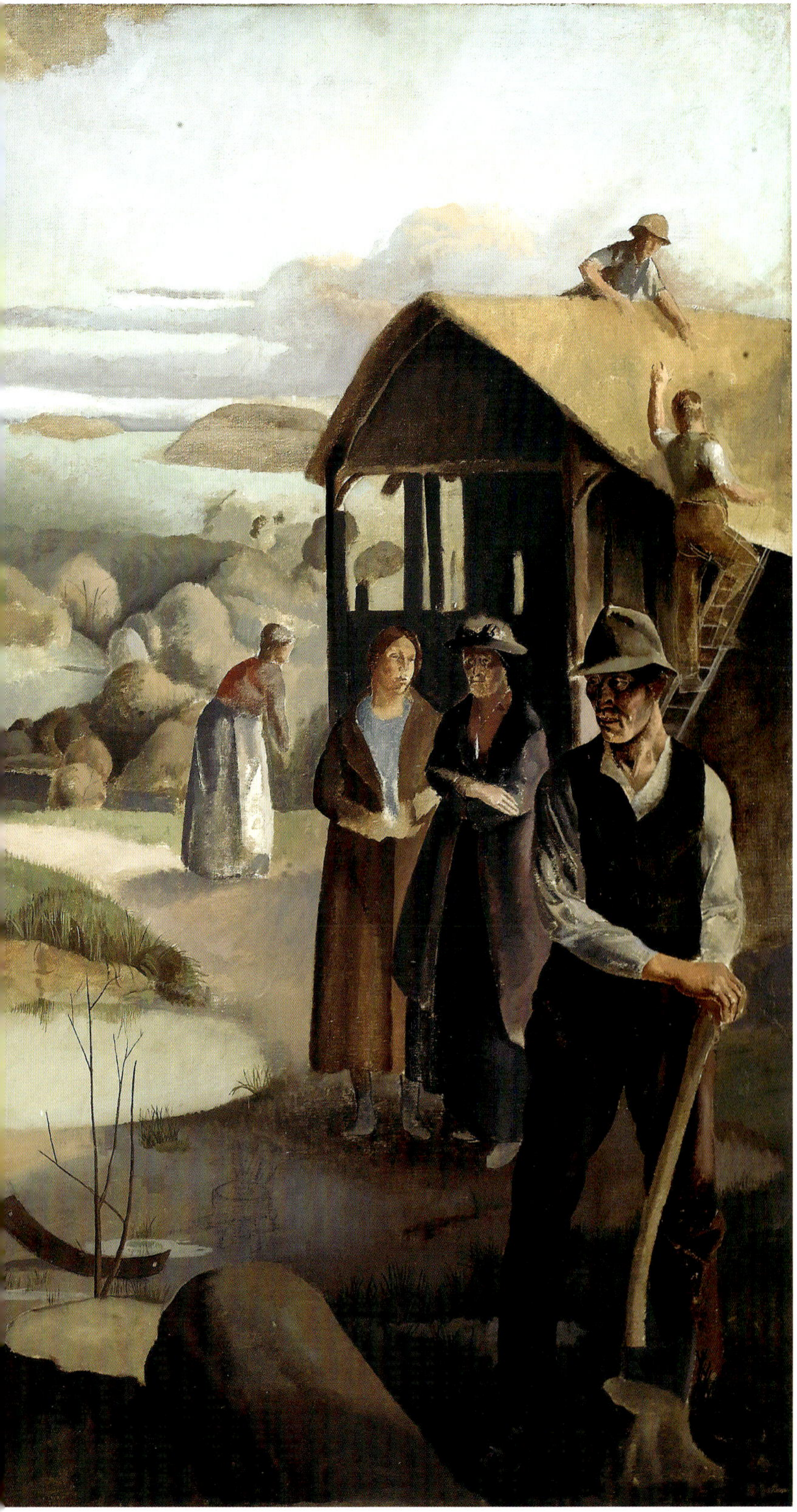

113
Winter, 1922
oil on canvas, 122 x 216 cm (48 x 85 in.)

The following spring he began work on the studies that would eventually be used for the painting now known as *Allegory*. An intensely personal project, closely bound up with his marriage in April to his fellow Rome Scholar, Winifred Knights, the studies and other preparations for this large work took up much of Monnington's time in 1924. When he applied for an extension of his scholarship later in that year, as was customary an outside assessment of his progress was required; Charles Ricketts and Charles Shannon, having seen his work at the School, supplied a very positive endorsement:

> ... the cartoon and studies he has made for a decorative picture are characterised by the utmost thoroughness and care, some of his pencil drawings of hands, feet, plant form etc being quite notable in their sense of finish and beauty. We both found him keenly alive to the merit of the masterpieces he had seen in Italy and alive to the technical practices of the masters.[6]

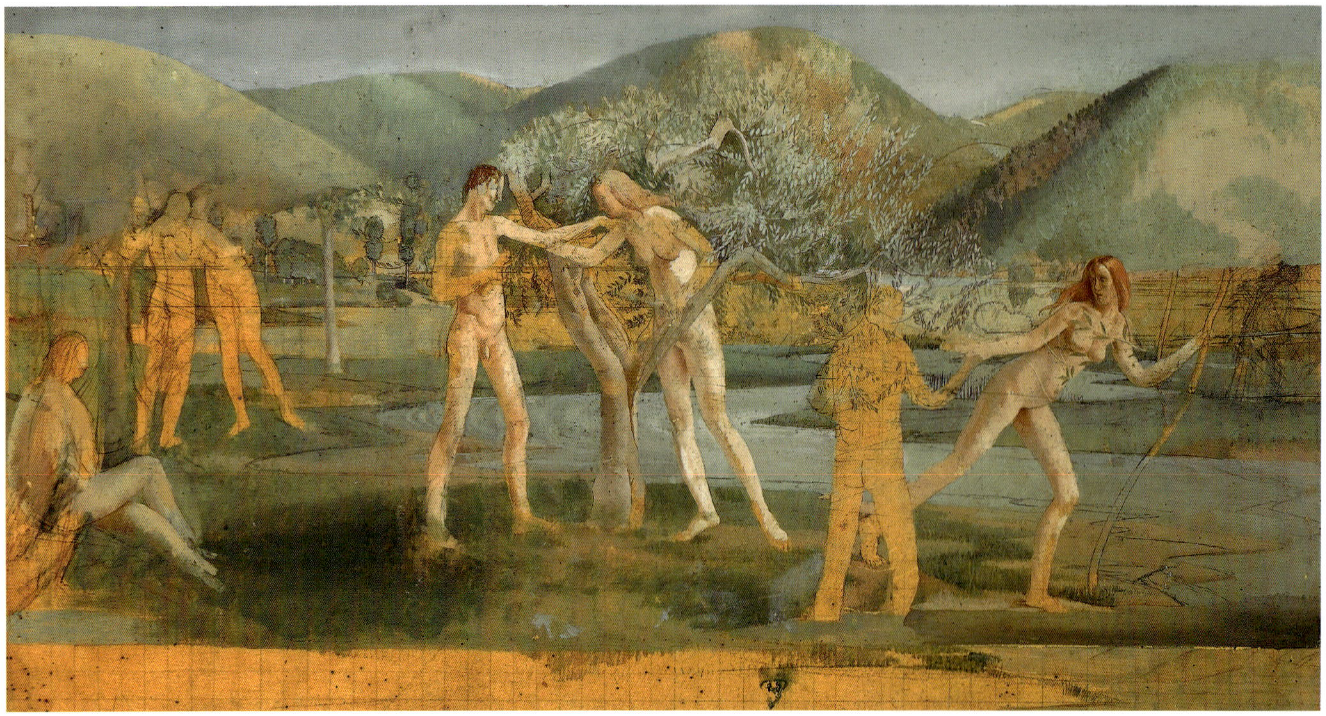

114
Study for *Allegory*, 1924
oil on tracing paper
laid on board,
squared for transfer,
31.7 x 57.2 cm
(12 ½ x 22 ½ in.)

The actual painting was executed from March to September 1925, although it was never completely finished. Something of the difficulties this work caused Monnington is captured in a letter he wrote to his brother, Meredith, in March 1925:

> Yesterday I began to paint my big picture, almost a year after I started the first sketches. I painted the sky, having spent the previous day from early morning to 6 p.m. mixing the paint. Today I am painting on the clouds. It requires considerable concentration since one dud stroke of the brush might necessitate repainting all the sky.[7]

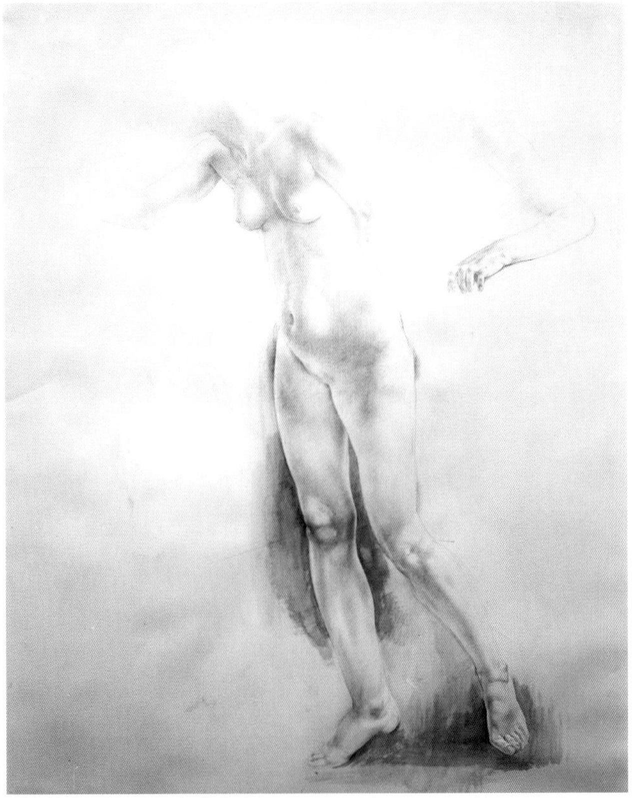

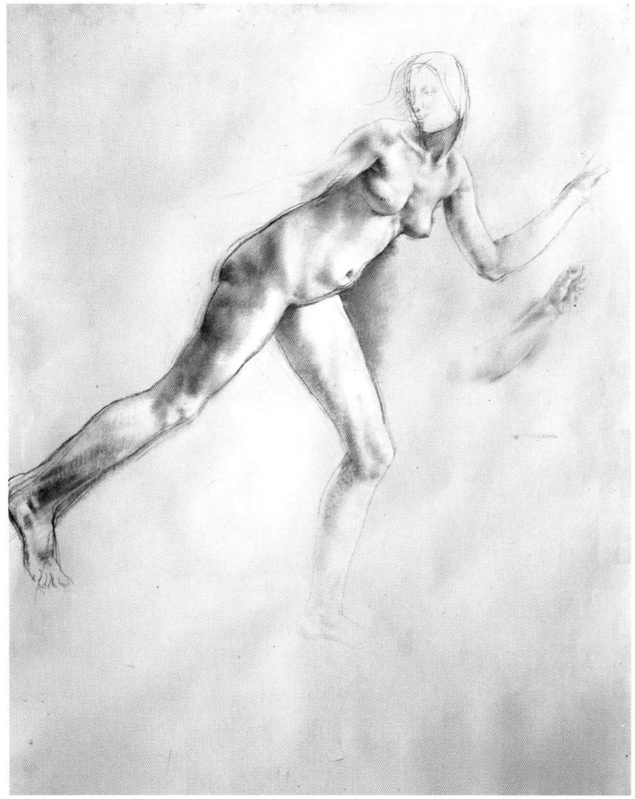

115 & 116
Two preparatory drawings for *Allegory*, photographed c. 1924, pencil on paper, whereabouts of drawings unknown

The picture was the most significant result of all the work he produced in Italy and was bought in Rome by Jim Ede for the Contemporary Art Society, the negotiations taking place in March 1925 while it was still not complete and indeed it was still unfinished when Monnington handed it over to the Society. It was presented to the Tate in 1939, the first of his works to enter the collection. Its current name is, in fact, inexact; Monnington had always referred to it simply as *Decoration* and the title of *Allegory* was given to it by the Tate in the 1950s, after they had requested Monnington to explain its subject and his answers had proved elusive.

As Monnington worked on it, the painting developed towards a timeless presentation, with the use of contemporary dress in some of the earlier studies quickly abandoned. Although he was guarded about its meaning, it is legitimate to think of the two figures as personifications of Monnington and Knights and the picture as a whole to represent their love for one another. The nakedness of the man and the woman is perhaps to be understood as both physical and spiritual, for this is a mystical painting which, as Monnington said, 'was an attempt to express in pictorial form my attitude to life – almost my faith.'[8] Iconographically, there are connotations of the Garden of Love, Adam and Eve in the Garden of Eden, Apollo and Daphne and even the Fountain of Youth and there are stylistic references to Botticelli and to Piero della Francesca, but the composition as a whole is much more than a pastiche of Quattrocento motifs and style.

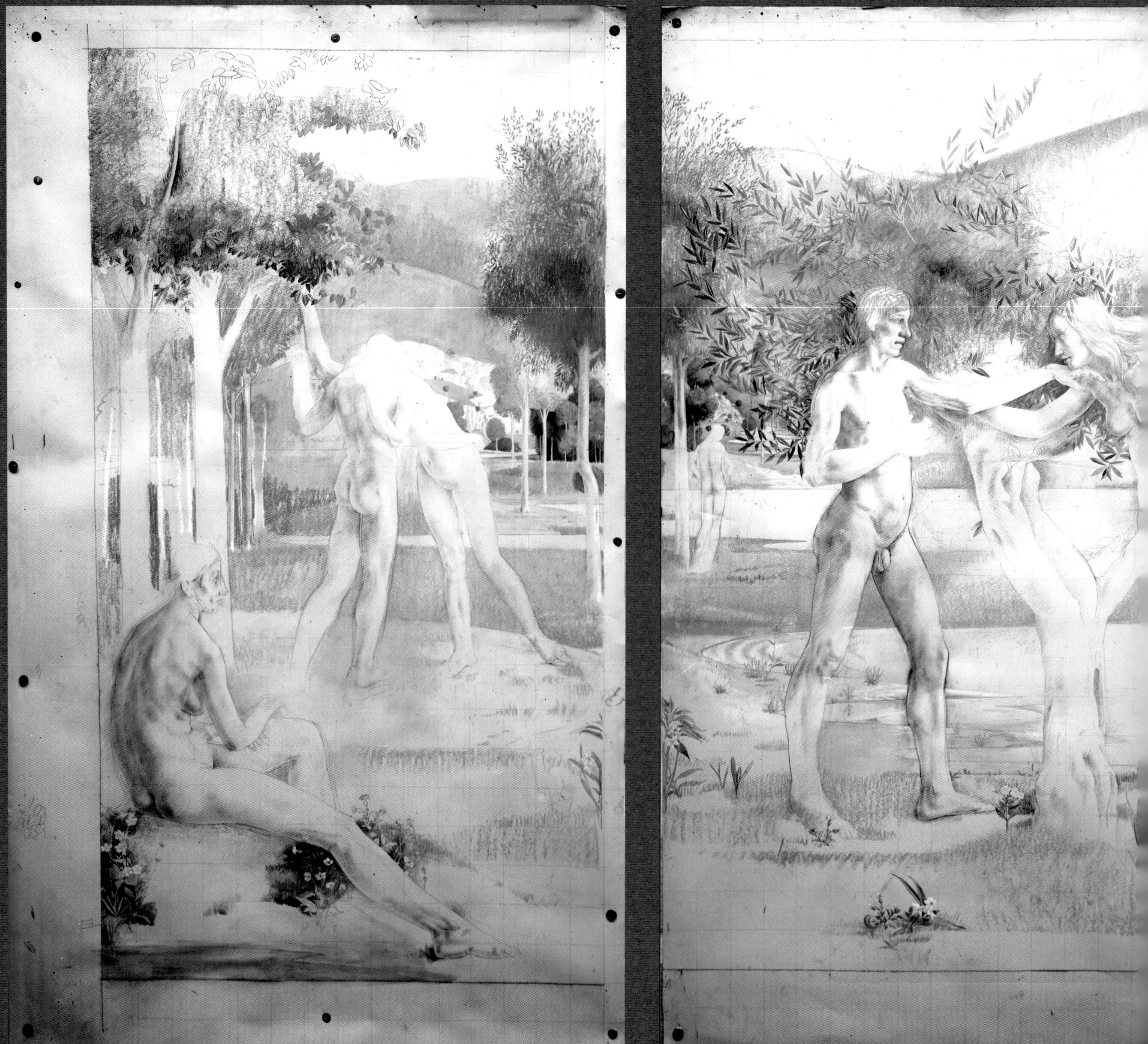

117 Cartoon for *Allegory*, most likely photographed in Monnington's studio c. 1924, pencil on paper, squared

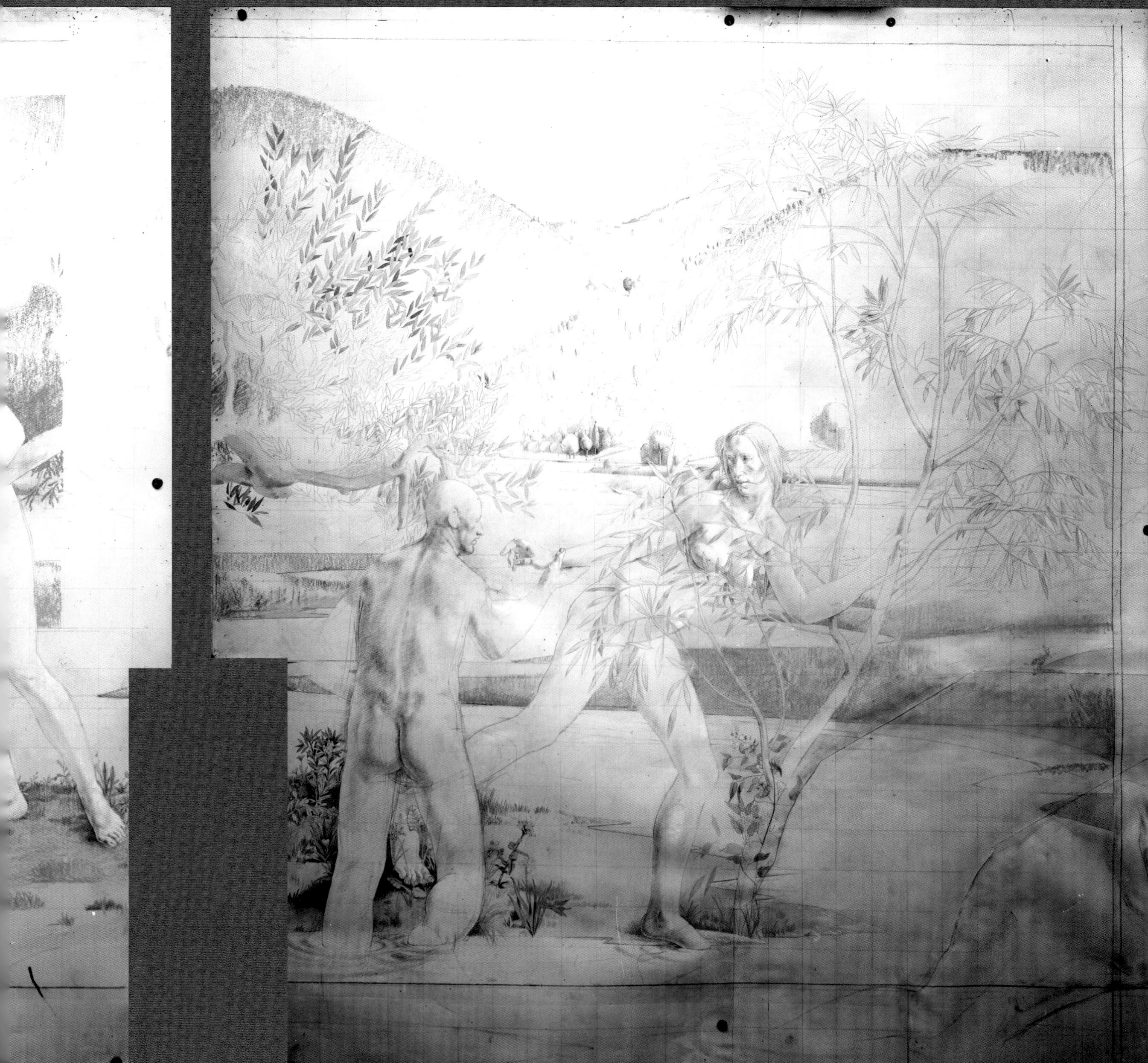

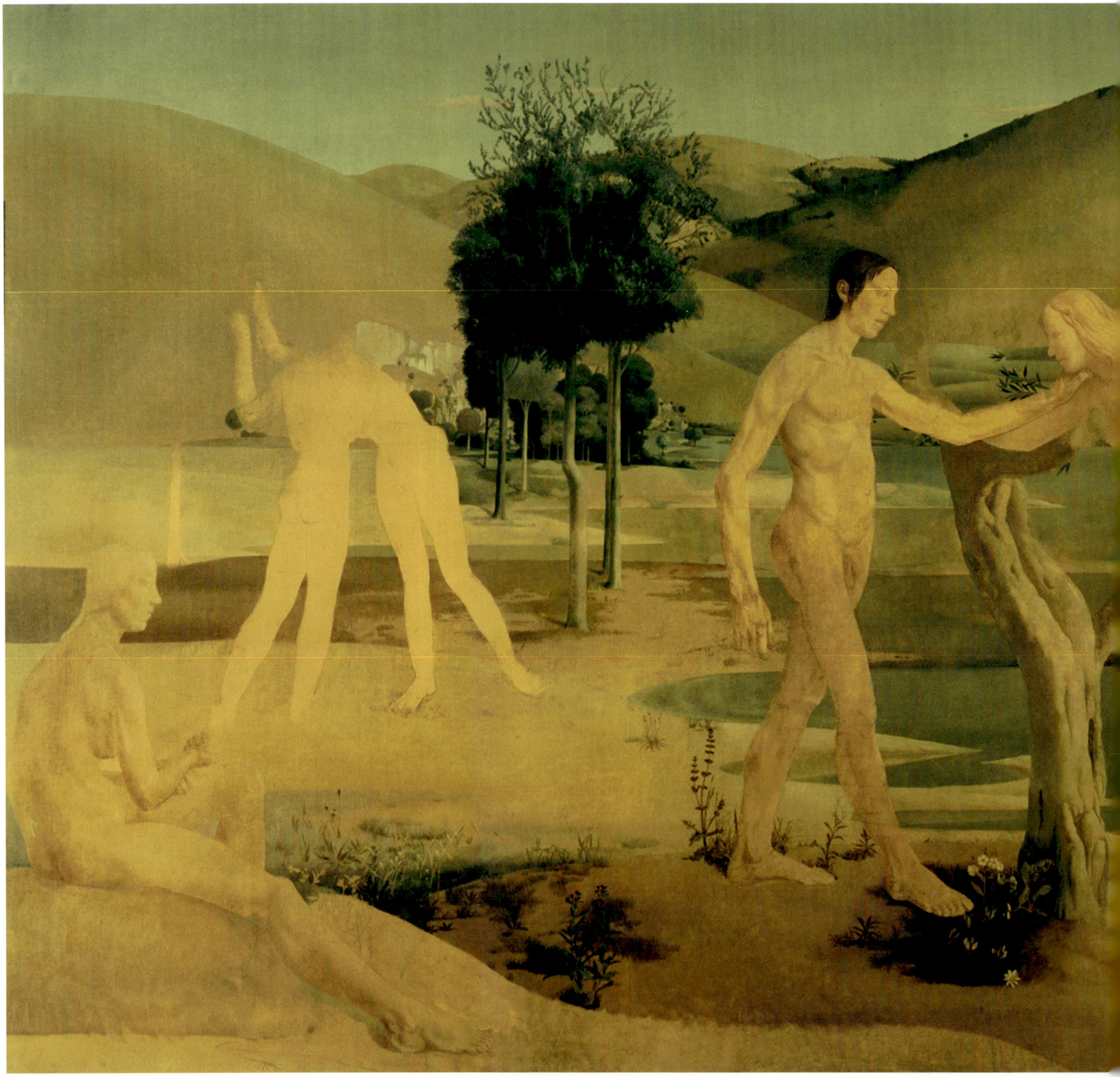

118 *Allegory*, c. 1924, egg tempera on canvas, 125.7 x 276.8 cm (49 ½ x 109 in.), © Tate, London 2012

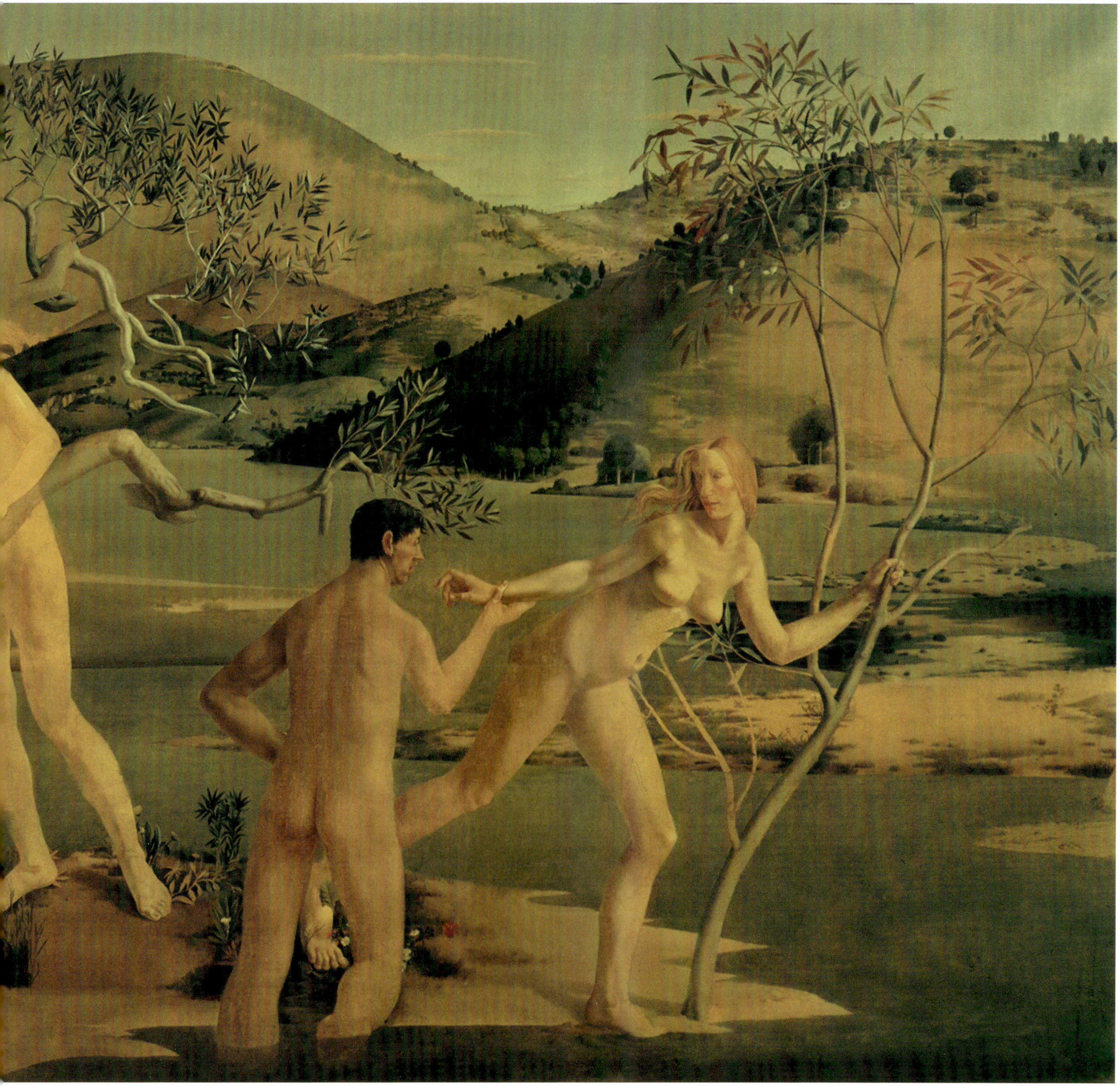

Another product of Monnington's studies in Italy was titled *Annunciation* when it was exhibited at the Royal Academy in March 1926.[9] This was presumably the picture he mentioned in December 1924 as 'another smaller picture, some work for which I have already done'[10] and which Jim Ede thought of inspecting the following March but noting 'as yet it is hardly begun.'[11] However, the subject of the *Annunciation* is not justified iconographically here. The woman on the right, whom we must assume is Mary, is clearly several months pregnant and the figure talking to her is depicted as a mature woman, rather than an ethereal angel. The composition of these two central figures bears a close relationship to a watercolour by Monnington now at Kettle's Yard, entitled *The Meeting of Anna and Mary.*[12] This title is probably erroneous, for the figures appear to be of similar ages, and the subject better represents the meeting of Elizabeth and Mary, a much more familiar narrative and widely treated in the history of art. It seems plausible to suggest that the picture exhibited in 1926 as *Annunciation* was also originally a treatment of the meeting of Elizabeth and Mary, when both were pregnant, Elizabeth with John the Baptist and Mary with Jesus. Monnington's work on the picture incorporated several changes of mind, as is clearly visible in the ghostly presence of other figures and the variations of narrative they imply. It may have been at a relatively late stage that he settled on *Annunciation* as its title.[13]

After his return to England in 1925 Monnington embarked on a professional career, including working as an art teacher at the Royal College of Art and then the Royal Academy and he also won commissions for portraits and large decorative schemes, such as St Stephen's Hall, Westminster (1926-27) and the Bank of England (1928-37).[14] The Bank of England designs, in particular, show how his subsequent work developed a more nuanced use of the lessons imparted by the balance and proportion of the Renaissance. After working as a war artist in the Second World War, some of Monnington's work in the 1950s began to incorporate complex geometric compositions, entirely non-figurative but alluding to the forces of nature at both micro and macro levels (the movement of waves and particles as well as the movement of the planets). Here too, however, the inspiration of the Renaissance can be detected in the idea that the systematic and rational exploration of the physical world finds its corollary in the disciplined control of pictorial space.

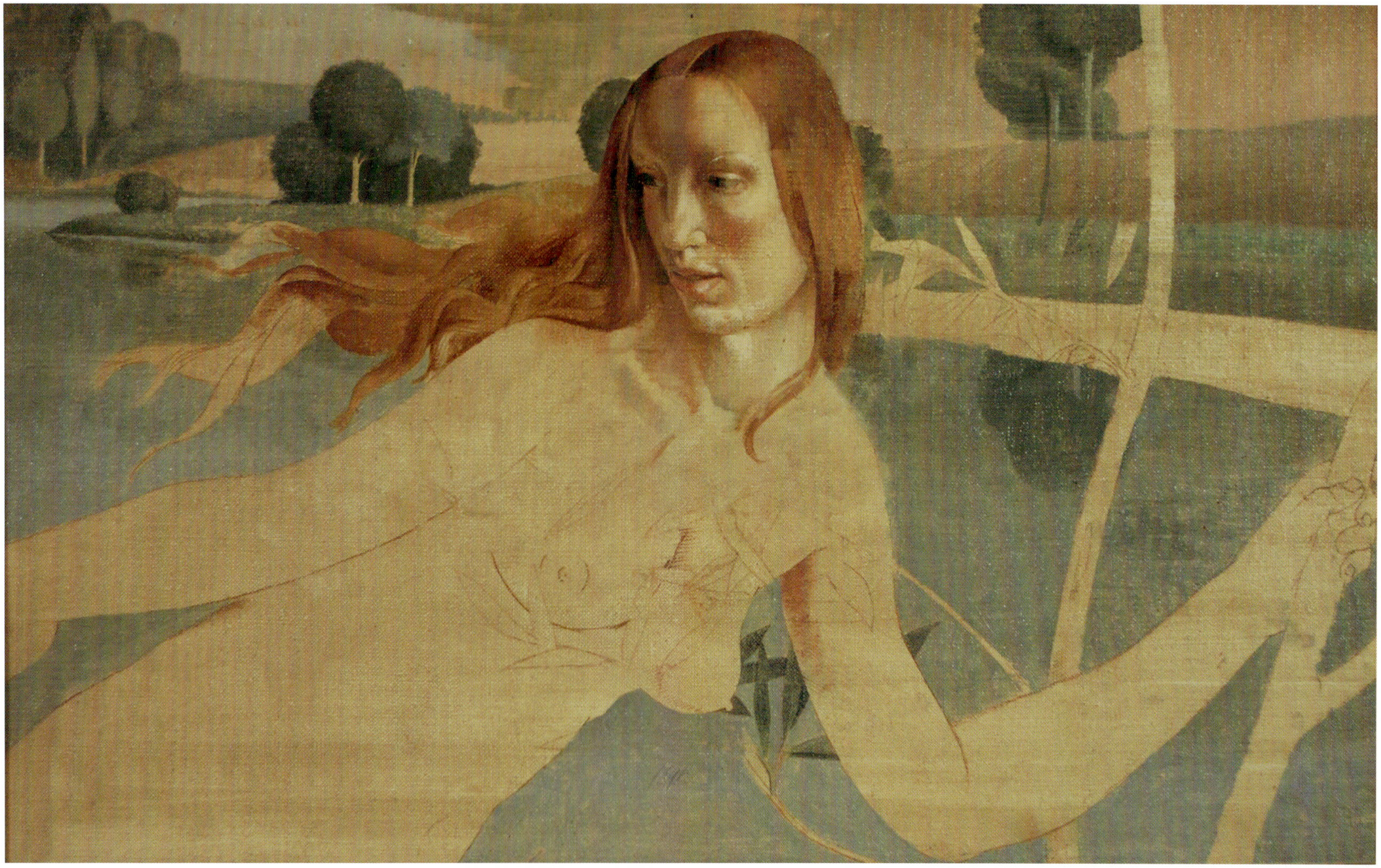

119 Study for *Allegory*, c. 1925, oil on canvas, 28 x 48.2 cm (11 x 19 in.)

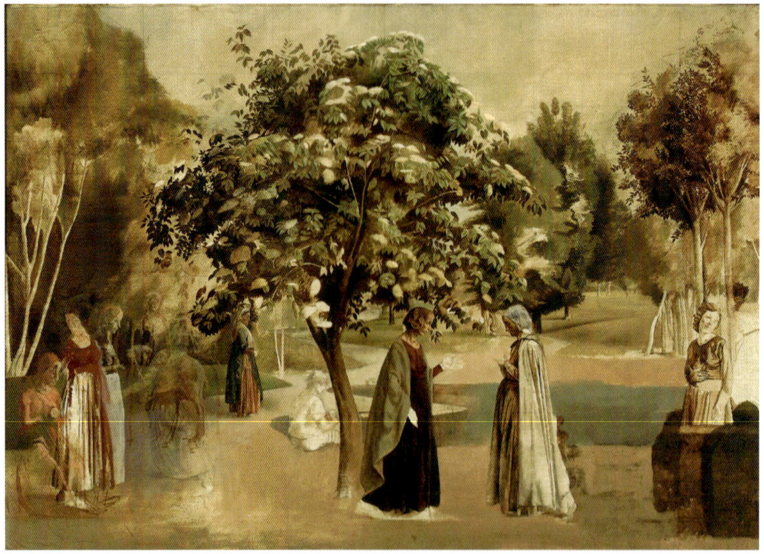

120
Annunciation, c. 1924-25 oil on canvas,
99 x 145 cm (39 x 57 in.)

ENDNOTES

1 The British School at Rome archive reveals that the full scholarship was withheld in 1922 and Monnington received initially a lesser award. He was awarded the full scholarship (backdated) on January 11, 1924. My thanks to Sacha Llewellyn for allowing me to make use of her BSR archive notes throughout this essay.

2 See David Boyd Haycock '"A Crisis of Brilliance": C.R.W. Nevinson, Henry Tonks, and the Slade School of Art, 1909-12' in Michael J.K. Walsh (ed.) *A Dilemma of English Modernism: Visual and Verbal Politics in the Life and Work of C.R.W. Nevinson (1889-1946)*, Newark: University of Delaware Press, 2007, pp.36-46.

3 See Hayden B.J. Maginnis 'Reflections on Formalism: the Post-Impressionists and the Early Italians,' *Art History*, vol. 19, no. 2, June 1996, pp. 191-207.

4 Cited in Andrew Causey 'Wadsworth in the early Twenties' in Jeremy Lewison (ed.) *A Genius of Industrial England: Edward Wadsworth, 1889-1949*, London: Arkwright Arts Trust, 1990, p.42.

5 *The Observer*, February 22, 1923.

6 BSR archive. Letter dated December 22, 1924.

7 Letter dated March 5, 1925. Private Collection.

8 Letter April 2, 1957. Tate Gallery Archive.

9 'Exhibition of Works Submitted in the Preliminary Competitions for the Rome Scholarship of 1926, together with Some Examples of the Work of Rome Scholars', Royal Academy, March 1926. The painting was then in the collection of Mr Leverton Harris.

10 Monnington's report on his activities, December 23, 1924. BSR archive.

11 Ede letter, dated March 23, 1925. BSR archive.

12 Undated. Kettle's Yard, Reserve Collection, TM1; watercolour and gouache on paper, 266 x 218 mm. There is no surviving evidence to show when this drawing entered Ede's collection, but it is conceivable that he bought it from Monnington in 1925.

13 Monnington used the title *Annunciation* to describe this painting when proposing works to include in the Royal Academy exhibition. Hand-written list, dated January 27, 1926. BSR archives.

14 For St Stephen's Hall see Alan Powers 'History in Paint: The Twentieth-Century Murals', *Apollo*, Vol CXXXV : No 363 , May 1992, pp.317-21.

121
Annunciation
(detail)

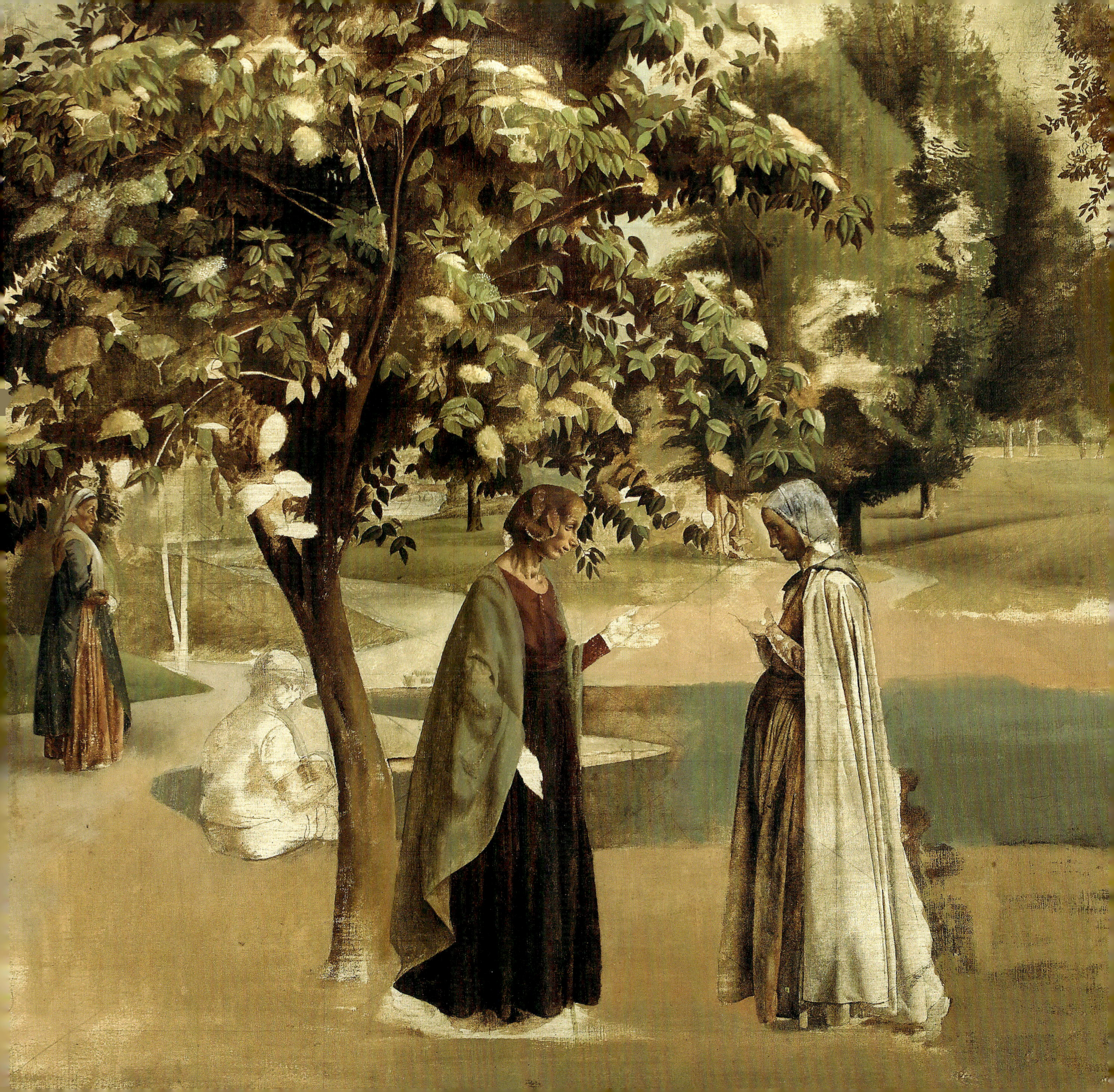

MURALS AND DECORATIVE PAINTINGS BY THOMAS MONNINGTON

1920 – *The Farm Stead*, oil on canvas, 122 x 91.4 cm (48 x 36 in.), Woverhampton Art Gallery and Museum

1922 – *Winter*, oil on canvas, 122 x 216 cm (48 x 85 in.), winning submission for the British School at Rome Scholarship in Decorative Painting, private collection

1923 – *The Wine Press*, oil on canvas, 101.6 x 151.1 cm (40 x 59 ½ in.), commissioned by Lord Balniel (later Earl of Crawford and Balcarres), private collection

1924 – *Allegory*, oil on canvas, 125.7 x 276.9 cm (49 ½ x 109 in.), purchased by Jim Ede for the Contemporary Art Society, before it was completed, and presented to the Tate Gallery in 1939
The Annunciation, oil on canvas, 99 x 114.8 cm (39 x 57 in.), private collection

1925 – *The English and Scottish Commissioners present to Queen Anne at St James Palace the Articles of the Agreement for the Parliamentary Union of the two Countries*, oil on canvas, 274.3 x 457.2 cm (9 x 15 ft.) St Stephen's Hall, Westminster, work began January 1926, unveiled June 27, 1927, still unfinished

1928 – Commissioned by Bank of England:
A Director Announcing the Bank Rate to the Chief Officials, exhibited RA 1932
The Doorkeeper Receiving a Message in the Entrance to the Parlours, oil on canvas, 233.7 x 132 cm (92 x 52 in.)
St Luke's Printing Works, completed in October 1937

1931 – *Summer at Emmaus*, oil on canvas, 53.3 x 190.5 cm (21 x 75 in.), Ormrod Chapel, Bolton

1939 – Altar piece for Church House

1953-56 – Ceiling of Conference Hall, new Council House, Bristol, tempera on fiberglass panels, 28.95 x 13.71 m (95 x 45 ft.)

1956 – Ceiling of Mary Harris Memorial Chapel, Exeter, acrylic on cedar, 34.13 x 8.53 m (112 x 28 ft.)
Stations of the Cross, Brede Parish Church

1960 – *Clematis*, acrylic on board, 130.1 x 92 cm (51 ¼ x 36 ¼ in.), private collection

1964 – Edwin Austin Abbey Trust for Mural Painting in Great Britain commission two murals for the University of London Students' Union mural, polyvinyl acetate on panel, 243.8 x 609 cm (8 x 20 ft.)

1966 – Design for the main staircase of The British Museum, never executed

1967 – *Square Design*, acquired by Tate

1968 – *Design on Root Five*, Towner Art Gallery

1969 – Second mural for University of London's Students' Union, acrylic on board, 274.3 x 182.9 cm (9 x 6 ft.)

1970 – *Reciprocity*, tempera on board, 91.4 x 132 cm (36 x 52 in.), private collection

Thomas Monnington (1902-1976)

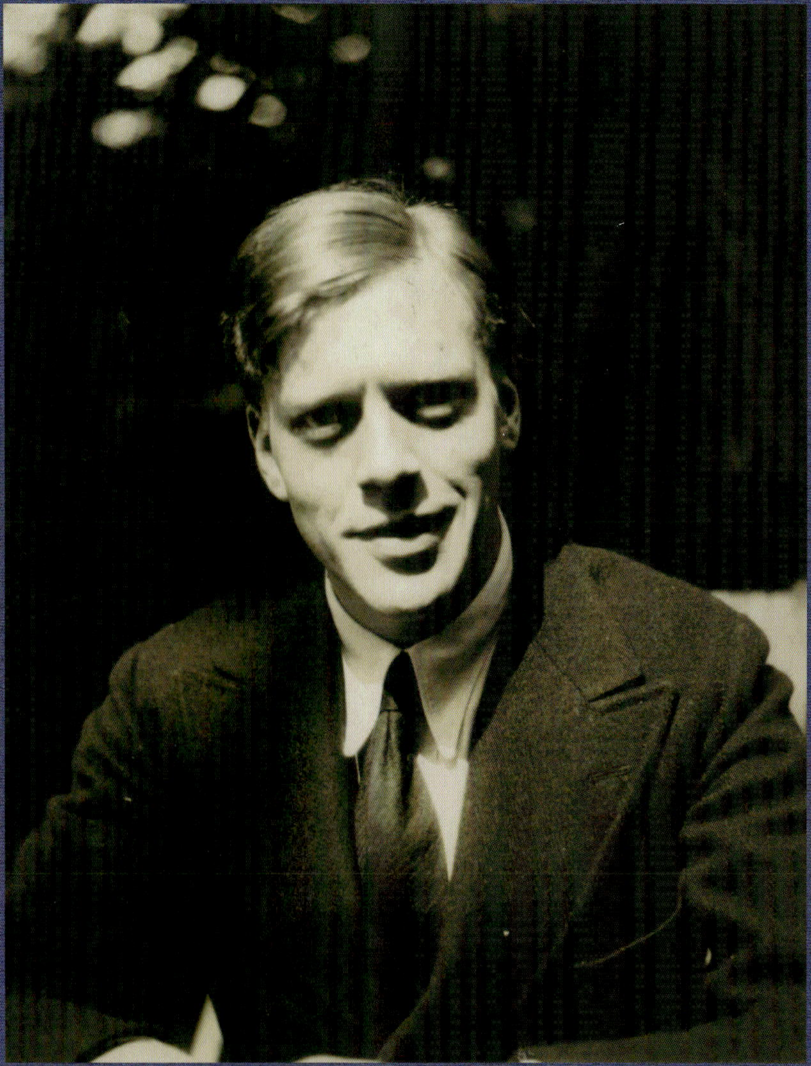

122 Thomas Monnington

SIR (WALTER) THOMAS MONNINGTON, PRA. Born London, died ? Painter and muralist. Studied Hassall's Drawing School, entered Slade School, London University age fifteen (1918-22), Rome Scholarship, British School at Rome (1923-25). Married Winifred Knights (qv) (1924). Appointed first Assistant Teacher of Painting at R.A. Schools (1931). Design team of the Civil Defence Camouflage Establishment, Leamington Spa (1939-43), Official War Artist 1943, spent winter of 1944 in Holland. Taught at Camberwell School of Art (1945-49), the Slade (1949-67). Elected P.R.A. 1966, Knighted 1967. Principal museum collections: Imperial War Museum; British Museum; Tate Gallery; University College; London; Royal Academy of Arts; Kettle's Yard, Cambridge; Wolverhampton Art Gallery.

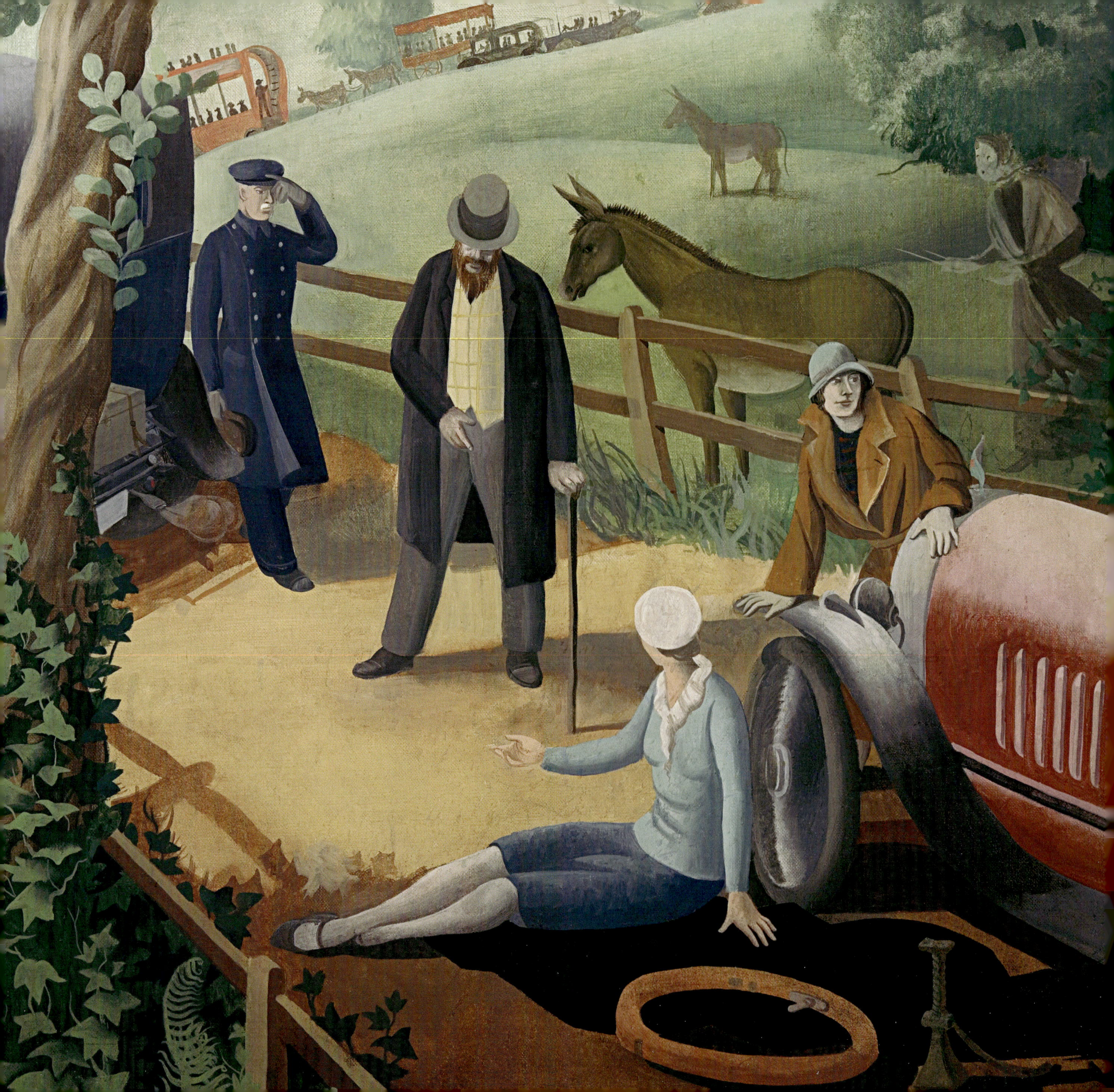

Mary Adshead
An English Holiday, 1928

Ann Compton

The Puncture and *Village Inn* are two of the eleven panels that make up *An English Holiday*. Today this is widely considered one of Mary Adshead's most engaging and important mural schemes but for many years more than half the paintings were thought to have been lost or destroyed. It was only in 2006 when *The Puncture* and *Village Inn* with four other panels turned up at auction that the ambition and importance of the work could be fully reassessed.[1] This happy conclusion to a checkered history makes a curiously fitting sequel to the events surrounding the mural's creation.

An English Holiday was commissioned by the press baron William Maxwell Aitken, first Lord Beaverbrook in early February 1928 to decorate a house he had recently acquired in Newmarket.[2] Each panel is a delightful, fully realized composition in its own right and collectively the mural depicts Beaverbrook's friends 'Going to the Races'.[3] Fitting the racecourse theme, many of the figures are on horseback or travelling in horse-drawn vehicles, whilst dashing touches are added by Winston Churchill arriving on an elephant and Lord and Lady Birkenhead yachting at sea. The overall effect is a seamless blend of historical fantasy and modern life, affirming Adshead's ability to 'treat the present as if it were a period, and make a telephone look sprightly'.[4]

In a surprising turn of events, Beaverbrook rejected the panels 'sight unseen' when they were close to completion in early August 1928 and cut Adshead's fee from £400 to £250.[5] His close friend Lady Diana Cooper is said to have told him to reject the paintings on the basis that they would cause quarrels amongst his friends.[6] At first sight this decision appears a puzzling, even slightly malicious, response to a charming and well-realised composition. Yet if we look in more detail at the lives of the people represented in the paintings and reconsider their connections to Adshead's patron, other readings of *An English Holiday* begin to emerge. These complex undercurrents are hinted at in *Newmarket Fair*, the panel featuring Beaverbrook. Here the newspaper magnate watches his employee at the *Sunday Express*, Lord Castlerosse, as he strikes a hammer at one of the sideshows. This testing of his strength makes play on the latter's position as the author of the first signed society column.[7] Readers of this 'Londoner's Log' would probably have been aware that Beaverbrook's circle of friends were a lively source of gossip and consequently understood that *An English Holiday*, far from being a straightforward and profitable commission, was something of a poisoned chalice.

123
An English Holiday – The Puncture, 1928
(detail)

It is unclear how far Adshead recognized the possible pitfalls of the project because some key decisions were made at meetings and only the correspondence in Beaverbrook's archive survives.[8] What these letters do reveal

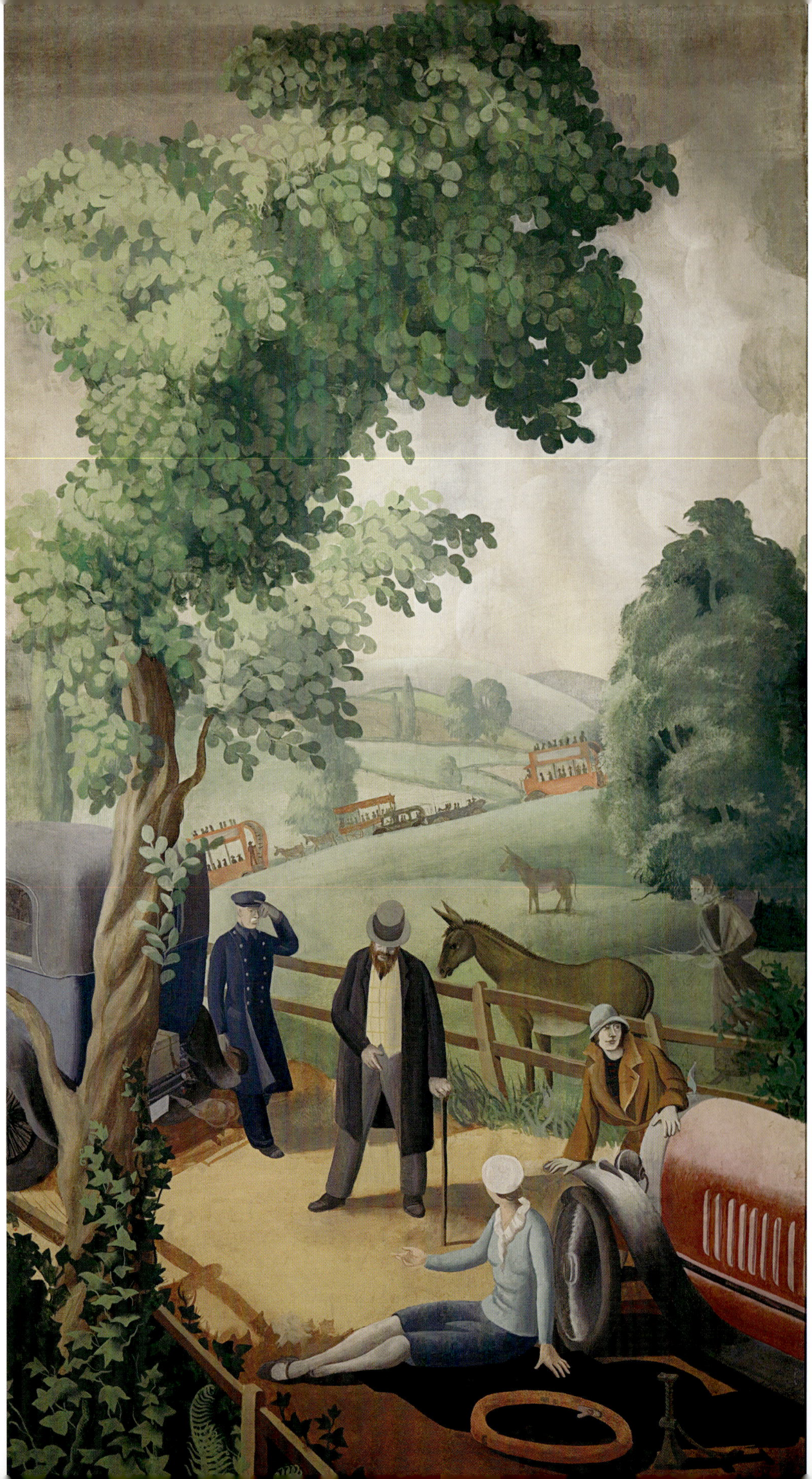

124
An English Holiday – The Puncture, 1928
signed lower left
oil on canvas, 217 × 121.5 cm (85 × 47 in.)

Exhibited: 'An English Holiday', Peter Jones department store, London,1930
Literature: M.H.Clough and A.Compton (eds), *Earthly Delights: Mary Adshead 1904-1995*, exhibition catalogue, University of Liverpool Art Gallery, 2005

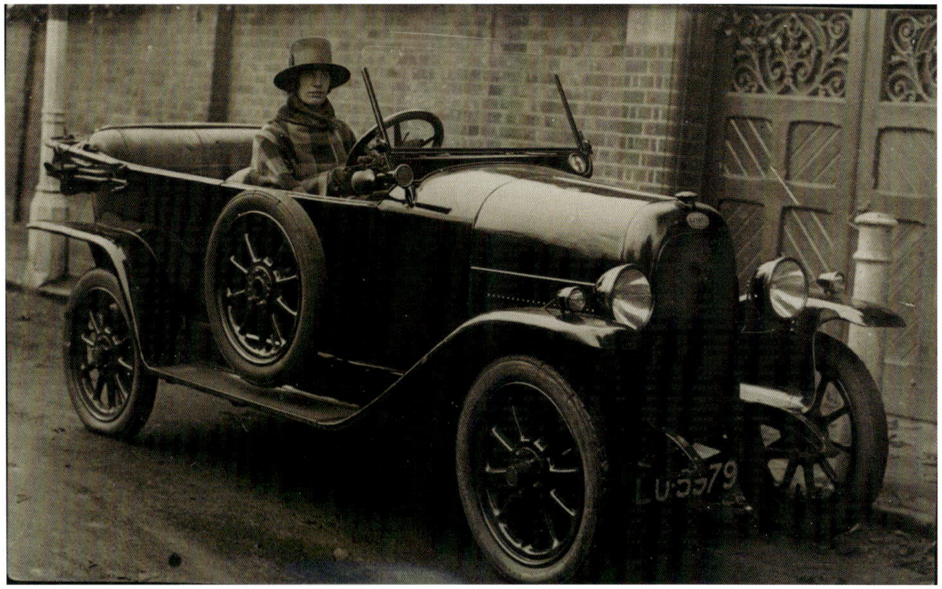

125
Mary Adshead in her first car, a Fiat 10HP

is that she approached the commission with a mixture of confidence, diplomacy and her characteristic 'cheerful up to date humour'.[9] Adshead selected the theme of 'Going to the Races' as well as devising many, if not all, of the 'amusing episodes'.[10] There is no sign in the correspondence that she objected to her patron determining precisely which people were to be represented in the paintings and how they were to be disposed across the panels. Perhaps Adshead made the reasonable assumption that because the subjects led colourful, high-profile lives, they would not object to a little teasing in the private setting of a friend's dining room.

In any case, some of the panels were not likely to cause any discomfort, as the subjects and settings were completely neutral. Amongst these is the *Village Inn*, which is simply a charming portrayal of a covered cart departing for the races with a pair of country lovers courting in the foreground. Other episodes made only very gentle fun of Beaverbrook's friends. *The Puncture*, for example, features Countess Edwina Mountbatten (1901-60) wife of Lord Louis Mountbatten (1900-79).[11] The innocent joke in Adshead's painting seems to be that this intrepid globetrotter has finally been halted in an English country lane by a punctured tyre. In *Gypsies on the Road to Newmarket*, the novelist and critic, Arnold Bennett plays a harmonium accompanied by a violinist whilst another man passes round the hat.[12] This musical recasting may refer to *Don Juan de Marana*, the opera Bennett and the composer, Eugene Goossens (1893-1962) published in 1923. A less flattering possibility is that portraying Bennett as a busker is a roundabout reference to the author's well-known commercial approach to his craft.

Other panels are more obviously open to uncomplimentary interpretations and may have caused Adshead to wonder how they would be received. One such is the painterly slap-stick in *Stable Yard* which shows Beaverbrook's childhood friend and international financier, Sir James Dunn, clumsily falling off his horse under the watchful eye of the wife of a highly successful English stockbroker, Mrs Norman Holden. In *Running Away From the Fair* the notorious womanizer Major 'Scatters' Wilson (Lieutenant-Colonel Sir Mathew Wilson) gallops off with the Spanish actress and singer, Raquel Miller. This echoes Wilson's real-life extra-marital affair with the heiress Lady Grace Curzon, whose considerable fortune they jointly squandered in the late 1920s, apparently much of it lost at the races. *The Winners' Enclosure* flatters Lord Derby whose horse Colorado had won the 2000 guineas (the principal Newmarket race) in 1926 but taunts another leading light of the Conservative party.[13] This is Reginald McKenna who is depicted being consoled by his wife after losing all his money at the races. The joke was unflattering given that McKenna was Chairman of the Midland Bank and a former Chancellor of the Exchequer who still nursed significant political ambitions.

We do not know what precise arguments Lady Diana Cooper used to persuade Beaverbrook that these imagined escapades might cause offence. One disinterested possibility is that she suggested *An English Holiday* was not in keeping with the ambitious political schemes the press baron was hatching in 1928. The following year he launched the Commonwealth Free Trade party in direct opposition to Stanley Baldwin, leader of the Conservative party. In the event, Beaverbrook's challenge was short-lived. Baldwin hit back, successfully fielding Duff Cooper (husband of Lady Diana Cooper) against Beaverbrook's candidate in the Westminster by-election of March 1931, effectively quashing the aspirations of the new party. But in 1928 it may have looked unwise or un-statesmanlike to have a mural scheme that celebrated scandal and ridiculed fellow political figures adorning his dining-room walls.[14]

Yet Beaverbrook does not seem to have been unduly concerned by social, or even political, niceties. A small but telling sign of this was a darkly humorous conjoining of puritan sensibility and racetrack fast living signalled by renaming his house at Newmarket, Calvin House.[15] It seems more likely that Beaverbrook was made to understand that he had offended Lady Diana Cooper by commissioning Adshead to paint a *Wayside Picnic* in which she appears with his mistress, Mrs Richard (Jean) Norton. The latter was Beaverbrook's lover from 1925 and, apparently, strongly disliked by Lady Diana Cooper. The rivalry between these women, and Beaverbrook's insensitivity to these tensions, was probably the reason *An English Holiday* was turned down.[16]

Intriguingly, rejecting the paintings was enough for Beaverbrook. He did not also prevent Adshead from exhibiting the murals. So the panels were shown as a group at the Peter Jones Department store in 1930. In retrospect this public, popular and leisure-driven venue presents a more fitting environment than a wealthy entrepreneur's dining room in Newmarket for Adshead's pictures. She had already completed a project for the Highways Boys' Club, Shadwell (1924) and two large works for Bank underground station (1925). From the early 1930s commercial or civic buildings provided the principal setting for Adshead's murals. By locating her work in these kinds of publicly accessible spaces, her painting acquired a level of social engagement between artist and public, or 'usefulness', which was considered a desirable dimension of art production around this time. Adshead may also have found civic and commercial buildings and the patrons who administered such commissions more sympathetic than autocratic business tycoons like Beaverbrook. Certainly public housing schemes and town planning were the milieu she was familiar with through the work of her father, Professor Stanley Adshead (1868-1946). He was an architect, town planner and university teacher who designed several housing projects, including landmark schemes in Kennington, Redcar and Stepney.[17] Creating murals for more obviously democratic spaces than the homes of wealthy individuals may also have fitted Adshead's burgeoning political tendencies. As the thirties advanced she would lean increasingly towards the left. In 1934 she joined the Artists International Association and together with her husband, the painter Stephen Bone (1904-58) and father-in-law the engraver Sir Muirhead Bone (1876-1953), Adshead campaigned against fascism and assisted in the resettling of European refugees.[18]

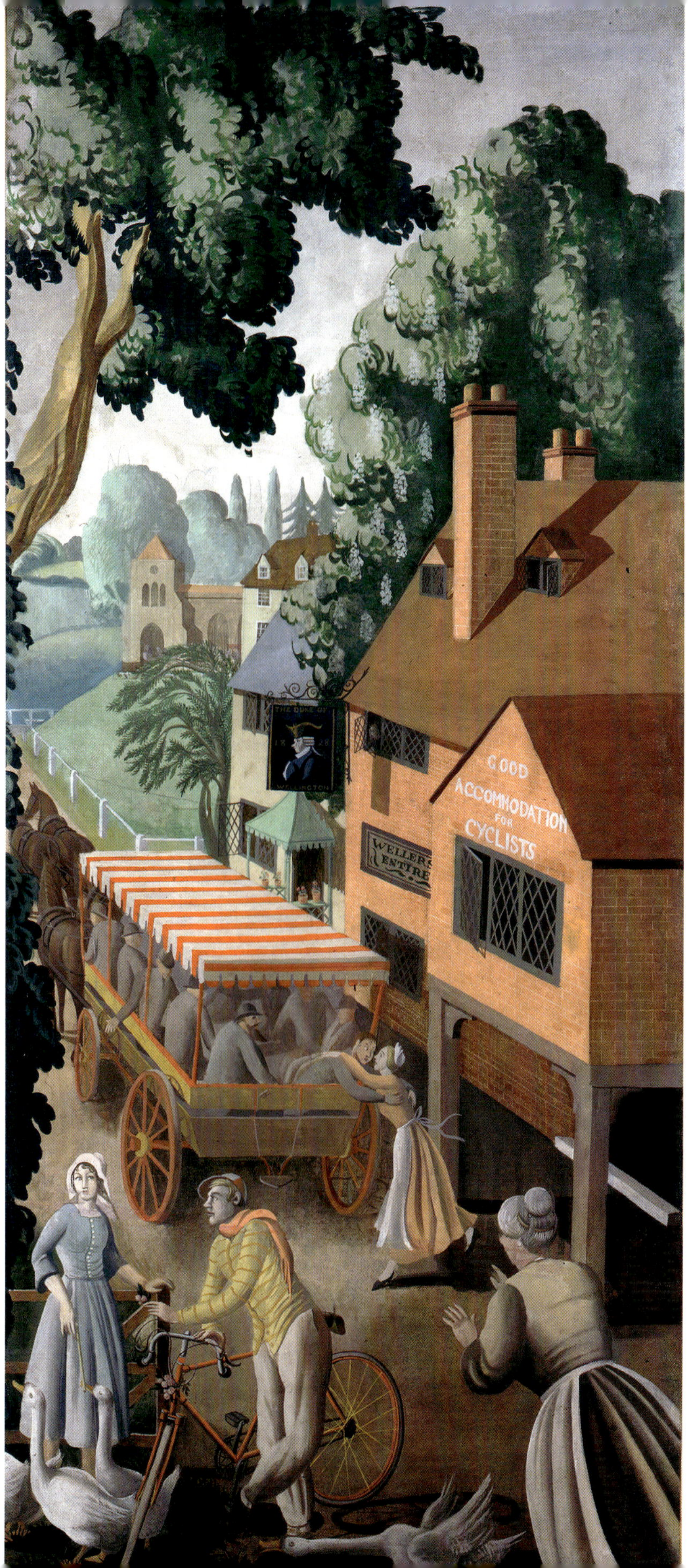

126
An English Holiday – Village Inn, 1928
signed lower left
oil on canvas, 217 x 96.5 cm (85 ½ x 38 in.)

Exhibited:
'An English Holiday', Peter Jones department store, London, 1930
Literature:
M.H.Clough & A.Compton (ed), *Earthly Delights: Mary Adshead 1904-1995*, exhibition catalogue, University of Liverpool Art Gallery, 2005

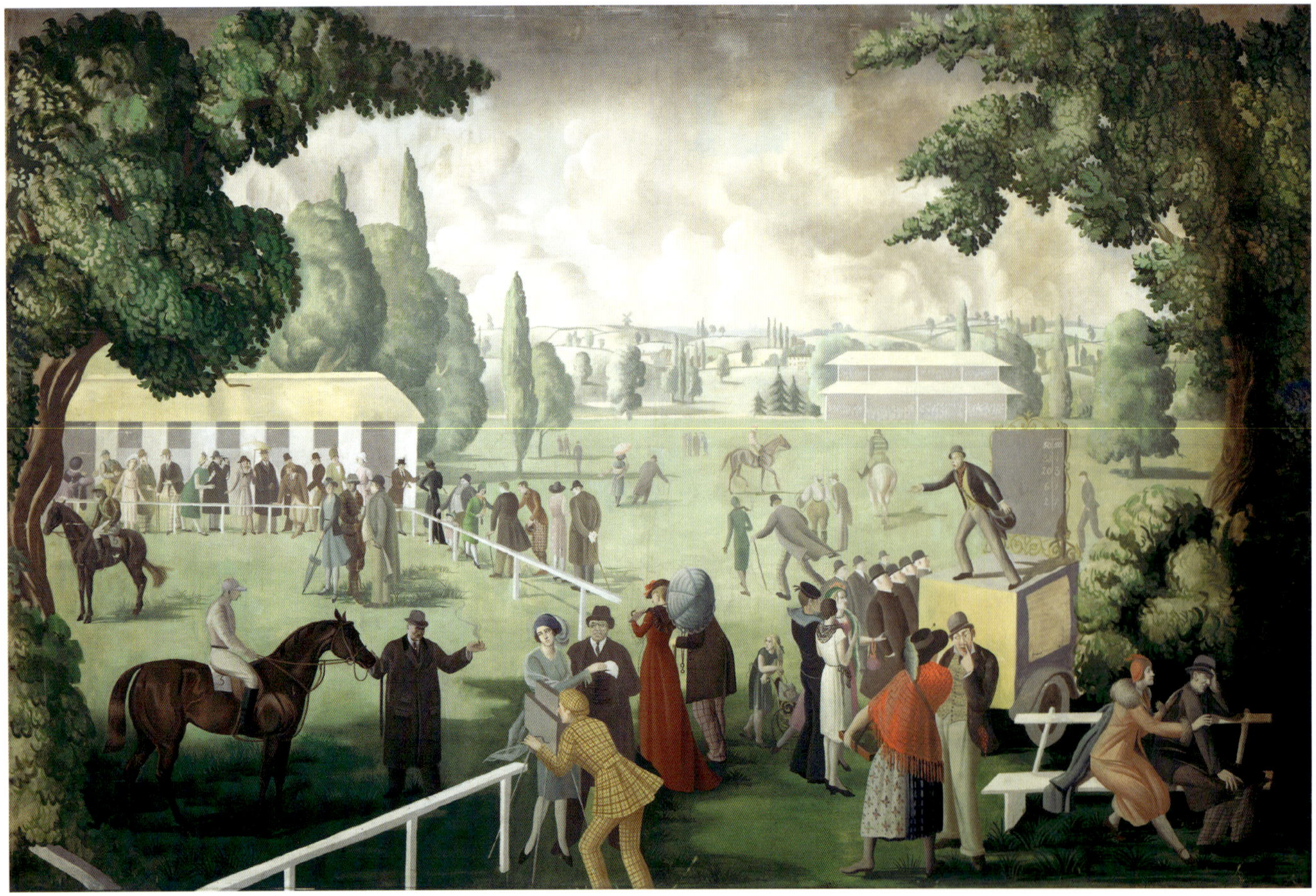

127
An English Holiday – The Winners' Enclosure, 1928
oil on canvas,
216 x 326 cm (85 x 128 ⅜ in.)

Yet in August 1928, the rejection of *An English Holiday* must have come as a blow to the young artist who had left the Slade only four years earlier. The reception of Adshead's murals sharply contrasted with the immediate acclaim given to Rex Whistler's *Expedition in Pursuit of Rare Meats* for Tate restaurant (1926-7). Their names were linked because of being contemporaries at the Slade and both receiving commissions for the Highways Boys' Club in 1924. Viewed in terms of financial remuneration, Adshead's commission from Beaverbrook was potentially more profitable than Whistler's mural for Tate.[19] Yet the inevitable comparison of theme between the race-goers' and gourmets' journeys, has often led to the conclusion that Adshead was the junior artist and that she was influenced by Whistler's skilful updating of the fête champêtre idiom. Whilst it is easy to imagine the two Slade students visiting the Wallace Collection to study works like Jean-Honoré Fragonard's *Le Petit Parc* (c.1762-3) and *The Swing* (1767), their practices followed different trajectories from an early stage. For Whistler the landscape and the creation of an Arcadia were always central preoccupations. In contrast, Adshead focused on the human presence – their bodies, emotions and actions were her over-riding interest. Whilst people might be shown, as in *An English Holiday*, behaving well or badly, primly or improperly, the accent remains the figures, not the pastoral setting. Indeed, her work embodies one of her former teacher, Henry Tonks' favourite dictums: 'Human beings, though lovely, must still have backbones secreted under their clothes…the artist enjoys all the fripperies of life, but must hang upon the foundation of being.'[20]

128
An English Holiday – Newmarket Fair, 1928
oil on canvas,
208 x 305 cm (82 x 120 in.),
(detail)

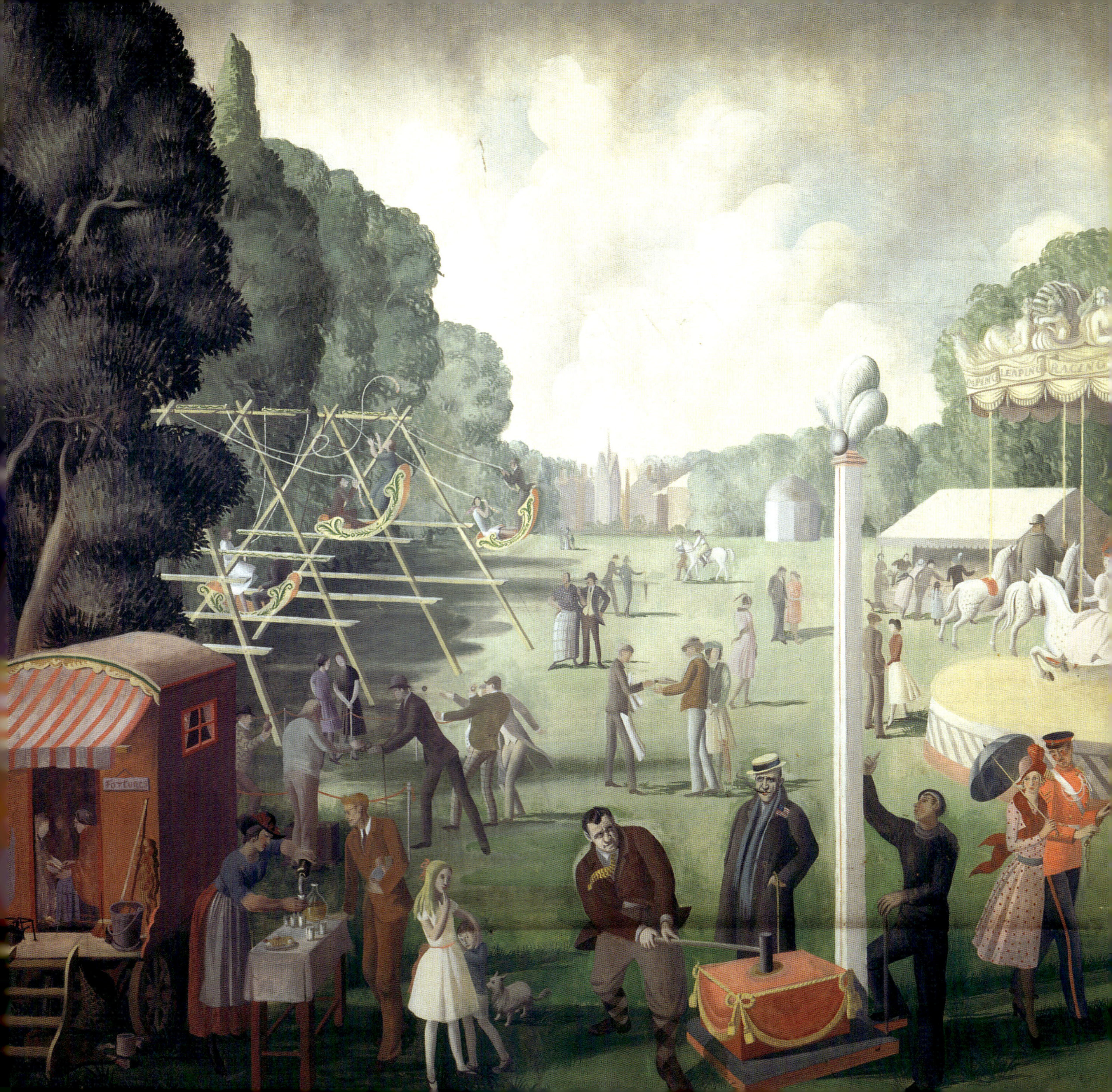
Fortunes
LEAPING
RACING

ENDNOTES

1 The panels from *An English Holiday* were stored in Mary Adshead's studio on Haverstock Hill and several were damaged in a fire, probably in the 1960s. *Newmarket Fair, The Winners' Enclosure* and *A Wayside Picnic* were sold at an exhibition in the 1980s. The remainder were disposed of when Mary Adshead's garage was cleared and a number of the panels were bought by a private collector on the Isle of Man. After the owner's death, six of the panels from *An English Holiday* were put up for auction at Sotheby's Olympia. (Conversation with Sylvester Bone, 6 August 2012.) Sale details: 20th Century British and Irish Works of Art, Thursday, February 16, 2006, sale number W06713, lots 47-52 comprising: *The Puncture*, lot 47, *Couple in the Rain*, lot 48, *Stable Yard*, lot 49, *Village Inn*, lot 50, *Dover Harbour*, lot 51, and *Running away from the Fair*, lot 52.

2 There are 19 documents relating to this commission contained in The Beaverbrook Papers 1869-1976 held by the Parliamentary Archives, ref: BBK/B/25 Correspondence: A, 1928.

3 Letter from Mary Adshead to Mrs Alexander (a secretary or assistant to Lord Beaverbook) dated February 15, 1928.

4 'Art Exhibition', *The Times*, February 11, 1930, p.12, this is a review of a joint exhibition also featuring the work of Elliott Seabrooke.

5 Correspondence between Mary Adshead and Lord Beaverbrook (or his representatives) dated August 1-22, 1928. In a letter dated August 1, 1928 to Lord Beaverbrook, Mary Adshead says: 'I have been rather surprised that you did not come and see the decorations in progress, as I imagined they would be of interest to you, and the odd panel put up at Newmarket, gave a very imperfect impression of the complete scheme.' p.1.

6 See Powers in Matthew Clough and Ann Compton, editors, *Earthly Delights: Mary Adshead 1904-1995*, University of Liverpool Art Collections, 2004, p.33. A letter from Adshead to Beaverbrook dated August 1, 1928 contains the following comment about Lady Diana Cooper: 'Mr Atkinson seemed to think, that Lady Diana Cooper – who is depicted in one panel – had been to see me at my studio but this is not so; I should very much like her to see them, however, as I have heard that she was very interested in some decorations of mine, which she saw during her recent visit to Liverpool.' This latter reference is to her panels for Sir Charles Reilly's dining room entitled *A Tropical Fantasy*, 1925.

7 Valentine Castlerosse, 6th Earl of Kenmare, was the author of the first signed social column 'Londoner's Log' in the *Sunday Express* from 1926.

8 See note 2.

9 As note 4, p.12.

10 As note 3.

11 From information supplied by Mary Adshead, the lady in *The Puncture* has been identified as Lady Louise Mountbatten, who was the wife of Crown Prince Gustaf Adolf (later King Gustaf VI Adolf) of Sweden. However, there is no documented connection between her and Lord Beaverbrook. It is more likely that Adshead intended to refer to Lady Louis Mountbatten, also known as Countess Edwina Mountbatten, who was a member of Beaverbrook's inner circle. For example, during 1928, Beaverbrook used his influence to get the Countess's name removed from a high-profile divorce case in America. See Anne Chisholm and Michael Davie, *Beaverbrook: a Life*, Hutchinson, London, 1988, p.265.

12 The young woman dancing to the music may be a portrait of Bennett's partner, the actress, Dorothy Muriel Cheston.

13 The Aga Khan who stands just outside the winners' enclosure in Adshead's panel won the 2000 Guineas in 1924 with Diophon (jockey G. Hulme, trainer R.C. Dawson). Lord Derby's horse, Colorado, was ridden by T. Weston, and trained by G. Lambton.

14 Other leading political figures shown in *An English Holiday* are the seventeenth Earl of Derby, Winston Churchill and Lord Birkenhead.

15 According to his biographer, A.J.P. Taylor, one of Beaverbrook's chief heroes was John Knox. Strict Presbyterians probably found his humour unpalatable. The original name of the house was Bedford Lodge. See A.J.P. Taylor, *Beaverbrook*, Hamish Hamilton, London, 1972, p.243.

16 Anne Chisholm and Michael Davie (as note 11) say that Jean Norton helped Beaverbrook furnish Bedford Lodge/Calvin House, as note 10, p.262. If so, this would have further fuelled the rivalry with Lady Diana Cooper. However, the personal diaries of Jean Norton, Lady Grantley 1928-31, which are also contained within the Beaverbrook Papers, Parliamentary Archives, BBK/K/2/179-182, do not offer any evidence that she was involved in redecorating the house at Newmarket.

17 Further details of Stanley Adshead's career can be found at Alan Powers, 'Adshead, Stanley Davenport (1868–1946)', *Oxford Dictionary of National Biography*, Oxford University Press, 2004 [http://www.oxforddnb.com/view/article/30344, accessed July 23, 2012].

18 For Adshead's, Stephen Bone's and Sir Muirhead Bone's involvement with the AIA see Lynda Morris and Robert Radford, *AIA: The Story of the Artists International Association, 1933-1953*, The Museum of Modern Art, Oxford, 1983, especially pp.51-2.

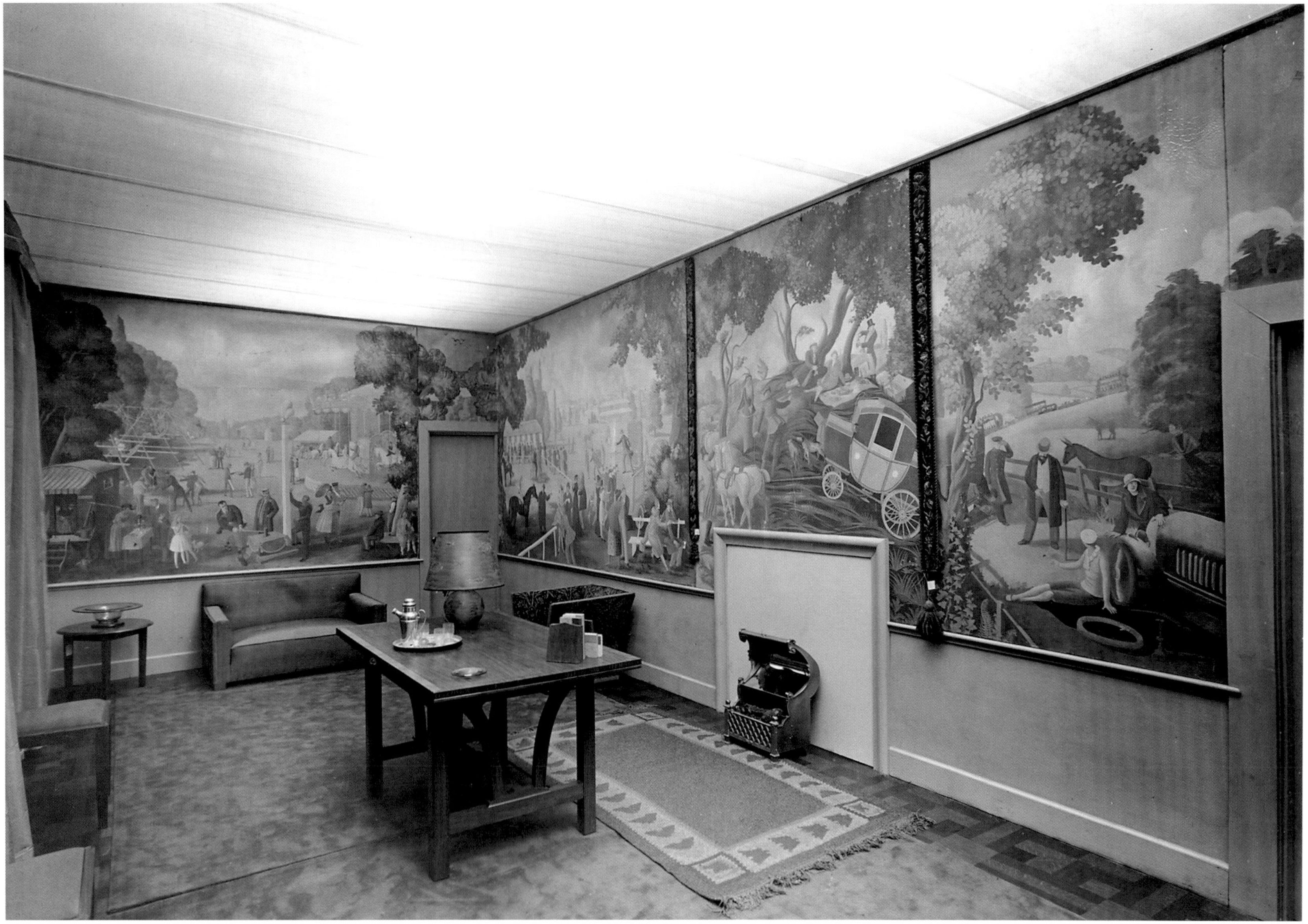

129 *An English Holiday Installation* – This image almost certainly shows the panels installed at Peter Jones department store, London, 1930

19 Whistler received £500 at £5 per hour over 18 months from Joseph Duveen for painting *The Pursuit of Rare Meats* (http://www.tate.org.uk/about/our-work/collection/about-the-collection/works-in-the-fabric-of-tate-buildings/rex-whistler-expedition-in-pursuit-of-rare-meats). Adshead worked on the Beaverbrook murals for about seven months between February and August 1928 and was to have been paid £400 which represents a significantly higher rate of pay. The reduction of her fee to £250 more or less equalized the payments (per hour of time) received by Adshead and Whistler. Both fees compare favourably with the annual stipend of £250 given to scholars at the British School at Rome.

20 Letter from Henry Tonks to Nan West quoted in Joseph Hone, *The Life of Henry Tonks*, Heinemann, London, 1939, pp.183-4.

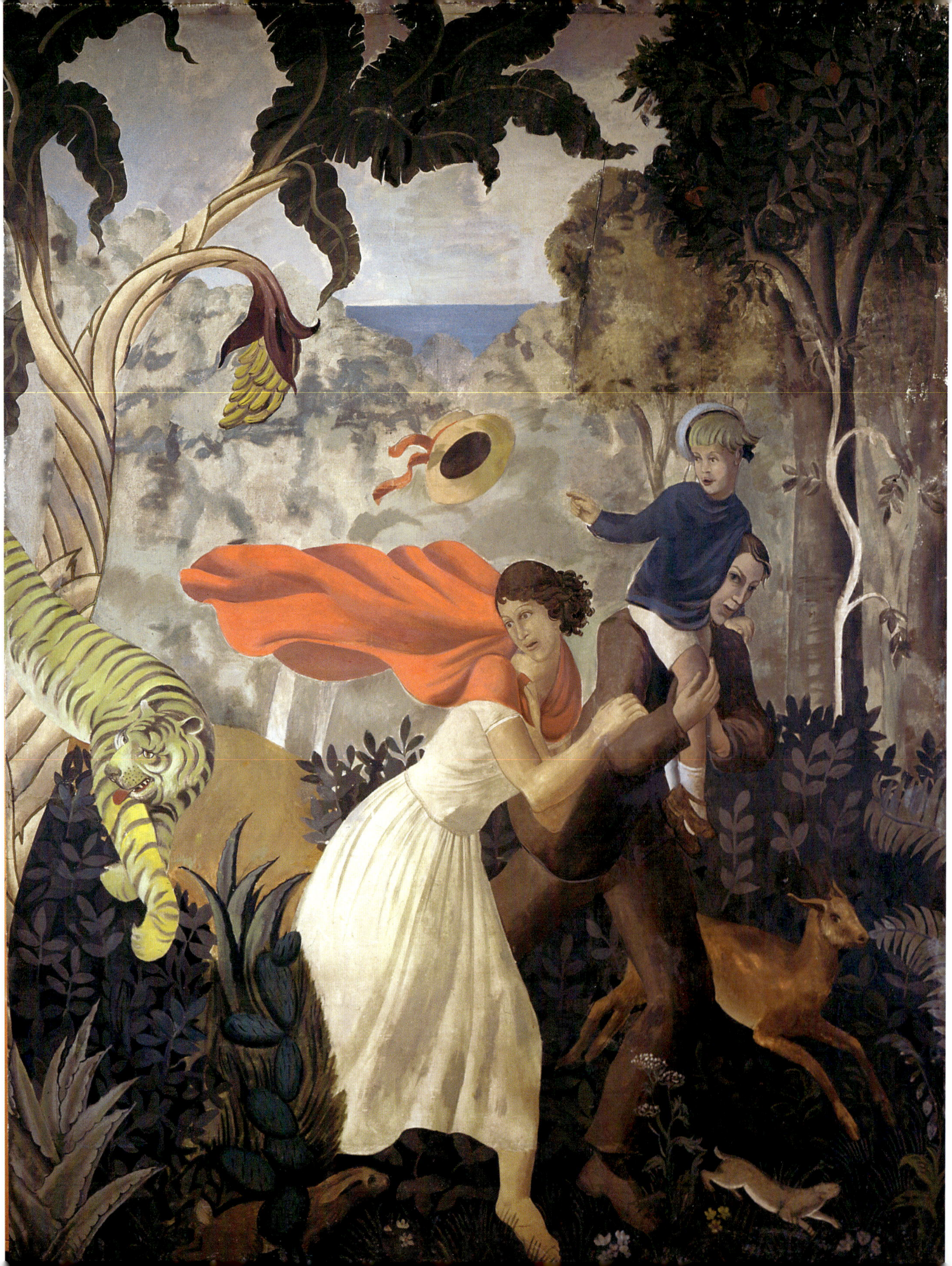

130
A Tropical Fantasy:
Charles Reilly's Dining Room Mural, 1926, (panel 3 of 6), oil on board, est. 244 x 190 cm (96 x 74 ¾ in.), University of Liverpool Collection

MURALS BY MARY ADSHEAD

Works that are extant, either in their original or other location, are marked *. Other murals have been destroyed or are presumed lost.

1924 – *The Joys of the Country*, Highway Boys' Club, Shadwell, London. Commissioned by Sir Joseph Duveen

1925 – *A Tropical Fantasy,** oil on canvas, 244 cm high, varied widths. Commissioned by Sir Charles Reilly for 71 Bedford Street South, Liverpool, Collection: Victoria Art Gallery & Museum, University of Liverpool

(March-May) – *Ripolin Paints*, Mural (advertisement), 2 panels, 226 x 467 cm and 223 x 452 cm, Bank underground station, London

(March-May) – *Remington Typewriters*, Mural (advertisement), 1 panel, 147 x 701, Bank underground station, London

1928 – *An English Holiday*, oil on canvas, dimensions vary. Commissioned by William Maxwell Aitken, first Lord Beaverbrook for the dining room at Calvin Lodge, Newmarket. Commission withdrawn in August 1928

*Newmarket Fair,** Lord Castlerosse testing his strength, Lord Beaverbrook looks on. Private collection
*Running Away From the Fair,** Sir Matthew Wilson (Major 'Scatters Wilson') on horseback running away with a gypsy (Raquel Meller)
*The Puncture,** Lady Louise Mountbatten has a puncture en route, Collection: Liss Fine Art
*Wayside Picnic,** Lady Diana Cooper with Mrs Richard Norton, Private collection
*Village Inn,** Collection: Liss Fine Art
*The Winners' Enclosure,** Lord Derby leads in a winner, Aga Khan looks on, Mr Reginald McKenna, Chancellor of the Exchequer – a ruined man being comforted by his wife
*Couple in Rain,** Picnicking under the umbrella, the couple who never go to the races owing to a deluge
*Dover Harbour,** Lord and Lady Birkenhead yachting
Gypsies on the Road to Newmarket, Arnold Bennett plays the harmonium. Presumed destroyed
*Stable Yard,** Mrs Norman Holden on horseback, Sir James Dunn falling off his horse
Elephant Hunt, Winston Churchill on elephant. Presumed destroyed

1930 – Music room, 47 Grosvenor Square,* Decorative scheme including murals commissioned by Stephen and Virginia Courtauld, Collection: Eltham Palace, Court Road, London SE9, under the care of English Heritage

1931-35 – *The Ascending Christ,** East wall, St Christopher's church, Withington, Manchester, Current location: St Columba's Church, Anfield, Liverpool where there is also Adshead's *The Nativity*, Lady Chapel, 1932, commissioned by the Lunt family

1934 – *The Pier Pavilion,** Colwyn Bay Pier, decoration of auditorium commissioned by Stanley Adshead

1936 – Lewis' Restaurant, Leicester

1937 – *Gastronomic Maps of Britain: Fruits of the Sea and Game*, British Pavilion, Exposition Internationale des Arts et Techniques dans la Vie Moderne (Expo 1937), Paris

1941 – Mural for British Restaurant, Leamington Spa
Mural for Factory Canteen, Rugby

1942 – *Welcome to Birmingham, Servicemen arriving, Servicemen Eating/Sleeping,* Columba House Services Club, Birmingham, murals in entrance and stairway
The World's Foods, British Restaurant, Granville Street, Birmingham
Mural for Staff Canteen, Vauxhall Motors, Luton

1946 – Cordon Rouge Restaurant, Sloane Street, London

1949 – Decorative Scene at Peter Robinson's, Oxford Circus, London

1949-50 – Mural for Tea-room, Luton Hoo House, Luton

1949-51 – The Jungle Restaurant, Fourth floor restaurant, Selfridge's, Oxford Street, London

1954 – Architectural Vista, Costain House, 111 Westminster Bridge Road, London

1957 – *Mid-Summer Eve Pageant of the Guilds of the Middle-Ages,** Pageant Restaurant and Food Hall, John Lewis' store, Cribbs Causeway Shopping Mall, Bristol
Totnes in Time, Totnes Civic Hall
Spencer House, 27 St James Place, Westminster, London

1958 – St Alban's Church, Warners End

1959 – Christie Hospital, Withington, Manchester

1961 – Barley Sheaf Pub, Plymouth
Maps of Kent, bar of Winter Gardens, Margate
Channel Islands panel, Commonwealth Institute, Kensington, London

1962 – *To the End of Time*, Saint Francis Church, Luton

1963 – Civic Centre – rear entrance to council chamber (galleons), Plymouth

1967 – Chapel of St Dunstan, St Peter's Church – St Dunstan reredos 1965-7
French Occupation of Guernsey, Commonwealth Institute, Kensington, London

1970 – Barge: canal scene, Post House, Leicester

1973 – Reception area, Champneys, Tring, Herts, 1972-3

1982 – Beatson walk, Rotherhithe Fighting Temeraire, Southwark, London

1985 – Plain tiles from mid-1980s, underpass, Elephant & Castle, London

Mary Adshead (1904-1995)

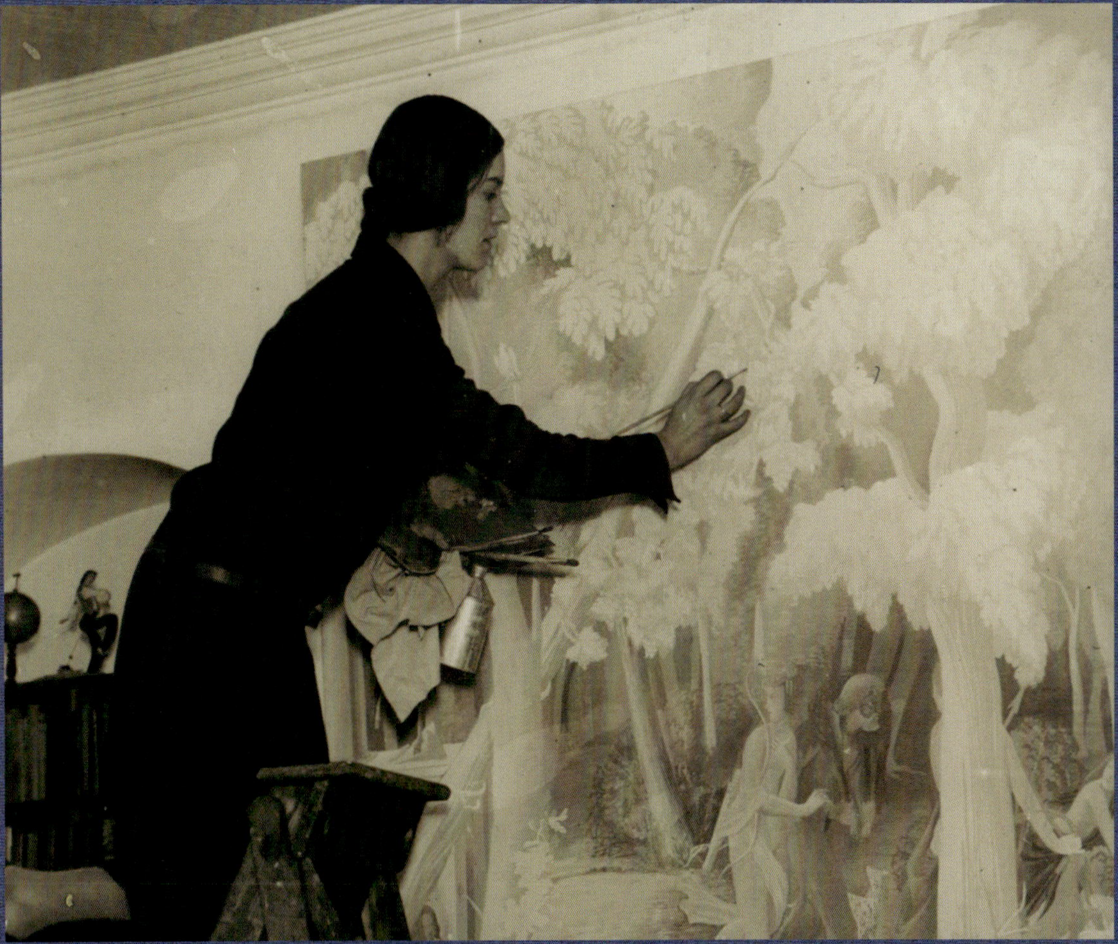

131 Mary Adshead at work on one of her murals

MARY ADSHEAD. Born and died in London. Mural painter, designer and illustrator. Daughter of Stanley Adshead (1869-1946), architect and town planner. Studied at Putney High School (1916-19), Lycée Victor Duruy, Paris (six months, 1919) and Slade School of Fine Art (1921-24). Student of Henry Tonks (1862-1937), (near) contemporaries at the Slade included Rex Whistler (1905-44), Colin Gill (1892-1940), Winifred Knights (1899-1947) and W.T. Monnington (1902-76). Married the painter Stephen Bone (1904-1958), son of Sir Muirhead Bone (1876-1953) in 1929. Collaborated on children's books with her husband and illustrated Mary Norton's *Bonfire and Broomsticks*, 1947. Elected member of the New English Art Club 1930. First solo exhibition, Goupil Gallery, 1930, thereafter exhibited regularly in London. Designed: theatre set 1924; advertisements from 1925; wallpaper 1945; window displays 1947; stamps 1948-63; and mosaics 1952-82. Member Society of Mural Painters, from 1939 and Honorary Secretary 1953-65.

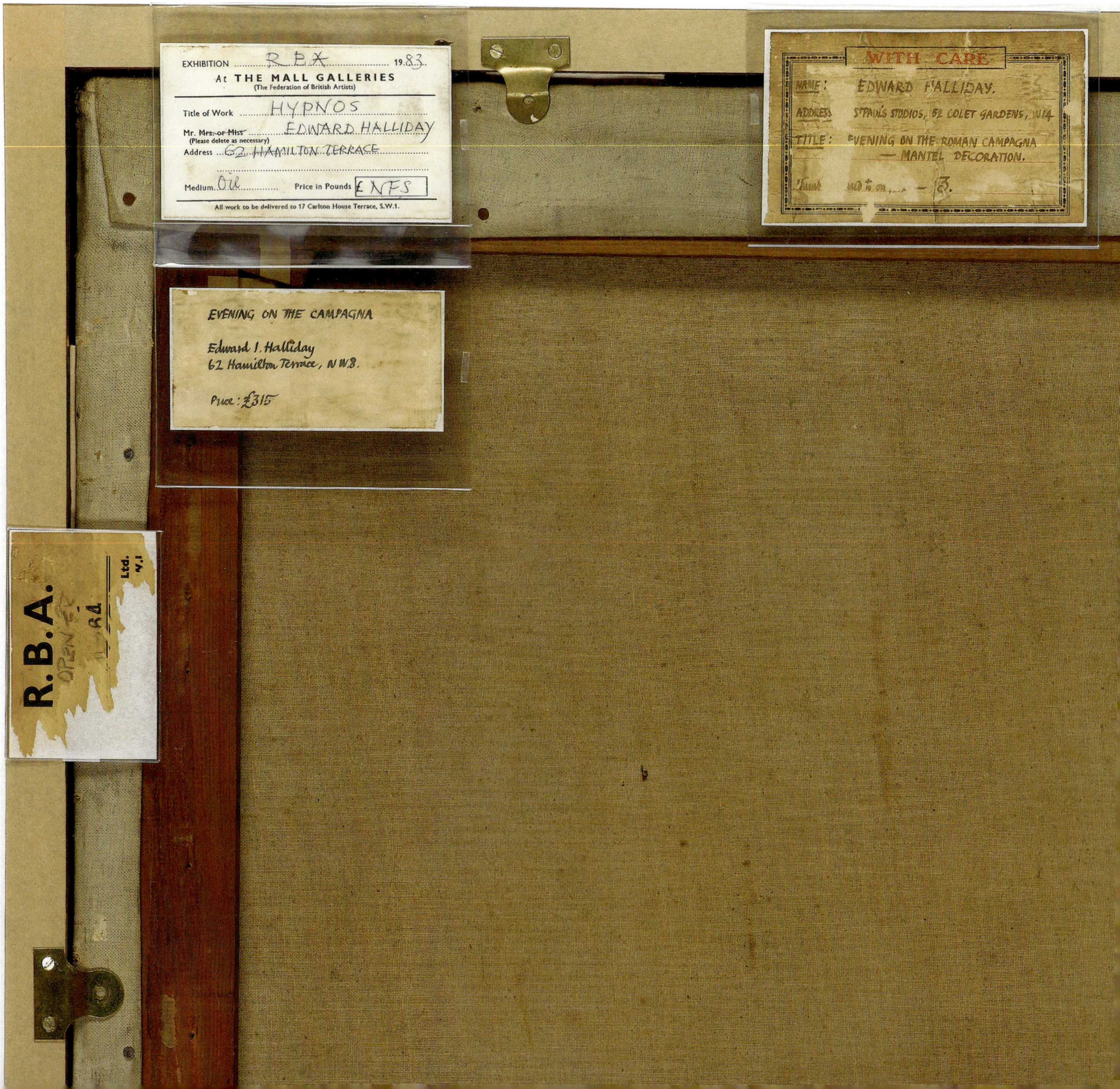

132
Reverse side of *Hypnos*

Edward Halliday
Hypnos, 1928

Ann Compton

The year *Hypnos* was painted – 1928 – marked a turning point for Edward Halliday (1902-84). His three-year scholarship at the British School at Rome (BSR) came to an end, concluding eight years of fine-art study.[1] At the same time, a new chapter in Halliday's domestic life opened when he married Dorothy Hatswell, a classicist and assistant librarian at the BSR.[2] The artist's return to England in late October 1928 therefore marked the formal commencement of his professional career and a fresh personal beginning. *Hypnos* provides a glimpse of Halliday's aesthetic and professional concerns at a pivotal moment.

This was the second work commissioned by Sir Benjamin Johnson (1865-1937) for his home, Abbott's Lea in Liverpool. Johnson was an industrial magnate who built up a successful family dyeworks into a national dry-cleaning company, which had its headquarters in Bootle, just north of Halliday's native city of Liverpool. In 1927 Johnson invited Halliday to paint a picture for his private library depicting the conversion of Lydia of Thyatira, who was a dye merchant, by St Paul the Apostle. The industrialist proved to be an important patron for the young artist because in 1928 he not only asked Halliday to paint *Hypnos*, but also to make a second, larger version of St Paul meeting with Lydia of Thyatira for the Bootle dyeworks and to execute three very large decorative paintings for the newly built Athenaeum club in Liverpool. In later years, there were further commissions for portraits of company staff. Johnson believed that art was as essential to life as 'earn[ing] one's daily bread' and tried to combine 'as far as possible, art and graces with business enterprise and endeavour'. He put this into practice by hanging over one hundred pictures from his own collection at the factory, organizing annual outings for his workforce to the Liverpool Autumn Exhibition, and regularly including items on art in the company magazine.[3]

Although Halliday stands out amongst his BSR peer group for securing an unusually large number of commissions whilst in Rome,[4] the principle of students taking on external projects during their scholarships was well-established. For example, Colin Gill (1892-1940) had painted *Canadian Observation Post* for the Canadian War Records Office in 1919; W.T. Monnington (1902-76) worked on a commission for the Contemporary Art Society in 1925; A.K. Lawrence (1893-1975) executed murals for the Laing Art Gallery in 1926; and Glyn Jones (1906-84) was commissioned to paint three scenes from the life of St Martin for a reredos in the Milner Memorial Chapel, Canterbury Cathedral in 1927.[5] The staff managing the BSR scholarships, particularly the secretary, Evelyn Shaw (1882-1974), and the Faculty of Painting (the panel of artists which selected scholars and monitored their progress) responded positively to students attracting patrons. Such projects provided independent validation that Rome scholars were promising young artists and also served a pragmatic purpose. The programme of self-directed study followed in Rome was intended to culminate in a scheme bridging architecture and fine art in fulfillment of the BSR's aesthetic ideals. However there were very few years in which the Faculty and director of the school had the resources (or sometimes the inclination) to offer scholars opportunities to carry theory into practice. Private commissions helped fill the gap. Both *Hypnos* and the panels for the Athenaeum Club met the requirement for an architectural scheme.[6]

The painting depicts fourteen rustic figures sitting, standing, dancing, playing music, or watching over their goats and cows in the foreground of an Italianate landscape. At the centre of the horizon looms a giant-sized lightly draped, youthful male – the eponymous god – allegorizing the descent of sleep during the siesta. This benign moment suited the work's original setting in the bedroom corridor of Johnson's home and gave rise to an alternative title – *Evening on the Campagna* – when Halliday exhibited the painting at the Royal Academy in 1939.[7] One of the painting's striking features is that Halliday has conceived the scene exclusively populated by men. It is also notable that the figures are grouped on a narrow piece of ground bounded by a river and channel. These details remind us that in classical mythology Hypnos lived in a cave close to the Lethe (one of the five rivers of Hades which induced forgetfulness) and is associated with tales of war, fitting his lineage as half-brother of Thanatos (death). Typical of these legends is a story from the *Iliad* in which Hypnos lulls Zeus into a deep sleep to assist the goddess Hera's machinations during the siege of Troy.[8] Although we should be wary of over-interpreting Halliday's intentions, there was certainly an appalling reminder of the consequences of the First World War during his time at the BSR. On March 29, 1928 Emile Jacot, the Rome Scholar in Sculpture for 1925, died in a sanatorium in Switzerland after a six-month fight against tuberculosis resulting from war wounds.

If *Hypnos* hints at darker themes, the compositional structure of the painting is designed to intrigue, or even mystify, the viewer. Halliday has sharply divided the space occupied by godly and human forms and in doing so has created a sense of dissociation between mythical and real, classical and modern (although this is tempered by the timelessness of the traditional dress worn by several of the figures). These discontinuities probably mirror the young artist's experiences whilst studying at the BSR. All scholars were expected to combine studio work with extensive study of art during their three-year scholarship. Halliday was particularly systematic about his researches, focusing first on Rome, central Italy and Sardinia, later venturing across Turkey, Bulgaria and Greece to pursue 'Byzantinology' and then in his final year visiting a dozen cities in north Africa, returning to Rome via the south of France.[9] Throughout these travels Halliday no doubt encountered repeated contrasts (and occasional continuities) between the classical past evoked by the historic sites he visited and the traditional customs of contemporary rural life. Amongst the many decorative schemes Halliday particularly admired were the richly painted interiors at the Villa Farnese, the Castello Orsini-Odescalchi in Bracciano and the Borghese apartments at the Vatican. The extraordinary visual wealth the young painter assimilated on his journeys emerges in *Hypnos* in the treatment of the figures, landscape and sumptuousness of Halliday's palette – the deep indigo sky, saturated green of the landscape and lush red highlights in the draperies.

133
St Paul Meeting with Lydia of Thyatira, 1928,
oil on canvas,
106 x 147cm
(41 ¾ x 57 ⅞ in.),
© The Artist's Estate,
photo: University of Liverpool,
(detail)

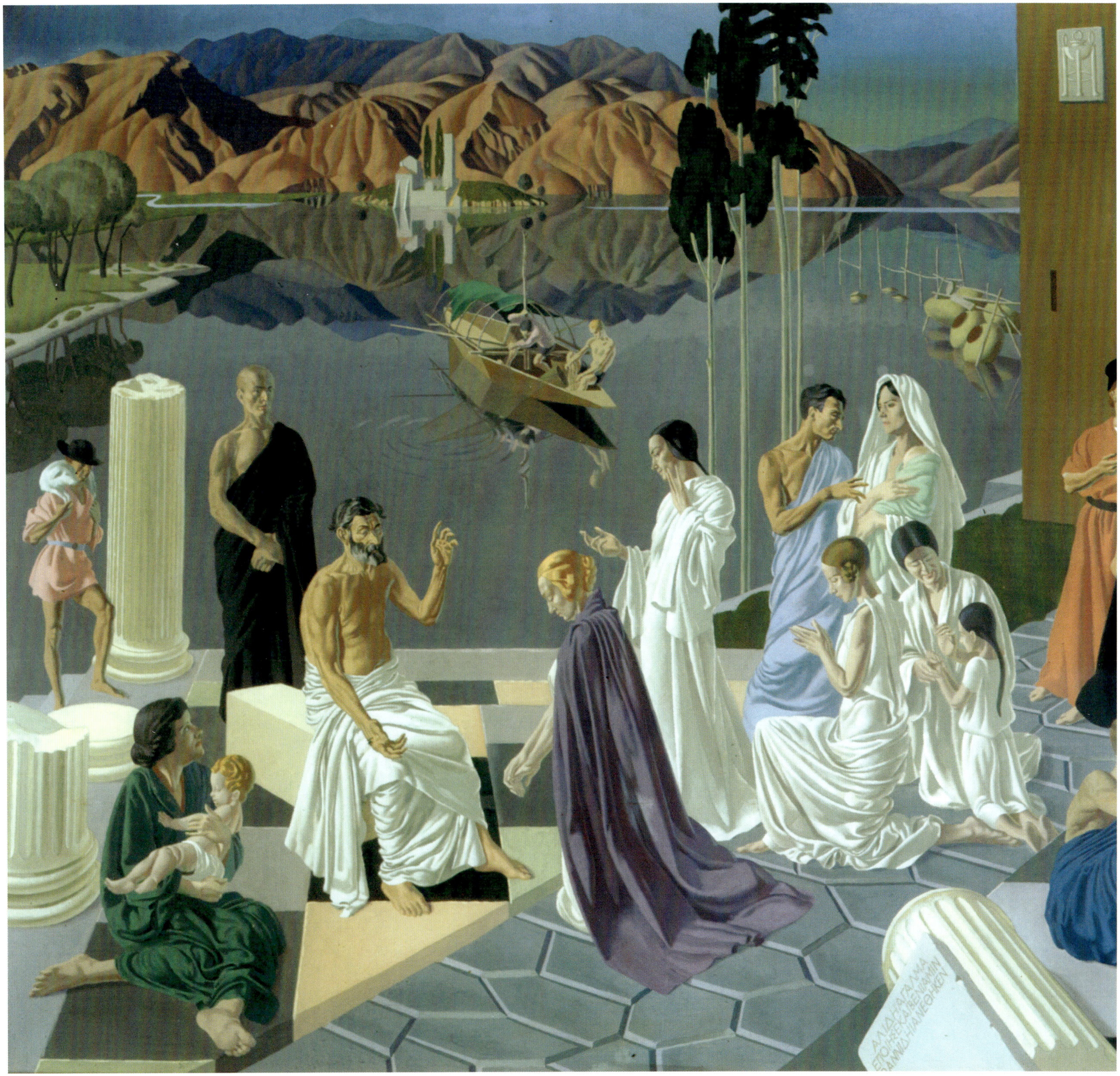

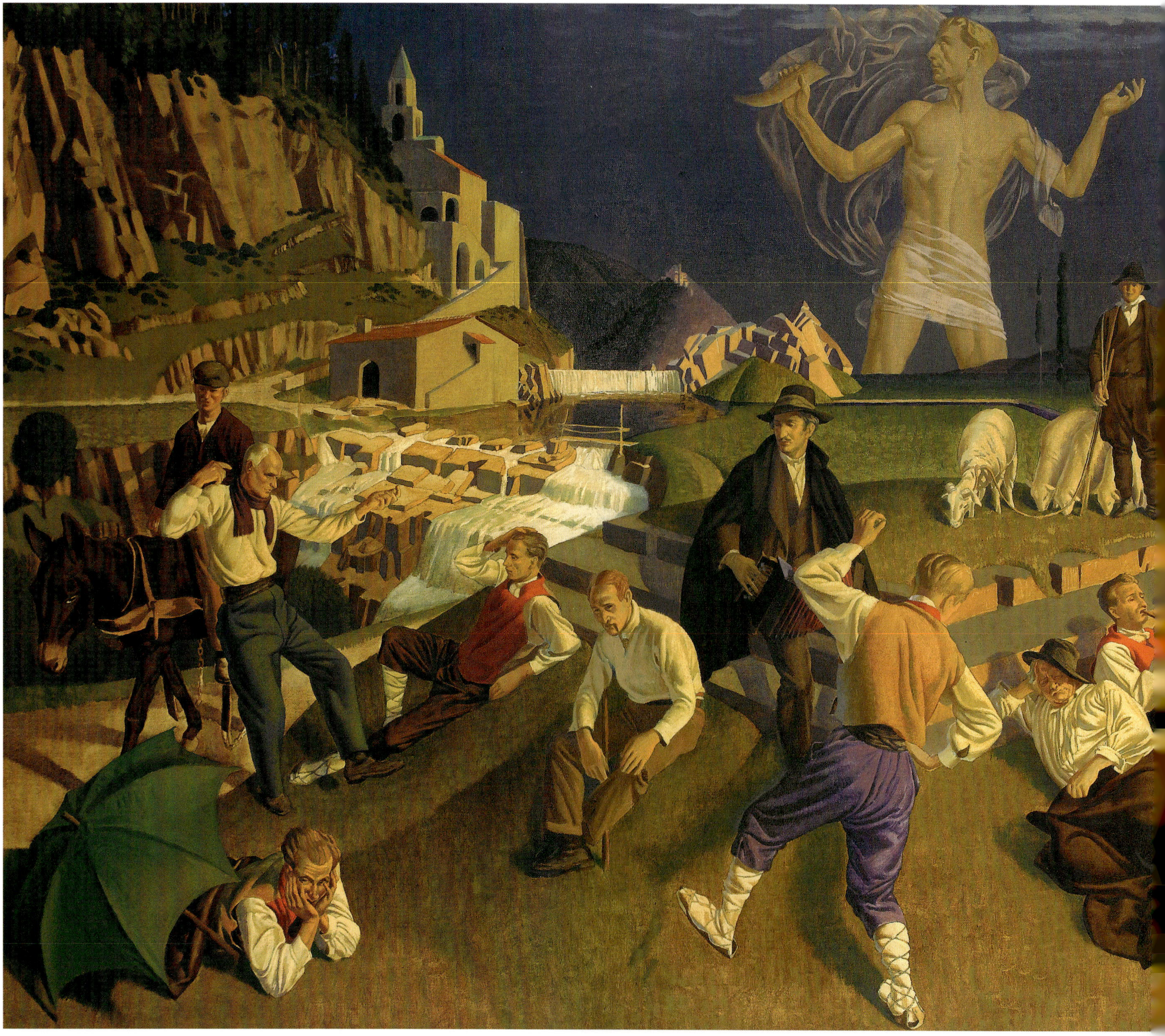

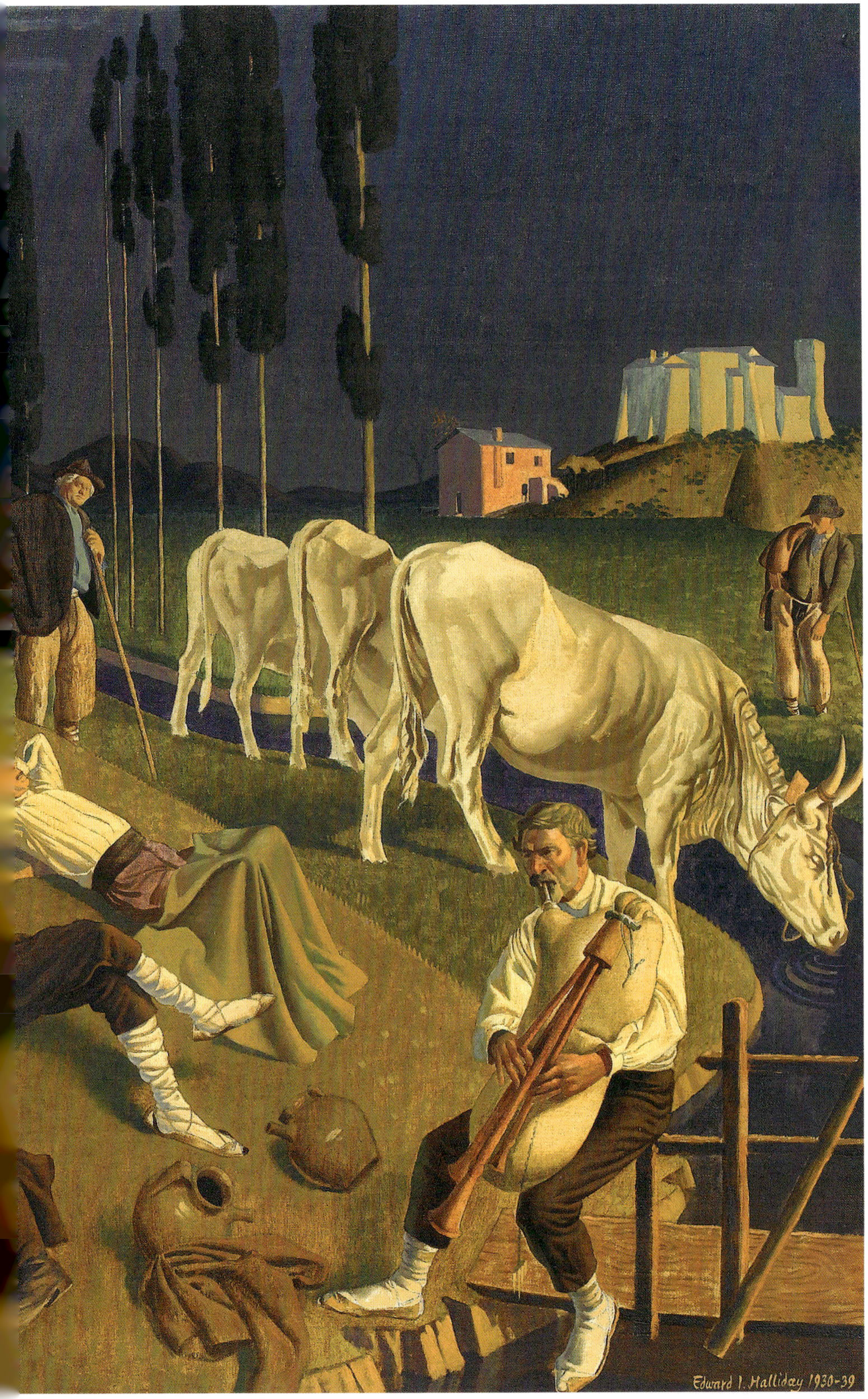

134
Hypnos, 1928
signed lower right
oil on canvas, 74.7 x 134.7 cm (30 x 54 in.)

Provenance: commission by Sir Benjamin Johnson for his house Abbot's Lea, Woolton, 1927. Completed in 1928; given to Halliday as a gift in 1937 upon the death of Johnson.

Exhibited: Royal Academy, 1939, under the title *Evening in the Campangna* (with new date added 1930-9 but no changes to the composition).

Literature: *Edward Halliday, Art for Life, 1925-1939*, Ann Compton, pp.18-21, reproduced p. 20 and on front cover.

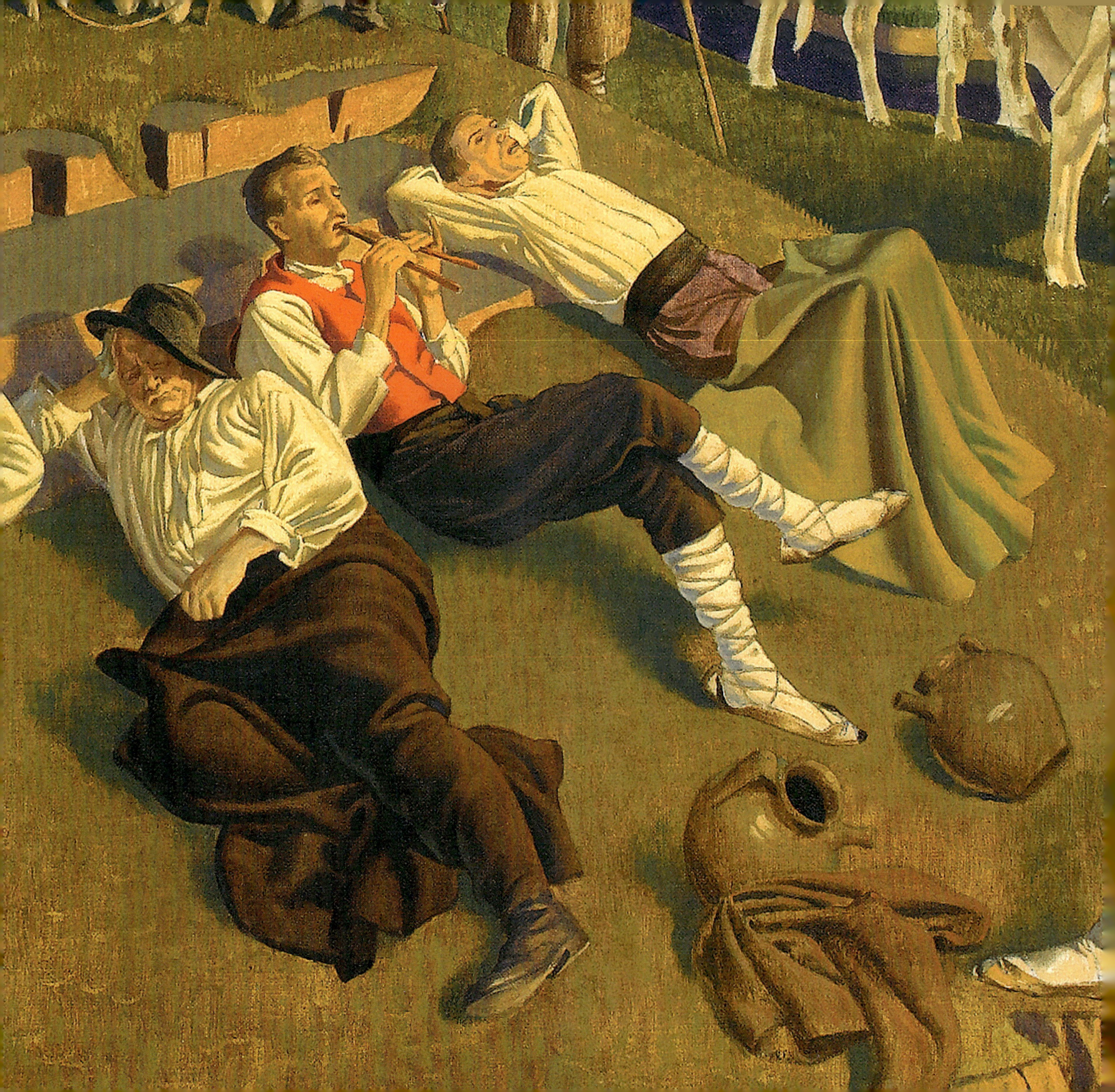

136
Portrait of R.P. Longden (Bobby Longden), 1928, from a photograph in The British School at Rome Historic Archive.

This portrait helped establish Halliday's reputation as a portrait painter when it was shown at the RA in 1929 and marked the start of a lifelong friendship. Bobby Longden was a classics scholar at the British School during Halliday's Rome Scholarship, and later became head of Wellington College. Longden appears to have modelled for several figures in *Hypnos* including the reclining figure in a red waistcoat playing the pipes.

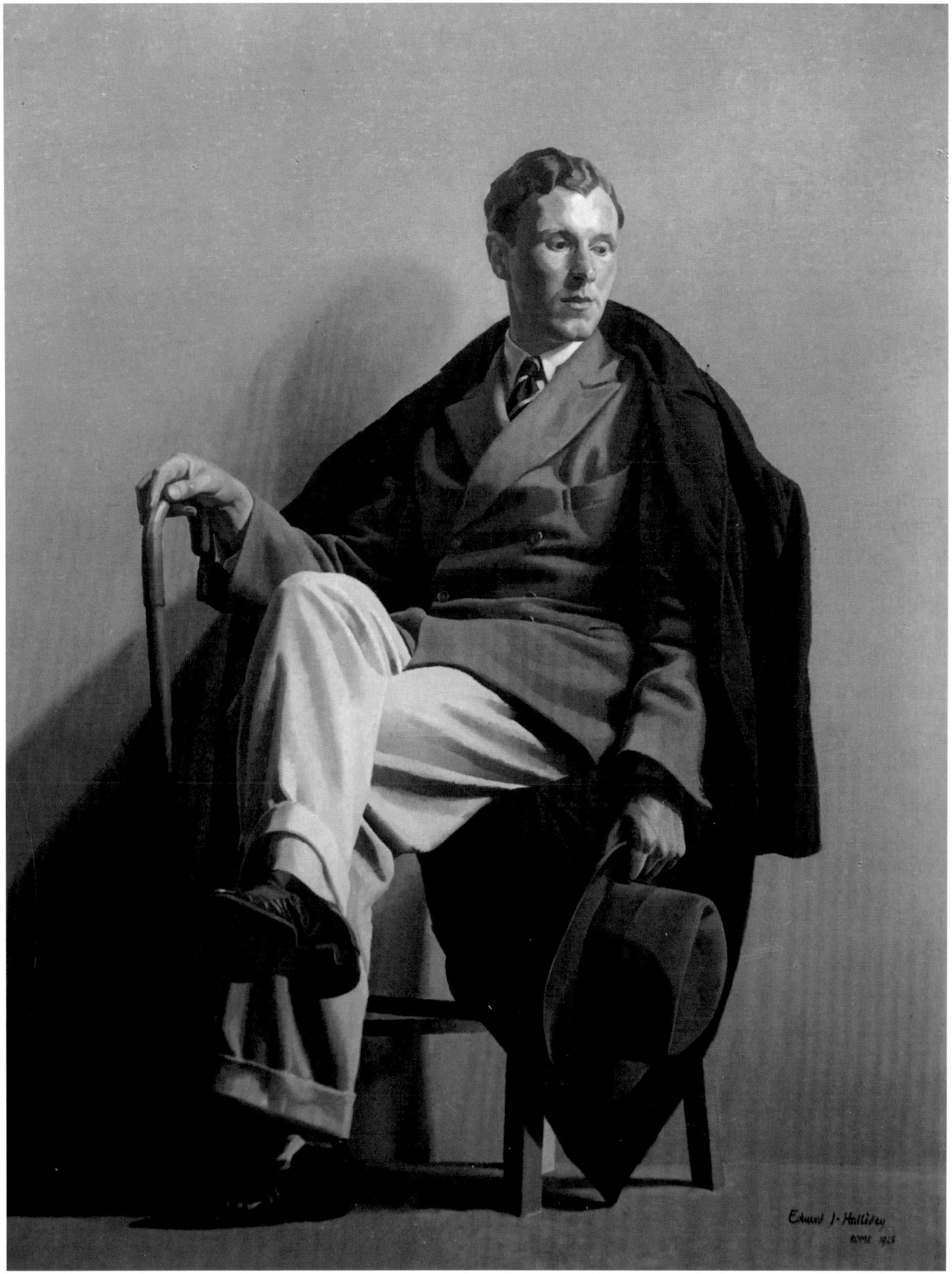

135 *Hypnos,* 1928 (detail)

Yet the painting is far more than a mere synthesis of historic exemplars, it also arises from more contemporary concerns. There are, for example, parallels to a still life, which also functions as a self-portrait, variously entitled 'Gulliver's Travels' and *Alter Ego* that Halliday was working on whilst painting *Hypnos*. This picture combines literary references with a play on scale and spatial relationships. Prominently positioned in the foreground of the still life are copies of Jonathan Swift's *Gulliver's Travels* and Wyndham Lewis's *The Enemy*. 'Sitting' or 'standing' beside the books are life-like marionettes, and in the centre of the canvas the artist is glimpsed at his easel via a reflection in a small mirror. The effect is both playful and disorientating. It echoes the confusion of large and small conjured by Swift in tales of Lilliput and Brobdingnag or, equally, by Halliday in *Hypnos* with its giant god and diminutive human figures. Another painting by Halliday of about 1928, *Group in Cortile*, represents the courtyard at the BSR with half a dozen fellow students standing, sitting, or playing music. Whilst familiar compositional devices (looks, gestures, and bodily positioning) make the group cohere, each person has the quality of being alone in his or her own space. This is also true of the figures in *Hypnos* who though clustered together appear oddly detached, even isolated. Here Halliday is following a tendency among his contemporaries at the BSR, notably Winifred Knights who created works in which this effect is even more pronounced.[10] A sense of self-containment also appears in the paintings of such prominent older generation artists as William Orpen (1878-1931), Harry Morley (1881-1943) and Halliday's tutor at the Royal College of Art and influential exponent of mural painting, Sir William Rothenstein (1872-1945).[11]

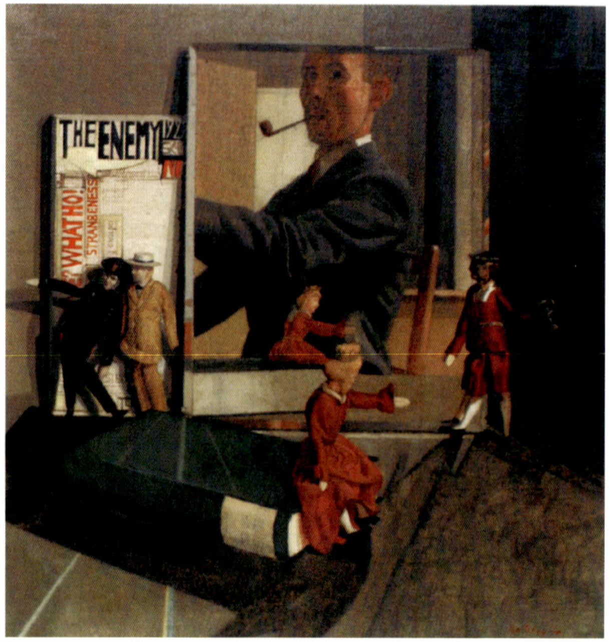

137
Gulliver's Travels or *Alter Ego*,
1927-28,
oil on canvas,
63.4 x 60.6 cm
(25 x 23 ⅞ in.)

When Halliday returned to London it was not just he who was at a pivotal moment, within two years the professional landscape of art practice had significantly changed. Although Jonhson's patronage and the panels for the Athenaeum provided a valuable commission that occupied Halliday during 1929, the stock market crash and subsequent economic depression produced a harsher, leaner climate for the aspirant decorative or mural painter. In the immediate term, Halliday worked hard to secure commissions for portraits recognizing this as a more assured source of income. However he did not altogether relinquish the BSR ideals of collaboration between the arts, rather he subsumed this within energetic campaigning for the Design and Industries Association and commissions for murals in leisure spaces in which he continued to bring painting into alignment with architecture and sculpture.

138
Study for
The Contest between Athena and Poseidon for the Patronship of Athens,
oil on panel,
40 x 37 cm
(15 ¾ x 14 ½ in.)
University of Liverpool Collection

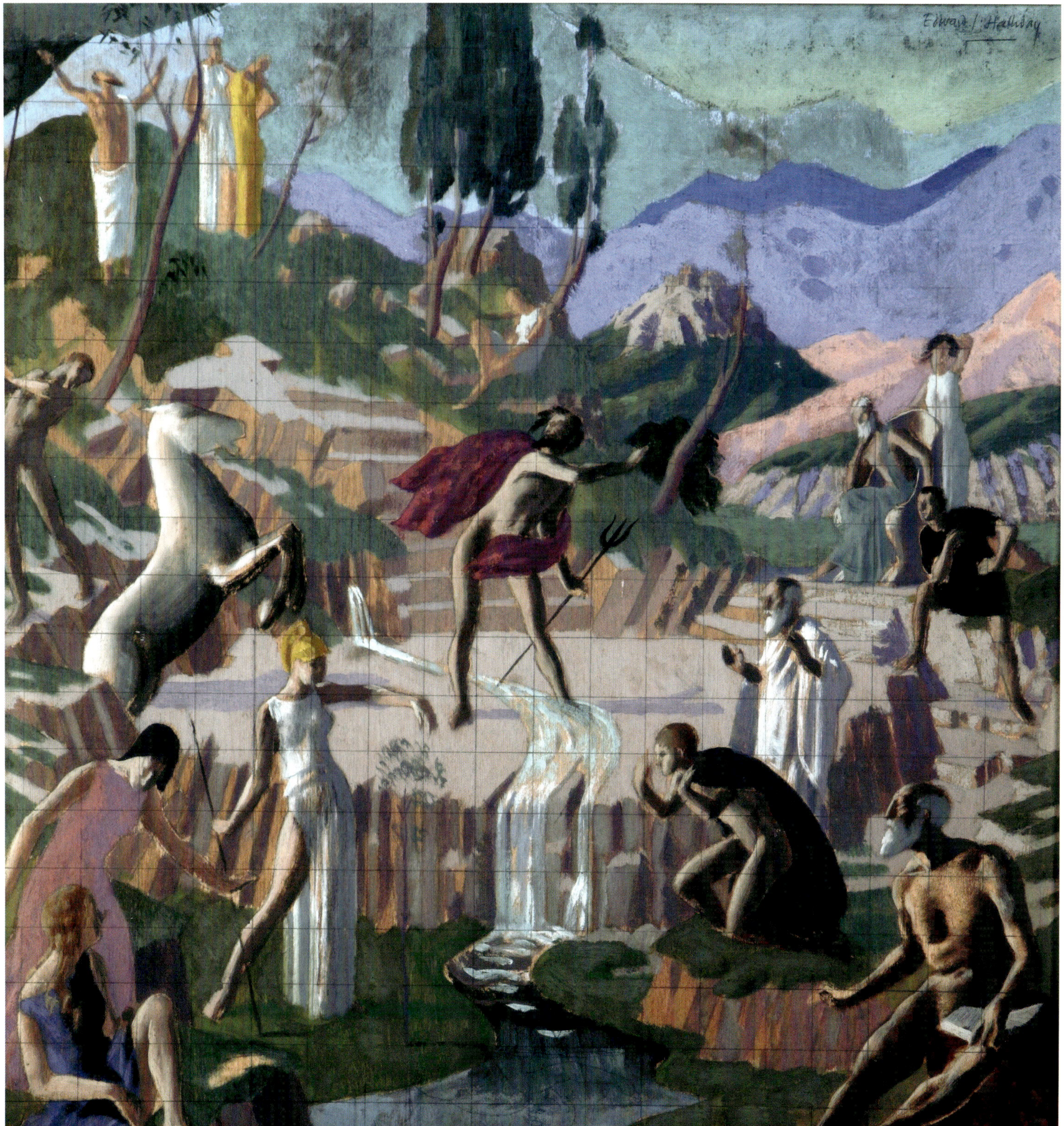

ENDNOTES

1 Details of *Hypnos* and Edward Halliday's tenure of his scholarship in Rome are largely drawn from his personal file, BSR Archive, Rome. There is a full account of Halliday's career in Ann Compton, *Edward Halliday: Art for Life, 1925-39*, University of Liverpool Art Collections, 1997.

2 Dorothy Hatswell replaced a Miss Hutton as librarian who had resigned because she was getting married. The rapid succession of assistant librarians contributed to a change of policy at the BSR which prevented scholars being married. Edward Halliday and Dorothy Hatswell's marriage was registered between July-September 1928 in London.

3 *The JB Journal: a monthly magazine published for and in the interests of Johnson Brothers (Dyers) Ltd and their employees*, first issue March 1907, multiple references to art throughout the remainder of Sir Benjamin's life. See especially no 46, December 1910. The connections between Johnson and Halliday are discussed in Compton, 1997, as note 1.

4 Halliday was also commissioned to make portraits of the Montserrat family and the diplomat, Lord Darling. Final annual report submitted by Halliday to the Faculty of Painting of the BSR for 1927-8, p.1.

5 These artists held the Rome Scholarship in Painting at the BSR for 1914, 1921, 1923 and 1926.

6 Halliday used this argument in correspondence with Evelyn Shaw, the Honorary General Secretary of the BSR, between January 29 and March 26, 1929 to leverage the last months of his scholarship money. The BSR attempted to retain this because he left Rome at the end of October 1928 to start work on the Athenaeum panels.

7 After the death of Sir Benjamin Johnson in December 1937 his daughter returned the painting to the artist.

8 Homer, *Iliad*, book 14, lines 231-354 for various references to the assistance Hypnos gave to Hera and the bargain they struck.

9 See annual reports submitted by Halliday to the Faculty of Painting of the British School at Rome for 1925-6, 1926-7 and 1927-8.

10 Particularly *Santissima Trinitia*, c.1924-30 which Knights had begun to work on before Halliday's arrival at the BSR. Possible connections between the figure lying under an umbrella in the front left of Hypnos and the use of umbrellas in *Santissima Trinita* have been noted by Sacha Llewellyn.

11 Halliday was particularly close to Rothenstein. The young artist delayed his departure for Rome in January 1925 so that he could accompany his former tutor as far as Rapallo (in Liguria). Rothenstein had been very ill and Halliday's task was to carry his luggage and ensure his companion's condition did not worsen on the journey. See *Since Fifty: Men and Memories, 1922-38: Recollections of William Rothenstein*, Macmillan Company, New York, 1940, p. 49 and letter from Halliday to Evelyn Shaw, January 6, 1926.

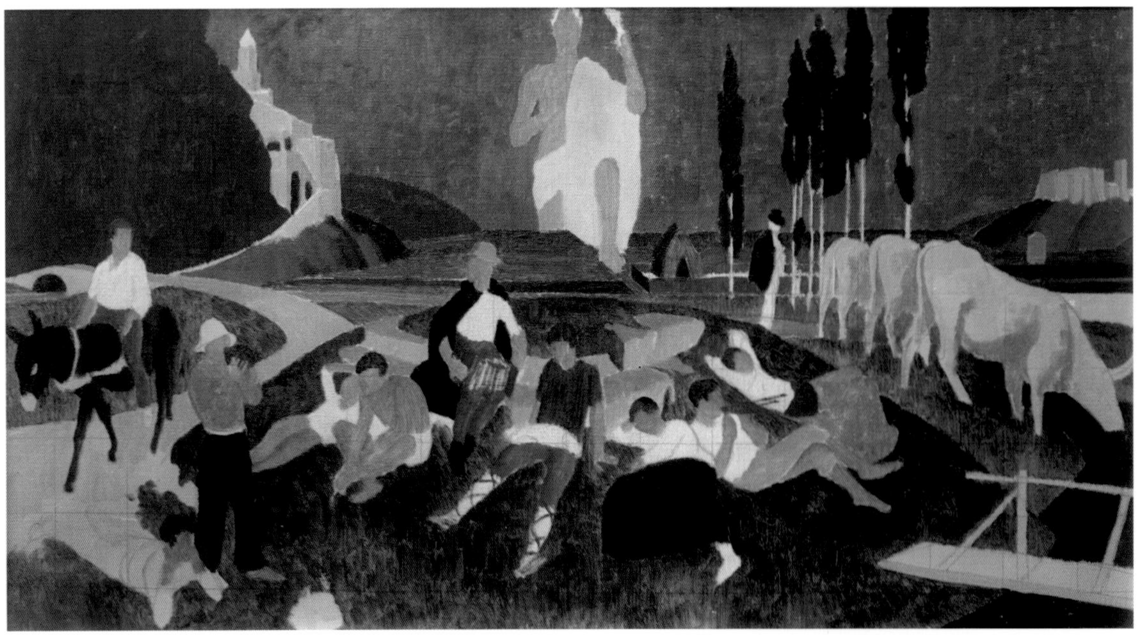

139
Study for *Hypnos,* 1928,
dimensions unknown

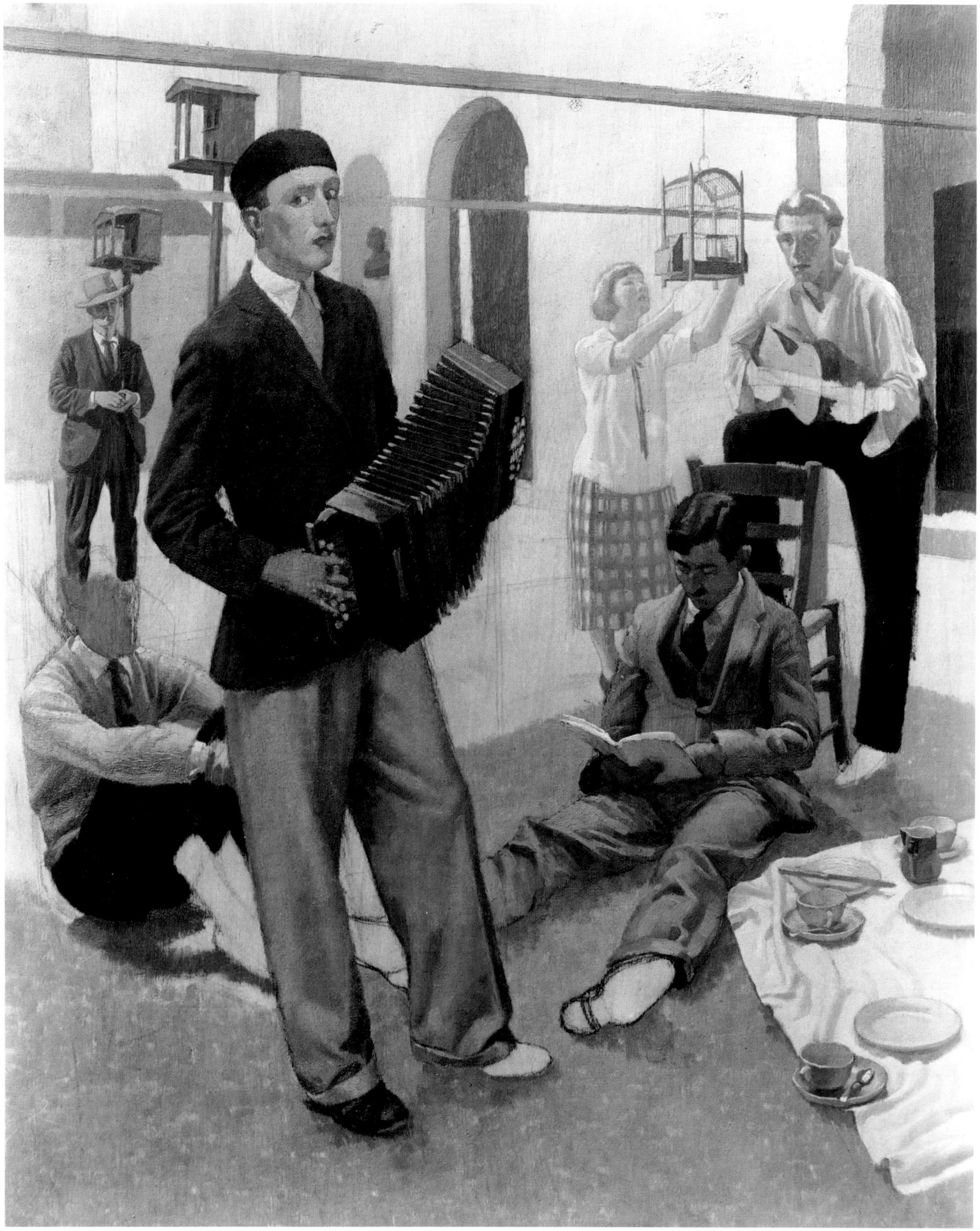

140
Group in Cortile, c. 1928
oil on canvas,
dimensions unknown

MURALS AND DECORATIVE PAINTINGS BY EDWARD HALLIDAY

Works that are extant, either in their original or other location, are marked *. Other murals have been destroyed or are presumed lost.

1927 and 1928 – *St Paul Meeting with Lydia of Thyatira,** oil on canvas, 56 x 81 cm (22 x 32 ⅞ in.) and 106 x 147 cm (41 ¾ x 57 ⅞ in.). Commissioned by Sir Benjamin Johnson (1865-1937), first version for his library at Abbott's Lea, Liverpool, second version for the headquarters of the Johnson company in Bootle.

1928 – *Hypnos,** oil on canvas, 74.7 x 134.7 cm (29 ⅜ x 53 in.). Commissioned by Sir Benjamin Johnson for the corridor, bedroom wing of Abbott's Lea, Liverpool. Returned to the artist after his death and exhibited under the title *Evening on the Campagna* at the Royal Academy in 1939. The work was then dated 1930-39 possibly in order to meet the rules for exhibiting recent works at the Academy.

Homeric Hymn to Hermes, oil on canvas, dimensions unknown. Commissioned by Dr Livesey for the music room at 10 Rodney Street, Liverpool.

1929 – *The Contest between Athena and Poseidon for the Patronship of Athens,** oil on canvas, 158.5 x 151.2 cm (62 ⅜ x 59 ½ in.), *The Story of Marsyas,** oil on canvas, 222 x 156.5 cm (87 ⅜ x 61 ⅝ in.) and *Athena and Arachne,** oil on canvas, 221.1 x 153.2 cm (87 x 60 ⅜ in.)

The three panels were commissioned by Sir Benjamin Johnson for the library of the new building for the Athenaeum, Church Alley, Liverpool, designed by Willink and Dod. Johnson's gift was made during his presidency in 1928-9. Halliday received the commission in October 1928 resulting in his leaving the British School at Rome two months before the official end of his tenure as Rome Scholar in Painting for 1925.

1935 – *Ulysses and Nausicaa*, oil on canvas (presumed), dimensions unknown
The Good Intent, mural, dimensions unknown

1937 – *Queen's Restaurant*, mural, dimensions unknown
The Departure of the Bath Coach, oil on canvas (presumed), dimensions unknown
*Map of the Thames, Seaside of Yesteryear,** *Seaside of Today,** murals, unknown dimensions, Dolphin Square, Pimlico, London

Edward Halliday (1902-1984)

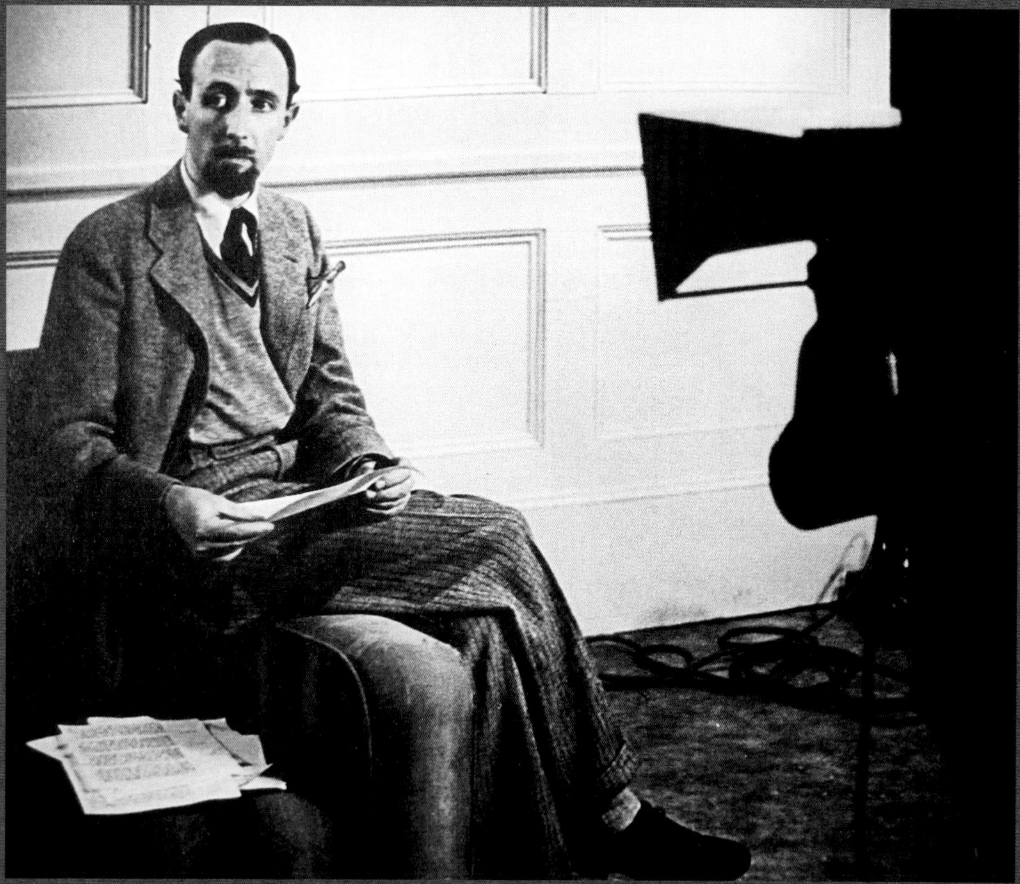

141 Edward Halliday in front of camera, 1938

EDWARD IRVINE HALLIDAY, FRSA, CBE. Born Liverpool, died London. Painter, mural painter, designer, interior decorator, broadcaster. Studied Liverpool School of Art, 1920-22, Académie Colarossi, Paris, 1922-3, Royal College of Art, 1923-5, and British School at Rome 1926-8. Worked primarily as a portrait and mural painter. Exhibited regularly at the Royal Academy from 1929. Designed furniture from c.1931, and all the decorative fixtures and fittings for Dolphin Square, Pimlico, London, 1937-38. Active member Design and Industries Association 1930 onwards. Radio broadcasts included 'Artists at Work', 1932 and 'Design in Modern Life', 1934. Television commentator from 1938, out-of-vision BBC newscaster from the early 1950s. Wartime occupations 1939-45, air traffic controller and 'black propaganda' for the Foreign Office. Co-founder Federation of British Artists, 1958, President Royal Society of British Artists, 1956-74, President Royal Society of Portrait Painters, 1970-75, Chairman Artists General Benevolent Institution, 1965-81, President Artists League of Great Britain from 1975.

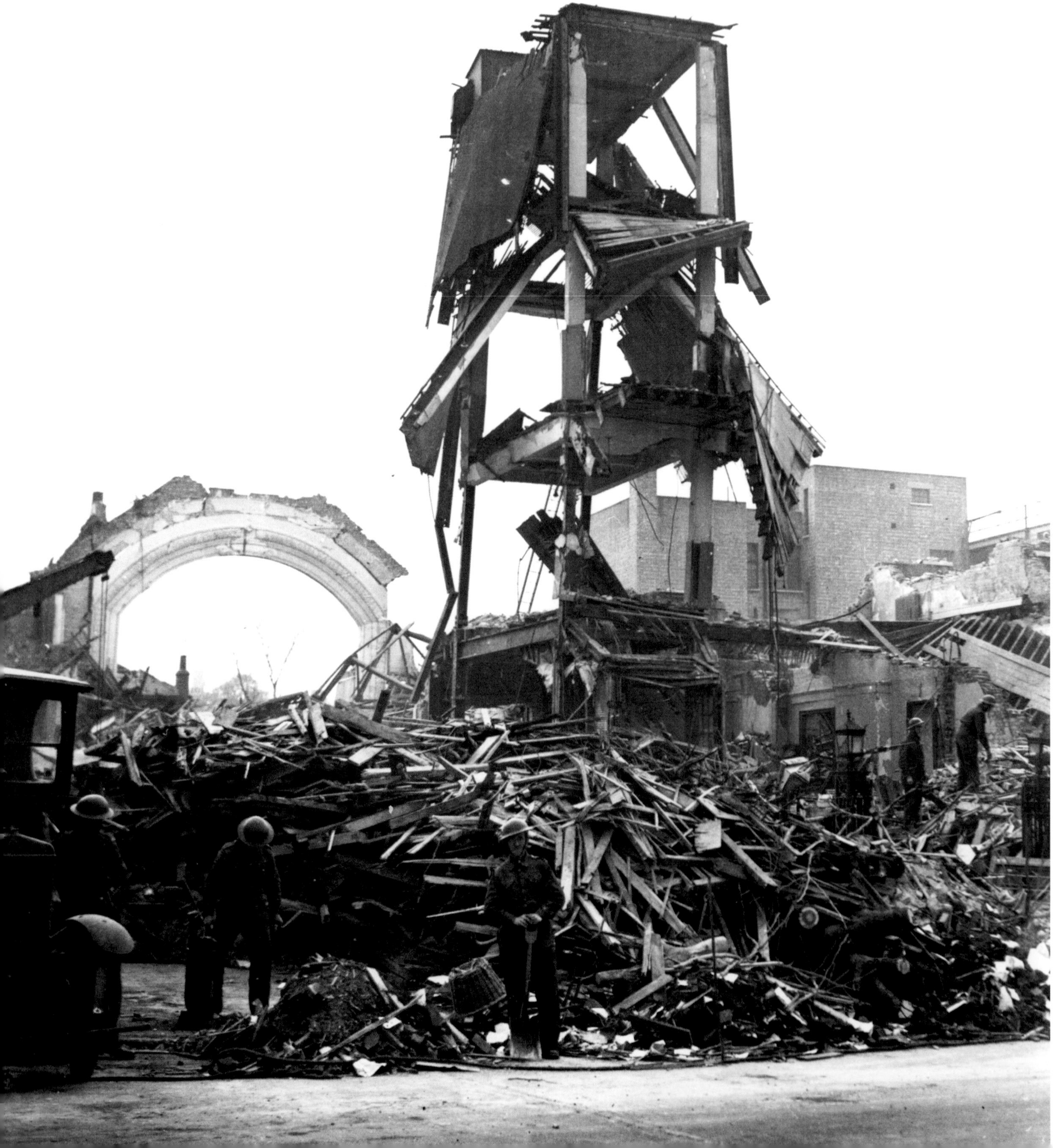

Charles Mahoney
Morley College, 1928-30 & Brockley School, 1932-36

Peyton Skipwith

In 1928 William Rothenstein, the Principal of the Royal College of Art, played an important role in the selection of three of his young former students – Mahoney, Bawden and Ravilious – to paint the murals at Morley College. While he appreciated to the full Bawden's and Ravilious's talent and 'phantasy', Mahoney's more direct and down-to-earth approach to painting had a greater affinity with Rothenstein's own work of this period, and although after graduation both Bawden and Ravilious taught at the College on a part-time basis, Rothenstein recruited Mahoney as an assistant tutor in the School of Drawing and Painting. It was in this rôle that he was selected four years later to decorate the Hall at Brockley County School, in which task he was assisted by three of his fourth-year female students – Evelyn Dunbar, Mildred Eldridge and Violet Martin.

Cyril Mahoney was quickly rechristened 'Charlie' on entering the College in 1922 by Barnett Freedman, a friend and fellow student, and it is as Charles that he is known to posterity. As a boy the young Cyril had lost the sight of one eye in a scuffle with one of his brothers over a pair of scissors, and this debilitation may to some degree have affected his manner of painting, particularly his use of tilted perspectives and shallow depth of field. The eye-surgeon, Patrick Trevor-Roper, in his book *The World Through Blunted Sight*, makes only passing reference to the effects of monocular vision on artists when commenting on the work of the seventeenth-century Baroque painter Giovanni Francesco Barbieri, better known as Il Guercino or 'the squinter'. Trevor-Roper notes that Guercino's paintings 'may be said to have a rather two-dimensional quality, as he could have painted with only one eye.'[1]

The Morley and Brockley mural cycles were separated in time by a mere four years, but it is difficult today to make a direct comparison, as the former was destroyed by bombs in 1940, and can be judged only from black-and-white photographs and some surviving mainly monochrome preparatory sketches. However, the general impression we get from this photographic evidence is that the Morley scheme – *The Pleasures of Life* – was classically Italianate and sculptural, emulating a frieze in low relief, in contrast to the more transparent ethereality of Mahoney's two large panels at Brockley.

142
Morley College after being bombed, 1940, © London Borough of Lambeth

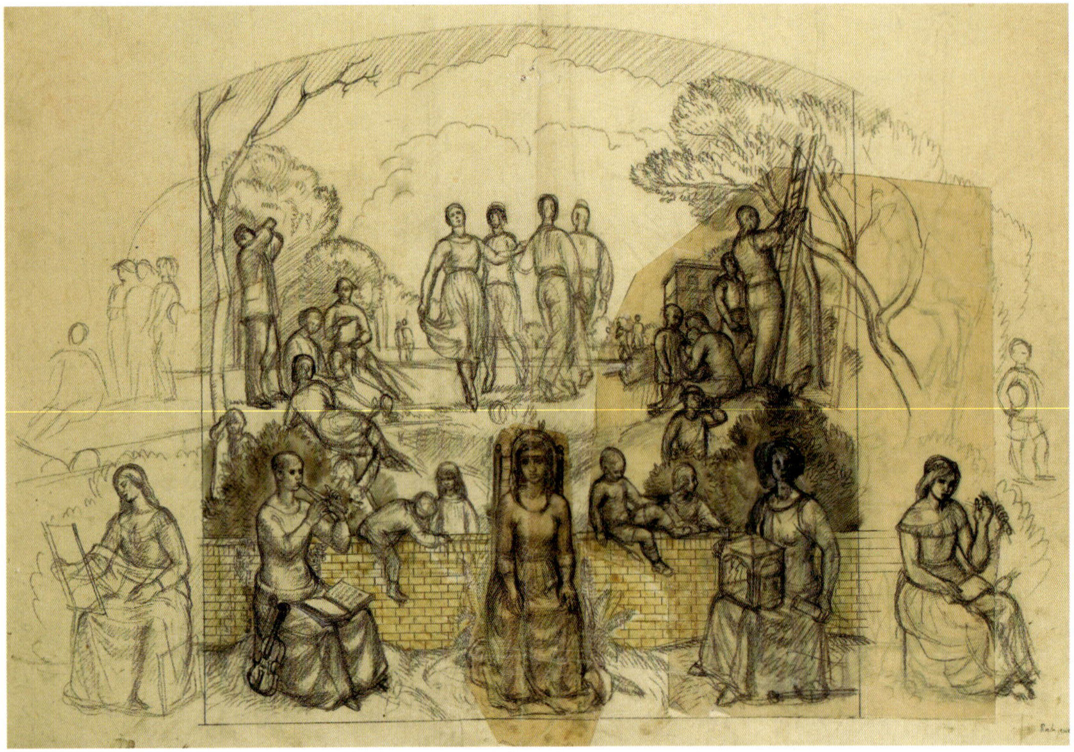

143
Compositional study for *The Pleasures of Life*, 1928-30,
pen and brown ink over pencil on paper,
47 x 65 cm (18 ½ x 25 ½ in.),
inscribed 'Rich jewels'

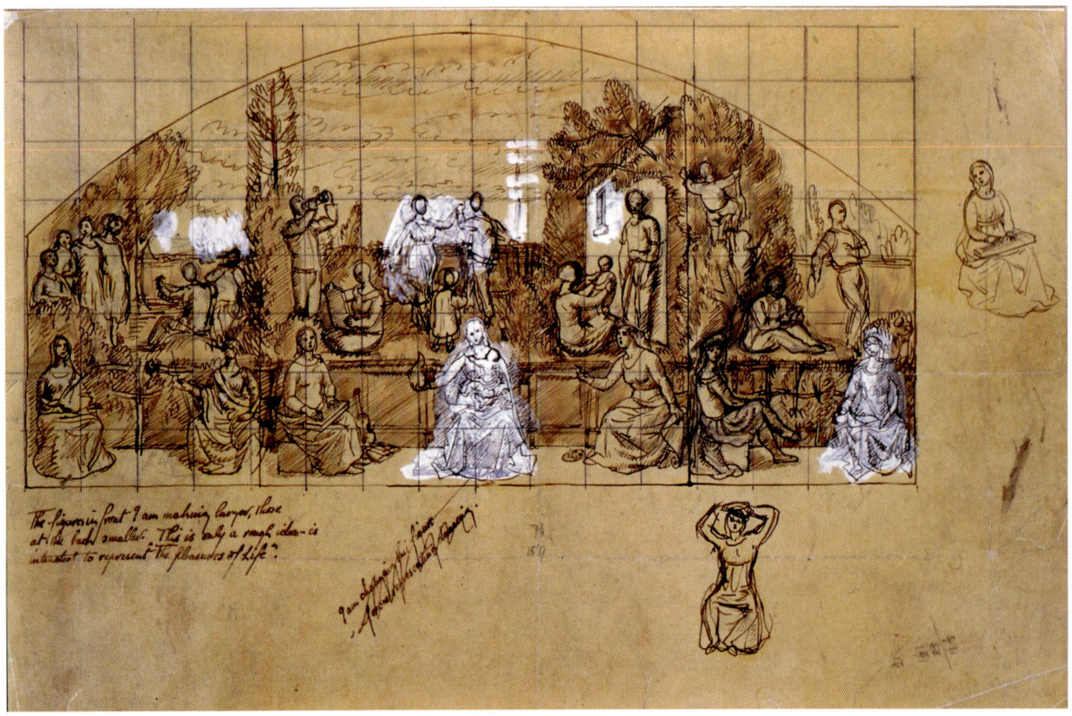

144
Compositional study for *The Pleasures of Life*, 1928-30,
pen and brown ink over pencil with areas of correction
in white, squared on tracing paper,
31.8 x 48.9 cm (12 ½ x 19 ⅛ in.)
inscribed 'The figures in front I am making larger,
those at the back smaller. This is only a rough idea – is
intended to represent "The Pleasures of Life" and I am
changing this figure for one representing dancing.'

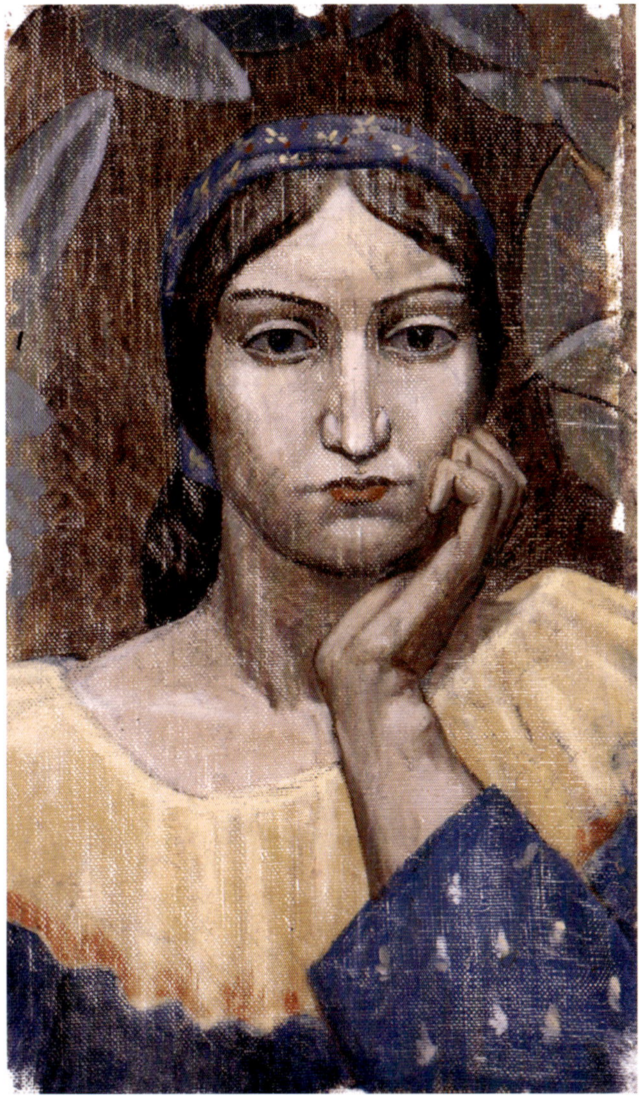

145
Muse: Study for Philosophy, oil paint mixed with wax on canvas, 58.4 x 35.6 cm (23 x 14 in.)

This fragment gives an idea of the original scale. The early compositional design indicates that this central figure was originally conceived as a Madonna.

The subject matter of Mahoney's large Morley mural, *The Pleasures of Life*, measuring 24 feet by 15 feet, was related directly to the setting in which it was to be viewed in the large Hall of the Georgian building in Lambeth, into which the College had moved in 1924. The Hall was used for all formal College functions, as well as for plays, choral and orchestral concerts and folk dancing, and its position immediately above and behind the stage largely dictated its character, if not its precise form. As John Rothenstein stated, the objective was to 'provide a decoration which would make the stage the centre of interest, without distracting the attention of an audience from any speaker or singer thereon. No dashing flights of fancy, therefore, nor humorous sallies were allowed him. In a word his painting had to be interesting but not arresting.'[2]

The challenge of producing a suitable and unified design was not made easier by the fact that the allotted space was both canted and divided into three parts. Mahoney's solution was to produce a two-tiered design in the manner of fifteenth-century Italian frescoes with a foreground frieze of seated statuesque figures set against a low wall: these seven figures represent the artistic and intellectual pleasures of life, namely Dancing and Plastic Art, in the left-hand section, Music, Philosophy and Drama in the centre, and Poetry and Prose to the right. The dividing wall against which they sit serves as a dividing wall against which they sit serves as a device for introducing realistically painted young children as interested spectators, and at the same time separates them from the bucolic pleasures of life, which are represented in the upper tier, where the composition is painted in a less formal manner. This section is centred on a quartet of two young men and two young women with linked hands dancing a pavane, while subsidiary groups of figures enjoy more relaxed country pursuits, including apple-gathering.

Sadly, no colour photographs of *The Pleasures of Life* are known to exist, but from the critic P.G. Konody we learn that blue and red were the key colours,[3] while it is clear from the excellent black-and-white photographs that Mahoney's brushwork was bold with each stroke making a telling and individual mark, like threads in long-stitch embroidery, in contrast to the smooth finish of Bawden's and Ravilious's murals in the refectory.

Rothenstein noted that *The Pleasures of Life* 'was planned somewhat after the fashion of a Florentine decoration of the fifteenth century.'[4] This historical reference back is entirely justifiable, but what no one seems to have commented on at the time is how in tune it was with some of Europe's most avant-garde art, particularly mural art, though Konody noted how the figures belonged 'to our own age and are English in type.' *The Pleasures of Life* fits precisely, in spirit and technique, into that sub-current of modernism – the return to classicism – which informed the work of artists such as Picasso, Mario Sironi, Carlo Carra and Giorgio de Chirico during the 1920s, and which has recently been so well exemplified in the Guggenheim Museum's 2011 exhibition *Chaos and Classicism: Art in France, Italy and Germany 1918-36*. If *The Pleasures of Life* existed today it would almost certainly rank alongside the best murals from Mussolini's Italy of the 1920s and those that were to adorn American post offices and other public buildings under Roosevelt's New Deal in the following decade. Although very different in subject matter there are affinities between Mahoney's mural and de Chirico's two decorative panels of *Gladiators at Rest* and *Gladiators (Triumph)* commissioned by Léonce Rosenberg, the Paris art dealer, at the precise moment that Mahoney undertook the Morley College commission. The Morley murals were unveiled by the future Prime Minister, Stanley Baldwin, on February 6, 1930.

Right:

148
The stage of the concert hall with *The Pleasures of Life*, Morley College, c. 1930, Courtesy of the Architctural Press Archive / RIBA Library Photographs Collection

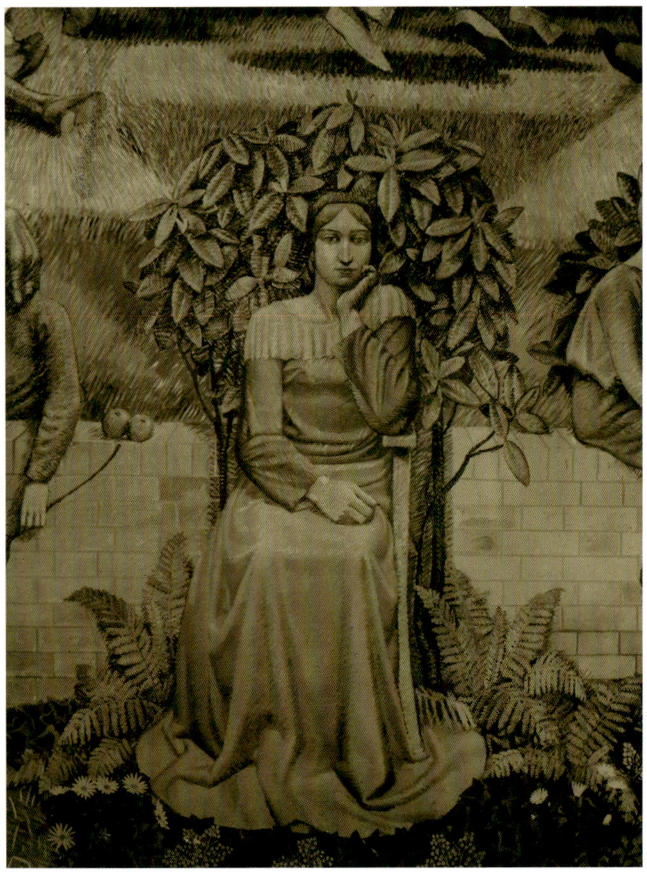

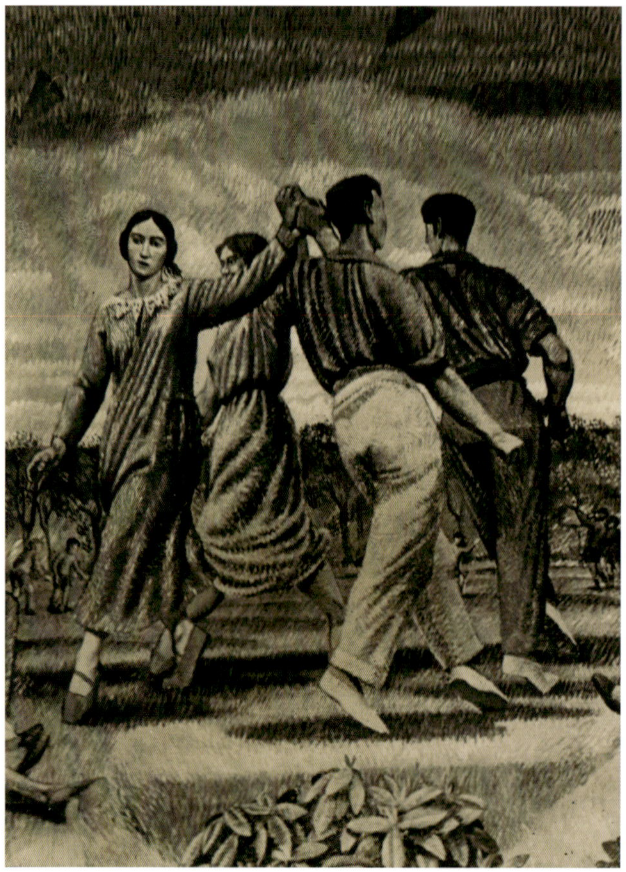

146 & 147
Two photographs taken of details of Mahoney's mural cycle *The Pleasures of Life*, at Morley College.
From a presentation album owned by Elizabeth Bulkeley

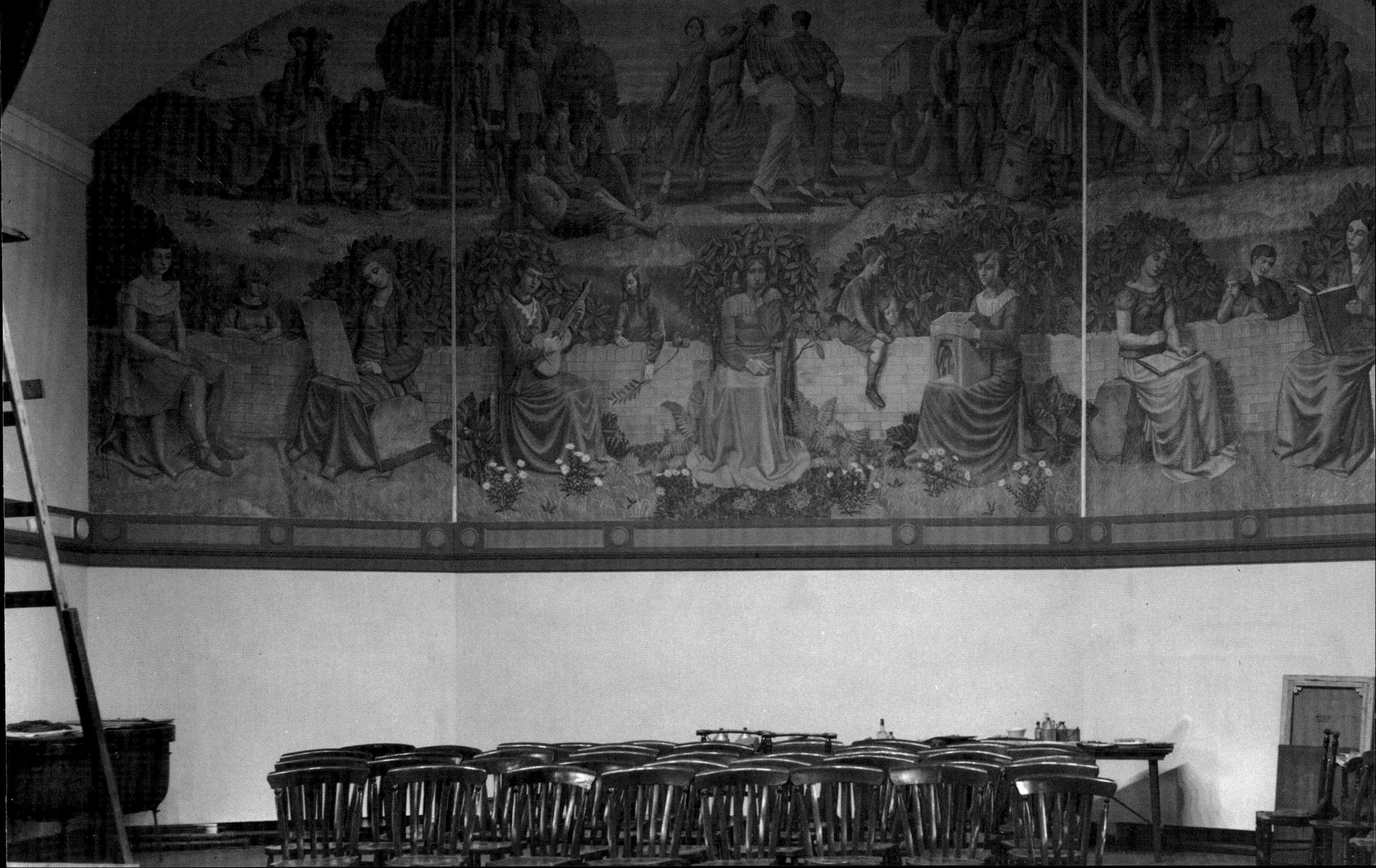

Three years later, when Mahoney began working on his designs for the murals at Brockley County School, both his approach and his technique had changed quite radically. The mythic quality of reality evident at Morley had now been replaced by a dreamlike vision of medieval legend, owing more to the embellishment of fourteenth-century north European Books of Hours than to fifteenth-century Florence. Some of the difference in effect can undoubtedly be attributed to the differences in preparation: at Morley the painting was carried out in oil colour mixed with wax on canvas which was fixed to the wall at an early stage, while at Brockley the murals were painted directly onto the walls. Happily, the April 1936 edition of the school magazine, *The Raven*, published shortly after the work was completed, gives a detailed account of the preparatory technique employed by Mahoney and his colleagues at Brockley: 'The surface was prepared with an absorbent coating of oil and white lead, covered with non-absorbent zinc white. Ordinary oil colours were used, but their surplus oil was removed by drying out on blotting paper. The resulting stiff colour was mixed with an emulsion of paraffin wax and turpentine to a very fluid consistency. Finally the paintings were varnished with beeswax.'[5]

The Hall, at what was then Brockley County School for Boys and is now Prendergast School for Girls, doubles up as both gymnasium and assembly hall, with a balcony at one end and five 12-feet-high arched spaces between the windows, which must have been crying out for decoration. The headmaster, Dr Sinclair, was aware of William Rothenstein's views on painting in public places and, in October 1932, proposed to the school governors the idea of decorating the hall with murals to be painted by R.C.A. students. The idea being approved, he contacted Rothenstein who

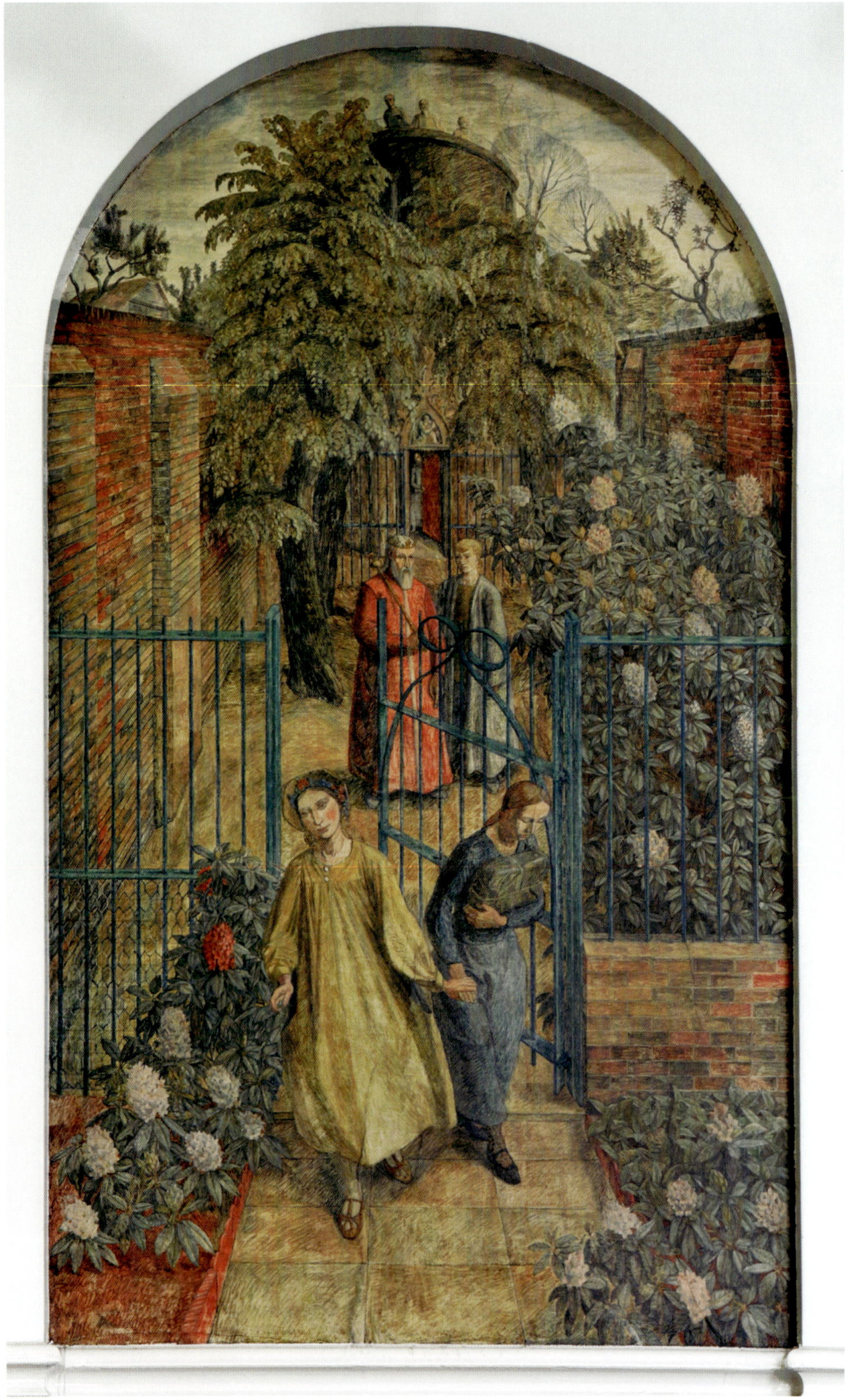

149 *Joy & Sorrow*, mural at Brockley County School, c. 1932-36

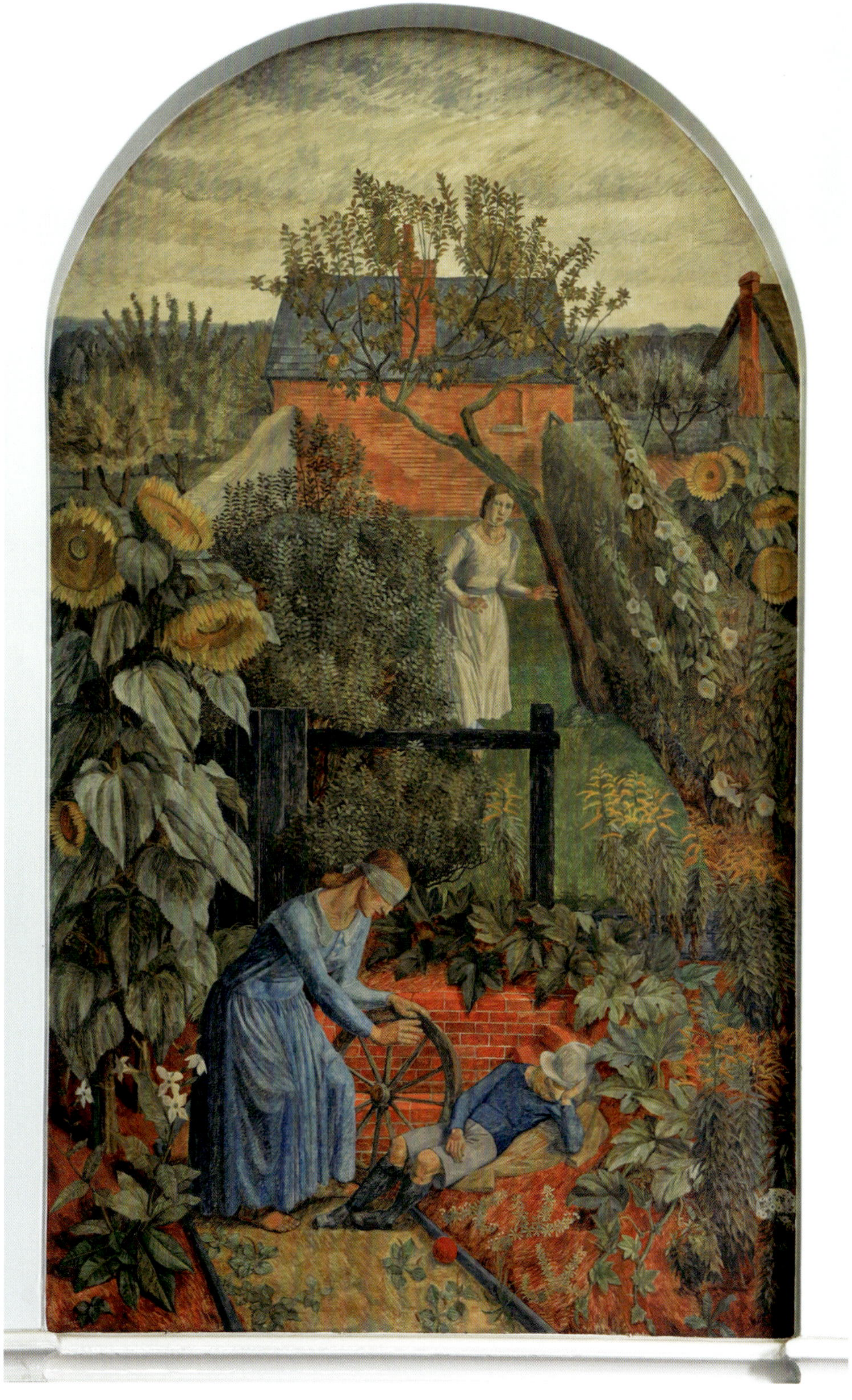

passed the matter over to Mahoney who, visiting the School and surveying the hall, suggested the idea of using fables from Aesop, Gay and other more obscure sources as a unifying theme. He undertook to decorate two of the large lunettes himself and allocated a third to Evelyn Dunbar, one of his most accomplished students. His chosen subjects were *Fortune and the Boy at the Well* and *Joy and Sorrow*, while Dunbar selected *The Country Girl and the Pail of Milk*. At a slightly later date two other younger students, Mildred Eldridge and Violet Martin were offered the two remaining lunettes on the opposite wall. Eldridge, who had just returned from a travelling scholarship at the British School at Rome, chose to create an amalgam of three fables – *The Birdcatcher and the Skylark*, *The Traveller and the River* and *The Farmer and the Cranes* – while Martin painted *The King and the Two Shepherds*. Under Mahoney's careful supervision these five large lunettes, each depicting figures in landscapes, were unified into a single decorative scheme.

The decoration of the balcony was largely carried out by Evelyn Dunbar with the front panels facing the hall providing the single largest surface measuring 39 feet wide by 8 feet high, for this she painted a panoramic view of the school in its fine semi-rural setting in Hilly Fields Park. Mahoney contributed two further fables in the spaces below the balcony, *The Clock and the Dial* and *The Butterfly and the Rose*, as well as a ceiling decoration, *The Four Winds of Hilly Fields*, on the underside of the gallery. The Brockley mural cycle stands out as one of the most important decorative schemes of the twentieth century in Britain, and the Hall was listed by the Department of National Heritage in April 1992 'solely because of the high quality and rarity of the mural paintings.'[6]

150 *Fortune & the Boy at the Well*, mural at Brockley County School, c. 1932-36

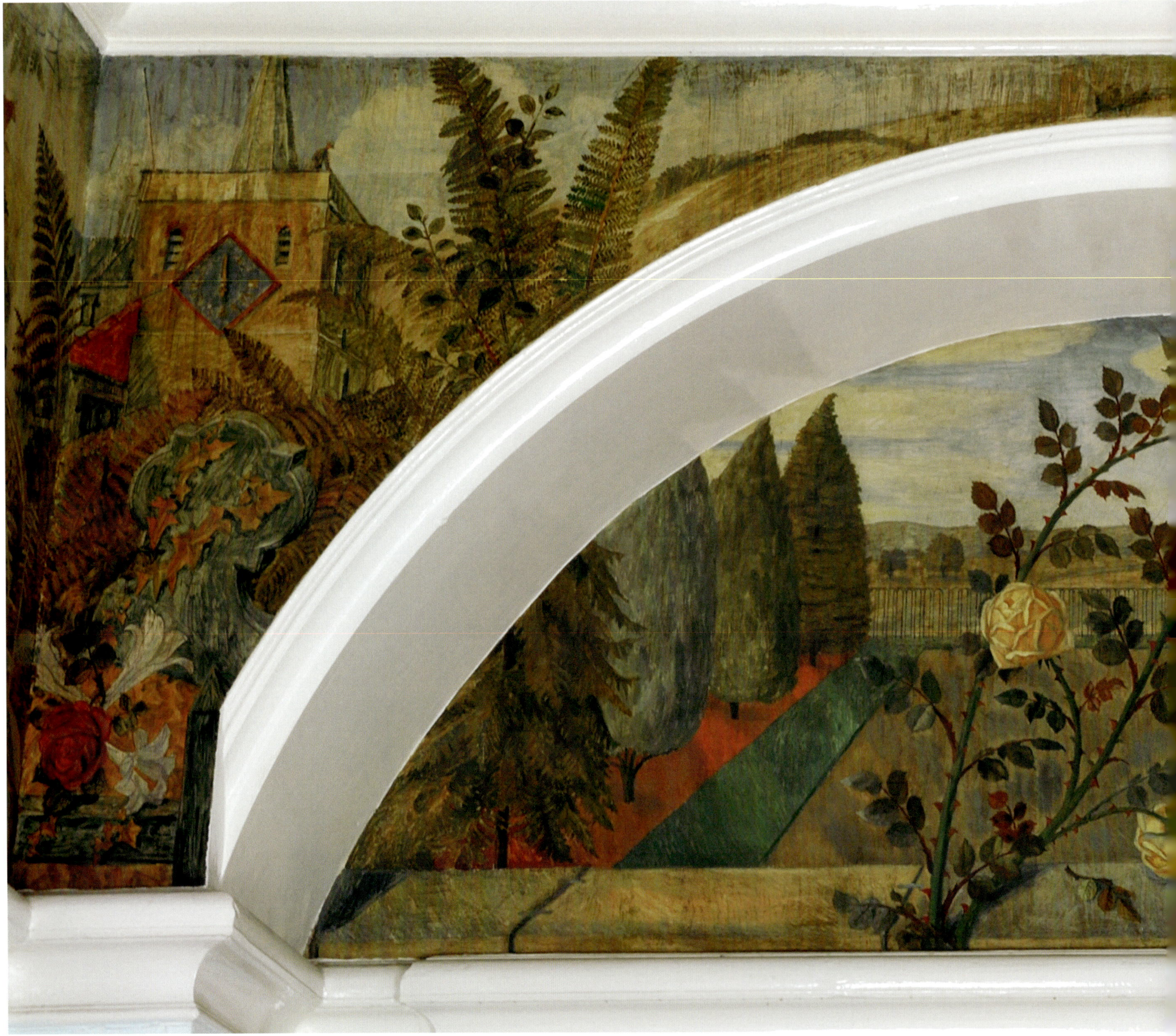

151 *The Clock and the Dial* and *The Butterfly and the Rose,* mural at Brockley County School in the spaces below the balcony, c. 1932-36

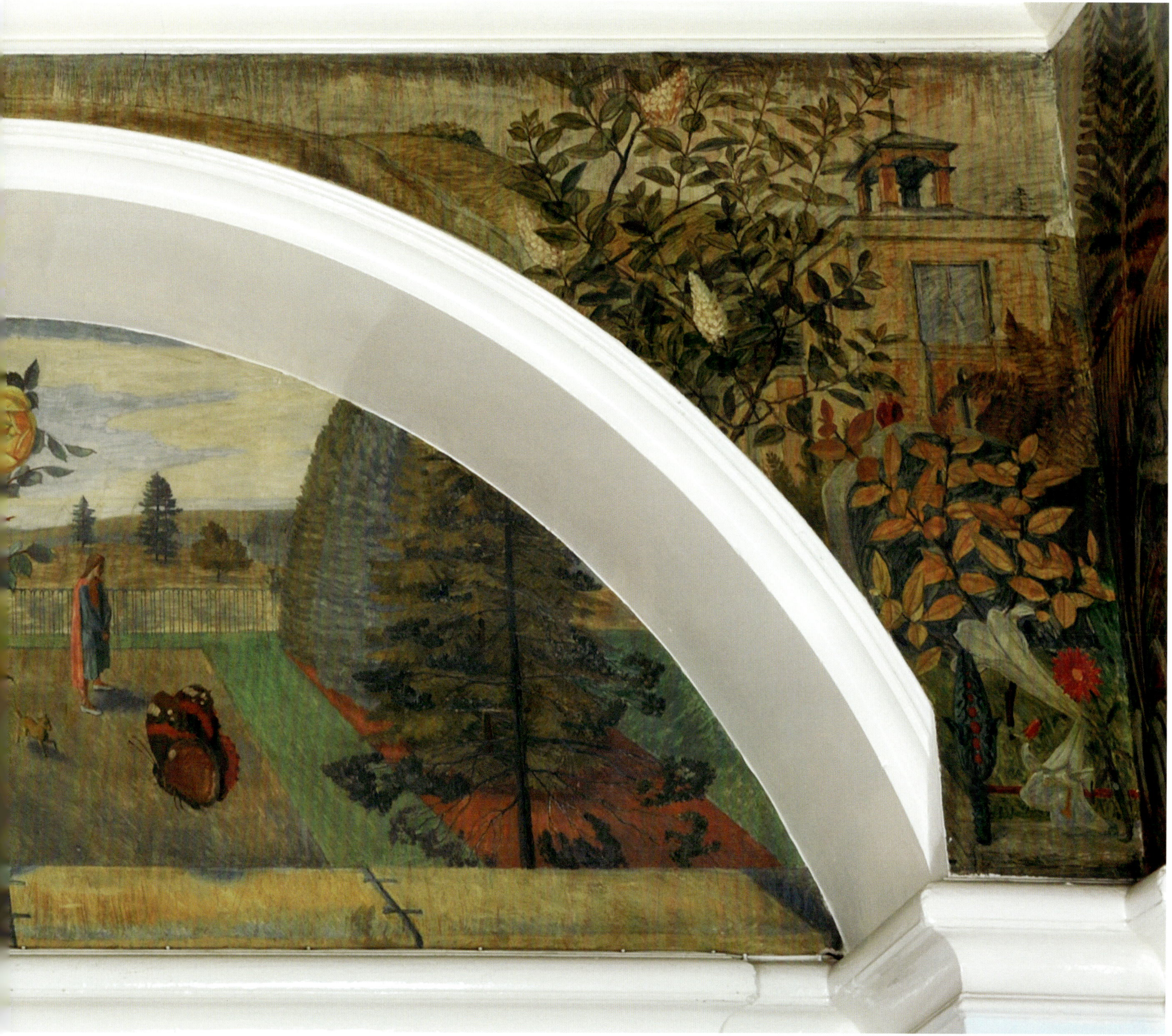

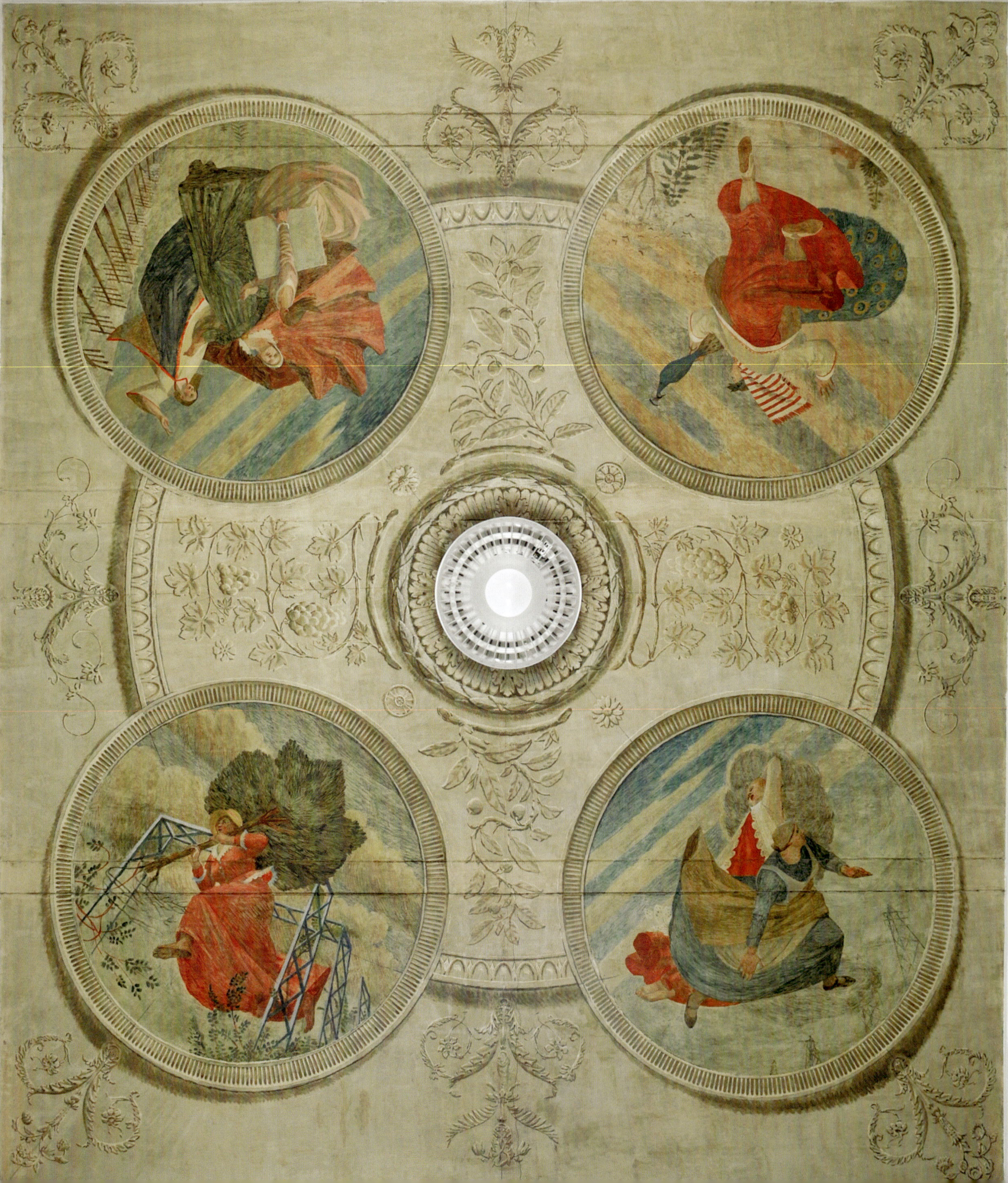

ENDNOTES

1 Patrick Trevor-Roper, *The World Through Blunted Sight*, London 1988, p.103.

2 John Rothenstein, 'The Mural Decorations at Morley College', *Studio*, xcix, 1930, p.430.

3 P.G. Konody, *The Observer*, 9 February, 1930, quoted in Alan Powers' 'Charles Mahoney as a Mural Painter' in the exhibition catalogue *Charles Mahoney, 1903-1968*, The Fine Art Society & Paul Liss, 1999, p.38.

4 *Studio*, op.cit.

5 *The Raven*, April 1936, p.136, quoted Gill Clarke, *Evelyn Dunbar: War and Country*, Sansom & Company, Bristol, 2006, p.26.

6 Quoted Gill Clarke, op.cit. p.24.

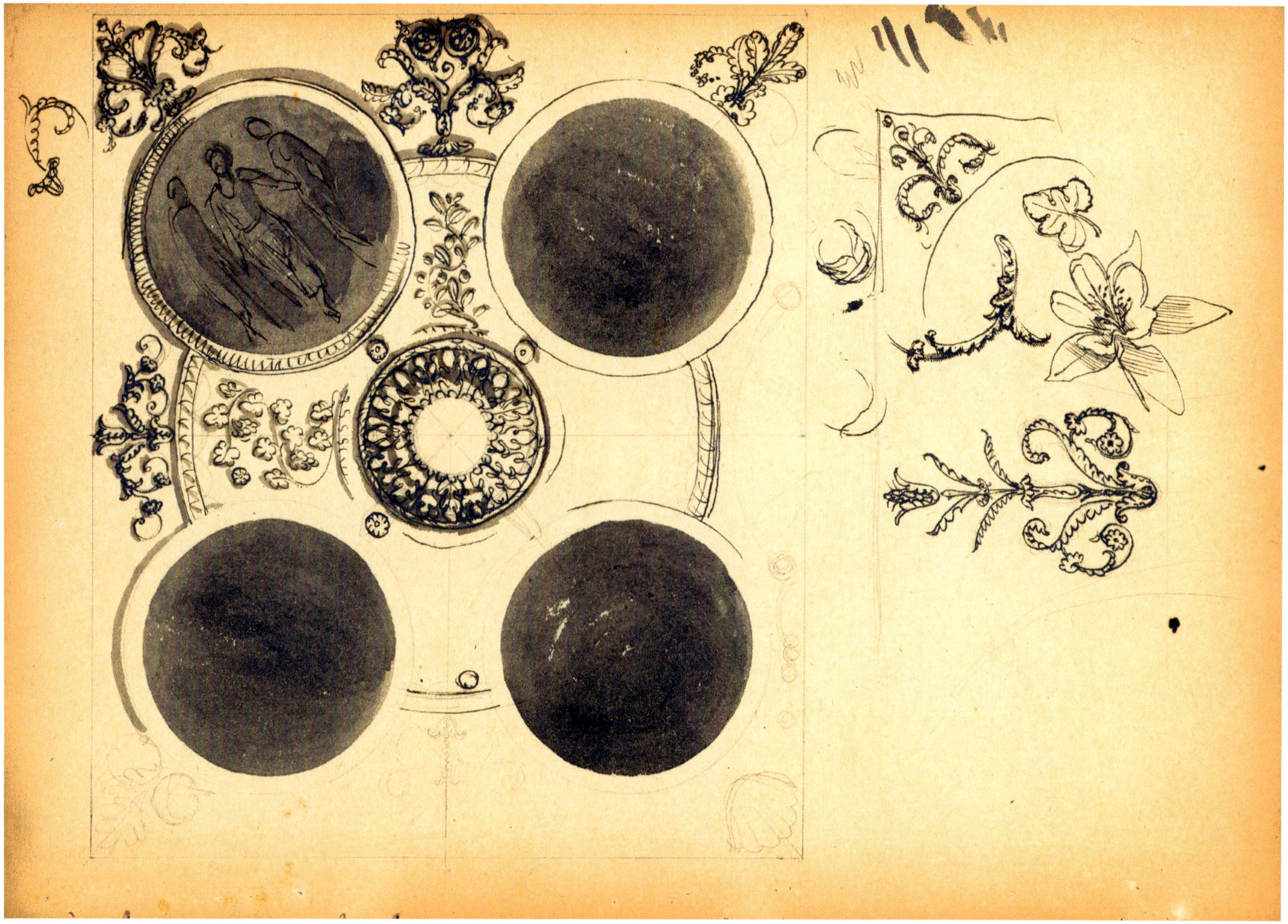

153 Study for *The Four Winds of Hilly Fields*, pencil, pen & ink and wash on paper, 39 x 28 cm (15 ⅜ x 11 in.), c. 1932-36

Left: 152 *The Four Winds of Hilly Fields*, a ceiling decoration at Brockley Country School, c. 1932-36

MURALS AND DECORATIVE PAINTINGS BY CHARLES MAHONEY

1928 – Morley College Murals – unveiled by Stanley Baldwin late 1930, destroyed by bombs in 1940

1932-36 – Murals for Brockley County School for Boys (now Predergast School for Girls)

1932 – *Thomas More* mural, Holy Redeemer Church, Chelsea

1936 – *The Expulsion from the Garden of Eden*, oil on canvas, 914 x 762 cm (359 ⅞ x 300 in.), Tate, London

1941-52 – Campion Hall. A house owned and run by the Society of Jesus, now part of Oxford University

1951 – *The Garden*, oil on canvas, 182.9 x 121.9 cm (72 x 48 in.), Festival of Britain: '60 paintings for 51'

Autumn, oil on board, 213.4 x 121.9 cm (84 x 48 in.), Exhibited: Society of Mural Painters Exhibition, Arts Council of Great Britain

1957 – Designs submitted to RA for rebuilt Morley College

1961 – Sketch Design for a Mural Decoration, Royal Academy

Charles Mahoney (1903-1968)

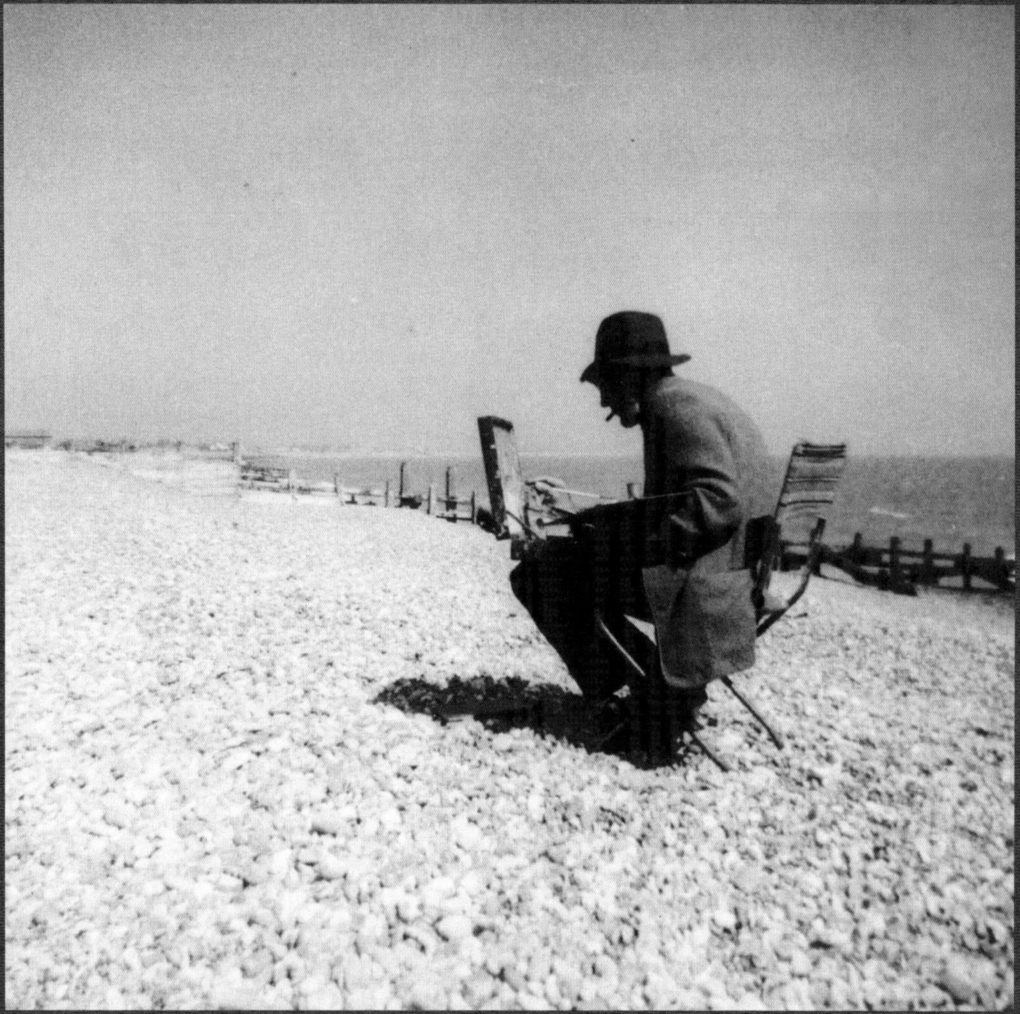

154 Charles Mahoney sketching on the shingle at Pevensey, 1958

CHARLES (CYRIL) MAHONEY, RA. Born Lambeth, died Chelsea. Draughtsman, painter and muralist. Studied Beckenham School of Art (1918-1922), Royal College of Art (1922-26), Art Workers' Guild (1942), NEAC (1950). Taught at the RCA (1928-53), Byam Shaw School (1954-61) and Royal Academy Schools (1961-68). Collaborated with Barnett Freedman on theatre designs for the Little Theatre, (1926) and with Evelyn Dunbar on *Gardeners' Choice* (Routledge, 1937). Evacuated with the RCA to Ambleside, 1940, resident master in charge of hostel for students. Married the calligrapher Dorothy Bishop 1941. His later life dogged by ill health. Museum collections: Tate Gallery.

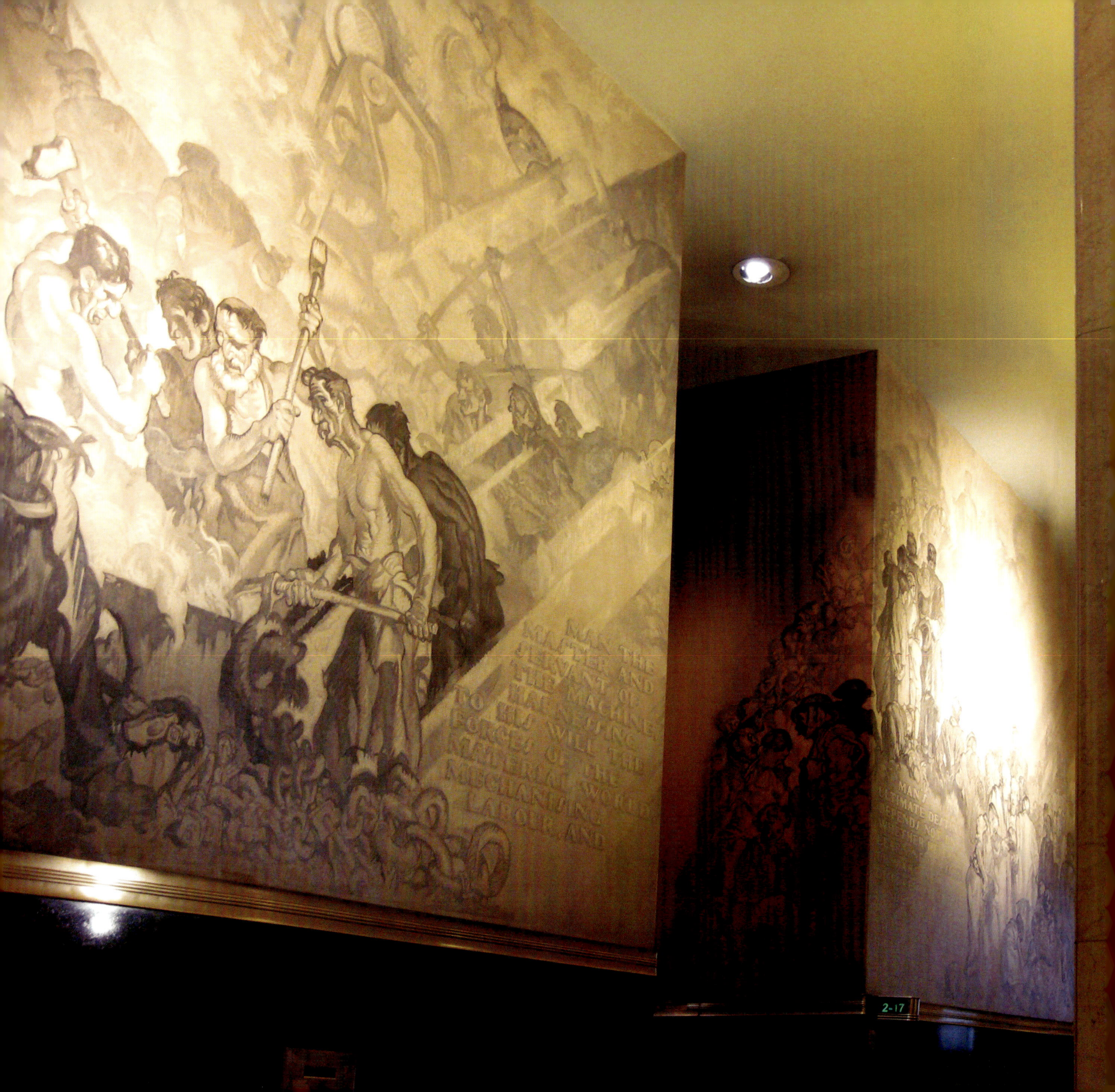
MAN THE
MASTER AND
SERVANT OF
THE MACHINE
HARNESSING
TO HIS WILL THE
FORCES OF THE
MATERIAL WORLD
MECHANIZING
LABOUR AND
2-17

Frank Brangwyn
Rockefeller Center, New York, 1932-1933

Libby Horner

The design of the seventy-storey Radio Corporation of America (RCA) building in the Rockefeller Center probably owed more to John R. Todd, the management guru for the Center, than it did to the architects whom Todd considered impractical and uppity. Todd was focussed on dollars and cents and claimed that ground space more than 30ft from a window was unrentable. As a result, the services and elevators were located centrally and as each lift shaft ended the building was set back, creating a false perspective and dramatizing the soaring façade, like a medieval church spire or a contemporary rocket, described by Le Corbusier as a 'machine aged temple'.[1] The lift shafts are a crucial element of the design and it was for this area that Brangwyn was asked to produce murals.[2]

John D. Rockefeller Jr desired a unified scheme of art and decoration for the Center's buildings which would somehow suggest a mixture of munificence, economic democracy, the glories of American civilization, intellect and spirituality. JDR was a member of the school of good taste and mediocrity in art, but his son Nelson was a collector of modern art and at his suggestion artists of international standing were approached to decorate the prestigious RCA concourse. The men who would have provided good propaganda, Matisse and Picasso, refused point blank (much to the amazement of the delegates who naively assumed that money could buy anything). However José Maria Sert took little persuasion and Diego Rivera was in accord until he learnt that Matisse and Picasso had withdrawn at which point the anarchic artist, source of future problems, had to be tempted back into the fold. Todd and Raymond Hood, who dominated the design team, visited Brangwyn in person in the autumn of 1932 and the artist, untroubled by artistic hierarchy, enthusiastically embraced the commission.

155 View of Frank Brangwyn's panels in the south corridor of the Rockefeller Center, New York

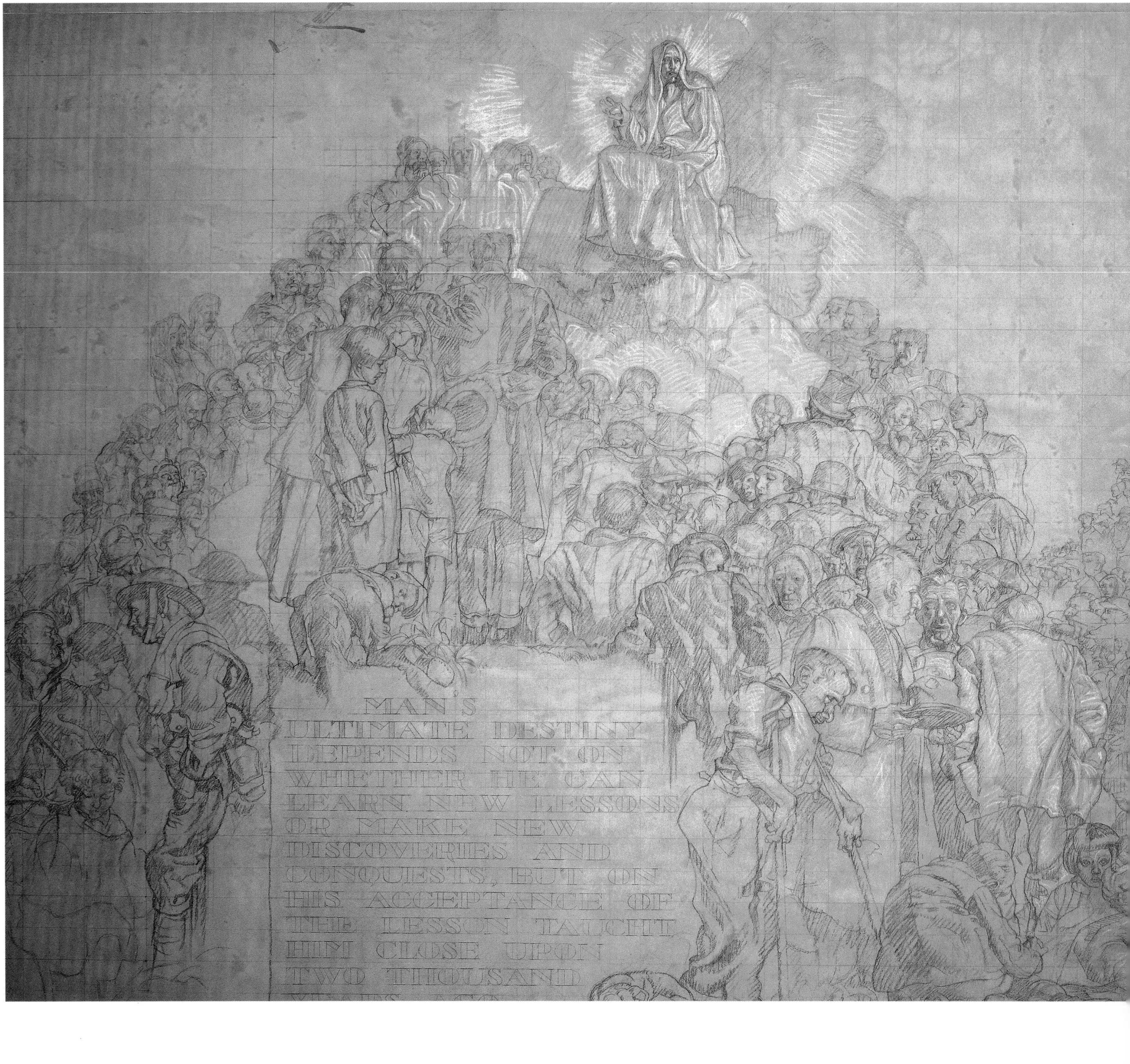
MAN'S
ULTIMATE DESTINY
DEPENDS NOT ON
WHETHER HE CAN
LEARN NEW LESSONS
OR MAKE NEW
DISCOVERIES AND
CONQUESTS, BUT ON
HIS ACCEPTANCE OF
THE LESSON TAUGHT
HIM CLOSE UPON
TWO THOUSAND

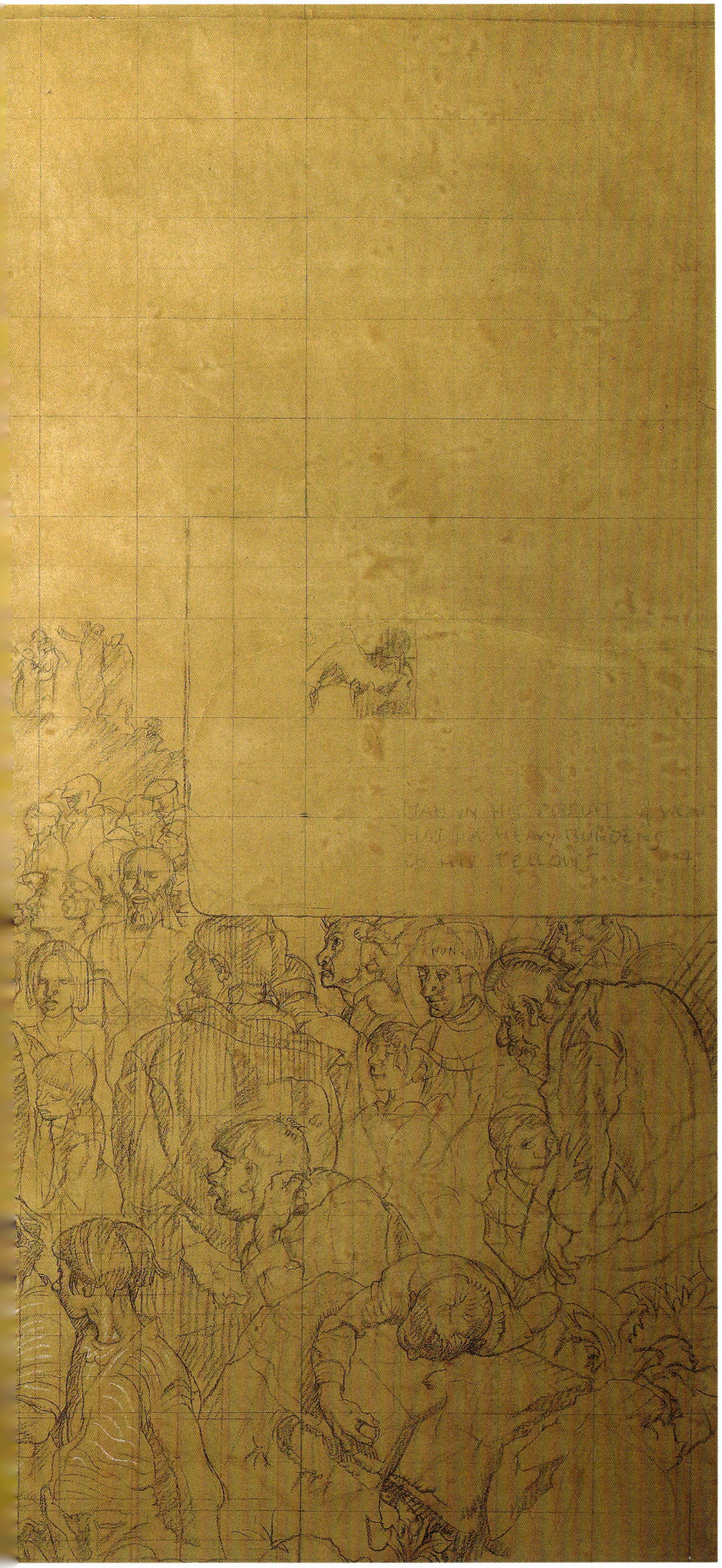

Brangwyn was instructed to produce four panels for the south corridor elevator banks, not more than 60-75% of the canvas was to be covered, lettering was to be included and the work was to be in black, white and brown – a limitation which did not disturb the artist since he had painted over 150 grisaille works for book illustrations and *The Graphic* magazine in the 1890s. Subtle sophistication was the effect aimed at – monochrome paintings, a black terrazzo floor, Champlain black marble walls and ivory paintwork elsewhere (unfortunately neither Rivera nor Sert adhered to the ban on colour). The panels were so large (17 x 25 ft) that Brangwyn had to hire exhibition galleries at Brighton where he worked with just one assistant Edward Kenneth Center.

Brangwyn was presented with the theme:
'Man's new relationship to society and his fellow man:

1 His Family Relationships,
2 His Relationships as a Worker,
3 His Relationships as a part of Government,
4 His Ethical and Religious Relationships,

the fourth being the dominating and controlling factor, without which the first three can only fail.'[3]

Todd also surprisingly suggested 'Christ's commandment "Do unto others as you would they should do unto you," and "The Sermon on the Mount."'[4] Surprising because the Rockefellers considered it unethical to display religious preferences in a commercial setting – faith-based institutions were not considered suitable tenants. Brangwyn had difficulty in interpreting the brief until his friend Philip Macer-Wright developed texts, all linked to Biblical quotations.

The scriptural references were disallowed and the final wording was as follows:

Man labouring painfully with his own hands; living precariously and adventurously, with courage, fortitude and the indomitable will to survive.

Man the creator and master of the tool. Strengthening the foundations and multiplying the comforts of his abiding place.

156 Cartoon for panel no. 4 of the Rockefeller Center, c. 1932, pencil on buff coloured tracing paper, squared, with highlights in white chalk, 152.4 x 213.4 cm (60 x 84 in.)

This cartoon is especially interesting because it illustrates Brangwyn's original proposal in that Christ is seen seated on a hill facing the viewer, before the Rockefeller fraternity disallowed any religious content. The area to the left of the lettering was also eliminated in the final work.

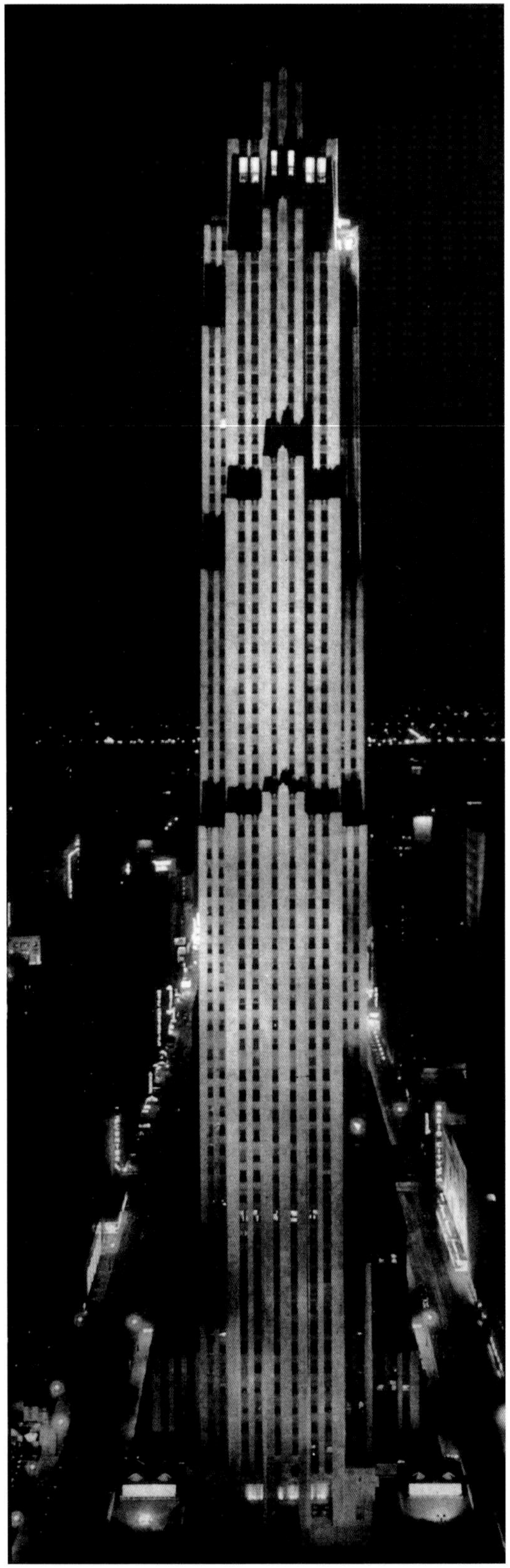

Man the master and servant of the machine, harnessing to his will the forces of the material world, mechanizing labour, and adding thereto the promise of leisure.

Man's ultimate destiny depends not on whether he can learn new lessons or make new discoveries and conquests, but on his acceptance of the lesson taught him close upon two thousand years ago.

This last panel, illustrating the Sermon on the Mount, was to cause Brangwyn the most problems. Diego Rivera, whose mural in the RCA building would link those of Brangwyn in the south corridor and those of José Maria Sert in the north corridor, was a committed Communist and as his work progressed it became apparent that a shadowy figure surrounded by peasants, workers and soldiers was to become a portrait of Lenin. Aghast, the leaders of capitalism demanded that the face be changed and a long battle ensued culminating in the removal and destruction of the entire mural. Having forbidden Lenin, it was felt that the leader of Christianity and arguably the original Communist, should not be portrayed. Rivera commented that:

'…it was a manifestation of certain laws of history that …the money-changers should now be taking belated revenge by expelling Jesus from their own Temple.'[5]

He added:

'The proprietors by forbidding a Christian painter to paint Christ and a Communist painter to paint Lenin prove that when they hire a painter they think they are buying him body and soul …They are mistaken.'[6]

As a Catholic and an increasingly religious and superstitious man, Brangwyn found it impossible to replace the figure of Christ with a suggested 'great light', and finally solved the dilemma by turning the figure round so that the onlooker sees only the back of Jesus, leading some people to remark that He had turned His back on New York.[7] Brangwyn explained that the depiction showed Christ 'looking over the world. There is a little of the world in the foreground, but the greater part is in the distance'.[8]

The 'little of the world' in the foreground was in fact populated by Ditchling inhabitants. On the left a small boy crawls over the grassy knoll. This is Leon Sinden, son of Alfred E. Sinden, the local pharmacist, who developed Brangwyn's photographs.

157 Night comes down on Rockefeller Center, highlighting the shaft of the 70-storey RCA Building (from *The Story of Rockefeller Center*, 1939)

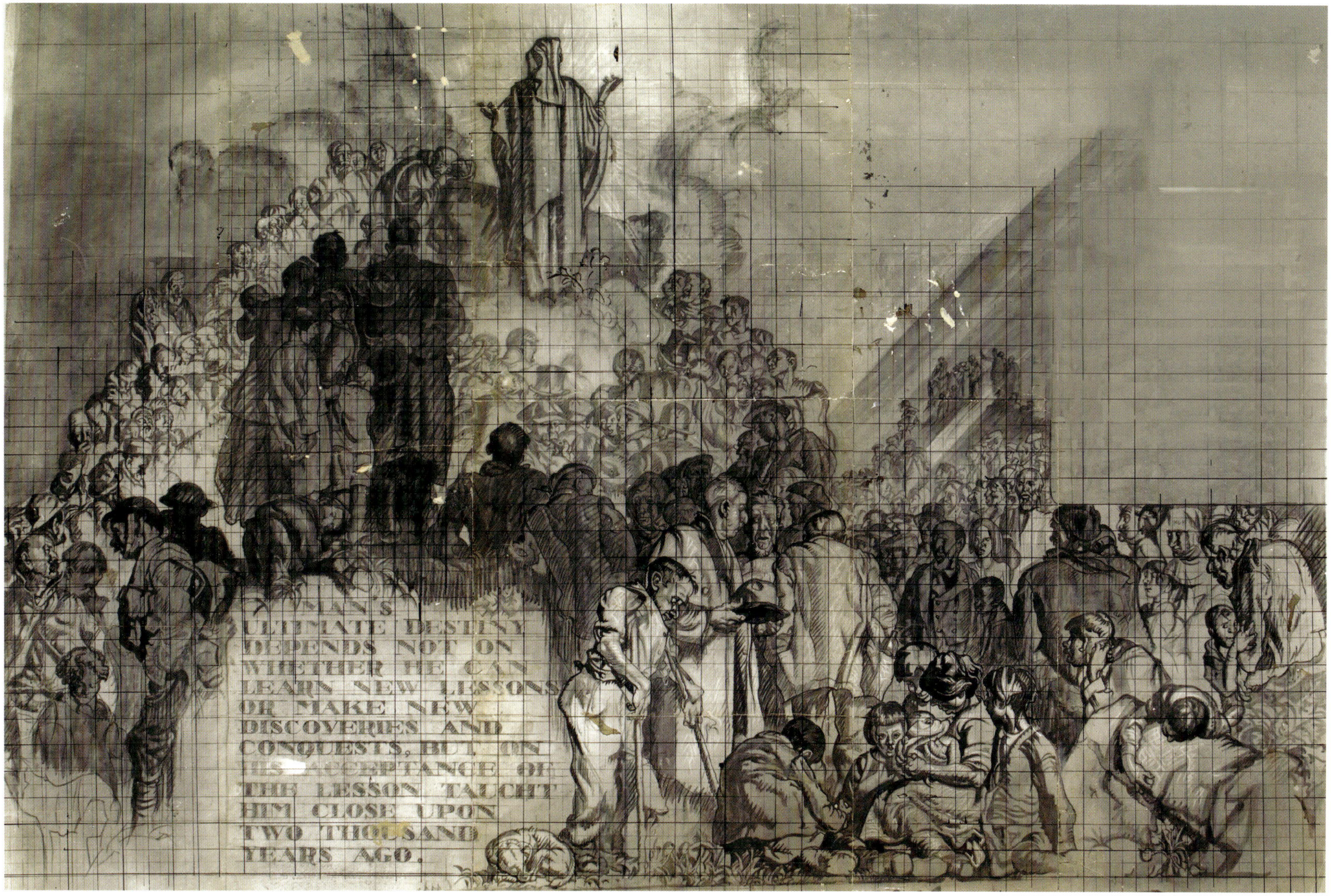

158 Working photomontage for *Man's Ultimate Destiny,* squared, with pen and ink and white oil paint highlights, 85 x 130 cm (33 ½ x 51 ⅛ in.)

This photograph forms the companion piece to the cartoon of *Man's Ultimate Destiny*. The only change in the composition is the figure of Christ. The photograph, which was probably developed by Alfred Sinden and was used by the artist himself, indicates Brangwyn's working methods in the multiple grids he has drawn for squaring and enlarging the image on to the final canvas. The cartoon from which the photograph is taken is one of four in the collection of the William Morris Gallery, London Borough of Waltham Forest.

Above Leon is a large standing group which comprises an amalgamation of three different photographs, the models being Mrs Sinden, Brangwyn himself, his housekeeper Lizzie Peacock, Tilly Cox who worked part-time for Mrs Peacock, together with her daughter Maud and baby Barry. The group on the right was inspired by a photograph of Mrs Cox with Barry, Maud, Lizzie Peacock and an unknown girl.

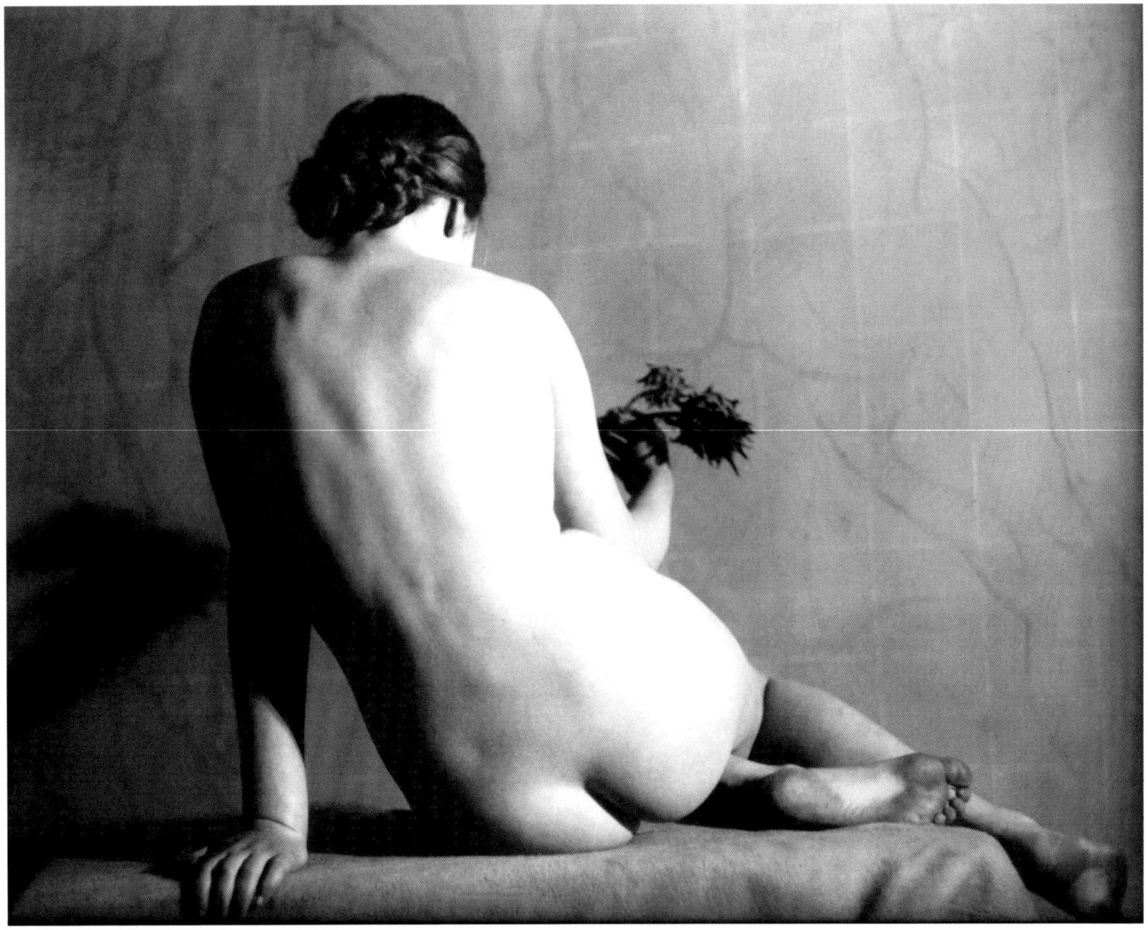

159 Joy Sinden modelling for *Man the Creator*, taken from the original glass plate held by Ditchling Museum

The press took great delight in an off-hand remark of Brangwyn's that he was searching for 'The Perfect Eve' but could not discover a woman model 'symbolic of her sex' among the 'flat-chested, narrow-hipped products of modernity'.[9] As Brangwyn explained to a friend, 'that lie the *Daily Mail* set going has given me some bother … about 300 letters from girls who seem game to sit … it was a shame making them think there was a chance for a job'.[10] *The Evening News* produced a cartoon showing a buxom Amazon being led into the studio by a thin and starched housekeeper (presumably Lizzie), and Brangwyn himself saw the humour of the situation, suggesting in a letter that the girls themselves should be brought together for an exhibition!

Finally the nineteen-year-old Miss Celia James of Brighton, who had been modelling for a year, and whose vital statistics were reported by the avid press to be 36 ½, 29, 37 was employed. The redoubtable Miss James can be identified in *Man the Creator* and in *Man Labouring Painfully*, together with baby.

Sir Donald Sinden also posed for Brangwyn and his sister Joy was a particular favourite as a nude model, her ample form conforming to Brangwyn's ideal – she appears to the right of the lettering in the panel *Man the Creator*.

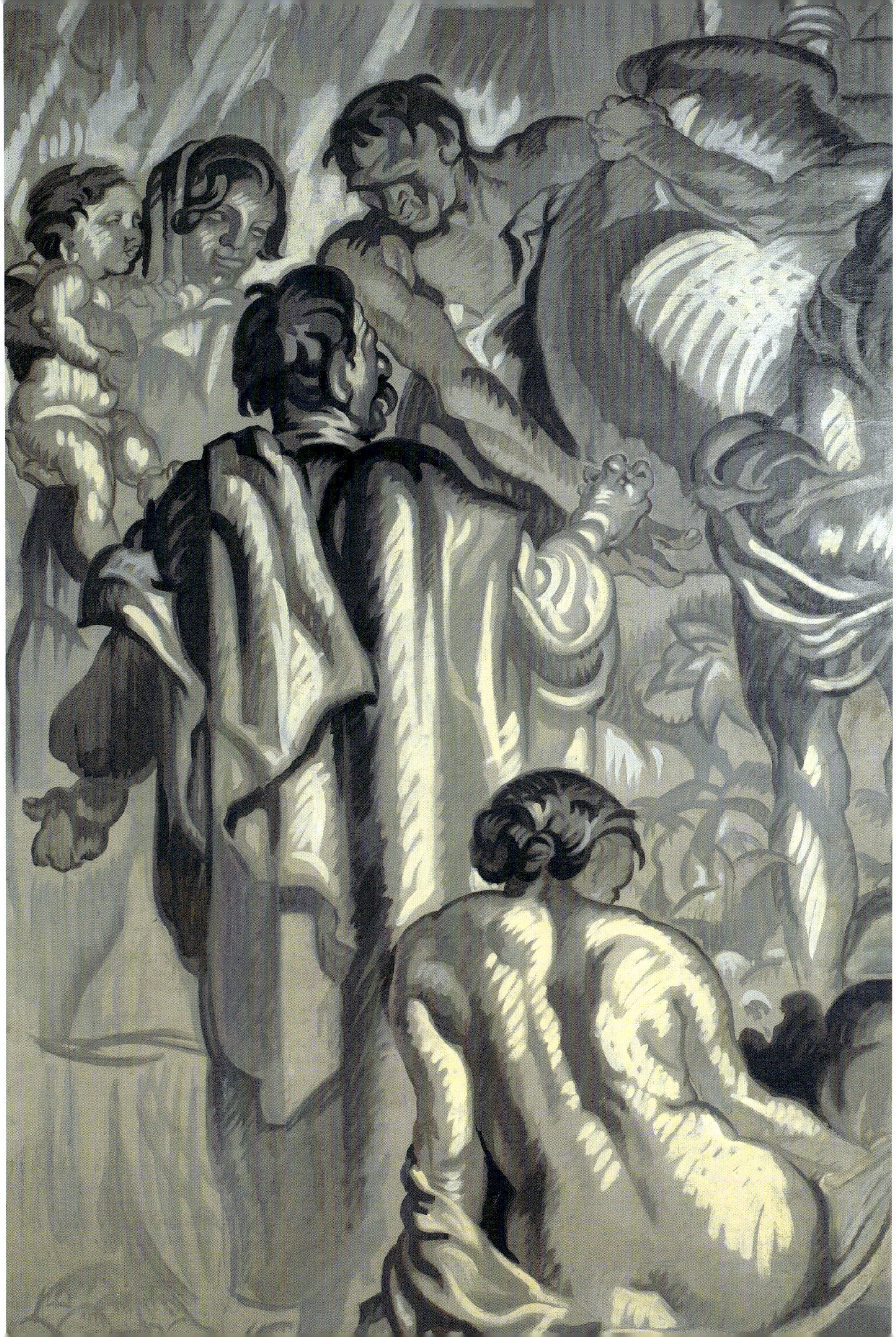

160
Study for Man the Creator, 1932
oil on canvas, 274.3 x 182.9 cm
(108 x 72 in.)

This study, like the one for *Man the Master,* would appear to be the same scale as the completed mural and was probably a preparatory exercise in colouring and shading techniques. In the final works the cross-hatching is slightly more detailed. It is interesting to note that as Brangwyn grew older (he was 65 when he painted these panels) his labourers also aged.

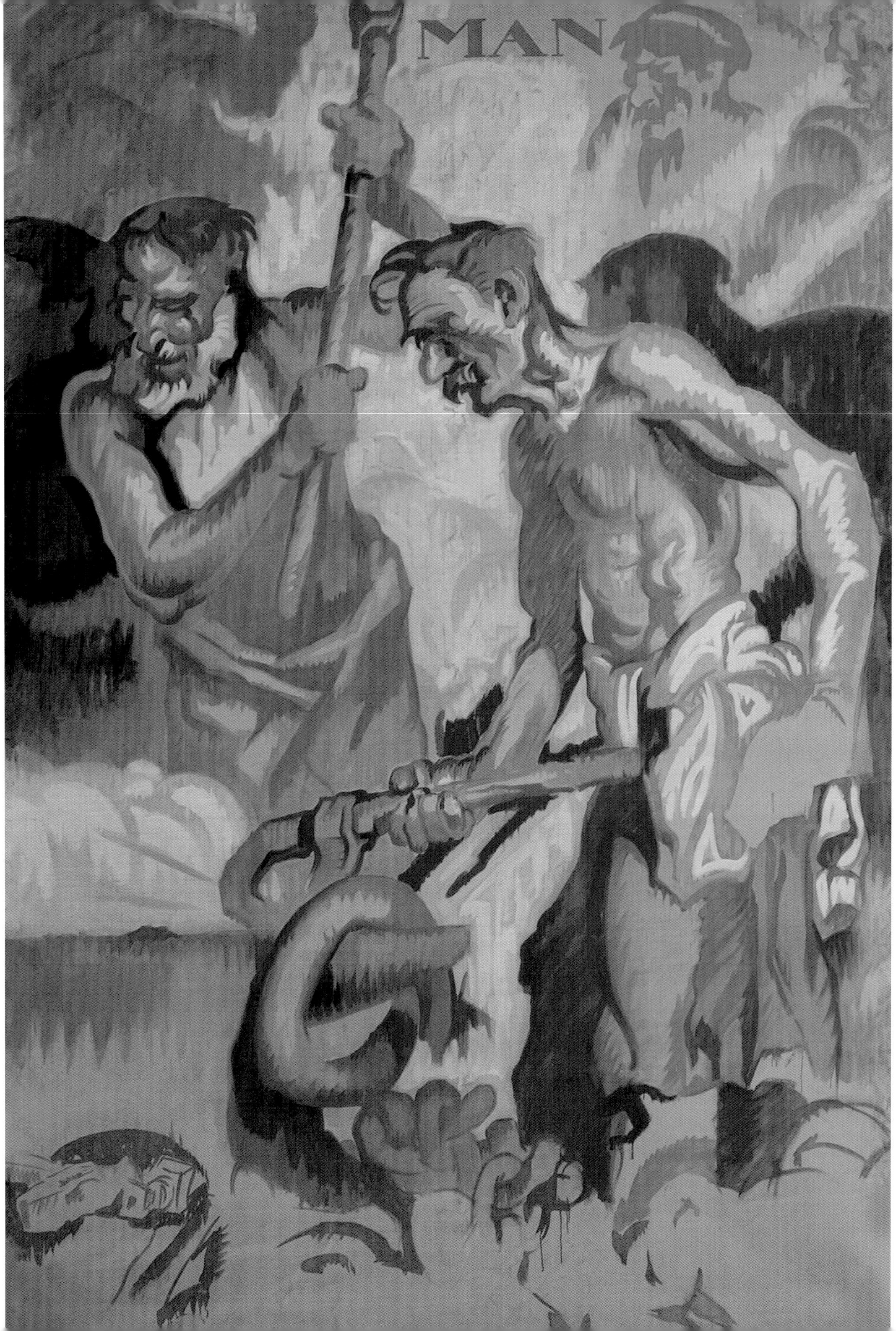

161
Study for Man the Master, 1932
oil on canvas,
274.3 x 182.9 cm
(108 x 72 in.)

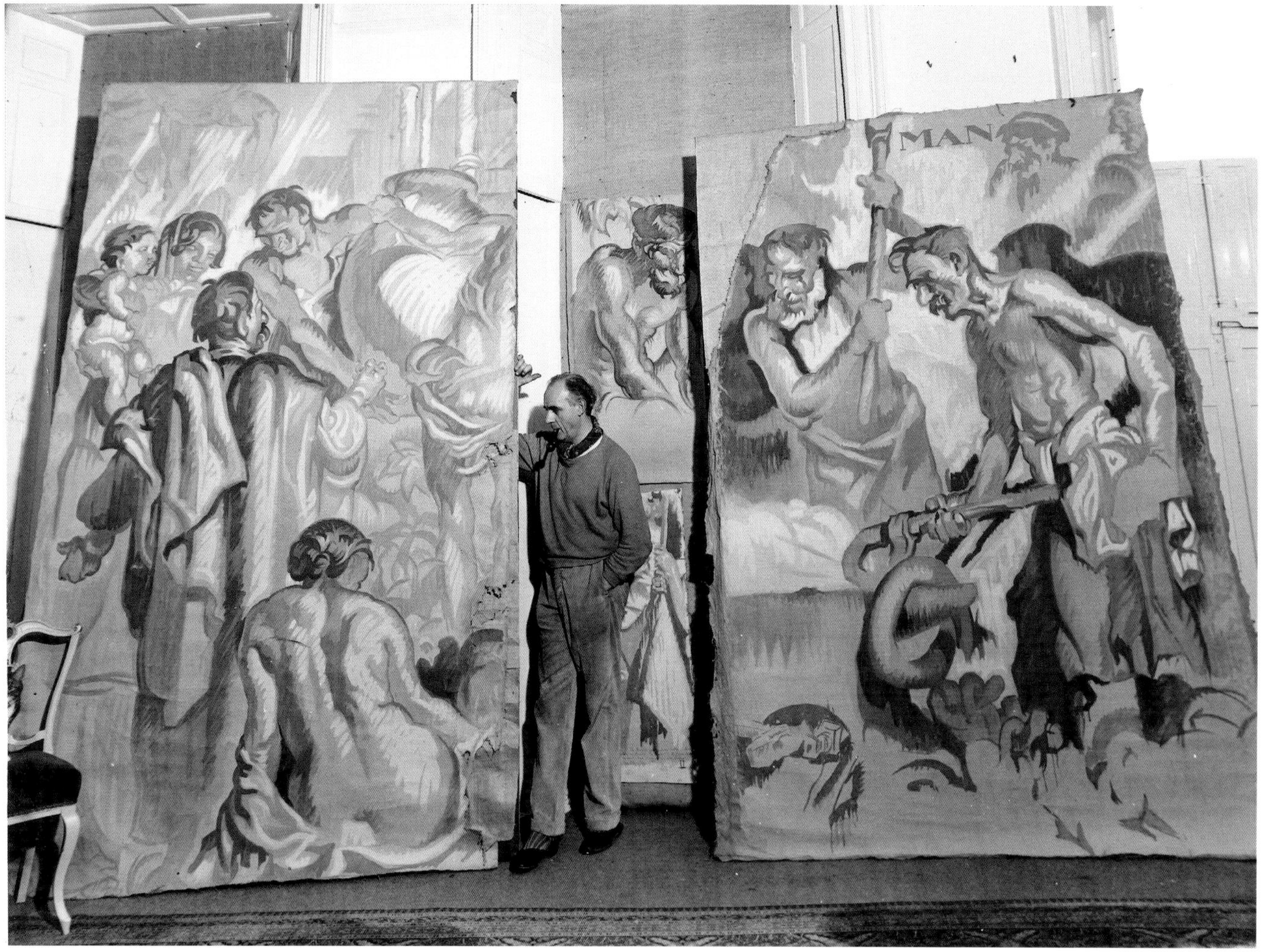

162 William de Belleroche with two of the 900 Brangwyn works he hoped to sell to Billy Butlin in 1961. In the hopes that Butlin would build a special gallery for the works, Sir Gerald Kelly became involved in negotiations and went down to Bognor to talk to the holiday camp owner who later spent 12 hours at Belleroche's Brighton home studying the paintings. Belleroche explained that 'Sir Frank, like Mr Butlin, was essentially a man of the people. If Mr Butlin had bought the paintings for his holiday camp he would have had a chance of educating the people in the appreciation of art'.

The panels were placed in position on December 5, 1933.

The difficulties the artist appeared to encounter in the planning of these panels are reflected in the final work which abounds in caricature and lacks the unifying elements of Brangwyn's earlier murals. Conversely the large-scale, powerful illustrations could be said to perfectly mirror the contemporary social consciousness resulting from the Depression, and, perhaps more interestingly, the efforts of commercial photographers, who in an attempt to boost magazine readership, found themselves preoccupied with 'the staging of stories, with narrative in its widest sense. A "living image" of the real world had to be presented if the photo-essay was to be seen as news, as compelling visual material with topical interest'.[11]

ENDNOTES

1 Alan Balfour, *Rockefeller Center. Architecture as Theater*, New York: McGraw-Hill Book Company, 1978, p.216.

2 The pride the developers felt for their lifts is indicated by the fact that a complete paragraph was dedicated to their statistics in *The Story of Rockefeller Center*, published in 1939: 'The interior transportation system of the RCA Building is of particular interest. The fastest cars, those serving the floors from the 53rd story to the 65th, operate at a speed of 1,200 feet a minute, and two of these eight high-rise cars are the fastest in the world, travelling 1,400 feet a minute. They cover the distance from the ground floor to the 65th floor in approximately thirty-nine seconds. It is estimated that when operating on a full schedule the elevators in the RCA Building travel a total of 2,100 miles daily between 8 A.M. and 3.30 A.M., a distance equal to that between New York City and the Grand Canyon.'

3 Philip Macer-Wright, *Brangwyn. A Study of Genius at Close Quarters,* London: Hutchinson & Co Ltd, 1940, p.222.

4 Philip Macer-Wright, op. cit., p.223.

5 Alan Balfour, *Rockefeller Center. Architecture as Theater*, New York: McGraw-Hill Book Company, 1978, p.189.

6 Alan Balfour, op. cit., 1978, p.189.

7 Alan Balfour, op. cit., 1978, p.189.

8 Philip Macer-Wright, 'The Artist's Delight', *News Chronicle*, December 6, 1933.

9 'We take our hats off to –', *The Sketch*, November 9, 1932.

10 Letter from Brangwyn to M B Walker, November 20, 1932, Birmingham Museum and Art Gallery.

11 *The Real Thing. An Anthology of British Photographs 1840-1950*, London: Arts Council of Great Britain, 1975, p.30.

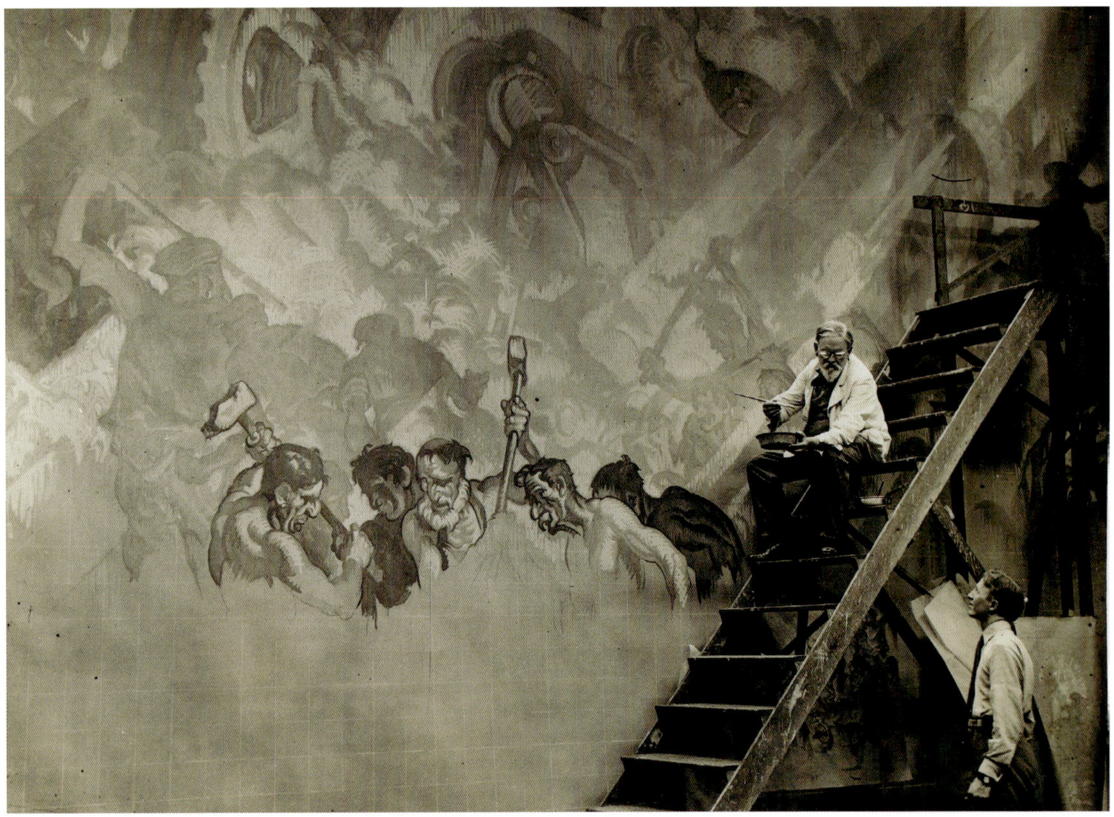

163
Frank Brangwyn and Kenneth Center working on *Man the Master*

MURALS BY FRANK BRANGWYN

1895 – Galerie L'Art Nouveau, 22 Rue de Provence, Paris commissioned by Siegfried Bing. Two friezes and stencil decorations on exterior of building, Keim's process on canvas, each frieze 5486 cm (180 feet) long

1899-1900 – bedroom murals, Lansdowne House, 11-13 Lansdowne Road, Kensington, London commissioned by Sir Edmund and Lady Davis

1907 – *Venetian Commerce*, *Venetian Serenaders*, *Agricultural Labourers*, *Miners* for interior of British Room, Venice Biennale commissioned by Antonio Fradeletto, General Secretary of Biennale Commission, oil on canvas, two panels measured 165 x 541cm (5 ft 5 in x 17 ft 9 in), two panels measured 165 x 206 cm (5 ft 5 in x 6 ft 9 in)

1908-1914 – *Dockside Porters*, Committee Luncheon Room, Lloyd's Register of Shipping, Fenchurch Street, London commission gained through Thomas Lane Devitt, oil on canvas, four panels measured 137 x1 22 cm (4 ft 6 in x 4 ft), four panels measured 137 x 244 cm (4 ft 6 in x 8 ft), two panels measured 137 x 91cm (4 ft 6 in x 3 ft), lunette measured 244 x 671 cm (8 x 22 ft)

1908-1916 – *Life of St Aidan*, St Aidan's, Roundhay Road, Leeds – commissioned by Robert Hawthorn Kitson, Rust's Vitreous Mosaic, 90 sq. m (900 sq. ft) apse, 90 sq. m (279 sq. ft) sea wall

1911-1915 – *King John Signing the Magna Carta*, Cuyahoga County Court House, Cleveland, Ohio, USA – commissioned by Charles F Schweinfurth, architect of the Court House, oil mixed with wax on canvas, 457 x 1524 cm (15 ft x 50 ft)

1912-1923 – *Mission and Expansion of Christianity, beginning with the Acts of the Apostles and leading to the Conversion of our own Islands, and Foreign Missionary Work for the Chapel*, Christ's Hospital, Horsham, Sussex, commission gained through Sir Aston Webb, architect of the chapel and school, egg tempera on canvas, fourteen panels x 244 x 427 cm (8 ft x 14 ft), two panels x 244 x 213 cm (8 ft x 7 ft)

1915 – Billiard room murals, Horton House, Northampton (panels divided and now at William Morris Gallery, London Borough of Waltham Forest; Graves Art Gallery, Sheffield; Dunedin Public Art Gallery, New Zealand and Te Papa Tongarewa, Wellington, New Zealand and a private collection) – commissioned by George Harold Winterbottom, oil on canvas, original size: 200 x 3744 cm (6 ft 7 in x 121 ft 2 in)

1915-1925 – *Missouri in Four Great Historical Periods*, dome and pendentives, State Capitol, Jefferson City, USA – flat oil on canvas, eye of dome 1097 cm (36 ft) in diameter; four pendentives each 732 cm (23 ft 9 in) high, 1463 cm (48 ft) wide at top and 457 cm (15 ft) wide at base; eight lower dome panels each approximately 488 x 853 cm (16 ft x 28 ft)

1918-1921 – *Canada's War Record*, Manitoba Legislative Building, Winnipeg, Canada – flat oil on canvas, 457 x 671 cm (15 ft x 22 ft)

1920-1921 – *Slave Market*, Arents House, Bruges, tempera on canvas, 145 x 158 cm (4 ft 9 in x 5 ft 2 in)
Swans, William Morris Gallery, London Borough of Walthamstow, oil on canvas, 149 x 161 cm (4 ft 9 in x 5 ft 3 in)

1920-1922 – *Stations of the Cross* for Leper Mission, Westfort, near Pretoria, South Africa (now in Church of the Beatitudes, Pretoria) - commissioned by Father Thomas Ryan, tempera on canvas, 14 panels x 81 x 104 cm (2 ft 8 in x 5 ft 1 in)

1920-1924 – *Stations of the Cross*, Arras Cathedral (unfinished although some Stations exist and are in private collections) – commission gained through Theophile Steinlen, oil on canvas, 14 panels x 104 x 142 cm (3 ft 5 in x 4 ft 8 in)

1921-1923 – *Trade of the World*, Dome, Selfridges', Oxford Street, London (unexecuted) – commissioned by Harry Gordon Selfridge, mosaic mural, dome measured 21 metres (70 ft) in diameter

1925-1932 – *British Empire Panels*, Brangwyn Hall, Guildhall, Swansea (originally intended for Royal Gallery, Westminster) – commissioned by Lord Iveagh, oil and tempera on canvas, ten panels x 365 x 365 cm (12 ft x 12 ft), six panels x 610 x 396 cm (20 ft x 13 ft)

1935-1936 – *The Printed Word Makes the People of the World One*, Odham's Press, Long Acre, London (now in private collection) – commissioned by Lord Southwood, oil and tempera, 396 x 549 cm (13 ft x 17 ft 2 in)

1930-1931 – *A Vision of the Lavish Gifts of Mother Earth*, Salle Jacques Cartier (1st class dining room), SS *Empress of Britain*, Canadian Pacific Line commissioned by E W Beatty, President of Canadian Pacific, oil paint on panels covered with silver leaf, varnished with gold size and lacquered, three panels measured 402 x 150 cm (13 ft 2 in x 4 ft 11 in), two panels measured 401 x 118 cm (13 ft 2 in x 3 ft 11 in), one panel measured 196 x 305 cm (6 ft 1 in x 10 ft) with further paintings measuring 226 x 726 cm (7 ft 5 in x 23 ft 10 in)

1932-1933 – *Man's new relationship to society and his fellow man, his family relationships, his relationships as a worker, his relationships as part of government and his ethical and religious relationships*, GE (previously RCA) Building, 30 Rockefeller Plaza, New York, USA, commissioned by John D Rockefeller Jr., tempera on coarse canvas, four panels measure 518 x 762 cm (17 x 25 ft)

1939-1945 – *Last Supper*, Holy Name of Mary Church, Middlesbrough – commissioned by Father John Jones, oil on canvas, 94 x 387 cm (3 ft x 12 ft 6 in)

1946-1947 – *Last Supper*, St Joseph's, Stokesley commissioned by Father John McDonnell, oil on canvas, 137 x 401 cm (4 ft 6 in x 13 ft)

Frank Brangwyn (1867-1956)

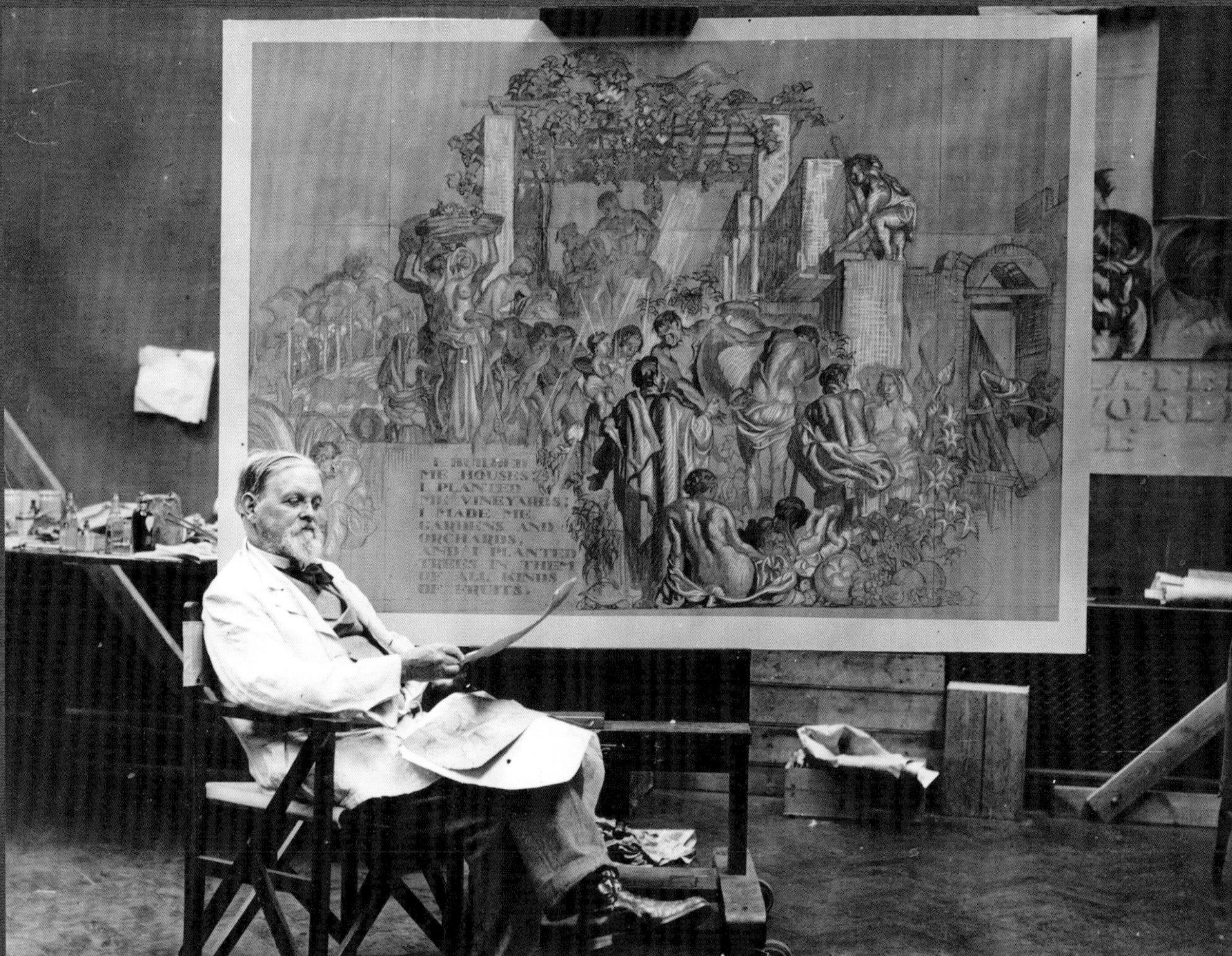

164 Frank Brangwyn at work in his studio

SIR FRANK BRANGWYN, RA. Born Bruges, Belgium, died Ditchling, Sussex. Painter, etcher, muralist, stained glass designer and designer of furniture, carpets, etc. Brangwyn received no formal training but worked with William Morris in the early 1880s. Travelled widely from 1891 onwards visiting South Africa, Spain (with Arthur Melville), Morocco, etc. Decorations for Bing's L'Art Nouveau, Paris, 1895. Founder member Vienna Secession 1897. 1909 in Sicily designs Casa Cuseni and paints the devastation caused by the Messina earthquake. During the ensuing years receives official honours Austria, Italy, Germany, Belgium, and France. Retrospective Exhibition, Queen's Gate, London, 1924 opened by Prime Minister Ramsay MacDonald. Pollard Exhibition 1930 – complete room settings designed by Brangwyn including furniture, light-fittings, carpets, glass and crockery. Brangwyn Museum, Bruges, opened 1936: created Grand Officer of the Order of Leopold II. Knighted 1941. Work represented in most major museums and art galleries in Britain and the Commonwealth as well as the William Morris Gallery, Walthamstow, and the Brangwyn Museum, Bruges.

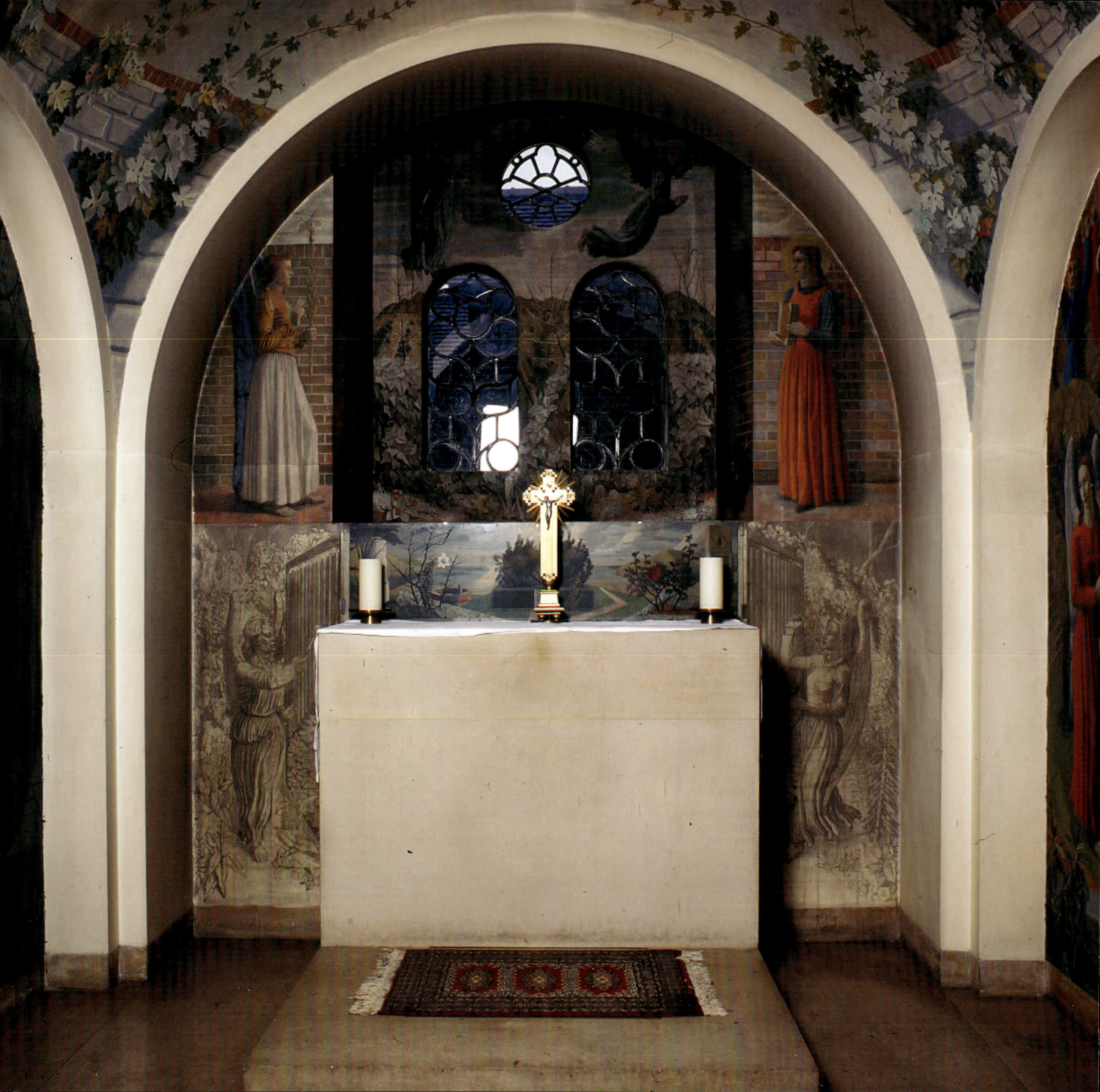

Charles Mahoney
Campion Hall, 1941-52

Elizabeth Graffius

The murals by Charles Mahoney in the Lady Chapel at Campion Hall, Oxford, are almost unknown outside Jesuit circles. The murals themselves were never finished and, therefore, never officially publicised. Mahoney worked on them during his teaching holidays for over ten years, but in the end abandoned the scheme in 1952 owing to illness. The murals are also unknown because of their location in the chapel of a private Jesuit Hall in Oxford.

Campion Hall was the first Catholic Private Hall to be established in the University of Oxford, founded by Fr Richard Clarke SJ in 1896.[1] Fr Martin D'Arcy, who commissioned the murals, considered the Hall 'as a shrine of Christian Civilisation – something that Oxford had once been and was no longer'.[2] Charles Mahoney's mural paintings for the Lady Chapel were part of this vision for Campion Hall. John Rothenstein wrote of the Hall that 'were it rumoured that someone of outstanding interest was visiting Oxford, it was likely that he would be found dining at the high table at Campion Hall'.[3] This was made possible by the extraordinary character of its master at that time, Fr Martin D'Arcy. D'Arcy has been described as:

> a man of great intellectual energy and passionate convictions, he was a fascinating conversationalist, a superb raconteur, a master at introducing and guiding discussions… He was kind by nature, thoughtful of others, courteous and beautifully mannered.[4]

D'Arcy was a well connected man. He was particularly well associated with those involved in the English arts, such as Evelyn Waugh, Augustus John, Eric Gill, and John Rothenstein. Most of these contacts were Catholics, many recent converts.

It has been written of England in the thirties that 'there developed a very strong sense of the Catholic intellectual community, self-confidently speaking of "the Catholic Revival", sunning itself at country houses or at Campion Hall'.[5] D'Arcy, often compared to Cardinal John Henry Newman, was at the centre of this group of Catholic intellectuals to such an extent that he was criticised for using his position 'as a power base for merely worldly exploits'.[6] These Catholic connections were key to his collecting and commissioning of art. He was an avid collector, which he wrote about in his memoirs *Treasure Hunting*. He explains that: 'Once excited by

165
The altar and Mahoney's murals in the chapel at Campion Hall

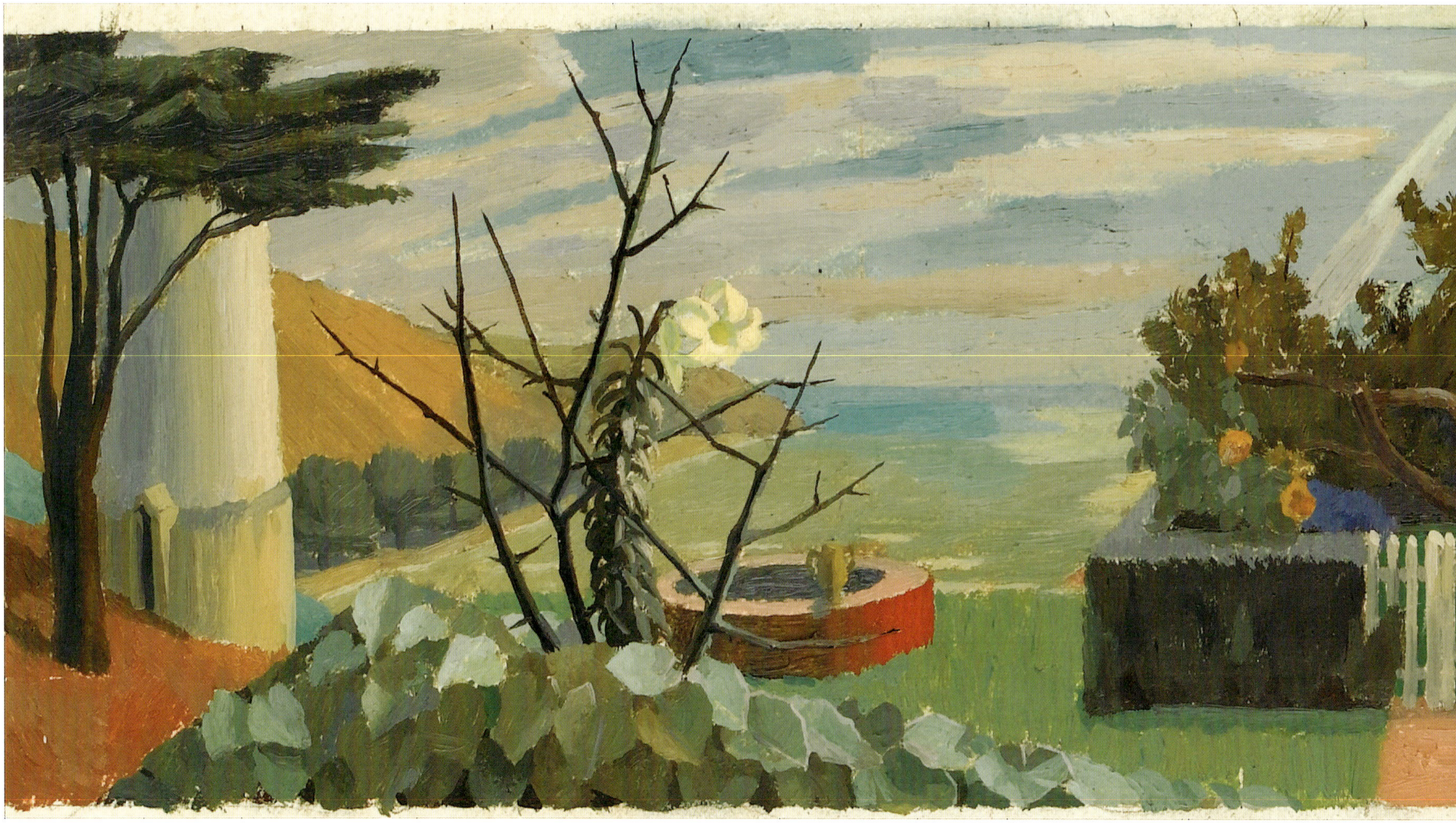

166 Design for Campion Hall, *The Symbols of Mary*, mid-1940s, oil on paper, 19 x 76.2 cm (7 ½ x 30 in.)

the thought of beautiful objects, my desire grew almost daily'.[7] D'Arcy pursued this desire as master of Campion Hall and filled the Hall with Italian Renaissance paintings, historic religious artefacts, textiles and contemporary commissions. These objects were known fondly by those connected to Campion Hall as 'Objets D'Arcy'.[8]

D'Arcy was a resourceful collector. As a Jesuit he had no money of his own, but managed to obtain many of these items at a minimum cost through his connections and generous donations from wealthy Catholic friends. It was Evelyn Waugh who was responsible for funding the decoration of the Lady Chapel. D'Arcy met Waugh on a Mediterranean cruise. Though this was before Waugh converted to Catholicism, D'Arcy and he bonded over religious and philosophical debates. D'Arcy was Waugh's spiritual director when he was received into the Catholic Church on September 29, 1930, and the pair became close friends.[9] In 1935 Waugh wrote a biography of the Jesuit English martyr St Edmund Campion (1540-81), to mark the building of Campion Hall. He donated the royalties from this book to the Hall.[10]

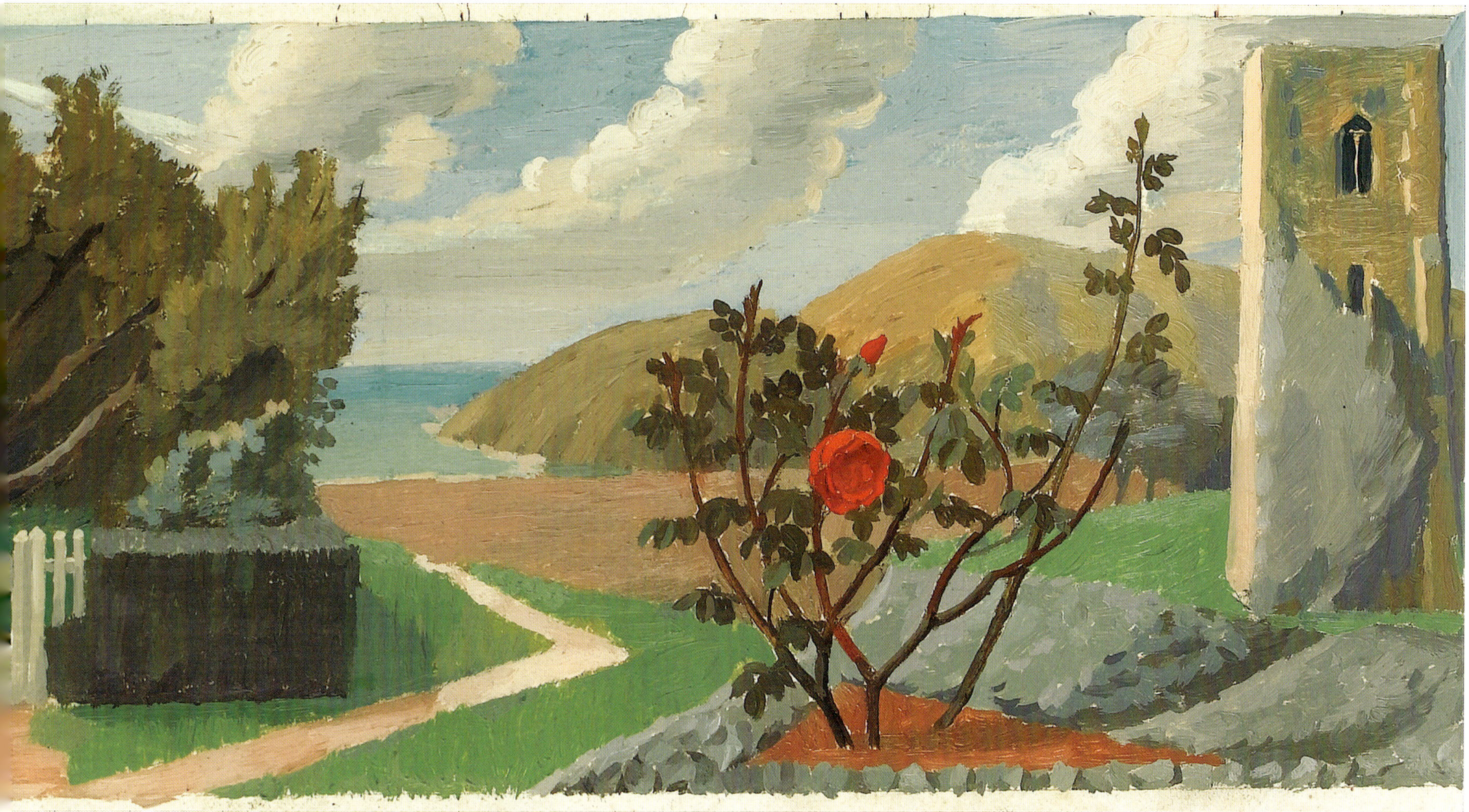

D'Arcy had strong opinions on the use of art in Catholic devotional space. He was embarrassed by the repository artworks displayed in most Catholic Churches, and wanted to prove that contemporary Catholic art could be tasteful. D'Arcy also wished to prove that Jesuit art in particular could be done in good taste. As he wrote in his memoirs:

> The Jesuits have been so often denigrated – at times quite unfairly – for their lack of taste, more barberi even than Barberini. Campion Hall would prove that this bad taste is not so common as believed in the works of the Society of Jesus.[11]

D'Arcy would have envisioned this commission for a contemporary painted chapel in the Jesuit Campion Hall as a chance to redeem the reputation of both. However, D'Arcy was not only interested in the reputation generated by art. He was also philosophically concerned about its importance and use for religious purpose:

> Beyond these considerations there is that of the vast importance beauty does and should play in the

> Catholic faith. Possibly more glimpse the truth and reality of the Christian religion and its liturgy and devotions through beauty than by reason. Art is man's contrivance for making real to himself what reason leaves in the abstract…In surrounding God with all the human splendour we can find, we pay our due homage and make public our sense of his majesty. Simple souls, as well as the cultured, realise that in so doing we are made more aware in ourselves how great our God is.[12]

The idea of a complete painted scheme would fit in well with this desire to praise God through works of art and beauty. Additionally, the fact that the Hall was full of young Jesuits in formation made it the perfect place to instil in new generation of priests a taste for 'good' religious works of art.

In 1938, D'Arcy approached his friend William Rothenstein, the Principal of the Royal College of Art, and his son John, the director of the Tate Gallery, to ask their advice on an English mural painter for the chapel. They both recommended Stanley Spencer as the 'leading religious painter in the country at the time'.[13] When Spencer arrived at Campion Hall D'Arcy was rather taken aback by his appearance and behaviour. He wrote an amusing and telling account of Spencer's stay at the Hall:

> So diminutive as to almost be a dwarf in labourer's clothes with a dirty sachel containing all his belongings, he was no ordinary guest. We got on, however, quite well until he started making models for his work. The figures of Christ were gross distortions, hideous looking barrels and an unexpected element of obscenity itself. The truth was he was going through a crisis of middle age, and his earthly but mystical religious vision was now crowded out by sexual images...He was for this period almost demented.

D'Arcy decided not to give the commission to Spencer. Thus, upon further discussion with the Rothensteins, D'Arcy invited Charles Mahoney to send some of his works for consideration.[14] D'Arcy was clearly pleased with the examples of work that Mahoney sent, crediting him with a 'wonderful sense of colour'.[15] Perhaps he was also keen to accept Mahoney, believing him to be a Catholic. 'From his name I assumed that he was an Irish Catholic, at any rate by birth, but he proved to be completely ignorant of the Catholic faith, indeed of Christianity, and was an agnostic socialist'.[16] However, D'Arcy was either unconcerned by this or was suitably impressed by Mahoney's skill as a painter to overcome his desire for the work to be done by a Catholic.

When Mahoney started on the commission he insisted on working *in situ* with only natural light, rather than painting the works on canvas in his studio and then installing them in the chapel.[17] However, he did not take into account the fact that the room was lit only by a small window on the east wall. This meant there was sufficient light for painting only during the spring and summer. Also, as Mahoney was a teacher at the Royal College of Art, which was located in the Lake District during the war, he could only work on the murals in the College holidays. Mahoney also had a very arduous and meticulous manner of working. Countless studies in a variety of materials bear witness to the care given to detail. Mahoney was also a perfectionist and had a habit of scraping back layers and starting again if he was not happy with the effect; 'frequently a painting which had apparently been finished would be found, much of its paint removed by swift swipes of his palette knife. He was seldom satisfied with his work'.[18] This, on top of Mahoney's increasingly fragile health, meant that the scheme took over ten years to reach a state of near completion, as it is now.

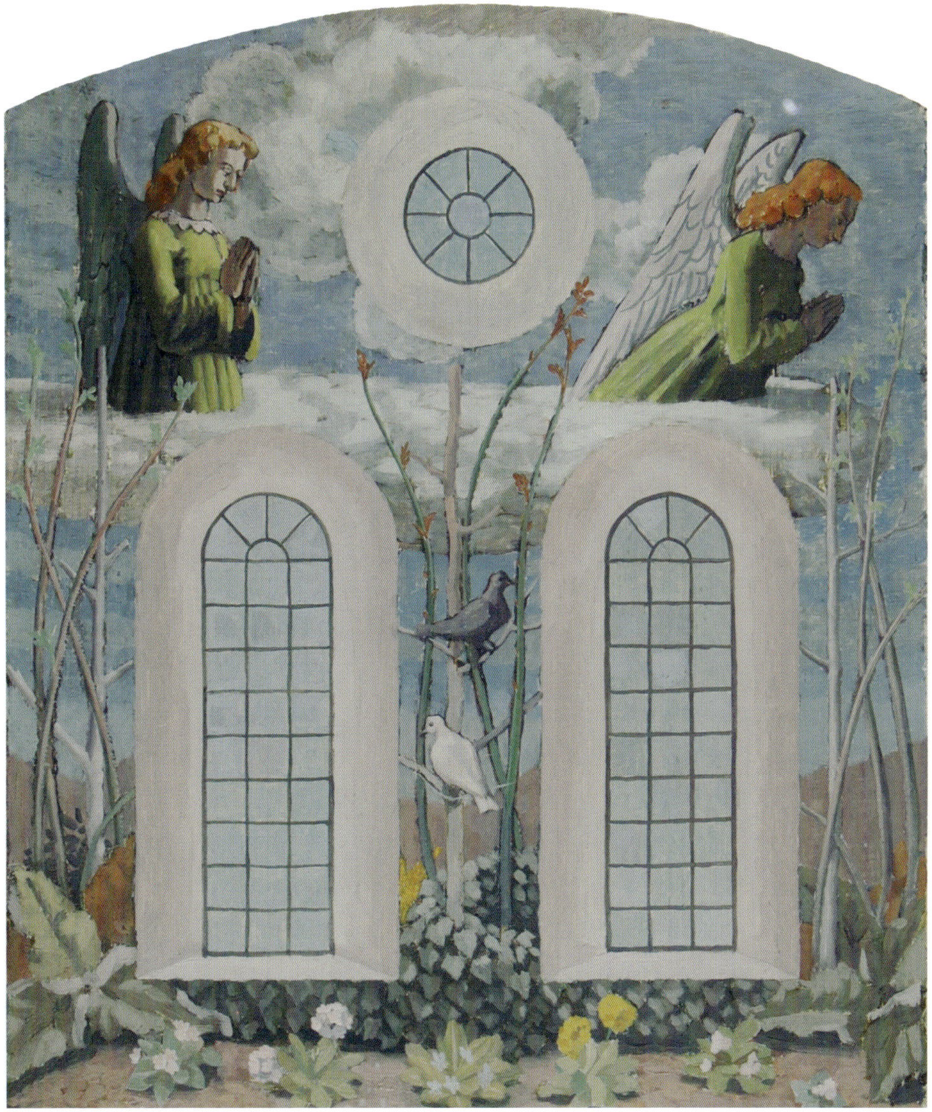

167
Design for the wall above the altar at Campion Hall, *Two Angels Overlooking a Garden,* oil on paper, 45 x 38 cm (17 ¾ x 15 in.)

The mural scheme can be divided into three parts: the east wall, the west wall, and the north and south walls. We can safely assume that Mahoney carried out the painting roughly in the order agreed in the contract, starting at the east wall and finishing at the west.[19] This can be seen in the different styles of each of the three sections. The east wall shows the Annunciation and a garden, separated by a recession with a window. Below is a panel depicting a rather unique selection of Symbols of Mary, from the *Litany of Loreto* and the *Songs of Solomon*. On either side of the altar are two unfinished panels showing angels playing musical instruments. The north and south walls contain three large images in arched recessions. *The Adoration of the Shepherds* is shown on the north wall, *The Coronation of the Virgin* on the eastern end of the south wall, and *Our Lady of Mercy* on the western end of the south wall. The west wall is divided into two sections. The upper half is a large semicircular section depicting *The Flight into Egypt.* The lower half on either side of the sacristy door is divided into four square panels which show different scenes from the life of Mary:

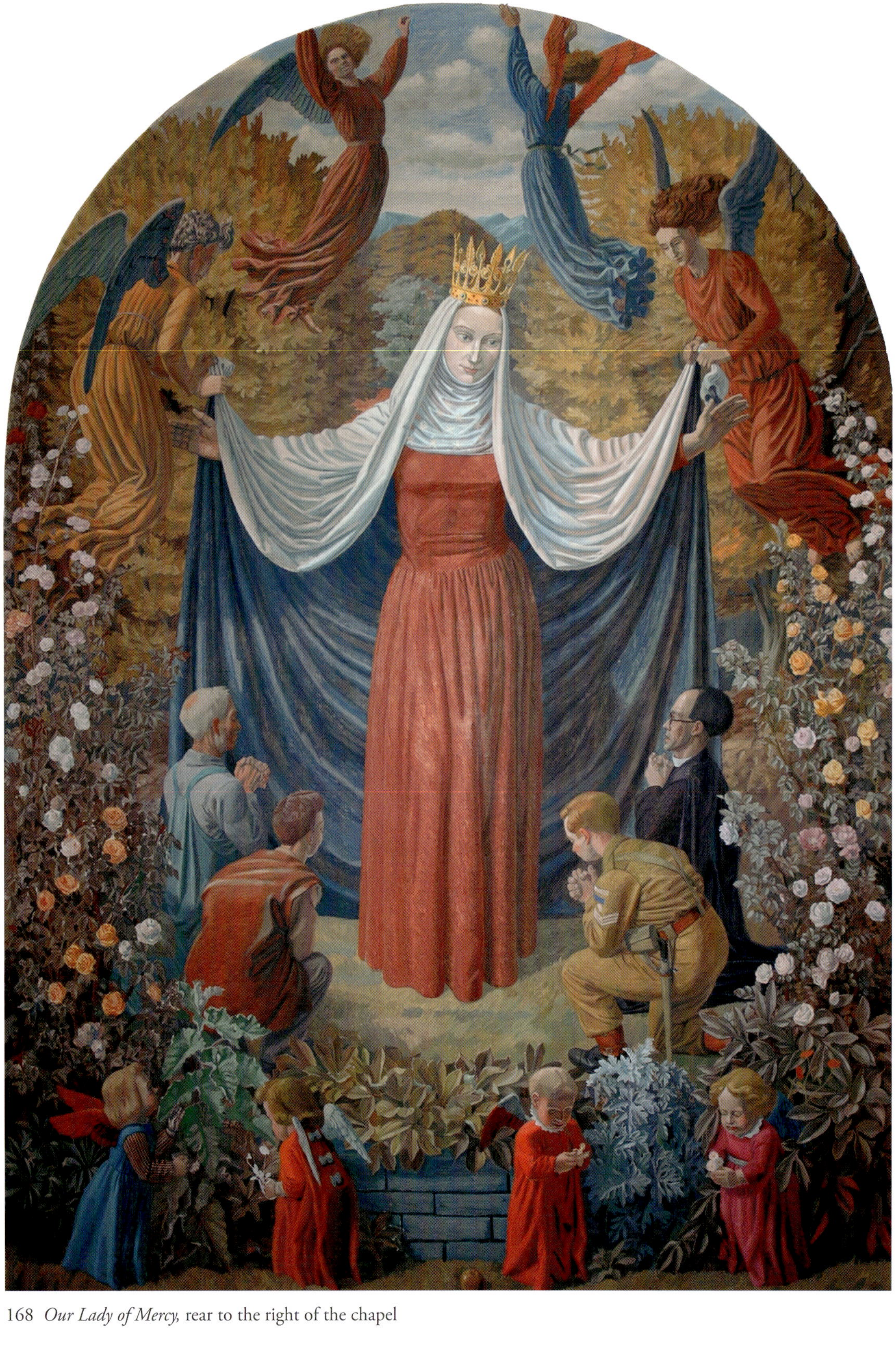

168 *Our Lady of Mercy,* rear to the right of the chapel

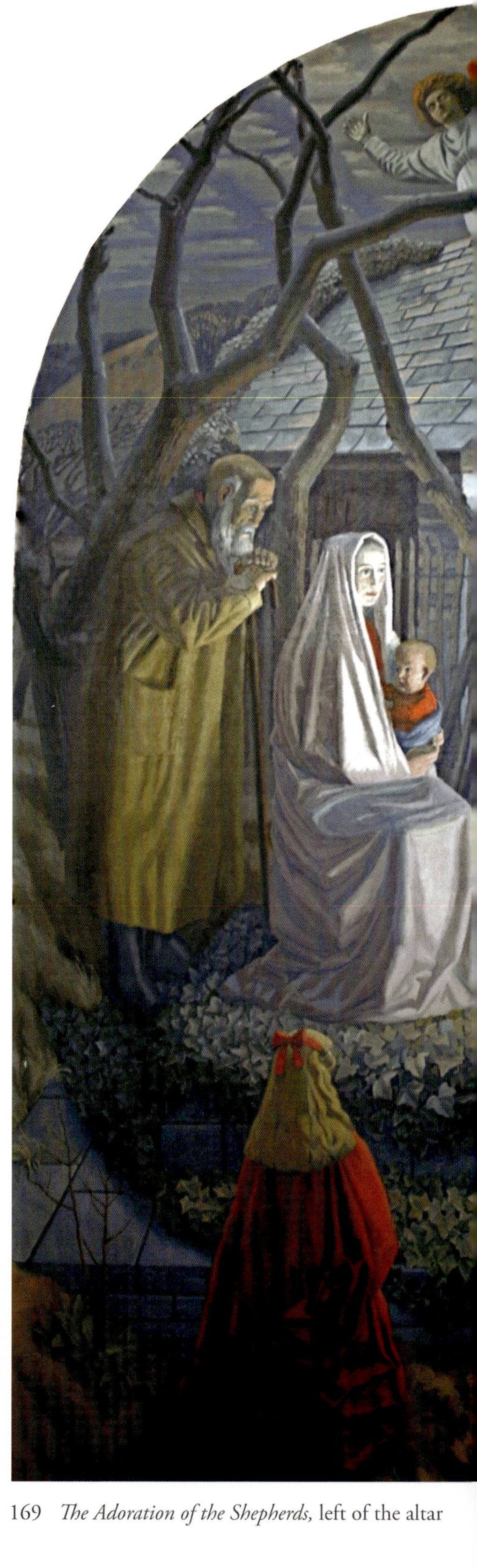

169 *The Adoration of the Shepherds,* left of the altar

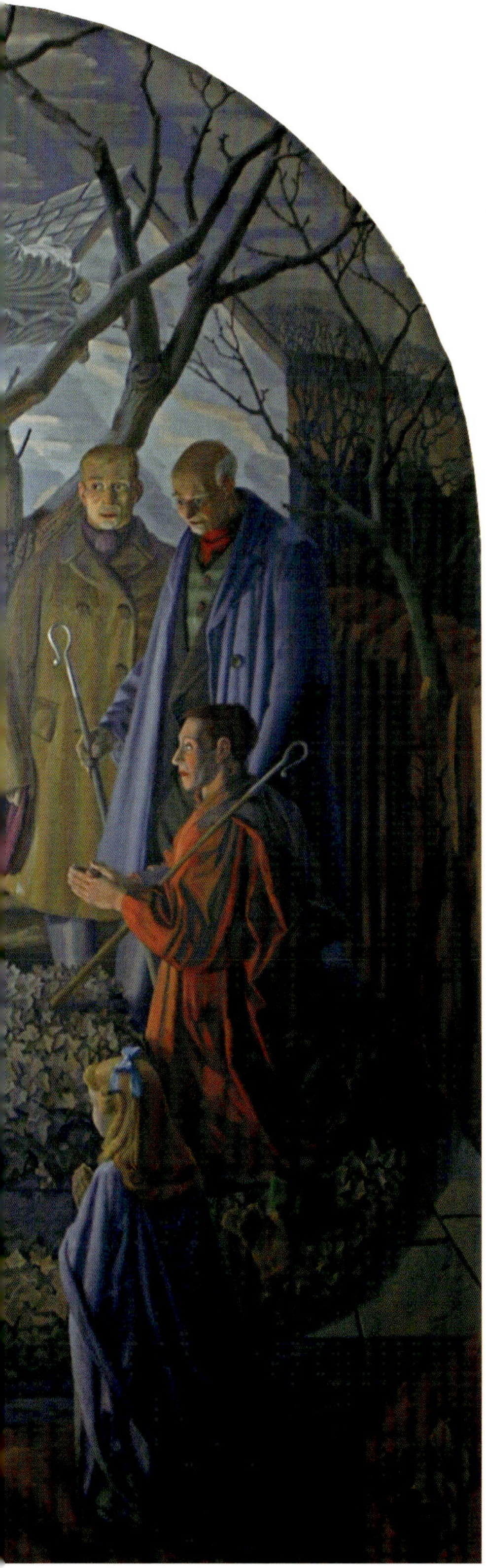

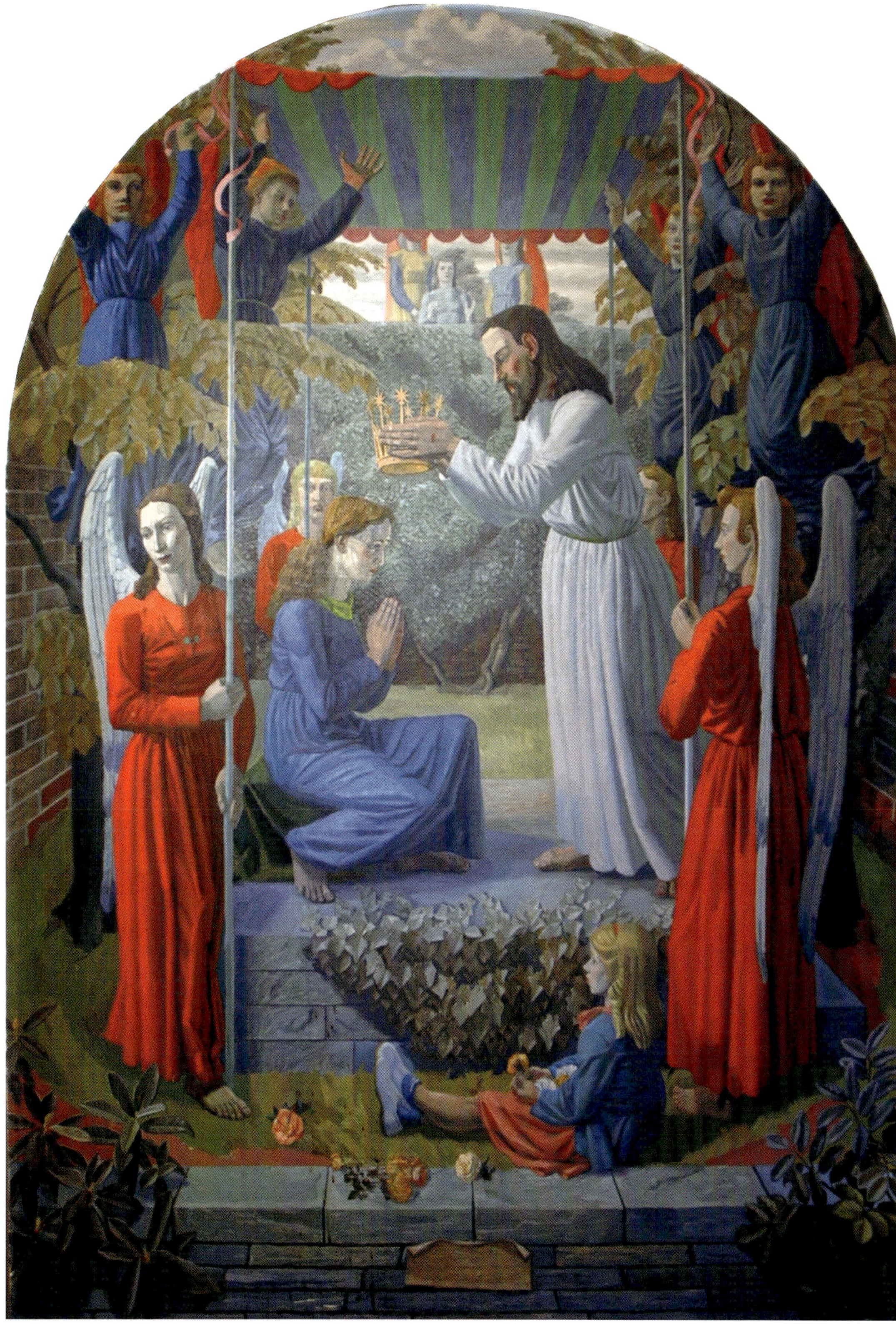

170 *The Coronation of the Virgin,* right of the altar

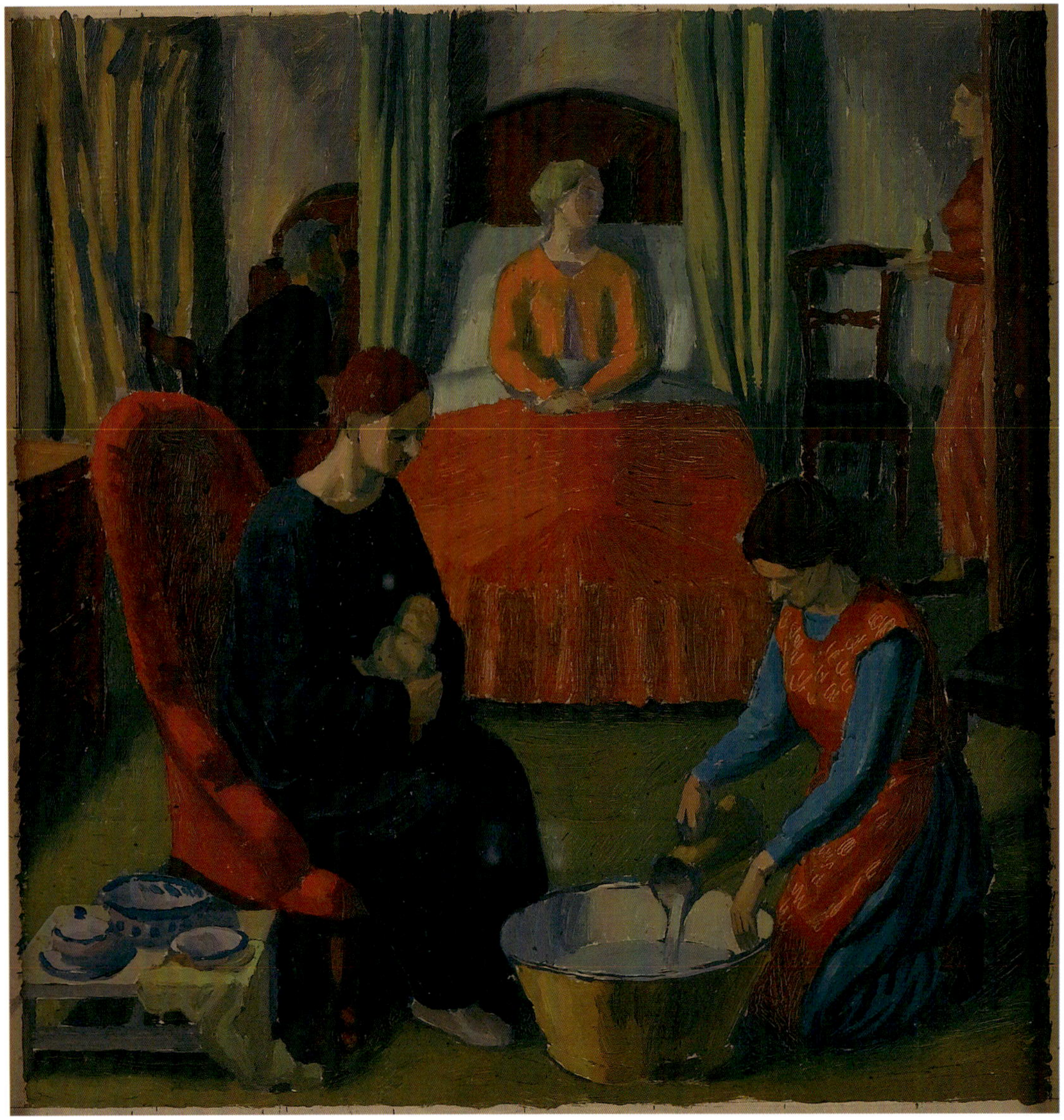

171
Study for
The Birth of the Virgin, c. 1942,
oil on paper,
29.2 x 28 cm (11 ½ x 11 in.)

The Birth of the Virgin, *The Betrothal of Mary and Joseph*, *The Visitation*, and *The Dormition*. Mary appears in every section of the chapel, a total of nine times, and yet Mahoney has not been so consistent in his representation of her in his paintings. There are similarities between certain images, for example the Mary of *The Annunciation* and that of *The Coronation of the Virgin*, but Mahoney doesn't seem to have used the same model.

The iconography of Mahoney's paintings is quite traditional. In *The Annunciation*, the Angel Gabriel carries a white lily and holds up his hand in a gesture of blessing and address. He also includes the iconography of the Hortus Conclusus, the enclosed garden which refers to Mary's virginity dating back to early gothic images. This can be seen in centre of *The Symbols of Mary* panel and *The Coronation of the Virgin*. In fact, Mahoney has made the whole Lady Chapel into one enclosed garden, with a stone wall running around the vaulting. Mahoney also seems to have drawn on the work of Piero della Francesca in this mural scheme, and makes many

172
Study for
The Visitation, c. 1942,
signed and inscribed on
a label to the reverse,
oil on paper,
squared in chalk
29.2 x 28.6 cm
(11 ½ x 11 ¼ in.)

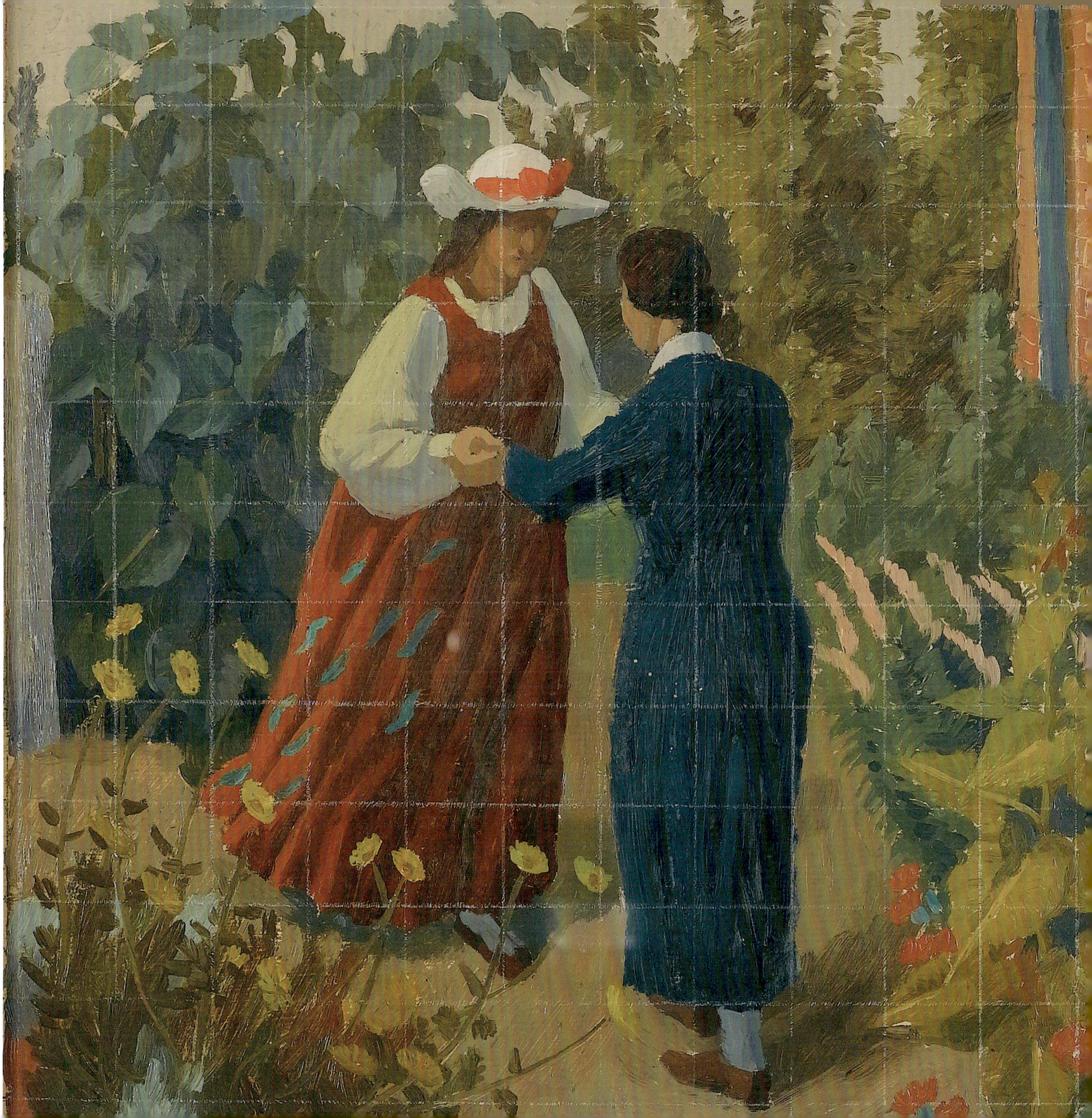

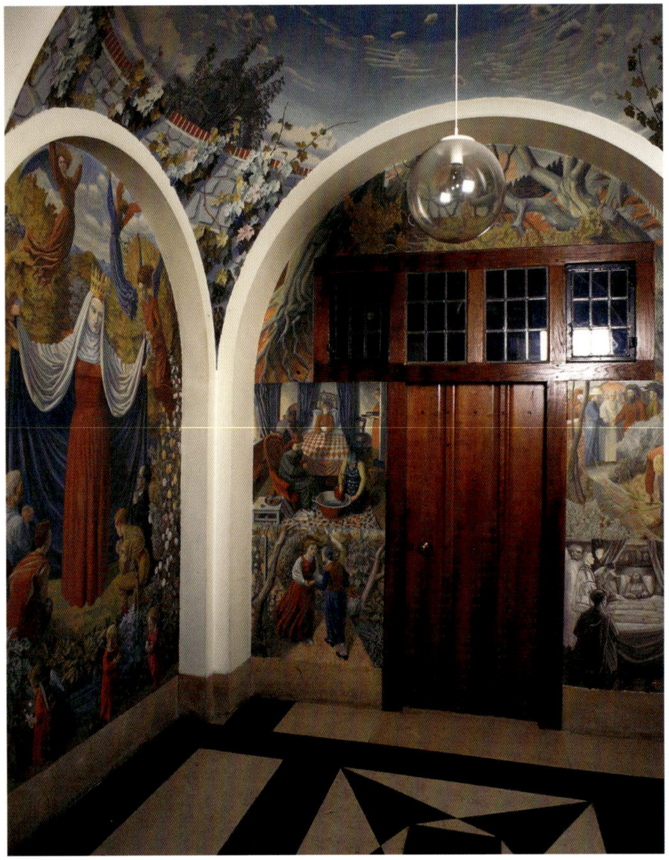

173 The Lady Chapel at Campion Hall

open references to the artist's work. The figures of Mary and Gabriel in *The Annunciation* are very similar to Piero's Annunciation panels in his *Misericordia Polyptich*. The figure of Mary in the painting of Our Lady of Mercy is also startlingly close to Piero's representation of her in the same *Misericordia Polyptich*. Mahoney's figures throughout the chapel have these similar qualities, found in earlier panel paintings, of solidity and very defined, heavy drapery. Perhaps this particularly drew D'Arcy to his work, as D'Arcy had a great love for Renaissance panel paintings.

Although in these elements Mahoney's approach to the murals has not strayed very far from more traditional Renaissance paintings of Mary, his work in the Lady Chapel exudes a strong sense of the artist's personal style. Mahoney was an avid gardener and botanist, which is apparent in his work for Campion Hall. The paintings are full of plants, trees, and flowers in bloom shown in very accurate detail. Mahoney seems to have chosen the flowers which he liked best, which were apart from those necessary for the iconography, rather than opting for any with a particular meaning pertinent to the subject depicted. His love of botany also shows itself in an overriding theme in the three large images found in the arched recessions in the north and south walls. These images are bound together by the theme of the Seasons. *The Adoration of the Shepherds* is set in a winter landscape, *The Coronation of the Virgin* represents the season of summer, and autumn is the setting for *Our Lady of Mercy*. These images include many flowers and plants appropriate to the season of the image and native to England.

Mahoney also displays his personal character in the general atmosphere of the murals. The images are imbued with an English, domestic, everyday beauty that Mahoney seems to have sought in all his works of art. This particularly complements that nature of the subject matter, making the legendary and religious become more accessible to ordinary people at the time that Mahoney was painting. This can be seen particularly in the scenes of the life of Mary on the west wall. One scene shows *The Birth of the Virgin* in a small bedroom furnished like a contemporary country cottage. Apart from the advanced age of the parents, there is nothing to suggest that this scene is anything other than a depiction of a normal birth. Mahoney used his daughter as a model for the baby and may have based the room on one in his own country cottage in Kent. In the Dormition scene Mahoney even includes portraits of the community at Campion Hall. The Jesuits stand crowded around the bed in whichMary lies, bringing this holy story directly into the present day. Edwin Lutyens, the architect of Campion Hall, and the patron Fr Martin D'Arcy are both identifiable in this image.

This section of the murals highlights the domestic 'Englishness' that is a predominant characteristic of Mahoney's paintings. Mahoney, who never once left Britain, was in love with the English plant life, houses and landscape. He instilled the Campion Hall murals with this love through the settings of the sacred story. This brings the stories alive and encourages the viewer to bring his or her experience of the world to these religious narratives. This is encouraged even more by the kneeling contemporary figures that appear in many of the images, who are contemplating the scene before them, and inviting similar behaviour from the viewer.

In the introduction to the 1976 Ashmolean exhibition – the first retrospective of Mahoney's work – John Rothenstein described the Lady Chapel Murals as second only to that by Spencer at Burghclere, adding that regrettably 'in spite of the high quality of much of [Mahoney's] painting and drawing, he is now best remembered as a teacher'.[20] Rothenstein put this lack of appreciation down to the fact that Mahoney's first major mural was destroyed (Morley College) and the other was virtually unknown (Campion Hall).[21] Mahoney's last major mural scheme, understood within its context as a unique example of intellectual interest in English Catholic art during the first half of the twentieth century, deserves to be better known and more fully appreciated.

ENDNOTES

1 H. E. Salter and M. D. Lobel (eds.), *A History of the County of Oxford: Volume 3*: The University of Oxford, Oxford, 1954, p.339.

2 H. J. A. Sire, *Father Martin D'Arcy, Philosopher of Christian Love*, Leominster, 1997, p.85.

3 J. Rothenstein, *Brave Day Hideous Night: Autobiography 1939-1965*, London, 1966, p.132.

4 H. J. A. Sire, op. cit., 1997, pp.xviii-xix.

5 Ibid, p.97.

6 Ibid. p.101.

7 M. D'Arcy, 'Treasure Hunting', MS in Campion Hall Archive 232/124/10, p.1.

8 *The Treasures of Campion Hall*, exh. cat., Oxford, 1996, p.5.

9 J. Brown, *Lutyens and the Edwardians: An English Architect and his Clients*, London, 1996, p.222.

10 H. J. A. Sire, op. cit., Leominster, 1997, p.82.

11 M. D'Arcy, op. cit., MS in Campion Hall Archive 232/124/10, p.2.

12 Ibid, pp.2-3.

13 Ibid. p.12.

14 Letter from John Rothenstein to Mahoney on November 23, 1940, in Tate Archive 4/2/661/1.

15 M. D'Arcy, op. cit., MS in Campion Hall Archive 232/124/10, p.12.

16 Ibid. p.12.

17 J. Rothenstein, *Charles Mahoney 1903-1968*, Oxford, 1975, p.11.

18 E. Bulkeley, 'Charles Mahoney 1903-1968', in P. Liss, *Charles Mahoney 1903-1968*, exh. cat., London, 1999, p.15.

19 'Statement of Agreement', in Campion Hall Archive 47/2/8.

20 J. Rothenstein, *Charles Mahoney 1903-1968*, (Oxford, 1975), p.5.

21 Ibid, p.5.

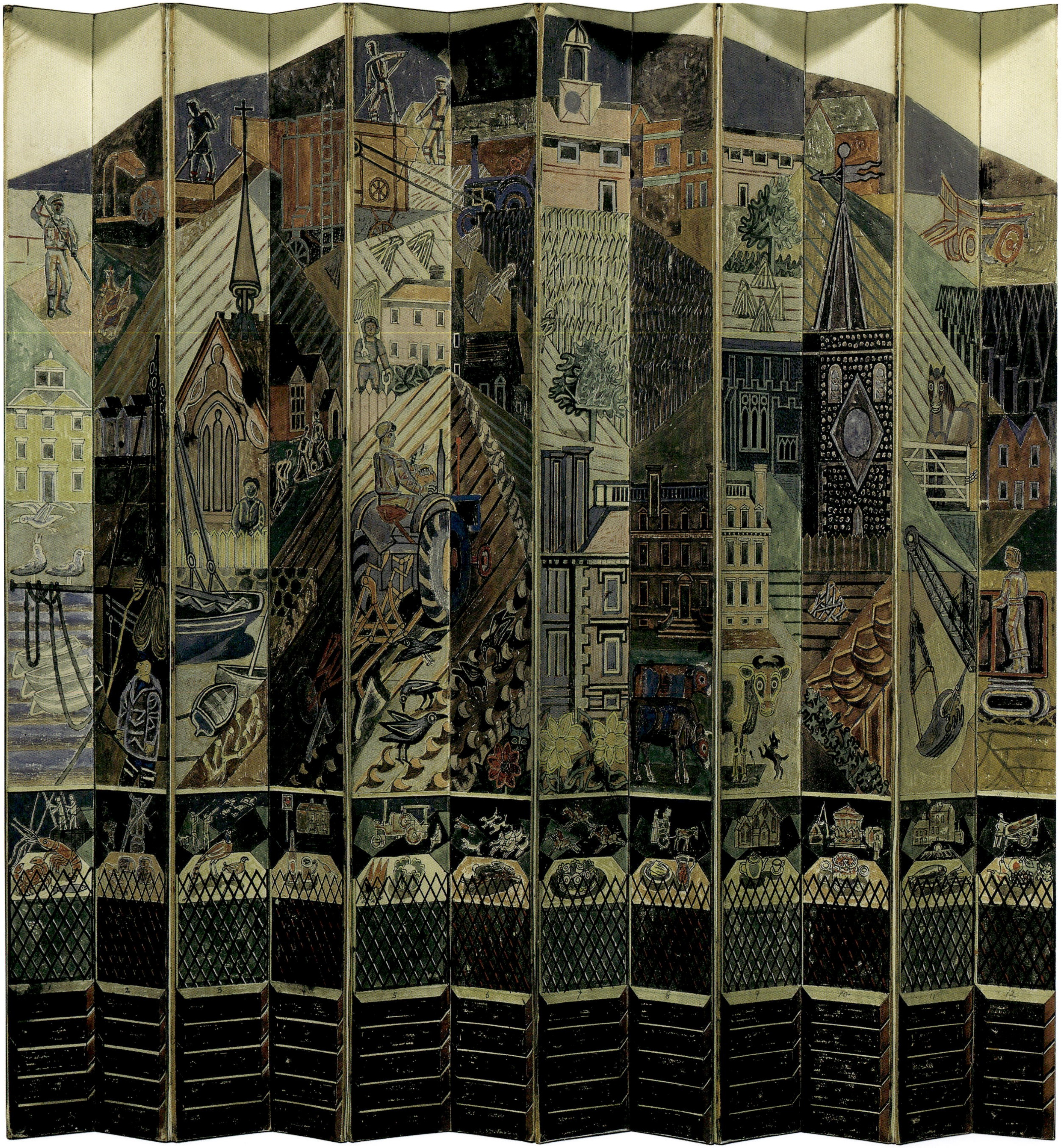

Edward Bawden and English Country Life

Peyton Skipwith

174
Country Life in Britain, cardboard and watercolour model for the free-standing mural commissioned for the Festival of Britain's Lion and Unicorn Pavilion, 1950-51

The Higgins Gallery Bedford, Bawden Gift

The high point of Edward Bawden's career as a muralist was achieved in the series of three murals – two for the Orient Line and one for the Festival of Britain – painted in the late 1940s and early 1950s, when his skill, wit and sheer inventiveness were at their peak. The earliest of the three was *English Garden Delights* commissioned by Sir Colin Anderson in 1947-8 for the first-class lounge of the liner *Orcades*. In solving the practical problems presented by the need to paint the mural off site, the intended location, and the installation requirements while the ship was still being fitted-out, Bawden hit on the idea of creating a nine-panelled screen. It was a device he was to repeat a few years later for the *Oronsay*, his second Orient Line commission, and exploit to great effect on a grand scale with *Country Life in Britain*, the vast, free-standing screen he painted for the 1951 Festival of Britain's Lion and Unicorn Pavilion on the South Bank. These three murals were united not only by their format but also by subject matter; both Colin Anderson and the organisers of the Festival set out to celebrate Britishness and to rejoice unashamedly in the fact that despite the depredations of war the country was once again reasserting its historic virtues, life and culture.

For Bawden the *Orcades* commission came at just the right time in his career; he had had in many ways a stimulating war with his duties as an Official War Artist taking him to Normandy and Italy as well as the Middle East where his area of operations extended from Cairo to the Euphrates, involving him in recording subjects as diverse as an open-air cinema, the Marsh Arabs of Iraq, the Sudan Defence Force at Omdurman and the Emperor Menelik's Palace in Addis Ababa. Returning to England on board the *Laconia* he was torpedoed and spent five virtually food and waterless days in an open boat before being rescued and interned in Morocco. Inevitably, after such experiences, he had returned to post-war Britain a changed man. His wartime work had been highly acclaimed but, despite the stimulus of the many exotic scenes he had witnessed and recorded, he had no desire for further travel, and was relieved to be back in Great Bardfield and to immerse himself once again in the gentle landscape of his native Essex.

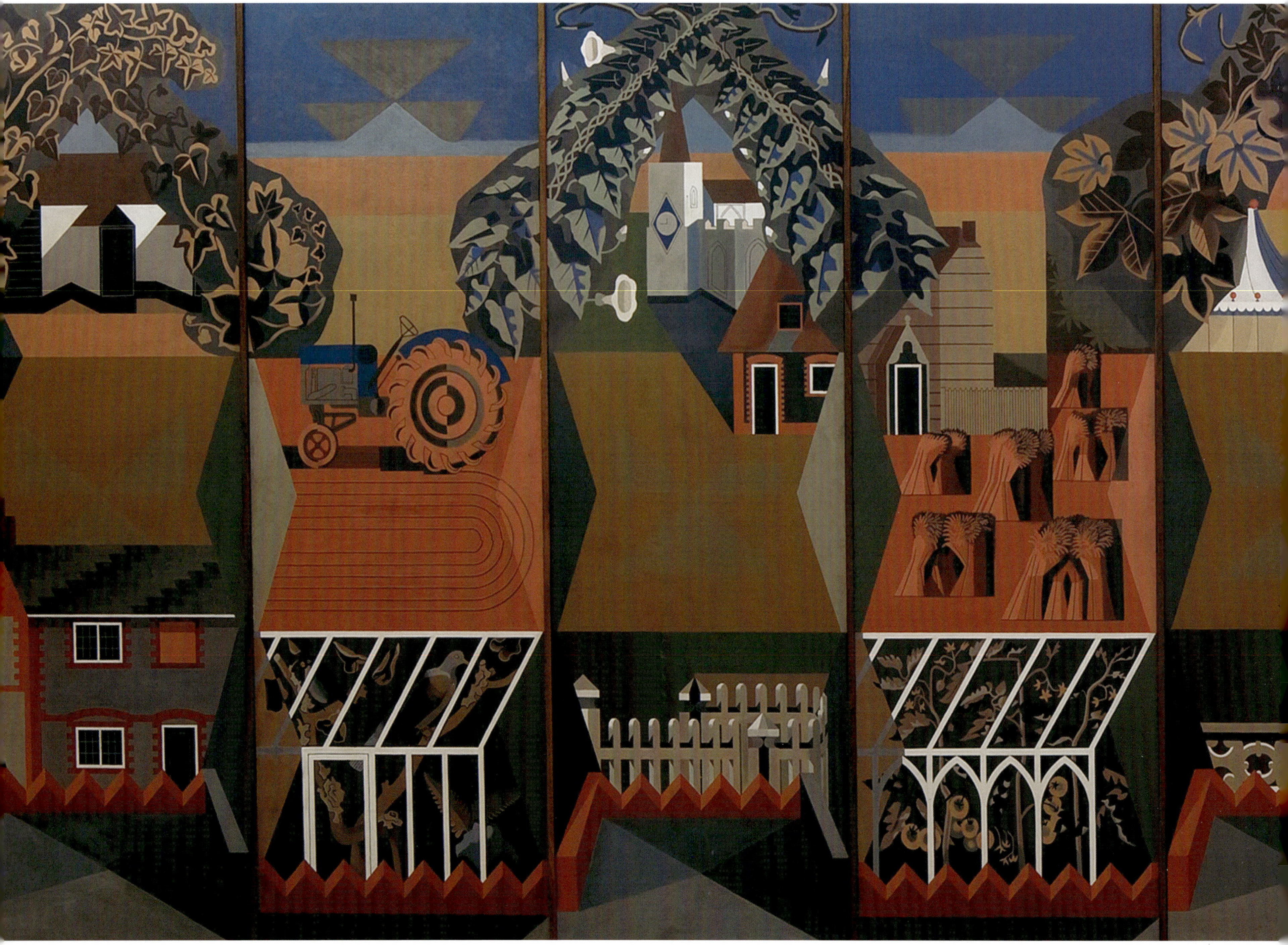

175 *English Garden Delights,* 1946, oil on panel, 2110 x 6480 cm (830 ¾ x 2551 ⅛ in.). Courtesy of Waddesdon, The Rothschild Collection (Rothschild Family Trust)

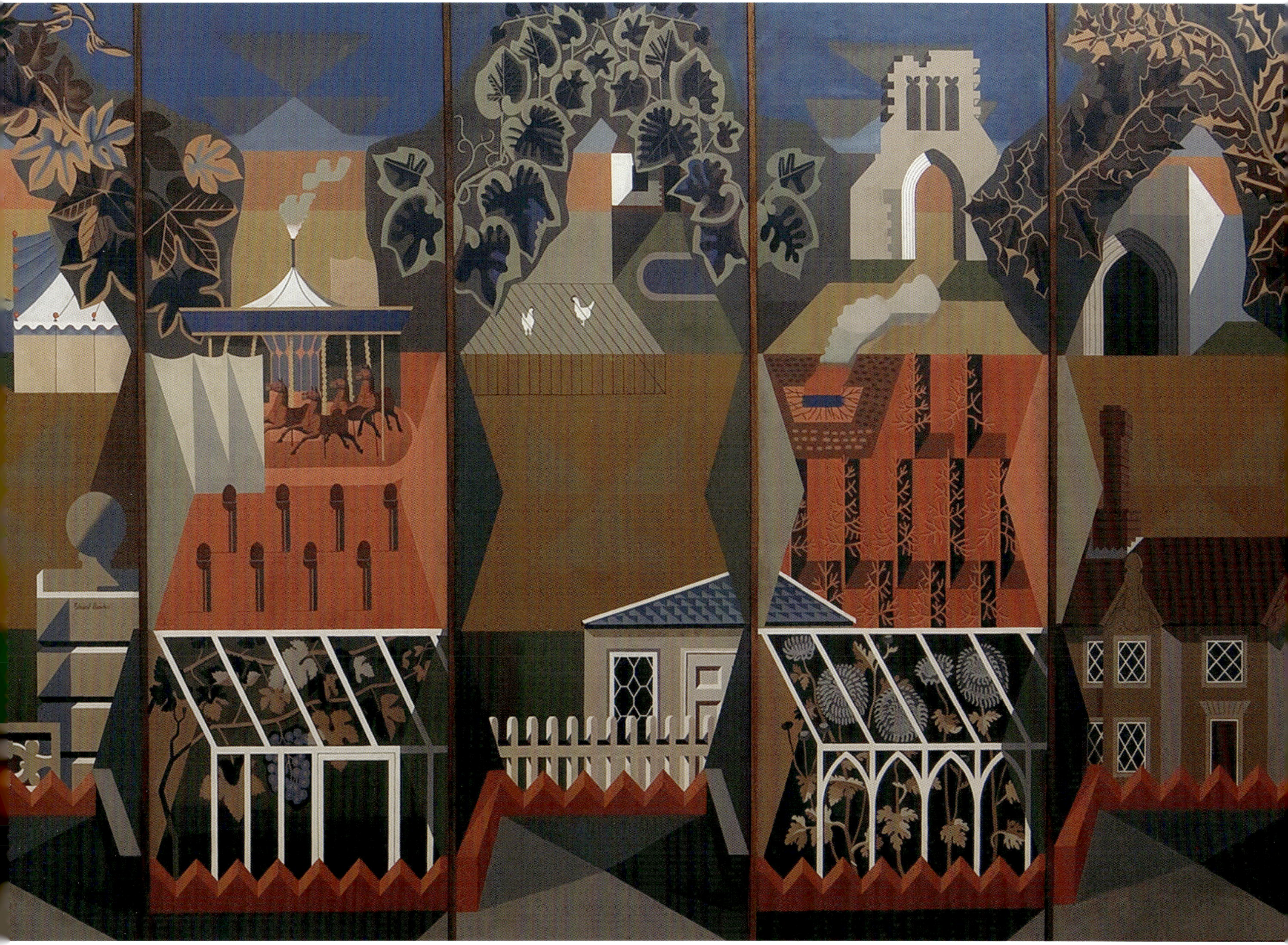

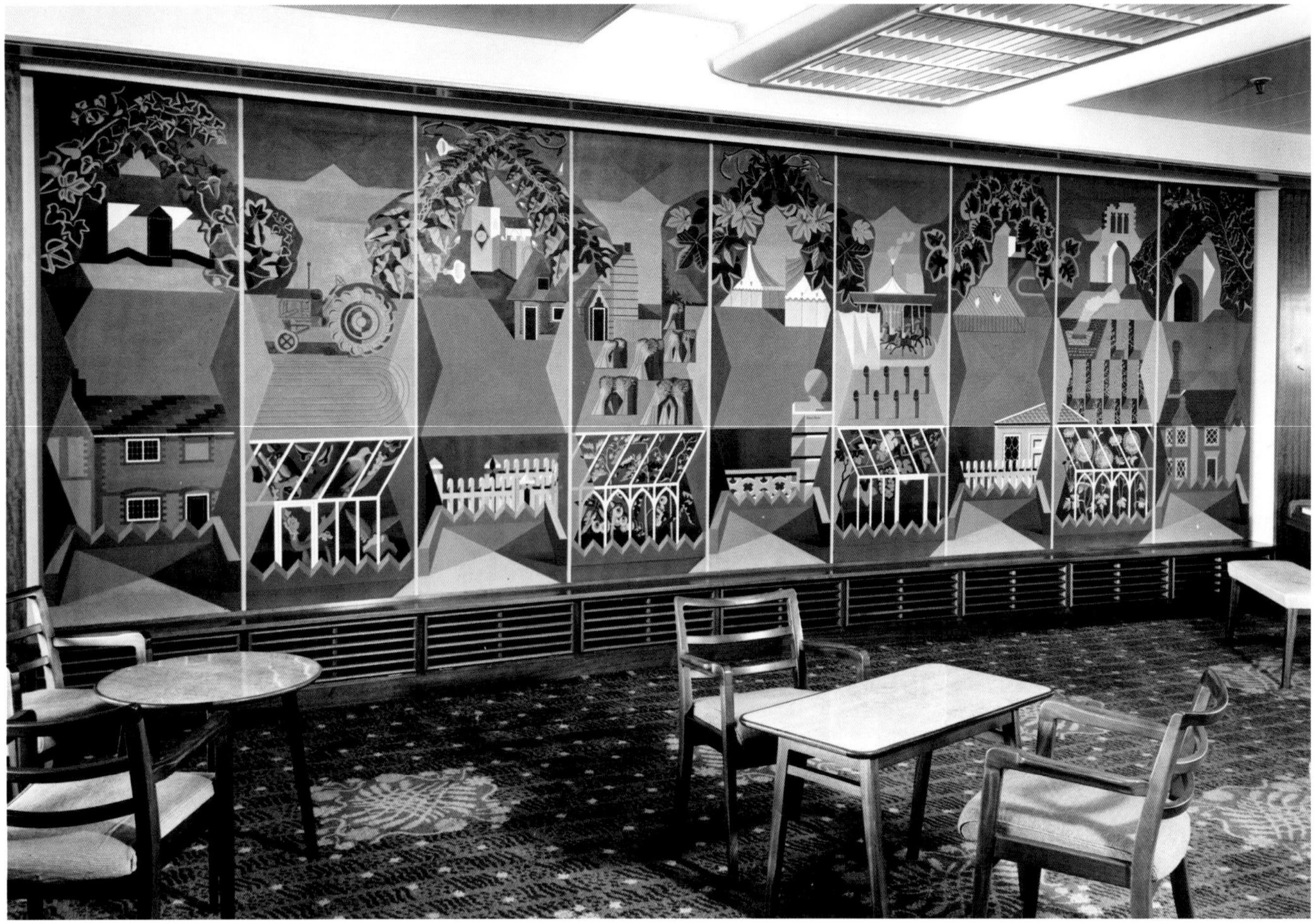

176
English Garden Delights in situ on board SS *Orcades,* (1948) in the 1st class lounge

Britain too had changed and Bawden, realising that the pastoral scenes of earlier days no longer chimed with public taste, was seeking a new way forward; he flirted briefly with 'the geometry of fear' creating a few spiky watercolours of bare trees and birds' nests, à la Graham Sutherland. These works are interesting but he was aware that they did not come from the heart, so was happy to undertake a commission to produce sixteen lithographs for Noel Carrington to illustrate the King Penguin book, *Life in an English Village* (published 1949). These delightful small-scale lithographs depict the mundane life of the tailor, the cobbler, the butcher, the baker as well as the church, pub and village store, with many of the Great Bardfield locals easily identifiable. Now, stimulated by Colin Anderson's commission for the mural, *English Garden Delights*, he turned away from such parochialism and drew inspiration for his design from the brightly coloured mosaics and tiles that he had seen in Addis Ababa, Cairo, Baghdad and other cities. He had always had an acute eye for pattern and through the alchemy of his very individual vision transformed these memories of exotic pattern into something quintessentially English. *English Garden Delights* is a sophisticated design – a geometric pattern of buildings and fields – with the sense of the changing seasons being conveyed through linking garlands of foliage, scenes of fairground, harvest and ploughing, and the four greenhouse structures in the foreground, symbolically representing spring, summer, autumn and winter. All this is evidence of the rich fruits of man's activity, but like its Islamic precursors there is no representation of the human figure.

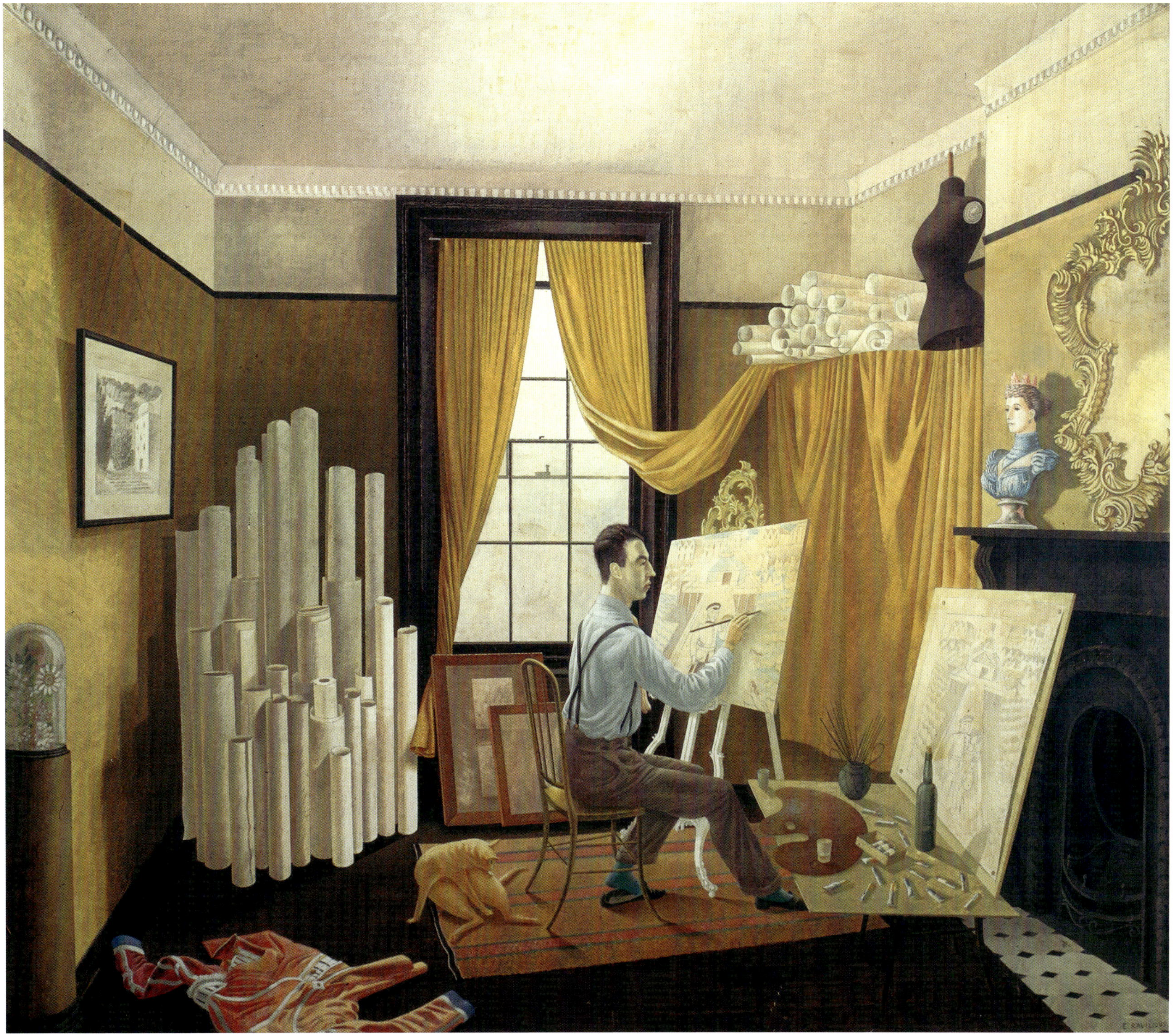

177 Eric Ravilious, *Edward Bawden Working in His Studio,* 1930, tempera on board, 79 x 92 cm (31 ⅛ x 36 ¼ in.)
Collection: Royal College of Art

The rolls of paper are cartoons and studies for the Morley College murals.

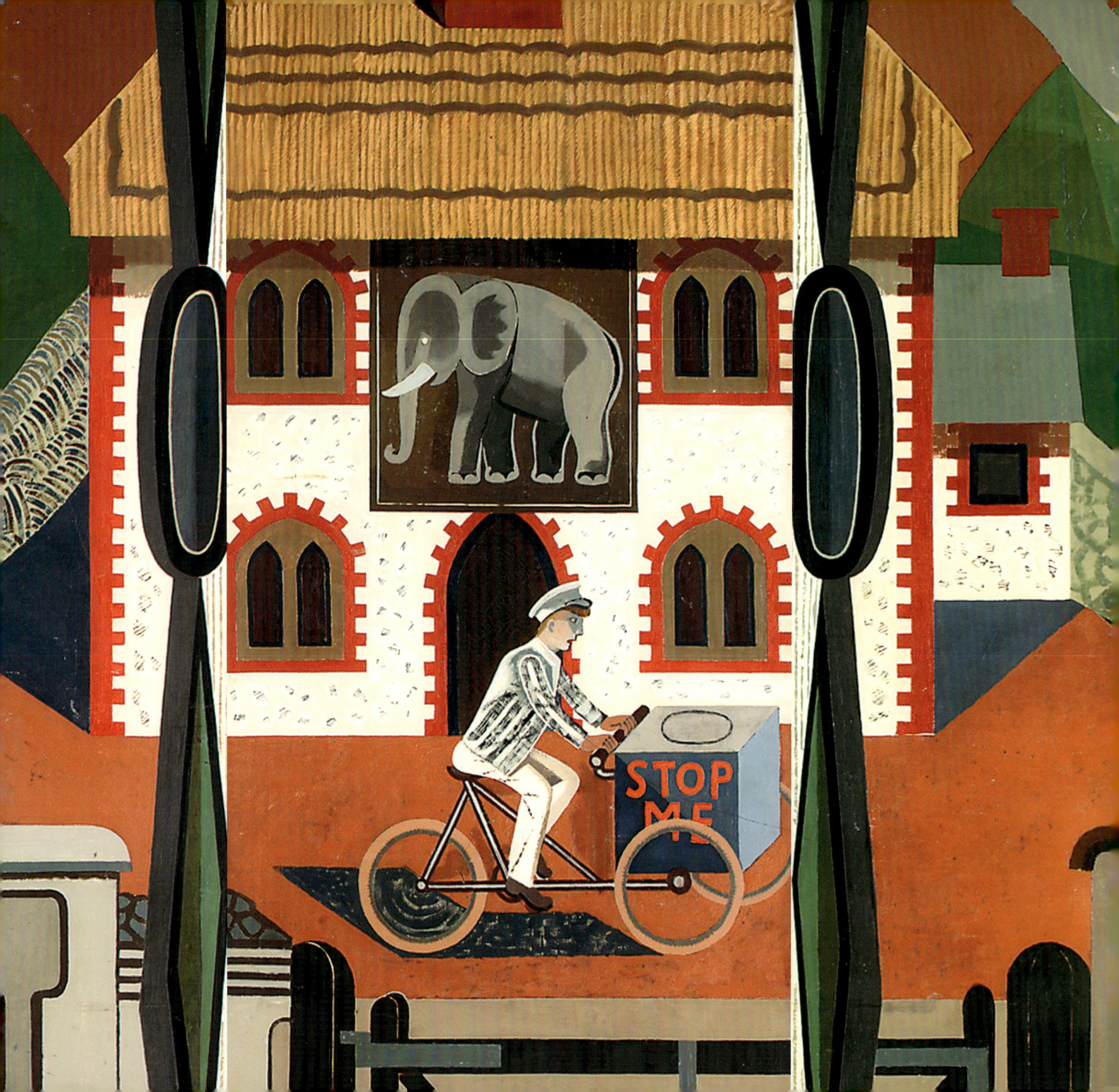
STOP
ME

For *The English Pub* – an eleven-panelled screen – building on his earlier success Bawden developed an even more sophisticated mosaic of buildings and landscape, though this time he allowed himself to include that quintessentially post-war figure – Stop Me And Buy One – the ice-cream man on his bicycle. Apart from this single individual placed at the centre of the composition, the animation of the scene is entirely achieved through the complex use of perspective: whereas in *English Garden Delights* he had linked the panels with foliage and a subtle abstract pattern of elongated lozenges, here he developed a dominant trellis-like device supporting traditional pub signs – Wheatsheaf, King's Head, Rose and Crown, etc. – and it is through this trelliswork that one views the scenes beyond.

Hugh Casson, the artistic director of the Festival of Britain, used his 1948 Christmas card, depicting the old Shot Tower on the south bank of the Thames, to announce to his friends and colleagues the proposed site for the Festival, for which Bawden was to be commissioned to paint a forty-five-feet high mural. This commission overlapped with that for the *Oronsay*, and to meet both deadlines Bawden employed former students as assistants for the first time, both a mark of his growing confidence and his mastery of design. E.W. Fenton and M. Hodell are acknowledged on the right-hand panel of *The English Pub*. William Fenton also assisted on *English Country Life* along with Walter Hoyle, Sheila Robinson, Roy Sharp and Bawden's daughter, Joanna. As Malcolm Yorke says, Bawden had planned *English Country Life* 'in such detail that they had very little to do except fill in the colours on the easy bits.'[1] The loss, through negligence, of the seventy-one panels on which the mural was painted, is a tragedy, but fortunately, being the fine craftsman he was, Bawden had made a beautiful small model, which shows precisely how the screen must have looked with its alternating facets of light and shade, and its many familiar details from Bawden's quirky repertoire. At 1620 square-feet it was Bawden's largest mural, though not his longest. In 1966 he received a commission from British Petroleum to paint a mural for the restaurant in their headquarters building, Britannic House, in the City of London: like *English Garden Delights* it was to contain no figures, but was to be an architectural fantasy, for which purpose BP sent Bawden and his wife on an all-expenses-paid trip to Isfahan and Mashad to study Saracenic architecture. The resulting mural, sixty-four feet in length, now rehoused in the Chelsea and Westminster Hospital, is an intricately patterned frieze of arches, domes and minarets set against a backdrop of distant mountains.

English Garden Delights, *The English Pub*, *English Country Life* and the BP mural were all painted in flat colours with a considerable use of masking tape to achieve the sharp edges he required, but for his final mural, painted at the age of seventy for Blackwell's bookshop in Oxford, he reverted to the more painterly style of earlier days. Just as his designs for the Festival of Britain and the Orient Line link together, so, too, do his designs for his 1928 Shakespearian fantasy at Morley College, his later (1958) *Canterbury Tales* mural for the rebuilt College, and his 1973 spoof history of Oxford, each of which is concerned with visual storytelling. Sadly, we know Bawden's original Morley College mural only from black-and-white photographs and preliminary studies, as is also the case with Charles Mahoney's *The Pleasures of Life*. (see pages 204-209) Bawden and Eric Ravilious worked together on the decoration of the refectory in Morley's newly acquired Georgian building in Lambeth, and because of the historic connection and close links between the College and the nearby Old Vic Theatre, a theme of Elizabethan drama was chosen. In addition to this, in one section, Ravilious painted the interior of a contemporary lodging-house opened out like a doll's house to enable one to view the furnishings and occupants of each room. Both Bawden and Ravilious treated their primarily Shakespearean subject matter with youthful levity and irreverence. As John Rothenstein commented: 'There would appear to be

178
The English Pub (detail)

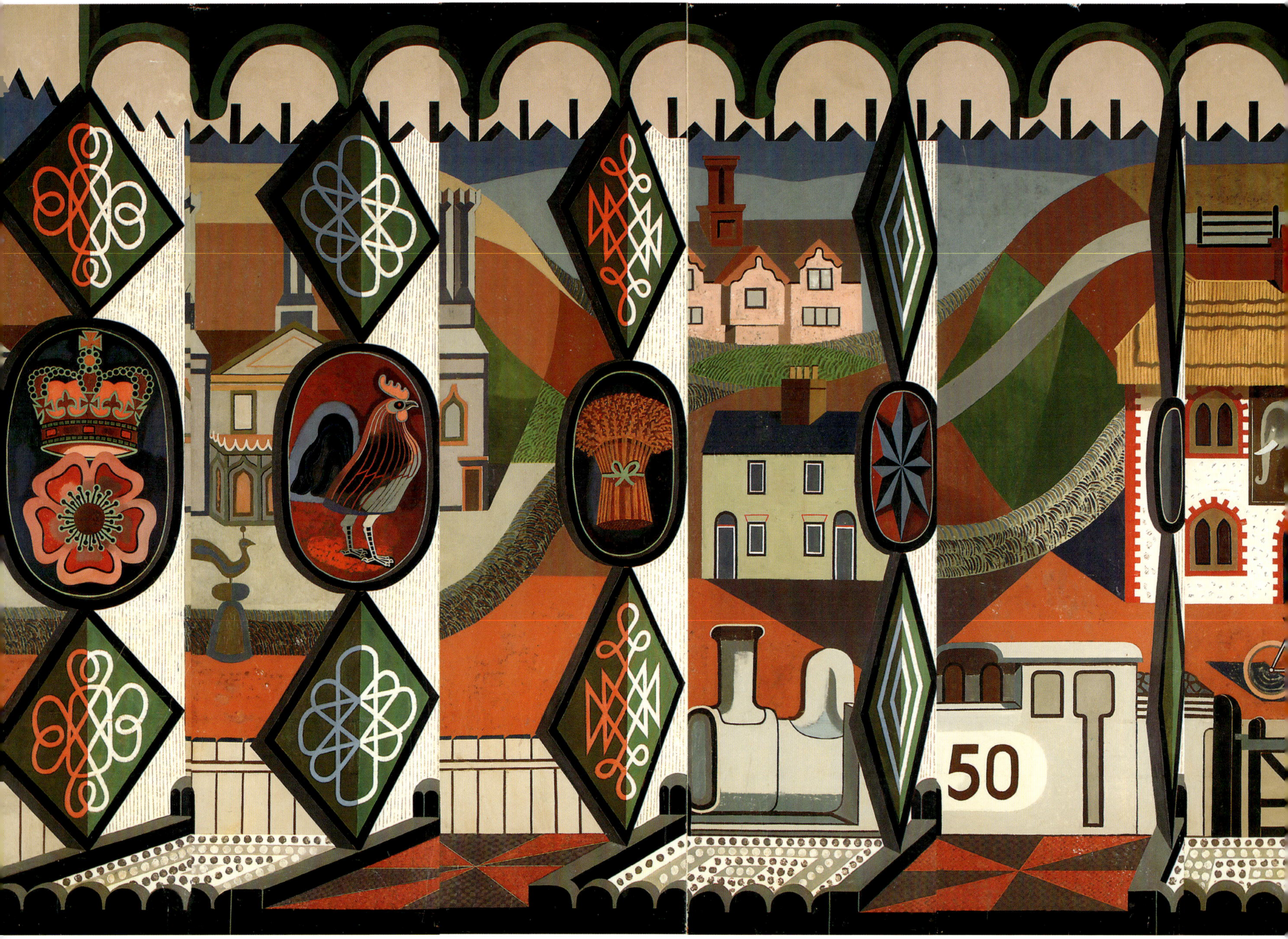

179 *The English Pub,* 1949-1951, oil on 11 panels, 176 x 539 cm (69 ⅜ x 212 ¼ in.)

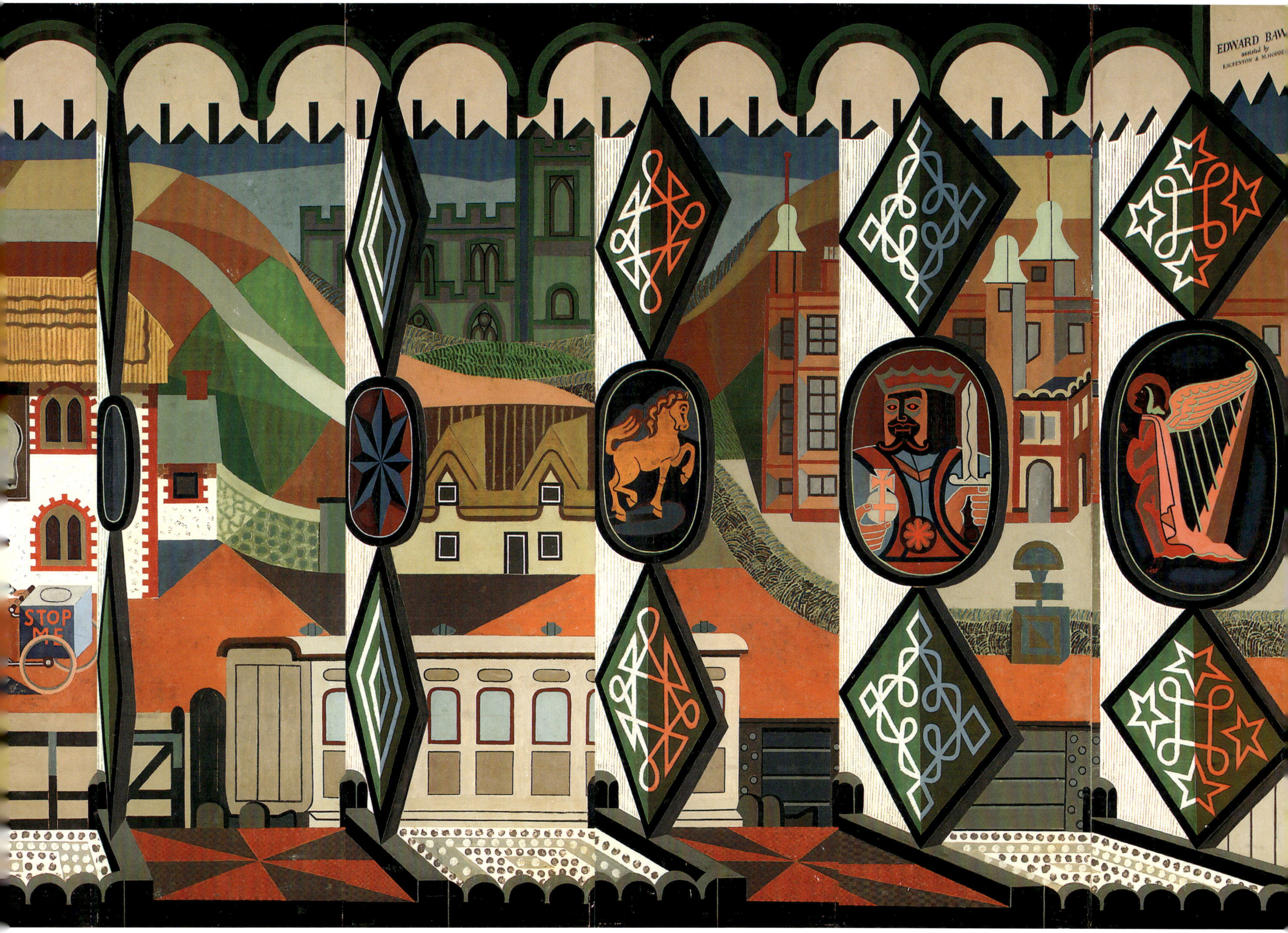
EDWARD BAW
assisted by
E.W.FENTON & M.HODDE
STOP ME

nothing from the paintings of the English primitives, engravings by Callot, and drawings by Cruikshank, to early Victorian gardening books and fashion-plates of the eighteen-eighties, that they have not ransacked.'[2] Forty-five years later at Blackwell's the levity may have subsided but the irreverence and humour – a little drier perhaps – are still in evidence in the glorious vignettes of the Scapegoat painting Holman Hunt, Ruskin painstakingly drawing one of the Seven Lamps of Architecture and Lewis Carroll photographing the White Rabbit.

Midway in time between the Orient Line and Festival of Britain commissions and Blackwell's, Bawden was asked to paint a new mural for the rebuilt Morley College. As before, for the new mural's subject matter he looked once again to local connections, selecting this time the College's location on the pilgrim route to Canterbury. He turned to Chaucer for his inspiration – and possibly to the Bayeux Tapestry also – and devised an unfolding narrative with mounted pilgrims in the foreground riding calmly past an animated backdrop of incidents from *The Canterbury Tales*, depicted as they might have been viewed in a multi-screen cinema. The macabre humour that he was later to exploit so outrageously in his lino-cut illustrations to *Morte d'Arthur* is already in evidence in several of these scenes.

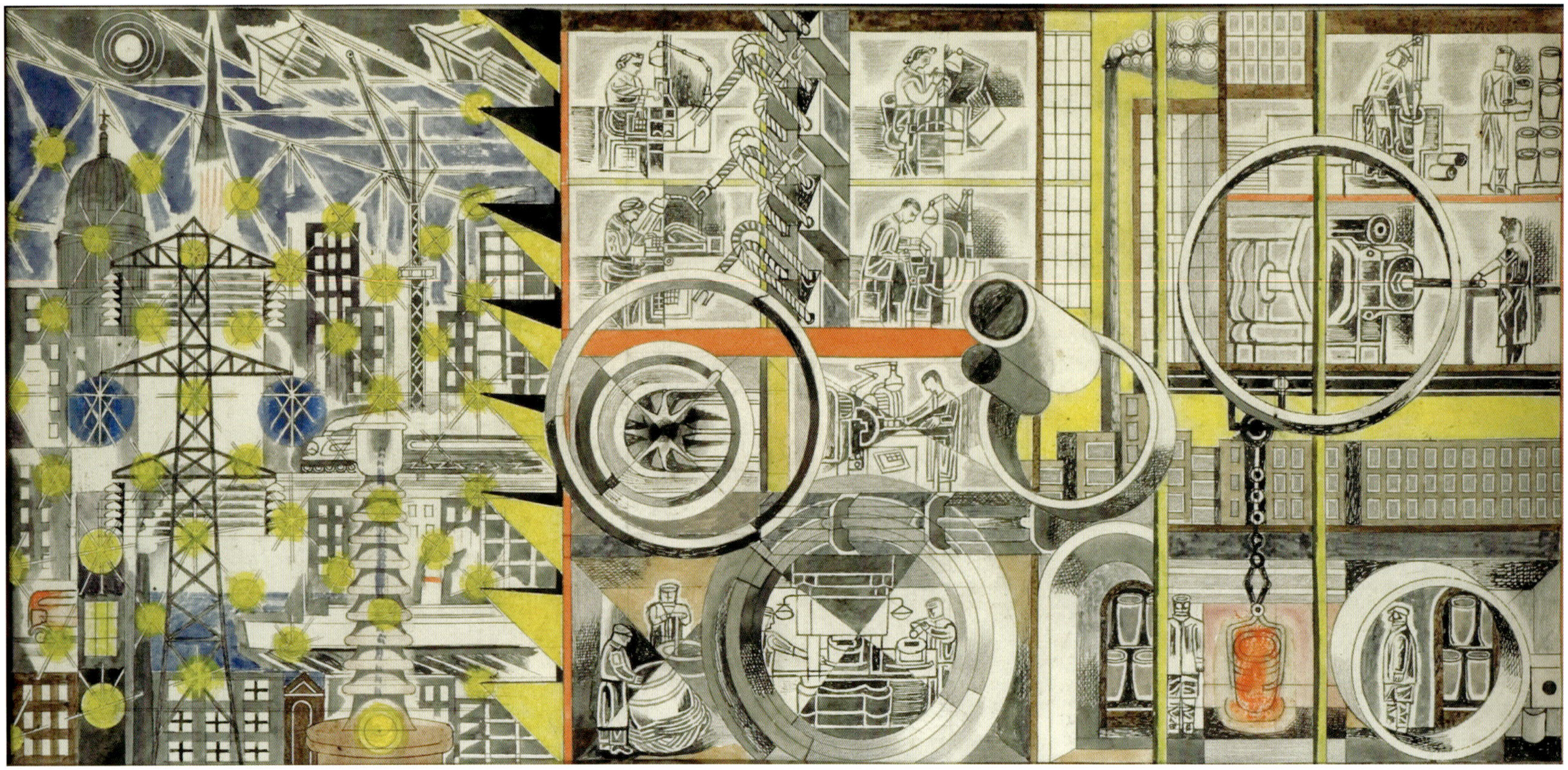

180 Design for mural commissioned by the Morgan Crucible Company for the entrance hall of their works on the South Bank of the Thames at Battersea, 1957-58, pen, ink, pencil and watercolour. The Higgins Gallery Bedford, Bawden Gift

181
Mural for British Petroleum at Britannic House, London, 1966, oil on panel, 412 x 914 cm (162 ¼ x 359 ⅞ in.)

Courtesy of Chelsea & Westminster Health Charity

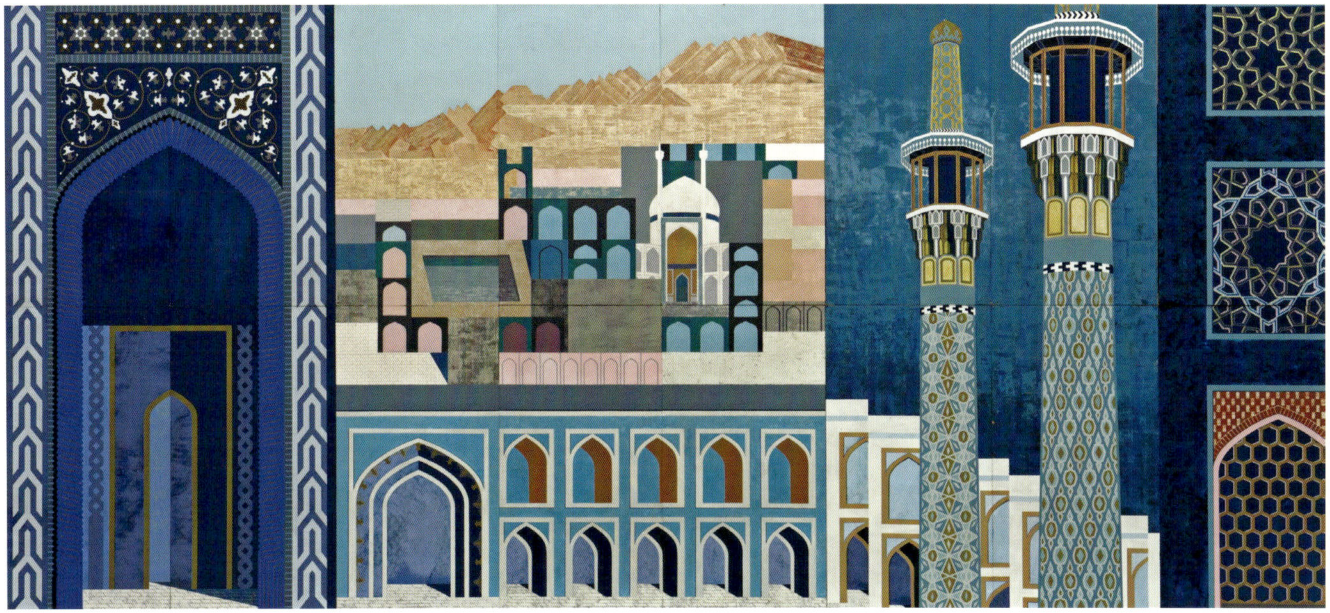

During his long life Bawden created more than a score of murals of one sort or another, some intended to be permanent and others, such as those for the Brussels International Exhibition and Expo '67 in Montreal, of a more transient nature. The modello for *English Country Life* is part of the extensive archive he selected and gave to the Cecil Higgins Museum, Bedford, along with sketches and models for several of his other murals including those for the Morgan Crucible Company, Associated Electrical Industries and Carr's Lane Congregational Chapel, Birmingham. The latter is perhaps his most extraordinary mural in terms of material, though not the most beautiful. It consists of three panels incorporating a mixture of collaged, painted and carved linoleum, wood, nails and drawing pins, and depicts broadly the earlier chapels that had stood on the site. The choice of nails – some 20,000 of them – was not symbolic, nor did it reflect the fact that his father had been an ironmonger, but was a pragmatic response to the starkness of the brick wall it was to adorn, and the raking light in which it would be seen. Every commission he undertook he approached with an open mind and was quite prepared to use unconventional materials if they helped achieve the desired effect.

ENDNOTES

1. Malcolm Yorke, *Edward Bawden & His Circle*, Woodbridge, 2007, p.168.

2. John Rothenstein, *Studio*, 1930.

MURALS BY EDWARD BAWDEN

1929-30 – Morley College – *Fantasy on Elizabethan Literature* – unveiled by the Rt Hon. Stanley Baldwin, February 5, 1930 (Destroyed by enemy bombs 1940)

1934 – Pavilion Hotel, Scarborough

1937-8 – International Building Society Club dining room, Park Lane, London - English Pastoral - Over-painted during the 1940s

1947-8 – *English Garden Delights*, first-class lounge on P & O Liner RMS *Orcades*

1950-1 – *The English Pub*, for first-class lounge on P & O Liner RMS *Oronsay*
Country Life in Britain, Festival of Britain, Lion & Unicorn Pavilion. Dismantled after the close of the Festival, missing

1957-8 – Morgan Crucible Company, Battersea, Entrance Hall – industrial design showing uses of the Company's products – Building demolished, mural believed to be in store

1958 – Royal Arms for Brussels International Exhibition
Morley College (new building) – *Canterbury Tales*

1960-1 – Canadian Pacific Liner, *Empress of Canada*

1963 – Associated Electrical Industries, Small Board Room – *The Power of Light Over Darkness*. Fate unknown
Hull University, Physics Block – Abstract Design based on Molecular Forms

1965 – Microbiology Laboratory, Queens University, Belfast – Molecular Structures
Mural for Boardroom for Pilkington Bros., St Helen's, Lancashire

1966 – British Pavilion, Expo '67, Montreal

1966-7 – Britannic House for British Petroleum – Saracenic Architecture – since relocated to the Chelsea & Westminster Hospital

1968 – London Underground, Victoria Line, tile panels for Victoria, Kings Cross, Highbury & Islington and Tottenham Hale Stations

c. 1970 – St George's Hospital, Hyde Park Corner – since relocated to St George's Hospital, Tooting

1971 – Carr's Lane Congregational Church, Birmingham
Wyvern Theatre and Arts Centre, Swindon

1973 – Blackwell's Bookshop, Oxford – fantasised history of Oxford

Murals for which date of execution is unknown:

Mosaic for High Commissioner's House, Lagos, Nigeria
Mural for *Empress of France*

Edward Bawden (1903-1989)

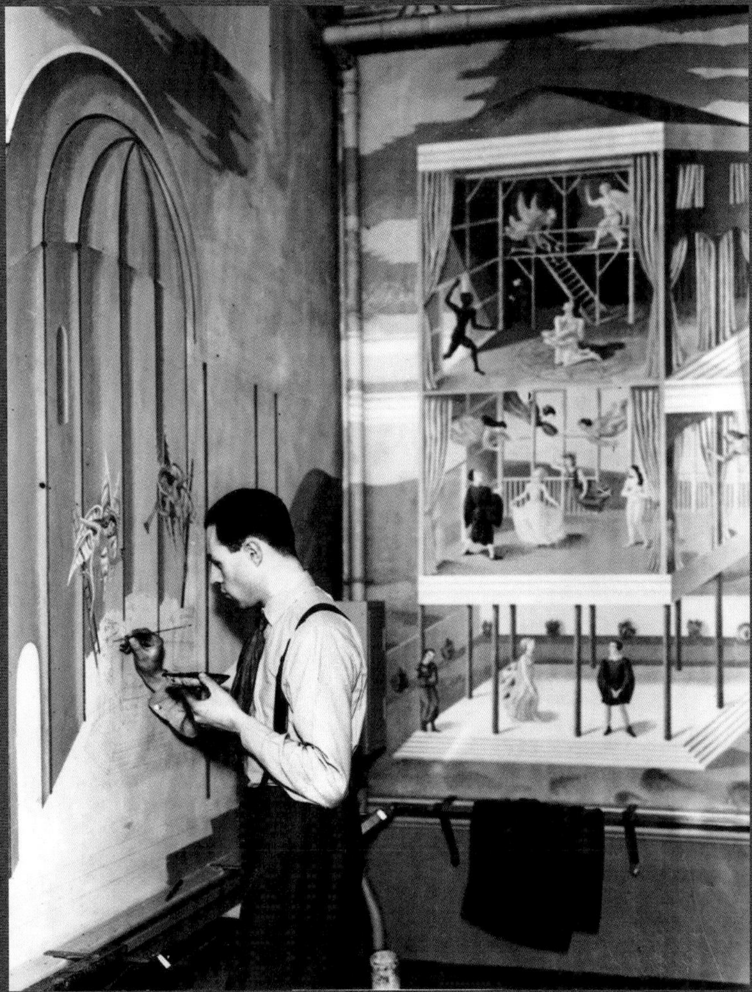

182 Edward Bawden at work on the Morley College murals, c. 1930

EDWARD BAWDEN, CBE, RA. Born Braintree, died Saffron Walden, Essex. Draughtsman, watercolourist, printmaker, illustrator and muralist. Studied Cambridge School of Art (1919-22), Royal College of Art (1922-25), Official War Artist (1940-45), Royal Designer for Industry 1949. Worked with the Curwen Press producing wallpapers and advertising material for London Transport, Fortnum & Mason and Twinings, as well as illustrations for Ambrose Heath's cookery books. As a war artist he travelled principally in the Middle East recording events in Egypt, Iraq, Persia, Abyssinia and Saudi Arabia. Torpedoed on the SS *Laconia* 1942 and later interned. Post-war he carried out mural commissions, designed china for the Orient Line and textiles for Time-Life, London. Guest Instructor Banff School of Fine Art, Canada, 1949. One-man exhibitions at the Leicester Galleries and The Fine Art Society, London. Principal museum collections: Imperial War Museum; Tate Gallery; Higgins Gallery, Bedford and Fry Gallery, Saffron Walden.

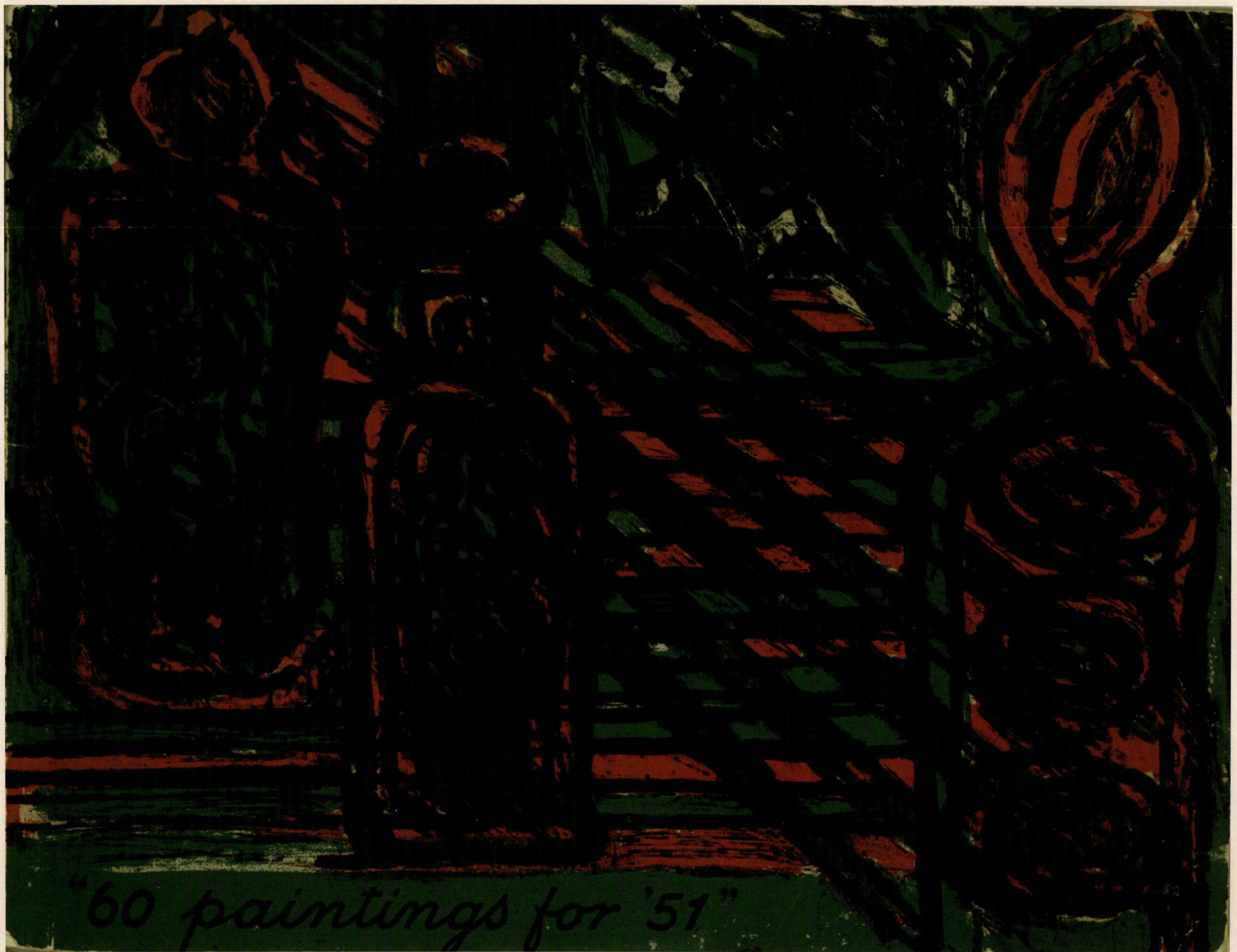

183 Cover of the catalogue for the Festival of Britain '60 Paintings for 51' exhibition

Confrontation: The Festival of Britain '60 Paintings for 51' Exhibition

Robert Upstone

In March 1951 the Arts Council opened an ambitious survey of contemporary British painting intended as a significant cultural component of the Festival of Britain. It was shown at the Society of British Artists galleries in Suffolk Street, near the National Gallery, and also in an extensive nationwide tour of eleven venues.[1] Sixty leading British artists were invited to submit works on a large scale – a minimum of 45 x 60 inches, but with no maximum size restriction. The show was consciously planned to mark and celebrate the quality and ambition of British contemporary art, and the scale of the works was meant to reflect this. They were not murals in the strict sense, being painted in oils on stretched canvases, but it was hoped and intended they would be used for public decoration, so fulfilling the same essential function. This was a distinction raised positively by *The Times*, which noted that if directed towards murals in tempera 'The painter in oils may be unhappy outside the medium he knows … Easel paintings are as proper an ornament for civic buildings as murals'.[2] Many of the painters involved made epic-scaled canvases that were the largest they had ever tackled. Ivon Hitchens's *Aquarium Nativity* was the biggest item in the show at over eighteen feet long. Hard to come by in post-war austerity Britain, the Arts Council undertook to supply and pay for the canvas the works were to be painted on, further encouragement for the artists not to limit the scale of their work.

It was expected that these canvases would be bought for the institutions of the new Welfare State, for schools, hospitals and New Town civic buildings, and also for factories, offices and workplaces. The Arts Council wrote to almost every major manufacturer and business throughout the country inviting them to a special private view on 17 and 18 April in the stated hope they would purchase a picture. They wrote also to the heads of major advertising companies recommended by Marcus Brumwell (the advertising executive, modernist art collector, supporter of Ben Nicholson, Barbara Hepworth and Henry Moore, and head of the Design Research Unit, which was a moving force in the Festival of Britain) asking if they had clients who might be purchasers.

The show was to be a competition, with five winners chosen who would each receive a prize of £500, a very significant sum in 1951. Most of the best painters then working contributed, but the outcome was not quite what was intended when the competition became mired in a bitter public controversy about the validity of abstract art and the misuse of public money.

ARTS COUNCIL FESTIVAL PURCHASES: CONTEMPORARY BRITISH PAINTINGS.

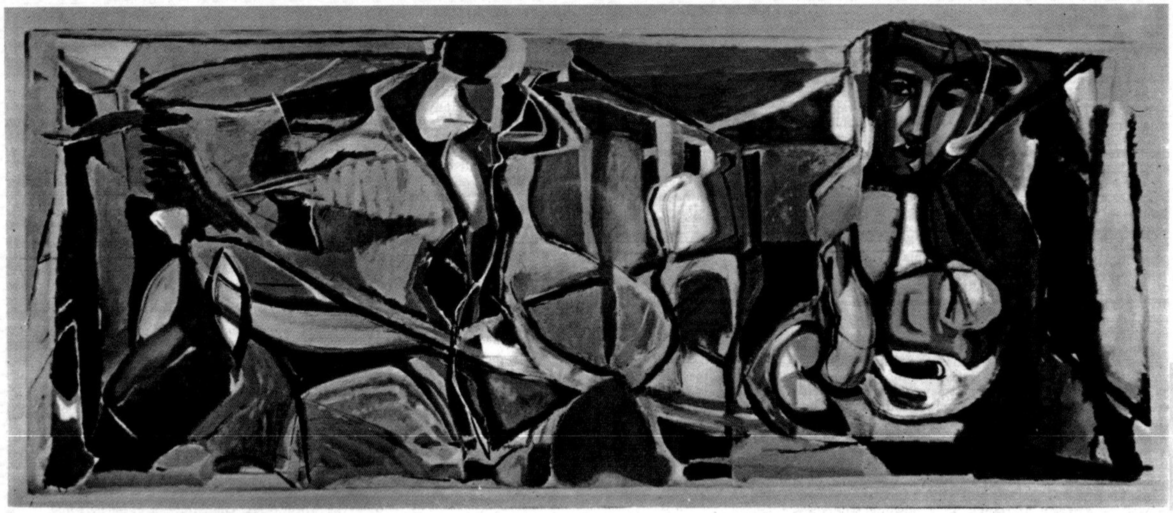

"AQUARIAN NATIVITY": BY IVON HITCHENS, b. 1893, WHO IS REPRESENTED IN THE TATE, THE VICTORIA AND ALBERT, AND OTHER GALLERIES. HE STUDIED AT THE ST. JOHN'S WOOD SCHOOL AND THE R.A. SCHOOLS.

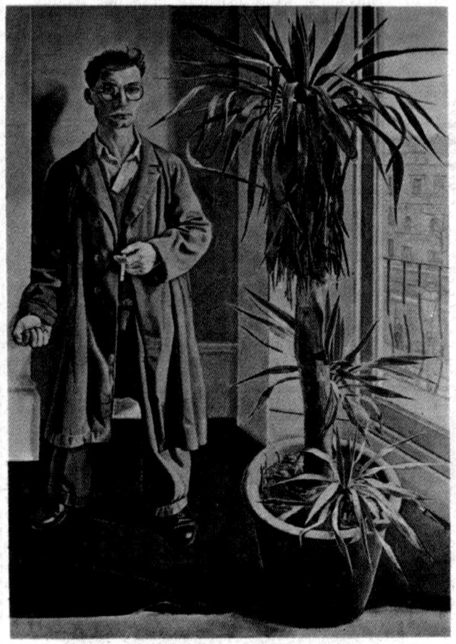

"INTERIOR NEAR PADDINGTON": BY LUCIAN FREUD (b. 1922). HE IS A TEACHER AT THE SLADE SCHOOL, AND HELD HIS LAST ONE-MAN SHOW AT THE HANOVER GALLERY IN 1949.

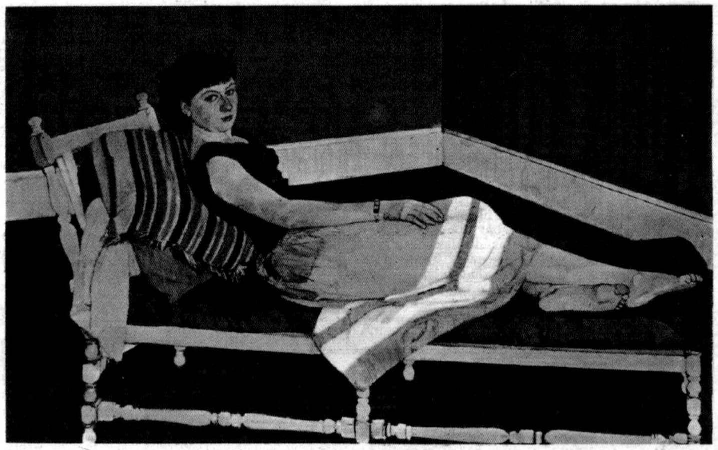

"MISS LYNN": BY CLAUDE ROGERS (b. 1907). HE IS A TEACHER AT THE SLADE SCHOOL, WHERE HE WAS ORPEN BURSAR AND ROBERT ROSS LEAVING SCHOOL. HE WAS ONE OF THE FOUR FOUNDERS OF THE EUSTON ROAD SCHOOL.

To mark the Festival of Britain, the Arts Council invited sixty artists to paint a large work on a subject of their own choice. Fifty-four paintings were completed, and the exhibition, entitled "Sixty Paintings for '51," due to open in Manchester on May 2, will be in London at the R.B.A. Galleries from June 22 to July 31, before touring the provinces and Scotland. We illustrate the five paintings selected for purchase by the Arts Council for £500 each, by Jhr. W. Sandberg, Director of the Municipal Museum, Amsterdam, Mr. Alan Clutton-Brock, art critic of *The Times*, and Mr. A. J. L. McDonnell, purchaser for the Felton Bequest to the National Gallery of Victoria, in Melbourne, who acted as judges. Mr. Ivon Hitchens, a member of the Seven and Five Group, held his first one-man show in 1925; Mr. Robert Medley, a member of the London Group, held his last exhibition at the Hanover Galleries in 1950; and the Tate Gallery purchased a painting from it. Mr. William Gear, son of a Fife miner, studied in Edinburgh. His war service lasted from 1940 to 1947, and he then worked in Paris.

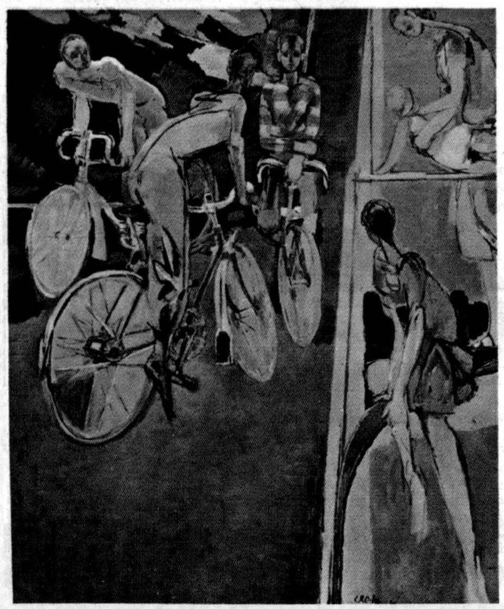

(LEFT.) "BICYCLISTS AGAINST A BLUE BACKGROUND": BY ROBERT MEDLEY (b. 1906), WHO STUDIED AT THE SLADE.

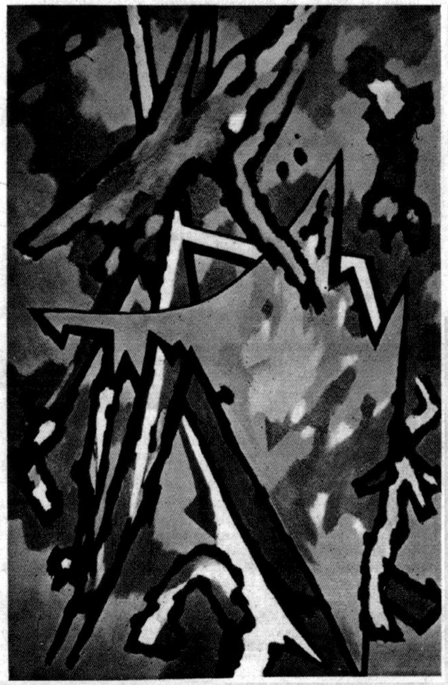

(RIGHT.) "AUTUMN LANDSCAPE": BY WILLIAM GEAR (b. 1915). A ONE-MAN SHOW OF HIS RECENT WORK IS IN PROGRESS AT THE GIMPEL GALLERY.

184
The Illustrated London News,
April 28, 1951

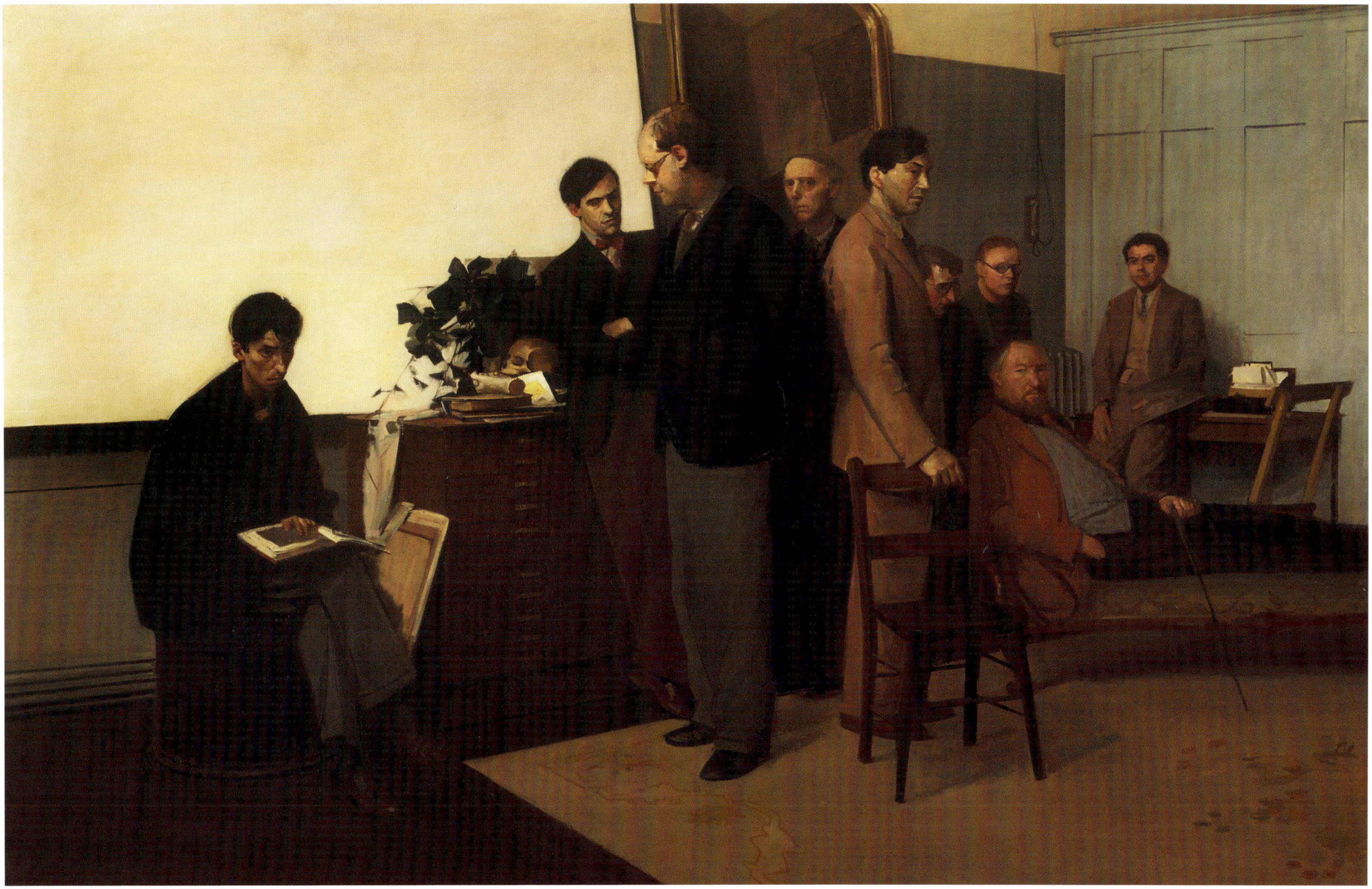

185 Rodrigo Moynihan, *Portrait Group*, 1951, oil on canvas, 213.4 x 334.6 cm (84 x 131 ¾ in.), © Tate, London 2012

The original idea appears to have been that of Philip James (1901-74), Director of Art at the Arts Council, who subsequently masterminded and organised the exhibition. The project ran into difficulty even before it started. In October 1949 the Arts Council's Art Panel had decided to commission five paintings for £500 each for the Festival. Panel members were asked to submit five nominations, but in the event none of them could agree a short list. So the compromise position was to hold a competition instead, and invite a wide selection of British painters of all ages and styles to contribute, chosen from a list of 145 names suggested by the Art Panel and members of the Art Department. The oldest painters invited were William Gillies, born in 1878, and Vanessa Bell and Matthew Smith, both born in 1879, and many others were similarly born in the nineteenth century, albeit including the artist at the epicentre of British Modernist art, Ben Nicholson. This was balanced by a good showing of younger, newer painters who worked to different degrees in an advanced style: Peter Lanyon, Victor Pasmore, William Gear, Lucian Freud, Keith Vaughan, William Scott, Bryan Wynter and Patrick Heron, among many others. The show successfully surveyed the variety of

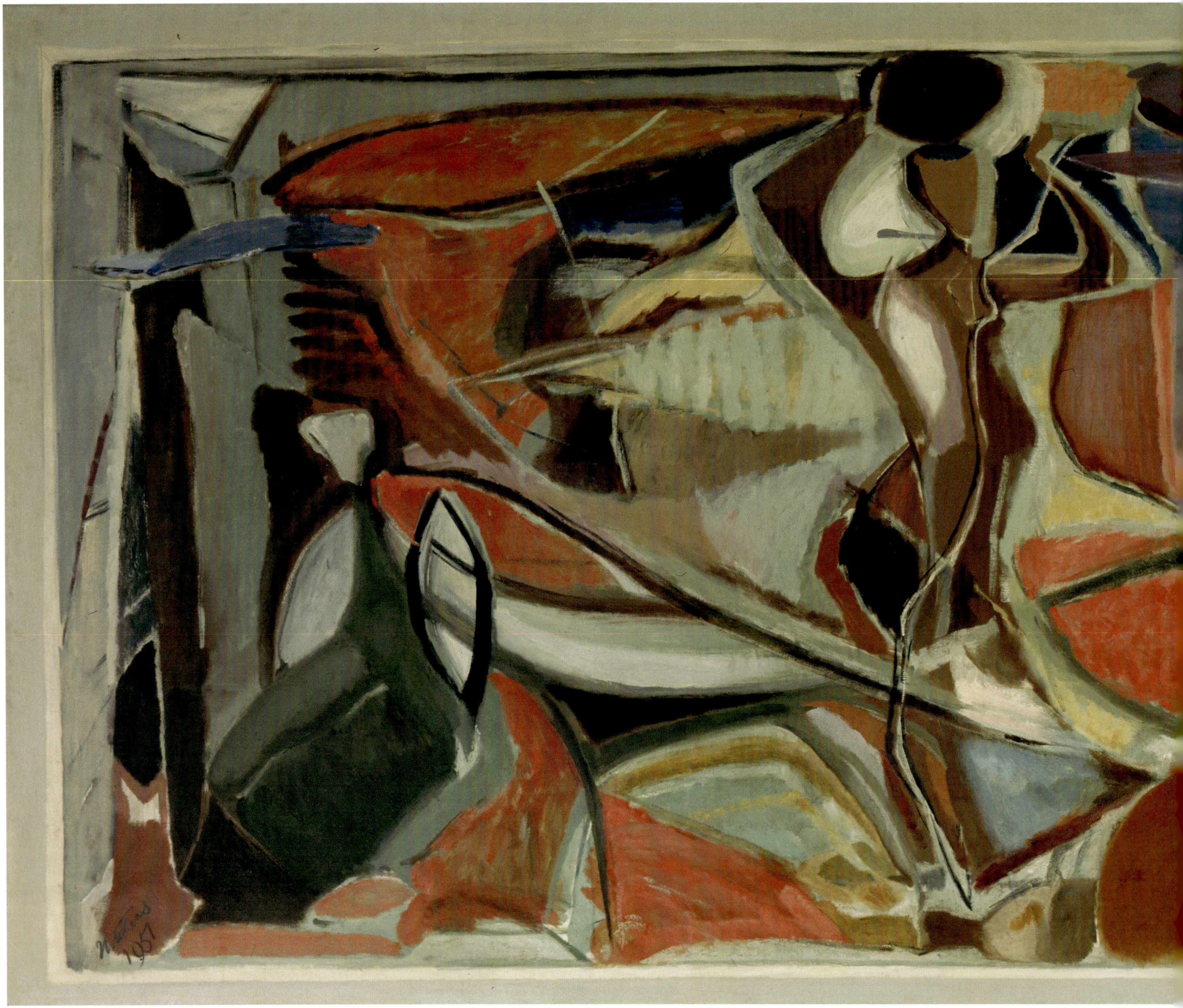

186 Ivon Hitchens, *Aquarium Nativity*, 1951, oil and wax on canvas, 210.9 x 566.4 cm (83 x 223 in.), © Ivon Hitchens' Estate/Jonathan Clark & Co., collection: UCL Art Museum

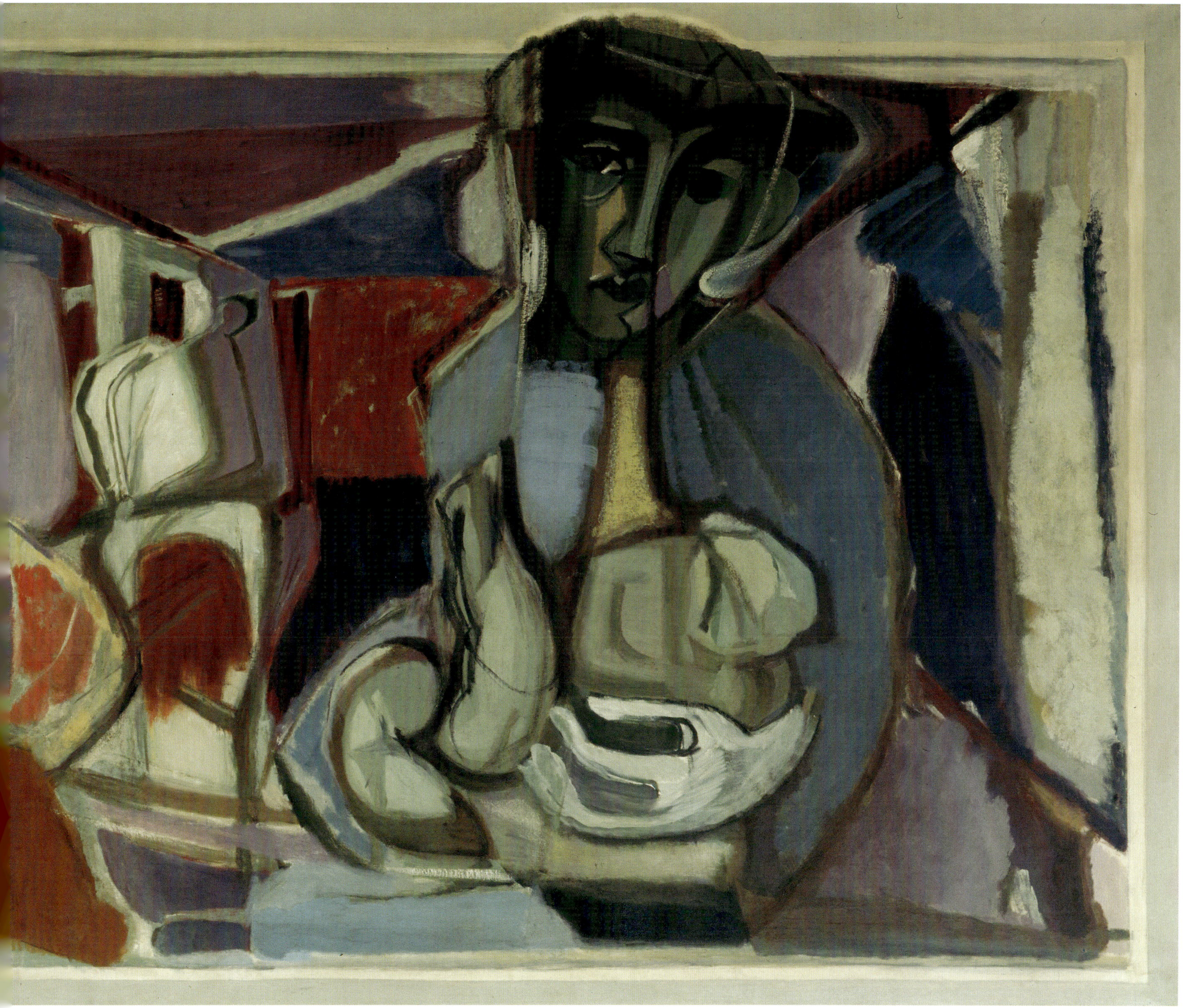

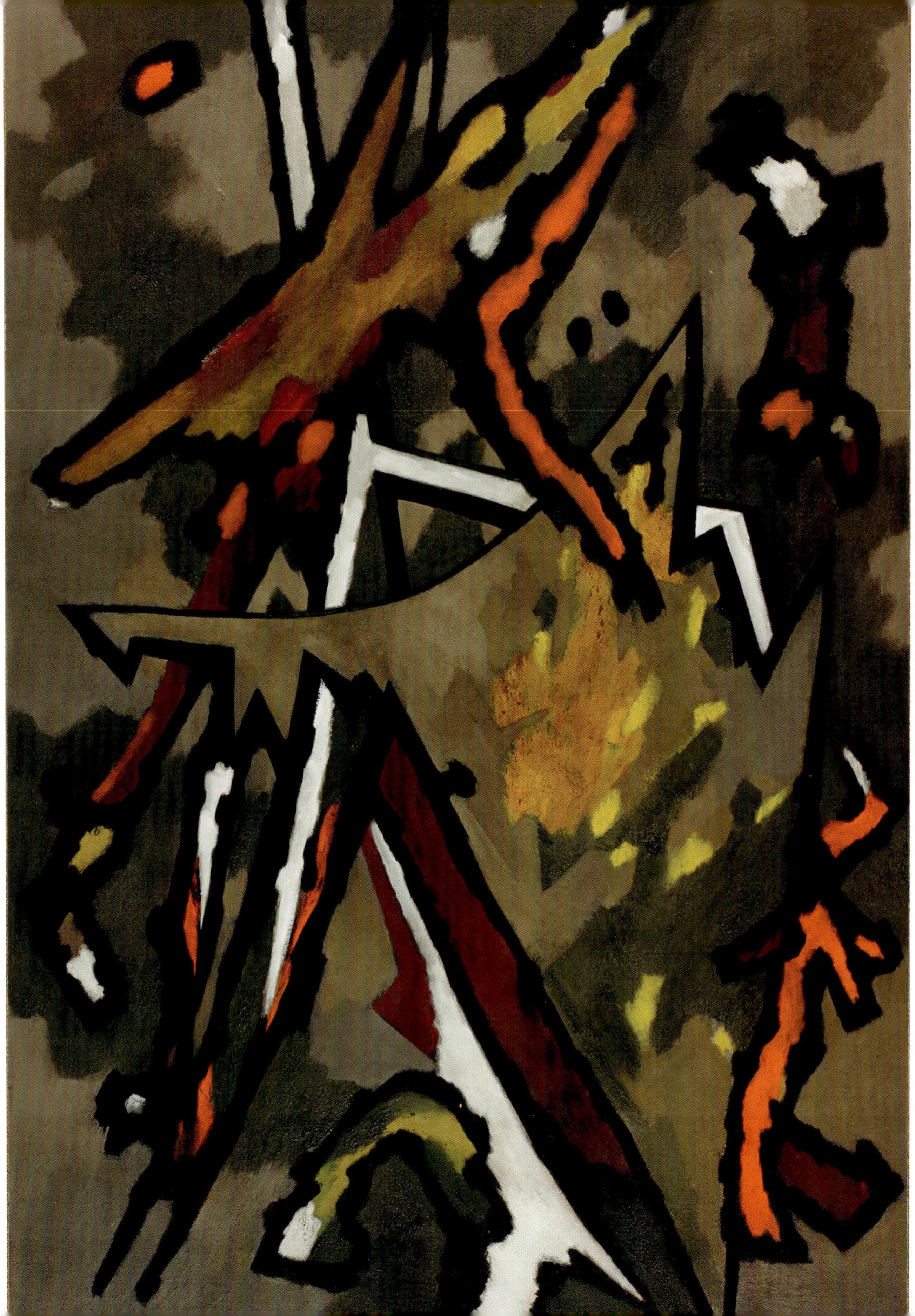

187
William Gear,
Autumn Landscape, 1951
oil on canvas,
127 x 183.2 cm
(50 x 72 ⅛ in.),
© The Estate of William Gear
Courtesy of the
Arts Council Collection

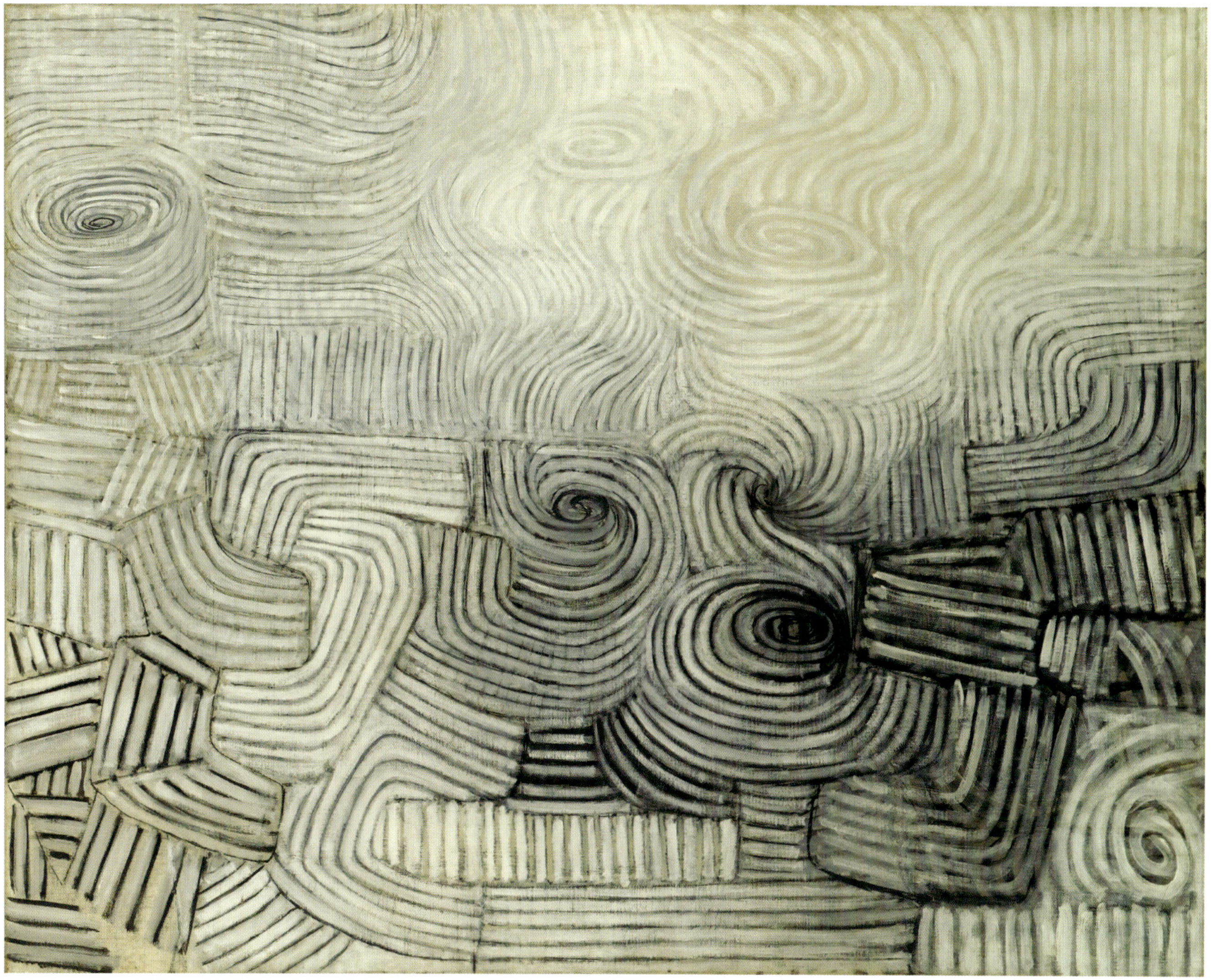

188
Victor Pasmore,
The Snowstorm: Spiral Motif in Black and White,
1950-51, oil on canvas,
119.4 x 152.4 cm
(47 x 60 in.),
© Victor Pasmore Estate,
Courtesy of the
Arts Council Collection

modern styles then being followed in British painting – the concise figuration of Freud, Lynton Lamb, Rodrigo Moynihan, Claude Rogers, Gilbert Spencer and Carel Weight; the Picasso-esque stylisation of Colquhoun and McBryde, and the Braque-inspired simplification of Wynter, de Maistre and Heron; the greatly differing degrees of expressive, painterly gesturalism found in the work of Peter Lanyon, William Gear, Ceri Richards and Robert Medley; or the highly refined, more advanced abstraction of Ben Nicholson and Victor Pasmore.

Critical reactions to the show were without unconditional praise and most addressed the question of appropriate scale. John Russell writing in *The Times* admired the ambition of the project but commented that several 'miniaturists' had found themselves out of their depth and that 'Size is out of fashion … current taste inclines to the small, the intimate, the incomplete'. It was, he judged, 'an exhibition where everybody has staked everything; and if a great many people have also lost everything, at least the disasters are of a heroic scale.'[3] However, individual works had been singled out for praise by *The Times* two days earlier, especially Freud's portrait of Harry Diamond which was described as being 'painted with a malignancy in minute observation

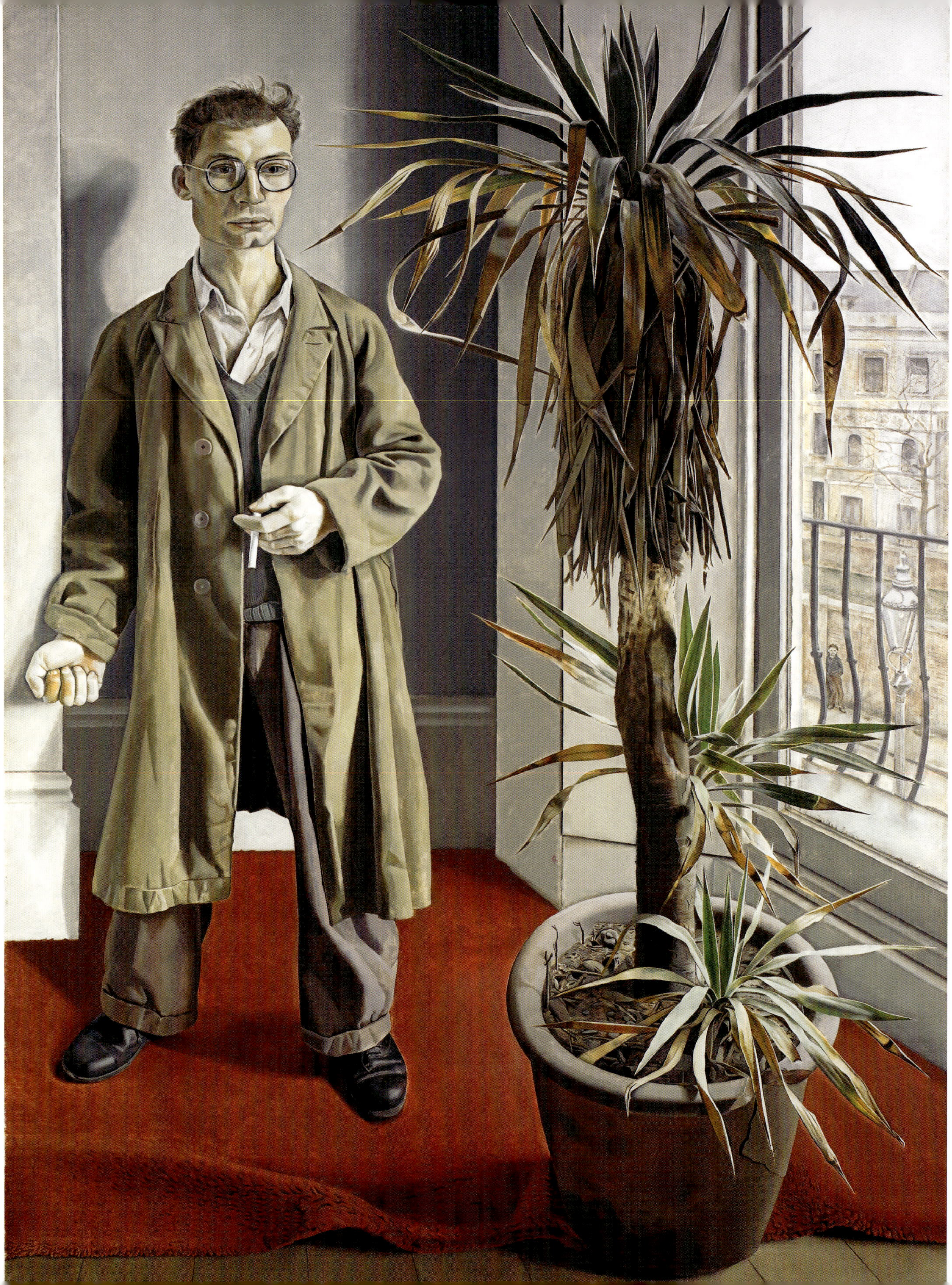

189
Lucien Freud,
Interior Near Paddington,
1951,
oil on canvas,
152.4 x 114.3 cm
(60 x 45 in.),
National Museums
Liverpool/Walker Art
Gallery

which even he has seldom surpassed; but it will be seen that there is no loss of unity because of the detail and that the curious colour has a real subtlety'.[4] The twenty-seven-year-old David Sylvester also questioned the suitability of large-scale paintings, writing in *The Burlington Magazine* that 'the best painters since the death of Turner have expressed themselves most naturally on a limited scale' and that 'nearly all' the pictures in the Arts Council exhibition 'seem to have been conceived on a scale not commensurate with their dimensions'.[5]

The winners of the competition were announced on 21 April 1951 with prizes going to Lucian Freud, Ivon Hitchens, Robert Medley, Claude Rogers and William Gear. Sir Alfred Munnings, former President of the Royal Academy and with a deep hatred of advanced or abstract art immediately wrote to the *Daily Telegraph* attacking William Gear's abstraction and challenging the spending of public money on a work he described as a 'scheming, self-conscious, anglicised 50-year old repetition of the Ecole de Paris'.[6] This was the beginning of a two-month battle in the *Telegraph* letters column lambasting the integrity of abstract art and questioning whether public money should be spent on it. Munnings had called for voters to demand their MPs ask questions in Parliament about the prize. Edgar Granville (1898-1998), Liberal Member for Eye in Suffolk, tabled a written question to the Chancellor of the Exchequer, Hugh Gaitskell, asking if 'he is aware that the recent purchase by the Arts Council of [William Gear's] "Autumn Landscape" and three other paintings is causing dissatisfaction; that these paintings are not representative of British art; and who was consulted before the paintings were purchased.' Granville's representation of a constituency in Suffolk must raise the possibility of some contact between himself and Munnings. Gaitskell's response was firm: he was quite aware of the criticism and 'I am assured that, taken together, these pictures are widely representative in style and cover various aspects of contemporary British painting. They were purchased on the recommendation of three persons with wide knowledge of modern art and diversity of tastes'.[7]

When James sent Gear his prize money he wrote: 'I do hope that the public reaction does not make you feel that you have earned your £500 too dearly'.[8] Gear replied hoping that those who had written to the newspapers to complain 'will change their minds when they see the original painting. I think myself it is the best thing I have ever done' and hoped the controversy would at least guarantee good attendance for the tour. Ultimately he believed 'The Munnings's of this world are fighting a losing battle'.[9]

Ben Nicholson took up the fight in the *Daily Mail*, which had attacked Gear on its front page. Under the title 'Defending Modern Artists' Nicholson wrote an article that was calmly persuasive and empathetic. 'The attack on modern art', he wrote

> is usually made on the ground that it is something that the ordinary man finds difficult or even impossible to understand. I can sympathise with the public in their difficulty in understanding what is, in fact, a new language, because at first I myself found it very difficult to understand. It was only because I took the line that the fault in understanding might be in me and not in the language, and because of this persisted, that I did eventually discover what this new development is that had been taking place … People to whom this new freedom in painting and sculpture is new ask: 'But what is it supposed to represent?' The answer to that is very much the same that one might give if asked what a flower is supposed to represent. Each flower exists *in its own right.*

Nicholson's article ended more sternly. Noting that the previous and current Directors of the National Gallery, Kenneth Clark and Philip Hendy, 'have done a great deal to encourage modern art', he warned: 'So when "the public" read one of these writers who attack all modern art, let them remember that *the experts do not agree with him*, and that it is well worth their while as intelligent members of the community to try to discover, quite humbly, what it is all about.'[10]

The issue of the amounts of money involved did have some validity. While the prices the artists set for their pictures varied widely, all were costly. Moynihan's *Portrait Group* (84" x 132") was the most expensive at £1,000 followed by Nicholson's *Still Life* (80" x 90") at £800. Many were pitched at the same £500 price as the prize, such as John Armstrong's *Storm* (45" x 60"), Duncan Grant's *The Arrival of the Italian Comedy* (72" x 90") and Victor Pasmore's *The Snowstorm: Spiral in Black and White* (47" x 60"). Others – Merlyn Evans, Claude Rogers, Gilbert Spencer – priced their pictures at 500 guineas. The cheapest work was Winifred Nicholson's *Fowl that fly in the Firmament* (46" x 63") at £100. There may have been the hope among many of the artists that pictures would be bought without demur with public money for public spaces. 'If we are to survive as painters', Winifred Nicholson wrote to James, 'we must find public bodies for our patrons; the private individual can no longer support us', and speculated that her contribution would be ideally suited to 'a new Secondary School or public hall – or village community centre'; she had not made it abstract because 'we must I think try to meet the average taste … if they once start accepting paintings they may accept more advanced vision later.'[11]

Other painters had some degree of confusion about prices. Vanessa Bell wrote: 'thinking £500 was the price to be paid for any [work] that might be chosen, I put that price on mine … In fact … I should be glad to ask much less, say £200 or £250, or to consider any offer'.[12] In any event, these were all significant amounts in post-war economic austerity Britain and served as a background to the complaints about the amount of public money being spent on the winners. Many of the artists were as flexible as Bell on their prices. Moynihan eventually accepted £250 from the Arts Council – a quarter of his original price – and the picture was presented to the Tate Gallery.

Privately there were also concerns about the judging. The judges appointed were Alan Clutton-Brock (1904-1976), art critic of *The Times*; Jonkheer Sandberg (1897-1984), Director of the Stedelijk Museum; and A.J.L. McDonnell, purchaser for the Felton Bequest to the National Gallery of Victoria in Melbourne. The plan was to appoint a critic, a collector and someone from abroad. Kenneth Clark 'was very anxious we have Alan Clutton-Brock', James wrote to his friend the patron Colin Anderson, 'Our first choice for the collector … was Robert Sainsbury', who turned down the opportunity because it was paintings rather than sculpture.[13] The Art Panel had originally invited the Cubist painter and writer on art André Lhote (1885-1962) 'as the Council thought it

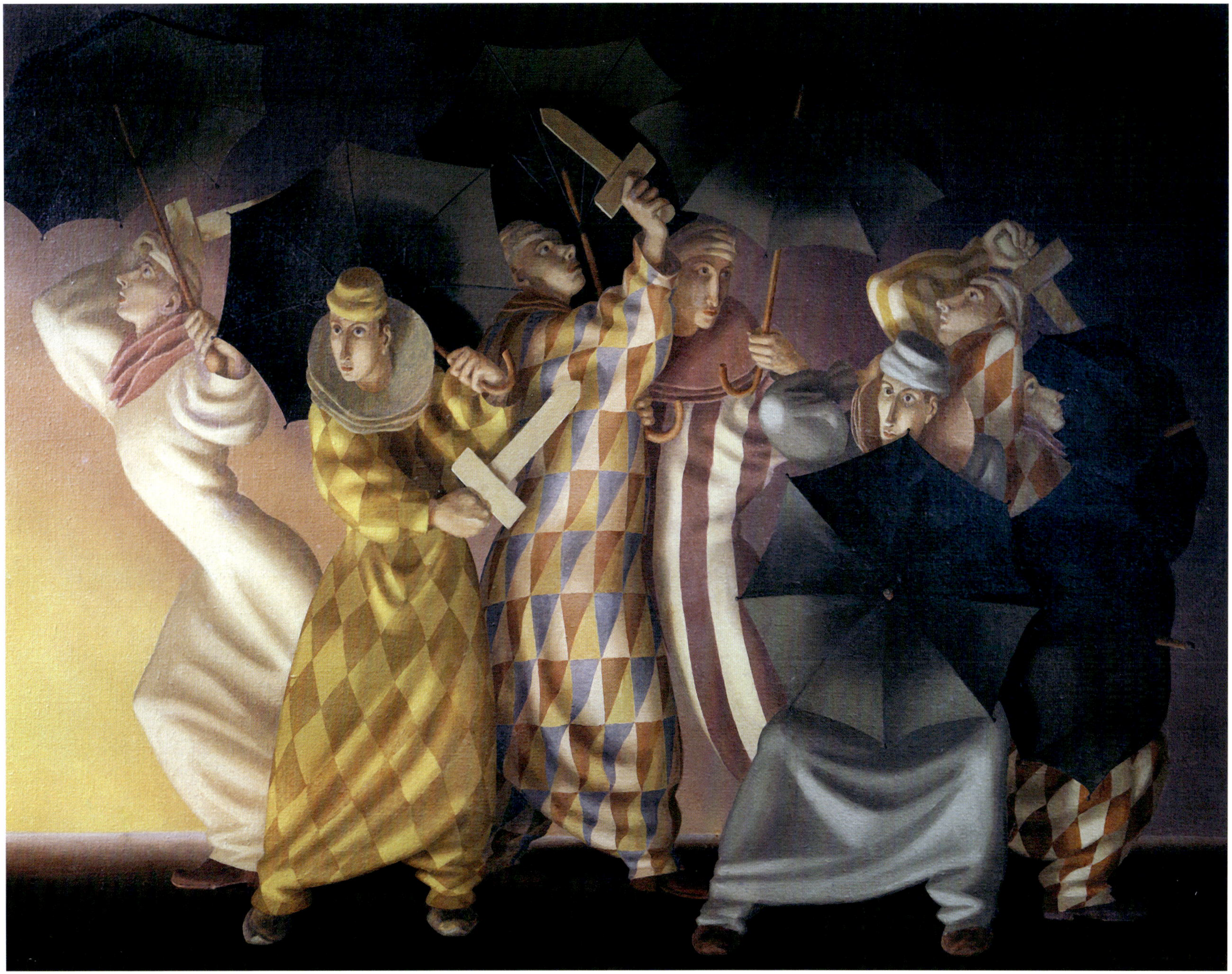

190 John Armstrong, *Storm,* 1951, oil and wax on canvas, 114.3 x 152.4 cm (45 x 60 in.)

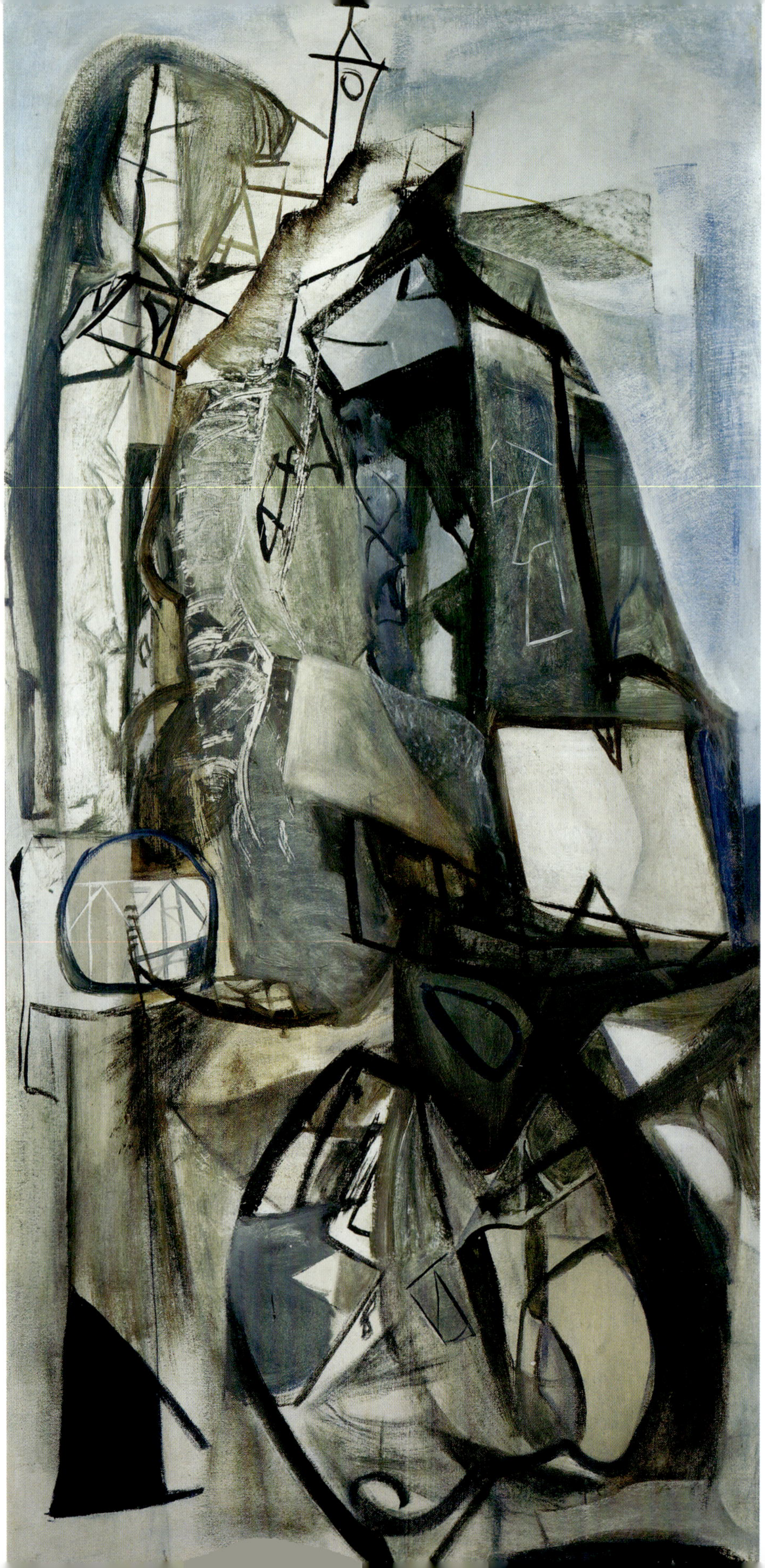

191
Peter Lanyon,
Porthleven, 1951
oil on board,
244.5 x 121.9 cm
(96 ¼ x 48 in.),
© Tate, London 2012

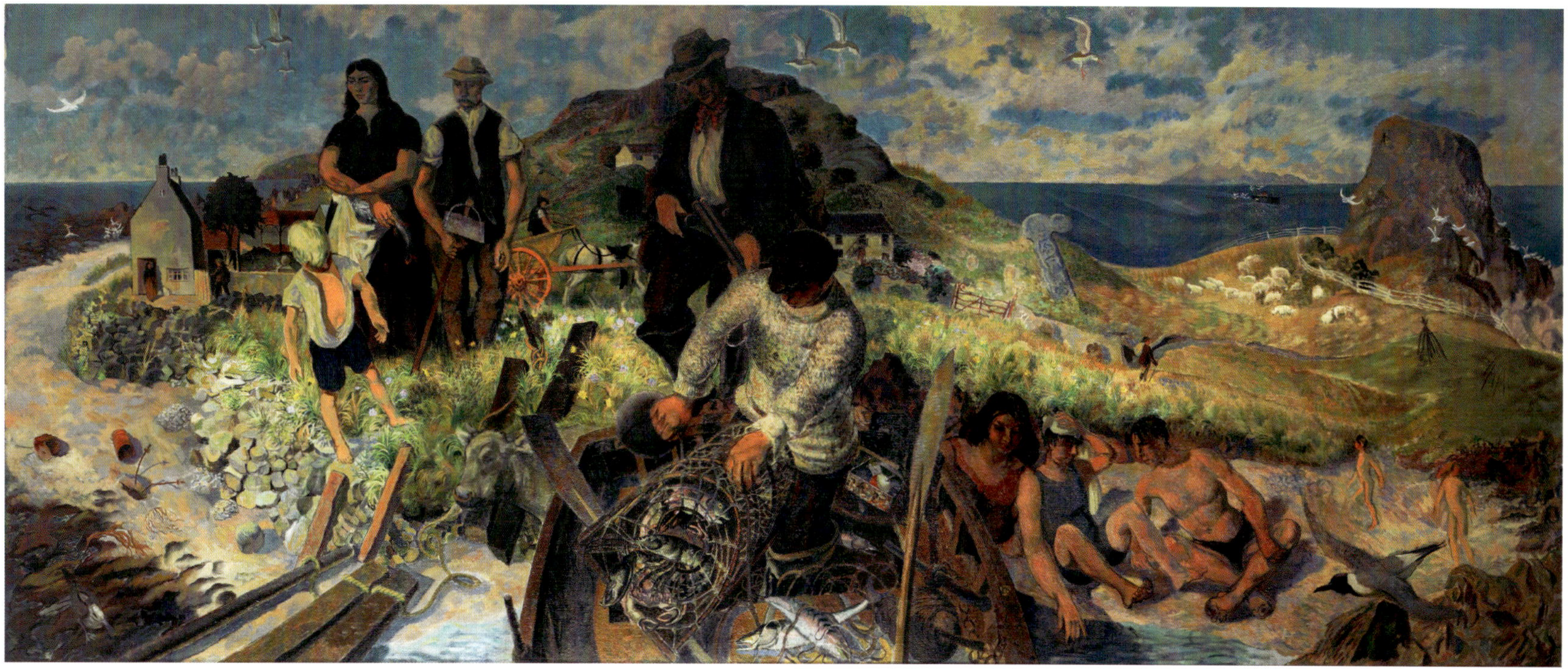

192 Gilbert Spencer, *Hebridean Memory* 1951, oil on canvas, 127 x 297 cm (50 x 117 in.) © Estate of Gilbert Spencer,

'desirable to have one distinguished foreigner on the panel';[14] McDonnell was his substitute. The judges' scoring sheet still remains, and it is clear they all disagreed quite profoundly as to the order of preference. They drew up a shortlist of eight finalists placed in order, but whereas Victor Pasmore was Clutton-Brock's favourite, he was Sandberg's least favourite, and so on. As winners Claude Rogers, Ivon Hitchens and Robert Medley do not feature on this scoring list, it must be assumed this was an exercise to decide the winners among the most advanced painters in the competition. This is strengthened by the separate listing of the names Pasmore and Gear, with a tick against the latter, as if it were a choice between the two of them for the position of winner in some abstract category. James's Assistant Director, Gabriel White, claimed in the 1980s that Jonkheer Sandberg thought only Gear's *Autumn Landscape* was any good, and all the other pictures were 'awful'.[15] However, the judges' marking sheet shows otherwise, with Sandberg placing Gear in sixth position, and William Scott his first choice.

There was internal controversy even before the judges reached their decision. Kenneth Clark, as an Art Panel member, had objected on April 10 – a week before the judges met – that the winners were not to be decided by the Panel.

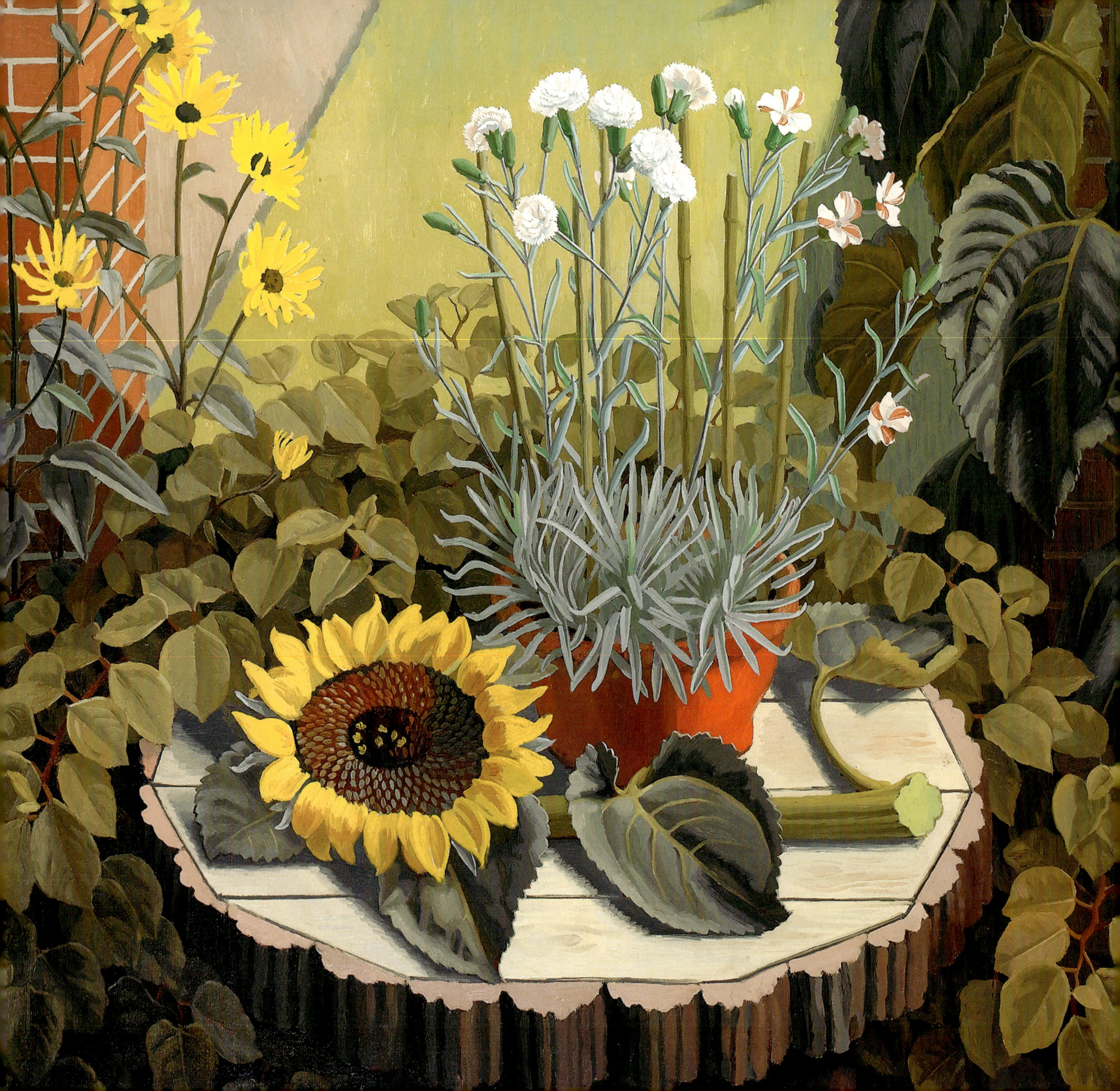

Ben Nicholson complained quite explicitly in a letter to James about the ability and outlook of the judges. His understanding of the competition:

> led me to trust the AC to make a responsible & progressive decision as to the judges to be appointed – & I feel that I was led up the garden path. Certainly had Clutton Brock's name originally appeared as one of even 5 judges I would have tapped my head to see if I was (still) sane! And since foreign judges were being selected why no one from say the heads of museums in Paris? (& why in heaven's name an Australian!) It seems to an outsider like myself a most haphazard selection & the kind of safety-first policy which one would expect from a Government Dept. & not from an enlightened Arts Council. Of course there are many points of view on painting but in the circles in which I move in London & here [Cornwall], I have yet to meet a single person who does not feel as I do about the selections.

Nicholson perhaps rightly drew comparison with the different way the sculptors included in the exhibition – Robert Adams, Reg Butler, Lynn Chadwick, Karin Jonzen, F.E. McWilliam, Bernard Meadows and Eduardo Paolozzi – were paid directly for making their work, while the painters only had their work offered for sale. His conclusion was that: '"advanced" painting has been discouraged while "advanced" sculpture has been encouraged, with no direct commissions to the painters followed by the appointment of this astonishing committee of three.'[16] In the Arts Council's file James's reply has had the first two thirds physically cut away, one must suppose because he entered into discussion of the judges' merits himself. He concluded: 'I don't think you would say as a result of these activities of ours "advanced painting" had been discouraged, if you had seen my post-bag during the past fortnight. We have never before received so much abuse for supporting advanced art.'[17] Other reactions to the exhibition or its judging may have been forthright. Access to the Arts Council file is restricted until 2033, and inserts indicate that several artists' letters have been removed to maintain privacy under the Freedom of Information Act.

The story of the exhibition and the responses to it mark an interesting battle for the acceptance of advanced art in Britain. Ultimately its success must be measured by the extraordinary achievement of bringing together such a large number of artists with works of such a grand scale, and it can also be assessed by the intense interest and vigorous discussion it stimulated. In the first month of its run alone the show was seen by a staggering 30,889 people at Manchester City Art Gallery.

ENDNOTES

1 Manchester, London, Leicester, Liverpool, Bristol, Norwich, Plymouth, Leeds, Newcastle, Brighton, York and Preston.

2 'Large Pictures', *The Times*, June 22, 1951, p.7.

3 John Russell, 'Big Pictures', *The Times*, June 24, 1951, p.8.

4 'Festival Paintings: Large Canvases on View', *The Times*, June 22, 1951, p.3.

5 A.D.B. Sylvester, *The Burlington Magazine*, October 1951.

6 *Daily Telegraph*, April 14, 1951.

7 Hansard, May 3, 1951, vol.487, c164W.

193
Charles Mahoney,
The Garden, 1950,
(detail)

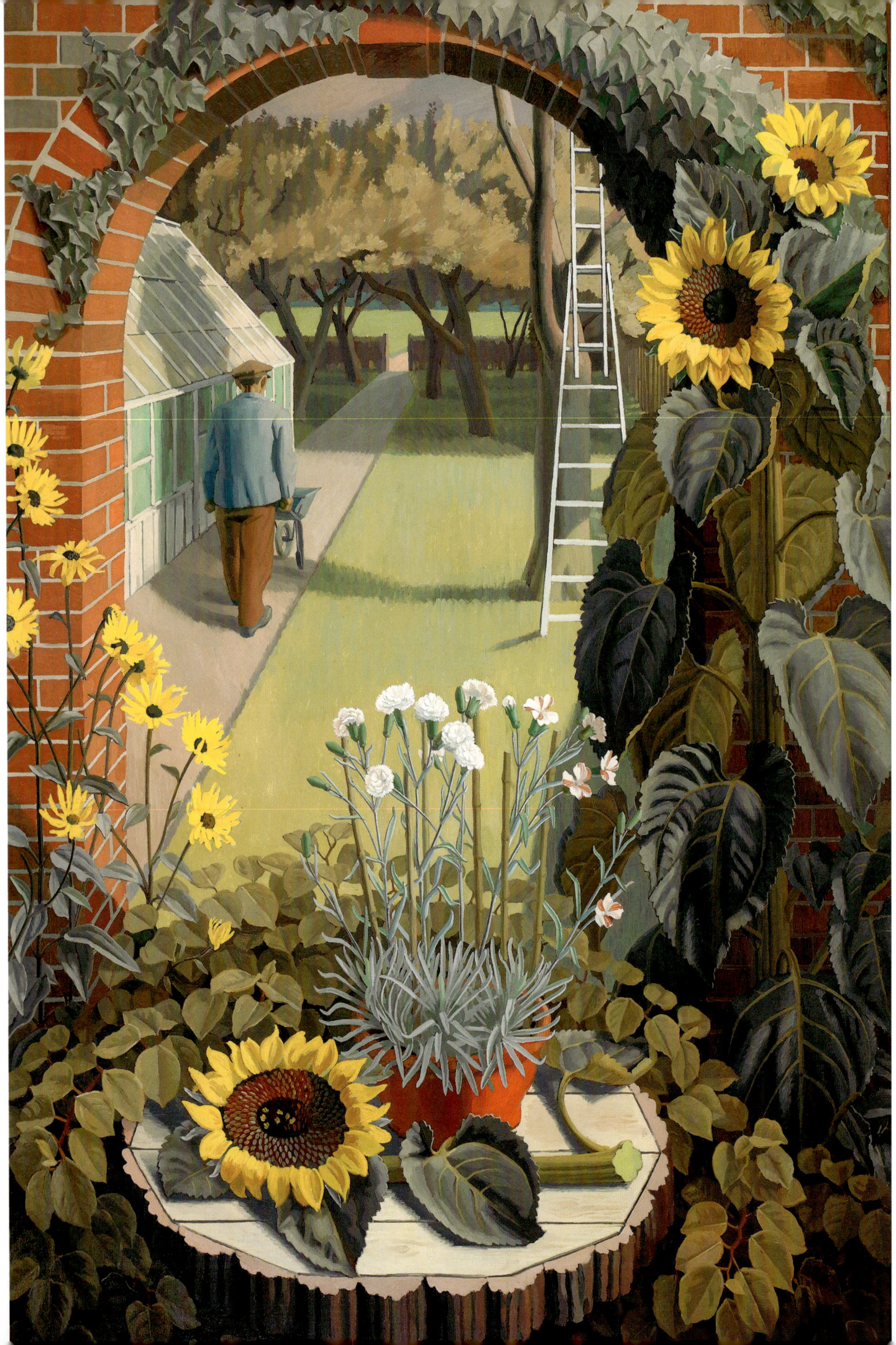

194
Charles Mahoney,
The Garden, 1950
oil on canvas,
182.9 x 121.9 cm (72 x 48 in.)

8 Letter from Philip James to William Gear, April 26, 1951; ACGB/121/953.

9 Letter from William Gear to Philip James, April 28, 1951; ACGB/121/953.

10 Ben Nicholson, 'Defending Modern Artists', *The Daily Mail*, August 7, 1951.

11 Letter from Winifred Nicholson to Philip James, February 22, 1951; ACGB/121/953.

12 Letter from Vanessa Bell to Philip James, May 13, 1951; ACGB/121/953.

13 Letter from Philip James to Colin Anderson, March 17, 1951; ACGB/121/953.

14 Letter from Philip James to A.J.L. McDonnell, March 20, 1951; ACGB/121/1953.

15 *25 from 51: 25 Paintings from the Festival of Britain*, 1951, exhibition catalogue, Mappin Art Gallery, Sheffield, 1978, p.7.

16 Letter from Ben Nicholson to Philip James, May 2, 1951; ACGB/121/953.

17 Undated letter [May 1951] from Philip James to Ben Nicholson; ACGB/121/953.

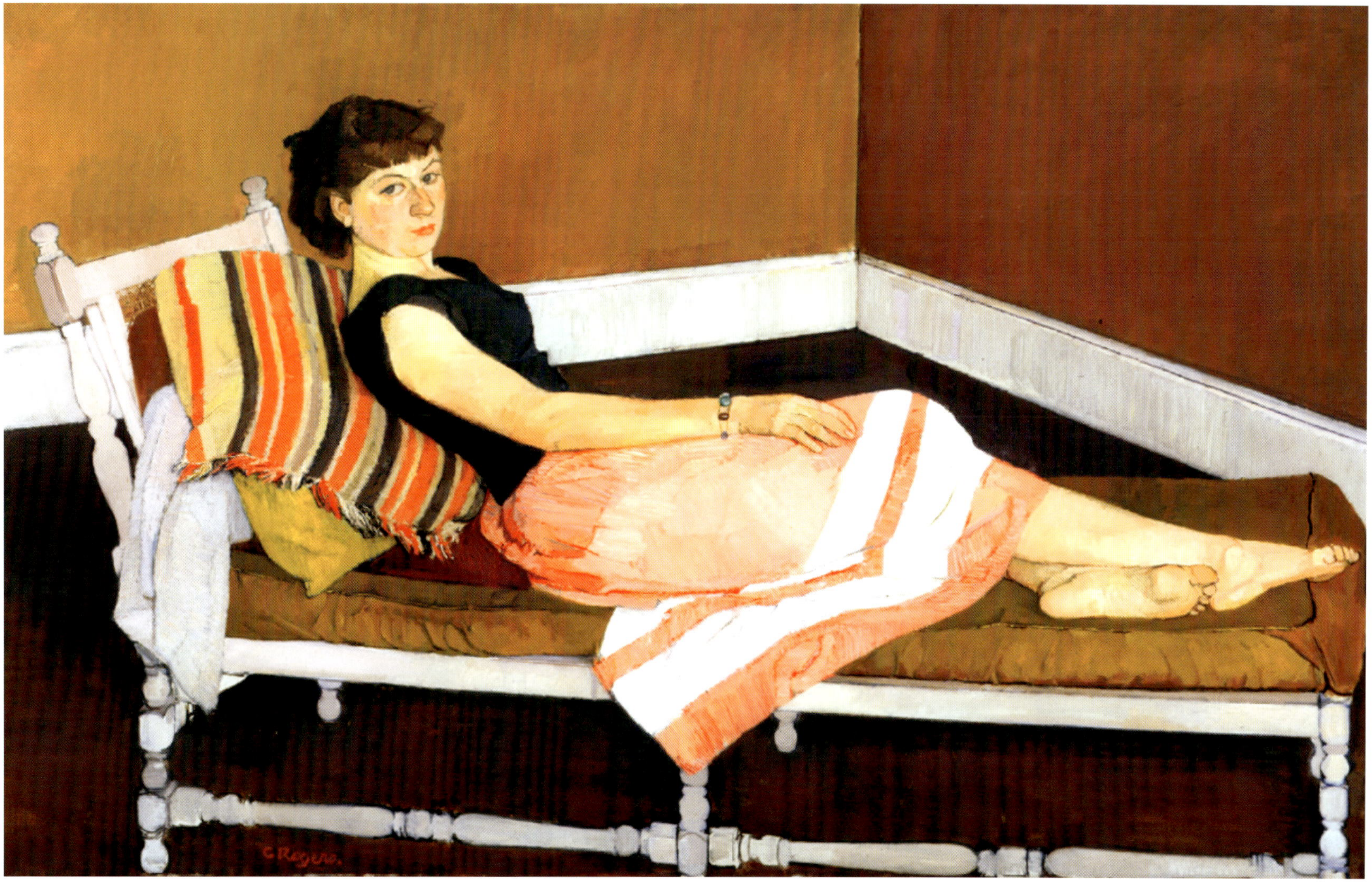

195 Claude Rogers, *Miss Lynn*, 1951, oil on canvas, 108 x 177.3 cm (42 ½ x 69 ¾ in.), © Crispin Rogers, collection: Southampton City Art Gallery

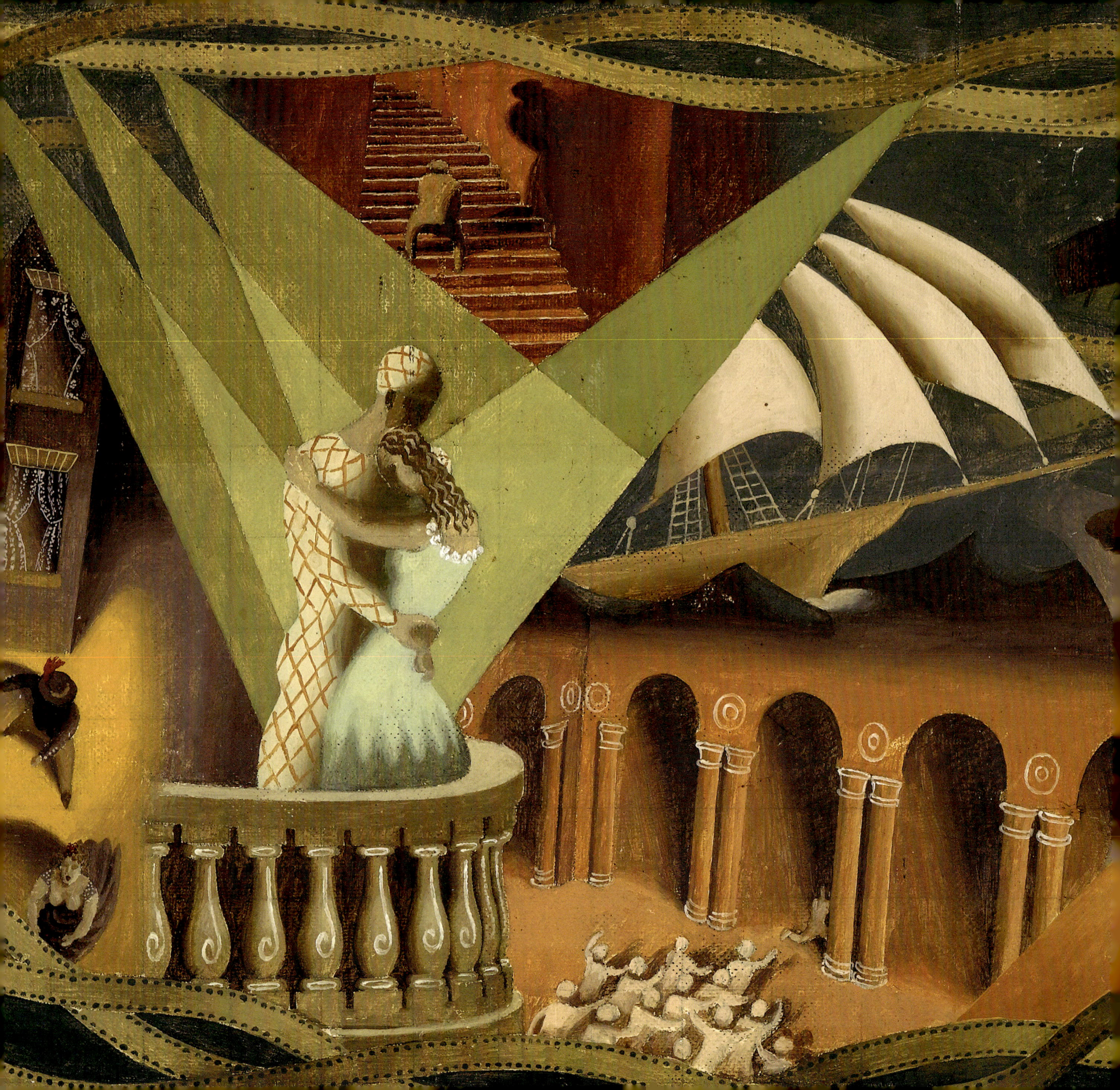

The Murals of John Armstrong

Andrew Lambirth

Wall painting was fundamental to John Armstrong's approach to art. His early paintings resemble *trompe l'oeil* frescoes, he executed a number of mural decorations for private houses and hotels, his work as a poster designer for Shell approached the mural in the scale of these billboard or lorry-board advertisements, and he executed a whole series of easel paintings inspired by Graeco-Roman wall decorations and ancient rock and cave paintings. He always said that his favourite decorative scheme was the series of panels he painted for Shell-Mex House in 1933, but there are better-known mural projects also to his credit. In 1951 he designed a mural for the Telecinema on the South Bank as part of the Festival of Britain celebrations, and in 1954-5 he painted the ceiling of the Bristol Council Chamber. And there were other schemes, imaginative and ambitious, of which only fragments remain today.

Right from the beginning of his career Armstrong worked as a mural painter, though nearly all his commissions for interior decor have long since vanished, recorded only in tantalizing black-and-white photographs. Considerable experience as a theatre designer made him a versatile manipulator of figures in space, and in the late 1920s he gained something of a name for himself as a painter of light-hearted and sophisticated Art Deco murals. For instance, when the fabric manufacturer Samuel Courtauld bought Home House in Portman Square, he commissioned Armstrong to paint murals for his wife's studio and bathroom. For the studio Armstrong produced a *trompe l'oeil* figure descending a staircase, while for the bathroom walls and ceilings he designed a tableau of jugglers and dancers. Armstrong's imagery at this period frequently featured circus performers and acrobats: muscular and slightly schematized bodies in extreme poses.

The Home House commission led to others, such as mural decorations for Sir Geoffrey Fry's flat in Portman Court, and later for the Labour MP, Russell Strauss, a dining-room mural and a frieze of dancers in the ballroom of his Kensington Palace Gardens home. Interior design proved a fruitful source of income for Armstrong in an uncertain period, and he was obligingly versatile in accepting work. This adaptable attitude led to a lengthy period of work as a designer for films (mostly working with Charles Laughton and Alexander Korda) which might have sidetracked him entirely from his primary calling as a painter. He also painted room-dividers for Charles Laughton's London flat and murals for Tom Laughton's hotels in Scarborough. None of these schemes is still extant, though photographs and preliminary drawings give some idea of their high quality. The initial design for the American bar in the Royal Hotel, Scarborough for instance, dating to 1935-6, is a lively white line on blue gouache study of sailors and girls dancing. Although there is something of the flavour of Christopher Wood and Edward Burra about it, this intricate linear decoration has a formidable crispness and structure to it, a pictorial logic, which is Armstrong's own.

196
Design for Telecinema Mural, South Bank, 1951 (detail)

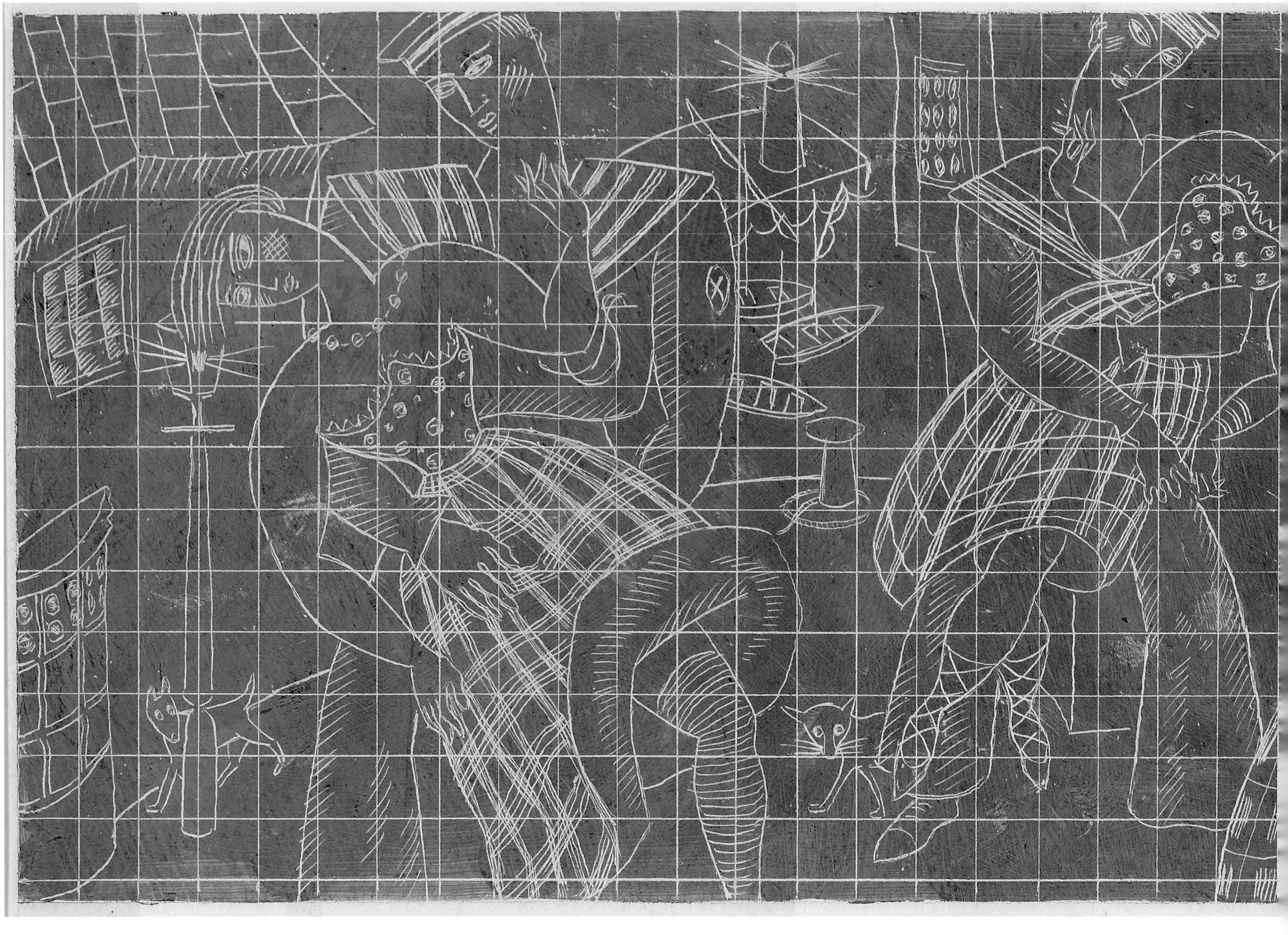

197 *Sailors and Girls*, design for the American bar in the Royal Hotel, Scarborough, 1935-6, signed with initials JA lower right, gouache on board, 18.5 x 54.6 cm (7 ¼ x 21 ½ in.)

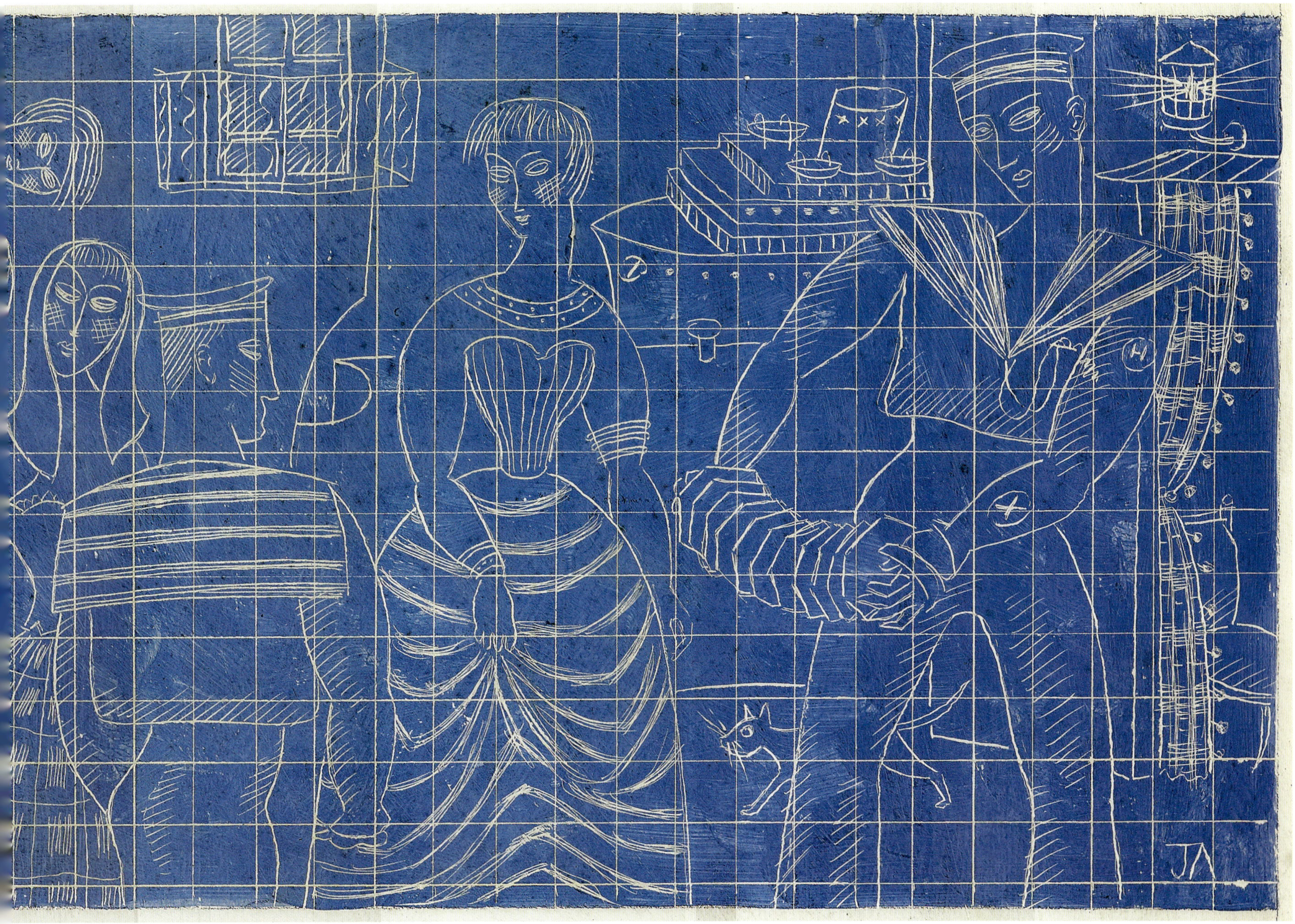
JA

Armstrong was widely praised for his wit and originality, and as early as 1929, the prominent critic R H Wilenski was drawing attention to Armstrong's 'architectural attitude of mind' and strong decorative impulse. These attributes led him in the early 1930s to experiment with abstraction, and to join the group of artists led by Paul Nash in the venture known as Unit One. This was an exhibition and a book rather than a movement, but part of Armstrong's statement in the Unit One book (1934) is worth quoting. Summarizing his own career and approach, and in particular his new-found abstraction, he had much to say about the relationship of art to architecture. He wrote:

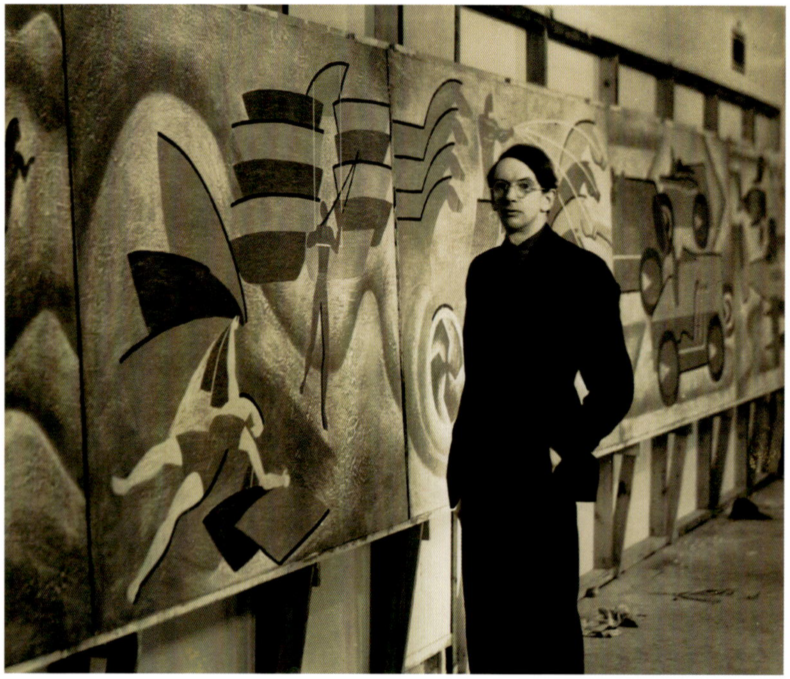

198
John Armstrong standing beside the Shell-Mex panels, 1933

> To some painters, certainly, it has been possible to absorb the structure of natural objects and create an independent edifice which can be looked at without regard to its surroundings, but to the painter engaged in the study of abstract form, position and relation to environment are all important.
>
> Architecture, on which these necessities depend, has never been so favourably placed to lead the artist as it is now. Having no longer any urge to blossom into bubbles or spires to cover the hot air of vain hopes, it is in its turn dictated to by practical human necessities, and the more it submits to them and the more closely it works with that force of scientific discovery which serves the same ends, the more it will tend towards the truth and the better guide it will be to those it leads.
>
> As a painter my ideal opportunity is wall-space and plenty of it. That is not easy to come by; architecture in this country has been slow in getting going, but it has begun. In the meantime it has only been by observing its tendencies of line and structure, and by sympathy with them, that I have been able to express myself. It was largely to develop the understanding of that sympathy, common to the members of the group, in the public at large, that Unit One was formed.

How close in fact was the relationship between Armstrong's work and architecture? The abstractions of the Unit One period rely heavily for their imagery on walls and architectural form, and this is a preoccupation which extended into his later work, whether figurative or abstract. Certainly a number of his 1930s paintings depict buildings with walls in various states of ruination and decay, frequently half-covered with peeling wallpaper or posters. *Invocation* (1938), for instance, depicts a substantial fragment of wall with the remains of an Egyptian-style fresco cracking off it. In the strange and haunting *Leda* (1952), girl seeks the solace of swan in a fraying poster peeling from a suburban brick wall, while the loosening poster image reaches its apogee in *The City* of the same year.

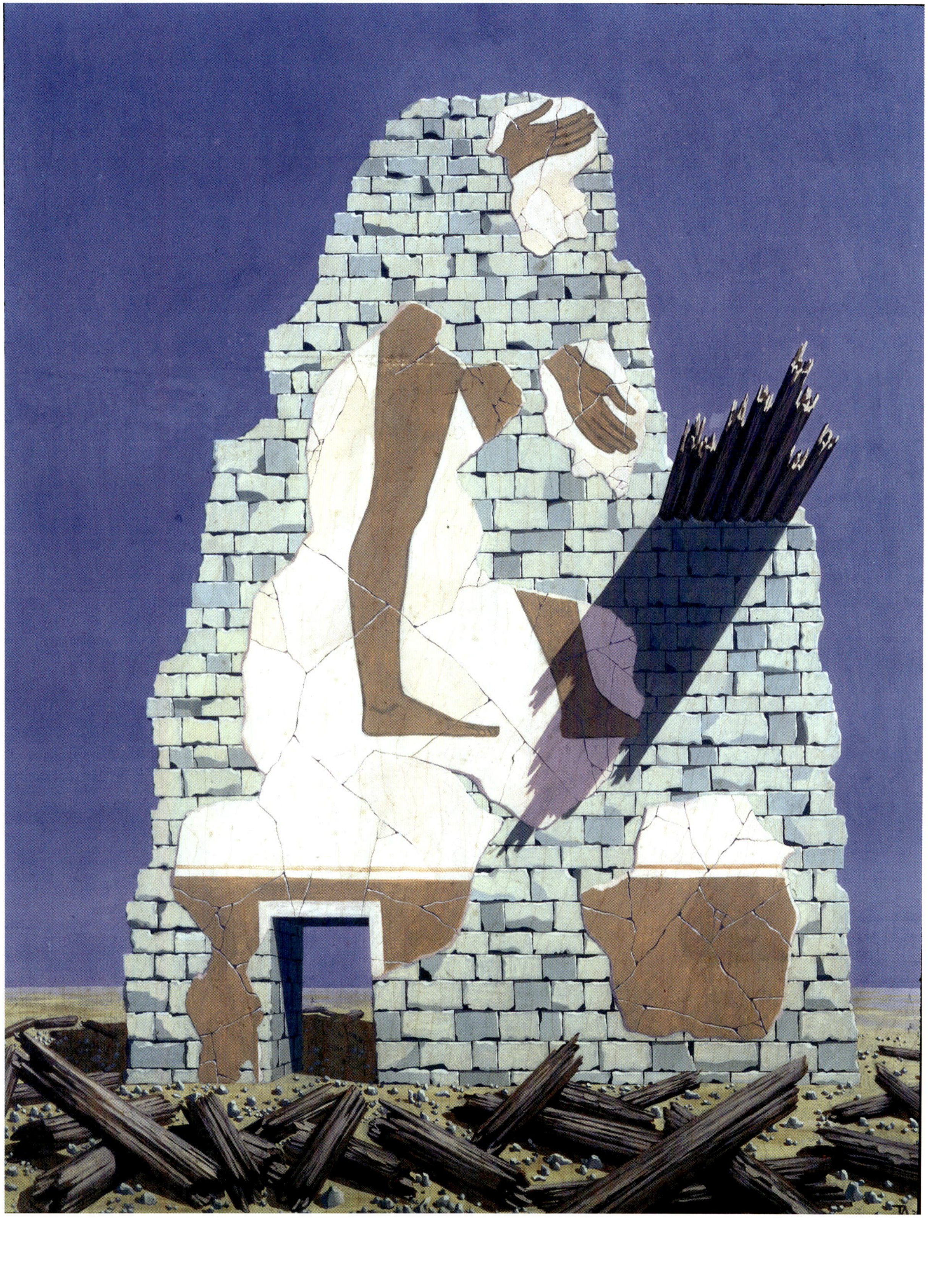

199
Invocation, 1938,
tempera on plywood,
71.1 x 54.6 cm (28 x 21 ½ in.)
National Gallery of Victoria,
Melbourne

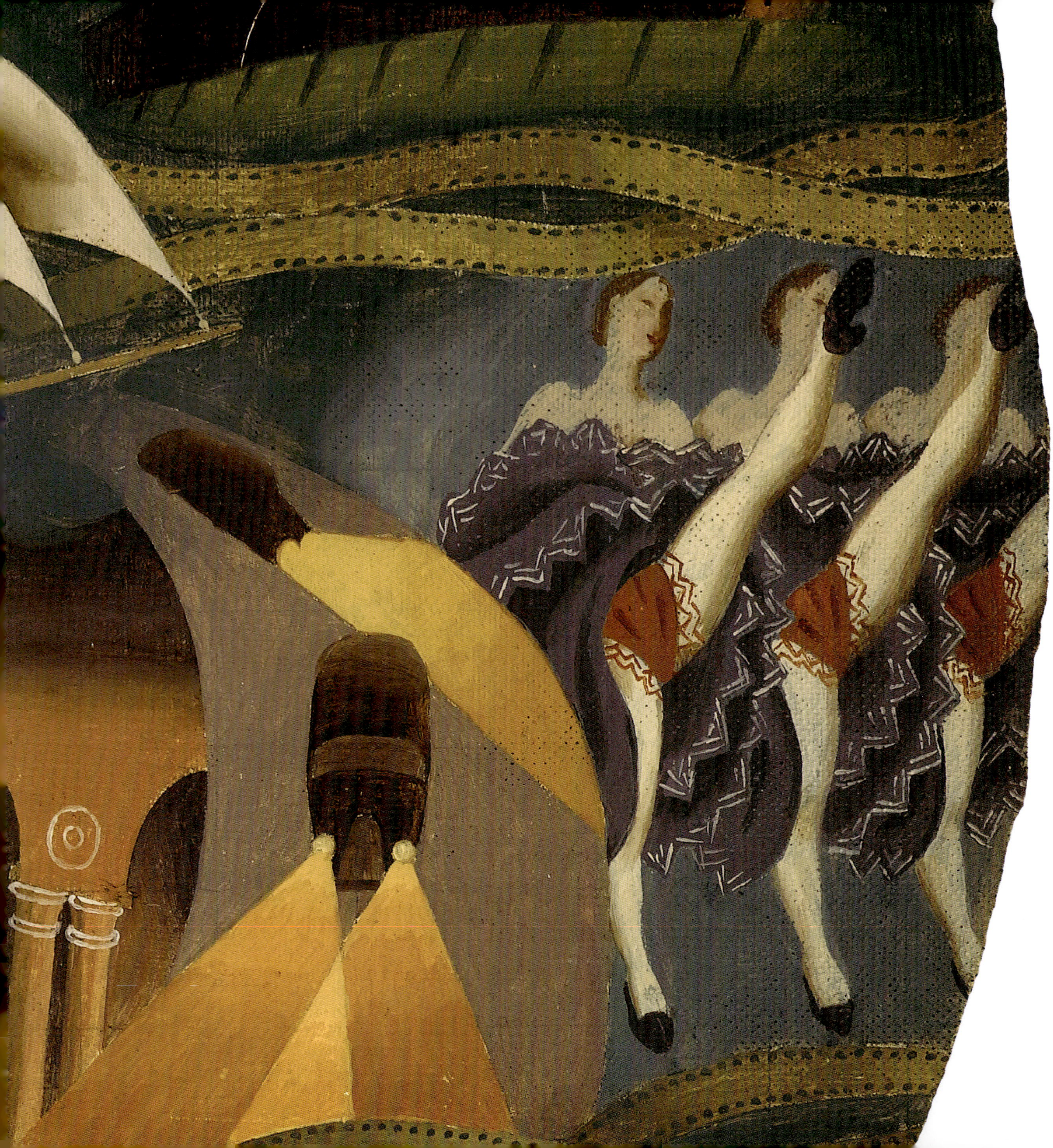

Armstrong's artistic versatility in the 1930s as a strategy for survival led to various engagements, chief amongst which were advertising and poster design. One of his most important patrons was Jack Beddington, publicity manager of Shell-Mex, for whom Armstrong designed five posters between 1932 and 1952. In addition, in 1933 Beddington commissioned Armstrong to design and paint an eight-panel mural for the staff dining-room at Shell-Mex House. The theme was 'Before and after Petrol', and featured various modes of transport through the ages, from Icarus and Daedalus with their home-made wings, to the rowed boat, the automobile, the aeroplane and the ocean liner. The drawing of these designs is highly simplified and formalized, in what might be called a curvy machine-made style. Painting on gesso on plywood, Armstrong restricted his palette to greys, whites and reds.

Hans Feibusch in his idiosyncratic monograph *Mural Painting* (1946), singled out Armstrong's Shell-Mex murals for praise: principally for their economy of means and their 'strong imaginative and dynamic quality'. Feibusch, writing just after the war, identified an impetus towards simplicity in contemporary wall decoration which these particular designs by Armstrong certainly exemplify. The rowing figures, for example, are schematized into curves (head, neck, back) and angular blades (muscular arms at work), in a manner reminiscent of the Grosvenor School of linocuts. This was not, however, to be a style that Armstrong was to pursue in later mural work, being more in the nature of a one-off experiment, although he professed himself very satisfied with the result.

It's clear that images on walls were of deep import to Armstrong. When he moved out of London to Essex at the beginning of World War II, he didn't feel settled in his new home at Tilty until he had painted murals in the hallway; the naturalness of this act reflects his priorities. In the late 1930s he was also painting a number of tempera panels of classical scenes, inspired by Greek or Roman frescoes, many of them depicting animals in heraldic profile: deer and horses a speciality. These rhythmic and decorative compositions look like fragments from worn and abraded murals, evidence of Armstrong's enjoyment of the 'painting within a painting' conceit. It seems he painted them as much from archaeological interest as from sheer pleasure; there is no hidden meaning or symbolic significance here, beyond the stylized decorative potential of interlocking gazelles or prancing stallions, and the knowledge of being part of a great tradition that stretched back to the prehistoric cave painters.

At the end of the war, Armstrong moved down to Cornwall, to Lamorna, while retaining his working contacts in London. Various design projects helped to keep him solvent and then in 1951 came a commission for a mural for the Festival of Britain, that much-trumpeted 'tonic to the nation'. Armstrong was asked to compose a mural for the foyer of the Telecinema, one of the buildings devoted to the moving image in the Television piazza on the South Bank. With his extensive experience as a designer for film, Armstrong was the obvious choice. The Telecinema became the first National Film Theatre but was later demolished when the lease on the site expired. Armstrong's mural disappeared, presumably destroyed.

200
Design for Telecinema mural, South Bank, 1951 (detail)

How do the designs for the Telecinema fit into the stylistic pattern of Armstrong's murals? In many respects, they are a logical development of the earlier interior decoration work, with an added focus on content. At last here was a subject which demanded a specific theme which was not simply decorative. Armstrong painted two alternative designs, one of which was chosen to be squared up and painted full-size. The successful cartoon is an unevenly shaped image, like a vignette, as if torn or roughly cut from a larger sheet. It brings together all the favourite clichés of the cinema: from spot-lit lovers on a balcony at its centre, to dancing girls, a car chase, a man in wait on shadowy stairs, a thundering train, a man pursued through a colonnaded square by a crowd, a woman pursued by a man, a pirate ship in full sail, a cowboy and his destriers. The composition is fractured, centrally by pale yellow-green triangles of light, less obtrusively elsewhere as the various scenes abut and overlap. At top and bottom, silver ribbons of film (straight from the Silver Screen) slinkily interweave. Most of these images are about rapid movement and pursuit: essentially about drama. The calmest snapshot is the 'still' of lovers embracing centre stage. Romance and mystery – Armstrong has packed his composition with action. All the main themes of popular movies are here.

Of course he would have been all too aware that he was making a static image of a moving medium, but his jump-cutting and juxtaposition give a very effective impression of movement, with the eye shifting about the surface of his design without finding rest. (The ribbons of film do, however, provide a degree of continuity.) Armstrong has managed to convey the sense of restless excitement the average filmgoer feels (or perhaps felt, in the days before image-overload) at the thought of viewing a new release. Yet at the same time he has made a cunningly unified image which suggests different lines of narrative which the prospective filmgoer might enjoy.

The first version, which is the smaller of the two, and was rejected as perhaps too surreal, is less worked up and complete in conception. It's as if Armstrong abandoned it before resolving it – perhaps he was advised to? – or else he himself decided to rework it in a slightly more cheerful spirit. Although fundamentally the same as the second, the first version is less tightly constructed and less emphatic in its meanings. Reading from the left: the two horses emerging from behind the stage flats are rider-less, which makes them look like stampeding beasts rather than essential servants of man in the historical sagas so much a part of movie narrative. The searchlights and lovers are much the same, though the figures are less thoroughly and convincingly realized.

The other elements (ship, train, car chase, crowd scene) appear in both versions largely unchanged, with one exception. The can-can girls, who provide a brilliant dynamic movement out of the scene to the right in the second version, and thus extend the vignette into our space, do not appear in the first version at all. Their place is taken by a troupe of nine disembodied heads, flowing round in an arc between the car chase and the colonnades. They look like a melancholy conclave of the masks of tragedy (and are thus reminiscent of Armstrong's painting *Two Heads*, c. 1928, in the Courtauld), and it's not surprising that he decided to do away with them altogether. The dancers are a much better solution. And finally, the framing strips of film look very different in the first version: without their ratchet holes they are mere fluvial decoration, not immediately to be recognized as film at all.

In these various ways it can be seen that Armstrong tightened up his design for the Telecinema and produced a vibrant piece of work which was well-received. According to Armstrong's widow Annette, Wells Coates, architect of the Telecinema building, was full of praise for the mural which he thought most brilliantly adapted for its role and context. The two men were old friends and colleagues: they had both been signatories to Unit One, and Wells Coates had undertaken the conversion of Russell Strauss' home at 1 Kensington Palace Gardens, where Armstrong had painted some of his earliest murals. Their fellowship of thought enabled them to work together very effectively.

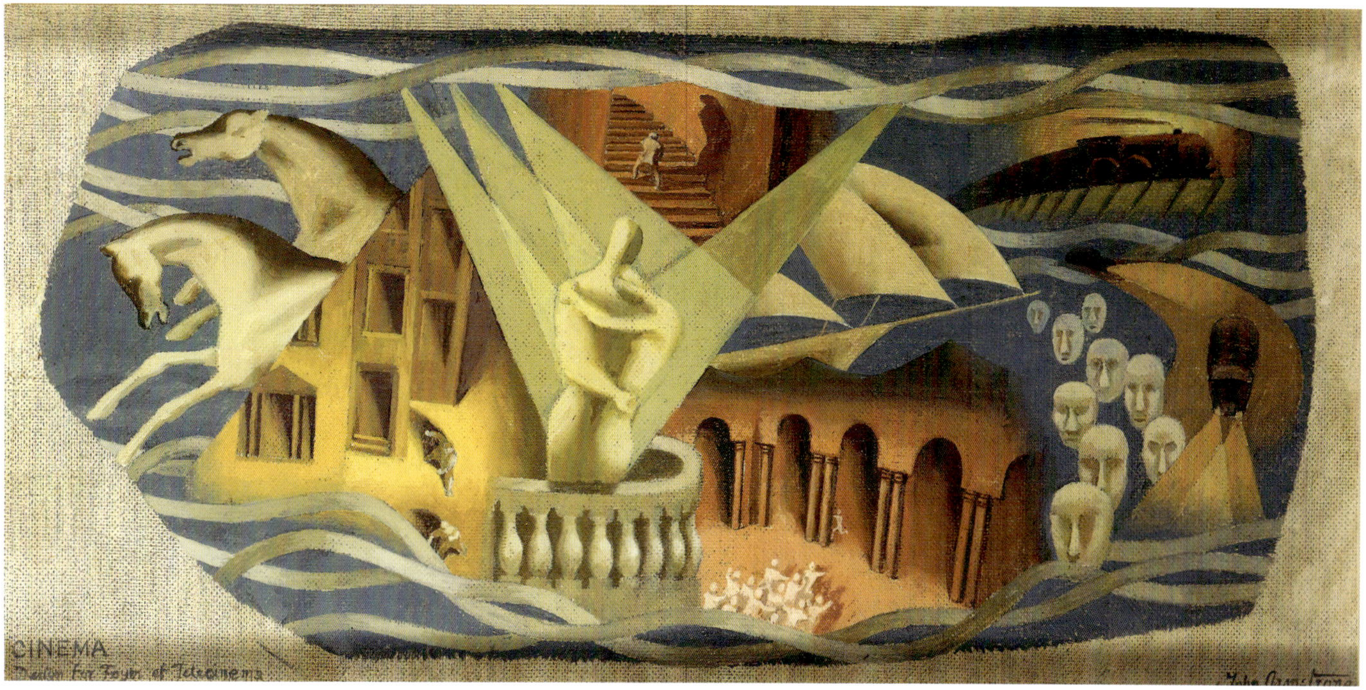

201 Design for Telecinema Mural, South Bank, 1951, inscribed on reverse: Design for Foyer of Telecinema, oil on board, 34.3 x 70 cm (13 ½ x 27 ½ in.)

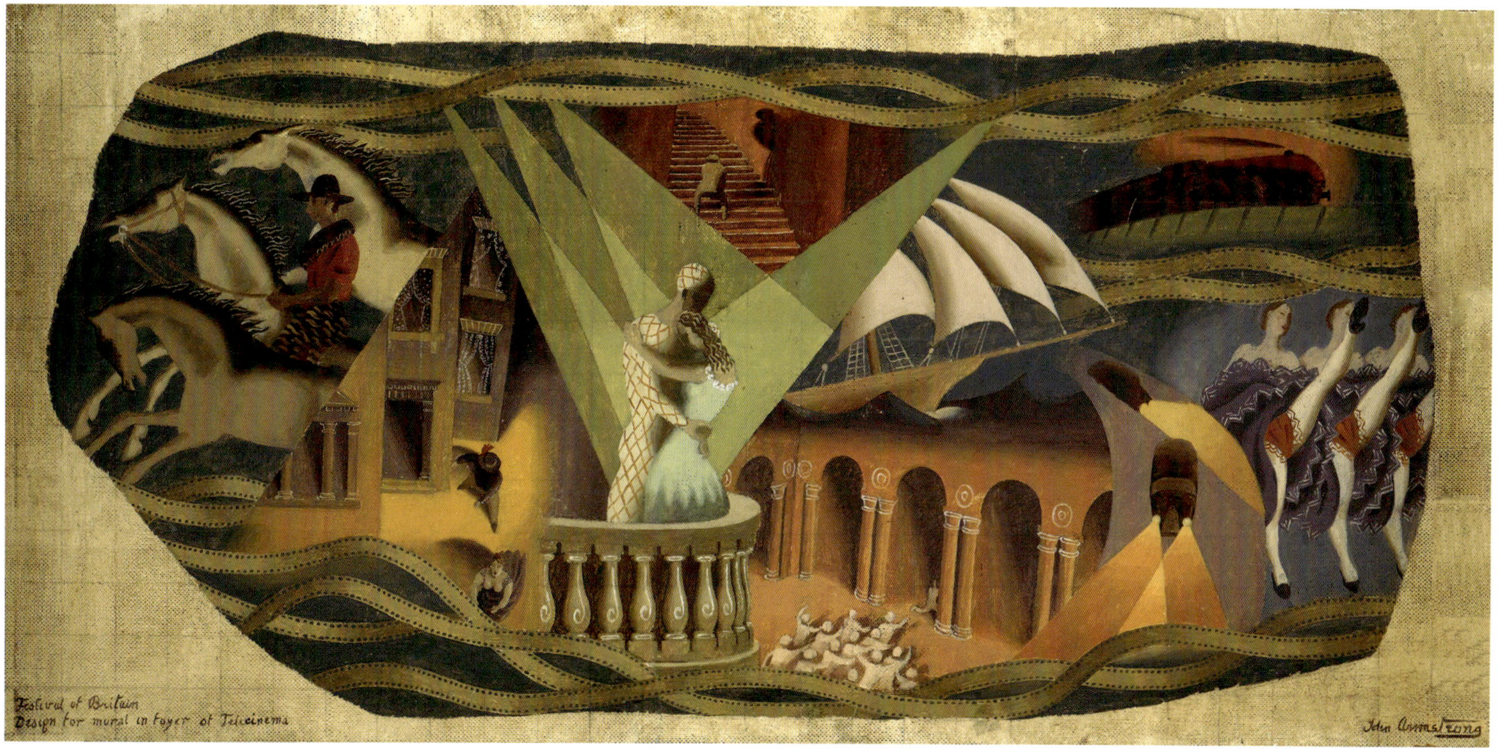

202 Design for Telecinema Mural, South Bank, 1951, oil on board, 40.5 x 76.2 cm (16 x 30 in.)

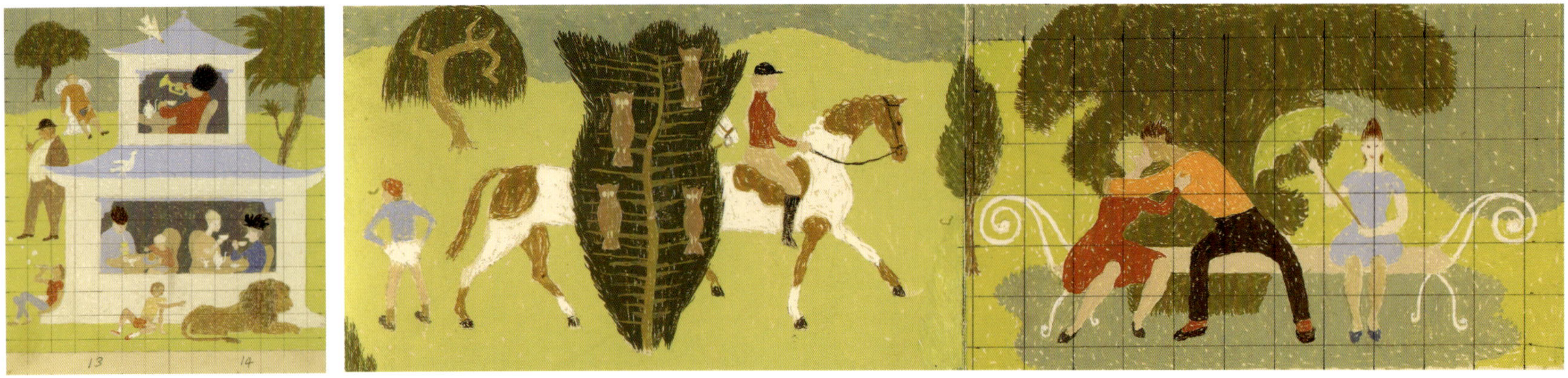

203 Studies for Royal Marsden Hospital in Sutton, Surrey, 1961, gouache on paper, 21 x 17.8 cm (8 ¼ x 7 in.) and 11.7 x 31.3 cm (4 ⅝ x 12 ⅜ in.)

Two years later, in 1953, Armstrong was commissioned by the Edwin Austin Abbey Memorial Trust to paint a decorative scheme for the ceiling of Bristol Council Chamber, at the same time as Thomas Monnington was commissioned to decorate the ceiling of the adjoining Conference Room. (see pages 55-57) At some thirty by sixty feet, this was a vast undertaking, and for the first time in his life Armstrong employed an assistant, a young art student called Mary Collett. The wonderfully elegant composition of boats and buildings that resulted was painted on sections of canvas in the Newlyn Gallery in Cornwall, because Armstrong couldn't face the physical strain of working directly onto the ceiling *in situ*. He produced a design in predominantly blue, white, terracottas and ochres, of a sailing fleet surrounded by historical buildings (both real and imaginary) and bonded warehouses, with classical allegorical figures at each corner: Industry, Navigation, Wisdom and Enterprise. The image has a natural sense of dignity fitting for a Council Chamber, whilst also employing enough movement and asymmetry to prevent it from being too formal.

In 1961, Armstrong received his last mural commission, once again from the Edwin Austin Abbey Memorial Trust Fund, to decorate a reception area in the Royal Marsden Hospital in Sutton, Surrey. The whole scheme took him two years to paint on canvas panels, squared up from small oil-on-card designs. The mural was subsequently destroyed, but the designs remain to demonstrate the humour and vitality, the inventiveness and visual wit, that Armstrong brought to their conception. Entitled *The Fantastic Park*, the subject resembles one of the mythical settings from P. L. Travers' Mary Poppins books, where normal rules don't obtain, and anything can happen (and probably will). The bright colours (sap green, scarlet, mauve) add to the air of celebration and unreality, and Armstrong subverts the usual park activities, with children riding on the lake on real swans, regaled by a trombonist in a busby, up to his thighs in water.

Armstrong wrote a detailed commentary on the composition: 'Bandsmen and children everywhere, that is the keynote of the Park. The bandstand is too small, it will hold only the conductor and the big drum. The rest of the band sit here and there wherever they feel disposed, with a kind of stereophonic effect.' Besides the P. L . Travers reference, there's a Dylan Thomas-ish *Under Milk Wood* feeling to the events. A little girl brings goldfish for her grandfather to catch. 'He has been fishing all morning,' wrote Armstrong, 'and has had no luck. Her aunts are also bringing the stuffed fish off the chimney-piece.' Frivolity meets anarchy in mutual admiration: there's a Stanley Spencer-ish note to the festivities, a breath of unexpected love among the participants.

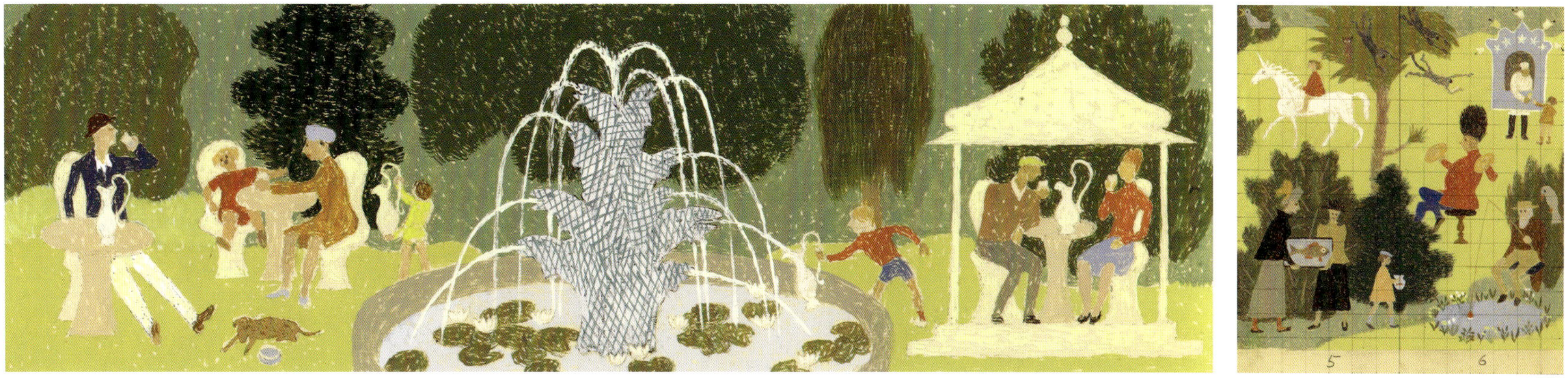

204 Studies for Royal Marsden Hospital in Sutton, Surrey, 1961, gouache on paper, 11.7 x 30.5 cm (4 ⅝ x 12 in.) and 21 x 17.8 cm (8 ¼ x 7 in.)

Armstrong's text concludes: 'On the left a bandsman gives up and wipes his forehead. He has got a pint from somewhere.... The lake mermaid has come out to have a better view and has found a boy-friend. On a seat the poet and his muse meditate.'

There is much to delight the eye and gladden the heart in these nine images of carousel in a modern sylvan setting – a sort of Watteau for the twentieth-century English suburbs. Friend Monkey leaps from a tree and a unicorn trots by. This is a very different world from the Art Deco designs of his first murals, or the chic-ly stylized clichés of his Telecinema image. The gentler, more playful imagery of *The Fantastic Park* doubtless owes something to the presence of a child in Armstrong's life, his daughter Catherine, born in 1959. This new serenity of mood seems to unite the apparently contrary impulses towards classic stylization and romantic particularity which run through Armstrong's career. His wall paintings remain at the centre of a diverse achievement, and form a bench-mark by which to judge and interpret his other activities. Not often was he given 'wall-space and plenty of it' but when he was, he took full advantage of the opportunity and created memorable designs of lasting interest.

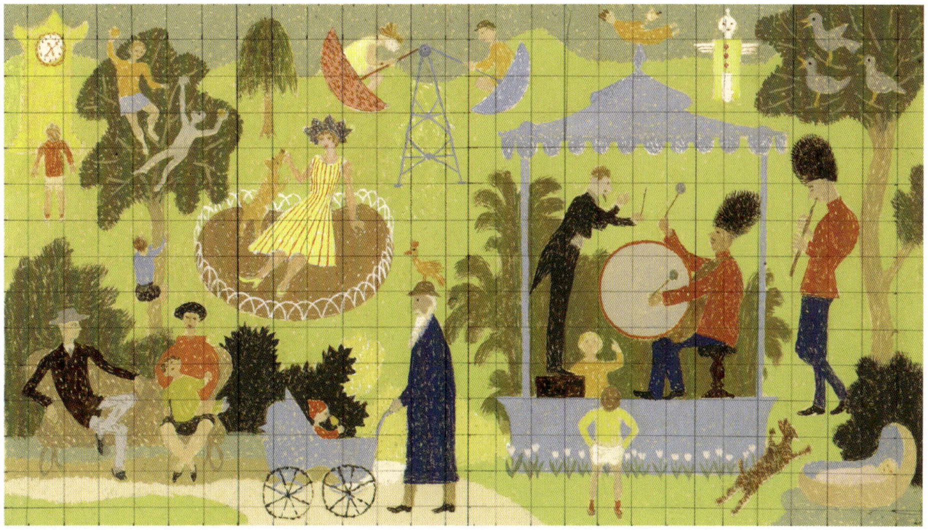

205
Study for Royal Marsden Hospital in Sutton, Surrey, 1961,
gouache on paper,
21 x 34.5 cm (8 ¼ x 13 ½ in.)

MURALS BY JOHN ARMSTRONG

1920s – Interior of Home House, Portman Square, London, for Samuel Courtauld. Destroyed

1920s – Interior of flat in Portman Court, London, for Sir Geoffrey Fry. Destroyed

1920s – Interior of house in Kensington Palace Gardens for Russell Strauss. Destroyed

1933 – Murals for Shell-Mex House, London. Now in BP Archive at the National Motor Museum, Beaulieu

1930s – The Pavilion Hotel & The Royal Hotel, Scarborough, various murals and decorations. A single panel, *Venetian Scene*, survives from the dining room of the Pavilion Hotel

1951 – Telecinema, South Bank, London. Possibly extant – whereabouts unknown

1954-5 – Ceiling for Bristol Council Chamber. Extant

1961 – Royal Marsden Hospital, Sutton, Surrey. Destroyed

John Armstrong (1893-1973)

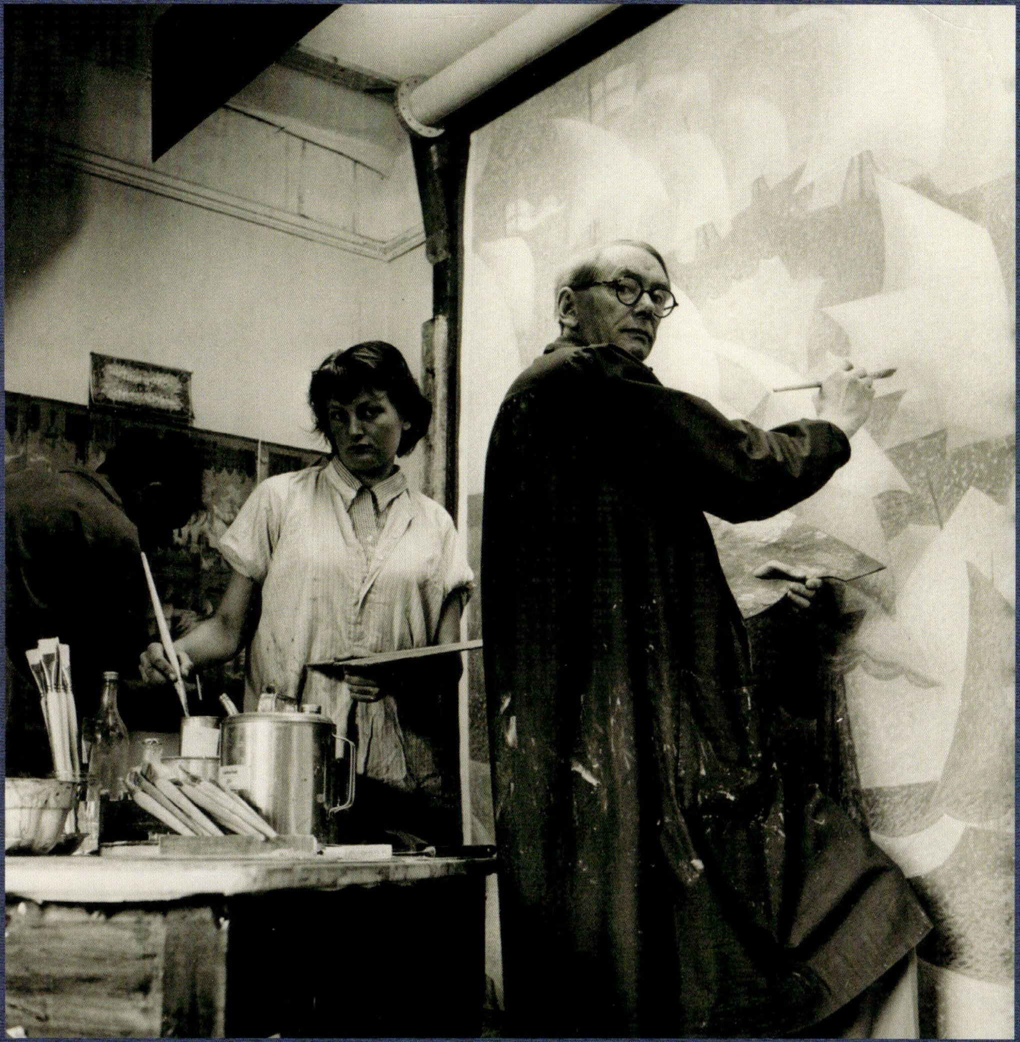

206 John Armstrong with Mary Collett, c. 1953

JOHN RUTHERFORD ARMSTRONG, ARA. Born Hastings, Sussex, died London. Painter, muralist and designer. Studied law, St John's College, Oxford, (1912-13), St John's Wood School of Art, (1913-14). Served in the Royal Field Artillery (1914-18). First solo exhibition Leicester Galleries, London (1928). Designs for the ballet, *Façade*, (1931) and the Old Vic/Sadler's Wells 1933-4 season. Regularly designed costumes for Alexander Korda's films, as well as posters for Shell, ICI and the GPO, and tableware for the Royal Staffordshire Pottery. Official War Artist (1940-44) working on the Home Front producing a series of disturbingly surreal images. After the War settled in Cornwall before moving back to London in the mid-1950s. Principal museum collections: Tate Gallery; Victoria & Albert Museum; Imperial War Museum; Courtauld Institute; RAF Museum, Hendon; National Museum of Wales; Manchester; Birmingham; Aberdeen; Bristol; Portsmouth; York; University of Hull; Leeds; Melbourne, Australia; Israel Museum, Jerusalem.

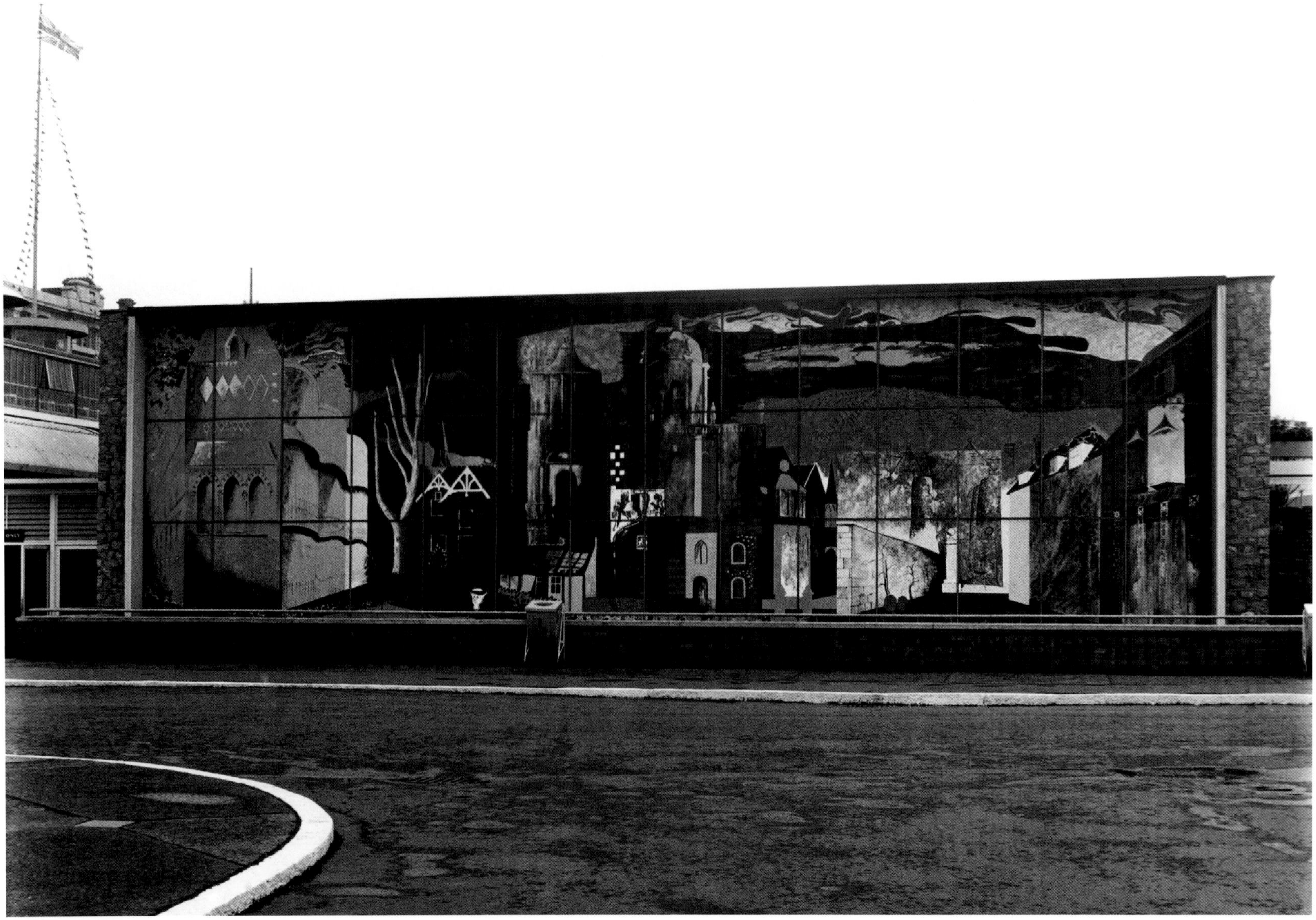

207 *The Englishman's Home* at the Festival of Britain, 1951. Courtesy of the Design Council Archive / University of Brighton Design Archives.

John Piper
The Englishman's Home, 1950-1951

David Fraser Jenkins

This out-of-doors mural was commissioned by Hugh Casson, Director of Architecture at the Festival of Britain, for the river side of the Homes and Gardens Pavilion, in a prominent place beside the main route through the Festival, Belvedere Road. It was painted on an array of forty-two plywood sheets, each about five foot by four, which must have been a daunting sight when they were installed ready-primed for painting in the former farmyard of the Pipers' house near Henley-on-Thames. There was an old wooden barn there which had recently been damaged in a fire, and while it was being re-built Piper had the mural panels set up leaning against it, with a two-storey scaffolding walkway in front. Overall, this measured about sixteen by sixty feet.

Piper knew Casson, though not particularly well, and the essentials of the commission were probably agreed in conversation. The Festival committee had first thought of getting him to paint a 'diorama of Stonehenge', but changed their minds, and requested *The Englishman's Home*. Piper recalled afterwards that Casson had asked merely for 'some kind of architectural congeries'. It seems likely that Casson was thinking of the five large paintings of Regency town buildings that Piper had made for the British Embassy in Rio de Janeiro, and which had been shown at the V&A in autumn 1949. But Piper was very well known as an architectural painter, and it is in terms of the architecture of the Festival that this mural needs to be understood, particularly as its location was in a general area, not part of some themed pavilion. The fee was to be £1,200, which was a slight reduction from the standard of 'thirty shillings a square foot'. He submitted his designs in November 1950, and painted it by the following April, probably in February, using some household paint such as Ripolin.

John Piper had tried out a design full of little incidents in several over-large prints before the war, a long *Nursery Frieze* (1936) and a *Panorama of Cheltenham*, the latter a concertina lithograph bound into *Signature* magazine in January 1940. The tricky issue in making such a thing bigger is then the sense of scale, since things that are small do not necessarily look acceptable when enlarged. A mural has to take on features of its place, and is an 'architectural painting' which is not at all the same thing as a 'painting'. Piper may

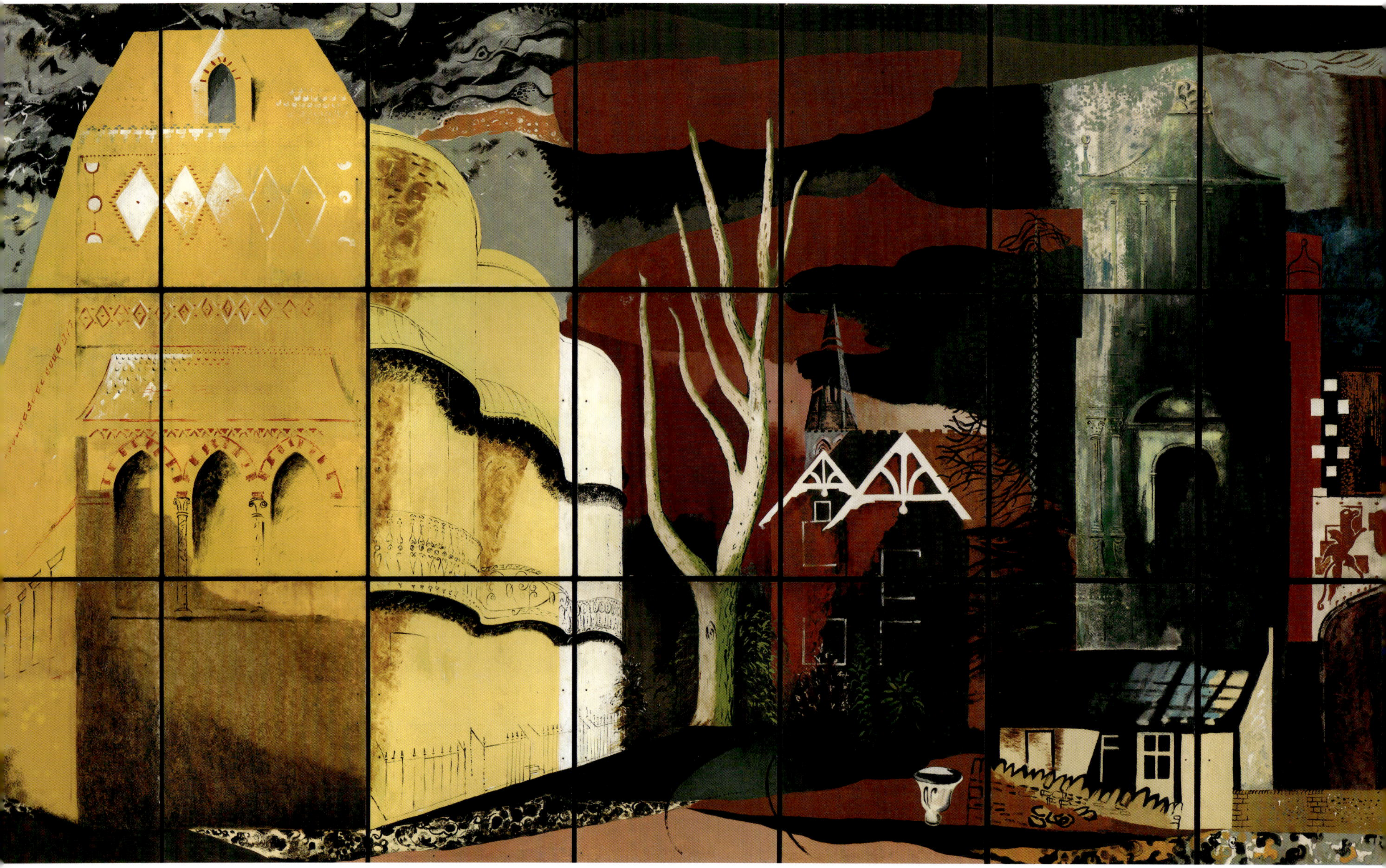

208 *The Englishman's Home*, 1951, oil on plywood, 42 panels, each panel 159 x 119 cm (62 ½ x 46 ⅞ in.) Overall size: 477 x 1547 cm (187 ¾ x 609 in.)

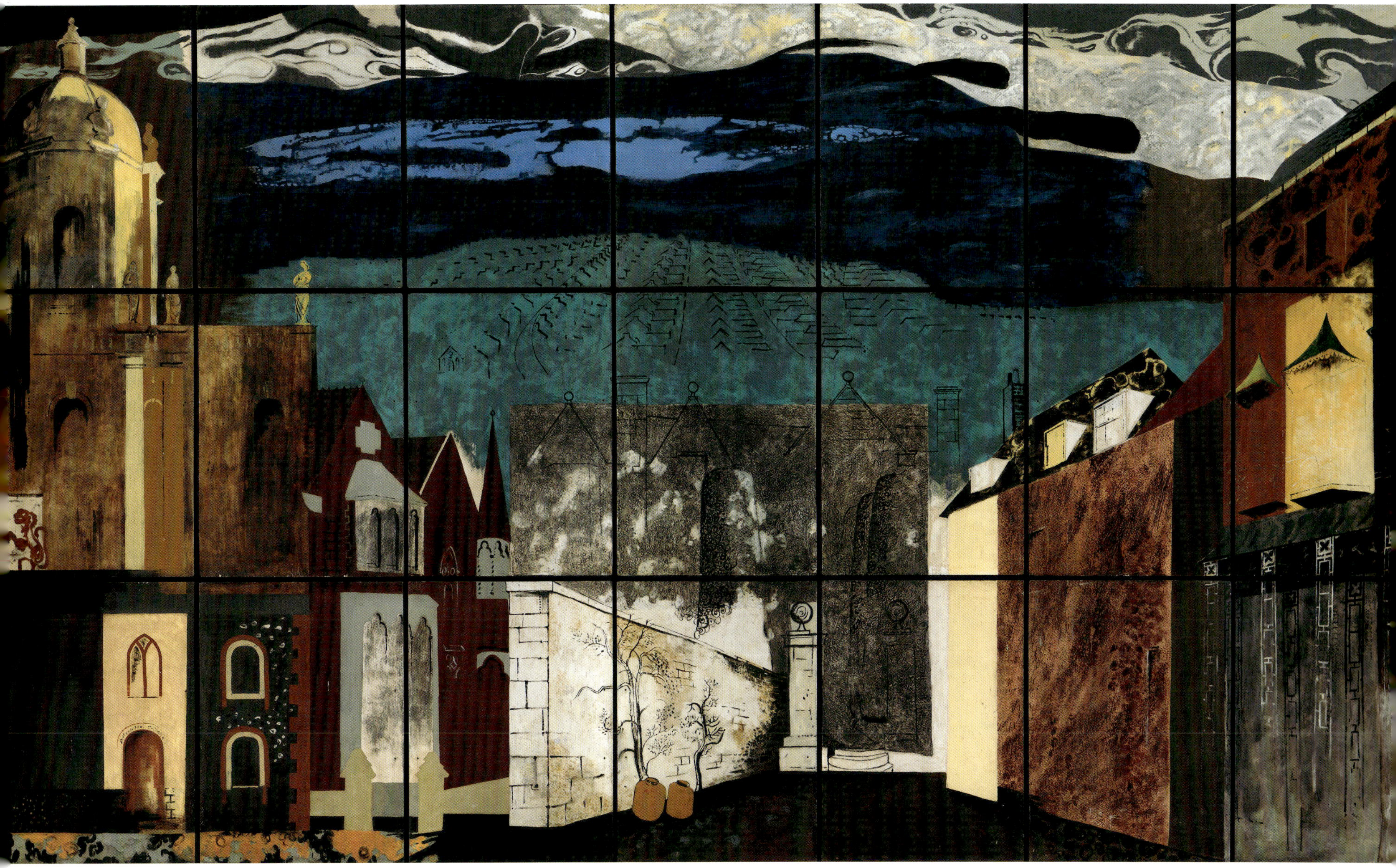

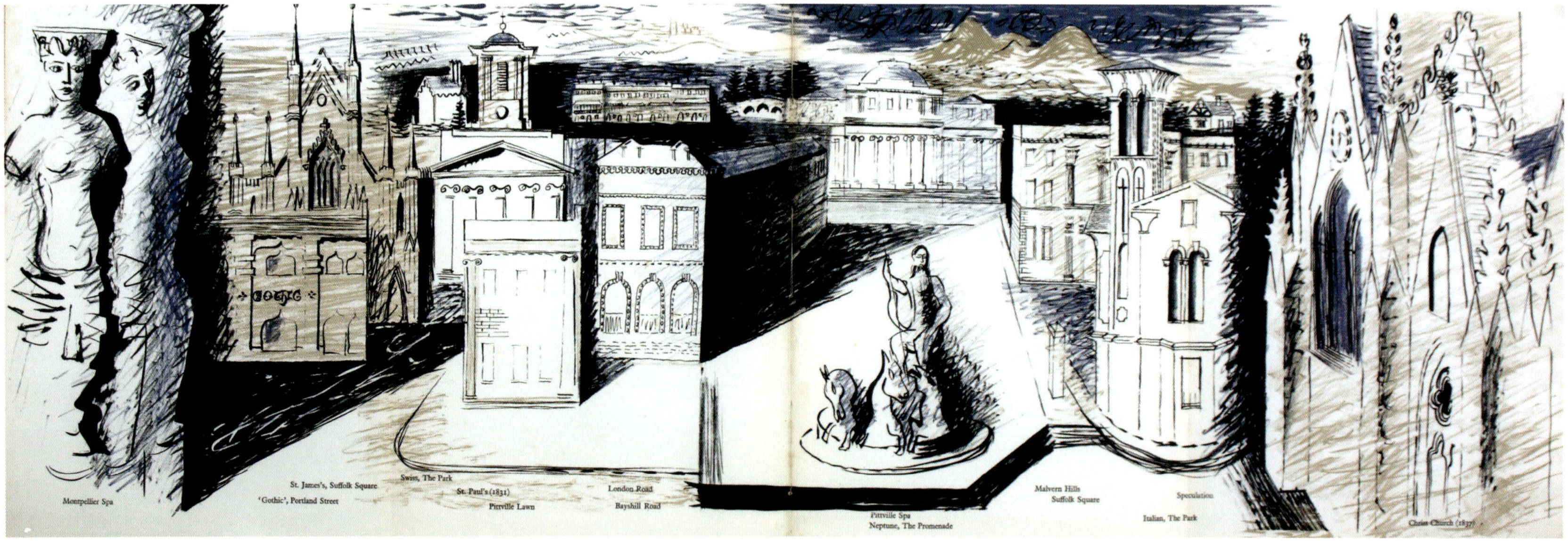

209 *Cheltenham,* 1940, autolithograph, 24.6 x 71 cm (9 11⁄16 x 27 15⁄16 in.) Curwen Press, appeared in *Signature,* No. 13, January 1940, a fold-out lithographic panorama of Cheltenham with printed descriptions, to accompany an article on Cheltenham by John Betjeman

have made more large paintings than any of his contemporaries. He knew what to do, and knew that the secret is to paint a few large things, without too much detail. In writing to Casson on November 24, 1950, he listed 'the degree of abstraction', 'the degree of elaboration' and 'strength of colour' as the critical elements. Piper worked for opera and ballet design, for stained-glass windows in churches, and for mosaics and tapestries. These were made by specialists, but Piper usually made designs full size in collage and watercolour, and preferred not to use a system of massive scaling up (although that inevitably happened in the theatre, where skilled scene painters enlarged freehand). But otherwise he preferred to make his designs actually in the size they were to be seen, and later on liked to point out the differences between his method and Graham Sutherland's studies for his tapestry in Coventry Cathedral (1953-8). Piper's paper collages for his stained glass mostly still exist, and are wonderful, but were made for the more intense colouring of sunlight. His painted murals, six of which still exist, are the only large-scale work of his from his own hand and in its final form.

It is habitual of Piper's painting that it delivers a double impact, both immediate and longer term. The quick effect of *The Englishman's Home* is a delight, as it is an imagined street scene that includes both town and country, grouped around plunging perspectives at each side. But the most extraordinary thing about the mural is that although the Festival was devoted to the nation's recovery after victory, and the Homes and Gardens Pavilion was all about a new kind of interiors and gardens for modern life, it includes nothing in the slightest new, or even nearly-new. It is not even a survey of great domestic buildings, but a very individual selection, mostly of eighteenth-century buildings of the almost-well-known kind that are a challenge to identify.

The given subject is of course a popular phrase, ending '… *Is His Castle*', but it also picked up for Piper the same words in the title of the first chapter of a remarkable book by his close friend the architectural critic J M Richards, *The Castles on the Ground* (1946). Piper had illustrated this, and copied his frontispiece in the

Festival mural, the two gables of a suburban house near his childhood home in Epsom. Richards had argued for the virtues of this ordinary suburban style of architecture, which was a dramatic reversal of the taste for thirties streamlined modernism that he had previously favoured. Like this first chapter, Piper's mural thrusts forward a rather unconfident kind of vernacular building, a shack and a house in the country, perhaps a pub, as if they were being promoted into prominence by the ins and outs of the enthralling tradition of the eighteenth century.

The most recent of the background buildings, the house at Epsom, is ostentatiously cut short of any development by a vast dead tree, a peculiar thing to show in such a summer display. But the message is like Richards's, that the Edwardian suburb is fine in principle, but is now a dead end in the way it looks. The new English style must grow out of the two ordinary little buildings in front, the only ones with what might be open windows, and the only ones that look inhabited. The mural is a narrative of architecture that is about-to-be. And this new architecture will not, it is hoped, be like the suburbs of Brighton, barely visible top right disappearing into the background. The mural may be a gallery of personal favourites, but it is not a version of picturesque Stourhead or of John Soane's watercolours by Joseph Gandy, and it is not a Poundbury of those days. These old things are over, and even Piper's much beloved Kirby Hall appears in black as if at a funeral.

There is a hiatus in the mural, between the grand buildings and the two little ones in the foreground. Something is missing. A year earlier Piper had illustrated the cover of the American *Fortune* magazine for May 1950 over the title *Britain's Road Back*. This implies a recovery, but his illustration was again not of anything new but of the Sheldonian Theatre and the centre of historic Oxford, in his style of 1939. It is implied here that the post-war recovery will start not from 1945, but instead will pretend that nothing since 1939 had happened, as if progress could re-start by simply forgetting the war. This is one message of the mural, that there exists this tradition, and the development of architecture in Britain must start anew while still acknowledging it. This sense that the past must endure in the future was the great bequest of Piper's career.

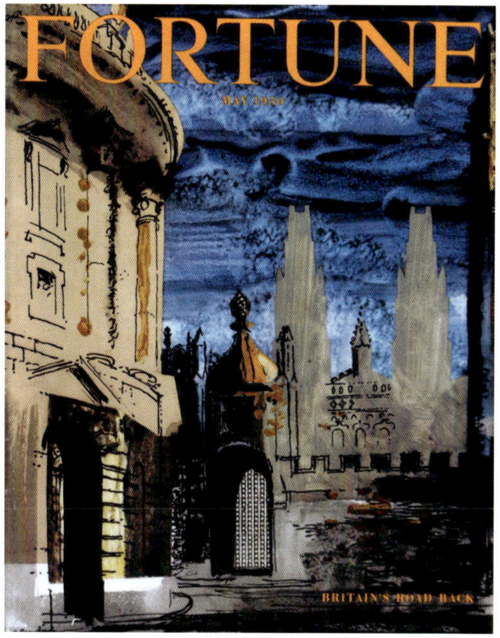

210 Cover of *Fortune* magazine, May 1950

Lionel Brett, reviewing the architecture of the South Bank, pointed to the way that the open vistas linked it all visually to the Houses of Parliament and other famous buildings nearby. He admired not just 'the flower of modern architecture' but 'the interplay between past and present', and this is exactly what Piper was showing. Yet this relation between past and future is neither obvious nor simple, and not at all a matter of unchanging continuity. It was the same man who commissioned and championed this mural who also commissioned Powell and Moya's *Skylon* and Ralph Tubbs's *Dome of Discovery*. Piper was always a modernist, despite appearances, but confounded the idea that the new means a rejection of the old. This mural celebrates variety and the extreme, and might as well be saying 'Pray God, whatever it is, make sure that the new building will be as thoroughgoing as this, and as individualistic, and as prepared in due course to cede its place'. As Piper wrote a few years later, 'the Englishman has always been eclectic in his tastes and eccentric in the expression of them'.

The productivity of Piper in these years is astonishing. In this same year he was painting in Snowdonia, Portland Bill and the Isle of Wight, designing *Don Giovanni* for Glyndebourne, *Billy Budd* for Covent Garden, Britten's version of Monteverdi for the Lyric Hammersmith and a ballet for John Cranko, publishing books and illustrations, and exhibiting in London and New York.

SOURCES

Casson papers, Archive of Art and Design, V&A.

Festival of Britain papers, The National Archives, Kew.

Lionel Brett, 'The South Bank Style', *Observer,* May 6, 1951.

John Piper, *What they stand for*, Ambassador, Coronation Edition 1953.

Mary Banham and Bevis Hillier, eds., *A Tonic to the Nation, Festival of Britain 1951*, 1976.

Alan Powers, 'Home from Home', *History Today*, May 2011, pp. 51-3.

Geoff Colton, letters, *History Today,* August 2011.

212
The Englishman's Home, 1951.
(detail)

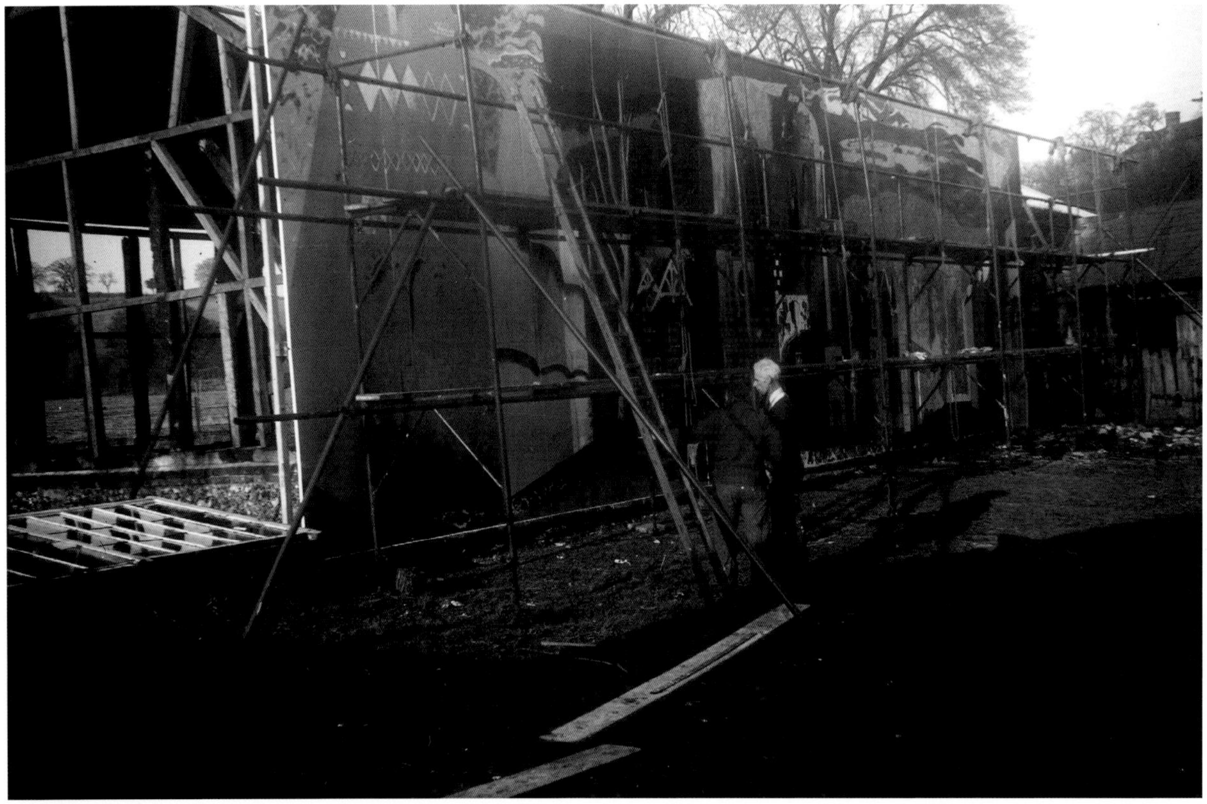

211
The Englishman's Home
being painted at Fawley
Bottom Farmhouse, 1951

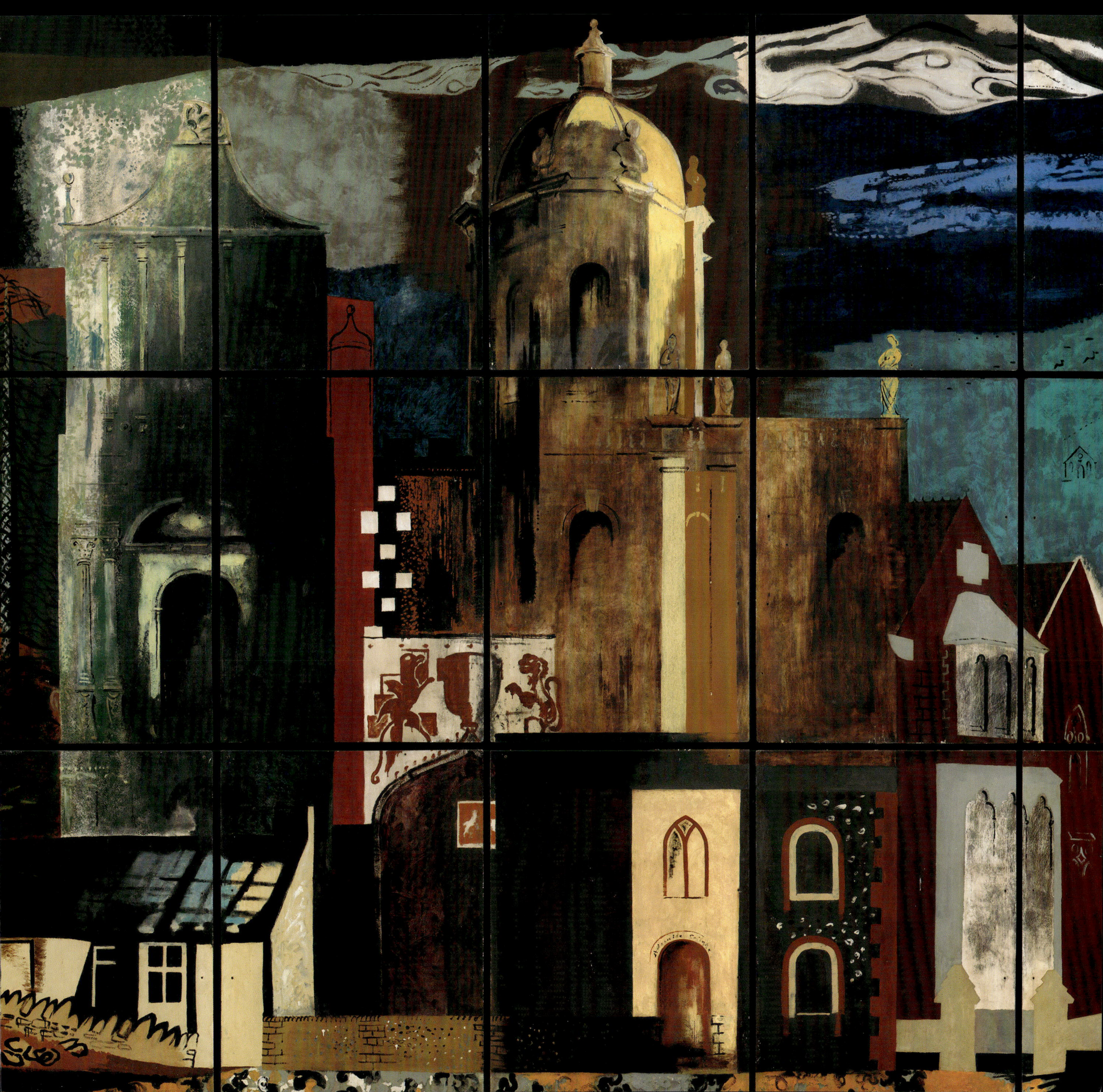

MURALS AND DECORATIVE PAINTINGS BY JOHN PIPER

The following list does not include designs for stage, stained glass, mosaic or tapestries

1938 – Untitled abstract commissioned by the architect Francis Skinner for a room in his own flat in Highpoint One, London. Oil on canvas attached to wall, about 244 cm (96 in.) square. Destroyed

1949 – *Regency Towns*: five large paintings commissioned by Ministry of Works for British Ambassador's dining room, Rio de Janeiro, Brazil. Oil on canvas, each painting about 259 x 137 cm (102 x 54 in.)
Government Art Collection (part loan to British Embassy, Washington)

Cheltenham: Montpelier Walk
Bath: Composite of Bath Street, corner of Camden Crescent
Cheltenham: Composite of Houses in Priory Parade and elsewhere
Brighton: Regency Square
Bath: Grosvenor Crescent

1950-51 – *The Englishman's Home*. Commissioned by Festival of Britain for exterior of Homes and Gardens Pavilion, South Bank. Oil on plywood, 42 panels, 477 x 1547 cm (187 ¾ x 609 in.). Private collection

1955 – *Man's Relation to Nature*. Commissioned by Mayo Clinic, Rochester, Minnesota, USA, as part of 'Mirror to Man'. Oil on canvas 396 x 1219 cm (156 x 480 in.). *In situ*

1958 – *Nailsworth Mill*. Commissioned for Common Room, Morley College, Lambeth. Oil on canvas. *In situ*

About 1959 – *Christ in Majesty*. St Bernadette's church, Bowerham Road, Lancaster. *In situ*

1960 – *Two Seasons*. Commissioned by P&O Liners for first-class 'Princess Room', RMS *Oriana*, private collection

John Piper (1903-1992)

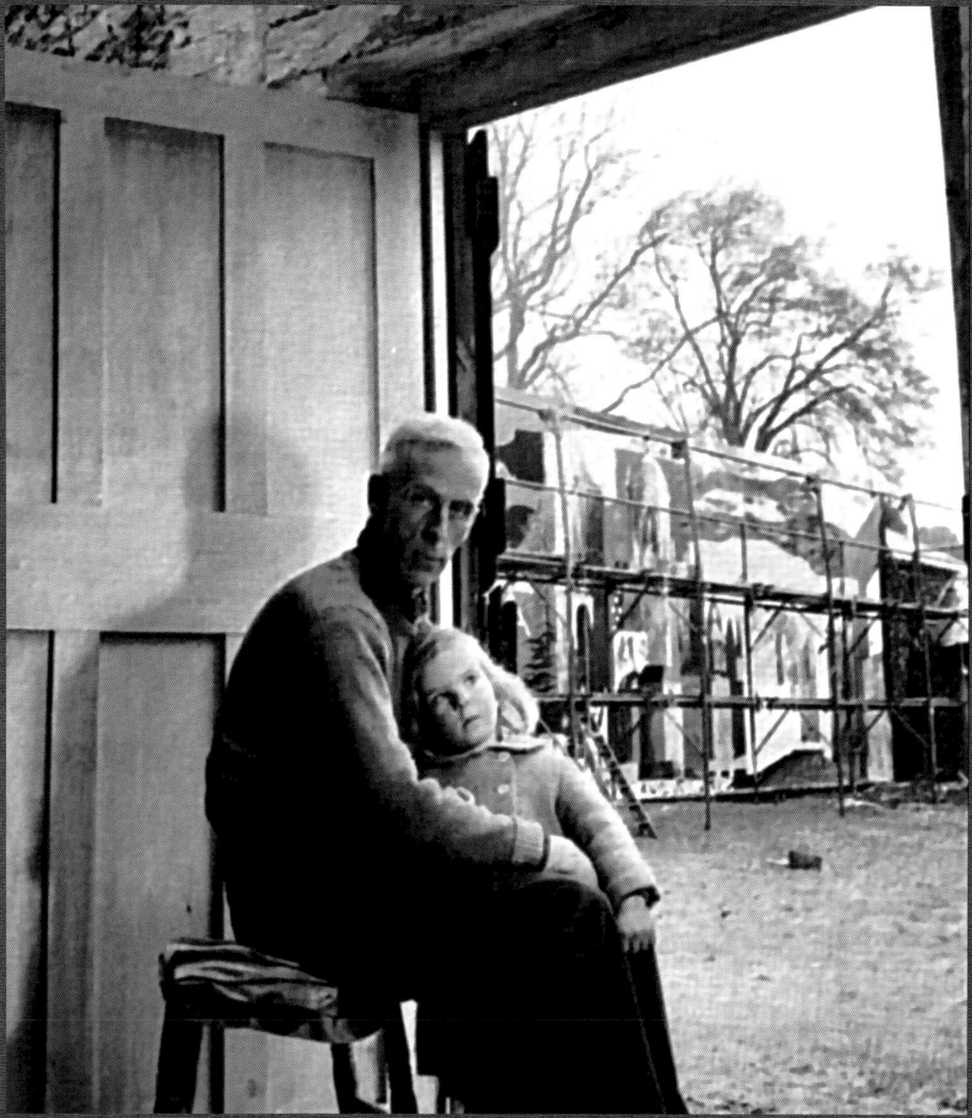

213 Piper and his daughter Suzannah sitting in front of the mural while it was being painted in 1951

JOHN PIPER. Born in Epsom, Surrey, and died in Fawley Bottom. Painter of landscape and architecture. Educated at Epsom College, Richmond School of Art and later the Royal College of Art. Appointed an official war artist from 1940-1942. Collaborated with numerous other artists such as the poet John Betjeman and the painter Ben Nicholson. Produced many limited-edition prints, designed the stained-glass windows for the new Coventry Cathedral as well as other churches, created tapestries and was a set designer for theatre and opera, notably for Benjamin Britten. Wrote extensively on modern art and founded *Axis* with his wife, Myfawny Piper.

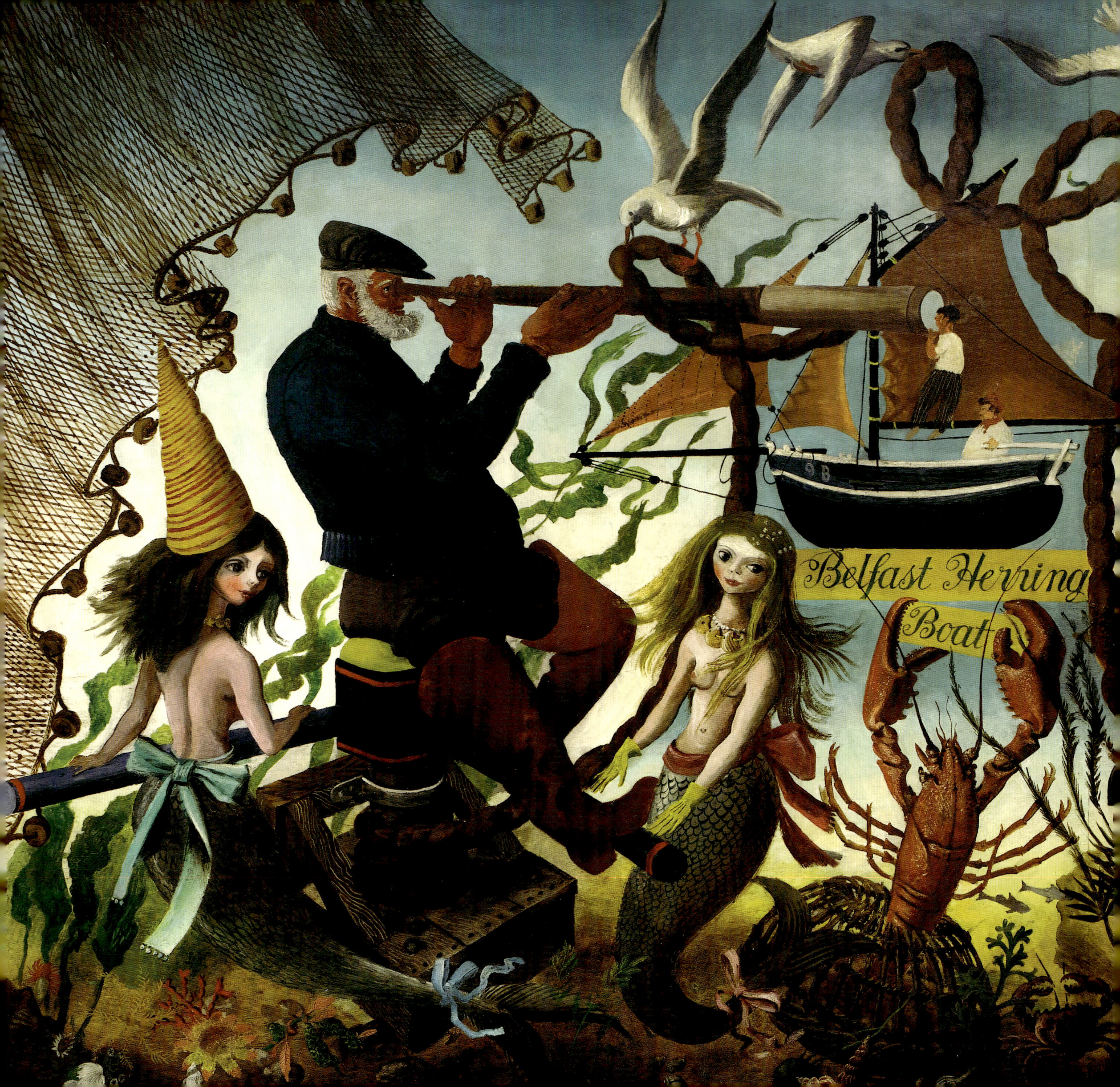
Belfast Herring
Boat

Alan Sorrell
Working Boats from Around the British Coast, Mural of the Nelson Bar, HMS *Campania*, 1951

Alan Powers

Alan Sorrell is best known for his poetic yet accurate renderings of castles and other archaeological sites, showing them reconstructed as they might have been at a particular moment in time. Like many artists of his generation, however, he went through a phase in which he considered himself a mural painter, although his mural works are less well known.

Sorrell grew up in Southend, where he studied at the Municipal School of Art. He went to the Royal College of Art in 1924, when mural painting was still a dominating activity and in 1928 he was the winner of the Rome Scholarship in Decorative Painting.[1] His two years in Rome were probably more decisive for his future direction than for any other Rome Scholar, as here he met archaeologists on whose discoveries he later so successfully built his career.

While teaching at the RCA on his return in 1931, Sorrell offered to paint four tall panels in Southend Public Library. While he wanted to show modern life subjects, his patron, the Mayor, preferred local historical ones in real settings, so that Sorrell almost accidentally fell into his future manner, including the high viewpoint that worked so well for depicting historic sites. His notes show the depth of his preparations and research, studying all the details of buildings and ships as well as the position of the landmarks and realistic light conditions.

Sorrell wrote an account of the commission during the war, stressing his pleasure in serving the community and feeling wanted, in contrast to the pose of alienation common among recent graduates.[2] In following the brief, he was happy to risk the criticism of being a 'mere illustrator', and his account offers practical advice as well as honestly admitting his own anxieties and difficulties. Clearly, the first panel of *The Refitting of Admiral Blake's Fleet at Leigh* taught him a great deal about using a more varied painting technique to achieve unity in a large canvas, which he completed in time for exhibition at the Royal Academy. Taking inspiration from John Constable, it is less glacial than the work of other Rome Scholars, with a lively quality of light in the choppy sea, flying clouds and moving light.

214
Working Boats from Around the British Coast, Mural of the Nelson Bar, HMS *Campania*, 1951 (detail)

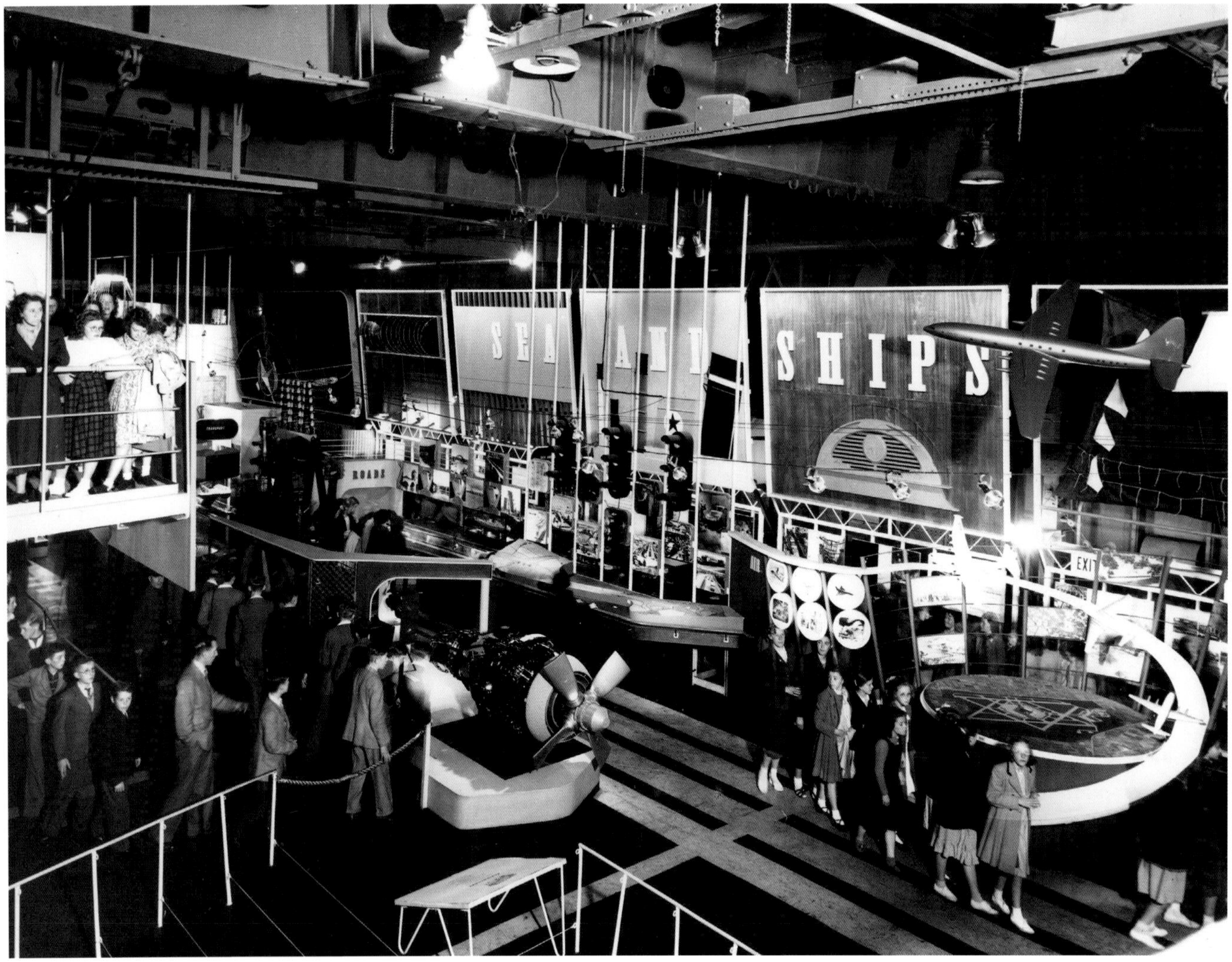

215
The *Campania* exhibition ship, Festival of Britain touring exhibition: general view from Gallery deck looking at Hangar deck, 1951

Courtesy of the Architectural Press Archive / RIBA Library Photographs Collection

As Mark Sorrell, the artist's son, wrote in 1981, 'all the elements that characterize his later work are already at play in this first unconscious exercise. His ambition was still to be a mural painter, but he was already discovering that his sure strength lay as a draughtsman and this and necessity impelled him to other possibilities.'[3]

After war service as a model-maker in the RAF and in camouflage, Sorrell picked up his career, having been purged from the teaching staff at the RCA in 1948 by Robin Darwin. His work with archaeologists now began in earnest, including the commissions for the Ministry of Works to illustrate monuments in the care of the state as they might have been in their prime, for which he is most widely remembered. There was an interval in the early 1950s, however, when he executed several murals among them the commission for panels in the Nelson Bar of the Festival of Britain 'Sea Travelling Exhibition', on board the HMS *Campania*. The ship was laid down in 1941 as a cargo ship but converted for wartime use into an aircraft carrier. The Festival organisers were keen to reach as wide a section of the public all over Britain as possible, so the *Campania* toured different ports around the coast, carrying an exhibition display by James Holland, which was a microcosm of the South Bank.[4] The commissioning of the mural was in the hands of Design Research Unit, the multi-disciplinary practice founded in 1943 by Herbert Read, Marcus Brumwell, with the designers Misha Black and Milner Gray.[5] For the 30ft by 4ft mural, Sorrell received a fee of £15. The specification asked for it to be 'carried out in the Fair ground technique to resist exposure to the weather.'[6]

Ships and the sea featured largely in the Festival, partly because of their decorative and dramatic appeal, and partly in response to a romantic sense that they defined English character, while at this period also playing an important and varied role in national economic life. Sorrell's theme for the *Campania* was the traditional small working boats around the coast of Britain. The details of sails and rigging look very expert, and after Sorrell's careful research on the Southend murals, we can trust him to get these details right, although the figures on board the boats are much enlarged in scale, making the boats, which float in air rather than water, or stand upright on sand, seem more toy-like.

What is unusual for Sorrell is a broad vein of comedy traditional to the theme of seafaring subjects, whether in the saucy mermaids supporting the extreme ends or the cattle and single sheep on board the Norfolk wherry. The 'old salt' at the left-hand end looks through his telescope, at the other end of which a sailor peers back from the far end of the frieze. These figures are similar in character to those with which Rowland

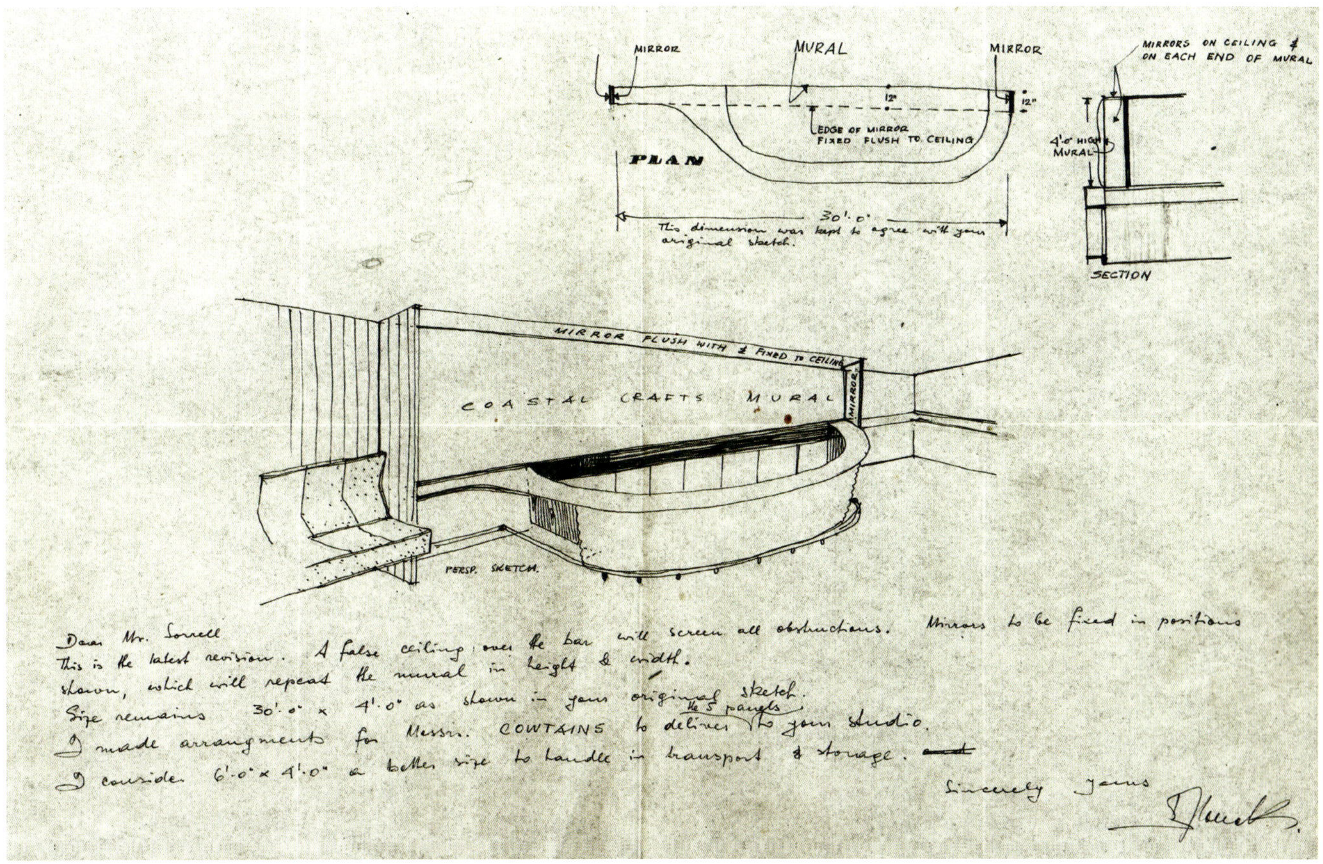

216
Drawing of Nelson Bar sent to Sorrell by the bar's designer, Ernest Pollak, c. 1951

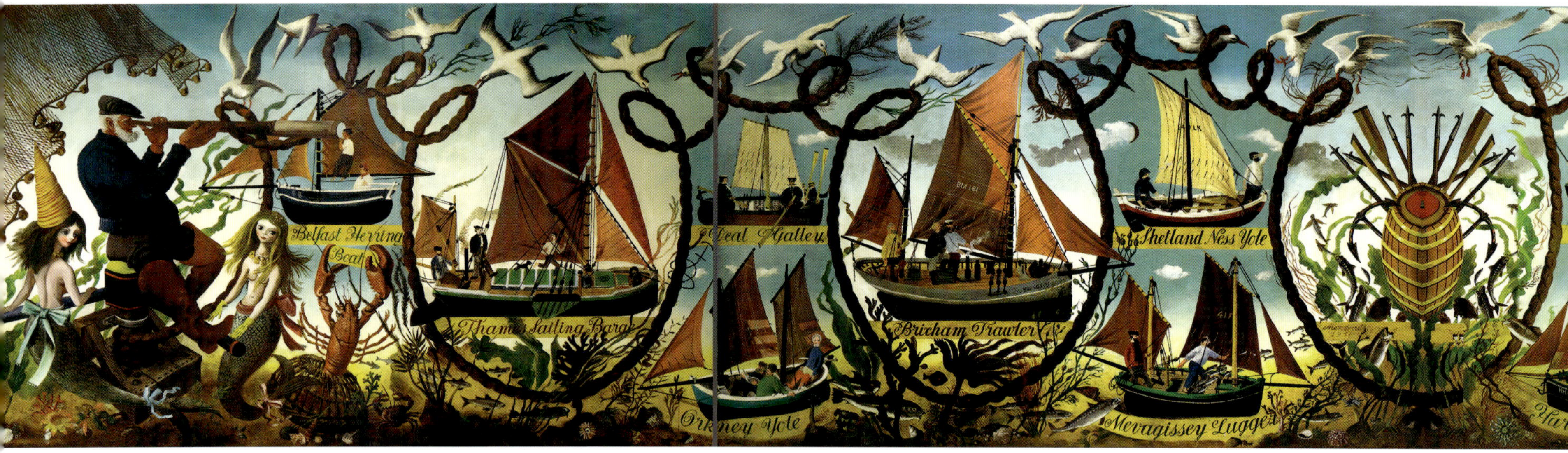

217 *Working Boats from Around the British Coast,* Mural of the Nelson Bar, HMS *Campania*, 1951, signed, oil on 5 panels, 122 x 914.4 cm (48 x 360 in.)

Emmett populated his cartoons in *Punch* at the time. The colour contrast between the blue background and the ochre sails is effective, with the shapes inside the curling ropes slightly darker in tone to establish a spatial differentiation between two alternating sets of subjects. The signwriter's lettering adds just the right folk-art quality.

The design drawing for the installation shows the mural running in one continuous piece across the back of the bar, within a mirrored frame. This must have been deemed impractical, and the photographs show that the bar has a back fitting with holes in which bottles are stored. The mural was divided in half, and instead of facing the customers at the bar formed a frieze above the bench seating on either side, which would have diminished the continuity of the design and presumably accounts for the fact that a small section seems to be missing from the centre, as the two halves fail to meet.

The mural, helped no doubt by its location, seems to have been popular. In June 1951, James Holland wrote to Sorrell, 'The bar, by the way, is doing a roaring trade at Newcastle; we have now had 300,000 visitors to the ship.'[7] Sorrell hoped that the brewers Ind Coope, who managed the bar, might buy it, or that it might bring him more work for ships. Neither of these things happened, but the panels were transferred to the Harlow Arts Trust, effectively disappearing from view until recently.

Prior to the Festival, Sorrell painted panels for the canteen of John D. Francis Ltd in Fazakerley, Liverpool. The four panels frame distant landscapes with buildings, mountains, rocky coastlines, a cathedral and a fairy-tale castle. The foregrounds are crowded with associational objects, while the top of each panel is framed with a festooned red curtain like the opening of a theatre proscenium, with a ledge at the base on which *trompe l'oeil* objects are displayed. There is a touch of Rex Whistler about these works, although the painting style is heavier and more like a Shell advertisement from the 1950s. In addition, he designed colour schemes for the factory.[8]

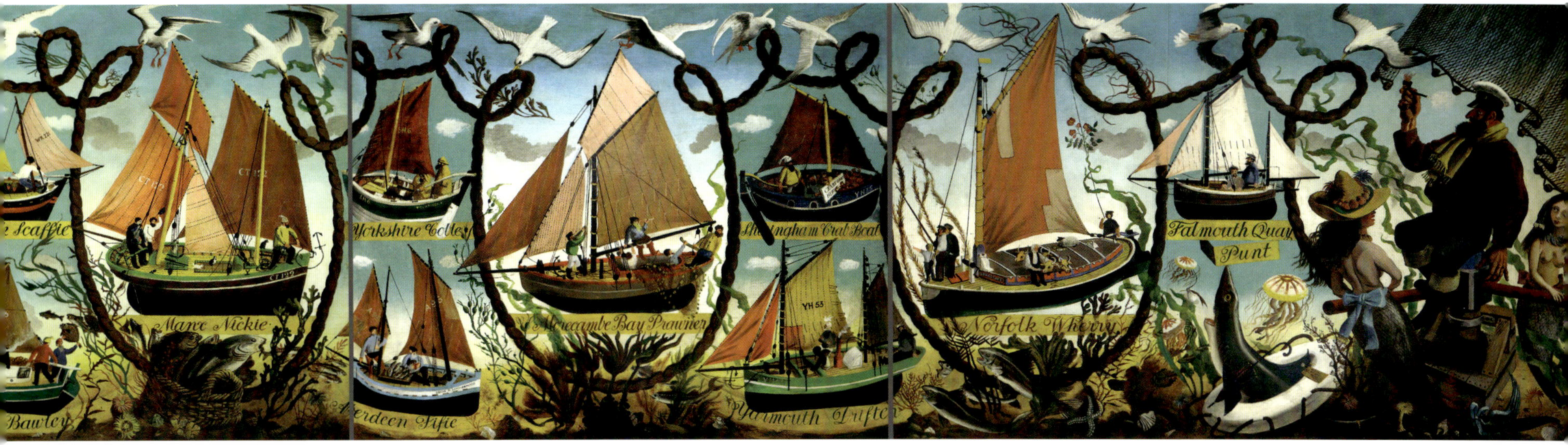

A reflection that Sorrell wrote in a sketchbook seems to relate to this subject, 'There are so many possibilities – there is the dummy window: the window sill with objects on it, all sorts of attractive and improbable objects, and the vertical thickness of the wall, and beyond that, the new outside a fantastic landscape perhaps, a coastline, with a ship putting into harbour. Why be serious subjectively? The artist is always serious artistically of course, but that does not mean that subjectively a new work cannot be objectively serious too. Fantasy plays an important part in decoration today and the reasons are not difficult to understand. There has been in the past so much pomposity in wall painting, so much seriousness of subject so often misplaced, that a reaction is not very surprising.'[9]

More murals followed the Festival, beginning in 1951 with the spandrels of a Gothic arch at St Peter's, Old Bexhill, one of Bishop George Bell's commissions. At Oken School, Warwick, he and his wife, Elizabeth joined the many artists contributing to the post-war school building programme. Their panorama of the seasons, over 50ft in length, was inspired by Breughel, with a combination of different historic periods in one continuous landscape, full of details likely to appeal to children, but not simplified in any childish way. Groups of figures symbolize the transition from youth to age as well as the Four Seasons. The painting, completed in a period of ten weeks 1953, is executed in oil directly onto plaster.[10] In 1956, for a local ironmongers' shop, Turners in Southend, Sorrell painted a cheerful modern scene, *Summer Scene Triptych*.[11] Several more commissions for major companies reflected the way that business liked to encourage artists during the post-war decades, including one for Bovril in the late 1950s and one for the shipping company, Balfour Williamson, showing Roman London. He also painted two further church commissions.

Sorrell's work has either been largely forgotten, or is remembered only in terms of archaeological reconstructions. It was never without imagination or a sense of carefully controlled design. Prior to this book, it seems that no colour image of the the *Campania* mural has been published. His surviving murals deserve to be better known and celebrated.

ENDNOTES

1 Sorrell's submission of a lunette showing a modern life subject, dramatically lit, is reproduced in *Architect and Building News*, July 27, 1928, p.117.

2 Alan Sorrell, 'Mural Painting from A to Z', *The Artist*, December 1942, pp.86-88; January 1943, pp.104-05; February 1943, pp.136-37; April 1943, pp.46-48; May 1943, pp.64-65.

3 Mark Sorrell, *Alan Sorrell: Reconstructing the Past*, Batsford, 1981, p.11.

4 See James Holland, 'Britain in Festival Guise', in Mary Banham and Bevis Hillier, eds., *A Tonic to the Nation*, London, Thames & Hudson, 1976, pp.150-1.

5 The correspondence between Sorrell and DRU also contains details of three paintings made for the Dome of Discovery on the South Bank of Jericho, Mohenjodare and Ur, under the direction of the archaeologists Sir Mortimer Wheeler and Sir Leonard Woolley.

6 Contract issued by Festival of Britain, September 4, 1950. Courtesy of the Sorrell family.

7 James Holland to Alan Sorrell, June 15, 1951. Courtesy of the Sorrell family.

8 The four panels are illustrated in *Journal of the Royal Institute of Architects*, Third Series, Vol.57, 1950, pp.446-7.

9 Family archive, quoted on http://www.alansorrell.ukartists.com/index_files/Page537.htm.

10 Part of the painting is illustrated and the commission discussed in Percy Horton, 'Alan Sorrell R.W.S.', *Studio*, vol.150, July 1955, pp.18-21.

11 Collection Southend Museums Service, Beecroft Art Gallery.

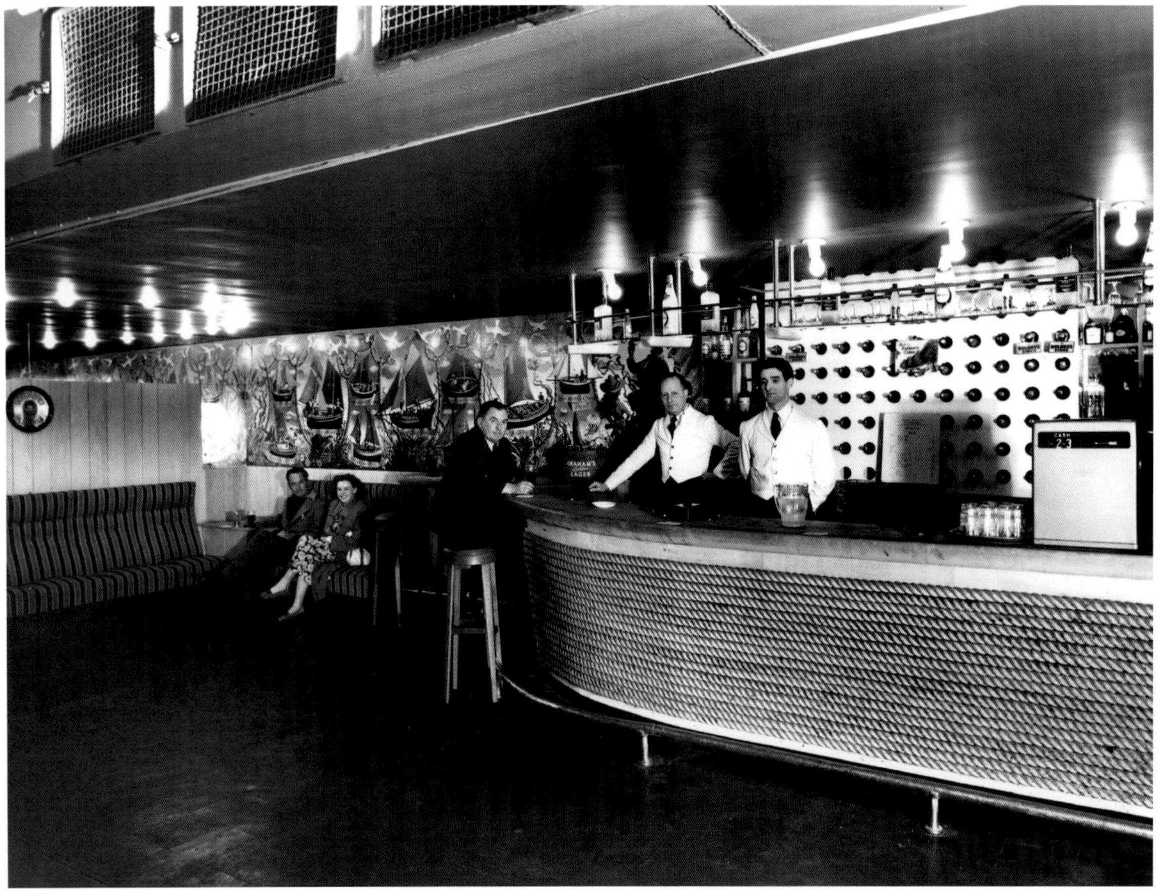

218
The *Campania* exhibition ship, Festival of Britain touring exhibition: Lord Nelson Bar, 1951

Courtesy of the Architectural Press Archive / RIBA Library Photographs Collection

219
Working Boats from Around the British Coast, Mural of the Nelson Bar, HMS *Campania*, 1951 (detail)

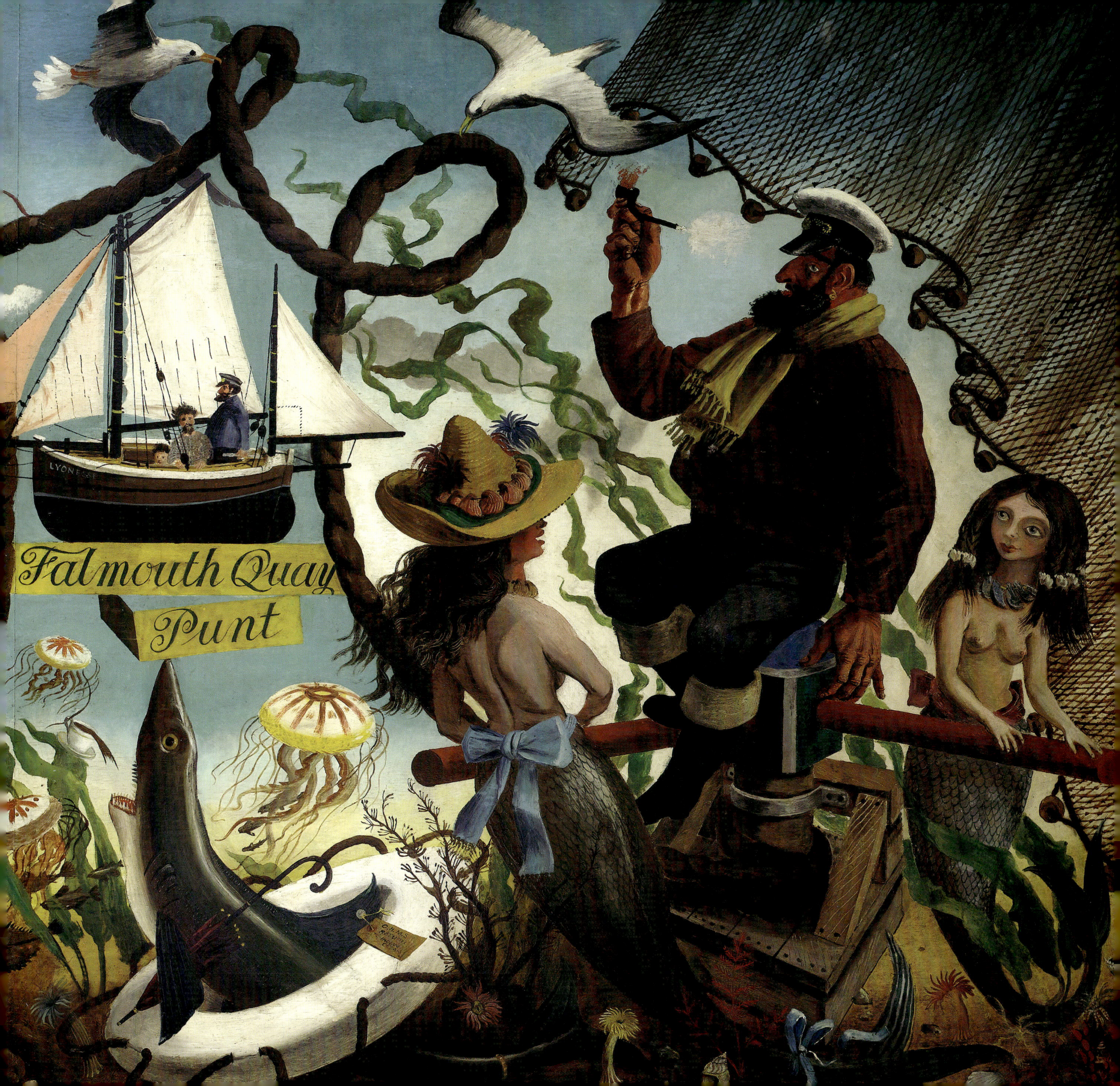
Falmouth Quay
Punt

MURALS BY ALAN SORRELL

1932-36 – Decorative scheme for the central library in Southend-on-Sea, four tall panels with historical subjects, one of which was *The Refitting of Admiral Blake's Fleet at Leigh, 1652*

late 1940s – Mural for ICI Middlesbrough

1950 – Panels for the canteen, John D. Francis Ltd., Fazakerley, Liverpool

1951 – *Working Boats from Around the British Coast,* Mural of the Nelson Bar, HMS *Campania,* Festival of Britain

Spandrels in nave arcade, St Peter's Church, Old Bexhill, East Sussex

1953 – *The Seasons,* wall-length mural for the entrance hall of Warwick Oken County Secondary School (now Myrton School)

1956 – *Summer Scene Triptych*, Turner's Ironmongers, Southend-on-Sea

1962 – Argentine scene, Head Office, Bovril Ltd

1963 – *Londinium Romanum*, Balfour Wiliamson & Co

1964 – Medieval banking scene, Lloyd's Bank, Southend-on-Sea

Alan Sorrell (1904-1974)

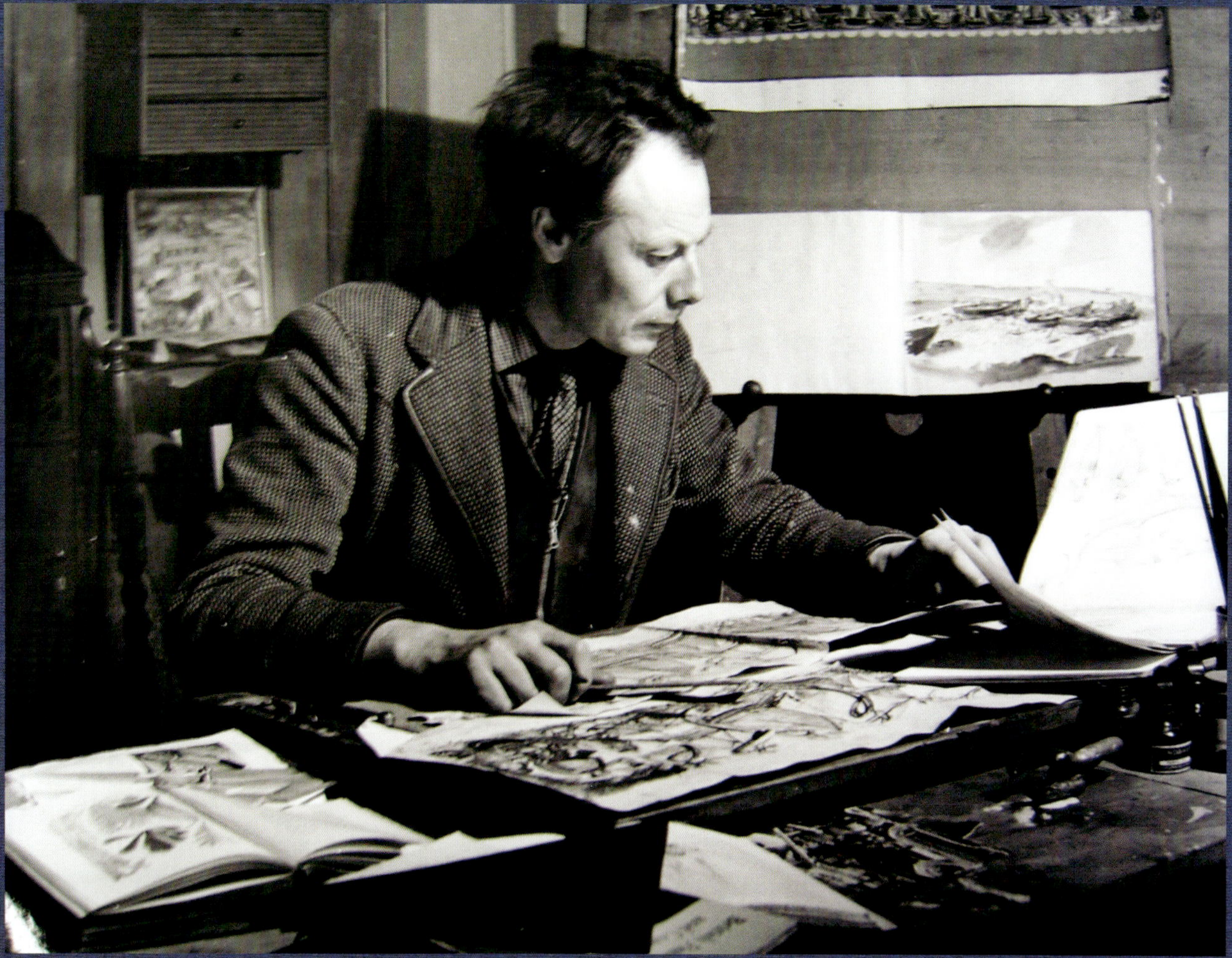

220 Alan Sorrell working on his Festival of Britain designs. c. 1950

ALAN SORRELL, born in Tooting, London, died in Southend-on-Sea. Trained at the Southend Municipal School of Art and at the Royal College of Art (1924-8) where he met William Rothenstein, the principal, who became a good friend. Won the Prix de Rome in mural painting in 1928 and spent until 1931 at the British School at Rome. Returned to England in 1931 and was invited by Rothenstein to join the teaching staff as a drawing-master at the RCA (1931-48). Executed his first reconstruction drawing of the Roman 'basilica' at Leicester in 1936 and continued producing these for nearly forty years. Journeys abroad to Iceland (1935), to Greece and Istanbul (1954) and to Egypt and Nubia (1962). Mural painter and member of the Royal Society of Painters in Watercolour. Exhibited regularly at the Royal Academy. His work is represented in many public and private collections.

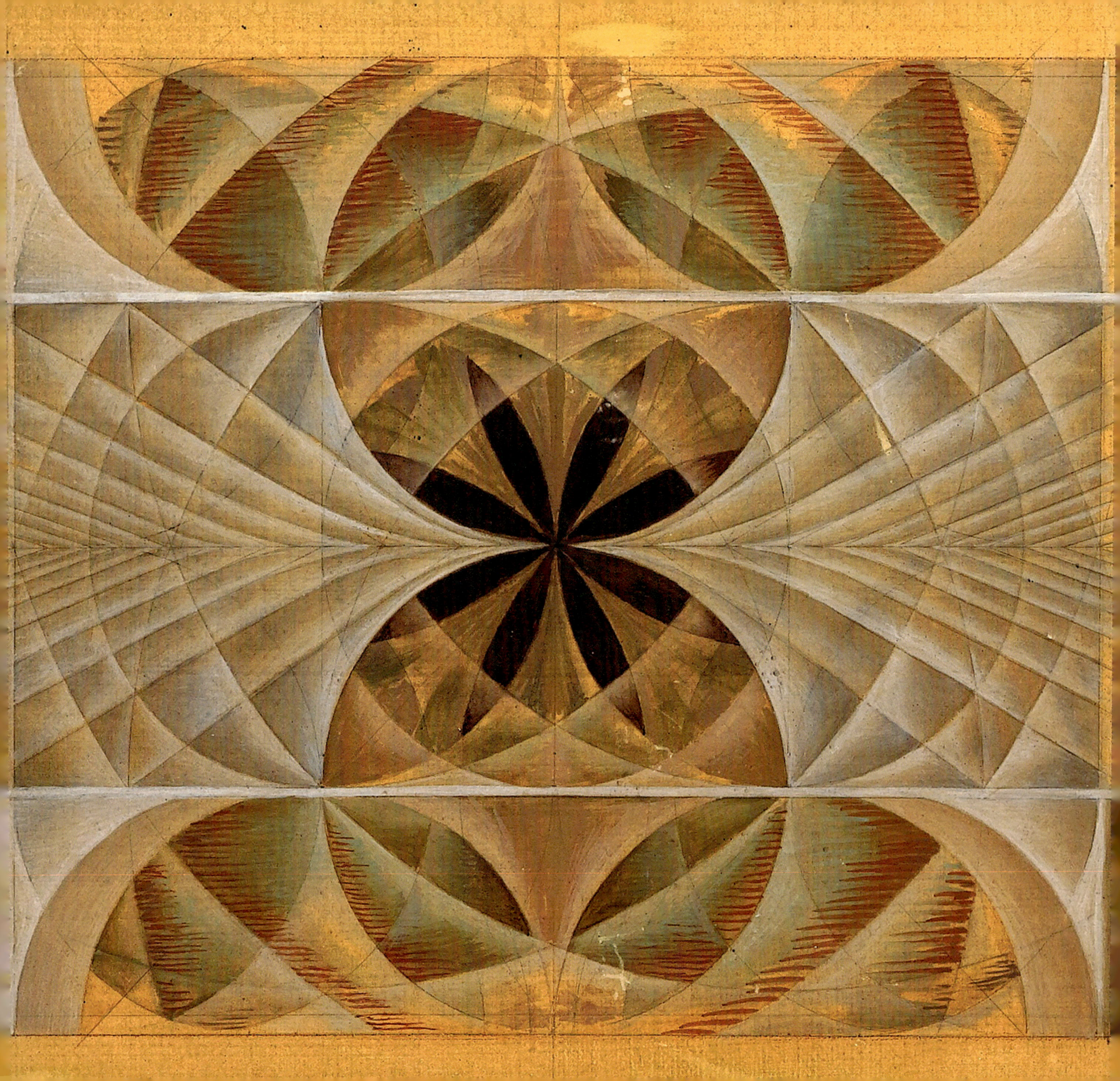

Thomas Monnington

The New Council House, Bristol, 1953-56 & The Mary Harris Memorial Chapel of Holy Trinity, University of Exeter, 1956-57

Paul Liss

The ceilings at Bristol and Exeter have matured well – unlike the earlier St Stephen's Hall – and can safely be hailed as twentieth-century masterpieces, and the studies for them, prepared with the precision and patience of a master, appear today both strong and vital.[1]

The commission to paint the ceiling of the Conference Hall of the new Bristol Council House (1953-56), marked a turning point for Monnington. The success of his early work – star student at the Slade (1918-22), Rome Scholar (1922-25) – had begun to wane.[2] Murals for St Stephen's Hall (1927) and the Bank of England (1932) were greeted with muted praise – the air of costume drama of the former and staid models of the latter resulted in paintings which looked dated even when they were unveiled.[3] In the 1930s – in spite of occasional flashes of inspiration – Monnington's star no longer seemed to be ascending.[4] In his private life his failing marriage to Winifred Knights also weighed down on him (ending in their eventual separation in 1945).

In July 1943 Monnington (aged 42) wrote to his friend, Lord Balniel (later the 28th Earl of Crawford and 11th Earl of Balcarres), 'I don't suppose you know of a job for an old man like myself. Interest (apart from painting which I do not believe I shall ever be able to do all day and every day) any form of social work which will be a step to assuring that the next 20 years will not be like the last 20 years'.[5] Monnington spent the first half of the war working for the Directorate of Camouflage and by 1943 had completed over 600 hours of aerial surveillance, an activity which he found so engrossing that 'all thought of painting had been put out of my head'.[6] He was especially inspired by a collaboration with Barnes Wallis (inventor of the Wellington bomber and the bouncing bomb), who, appreciating Monnington's experience as both a pilot and an artist, asked him to improve the appearance of a heavy bomber that was being developed at the time.[7] In November 1943 a successful application to become an Official War Artist showed a keenness on Monnington's part to re-engage with painting:

221
Design for ceiling of the Mary Harris Memorial Chapel of Holy Trinity, University of Exeter, c. 1956 (detail)

'From the limited amount of war painting which I have seen, it does not appear to me that the war in the air, as seen from the air, has been recorded in a way comparable with the significance which this aspect of the war deserves'.[8] Monnington's appointment resulted in a series of inspired compositions which demonstrate a renewed sense of purpose – *Battle Area, 15,000 ft* (1943), *Flying Fortresses over Europe* (1943), *Radar Aerials and Type 70, Tempests Attacking Flying Bombs, Halifax* (all 1944). These paintings represent a fusion between his love of the English Pastoral tradition and a fascination with modern science, on which the war had acted as a catalyst, soon to flower in his post-war geometric designs. These paintings, a celebration of the new horizons Monnington experienced at first hand as a pilot, formed the prelude to, and offer a context for, his remarkable design for Bristol.

The architect of the new Bristol Council House was Vincent Harris RA. The foundation stone was laid in 1938 and the building was opened by the Queen in 1956. In 1953 The Edwin Austin Abbey Trust for Mural Painting in Great Britain commissioned two artists, John Armstrong and Monnington, to paint ceiling designs for two adjoining rooms. Armstrong was asked to paint the ceiling of the Council Chamber and Monnington that of the larger, adjoining, Conference Hall which measuring 95 x 45 feet was to become one of the largest post-war painted ceilings in Europe.

The subject suggested by the Bristol city fathers was, 'something connected with the Merchant Adventurers.'[9] Armstrong responded by depicting Bristol buildings around the parameters with sailing ships from different periods of Bristol history in the centre and allegorical figures of Enterprise, Wisdom, Industry and Navigation in the corners. Monnington declared himself 'very reluctant to get involved in an imitation of nature' and determined that his design should instead commemorate those scientific achievements which future Bristolians would associate with the mid-twentieth century.

Monnington resolved to divide the ceiling into a double square subdivided into a series of octagons, rectangles, lunettes, and corner squares. His approach drew inspiration from Piero della Francesca's treatise *De Prospective Pingendi* (circa 1470) a theoretical study of perspective which attached paramount importance to geometry.[10] In the centre Monnington represented the earth with planets and electrons orbiting round a nucleus of radio-active atoms. Judy Egerton has noted that the scheme might be read as a visual equivalent to Gustav Holst's *Planets Suite*, 'painted in subtly graduated shades of ochre, light red, umber and blue….an effect which is mystic and ethereal.[11] The corner squares refer to nuclear physics, electronics, biochemistry and aeronautics – subjects which offered Monnington a new visual vocabulary. Monnington was especially inspired by an encounter with Nobel Prize-winning scientist Sir Joseph Thomson (whom he had painted for the National Portrait Gallery in 1932) which gave him a profound insight into the field of nuclear physics.[12] The corner square for electronics was inspired by a photograph taken looking upwards inside the Crystal Palace television mast (reproduced on the cover of the *Radio Times*).[13] Enlarged photographs of recent research in the field of bio-chemistry revealing amazing patterns caused by cellular mytosis provided Monnington with the inspiration for his representation of bio-chemistry. The corner square for aeronautics was inspired by pictures of supersonic wind-tunnel experiments on aerofoil sections provided by Barnes Wallis (et al).

Monnington started work in April 1954 and it lasted for two years. As Judy Egerton notes, 'the subject Monnington chose might have belonged to the nuclear age but the technique was entirely traditional.'[14] The

222
Fighter Affiliation : Halifax and Hurricane aircraft co-operating in action, 1943
oil on canvas,
46.3 x 41.2 cm
(18 ¼ x 16 ¼ in.)

Courtesy of
Imperial War Museums
© IWM

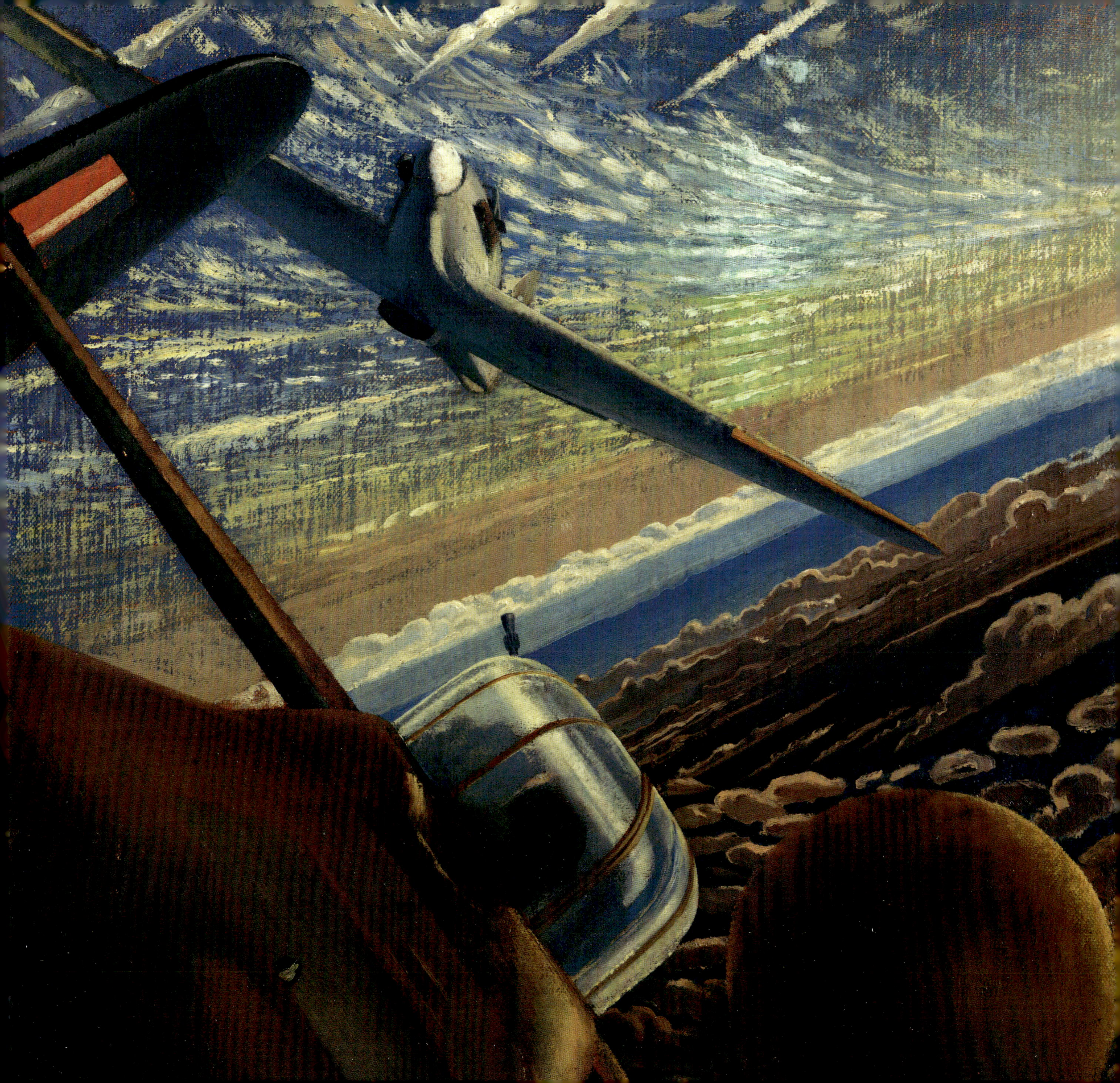

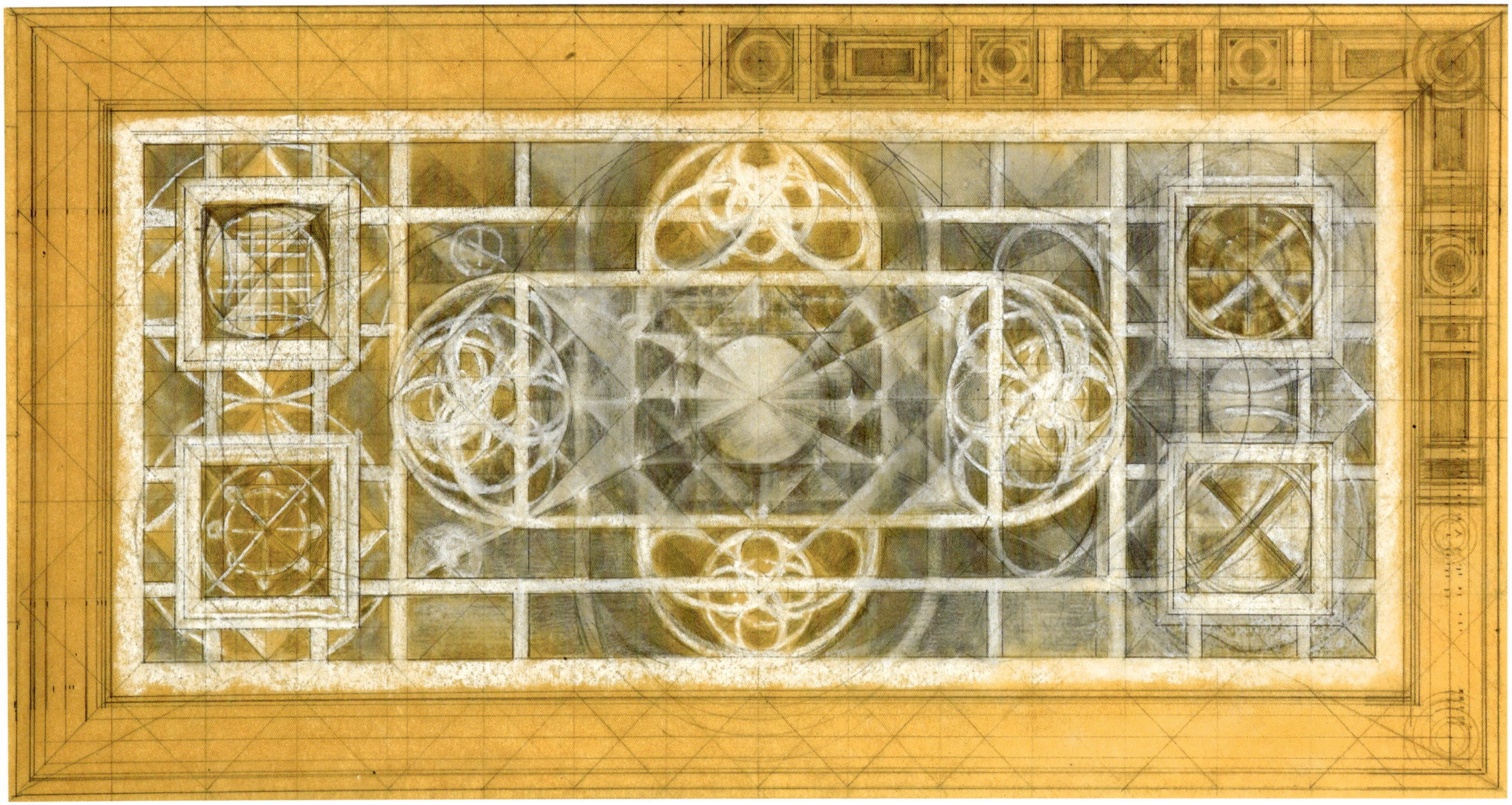

223 Design for Bristol Council House Ceiling, c. 1953, pencil and chalk on tracing paper, 61 x 33 cm (24 x 13 in.)

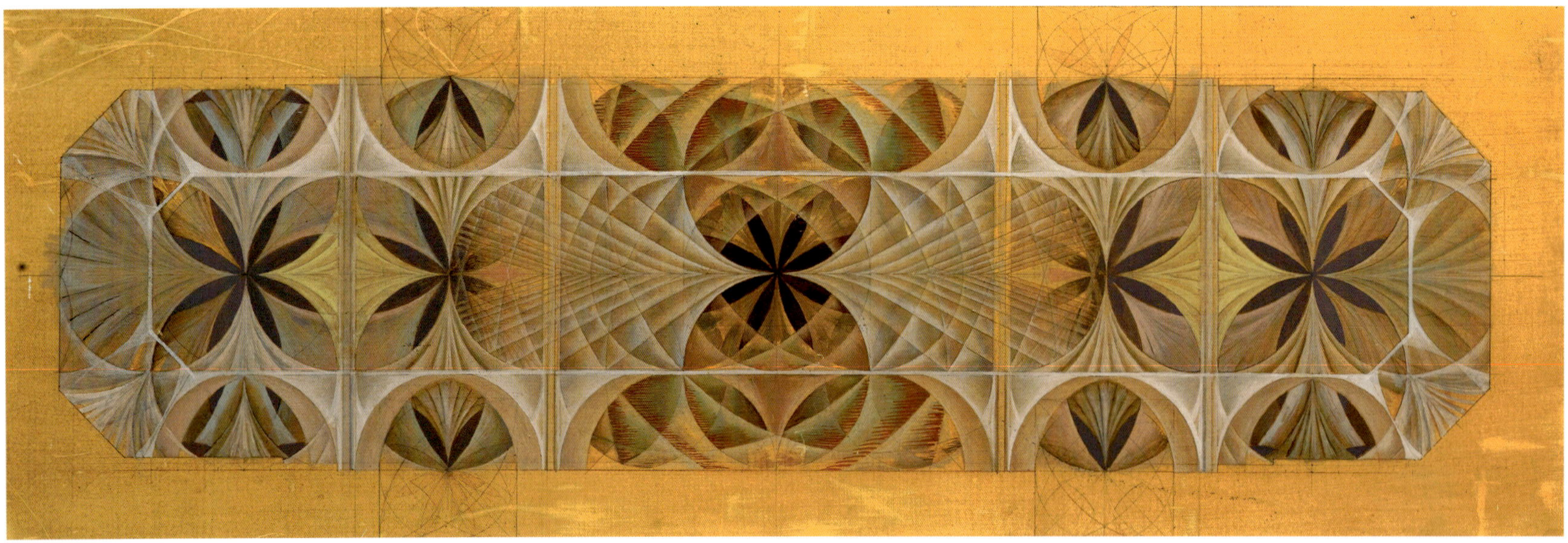

224 Design for ceiling of the Mary Harris Memorial Chapel of Holy Trinity, University of Exeter, c. 1956, oil on board, 123 x 49 cm (48 ½ x 19 ⅜ in.)

entire ceiling was sized with calcium and rabbit-skin glue and a platform was erected some six feet below. The design was laid out from Monnington's detailed and precisely-measured working drawings using string rubbed with charcoal. The medium of the Bristol ceiling is tempera and Bristol's Clerk of Works delivered baskets of eggs daily.[15] The colours were ground and mixed with an emulsion of eggs, chalk and water. Scott Medd, one of Monnington's former RA students, was his chief assistant;]ohn Monnington, his elder son, helped to mix the size and the paint. Unlike Armstrong who painted his ceiling design in his studio in Cornwall and delivered it in a van in ten-foot strips, to be rolled onto the ceiling with adhesive, Monnington insisted on working *in situ* with 'a routine of starting work at 6 am and going to bed at 9 pm. The platform prevented any chance to judge progress at ground level; only for the final stages of detail were mobile scaffolding towers used. Vision was restricted to a small area around the brush, the head always upwards'.[16]

Monnington's triumph was not without its price – before the much acclaimed ceiling was unveiled, he suffered a heart attack. In spite of this a further commission from Vincent Harris, for the ceiling of a chapel in memory of Harris' mother, proved an immediate temptation. For this Monnington employed two full-time assistants: Scott Medd and W.B. Peter Lowe, and elected to use oil not tempera. The 112 x 28 ft. ceiling – with eight sloped areas and four alcoves – took 11 months to complete.[17]

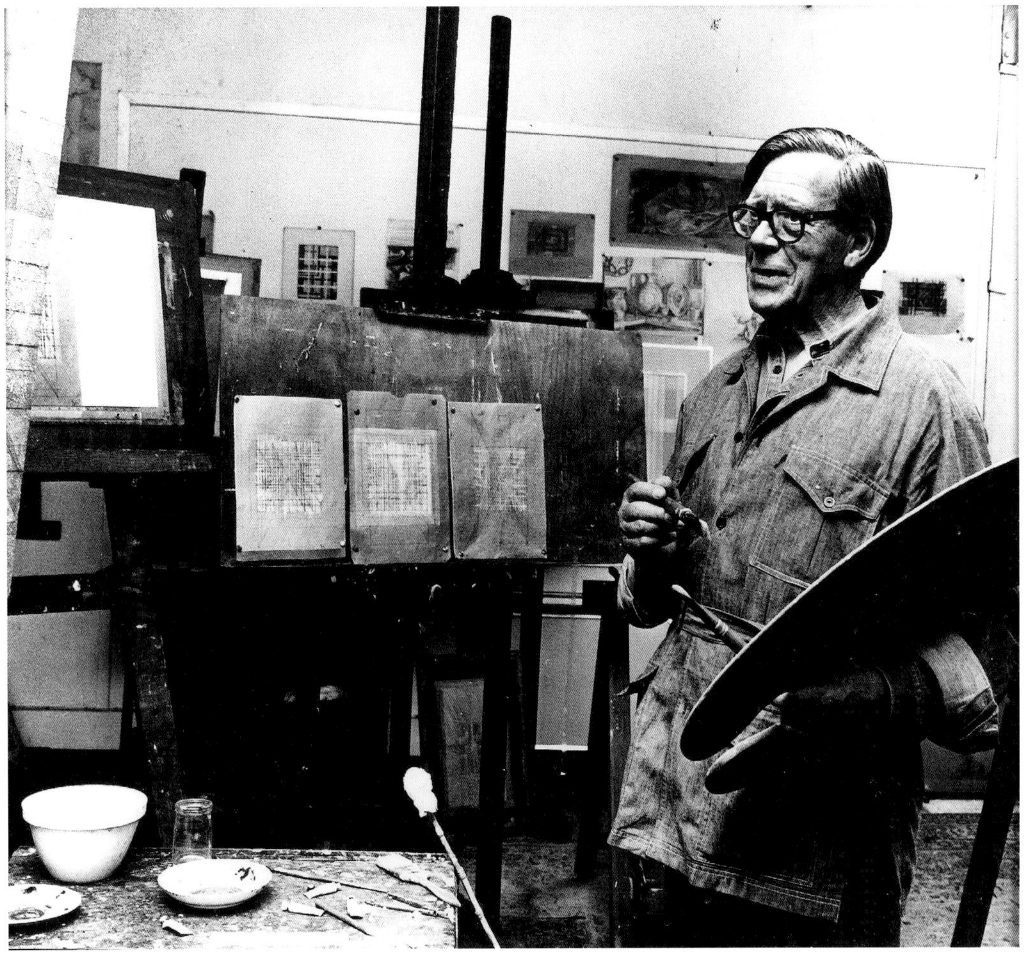

225
Thomas Monnington in his studio at Leyswood, c. 1967

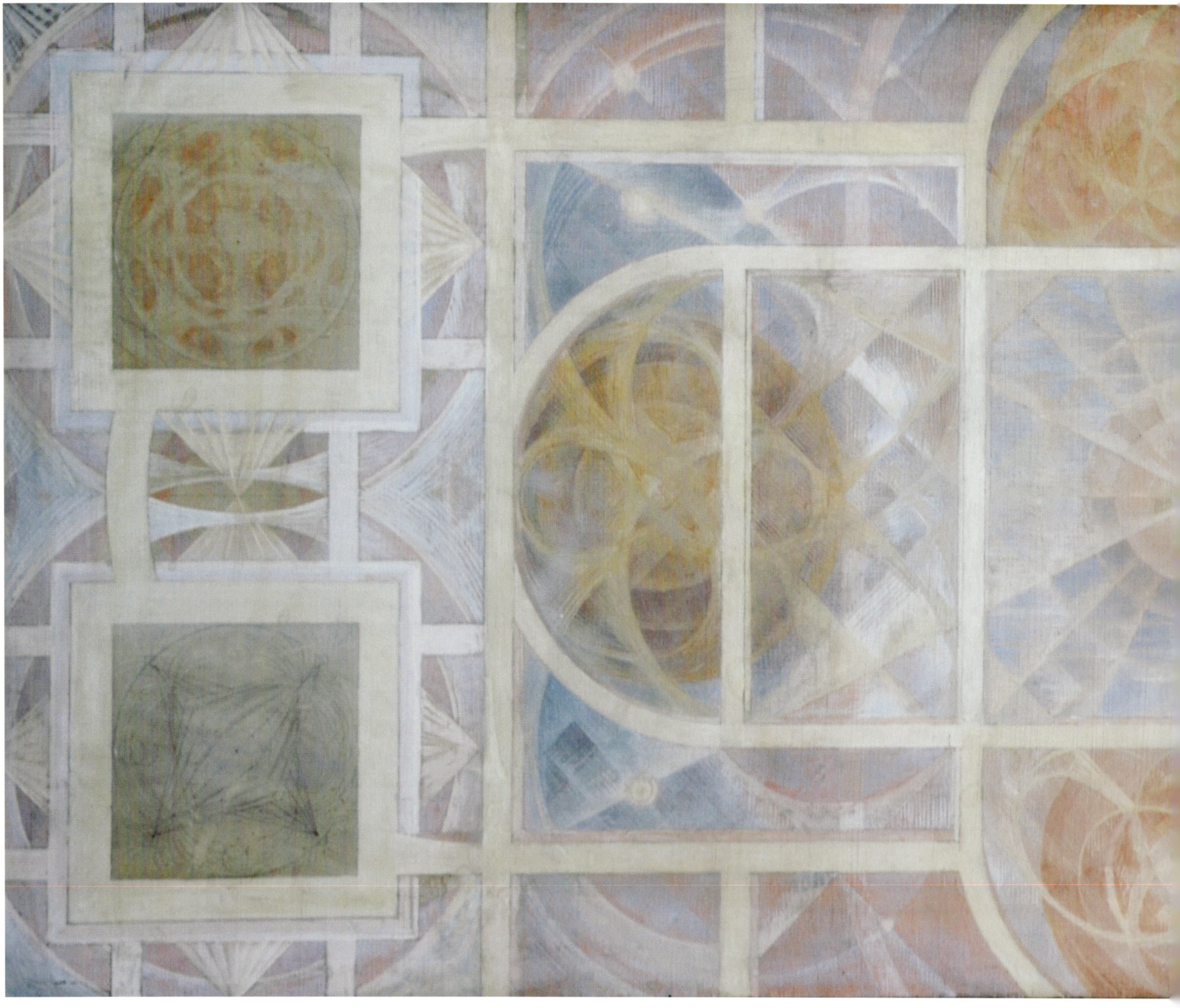

226 Design for Bristol Council House Ceiling, c.1953, inscribed on the reverse, 'working study', tempera over pencil on a gesso ground, 76.2 x 193 cm (30 x 76 in.)

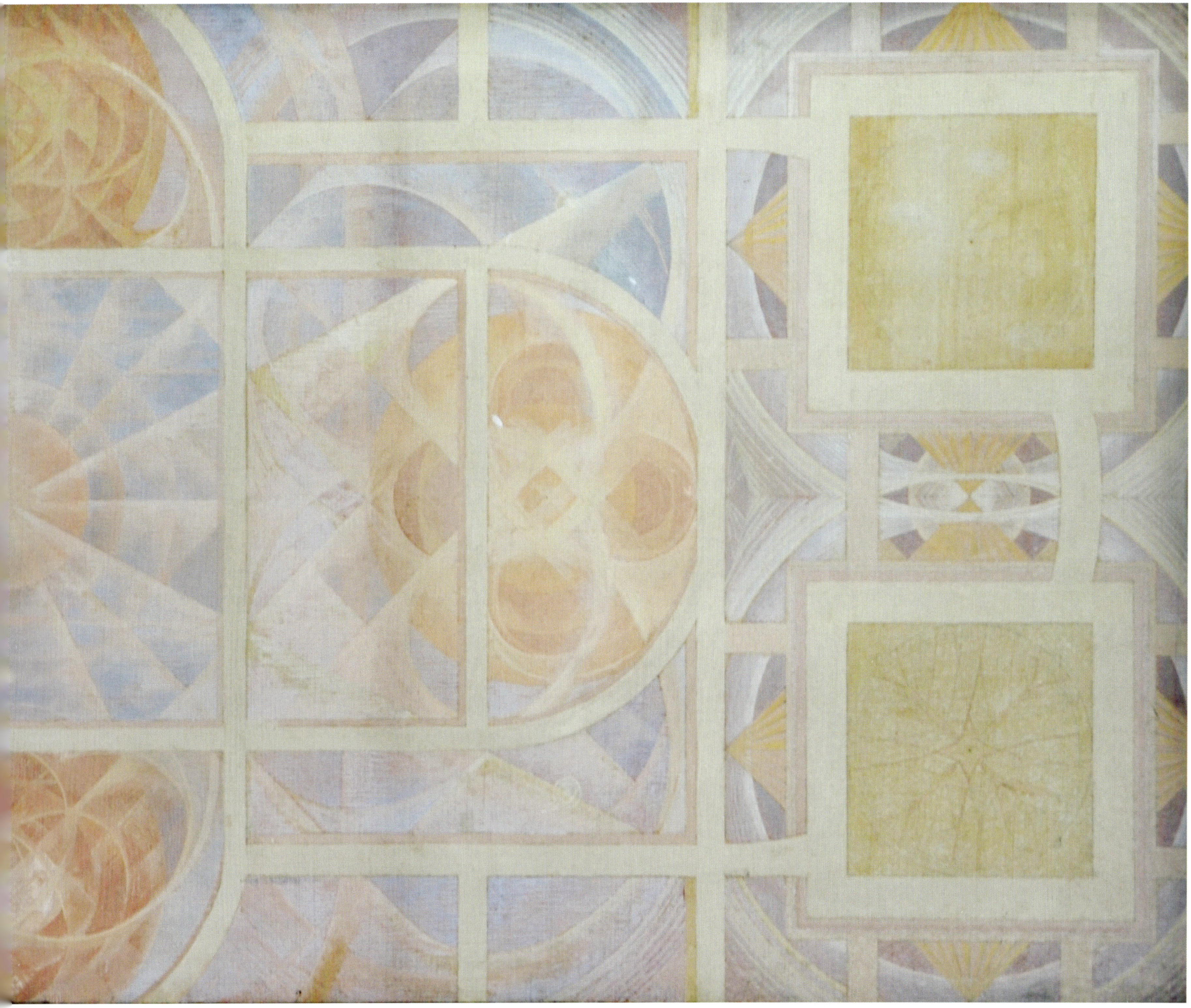

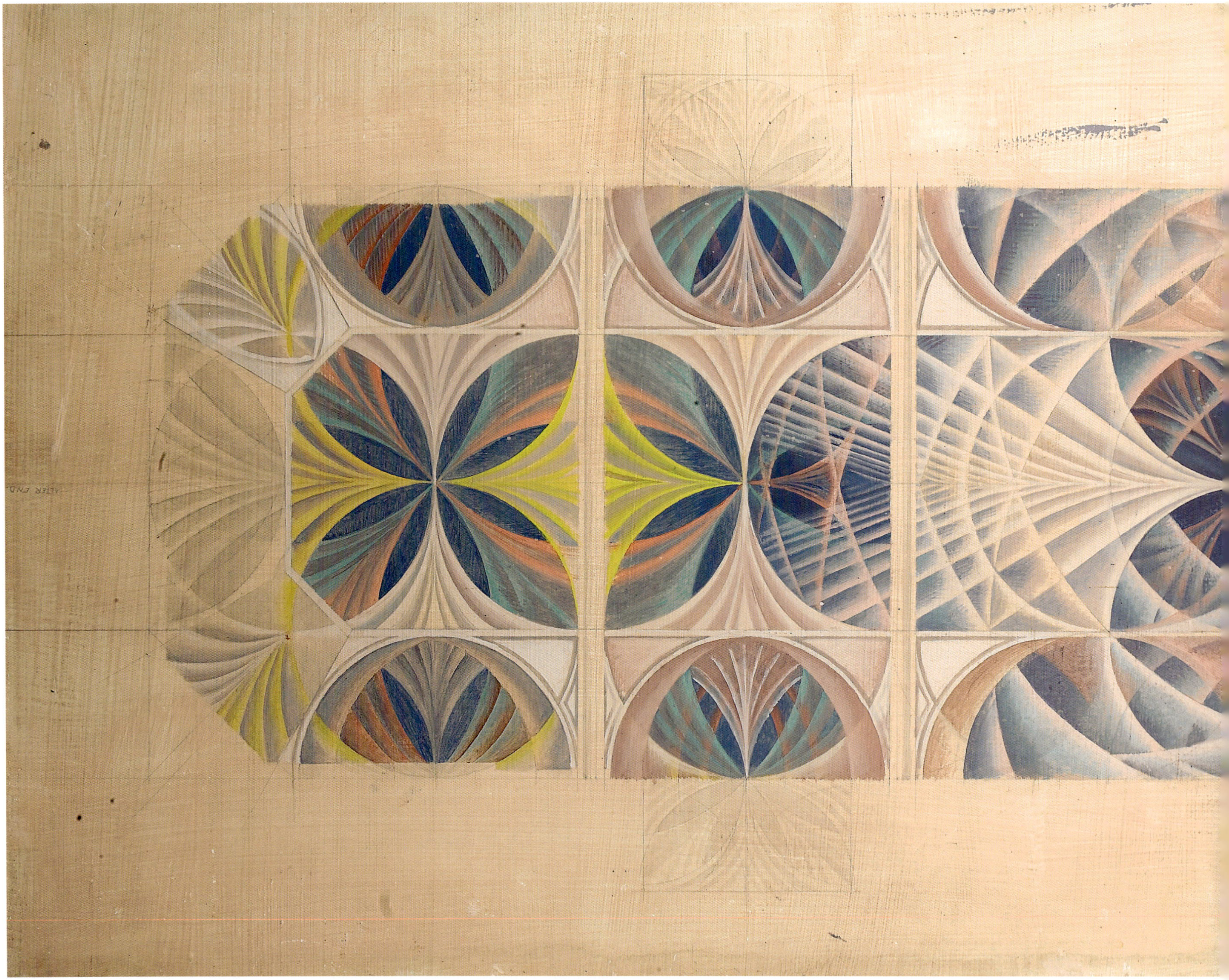

227 Design for ceiling of the Mary Harris Memorial Chapel of Holy Trinity, University of Exeter, c. 1956, oil on board 43.7 x 122 cm (17 ¼ x 48 in.)

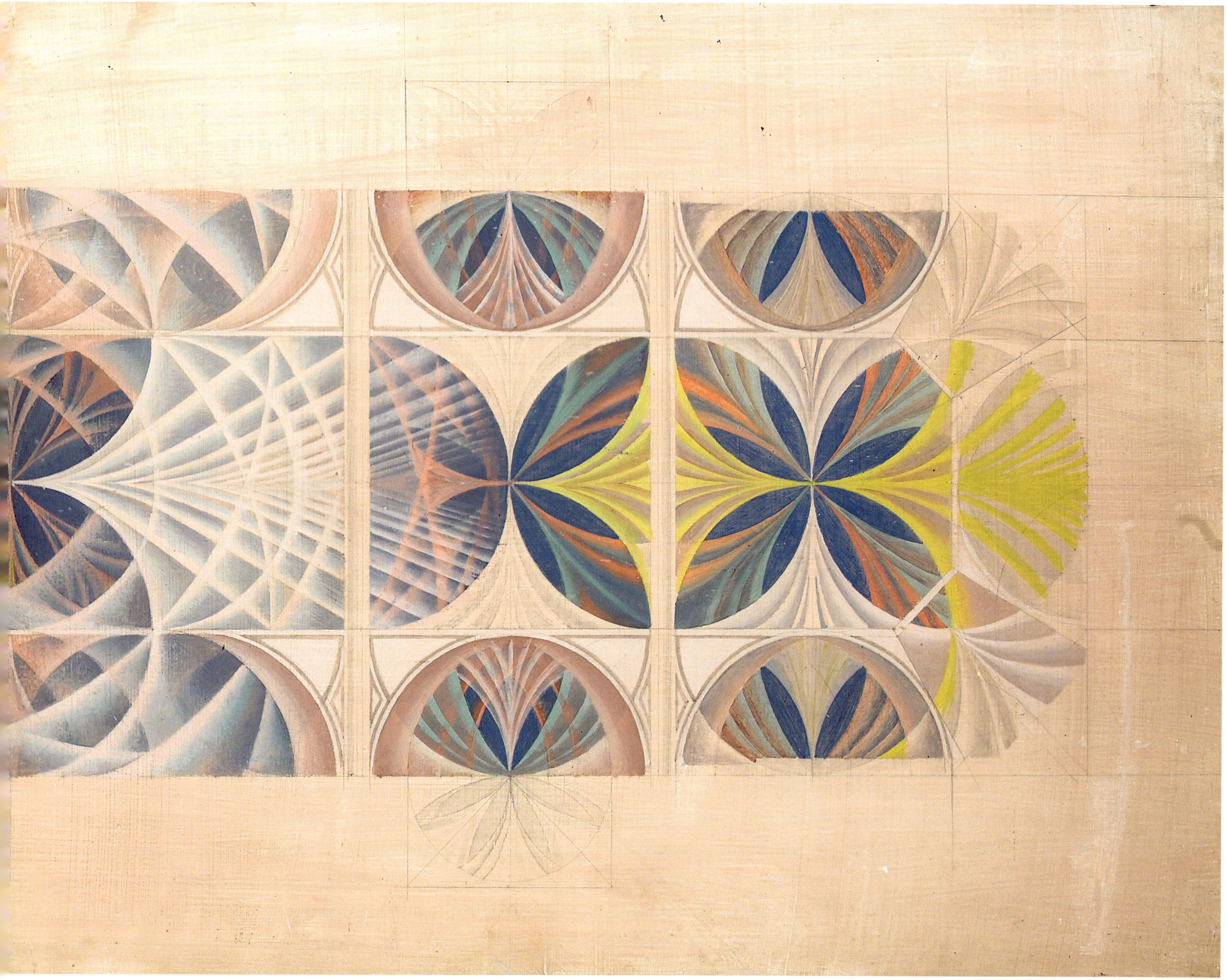

An account by W. B. Lowe records that, 'before the oil paint was applied the whole design was carried out in a monochrome watercolour. We were reluctant to cover this up because it looked enchanting. The problem with oil paint is its tendency to look heavy in a ceiling and its habit of reflecting light in an unpredictable way. To counter this the colours are very light in tone and the ridges that oil encourages were brushed out to form a matt finish....Tom maintained that it was difficult to draw angels in the twentieth century, and was comforted by the enduring qualities of geometry and light. The design, based on simple geometry, was visualised as overlapping webs of transparent light extending into and partly veiling the mysteries of space.'[18]

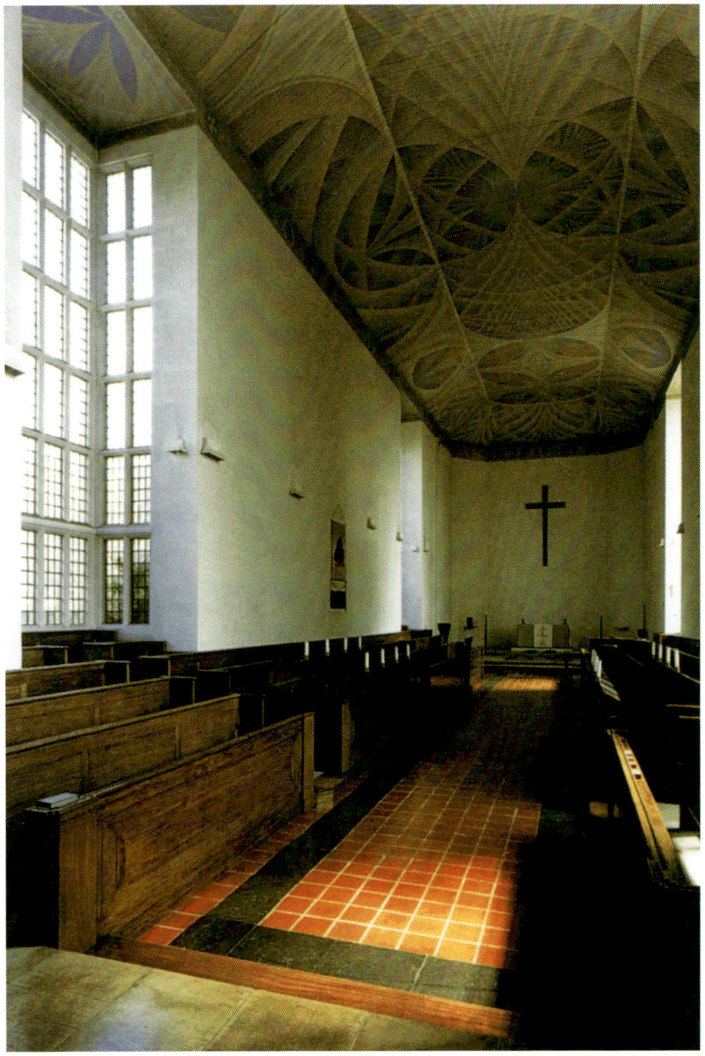

228
View of
Mary Harris Memorial
Chapel of Holy Trinity,
University of Exeter

Other commissions followed. In 1964 The Edwin Austin Abbey Trust requested two further murals for the University of London Students' Union. The first was executed *in situ*, in polyvinyl acetate, on a 8 x 20 ft. panel. Monnington's design for this contrasts with the florid *Scholar Gypsy* painted by Gilbert Spencer R.A. (1957), also commissioned by the Abbey Trust, on the floor below. Monnington's second mural, measuring 9 x 6 ft. in acrylic on linen, was not started until 1969 – the commission being delayed by his surprise election, in 1966, as President of the Royal Academy.[19] At the Academy most of Monnington's energies were consumed in trying to reverse the fortunes of an ailing institution facing financial ruin.[20] In addition to resolving the Academy's financial dilemmas Monnington can also be credited with persuading a largely sceptical British public to consider embracing – somewhat late in the day – the mainstream developments of twentieth-century art: 'surely what matters,' he declared, 'is not whether a work is abstract or representative, but whether it has merit...is this work distinguished or is it commonplace? Fresh and original or uninspired, derivative and dull? Is it modest or pretentious?'[21] Monnington never liked referring to his own paintings as abstracts but rather as geometric paintings which he considered were born out of the same preoccupations as those which had defined Cézanne's art.

Monnington's post-war art has yet to receive the attention that it merits. As President of the Royal Academy he is remembered as a significant administrator but little is made of the fact that he was the first president to exhibit abstract art. The Tate purchased his *Square Design* in 1967 – presumably as an acknowledgement of his

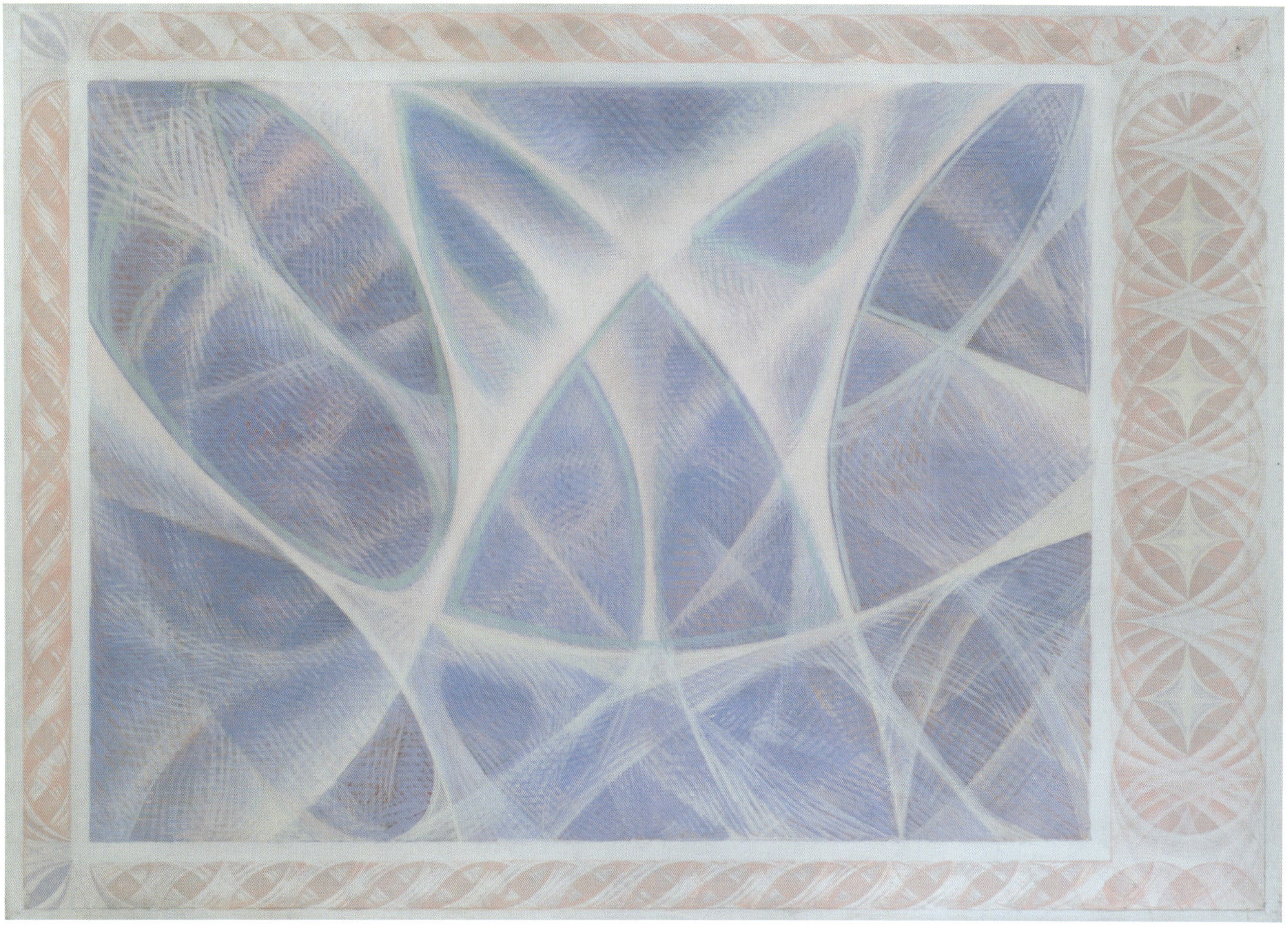

229
Clematis, c. 1960,
acrylic on board,
130 x 92 cm
(51 3⁄16 x 36 ¼ in.)

recent appointment as PRA – but there is no record of its ever having been shown in public.[22] Both of his murals for University of London Students' Union were removed within a short period of his death and are assumed to have been destroyed.[23]

It is curious that Monnington has been consistently written out of accounts of British Art in the second half of the twentieth century. His geometric paintings emerged at the same time, if not necessarily from the same context, as the Op Art movement. In common with artists such as Victor Vasarely (six years his junior) or Bridget Riley (30 years his junior) Monnington's painting shares a clarity of design which concentrates on the representation of space and depth. Indeed Terence Mullaly's withering remark that he could 'only recommend Monnington's designs to some linoleum manufacturer' might easily have been levelled at an entire generation of artists who had emerged out of Constructivism into the Op Art movement.[24] At the same time it is clear that Monnington fails to fit comfortably in any post-war box, nor was he part of any post-war movement. He might have understood the principles of Op Art but his paintings are far more intellectual.[25] Whilst he arrived at Abstraction some 20 years later than his contemporaries – Nicholson or Moore – his works from the 1950s onwards are not simply those of an ageing artist trying to catch up. On the contrary by engaging with an emerging vocabulary inspired by nuclear physics, biochemistry and aeronautics he was in many ways ahead of his time.[26]

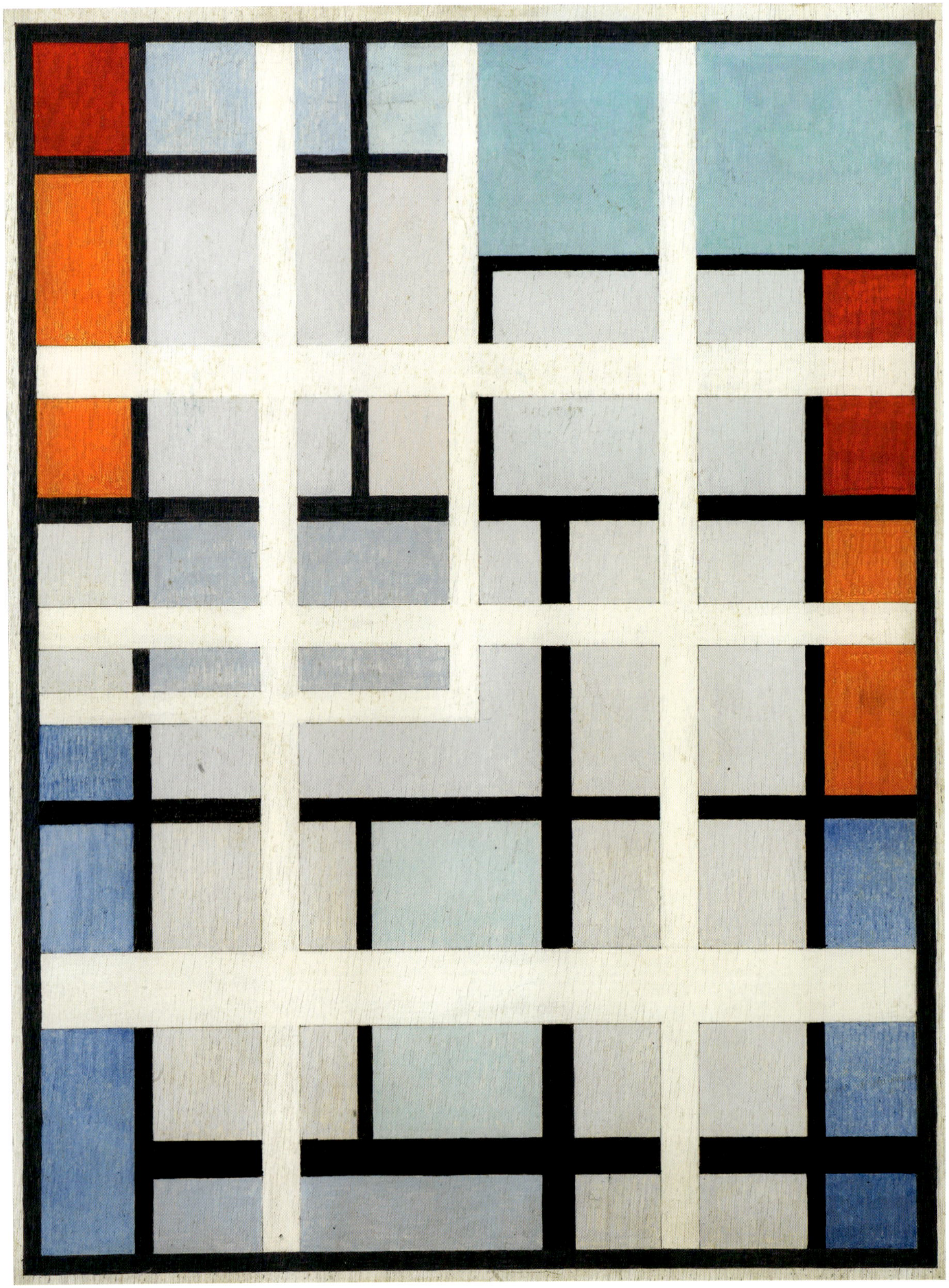

230
Design for Students' Union,
University of London, c. 1969,
acrylic on board,
43.2 × 33 cm (17 × 13 in.)

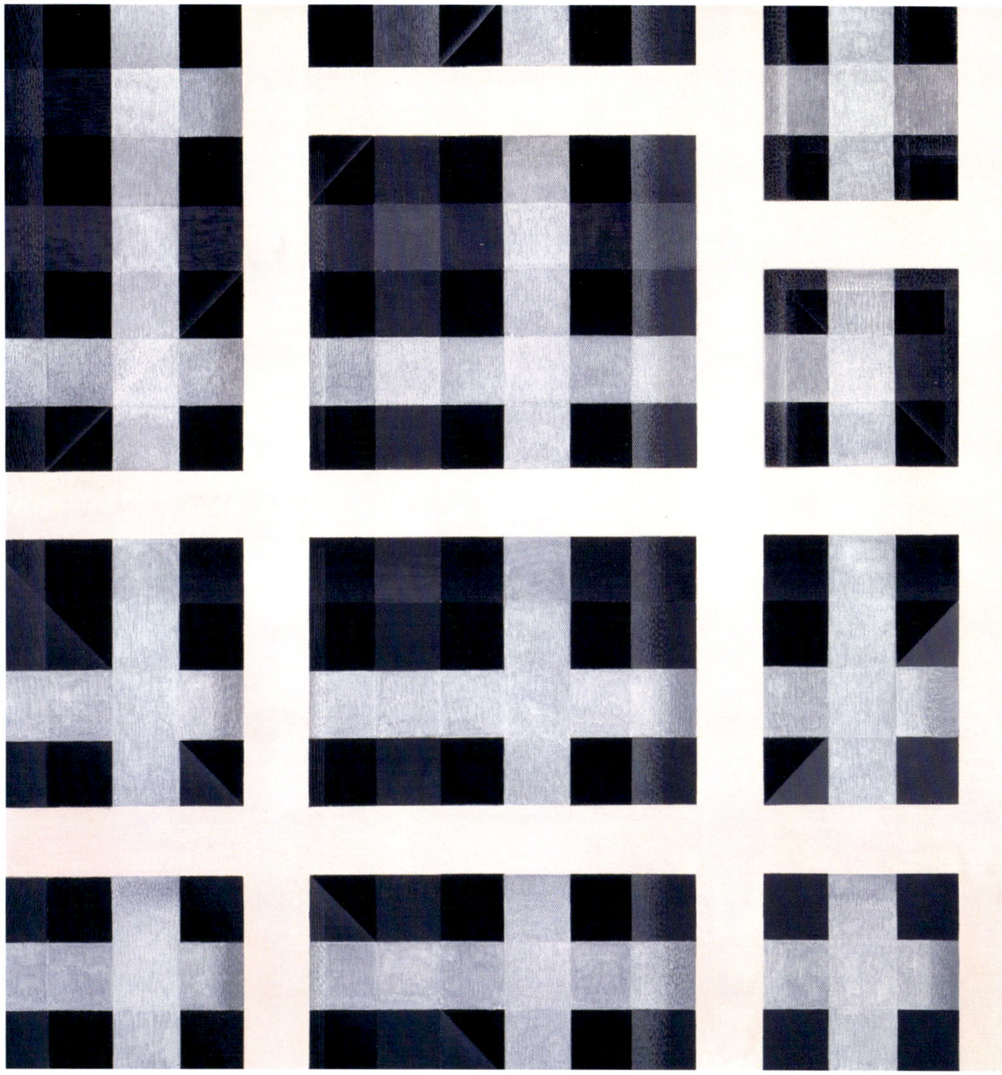

231
Square Design, 1966,
oil on canvas,
93 x 92 cm
(36 ¼ x 36 in.),

It is perhaps in the apparent anachronism of Monnington's working methods that his art can best be understood. Conceived through complex mathematical calculations and crafted through painstaking preparations in chalk and tempera Monnington saw no conflict in pursuing in the twentieth century methods and ideals to which Piero della Francesca would have been no stranger. Ultimately all that mattered was what Monnington termed 'honesty of purpose' – a quality which applies as well to his Tate *Allegory* (1924) as it does to his Tate *Square Design* (1976). The visual difference between the two is not as large as it at first appears. As Alan Powers notes, whilst Monnington's earlier subject paintings are 'extraordinarily abstract' and generalized in their narrative, the Bristol ceiling, 'the first indication of his new post-war direction, is, on the other hand, quite specific in its content.'[27]

'I have never liked what I have done enough to look at it' Monnington said with characteristic modesty when interviewed in the *Sunday Mirror* shortly after his election as PRA. Perhaps it is time for Monnington's work – and especially his post-war work – to be reconsidered.[28]

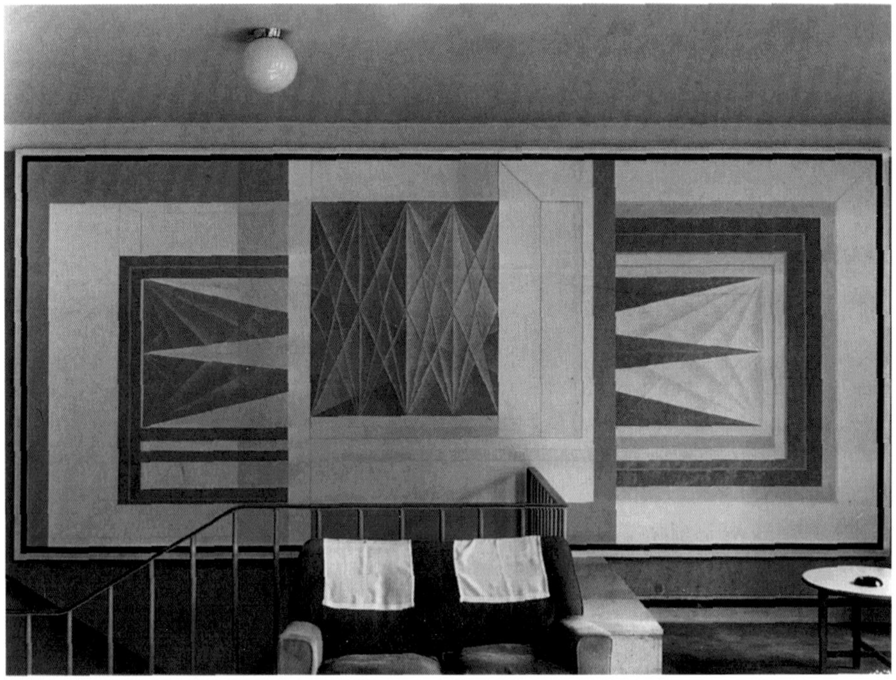

232 Monnington's University of London Students' Union Mural *in situ* c. 1964

ENDNOTES

1 Peyton Skipwith, quoted in *Thomas Monnington,* (exhibition catalogue), Paul Liss and The Fine Art Soceity, 1997, p.9.

2 Monnington was one of Tonks' favourite students. He enrolled at the Slade at the age of 15. He was awarded First Prize For Figure Painting in 1921 and First Prize For Head Drawing in 1922. In the same year Monnington was awarded The Rome Scholarship in Decorative Painting.

3 The reception of both murals, when unveiled, was largely unenthusiastic. Of the Bank of England murals Monnington confided to his brother: 'they certainly look shocking and I forgive any criticism,' (letter to Meredith Monnington, 6th May 1932).

4 In his *Supper at Emmaus*, 1931, for the Ormrod Chapel of St Peter's Parish Church, Bolton, 'the deliciously painted and very English landscape background' was singled out for praise and Monnington was deemed to be the only 'modern Religious painter,' who achieved 'the same note of sincerity' as Stanley Spencer ('N' reviewing Monnington's work in an unidentified newspaper cutting, collection of the author).

5 Crawford Papers, National Library of Scotland, 101/61, quoted in 'Thomas Monnington: Remarking a Picture of English Art', Alan Powers, p.13, published in *Thomas Monnington* by Paul Liss in association with The Fine Art Society, p.13.

6 *Thomas Monnington,* (1997), p.49.

7 Monnington had a life-long fascination with flight. He learnt to fly in the early 1930s and began working for the design team of the Directorate of Camouflage even before the war broke out, first at the Brooklands Race Track, and then at Leamington Spa. The Vickers Air Works – where Barnes Wallis worked – were situated in the middle of the Brooklands Race track, hence the priority for creating camouflage at this strategically sensitive area. Two drawings relating to Monnington's collaboration with Barnes Wallis are in the collection of the V&A (Department of Prints and Drawings).

8 *Thomas Monnington,* (1997), p.49.

9 Op. cit., p.21.

10 Monnington was deeply impressed by Sam Carter, Professor of Perspective at the Slade, who expounded upon Piero's contemplative approach to painting through the study of perspective.

11 *Drawings and Paintings by Sir Thomas Monnington P.R.A. 1902-1976*, Royal Academy of Arts, 1977.

12 Thomson had discovered the electron as a constituent of the structure of matter.

13 Monnington had been enthralled by the taut curves and economic cross-bracing of radio masks and later in radar equipment, (see *Radar Aerials and Type 70*, 1944, IWM).

14 *Thomas Monnington* (1997), p.21.

15 Only small quantities of paint could be mixed at a time: it soon lost its virtue, and began to smell evilly. Rapidity and continuity of work were essential; tempera dries within minutes, making it practically impossible to merge colour or to correct a mistake ('One dud stroke', Monnington had commented when painting *Allegory* thirty years earlier, might necessitate repainting a whole area). While they were painting, the artists camped out in an empty room in the Council House. The physical exertion was considerable, especially as Monnington was still teaching two days a week at the Slade.

16 *Thomas Monnington* (1997), p.22.

17 'Apart from all the problems of organization and design, Tom had an additional worry. He had to entrust the execution of his brilliant idea to others. His health at that time was not robust and he was discouraged from climbing ladders. Much of the paint was mixed by him – down below on trestle tables.' op. cit., p.23.

18 Alan Powers has noted that the design could be seen as a commentary on the statement of Proclus that 'Space is nothing other than the finest light'. Proclus, *Elements of Physics*, 1422. This would be entirely appropriate for a memorial to Harris's mother who was called Mary: a fitting stage set for her Ascension.

19 Monnington was elected PRA in 1966 when a run-off between him and the two favourites Fitton and Weight resulted in a surprise victory for Monnington who had only presented himself to make up numbers. The Academy was in a grave financial situation.

20 Monnington's period in office coincided with inflation and recurring financial problems for the Academy.

21 Interview in *The Christian Science Monitor* 29.5.67.

22 Records at Tate Britain going back to 1985 show that this painting has not been on public display for at least nearly 30 years.

23 The mural was completed and installed in the early 1970s but later removed from the Students' Union and is assumed to have been destroyed. The earlier mural has within the last three years suffered a similar fate. The Gilbert Spencer mural has fared only slightly better – it has remained *in situ*, but covered over.

24 'The President is indeed a charming man but his work is an embarrassment. I can only recommend it to some linoleum manufacturer,' Terence Mullaly, reviewing the Royal Academy Summer Show (*Daily Telegraph*, April 28, 1967).

25 When the Tate purchased Monnington's *Square Design* (1967) he spoke of his abstract paintings as 'direct descendants from my ceiling painting in the Council House, Bristol, which was my first departure from purely representational painting. Since then I have been increasingly interested in the subdivisions of surface areas contained in equilateral rectangles (squares) and rectangles derived from square roots. These two-dimensional mathematical relationships suggest to me dimensions in depth, and provide a discipline which at the present time I find as necessary and interesting as that imposed previously in representational painting... You can cut out the blurb if you wish, but I was trying for my own edification to put into words what I think I have been trying to do in the last ten years'. (letter of June 12, 1968).

26 Alan Powers points out: 'Monnington came to abstraction by his own path via Quattrocento Italian painting and science, and he came to it relatively late. Although undoubtedly aware of the work of Ben Nicholson and others during the 1930s, he did not share their particular intellectual pursuits. It was only in the post-war years – after a prolonged period of artistic importance – that he was stimulated again; this time by discussions with Sam Carter, Professor of Perspective at the Slade and the challenge of the Bristol ceiling.' Gordon House recalled that 'for Monnington the Golden Mean of Piero della Francesca reconsidered with the experience of the twentieth century had bought him to the fringe of modernity. He spoke to me of the "magic section" and had obviously taken in Ghika's Dynamic Symmetry without missing along the way Mondrian's Broadway Boogie Woogie', letter to Paul Liss, cited Skipwith p.9.

27 *Thomas Monnington,* (1997), p.11.

28 *Sunday Mirror*, April 16, 1967.

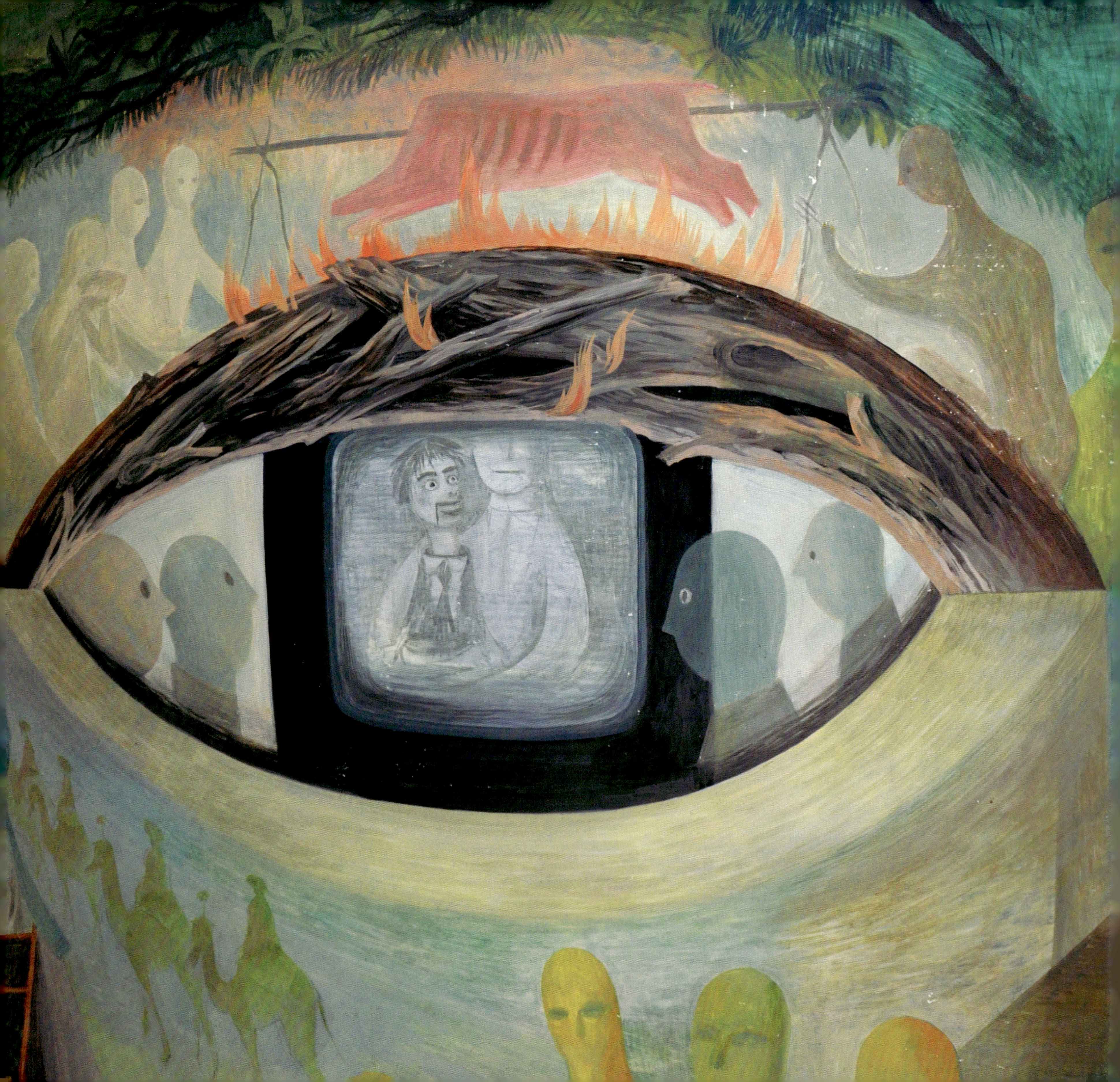

The Murals of Barbara Jones

Ruth Artmonsky

233
Mural based on the theme 'Man at Work – a century of technical and social progress' (detail)

Barbara Jones was reluctant to be pigeonholed, to be seen as a specialist. In her forthright manner she declared that specialization was 'death to creativity' and that artists should continually be moving on 'to the next idea, or etching or beer mat'. So although she can validly be described as a mural artist in that she produced a considerable number of 'murals' and frequently showed with the Society of Mural Painters, she might equally be seen to be a graphic artist, extremely active in the Society of Industrial Artists and Designers, a water colourist (she produced prolifically for the Recording Britain scheme), a social historian for her evangelism on behalf of the 'popular' arts, or, for that matter, an architectural historian for her gazetteering of 'follies'.

However, it was while she was at the Royal College of Art that she fell in love with mural painting. She had felt considerable constraint in her first year at the College, in the mid-1930s, trying to tackle the painstaking requirements of etching, suited neither to her talents nor her personality. Transferring to the Department of Mural Decoration she described herself as feeling immediately at home. It has been said of her that spontaneity was her style rather than laborious effort and she found that working with the expanse of large canvases rather than with small plates gave her the freedom of expression she needed.

Her first two commissions, on leaving college in 1937, were for murals, for a nursery in a private house, and for decorations for the walls of a hotel restaurant. These were quite modest career beginnings but, nevertheless, her nursery piece was of a sufficient standard to be included in the Tate Gallery Exhibition 'Mural Painting in Great Britain 1919-1939'; and her vignettes for the Jules Hotel in Jermyn Street received an accolade from *The Times* [December 12, 1939]:

> Lively in manner, they have an effect of ease which accords well with the subjects and they set an example that might well be followed by other places of entertainment. They take the solemnity out of the mural.

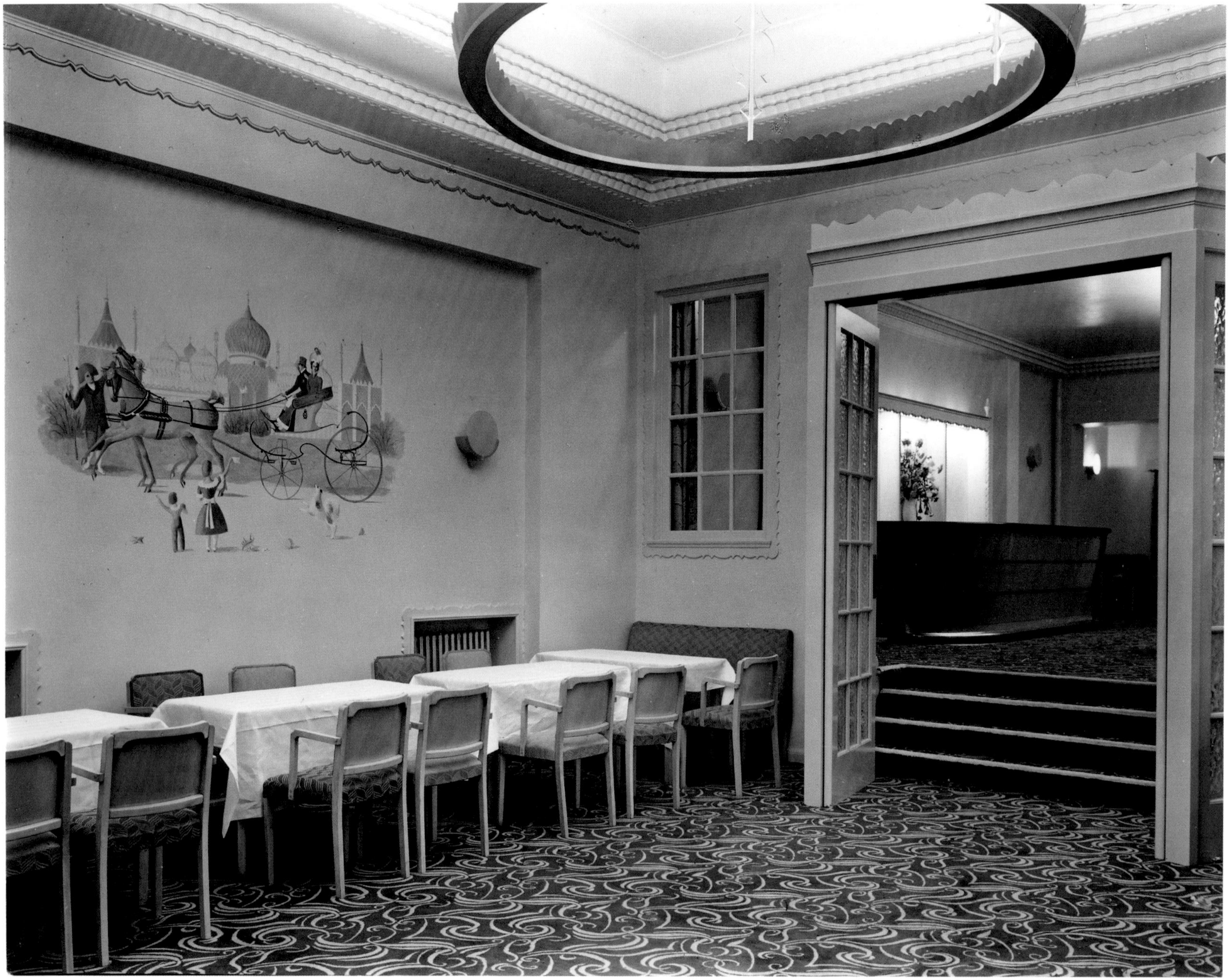

234 Murals painted for the Jules Hotel, Jermyn Street, London, 1939-1943. Referred to in *The Times* in 1939, the work was repainted after bombing in 1943.

Although these murals had a Bawdenesque, whimsical lightness to them, Jones was yet to develop her own brand of humour, which was to be altogether more sharp and dark, veering at times to the grotesque. Early on she declared that as far as she was concerned the allegoric men and women, traditional mural figures were 'out' – 'all those boring creatures are dead now and we can safely forget them.' A hint of what was later to be characteristic of her quirky work was shown in her numerous topographical watercolour paintings for the wartime 'Recording Britain' scheme, for which artists were left relatively free to choose which subjects they would; Patrick White referred to Jones's choice as representing England as full of 'follies, eccentric ornamentation and Gothic neglect'.

Barbara Jones's post-war mural works fall roughly into three phases of decreasing ephemerality – her exhibition work largely carried out with James Gardner, her ships' murals for Colin Anderson of the Orient Line, and her work for 'solid' structures both public and commercial buildings along with some private houses.

From the late '40s to the early '50s Britain was focused on reconstruction and there was a plethora of exhibitions, trade shows and fairs often frantically assembled with the aim of revitalizing exports, even when merchandising was still scarce and wartime restrictions on materials still in place. The haste with which the 'Britain Can make It' exhibition was mounted by the newly established Council of Industrial Design (1946) is well documented. Jones was given about two months to design and construct a series of panels illustrating the old rhyme 'Monday's Child'. A note on an archived photograph of her work describes it as 'striking'.

Further exhibitions with Gardner followed – the Council of Industrial Design 'Design Fair' (1948) and its Scottish Committee's 'Enterprise Scotland' the previous year. At about the same time she received a commission to provide ten panels for Shell-Mex for an agricultural show (1948), illustrating agricultural machinery, presumably those using Shell products – ploughing, harvesting, and so on – at different times of the year. Jones did not shy away from what would have been considered a subject suited to a male designer, and her efforts were so admired that Shell continued to use the panels at a number of later shows.

By the time the Festival of Britain was being planned Jones had built a sufficient reputation as a muralist to have her name put forward, along with the likes of Hans Feibusch, Hans Tisdall and Edward Bawden, as falling into a Class I category – 'Very Good People' as assessed against the criteria of economic work, colour, and a gay and light approach. Besides her contribution to the Battersea site 'fairground' Jones supplied murals on the South Bank for *The Coastline of Britain* display and for the Television Pavilion. In her account of her work for the Festival she illustrates her focused planning and her high energy level which continued to enable her, throughout her career, to keep a number of balls in the air at the same time:

> But I did set up one of those charts of times and jobs that are now called critical path analysis, below the South Bank jobs came various capers at Battersea Gardens, an exhibition at the Whitechapel Art Gallery called 'Black Eyes and Lemonade', its poster and catalogue, and an illustrated book on the same theme to be published at the same time.

The second phase of Jones's mural output spans the late '40s into the middle '50s, when she worked on a number of murals for Colin Anderson's post-war cruising ships for the Orient Line. Although his own personal taste inclined to Art Nouveau, for his ships his preference was along Bauhaus lines – 'fitness for purpose' – clean, unornamented modernism. Jones's contributions were anything but this and can only be described as 'wayward'. Their subject matter was almost entirely drawn from 'popular' art ephemera which by now had become an obsession with her. The incongruity of her use of a government booklet of 1894 entitled *Inspiration in Dr. Sylvester's Method* – showing a man in a boat receiving artificial respiration – seems neither to have occurred to her nor to Anderson, neither for its clash with its modernist surroundings, nor as an unsuitable stimulus for jaded passengers' conversations whilst they ate. She provided similar murals, derived from Victorian and Edwardian ephemera, for four ships in all – SS *Orcades* (1948-9), SS *Oronsay* (1952), SS *Orsova* (1954) and SS *Oriana* (1960).

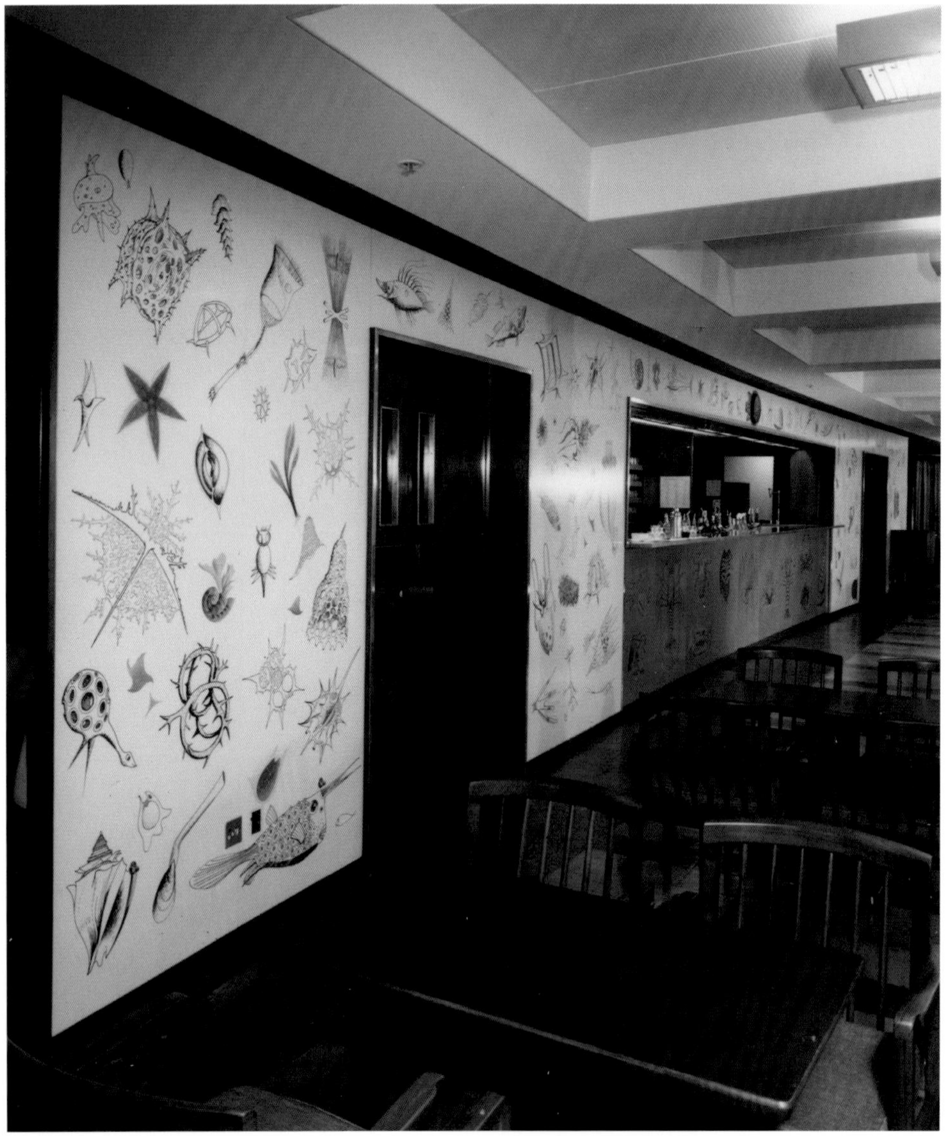

235
Ocean Life, 1960,
The Ocean Bar of the SS *Oriana*, the last of the Orient Steam Navigation Company's ocean liners

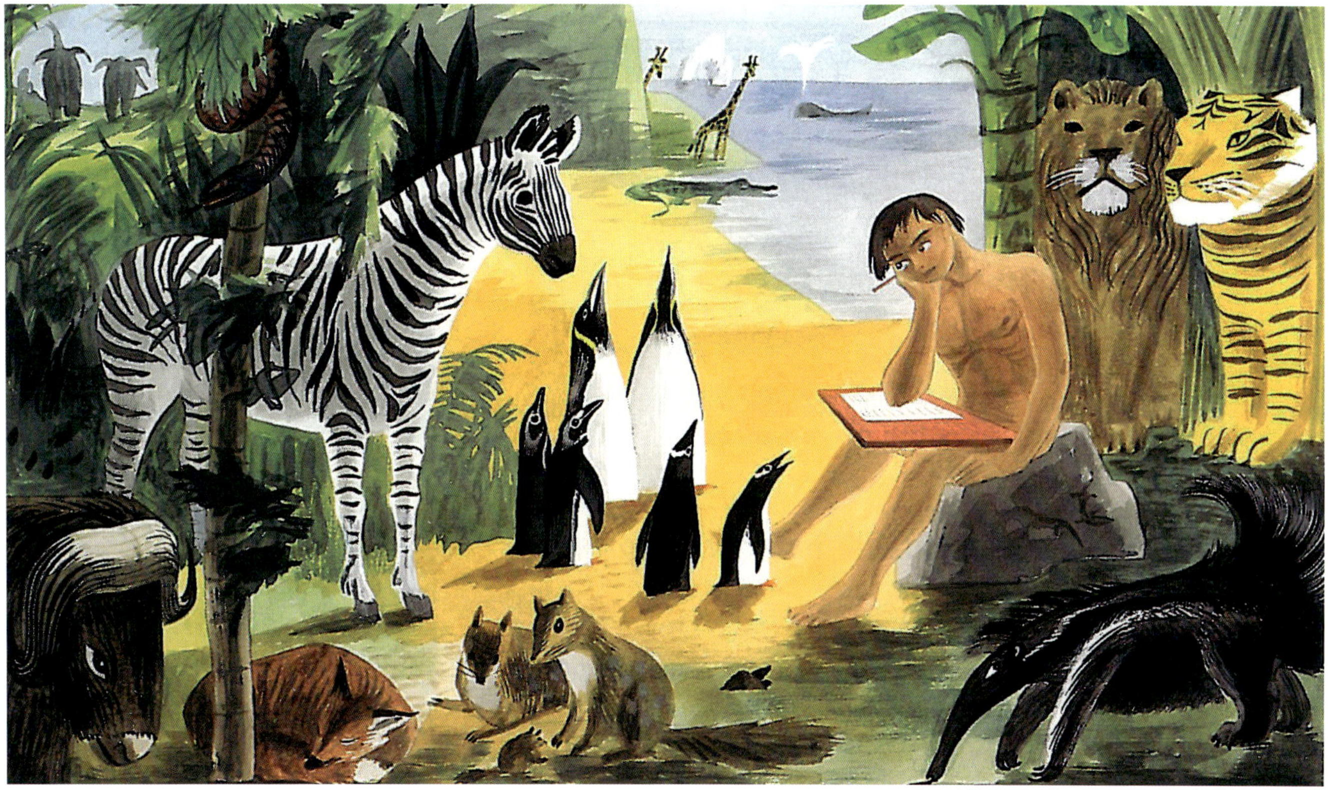

236
Adam Naming the Animals,
Sketch for the mural for Yew Lane School, Sheffield, 1959

The third phase continued to carry Jones's quirky subject matter but now for altogether more solid structures including Crown Buildings in Uxbridge, department store restaurants in Bristol and London, and schools in Shropshire and Sheffield. What children in Sheffield made of her curiously static animals, some with quite 'knowing' looks, placed awkwardly around a young Adam, pondering what names to give, is not recorded; but the worthy governors of the school are known to have been alarmed at the cost of the piece and were later to have it walled-up for its 'protection' when some rebuilding was taking place. It was eventually demolished.

For three of her later murals Jones was to work with one of her teaching colleagues at Hornsey School of Art – Richard Parkinson, the ceramicist. For two of these she was certainly out of her 'comfort zone' – the Cheshire County Police Headquarters (1964) and Portcullis House for the Customs & Excise in Southend (1966) as for these the brief was for abstracts, which allowed Barbara little scope for her preoccupations. The results were consequently unimpressive, although she managed to introduce some glitzy jeweller's enamels in her representation of road intersections in the police headquarters, presumably desperately straining for some personal touch.

Jones was back on home ground tackling a commission for a new Cake House in St James's Park for her brief was broad – the history of the park – which allowed her to draw on her, by now, extensive knowledge of 'popular' art; she chose to include images of cows being milked, firework displays and the park's menagerie. The task was Herculean – to cover a space 40ft by 10ft – and she called upon Tony Raymond, one of her Hornsey students, to help her. They took some two months to complete it, working on cartridge paper with blue and platinum lithographic chalks which Richard Parkinson then transferred on to tiles.

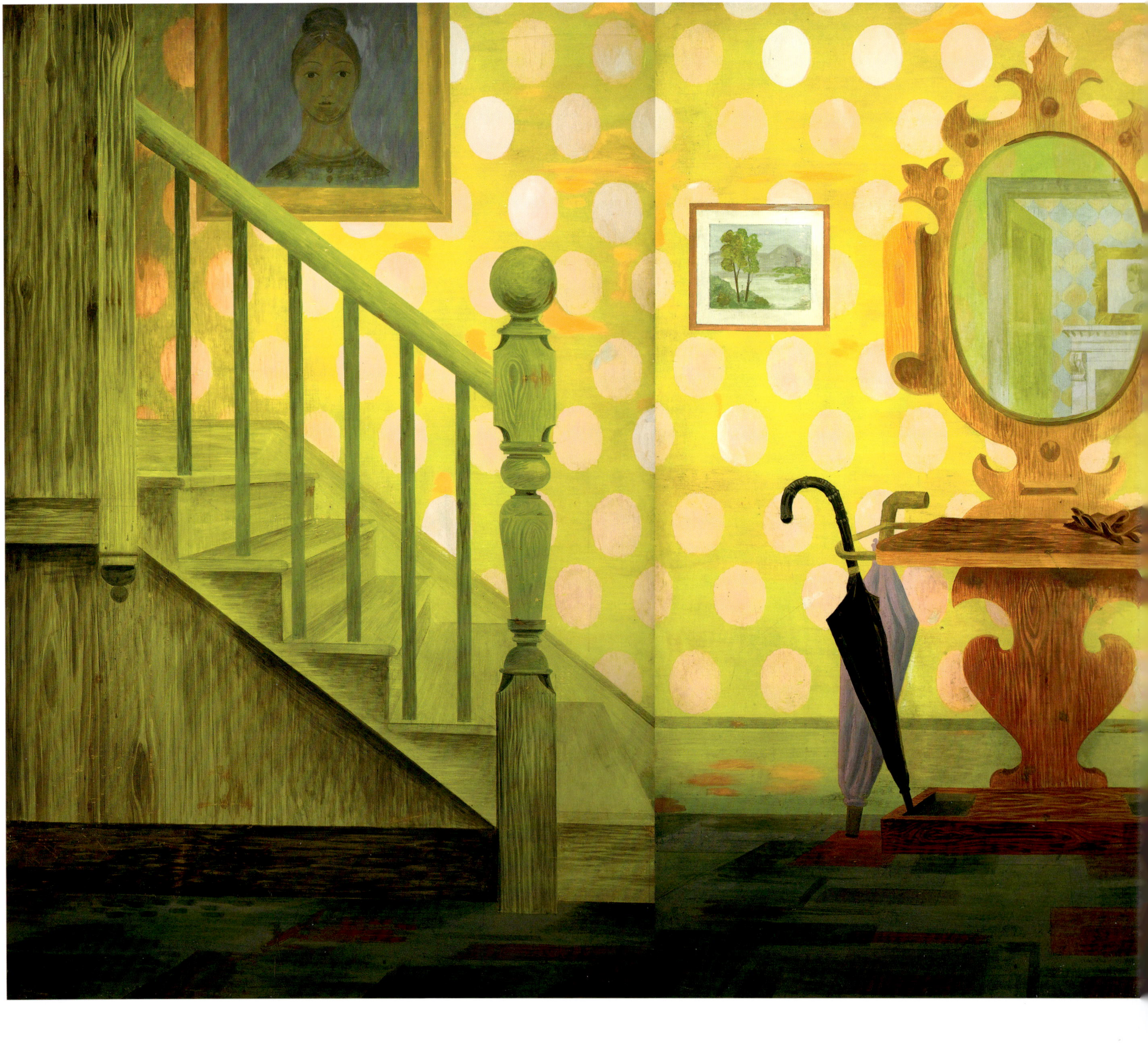

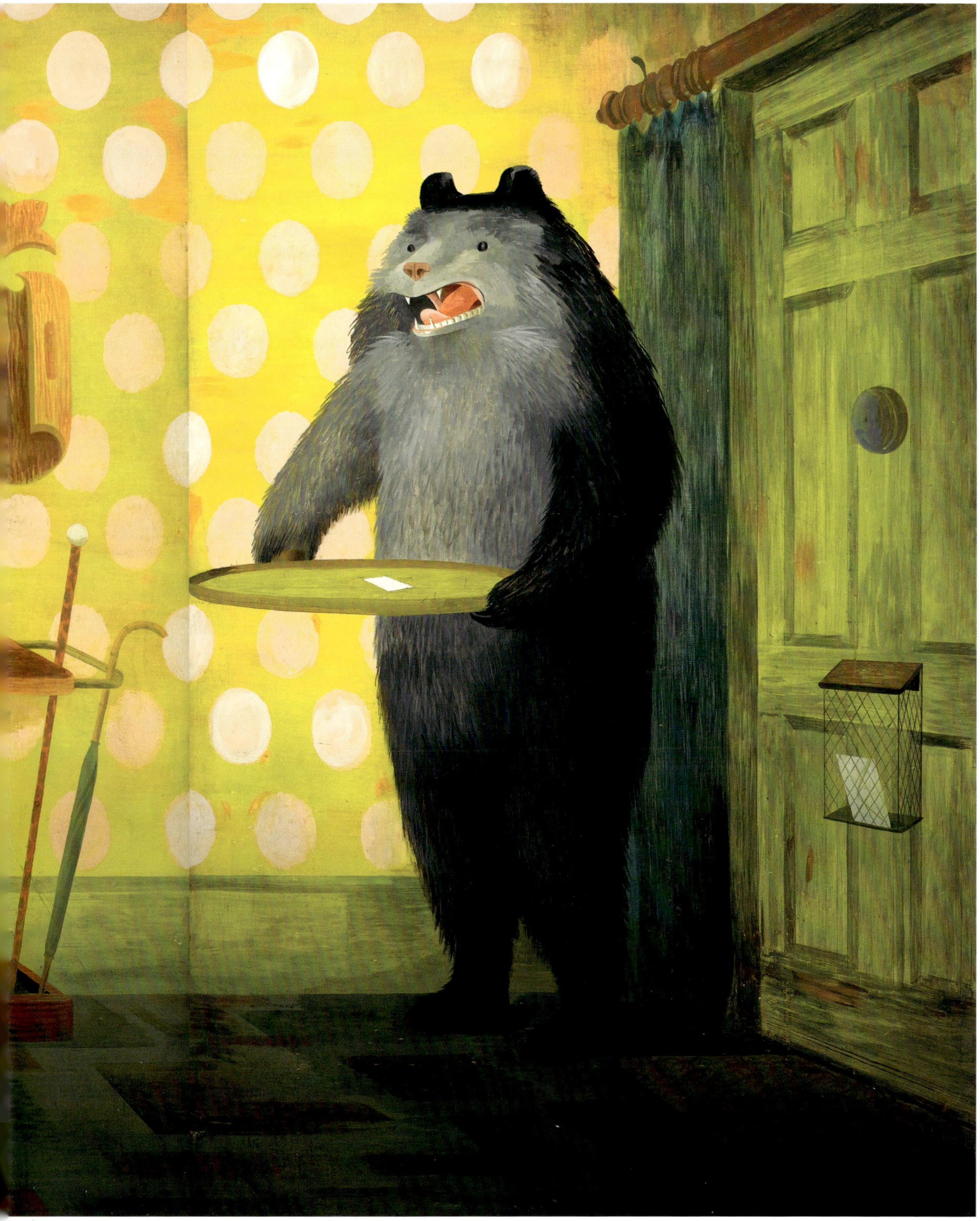

237
Out in the Hall, 1960,
Oil and wax, three panels, 183 x 365.8 cm (72 x 144 in.)

In *Out in the Hall* Jones showed her creative confidence in caricaturing an Edwardian house entrance hall, along with compulsory hatstand and family portrait; yet dominating the scene is a large stuffed bear carrying a tray! The whole image was built up over three panels, some 12ft in length, and much resembles the hallway to Barbara's own house, filled as it was with macabre miscellanea.

Provenance: The Artist's Studio
Exhibited: Victoria & Albert Museum,
'Mural Art Today', 1962, no. 18.

The two most impressive murals Barbara Jones produced were of gigantic heads, the first commissioned by the Central Office of Information for an International Labour Office exhibition in Turin celebrating the centenary of the Italian State (1961), the other for Philips Research Laboratory in Eindhoven (1966). These were not only striking because of their size but because of the way Jones chose to interpret her briefs. The Philips' mural, entitled *Man and his Senses*, is a relatively straightforward strong image, with enlarged fingertips, mouth, nose, eyes and ears filled with patterned neurons and synapses, only weakened by the somewhat sentimental placing of a rose outside the head. The Turin head is altogether more problematic carrying numerous ghostly figures not easily discerned at a distance. The theme was 'Man at Work – a century of technical and social progress' with which Barbara seems to have been at her most capricious. A very close inspection shows that at least some of the figures have at least a tenuous connection to the title – a board meeting, some agricultural scenes, coal miners with lamps and canaries, and, in the right ear of the head, a dentist with his patient! However, these few scenes are completely overwhelmed by a plethora of Jones's preferred subjects – a coffin, two couples embracing, a skeleton, a tiger atop a crocodile, and, her very favourite – an owl.

It is not surprising then that Barbara declared the Turin head the work of which she was most proud, and she went to considerable lengths and expense to buy it back and to return it to her studio, where it remains, her only extant mural of any note. The work epitomizes her approach to mural commissions, which can only be described as that of a maverick. She was sufficiently competent, charming and astute to attract commissions, and to know when, and how far, to compromise with briefs, but would seize any possibility to slip in her own quirky obsessions.

She has occasionally been described as a surrealist, but Jones ploughed her own furrow. She saw herself as essentially a 'jobbing' artist with little interest in 'fine' art. She aligned herself to no school or group of painters, was not a visitor to art exhibitions, did not mix socially with painters, and had barely any concern for such wider considerations as to what art was all about. When she made use of an assortment of objects for her murals, they can more aptly be described as 'assembled', sometimes without a strong overall design, and not as given any unconscious, symbolic or analytic meaning as with surrealistic works; their only linkage seems to be that the artist liked them …

Whatever assessment is made of Barbara Jones as a mural artist, her standing with her contemporaries was such that she was regularly included in the Society of Mural Artists exhibitions; and she was accepted as having proved herself as a muralist of a 'very high order' by the Edwin Austin Abbey Memorial Trust Fund for Mural Painting in Great Britain who were known to embrace only the best.

238
Mural based on the theme 'Man at Work – a century of technical and social progress' for the International Labour Exhibition, Central Office of Information, Turin, Italy, 1961, two panels, oil on canvas, 365.8 x 365.8 cm (144 x 144 in.)

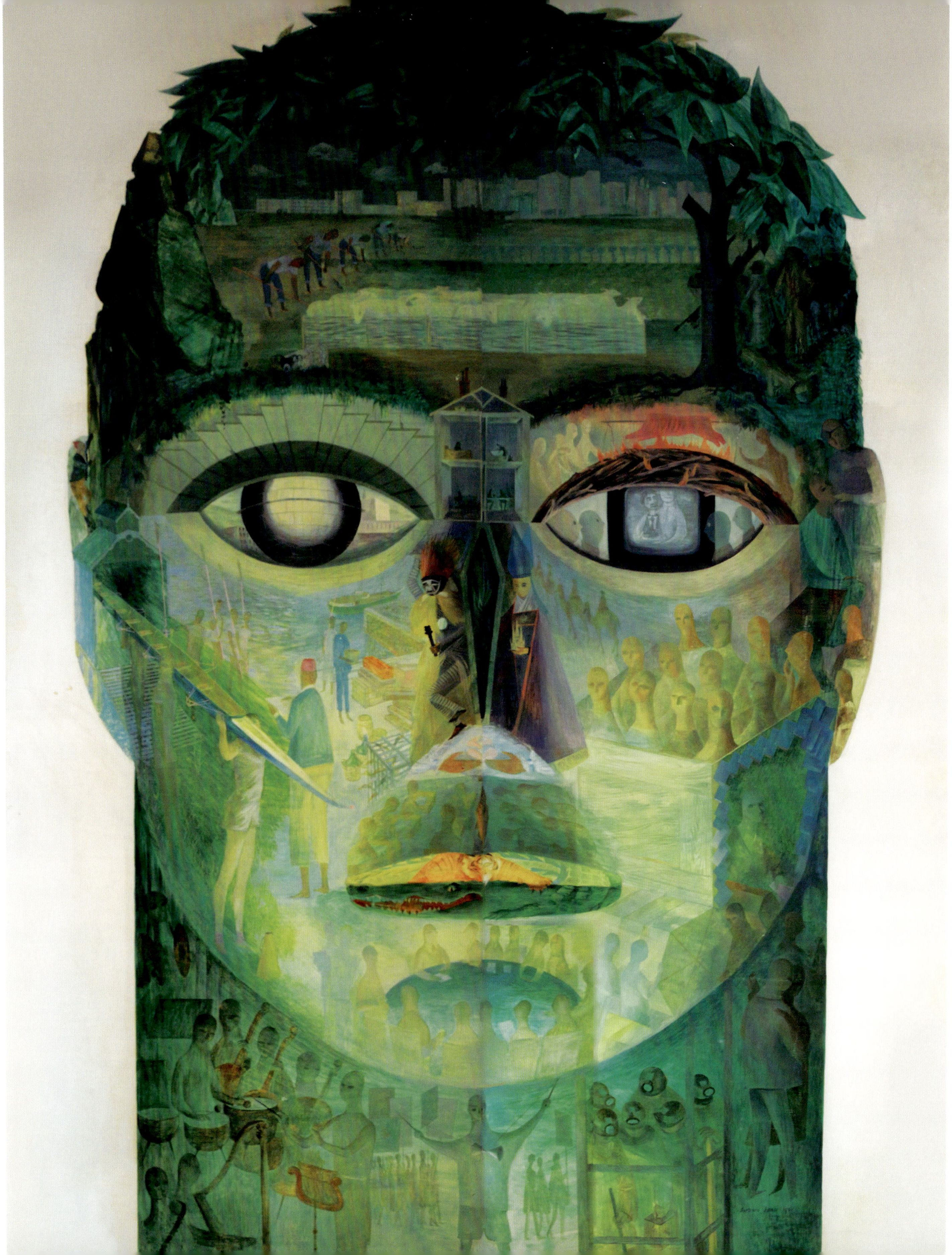

MURALS BY BARBARA JONES

1938 – Nursery, 20 Hill Street, London

1943 – Jules Hotel, London

1947 – *Monday's Child* (triptych). 'Britain can make it' exhibition
Royal Easter Show, Sydney, Australia
Enterprise Scotland exhibition

1948 – Council of Industrial Design fair
Shell-Mex Agricultural exhibition

1948-1949 – SS *Orcades*

1950 – First exhibition of the Society of Mural Painter

1951 – Festival of Britain. (Section Designer for the 'Seaside' section)
Shell-Mex and BP exhibition

1952 – SS *Oronsay*

1954 – SS *Orsova*

1956 – Crown Building, Uxbridge
Messrs. Lewis Restaurant, Bristol, department store ('The Bristol Traders')

1957 – St Martin's School, Shropshire

1958 – Orchard Restaurant, Selfridge's, London

1959 – *Adam Naming the Animals,* Yew Lane [now Yewlands], Sheffield

1960 – Exhibition of The Society of Mural Painters (*Out in the Hall* and part of the SS *Oriana* mural), V & A
SS *Oriana*

1960-1961 – Diorama painted on glass for East Pakistan display, Commonwealth Institute

1961 – Mural symbolising the social sciences (location unknown)
Mural based on the theme 'Man at Work – a century of technical and social progress' for the International Labour Exhibition, Central Office of Information, Turin, Italy

1962 – Gothic gazebo, Marston Hall, Lincolnshire

1963 – Murals for Sir Harry Oppenheimer's house, The Bishop's Avenue, London

1966 – Design for the entrance hall of Portcullis House, Southend, for the Customs and Excise

1971? – *Man and his Senses,* mural for Philips, Eindhoven, The Netherlands

197-? – Mural for Cheshire County Police headquarters (possibly illustrating tramways in Chester)

197-? – Mosaic mural for the new Cake House, St James's Park, London

Barbara Jones (1912-1978)

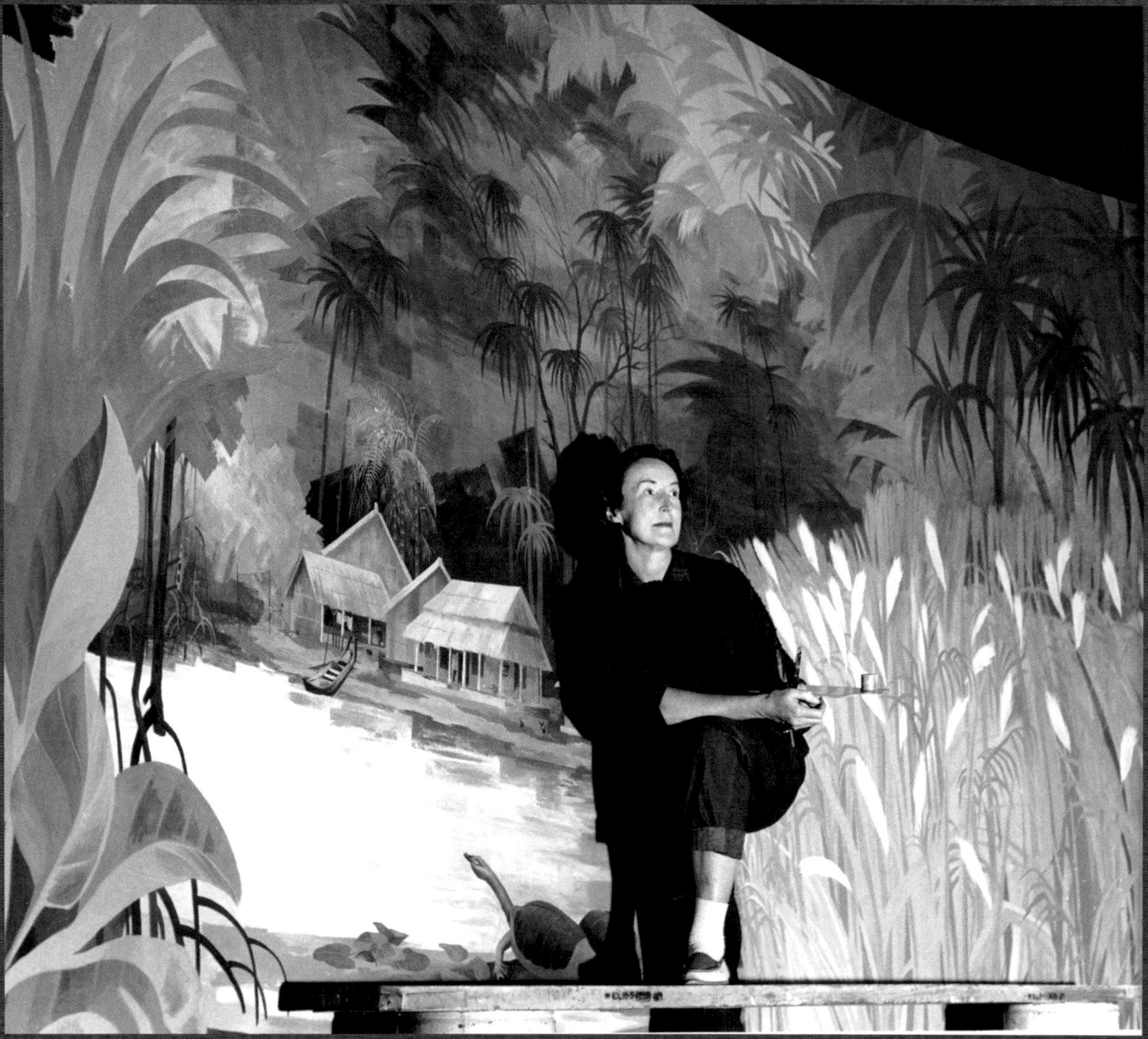

239 Barbara Jones at work on one of her murals

BARBARA JONES. Painter, designer, illustrator and author, born in Croydon, Surrey. First studied art at her local art school under Isabel Wrightson, 1931-33, before gaining a scholarship to the RCA, 1933-36, where she studied under Ravilious, Bawden and Charles Mahoney, in the mural painting school. Distinctive landscape painter and one of the strongest contributors to the World War II Pilgrim Trust Recording Britain project. Wrote and illustrated books on design history, dealing with subjects such as Grottoes and Follies, The Isle of Wight, and The Unsophisticated Arts. In 1951 was responsible for the Whitechapel Gallery exhibition 'Black Eyes and Lemonade', involved in the Festival of Britain, and produced her seminal book *The Unsophisticated Arts*. A retrospective exhibition was held at Katharine House Gallery, Marlborough, in 2000.

LIST OF ILLUSTRATIONS

42 Eric Ravillious, *Day*, Midland Hotel, Morecambe, Lancashire, 1933, (destroyed c. 1935), courtesy of the RIBA Library Photographs Collection
43 Eliot Hodgkin, mural for Geoffrey Jellicoe's Caveman Restaurant in Cheddar Gorge, 1934-35, 'Mural Decoration', *The Artist*, August 1935, p.192
44 Eric Gill and Denis Tegetmeier, *Neptune*, painted ceiling relief, Midland Hotel, Morecambe, Lancashire, c. 1933, photograph: Ian Thompson, Friends of the Midland Hotel
45 Eric Fraser, studies for murals for 'Fitter Britain' display, Empire Exhibition, Glasgow, 1938, gouache on card, approx. each 20 x 30 cm (8 x 12 in.), courtesy of the Artist's Estate, provenance the artist's son, until 1997, Laporte Corporate Art collection until 2003, private collection since 2004
46 Edward Wadsworth, study for mural at De La Warr Pavilion, Bexhill-on-Sea, 1935, 58.4 x 78.7 cm (23 x 31 in.), © The Estate of Edward Wadsworth. All rights reserved, DACS 2012
47 John Hutton, mural for the Sea and Ships Pavilion, Festival of Britain, 1951, *Penrose Annual*, 1952
48 John Cecil Stephenson painting the fluorescent mural for the Festival of Britain, April 5, 1951, courtesy of the Artist's Estate
49 John Cecil Stephenson, mural for British Pavilion at the Brussels Exhibition, 1958, courtesy of the Artist's Estate
50 Peter Yates, mural at Bevin Court Flats, Finsbury, 1953, photograph: Alan Powers
51 John Piper, panels for North Thames Gas Board, Fulham, (now Piper Building), 1963, photograph: Chris Gascoyne, courtesy of Liftschutz Davidson Sandilands
52 Victor Pasmore, murals in Rates Hall, Newcastle Civic Centre, 1968, photograph: courtesy of Elain Harwood
53 Victor Pasmore, Apollo Pavilion, Peterlee, County Durham, 1969, photograph: courtesy of Elain Harwood
54 Frank Brangwyn, British Empire panels as they would have looked in place, oil and tempera on canvas, total painted surface: 300 m^2 (3000 sq. ft.), ten panels measuring 365 x 365 cm (12 x 12ft.) and six panels measuring 610 x 396 cm (20 x 13 ft.), courtesy of Libby Horner
55 Frank Brangwyn, Casa Cuseni, Taormina, Italy, 1909-10, photograph: Charles Mapleston
56 Daphne Pollen, murals from the Church of All Hallows, Poplar, 1923-32 (destroyed by bombing), courtesy of Louis Jebb
57 Mary Adshead, altarpiece from St Christopher, Withington, 1931-35, (in original setting), source: Mary Adshead catalogue, © The Estate of Mary Adshead
58 Duncan Grant and Vanessa Bell, Berwick Church, Sussex, photograph: Alan Powers
59 Carel Weight, *Christ and the People,* Manchester Cathedral, 1963, photograph courtesy of Manchester Cathedral
60 Fyffe Christie, *Christ Feeding the People*, mural for the café set up in Glasgow by the Iona Community, signed and dated, oil on board, eight panels : 243.8 x 975.2 cm (96 x 384 in.), courtesy of Eleanor Christie-Chatterley, private collection
61 John Piper, *Landscape of the Two Seasons,* Princess Room, SS *Oriana*, 1959 (period colour photo), © P&O Heritage collection, courtesy Maritime Local Collections, Southampton City Council (original now on loan to Museum of the River and Rowing, Henley-on-Thames)
62 Mary Adshead, study for mural for tea room, Luton Hoo, Bedfordshire, c.1949, signed, gouache over pencil on card, 27 x 26 cm (10 ½ x 10 ⅜ in.), private collection
63 Edward Bawden, mural for International Building Club, London, 1939 (destroyed), *The Studio*, November 1943, p.141
64a Kenneth Rowntree, study for mural in British Restaurant, Acton, Middlesex, 1943 (destroyed), courtesy of Neil Jennings, All works by Kenneth Rowntree © Sasha Devas
64b Wartime booklet with photograph of Rowntree mural *in situ*, courtesy of Neil Jennings
65 William Nicholson, painting on glass for Edward Knoblock, Beach House, Worthing, early 1920s, © *Country Life*
66 A.K. Lawrence, *The Altruists,* British Pavilion, 1925 Paris Exhibition (first exhibited at British Empire Exhibition, Wembley, 1924, mural lost), *A Report on the Present Position and Tendencies of the Industrial Arts as indicated at the International Exhibition of Modern Decorative and Industrial Arts, Paris 1925*, London, Department of Overseas Trade, 1926
67 Jean Dupas, *Les Perruches,* panel installed in the suite of the Hôtel d'un Collectioneur, Paris, 1925
68 Glyn Philpot, *Oedipus and the Sphinx*, Drawing Room, Mulberry House, Westminster, 1931. © *Country Life*
69 John Armstrong, Dining Room for Sir Geoffrey Fry, Portman Square, 1920s (destroyed), Derek Patmore, 'Colour Schemes and Modern Furnishing', *The Studio*, 1945
70 John Armstrong, *The Fantastic Park*, study for murals for Royal Marsden Hospital in Sutton, Surrey, 1961, gouache on paper, 25.5 x 34 cm (10 x 13 ⅜ in.), private collection
71 Duncan Grant and Vanessa Bell, Music Room, gallery installation for Alex, Reid & Lefevre, 1932, Derek Patmore, 'Colour Schemes and Modern Furnishing', *The Studio*, 1945
72 Felix Kelly, mural on board SS *Windsor Castle*, 1959-60, courtesy of Donald Bassett
73 Edward Bawden, mural for Blackwell's Bookshop, Oxford, 1973, (*in situ* 2012), photograph: Rod Dorling
74 Evelyn Dunbar, left to right: *The Butterfly, the Snail and the Bee, The Cock and the Jewel, The Crow and the Pitcher,* murals at Brockley School (now Prendergast School, Lewisham), c. 1932-36, (*in situ* 2012), with kind permission of Prendergast – Hilly Fields College, photograph: Nigel Green
75 Brian Thomas, ceiling for Templewood, Northrepps, Norfolk, 1964
76 Winifred Knights, cartoon for *The Deluge*, c. 1920, pencil on tracing paper, 152.9 x 183.5 cm (60 ⅛ x 72 ¼ in.), private collection
77 Thomas Monnington, study for *Winter*, c. 1922, signed and dated, pencil and gouache on paper, squared, 21 x 37 cm (8 ¼ x 14 ½ in.), private collection
78a Mildred Elsie Eldridge, *The Dance of Life*, created for the canteen of a nurses' home at the Robert Jones and Agnes Hunt Orthopaedic Hospital at Gobowen, near Oswestry, completed c. 1955 (*in situ* at Glyndwr College Wrexham, 2012), photograph: Rod Dorling
78b Mildred Elsie Eldridge, *The Dance of Life,* (*in situ* at Glyndwr College Wrexham, 2012), photograph: Rod Dorling

NOTE: A large majority of the works which appear in Part II – Case Studies were photographed by Glynn Clarkson

Winifred Knights – *The Deluge*, 1920 All images by Winifred Knights are copyright Sacha Llewellyn on behalf of the artist's estate unless otherwise stated
79 *The Deluge,* (detail) © The Estate of Winifred Knights / © Tate, London 2012
80 *A Scene in a Village Street with Millhands Conversing*, 1919, tempera on canvas relined on board, 91.4 x 122 cm (36 x 48 in.) Courtesy of UCL Art Museum, University College London
81 *The Illustrated London News*, February 12, 1921
82 *Figure from Life,* 1920, oil on canvas, Courtesy of UCL Art Museum, University College London
83 *Waterfall at Roydon Weir*, 1920, Book of Studies for the Rome Scholarship, private collection
84 Full-scale drawing for *The Deluge*, pencil on paper, 152.9 x 183.5 cm (60 ⅛ x 72 ¼ in.) With the permission of The Wolfsonian – Florida International University (Miami, Florida)
85 Early study for *The Deluge*, pencil and watercolour, 23.2 x 29.1 cm (9 ⅛ x 11 ½ in.), Courtesy of the UCL Art Museum, University College London
86 Study for *The Deluge*, 1920, oil over pencil on paper, 32.5 x 26.5 cm (12 ¾ x 10 ⅜ in.), Courtesy of the UCL Art Museum, University College London
87 Compositional study for *The Deluge*, pencil and watercolour, 12.5 x 19 cm (5 x 7 ½ in.), private collection
88 Print after Nicolas Poussin's *Le Déluge,* c. 1810 – Louvre cycle *Les quatre saisons* of 1660-64
89 *The Deluge,* 1920, oil on canvas, 152.9 x 183.5 cm (60 ⅛ x 72 ¼ in.), © The estate of Winifred Knights / © Tate, London 2012
90 Vittorio Carpaccio, *St Jerome and the Lion*, c.1502, from the 1907 edition of Molmenti and Ludwig's *Life and Works of Vittorio Carpaccio*
91 Cover of the catalogue for the exhibition of the Nation's War Paintings at Burlington House, December 12, 1919-February 7, 1920
92 *Study of* Andrea Verrocchio's *Putto with Fish,* 1920, Book of Studies for the Rome Scholarship, private collection

93 Cartoon for *The Deluge*, pencil on tracing paper, 152.9 x 183.5 cm (60 ⅛ x 72 ¼ in.), (detail), private collection
94 Winifred Knights in her studio at the British School at Rome

Colin Gill – *Allegro*, 1921 All works by Colin Gill © The Estate of Colin Gill
95 *Allegro,* 1920-21, oil on canvas, 117 x 228.5 cm (46 x 90 in.), (detail), private collection
96 *Flora*, c. 1912, oil on canvas, 76.2 x 55.9 cm (30 x 22 in.), colour study submitted for the finals of the Rome Scholarship in Decorative Painting 1913, private collection
97 *Heavy Artillery,* 1919, oil on canvas, 182.8 x 317.5 cm (72 x 125 in.), Accession number: IWM ART 2274, photo credit: IWM (Imperial War Museums) © the copyright holder © IWM (Art.IWM ART LD 2274)
98 *Canadian Observation Post*, 1920, oil on canvas, 185.5 x 243 cm (73 x 95 ⅝ in.), CWM 19880266-003, Beaverbrook Collection of War Art, © Canadian War Museum Recto, lower right, in red paint: Colin; Gill; 1920, verso, on upper stretcher bar at centre, in black felt pen: Acc. 8967 (reads upside down); lower centre in black felt pen: Acc. 8967; OBSERVATION POST by GILL; directly on canvas at lower left in blue paint: THE WIDOW'S HOUSE COLIN GILL ROME 1920
99 *Allegro*, 1921, signed and dated, oil on canvas, 117 x 228.5 cm (46 x 90 in.), private collection
100 Colin Gill in his studio at The British School at Rome, 1920, private collection
101 Photograph of Winifred Knights, September 1920, private collection
102 Letter from Colin Gill to 'Jane' (Winifred Knights), private collection
103 *Study for Allegro, (sleeping nude*), 1921, signed, pencil on card, 54.6 x 61 cm (21 ½ x 24 in.), © Tate, London 2012
104 Mark Gertler, *The Fruit Sorters*, 1914, oil on canvas, 76.2 x 63.5 cm (30 x 25 in.), courtesy of Leicester Arts and Museums Service
105 Colin Gill's dedication to Winifred Knights ('Jane') inscribed on a photographic reproduction of his *Allegro*, May 1921, private collection
106 Colin Gill, Thomas Ashby and unidentified man in the Italian campagnia, c. 1920, © BSR AF Collection Asbhy LV1 52
107 *Portrait of Winifred Knights*, 1921, signed and inscribed 'Jane' on the original backboard, pencil on paper, 43.8 x 32.4 cm (17 ¼ x 12 ¾ in.), private collection
108 Colin Gill working in Whistler's old studio in Tite Street, Chelsea, c. 1938, photograph: *Picture Post*, November 5, 1938

Thomas Monnington – *Winter*, 1922 & *Allegory*, 1925 All works by Thomas Monnington ©The Estate of Thomas Monnington / Liss Fine Art
109 Study for *Winter*, c. 1922, signed and dated, pencil and gouache on paper, squared, 21 x 37 cm (8 ¼ x 14 ½ in.)
110 Works of the four finalists for the Rome Scholarship in 1922: John Bateman, John W. Widmer, Joyce Smith and Walter T. Monnington, Courtesy of the British School at Rome Historic Archive
111 Exhibitor's label for *Winter,* private collection
112 Cartoon for *Winter*, c. 1921, chalk and gouache on brown paper, 122 x 216 cm (48 x 85 in.), private collection
113 *Winter*, 1922, oil on canvas, 122 x 216 cm (48 x 85 in.), private collection
114 Study for *Allegory*, 1924, oil on tracing paper laid on board, squared for transfer, 31.7 x 57.2 cm (12 ½ x 22 ½ in.), private collection
115 & 116 Two preparatory drawings for *Allegory*, original photographs from c. 1924, pencil on paper, whereabouts of drawings unknown
117 Cartoon for *Allegory*, original photographs from c. 1924, pencil on paper, squared
118 *Allegory*, c. 1924, egg tempera on canvas, 125.7 x 276.8 cm (49 ½ x 109 in.), © The Estate of Sir Thomas Monnington, © Tate, London 2012
119 Study for *Allegory*, c. 1924, oil on canvas, 28 x 48.2 cm (11 x 19 in.), private collection
120 *Annunciation*, c.1924-25, oil on canvas, 99 x 145 cm (39 x 57 in.), private collection
121 *Annunciation*, c.1924-25, oil on canvas, 99 x 145 cm (39 x 57 in.), private collection (detail)
122 Thomas Monnington, courtesy of John Monnington

Mary Adshead – *An English Holiday*, 1928 All works by Mary Adshead ©The Estate of Mary Adshead / Liss Fine Art
123 *An English Holiday – The Puncture*, 1928 (detail)
124 *An English Holiday – The Puncture*, 1928, signed lower left, oil on canvas, 217 × 121.5 cm (85 × 47 in.), private collection
125 Mary Adshead in her first car, a Fiat 10HP
126 *An English Holiday – Village Inn*, 1928, signed lower left, oil on canvas, 217 x 96.5 cm (85 ½ x 38 in.), private collection
127 *An English Holiday – The Winners' Enclosure*, 1928, oil on canvas, 216 x 326 cm (85 x 128 ⅜ in.)
128 *An English Holiday – Newmarket Fair,* 1928 (detail), oil on canvas, 208 x 305 cm (82 x 120 in.)
129 *An English Holiday Installation*', most likely at Peter Jones Department Store, London, 1930
130 *A Tropical Fantasy:* Charles Reilly's Dining Room Mural, 1926 (panel 3 of 6), oil on board, est. 244 x 190 cm (96 x 74 ¾ in.), University of Liverpool Collection
131 Mary Adshead at work, source: Ann Compton

Edward Halliday – *Hypnos*, 1928 All works by Edward Halliday © Charlotte & Stephen Halliday / Liss Fine Art
132 Reverse side of *Hypnos,* photograph: Glynn Clarkson
133 *St Paul Meeting with Lydia of Thyatira,* 1928 (detail), oil on canvas, 106 x 147cm (41 ¾ x 57 ⅞ in.), photograph: University of Liverpool
134 *Hypnos,* 1928, signed lower left, oil on canvas, 74.7 x 134.7 cm (30 x 54 in.), private collection, photograph: Glynn Clarkson
135 *Portrait of R.P. Longden (Bobby Longden),* 1928, photograph: The British School at Rome Historic Archives (ref. FA 1968)
136 *Hypnos, Study for Reclining Figure,* 1928, signed and dated, pencil on paper, dimensions unknown, photograph: British School at Rome Archives (ref. FA 1972)
137 *Gulliver's Travels* or *Alter Ego,* 1927-28, oil on canvas, 63.4 x 60.6 cm (25 x 23 ⅞ in.)
138 Study for *The Contest between Athena and Poseidon for the Patronship of Athens*, oil on panel, 40 x 37 cm (15 ¾ x 14 ½ in.), photograph: University of Liverpool
139 Study for *Hypnos,* 1928, dimensions unknown, photograph: British School at Rome Archives (ref. FA 0228)
140 *Group in Cortile,* c. 1928, oil on canvas, dimensions unknown, photograph: British School at Rome Archives (ref. FA 1967)
141 Edward Halliday in front of camera, 1938, source: Ann Compton

Charles Mahoney – Morley College, 1928-30 & Brockley School, 1932-36 All works by Charles Mahoney ©The Estate of Charles Mahoney / Liss Fine Art
142 Morley College after being bombed, 1940, © London Borough of Lambeth
143 Compositional study for *The Pleasures of Life*, 1928-30, pen and brown ink over pencil on paper, 47 x 65 cm (18 ½ x 25 ½ in.), private collection

144 Compositional study for *The Pleasures of Life*, 1928-30, pen and brown ink over pencil with areas of correction in white, squared on tracing paper, 31.8 x 48.9 cm (12 ½ x 19 ⅛ in.), private collection
145 *Muse: Study for Philosophy*, oil paint mixed with wax on canvas, 58.4 x 35.6 cm (23 x 14 in.)
146 & 147 Two photographs taken of details of Mahoney's mural cycle *The Pleasures of Life,* Morley College. From a presentation album owned by Elizabeth Bulkeley
148 The stage of the concert hall with *The Pleasures of Life,* Morley College, c. 1930, photograph: courtesy of Architctural Press Archive / RIBA Library Photographs Collection
149 *Joy & Sorrow*, mural at Brockley Country School, c. 1932-36, with kind permission of Prendergast – Hilly Fields College, photograph: Nigel Green
150 *Fortune & the Boy at the Well*, mural at Brockley Country School, c. 1932-36, with kind permission of Prendergast – Hilly Fields College, photograph: Nigel Green
151 *The Clock and the Dial* and *The Butterfly and the Rose,* mural at Brockley Country School in the spaces below the balcony, c. 1932-36, with kind permission of Prendergast – Hilly Fields College, photgraph: Nigel Green
152 *The Four Winds of Hilly Fields*, a ceiling decoration at Brockley Country School, c. 1932-36, with kind permission of Prendergast – Hilly Fields College, photograph: Nigel Green
153 Study for *The Four Winds of Hilly Fields*, pencil, pen & ink and wash on paper, 39 x 28 cm (15 ⅜ x 11 in.), c. 1932-36
154 Charles Mahoney sketching on the shingle at Pevensey, 1958

Frank Brangwyn – Rockefeller Center, New York, 1932-1933 All works by Frank Brangwyn © David Brangwyn / Liss Fine Art
155 View of Frank Brangwyn's panels in the south corridor of the Rockefeller Center, New York, © David Brangwyn, photograph: private source
156 *Cartoon for Man's Ultimate Destiny,* © David Brangwyn, private collection, photograph: Glynn Clarkson
157 Night comes down on Rockefeller Center, highlighting the shaft of the 70-storey RCA Building (from *The Story of Rockefeller Center*, 1939)
158 Working photomontage for *Man's Ultimate Destiny,* © David Brangwyn, private collection
159 Joy Sinden modelling for *Man the Creator*, taken from the original glass plate held by Ditchling Museum
160 *Study for Man the Creator*, 1932, oil on canvas, 274.3 x 182.9 cm (108 x 72 inches), © David Brangwyn, private collection, photograph: Glynn Clarkson
161 *Study for Man the Master*, 1932, oil on canvas, 274.3 x 182.9 cm (108 x 72 inches), © David Brangwyn, private collection, photograph: Glynn Clarkson
162 William de Belleroche with studies for *Man the Creator* and *Man the Master,* 1961
163 Frank Brangwyn and Kenneth Center working on *Man the Master*
164 Frank Brangwyn in his studio

Charles Mahoney – Campion Hall, 1941-52 All works by Charles Mahoney © The Estate of Charles Mahoney / Liss Fine Art
165 The altar and Mahoney's murals in the chapel at Campion Hall, photograph: Richard Ivey
166 Design for Campion Hall, *The Symbols of Mary,* mid-1940s, oil on paper, 19 x 76.2 cm (7 ½ x 30 in.), private collection
167 Design for the wall above the altar at Campion Hall, *Two Angels Overlooking a Garden,* oil on paper, 45 x 38 cm (17 ¾ x 15 in.), private collection
168 Study for *The Birth of the Virgin*, c. 1942, oil on paper, 29.2 x 28 cm (11 ½ x 11 in.), private collection
169 Study for *The Visitation*, c. 1942, signed and inscribed on a label to the reverse, oil on paper, squared in chalk, 29.2 x 28.6 cm (11 ½ x 11 ¼ in.), private collection
170 *The Adoration of the Shepherds,* left of the altar
171 *Our Lady of Mercy,* rear to the right of the chapel
172 *The Crowning of the Virgin,* right of the altar
173 The Lady Chapel at Campion Hall, photograph: Richard Ivey

Edward Bawden and English Country Life All works by Edward Bawden ©The Estate of Edward Bawden
174 *Country Life in Britain*, cardboard & watercolour model for free-standing mural commissioned for the Festival of Britain's Lion & Unicorn Pavilion, 1950-51. © Bedford Gallery
175 *English Garden Delights*, 1946, oil on panel, 2110 x 6480 (830 ¾ x 2551 ⅛ in.), nine panels, each panel approx.: 2110 x 717 (830 ¾ x 282 ¼ in.), courtesy of Waddesdon, The Rothschild Collection (Rothschild Family Trust), on loan since 1998, Acc. no. 95.1998, photograph: Mike Fear
176 *English Garden Delights in situ* on board SS *Orcades*, (1948) in the 1st class lounge, © P&O Heritage collection
177 *The English Pub,* 1949-1951, (detail)
178 *The English Pub,* 1949-1951, oil on 11 panels, 176 x 539 cm (69 ⅜ x 212 ¼ in.), private collection.
179 Design for mural commissioned by the Morgan Crucible Company for the entrance hall of their works on the South Bank of the Thames at Battersea, 1957-58, pen, ink, pencil and watercolour, © Bedford Gallery
180 Mural for British Petroleum at Britannic House, London, 1966, oil on panel, 412 x 914 cm (162 ¼ x 359 ⅞ in.), courtesy of Chelsea & Westminster Health Charity.
181 Eric Ravilious, *Edward Bawden Working in His Studio,* 1930, tempera on board, 79 x 92 cm (31 ⅛ x 36 ¼ in.), collection: Royal College of Art, Accession number: RCA_CC_14
182 Edward Bawden at work on the Morley College murals, c. 1930

60 paintings for '51
183 Cover of the catalogue for the Festival of Britain '60 Paintings for 51' exhibition
184 *The Illustrated London News,* April 28,1951
185 Rodrigo Moynihan, *Portrait Group* 1951, oil on canvas, 213.4 x 334.6 cm (84 x 131 ¾ in.), © Tate, London 2012
186 Ivon Hitchens, *Aquarium Nativity*, 1951, wax & oil on canvas, 210.9 x 566.4 cm (83 x 223 in.), © Ivon Hitchens' Estate/ Jonathan Clark & Co., Courtesy of UCL Art Museum, University of London, photograph: UCL Art Museum
187 William Gear, *Autumn Landscape,* 1951, oil on canvas, 127 x 183.2 cm (50 x 72 ⅛ in.), © The Estate of William Gear, courtesy of the Arts Council Collection
188 Victor Pasmore, *The Snowstorm: Spiral Motif in Black and White,* 1950-51, oil on canvas, 119.4 x 152.4 cm (47 x 60 in.), © Victor Pasmore Estate, courtesy of the Arts Council Collection, acquisition date: 1951, ACC3/1951
189 Lucien Freud, *Portrait of Harry Diamond,* 1951, oil on canvas, 152.4 x 114.3 cm (60 x 45 in.), National Museums Liverpool / Walker Art Gallery
190 John Armstrong, *Storm,* 1951, oil and wax on canvas, 114.3 x 152.4 cm (45 x 60 in.), private collection
191 Peter Lanyon, *Porthleven,* 1951, oil on board, 244.5 x 121.9 cm (96 ¼ x 48 in.), © Tate, London 2012
192 Gilbert Spencer, *Hebridean Memory* 1951, oil on canvas,| 127 x 297 cm (50 x 117 in.), © Estate of Gilbert Spencer, All rights reserved DACS 2012, private collection
193 Charles Mahoney, *The Garden,* 1950, (detail)
194 Charles Mahoney, *The Garden,* 1950, oil on canvas, 182.9 x 121.9 cm (72 x 48 in.), private collection

195 Claude Rogers, *Miss Lynn*, 1951, oil on canvas, 108 x 177.3 cm (42 ½ x 69 ¾ in.), © Crispin Rogers, collection: Southampton City Art Gallery

The Murals of John Armstrong All works by John Armstrong © The Estate of John Armstrong

196 Design for Telecinema Mural, South Bank, 1951 (detail)
197 *Sailors and Girls*, design for the American bar in the Royal Hotel, Scarborough, 1935-6, signed with initials JA lower right, gouache on paper, 18.5 x 54.6 cm (7 ¼ x 21 ½ in.), private collection
198 John Armstrong standing beside the Shell-Mex panels, 1933
199 *Invocation*, 1938, tempera on plywood, 71 x 55.8 cm (28 x 22 in.), National Gallery of Victoria, Melbourne, Accession number: 2006.492, purchased with funds donated by Ian Hicks AM and Dorothy Hicks, 2006
200 Design for Telecinema Mural, South Bank, 1951 (detail)
201 Design for Telecinema Mural, South Bank, 1951, inscribed on reverse: 'Design for Foyer of Telecinema', oil on board, 34.3 x 70 cm (13 ½ x 27 ½ in.)
202 Design for Telecinema Mural, South Bank, 1951, oil on board, 40.5 x 76.2 cm (16 x 30 in.)
203 Studies for Royal Marsden Hospital in Sutton, Surrey, 1961, gouache on paper, 21 x 17.8 cm (8 ¼ x 7 in.) and 11.7 x 31.3 cm (4 ⅝ x 12 ⅜ in.), private collection
204 Studies for Royal Marsden Hospital in Sutton, Surrey, 1961, gouache on paper, 11.7 x 30.5 cm (4 ⅝ x 12 in.) and 21 x 17.8 cm (8 ¼ x 7 in.), private collection
205 Study for Royal Marsden Hospital in Sutton, Surrey, 1961, gouache on paper, 21 x 34.5 cm (8 ¼ x 13 ½ in.), private collection
206 John Armstrong with Mary Collett, c. 1953

John Piper – *The Englishman's Home*, 1950-51 All works by John Piper ©The Piper Estate

207 *The Englishman's Home* at the Festival of Britain, 1951, photograph: courtesy of the Design Council Archive / University of Brighton Design Archives
208 *The Englishman's Home*, 1951. Oil on plywood, 477 x 1547 cm (187 ¾ x 609 in.), private collection
209 *Cheltenham*, 1940, autolithograph, 24.6 x 71 cm (9 11⁄16 x 27 15⁄16 in.)
210 Cover of *Fortune* magazine, May 1950
211 *The Englishman's Home* being painted at Fawley Bottom Farmhouse, 1951, photograph: Janet Stone
212 *The Englishman's Home*, 1951 (detail)
213 Piper and his daughter Suzannah sitting in front of the mural while it was being painted in 1951, © reserved (we have attempted to trace the copyright holder and would be happy to clear rights with them should they come forward), photograph: Janet Stone

Alan Sorrell – *Working Boats from Around the British Coast*, Mural of the Nelson Bar, HMS *Campania*, 1951 © Richard, Julia & Mark Sorrell / Liss Fine Art

214 *Working Boats from Around the British Coast,* Mural of the Nelson Bar, HMS *Campania*, 1951 (detail), private collection
215 The *Campania* exhibition ship, Festival of Britain touring exhibition: general view from Gallery deck looking at Hangar deck, photograph: courtesy of the Architectural Press Archive / RIBA Library Photographs Collection
216 Drawing of Nelson Bar sent to Sorrell by the bar's designer, Ernest Pollak, c. 1951, courtesy of Richard Sorrell
217 *Working Boats from Around the British Coast,* Mural of the Nelson Bar, HMS *Campania*, 1951, signed, oil on five panels, 122 x 914.4 cm (48 x 360 in.), private collection
218 The *Campania* exhibition ship, Festival of Britain touring exhibition: Lord Nelson Bar, 1951, photograph: courtesy of the Architctural Press Archive / RIBA Library Photographs Collection
219 *Working Boats from Around the British Coast,* Mural of the Nelson Bar, HMS *Campania*, 1951 (detail), private collection
220 Alan Sorrell working on his Festival of Britain designs. c. 1951, courtesy of Richard Sorrell

Thomas Monnington – The New Council House, Bristol, 1953-56 & The Mary Harris Memorial Chapel of Holy Trinity, University of Exeter, 1956-57
All works by Thomas Monnington ©The Estate of Thomas Monnington / Liss Fine Art

221 Design for ceiling of the Mary Harris Memorial Chapel of Holy Trinity, University of Exeter, c. 1956, private collection (detail)
222 *Fighter Affiliation: Halifax and Hurricane aircraft co-operating in action*, 1943, oil on canvas, 46.3 x 41.2 cm (18 ¼ x 16 ¼ in.), courtesy of Imperial War Museums © Crown Copyright. IWM, catalogue number Art.IWM ART LD 3769
223 Design for Bristol Council House Ceiling, c. 1953, pencil and chalk on tracing paper, 61 x 33 cm (24 x 13 in.), private collection
224 Design for ceiling of the Mary Harris Memorial Chapel of Holy Trinity, University of Exeter, c. 1956, oil on board, 123 x 49 cm (48 ½ x 19 ⅜ in.), private collection
225 Thomas Monnington in his studio at Leyswood, c. 1967
226 Design for Bristol Council House Ceiling, c. 1953, inscribed on the reverse, 'working study', tempera over pencil on a gesso ground, 76.2 x 193 cm (30 x 76 in.), private collection, photograph: Evelina Llewellyn
227 Design for ceiling of the Mary Harris Memorial Chapel of Holy Trinity, University of Exeter, c. 1956, oil on board 43.7 x 122 cm (17 ¼ x 48 in.), private collection
228 View of Mary Harris Memorial Chapel of Holy Trinity, University of Exeter
229 *Clematis,* c 1960, acrylic on board, 130 x 92 cm (51 3⁄16 x 36 ¼ in.), private collection
230 Design for Students' Union, University of London, c. 1969, acrylic on board, 43.2 × 33 cm (17 × 13 in.), private collection
231 *Square Design,*1966, oil on canvas, 93 x 92 cm (36 ¼ x 36 in.), © Tate, London 2012
232 Monnington's University of London Students' Union mural *in situ* c. 1964

The Murals of Barbara Jones All works by Barbara Jones ©The Estate of Barbara Jones

233 Mural based on the theme 'Man at Work – a century of technical and social progress' (detail), photograph: Evelina Llewellyn
234 Murals painted for the Jules Hotel, Jermyn Street, London, 1939-1943, photograph: courtesy of Ruth Artmonsky
235 *Ocean Life,* 1960, The Ocean Bar of the SS *Oriana,* photograph: courtesy of John Maltby/RIBA Library Photographs Collection
236 *Adam Naming the Animals,* Sketch for the mural for Yew Lane School, Sheffield, 1959, photograph: courtesy of Ruth Artmonsky
237 *Out in the Hall*, 1960, oil and wax, 3 panels, 183 x 365.8 cm (72 x 144 in.), private collection, photograph: Glynn Clarkson
238 Mural based on the theme 'Man at Work – a century of technical and social progress', 1961, two panels, oil on canvas, 365.8 x 365.8 cm (144 x 144 in.), photograph: Evelina Llewellyn
239 Barbara Jones at work, photograph: courtesy of Ruth Artmonsky

INDEX

Note: Page numbers in *italic* refer to captions and illustrations; those in **bold** refer to major passages on individual artists or works

CONTRIBUTORS

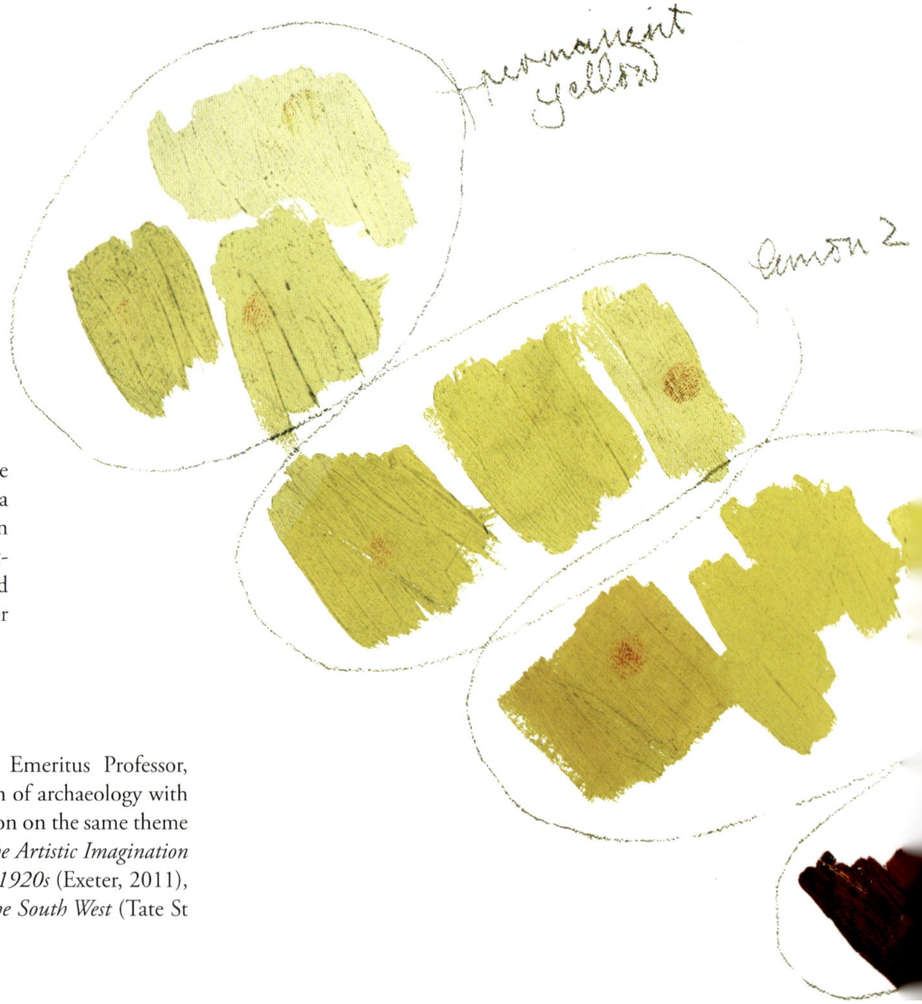

Alan POWERS is a specialist in the history of twentieth-century British art, architecture and design and has written widely on these subjects, as well as curating exhibitions at the Design Museum, Imperial War Museum, Kettle's Yard, the Royal Academy and the De La Warr Pavilion. His interest in murals began in the 1970s, when he began to research their history, rediscovering a number of almost forgotten artists. He has a long involvement with the Twentieth Century Society and is one of the editors of its journal. He taught at the University of Greenwich School of Architecture for many years, and is now an independent scholar, teaching at NYU (London) and working on a number of writing projects.

Sacha LLEWELLYN, art historian and exhibition organiser. Studied history of art at the University of East Anglia and the Courtauld Institute of Art. Joined Liss Fine Art as a Director in 1996. The first generation of Rome Scholars has been a focus of research resulting in exhibitions at the British School at Rome and museums in Britain. Currently joint-curating an exhibition on Alan Sorrell for Sir John Soane's Museum, London (autumn 2013) and curating an exhibition on Winifred Knights for Dulwich Picture Gallery (January 2016). Her monograph on Winifred Knights will be published in 2015.

Sam SMILES, Programme Director, Art History and Visual Culture, University of Exeter; Emeritus Professor, University of Plymouth. He has published widely on British art c. 1750-1950 and the collaboration of archaeology with the visual arts. He is currently completing a study of Turner's last paintings and preparing an exhibition on the same theme for Tate Britain (2014). He has curated numerous exhibitions, the most recent being: *Flight and the Artistic Imagination* (Compton Verney, 2012), *Into the Light: French and British painting from Impressionism to the early 1920s* (Exeter, 2011), *Sir Joshua Reynolds: The Acquisition of Genius* (Plymouth, 2009) and *Light into Colour: Turner in the South West* (Tate St Ives, 2006).

Ann COMPTON, writer, curator, project originator and director of the digital research project *Mapping the Practice and Profession of Sculpture in Britain and Ireland 1851-1951* (Glasgow University, Victoria and Albert Museum and Henry Moore Institute). Has curated numerous exhibitions of 19th- and 20th-century British art in Cambridge, London and Liverpool. Publications include: *Edward Halliday: Art for Life 1925–39*, Liverpool, 1997; *The Sculpture of Charles Sargeant Jagger*, 2004; and she was co-editor of *Earthly Delights: the Murals of Mary Adshead,* Liverpool, 2005. Forthcoming titles: co-editor, *Sculpture Journal*, vol 21.2 (special issue) and editor, *Garth Evans Sculpture: Beneath the Skin*, London, 2013.

Peyton SKIPWITH, fine art consultant and author, executor to the Estate of Edward Bawden. Joined the staff of Bond Street dealers, The Fine Art Society, in 1961, retiring as deputy managing director in 2005. Has curated many exhibitions concerned with British fine and decorative arts 1880-1945 in the UK and USA. Co-author with Brian Webb of seven monographs for ACC, including Bawden, Ravilious, Paul and John Nash, McKnight Kauffer, Lovat Fraser, David Gentleman and Peter Blake – John Piper is due out spring 2013 – as well as *Edward Bawden's London* (V&A Publications).

Libby HORNER is known for her efforts to resuscitate the fortunes of Frank Brangwyn, through exhibitions (the most recent being at the National Museum of Western Art in Tokyo, 2010 which won a prestigious award from the Western Art Foundation), lectures and publications (*Frank Brangwyn: Stained Glass.* A catalogue raisonné published in 2011 holds the unique distinction of being the first catalogue to be produced as a DVD, giving her the opportunity to interview experts and film the windows *in situ*). In recent years she has expanded her portfolio and having made films about John Piper and Patrick Reyntiens is now compiling a catalogue of the latter's stained glass windows and panels.

Andrew LAMBIRTH is a writer, critic and curator. He has written on art for a variety of publications including *The Sunday Times, Modern Painters* and *RA*, the Royal Academy magazine. Among his many books are monographs on John Armstrong, Roger Hilton, Maggi Hambling, John Hoyland, Margaret Mellis, Allen Jones, LS Lowry, David Inshaw and RB Kitaj. He is currently art critic of *The Spectator* and lives in Suffolk.

Elizabeth COHEN (née GRAFFIUS), read a BA in History of Art at the University of Cambridge between 2009 and 2012. Her third-year dissertation was entitled *The Lady Chapel Murals by Charles Mahoney at Campion Hall*, and is the basis for this essay. She was educated at the Jesuit boarding school Stonyhurst College, which is how she came to hear of the Campion Hall murals. She is now working as a teaching assistant in a primary school in London and hopes to train to become a teacher.

David FRASER JENKINS, art gallery curator at National Museum of Wales, 1969, Tate Gallery 1980, retired 2005. Has curated exhibitions of John Piper, Paul Nash, Gwen and Augustus John, Jacques Lipchitz and published extensively on modern art, especially British. He has recently completed a monograph on the art of John Piper.

Paul LISS, fine art dealer and exhibition organiser. Joined Sotheby's as a Bursary student prior to working for Hazlitt, Gooden & Fox. Founded Liss Fine Art in 1991. Has curated many monographic exhibitions – Winifred Knights (1995), Thomas Monnington (1997), Charles Mahoney (1999), Robert Austin (2001), Frank Brangwyn (2006), Michael Canney (2007), Cecil Stephenson (2009), Stanley Lewis (2010), John McKenzie and Victor Moody (both 2012). Thematic catalogues include Women Artists, the art of WW1 and WW2 and the British School at Rome. Currently joint curating an exhibition for autumn 2013 of the work of Alan Sorrell for the Sir John Soane Museum, London.

Robert UPSTONE is a Director of The Fine Art Society in London where he moved in 2010 after a long-standing career as a senior curator at the Tate. He is a well known specialist in Modern British art and has written and broadcast extensively in this area. Robert has curated several major museum exhibitions, including the survey of William Orpen held at the Imperial War Museum and National Gallery of Ireland (2005), 'Modern Painters: The Camden Town Group' at Tate Britain (2008), 'Sickert in Venice' at Dulwich Picture Gallery (2009), 'Cayley Robinson' at the National Gallery (2010) and 'The Vorticists: Manifesto for a Modern World' at Tate Britain (2011). He is currently working on exhibitions about Barbara Hepworth and Laura Knight, and writing a book about British art and the First World War.

Ruth ARTMONSKY started her career as a psychologist, a director of the premier psychometric worldwide consultancy. On retirement she ran an art gallery – Artmonsky Arts – and began to write books on a variety of subjects relating to design and the graphic arts including *The School Prints* and *'A Snapper up of Unconsidered Trifles' – a biography of Barbara Jones.* Her twelfth book *Designing Women* has just been published.

David MAES, painter and printmaker from Montreal, he has been living in Europe since 1987 and exhibits regularly in France and Spain. In 2002 he and Sylvie Cavillier created *le mariage des eaux*, a small publishing firm. He designs catalogues and books in France and the UK.

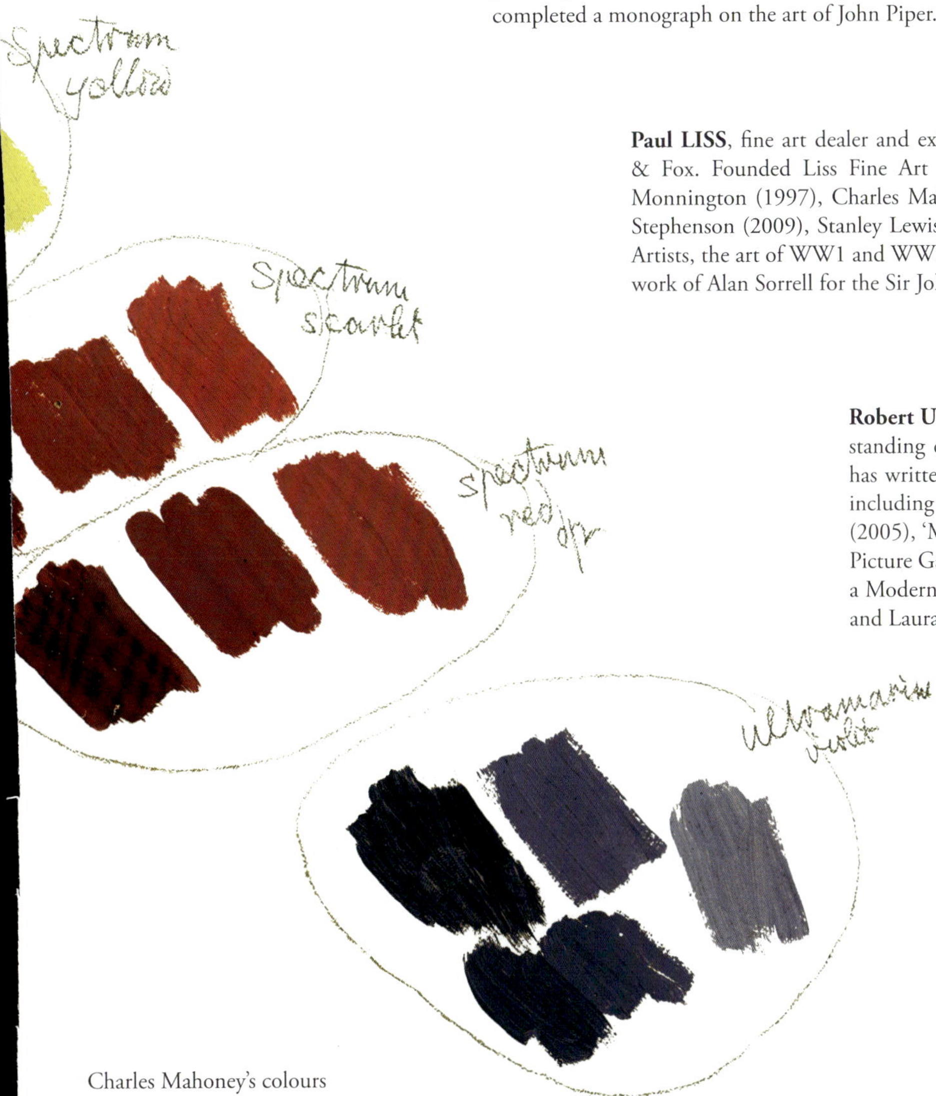

Charles Mahoney's colours for the murals at Campion Hall, 1940s

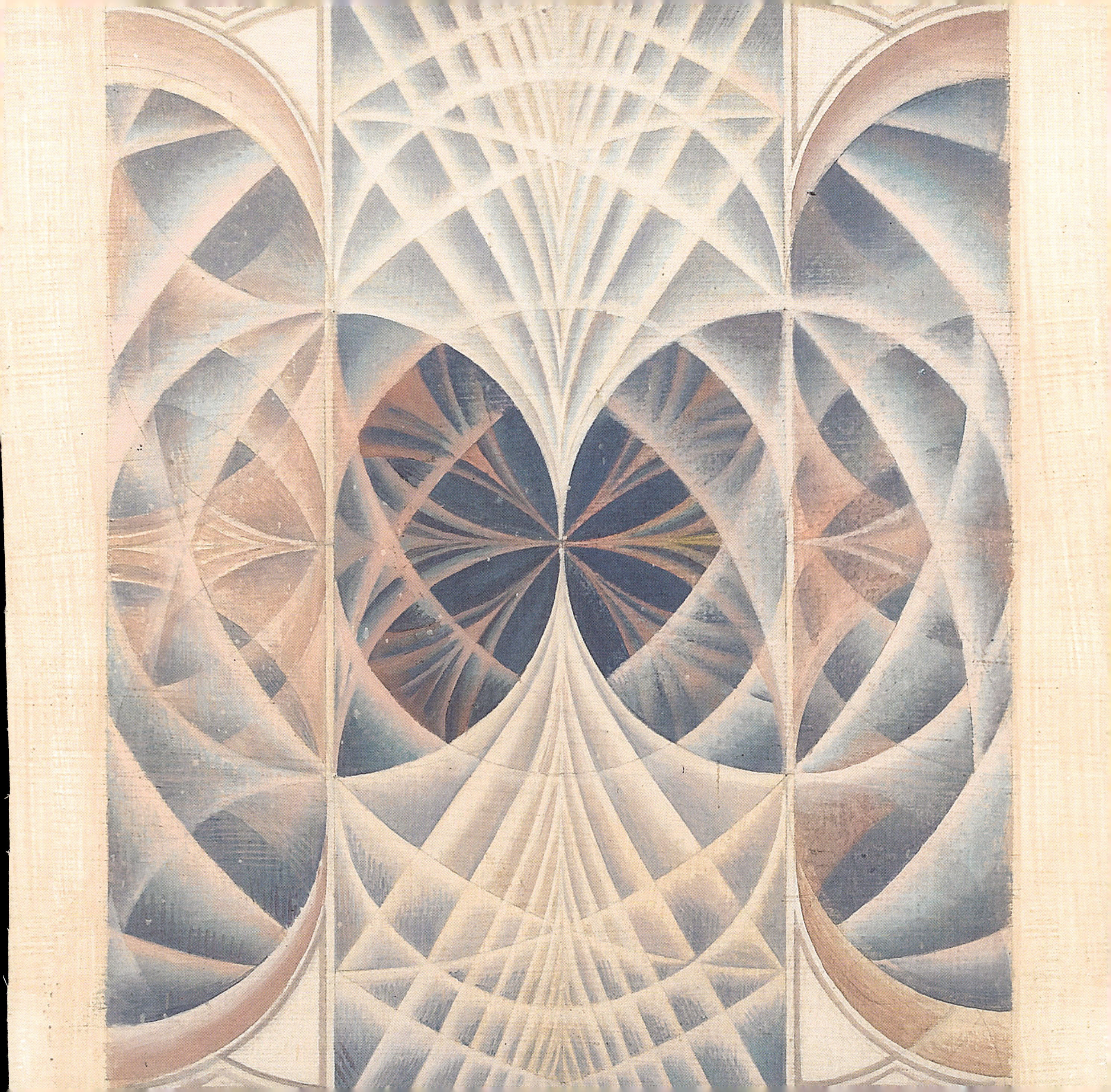

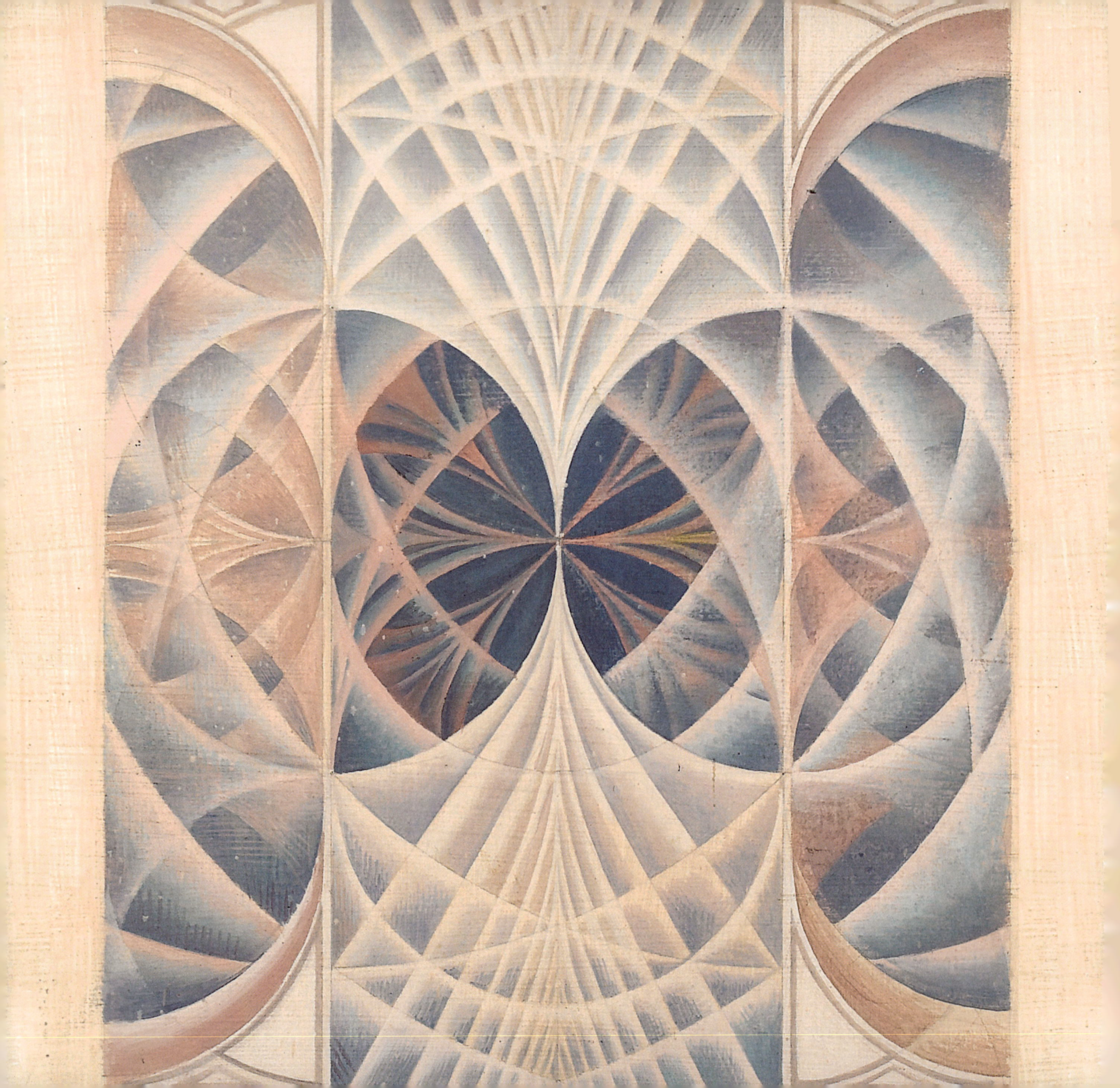